DATE DUE

DE ~~8 '01~~		
JA 23 '02		
MR 31 03		
NV 7 '03		
DE 5 03		
DE 7 '04		
JA 27 05		

DEMCO 38-296

International Organizations

A Dictionary

Fourth Edition

International Organizations

A Dictionary

Fourth Edition

Giuseppe Schiavone

STOCKTON

© Macmillan Press Ltd, 1997

First published in the United Kingdom by
MACMILLAN REFERENCE LTD 1997
25 Eccleston Place, London, SW1W 9NF
and Basingstoke

Companies and representatives throughout the world.

Distributed by Macmillan Direct
Brunel Road, Houndmills, Basingstoke,
Hampshire, RG21 2XS, England

ISBN 0-333-675916

A catalogue record for this book is available from the British Library.

Published in the United States and Canada by
STOCKTON PRESS, 1997
345 Park Avenue South, 10 Floor
New York, NY 10010-1707

ISBN 1-56159-195-5

Typeset by EXPO Holdings, Malaysia

Printed and bound in Great Britain by
Antony Rowe Ltd, Chippenham, Wiltshire

Contents

Introduction

The New Frontiers of International Organization

The goals, scope and activities of international organizations have been affected to a significant extent by the dramatic and unexpected events of the last decade of the twentieth century, with far-reaching repercussions at the global level (notably the UN and its system) as well as on a regional scale (notably the process of European integration).

The East–West confrontation – for decades a seemingly intractable issue shaping the agenda of international relations – appears to be a thing of the past now that the demise of communism is an accomplished fact in all but a few countries and the transition to multiparty democracy and a market-driven system is under way in Central and Eastern Europe and in the republics of the erstwhile Soviet Union. As the East–West conflict has disappeared, the North–South polarization has taken on new features characterized by a clear shift of the developing countries toward less interventionist government policies and an acceptance of the 'democratic model' prevailing in major industrial nations.

The traditional scenarios of bloc-to-bloc confrontation throughout the world have been replaced by a number of conflicts, interstate as well as intrastate, no longer directly inspired or controlled by the major powers. The variety of approaches and interests, largely unconditioned by traditional ideological tenets, presents unprecedented challenges to international co-operation in all areas, from security, trade and financial issues to environmental protection and drug abuse control. This is especially true with regard to the theory and practice of development in all its dimensions. It is now a widely recognized fact that economic growth does not automatically translate into a human progress which should ultimately lead to enlarging people's choices and putting the human being, not the economic system, at the core of the development process.

The concern about the rapid deterioration of the environment has contributed to the emergence of the notion of 'sustainable development' – that is, development that does not threaten the well-being and survival of humanity itself. Sustainable development involves, in fact, not only the protection of natural resources and the physical environment but also the protection of future economic growth and future human development. Radical changes will be necessary in both policies and institutions if the needs and options of unborn generations are to be taken into account.

The 1990s provide a decisive test for the capacities of international organizations to meet the challenge of sustainable development by taking stock of past experience and opening up new avenues for implementing global solidarity. The new spirit of co-operation among the 'great powers' and the growing awareness of the interdependence among all countries, large and small, should induce the international community to avail itself more extensively than in the recent past of the opportunities provided by international institutions at all levels and in all fields of activity.

The emergence and, particularly during the last decades of the twentieth century, the enormous expansion in number, range of tasks and functions of international organizations may be viewed as a response to the objective need for integration of international society at both the global (universal) and regional level.

It is important to emphasize, however, that the many and varied efforts towards integration have neither altered substantially the structure and dynamics of international society nor brought mankind any further towards the establishment of a world government within a more-or-less centralized international system.

Active nationalistic competition, fierce pressures for protectionism, and the stubborn defence of vested interests on a national scale, remain a constant feature of relations, even between countries such as those of Western Europe, which have set up supranational institutions endowed with very wide competences and far-reaching powers of co-ordination.

The proliferation of independent sovereign countries and the resulting sharp increase in membership of intergovernmental organizations are inevitably leading to the fragmentation of decision-making centres. Contrary to the widespread expectation of a gradual concentration of power in a few highly-integrated units, more and more countries are performing a significant role in the international system. The break-up of traditional alliances and support systems has often had an impact on the internal stability of both old and new states, which are now confronted with violent tensions of an ethnic or political/economic nature and with an increasingly organized criminality.

Despite the magnitude of the political, economic and social problems in the present phase of international relations, intergovernmental organizations stand a significant chance of improving the overall climate and of tackling successfully at least some aspects of major world issues on a multilateral basis. The heterogeneity of international society, made up of countries characterized by vastly different cultural backgrounds and huge variations in living standards, should not prevent the rational exploitation by all its members of the potentiality for co-operation provided by existing organizations. As in the past, the success of these bodies, born of good intentions but not by themselves representing a practical shortcut to world peace and stability, will ultimately depend on the resolve of member countries not to abuse a collective instrument for the mere pursuit of national interests and ends.

The Legal Framework of Inter-governmental Co-operation

From a legal point of view, international intergovernmental organizations are the products of treaties; the purely voluntary character of the participation of sovereign countries in international organizations and international co-operation efforts need not be emphasized. The formation of permanent international groupings, although almost inevitably involving a limitation of individual state sovereignty, cannot by itself be regarded as a preliminary stage towards the establishment of co-operative federal structures and the eventual institutionalization of world society. In fact, the majority of countries continue to emphasize the paramount value of the state, and obstacles to any larger role for international organizations are not diminishing.

The evolution of the international legal system invites comparison with the evolution of national legal systems; the present legal framework of world society then emerges as a relatively weak and primitive system bound to develop gradually into a strong and highly organized pattern of rules. Whatever the wisdom of such an assumption and its long-term implications, existing international organizations essentially represent a more sophisticated means of conducting interstate relations when national interests are better served through multilateral action or international concert.

In the absence of a generally agreed system of classification of international organizations, several possible criteria for distinction may be put forward, each concentrating on a specific feature or set of features. From a historical perspective, it can be observed that administrative and technical unions of fairly limited scope preceded the creation of institutions with broad political, economic and social aims. However, any clear-cut classification of organizations according to main objects of activity – preservation of peace and security, economic development, financial aid, technical, cultural and scientific exchange, humanitarian or military assistance – would prove to be less than accurate and lead to glaring inconsistencies in a number of cases, because of the overlap of functions and responsibilities.

A broad distinction may be made between organizations endowed with a wide array of powers (legislative, administrative and judicial) and with comprehensive competence and organizations with limited competence. Another suggested distinction is based on the global, regional or subregional scope of an organization. In a few cases the boundaries of a region are defined according to political or ideological rather than strictly geographical considerations. A further possible distinction – between supranational and non-supranational organizations – rests on the degree of integration which characterizes the organizations themselves and regards the nature and extent of the decision-making powers granted to particular organs. Supranational organizations have the ability to take decisions which are directly binding upon member states, and public and private enterprises as well as individuals within these states, whereas traditional organizations can act or execute decisions only by or through member states.

The basic purposes, functions and powers of international organizations are usually set out, in a general or specific way, in their constituent documents, which bear titles such as 'constitution', 'charter', 'covenant', 'statute' or 'articles of agreement'. Besides the functions and powers which are expressly mentioned in the relevant clauses of the basic instrument, it is generally assumed that an organization may be endowed with implied powers – that is, such powers as are essential to the adequate fulfilment of its appointed tasks.

As a rule, the constituent instruments of international organizations provide that the original signatories may become members upon ratification or acceptance of the instruments themselves, while other states may be admitted to membership by a special majority vote of the competent organs. Since legal rights and obligations are the same for both original and subsequent members, the distinction between the two categories is essentially of historical value. Although only states are normally envisaged as members, the constitutions of a number of organizations refer to 'governments', 'countries', 'sovereign countries' or 'nations'; these different expressions are of no consequence on the legal plane. Entities such as politically dependent territories or even independent and sovereign countries which are not acceptable as full members may be admitted to limited (associate) membership, usually without voting rights or representation in institutional organs. On occasion, organizations grant observer status to countries which may be admitted to membership at a later stage.

Loss of membership of international organizations may derive from a multiplicity of causes. The first step towards termination of participation may be represented by suspension of a member's rights and privileges, notably voting rights, as a sanction for the non-fulfilment of financial obligations or the serious breach of other membership obligations. Persistent violations of the fundamental principles of an organization may eventually lead to expulsion or compulsory withdrawal from membership. Voluntary withdrawal of dissident members is envisaged in the constitutions of several organizations, although special conditions may be prescribed. In many cases withdrawal does not take effect immediately but is subject to a period of notice ranging from a few months to one or more years.

The institutional structure of international organizations is generally based on a division of labour among three different types of organ: (a) a policy-making body in which all members are represented; (b) an executive or governing body of limited composition; and (c) a largely technical–administrative body made up of international civil servants and headed by a Secretary or Director.

The plenary organ – known usually as the Assembly, Conference, or Congress, and meeting at regular intervals ranging from one to several years – is the supreme body. It determines basic policies, adopts recommendations and decisions, draws up conventions and agreements, approves the budget and exercises any other power conferred upon it by the constituent instrument.

The smaller executive organ is usually elected by the plenary body from among its members according to varying criteria – such as the adequate representation of leading members or main geographical areas – and meets with relative frequency to ensure continuity of the work of the organization between sessions of the supreme organ. It carries out the directions of the plenary organ and is responsible to it, administers finances, and directs all activities relating to the fulfilment of the tasks of the organization.

The administrative organ, generally known as the Secretariat or Bureau, is in charge of the practical working of the organization. It performs various administrative, executive, technical and co-ordination functions, centralizes the handling of numerous questions, and collects and disseminates information and statistical data. Members are enjoined to respect the international character of the functions performed by the staff, whereas the civil servants themselves undertake not to accept instructions from outside authorities. Besides the standard principal organs, most organizations possess other lesser (subsidiary) organs designed to meet specific requirements.

The systems of representation and voting have played a crucial role in the decision-making process of international organizations, especially during periods of acute East–West or North–South confrontation. The basic principle of sovereign equality of all members should naturally lead to the one-country-one-vote procedure that is already enshrined in the constitutions of many organizations. However, in a number of cases, special consideration needs to be given to the different political, economic or financial weight and interests of members in order to ensure some kind of proportional representation. Weighted voting, veto rights and specific majorities are among the modes of decision which may be adopted with a view to balancing general equality against particular powers and responsibilities.

The majority principle is generally now applied in the decision-making process of international organizations, and unanimity is hardly ever prescribed, except in a handful of bodies of limited membership. In most organizations the basic voting rule is currently a simple majority of members, although a qualified majority – usually a two-thirds majority of those present and voting – may be required for important matters. None the less, full reliance on the results of formal voting may occasionally prove unrealistic, especially when a massive numerical majority forces through a resolution whose implementation depends largely on the goodwill and participation of a dissenting minority which happens to comprise some of the most important and influential members. More recent practices tend to avoid voting whenever a recorded vote would dramatically divide an organization or aggravate discord among members. Resolutions are therefore adopted – without taking formal votes – by acclamation, without objection, or by consensus. As a rule – and with the exception of supranational organizations – resolutions, recommendations, declarations and decisions are not legally binding upon members. Decisions in the substantive meaning of the term usually may be taken only with regard to the internal affairs of an organization.

It is generally held that international organizations enjoy some measure of international personality and are endowed with such treaty-making power as is necessary for the full performance of their functions. A fairly wide power has been expressly conferred upon the policy-making organs of certain organizations. Besides treaties concluded with both member and non-member countries, relationship and co-ordination agreements with other international organizations (in order, *inter alia*, to avoid unsound competition and duplication of efforts) may assume special relevance.

With a view to enabling them to fulfil their purposes and to exercise their functions in an impartial, independent and efficient manner, international organizations are ordinarily granted various privileges and immunities, such as inviolability of premises and archives; immunity from jurisdiction; freedom from direct taxes and customs duties; freedom of official communications; and special privileges and immunities for representatives of member countries and officials of the organization. These matters are dealt with in detail by separate agreements which supplement the general provisions contained in basic constitutional texts. Because of their functional basis, privileges and immunities are subject to waiver whenever the interests of an organization are not

prejudiced. Questions concerning the status of the headquarters or other offices of an organization are regulated by bilateral agreements with the host country. The location of the headquarters of an organization is normally fixed by the constitution, although on occasion the matter is left undecided for further consideration by members.

As regards budgetary questions, the estimates of future expenditure of an organization are generally prepared by the executive head of the secretariat and submitted for review and approval – either directly or through the executive organ – to the plenary policy-making body. The budget consists of the administrative costs of running the organization (salaries of staff and costs of the various services) plus the expenses incurred as a result of activities undertaken to implement decisions taken by the organization. As a rule, the total amount is apportioned among members on the basis of percentage quotas graduated according to specific criteria such as national income or population. Not all expenses are necessarily borne by members, since international organizations may derive an income from sources such as sales or investments. It should also be noted that certain activities may be financed as extra-budgetary programmes supported by voluntary contributions made by members, in addition to normal budgetary commitments.

The eventual dissolution of an international organization and the liquidation of its assets and affairs may be expressly regulated in the constituent instrument. This is generally the case for organizations of a transitional nature or created for a limited period, as well as for financial bodies. It is generally admitted that, even in the absence of any specific provision concerning dissolution, members of an organization are endowed with the implied power to dissolve it. Succession – which is not necessarily associated with dissolution – takes place when the functions, rights and duties of an organization are transferred wholly or partly to another existing or new organization. In a number of cases, the personality of the predecessor continues in the successor.

The Origin and Early Developments of Multilateral Institutions

In the course of history, the inadequacy of the traditional techniques of bilateral diplomacy to solve major problems involving the interests of more than two countries became evident as a result of the steady development of a complex web of relations between different peoples and between their rulers. From this state of affairs originated the international conference – that is, the gathering of representatives from several countries to discuss and negotiate the settlement of common problems, normally through the conclusion of a multilateral treaty creating legal obligations for the contracting parties. The great post-war settlements of modern history – from the Peace of Westphalia (1648) and the Final Act of the Congress of Vienna (June 1815) to the Peace Treaties concluded after the First World War at Versailles, St Germain, Neuilly (1919), and Trianon (1920) – emanated from international conferences.

After the Napoleonic Wars, the creation in 1815 of a new balance of power system between the five great powers ('pentarchy') – Austria, Britain, France, Prussia and Russia – represented a major effort to secure international peace and stability within a multilateral framework. Through the Holy Alliance, concluded in Paris in September 1815, the monarchs of Austria, Prussia and Russia (subsequently joined by other European rulers), committed themselves to govern their subjects 'as fathers of families' according to Christian principles, and to practice solidarity in foreign affairs, holding consultations and regular meetings ('congress system'), in order to safeguard the settlement of Vienna. Although regular congresses were convened only four times (between 1818 and 1822), and European solidarity was weakened by the formation of a 'liberal' bloc (Britain and France) opposed to a 'conservative' bloc (Austria, Prussia and Russia), the 'Concert of Europe' succeeded in surviving recurring tensions between its partners and remained in operation until the outbreak of the First World War.

The change from *ad hoc* to standing international conferences constituted another landmark in the development of international organization. From the 1850s, administrative international institutions, at both intergovernmental and nongovernmental level, began to grow at a remarkably rapid pace. Hundreds of private international associations or unions were formed during the second half of the nineteenth century and their spread to cover a wide variety of fields paved the way to the establishment of a number of intergovernmental organizations. Of special relevance was the foundation in 1863 in Geneva, where it still has its headquarters, of the *International Committee of the Red Cross (ICRC), a private institution acting as a neutral intermediary in humanitarian matters during international conflicts, civil wars and other internal disturbances.

The European Commission for the Danube (1856) was endowed with important administrative and legislative functions far wider than those entrusted to similar bodies responsible for other European rivers, such as the *Central Commission for the Navigation of the Rhine (1815). Several institutions were charged with co-ordination of the activities of national administrations and/or the performance of supplementary liaison, information and consultation tasks including: the Geodetic Union (1864); the International Telegraph Union (1865), later renamed *International Telecommunication Union (ITU); the International Meteorological Organization (1873); the General Postal Union (1874), later renamed *Universal Postal Union (UPU); the Metric Union (1875); the International Copyright Union (1886); the Central Office for International Railway Transport (1890); and the United International Bureau for the Protection of Intellectual Property (1893). Besides culture, sciences, transport and communications, intergovernmental co-operation gradually extended to other vital areas at the very beginning of the twentieth century: suffice it to mention the International Office of Public Health, established in 1903, and the International Institute of Agriculture, founded in 1905, which may be viewed as the forerunners of the *World Health Organization (WHO) and the *Food and Agriculture Organization (FAO) respectively.

The League of Nations was created in 1919 to promote international co-operation and to achieve world peace and security by ensuring the respect 'for all treaty obligations in the dealings of organized peoples with one another'. In principle it presented a unique opportunity to co-ordinate on a multilateral scale the activities of specialized unions and associations under the supervision of the League itself.

The League Covenant expressly provided that 'there shall be placed under the direction of the League all international bureaux already established by general treaties if the parties to such treaties consent'. Moreover, 'all such international bureaux and all commissions for the regulation of matters of international interest hereafter constituted shall be placed under the direction of the League'. For a number of reasons, the international bodies that were actually placed under the League's direction were comparatively few – only six, in fact, including the International Commission for Air Navigation (ICAN) and the International Hydrographic Bureau. Close co-ordination links existed with the *International Labour Organization (ILO), whose original constitution formed part of the Peace Treaties of 1919 and 1920, and whose connection with the League lasted until the mid-1940s.

The League never attained a truly universal character, its membership being confined mainly to Europe and gravely prejudiced by the non-participation of the USA, but its political failure should not lead to underestimating the importance of its undertakings in several non-political fields, and its overall contribution to the development of international organization as one of the salient features of interstate relations in the twentieth century. The steadily deteriorating political climate of the period after the First World War, and major crises in international economic and social affairs substantially reduced the opportunities and prospects for fruitful multilateral collaboration within institutionalized frameworks.

The need to alleviate human sufferings throughout the world, complementing the activities of the ICRC, led a number of national Red Cross societies to establish in 1919, in Paris, the League of Red Cross Societies, a non-governmental agency destined to become the forerunner of the *International Federation of Red Cross and Red Crescent Societies.

The gradual extension of government intervention to nearly all aspects of economic life and the need to protect and insulate national economies plagued by depression, especially in the late 1920s and early 1930s, led to extreme forms of economic nationalism and to the consolidation of major trends away from the basic principles of economic liberalism, such as the introduction of severe measures hampering the international circulation of goods, capital and manpower, the abandonment of the gold standard and the continued manipulation of exchange rates. The World Economic Conferences, held in 1927 and 1933 under the auspices of the League and with the participation of the USA, could not prevent the disintegration of the world economy by the out-

break of the Second World War. The foundation of the *Bank for International Settlements (BIS) in 1930 – with a view to solving, inter alia, the German reparations problem – may be regarded as one of the few notable achievements of international organization in the inter-war period. Another significant event was the adoption in 1931 of the Statute of Westminster, which is the basic charter of the modern Commonwealth.

The Flourishing of Global and Regional Co-operation in the Post-1945 World

The firm commitment of the Allies to reorganize the whole network of international relations in the post-war world on the basis of friendship, co-operation and equal opportunities for all nations was clearly expressed from the early 1940s, well before the end of the Second World War. The principles of the Atlantic Charter of August 1941 and the Joint Declaration of the United Nations at war (that is, the Allies fighting against the Axis Powers) of January 1942 were subsequently confirmed and supplemented in solemn declarations and treaties of the parties concerned.

As early as November 1943, the representatives of the 44 United Nations at war signed the Agreement establishing the United Nations Relief and Rehabilitation Administration (UNRRA) to provide assistance to the areas liberated from German domination. In May and June 1943, the United Nations Conference on Food and Agriculture, held at Hot Springs, Virginia, set up an Interim Commission charged with the responsibility of drawing up the constitution of the FAO. The creation of the *International Monetary Fund (IMF) and the *International Bank for Reconstruction and Development (IBRD) was the outcome of another major United Nations Conference, devoted to monetary and financial problems, summoned at Bretton Woods, New Hampshire, in July 1944. The *International Civil Aviation Organization (ICAO) was established under a Convention on International Civil Aviation concluded in Chicago in December 1944.

During that period, the features of the global institution to succeed the League of Nations were discussed and subsequently worked out in detail at Dumbarton Oaks, Yalta and San Francisco. At the San Francisco Conference held between April and June 1945, representatives from 50 countries eventually decided on the structure and mechanisms of the *United Nations (UN). The Security Council was entrusted with primary responsibility for the maintenance of international peace and security, while the Economic and Social Council, acting under the authority of the General Assembly, was to promote, assist and co-ordinate co-operation in the economic and social fields. The basic goal of a truly comprehensive and lasting peace had to be pursued in all its dimensions – political, economic, social, cultural and humanitarian. With a view to decentralizing the economic and social activities of the UN and making them more responsive to specific needs emerging at regional level, the following UN regional commissions were created between 1947 and 1974 and are currently in operation: the *Economic Commission for Europe (ECE); the *Economic Commission for Latin America and the Caribbean (ECLAC); the *Economic Commission for Africa (ECA); the *Economic and Social Commission for Asia and the Pacific (ESCAP); the *Economic and Social Commission for Western Asia (ESCWA). The latter two bodies replaced the Economic Commission for Asia and the Far East (ECAFE).

Functional international co-operation was to play a prominent role within the newly-created institutional framework through the Economic and Social Council. Specialized organizations, established by intergovernmental agreements and having wide international responsibilities in economic, social, cultural, educational, health and related fields had to be brought into relationship with the UN which would recognize them as its 'specialized agencies'. In addition to the FAO, IMF, IBRD and ICAO, other important specialized bodies were set up in the second half of the 1940s and entered into relationship agreements, following a similar general pattern, with the UN: the *UN Educational, Scientific and Cultural Organization (UNESCO); the WHO; the *World Meteorological Organization (WMO); the Intergovernmental Maritime Consultative Organization (IMCO) later renamed *International Maritime Organization (IMO). Similar agreements were also concluded by the UN with older international institutions, such as the UPU and ILO. In order to supplement the lending operations of IBRD and to meet a wider range of needs, with special regard to the developing countries, two more agencies

were set up: the *International Finance Corporation (IFC), in 1956, and the *International Development Association (IDA), in 1960. Together with the IBRD, these two institutions form the World Bank Group to which the *Multilateral Investment Guarantee Agency (MIGA) has been added in 1988. Another specialized institution with special status with the UN is the *International Atomic Energy Agency (IAEA), established in 1956 as a result of an International Conference on the Peaceful Uses of Atomic Energy.

While the basic principles of post-war monetary and financial co-operation were eventually embodied in the Bretton Woods Agreements on the establishment of the IMF and IBRD, the UN-sponsored plans to set the broad outlines for dealing with international trade issues failed to materialize and the creation of an agency especially responsible for trade matters proved impossible. The Havana Charter of 1948 – intended to serve as the constitution of the abortive International Trade Organization (ITO) – was never ratified by the signatory countries and an interim convention, the General Agreement on Tariffs and Trade (GATT), was virtually assigned the heavy task of promoting the gradual abolition of tariff and non-tariff barriers and improving the practices and mechanisms of international commercial relations through multilateral negotiations.

The Allies' comprehensive attempt to deal effectively with the vast economic, financial and social problems of the post-war era was largely based on the ideals and principles of economic liberalism rooted in an international structure that had long since ceased to exist. Failure to recognize the full impact of the shift from 'market economies' to 'command economies', and of the underlying forces which were to bring about dramatic changes in the pattern of international relations and the corresponding rules of the game (such as the formation in Eastern Europe of a group of countries within the Soviet sphere of influence and the emergence of scores of assertive developing nations) prevented a more far-sighted approach to the problems of the post-1945 world.

The overall commitment to universality and to an open international trade and monetary system was not seen as an obstacle to the conclusion of arrangements on a regional scale. The nations of the European continent appeared particularly well-suited to that end, once recovery from the devastation caused by the Second World War had been achieved. The launching in 1947 of the Marshall Plan, open to any country 'willing to assist in the task of recovery', followed by the establishment in 1948 of the Organization for European Economic Co-operation (OEEC), may be regarded as a turning point in the reconstruction process of the Western half of Europe. On the Eastern side, the creation in 1949 of the Council for Mutual Economic Assistance (CMEA; Comecon) represented the Soviet riposte to the Marshall Plan. The *Danube Commission was set up in 1949 to govern navigation on the river in its various aspects. On a broad political plane, the appeal of European unity stimulated the creation of the *Council of Europe which, according to the Statute signed in 1949, was intended to safeguard the common heritage as well as to facilitate the economic and social progress of the member countries. In 1952 Scandinavian countries established the *Nordic Council, an organ for consultation between national parliaments and governments.

The rapprochement of wartime enemies in continental Europe found a most significant expression in the signature, in 1951, of the Treaty setting up the earliest of the European Communities, the *European Coal and Steel Community (ECSC), by the representatives of the 'Six' – that is, France, the Federal Republic of Germany, Italy, and the Benelux countries. The Treaties of Rome establishing the *European Economic Community (EEC) and the *European Atomic Energy Community (Euratom) completed in 1957 the institutional framework for economic co-operation between the 'Six'. Following a British initiative, other European countries (the 'Seven') that were not prepared to accept the far-reaching political and economic objectives of the 'Six' founded, in 1960, the *European Free Trade Association (EFTA), largely conceived as an interim counterpart to the European Communities.

In 1960, the OEEC, which had virtually fulfilled its basic task of assisting in the reconstruction of Western Europe, was succeeded by the *Organization for Economic Co-operation and Development (OECD). The OECD had a larger membership than its predecessor, notably with the participation of Canada and the USA as full members, and broader aims, such as the achievement of the highest sustainable growth and the promotion of sound economic expansion in member as well as non-member countries in the process of economic development.

On the defence side, as a response to growing Cold War tensions, the North Atlantic Treaty, signed in 1949 by the representatives of Canada, the USA, and ten European nations, provided for mutual assistance should any one contracting party be attacked. In fact, the *North Atlantic Treaty Organization (NATO) appeared far more adequate from the standpoint of regional security than the Brussels Treaty Organization, established in 1948 by the Benelux countries, France and the UK. In 1954, following the rejection by the French National Assembly of the 1952 Treaty on the European Defence Community (EDC), a number of protocols were signed in order to transform the Brussels Treaty Organization into the *Western European Union (WEU), with the inclusion of the Federal Republic of Germany and Italy as full members.

Exports of strategic goods and technology that would contribute significantly to the military potential of socialist countries were to be kept under close control by the Co-ordinating Committee for Multilateral Export Controls (Cocom) established by the USA and its NATO partners in 1949.

The participation of the Federal Republic of Germany in the Western security system and the need to supplement bilateral military treaties prompted the USSR and its Eastern European allies to establish a joint military command under the Warsaw Pact of 1955, which obliged contracting parties to assist each other to meet any armed attack on one or more of them in Europe.

International co-operation on a regional or subregional scale also materialized outside Europe. In this connection, the Western Hemisphere offered several examples of varying kinds and levels of co-operation. The foundation of the *Organization of American States (OAS) in 1948 represented a milestone in the gradual development of pan-American policies involving all independent countries of the continent, with the exception of Canada. Three years later, a subregional agency, the Organization of Central American States (ODECA), was set up by five nations of the area.

The achievements of the European Communities induced Latin American countries to concentrate their co-operation efforts on trade and financial issues. As a result, the *Central American Common Market (CACM) and the Latin American Free Trade Association (LAFTA) were formed in 1960 to establish, by stages, subregional or regional 'common markets'. Development financing problems were to be dealt with on a continental scale by the *Inter-American Development Bank (IDB), set up in 1959 with the inclusion of the USA as a full member, and on a subregional scale by the *Central American Bank for Economic Integration (CABEI), established in 1960. Regarding the Caribbean specifically, an agreement establishing a subregional institution, the Caribbean Organization, was signed in 1960. To deal with the often serious liquidity problems of a number of debtor countries, mostly Latin American, the *Paris Club was set up in 1956 as an informal forum where developing countries unable to meet their official debt servicing obligations could negotiate a settlement with industrial creditor countries.

In 1945, representatives of independent Arab countries signed the Pact of the *League of Arab States (Arab League), an important though institutionally loose association favouring political and economic unity among member countries and promoting the adoption of common policies vis-à-vis non-member countries, notably on Middle Eastern issues. Another body, the Central Treaty Organization (CENTO), developed in 1955 out of the 'Baghdad Pact' between Iraq and Turkey, and was subsequently enlarged to include Iran, Pakistan, and the UK. Co-operation on military and political questions was expressly envisaged, without involving any mandatory form of mutual assistance. With a view to developing mutual economic links, the Regional Co-operation for Development (RCD) was established by Iran, Pakistan and Turkey in 1964.

In the Asian and Pacific region, various intergovernmental organizations had come into being from the early 1950s, especially in the fields of collective self-defence, economic co-operation and development assistance. The Security Treaty concluded in 1951 between Australia, New Zealand and the USA, generally known as the *ANZUS Pact, was intended to ensure mutual assistance should any signatory country be the victim of 'an armed attack in the Pacific area'. A more far-reaching collective security pact was signed in 1954 with a view to defending non-member countries in Indo-China and providing for the establishment of the South East Asia Treaty Organization (SEATO).

A very loose association for broad consultation on economic and social matters, the *South Pacific Commission (SPC), was founded in 1947 by six countries with dependent territories in the area. The *Colombo Plan for Co-operative Economic Development in South and South East Asia was launched in 1951 in order to provide capital and technical training to Asian countries closely associated with the UK. Both the membership and scope of the Colombo Plan were subsequently enlarged to include donor and recipient countries outside the Commonwealth.

The decolonization of Africa reached its climax in 1960 but the association of the newly-independent African countries with different and often rival political groups delayed the constitution of a truly pan-African institution – the *Organization of African Unity (OAU) – until 1963. The new regional institution was endowed with wide competence, despite its relatively weak institutional mechanism.

The foundations for a far-reaching change in the international political setting were laid in April 1955, when the leaders of 29 nations from the African and Asian continents meeting in Bandung, Indonesia, condemned colonialism, racial discrimination and atomic weapons, and refused to be politically or militarily associated with either the West or the Soviet bloc, thereby emerging as a third force in world affairs. The formal adoption of a 'non-aligned' attitude towards the Cold War confrontation between East and West was the outcome of the first Conference of the *Non-Aligned Movement (NAM) held in September 1961 in Belgrade, notwithstanding differences between moderate and anti-Western states. The 25 countries (mainly Afro-Asian) participating in the Belgrade summit meeting were shortly to be joined by Latin American countries, an event of the highest significance for the future of North–South relations.

Another significant event at the level of intergovernmental co-operation took place in 1960 when a group of oil exporting countries set up a cartel to regulate production and pricing of oil in the world market – the *Organization of the

Petroleum Exporting Countries (OPEC), destined to play a leading role in the 1970s.

The North–South Confrontation and the Challenges of Economic Development

The political and economic events from the early 1960s to the end of the decade emphasized the need for a fresh approach to some basic problems of international organization, either by adapting existing institutions or by establishing further bodies in order to respond effectively to new situations, especially in the developing world. The UN itself had to change greatly – not only because of the dramatic increase in membership – in order to meet many pressing needs through the improvement of 'special help' activities for children, refugees and disaster victims, and to respond to a variety of problems through initiatives ranging from promotion of a new international economic order to the encouragement of sound environmental practices, campaigns against the remnants of colonialism and apartheid, and the negotiation of treaties and other agreements on matters of global concern, such as the seas and outer space. A new specialized agency, the *World Intellectual Property Organization (WIPO), entered into relationship with the UN. The co-operative efforts of the UN and related agencies in the economic and social sphere were expanded and streamlined, priority being given to problems having a direct bearing on the conditions of the poorest segments of society within the framework of the UN Development Decades.

The special problems of trade in relation to development were entrusted to the *UN Conference on Trade and Development (UNCTAD), established in 1964 as a permanent organ of the UN General Assembly. Growing emphasis on direct field activities led to the creation in 1965 of the *UN Development Programme (UNDP) as the world's largest channel for multilateral technical and pre-investment co-operation. The *UN Industrial Development Organization (UNIDO) was set up in 1966 to foster and accelerate the industrial development of developing countries. With respect to food problems, the *World Food Programme (WFP) was founded in 1963, under the joint sponsorship of the UN and FAO, with a view to providing aid in the form of food. Financial resources for technical co-operation activities in the population field were provided through the UN Fund for Population Activities (UNFPA), created in 1967 and later renamed the *UN Population Fund but keeping the old acronym. For their part, the specialized agencies in relation with the UN were increasingly focusing on the promotion of sustained growth over the long term, with special regard to the needs of the poorer countries.

On the other hand, expenditure on arms and armies continued to grow throughout the world, consuming huge material and human resources that might have been employed for development purposes. In 1969, in an effort to slow and reverse the arms race, the UN General Assembly proclaimed the 1970s as a Disarmament Decade but little or no progress was actually made, despite a number of international agreements for the limitation and regulation of armaments.

The growing solidarity between developing countries and the ensuing pursuit of a unified approach to North–South issues represented one of the most significant features of international relations to emerge in the 1960s.

The cohesion of developing nations acquired a concrete operational meaning through the consultation and co-ordination procedures carried out within the NAM with regard to broad political issues and within the *Group of 77 (G-77) – which was founded at the time of the first session of UNCTAD in 1964 and took its name from the number of signatories to a declaration of common aims – with regard to economic issues and multilateral negotiations. In fact, owing to the relatively high degree of overlap in membership, it became possible for the two groups to establish an original form of 'division of labour' in advancing development goals.

One of the earliest successes for developing countries was the establishment of the Generalized System of Preferences (GSP). After negotiation on the principles of the GSP between 1968 and 1970 within the UNCTAD framework, national preference schemes were put into operation by virtually all developed countries in order to help developing countries to expand their exports of manufactured goods.

Co-operation at the regional and subregional level made significant progress in the 1960s in a relatively favourable international setting characterized by fairly high rates of growth of income in developed market-economy countries, and of world trade coupled with a reduction in international tension gradually leading to East–West *détente*.

In Western Europe, the EEC experiment progressed swiftly, achieving, *inter alia*, a customs union and free movement of workers between the 'Six', and developing step by step the essentials of the highly controversial Common Agricultural Policy (CAP). Within the CMEA area, efforts to improve monetary and financial relations eventually materialized in the foundation of the International Bank for Economic Co-operation (IBEC) in 1963, and the International Investment Bank (IIB) in 1970.

In Latin America, an important step was made in 1967 by the signing of the Treaty of Tlatelolco which prohibited nuclear weapons in the region and established *OPANAL as an Agency responsible for ensuring compliance with the obligations arising from the Treaty itself. Besides creating the first nuclear-weapon-free zone in a densely-populated area, the Treaty was the first arms control agreement whose implementation had to be verified by an international organization. On the plane of economic integration, LAFTA's failure to establish a common market on the European model induced Andean countries to form a subregional group of their own in 1969, the Andean Group based on the Cartagena Agreement. A limited but promising form of co-operation was inaugurated by the River Plate Basin Treaty, signed in 1969 and aiming to develop physical integration between countries drained by the River Plate and its tributaries.

After the dissolution of the Caribbean Organization in 1965, a Caribbean Free Trade Association (CARIFTA), following the patterns of LAFTA and EFTA, was set up in 1968. An autonomous financial body, the *Caribbean Development Bank (CDB; Caribank), was established in the following year.

In Africa, widespread dissatisfaction with the course followed by OAU in handling highly-sensitive issues such as the Congo crisis prompted a group of French-speaking African countries to form in 1965 the African and Malagasy Common Organization (OCAM) as an agency for promoting economic, social, technical and cultural development. Given the fact that small subregional groupings seemed to offer far more favourable prospects for co-operation in the economic and

financial sphere, a number of intergovernmental organizations were founded, such as the Maghreb Permanent Consultative Committee, the Customs Union of West African States (UDEAO), the Customs and Economic Union of Central Africa (UDEAC) and the short-lived Economic Community of East Africa. On a continental scale, the *African Development Bank (AfDB) was established in 1963 and entrusted with the task of dealing with development financing problems.

In the Asian and Pacific region, a significant achievement was the establishment in 1967 of the *Association of South East Asian Nations (ASEAN) to encourage subregional co-ordination and co-operation in economic, social and cultural matters and to ensure political stability. In 1965 the *Asian Development Bank (AsDB) had been created to serve as the region's development financing body.

Institutional Responses to the Economic, Monetary and Energy Crises of the 1970s

The monetary events of 1971 – the suspension of the convertibility of the dollar into gold and its subsequent devaluation – represented a turning point in the history of international monetary relations and radically altered the conditions under which the IMF had been operating since its foundation. A system of floating exchange rates gradually emerged, encouraging speculation, increasing economic uncertainty and instability, and seriously threatening the orderly development of world trade. The monetary turmoil was accompanied by rising prices for such essentials as food and fuel, notably oil under OPEC's pressure, and growing burdens of debt and trade imbalances.

The steady progression of the economic crisis had a substantial impact on the growth rates and development programmes of developing countries, with depressed prices for exports of primary commodities (other than oil), soaring prices for imports of manufactured goods, reduced flows of official development assistance (ODA) from industrial countries, high interest rates, limited access to international capital markets, and sharp aggravation of the external debt problem. In the developed countries, renewed protectionist pressures gradually led to the adoption of narrow and generally short-sighted nationalistic policies. Therefore, it became virtually impossible to deal effectively, in an integral and co-ordinated manner, with the vital questions concerning international trade and the global relationship between developing and developed countries.

At the political level, rising international tension in an ambience of escalating super-power antagonism and regional conflicts prepared the crisis of *détente*. In 1976, the meagre achievements of the first Disarmament Decade prompted the UN General Assembly to convene a special session, devoted entirely to the question of disarmament, which was held in 1978.

By the mid-1970s the increased awareness of the structural character of the rigidities and maladjustments of world trade and financial systems led to a drastic reappraisal of development policies and priorities. In the aftermath of the 'oil shock' of 1973, widespread concern that the experience of OPEC might encourage the producers of other commodities to form cartels to improve their terms of trade with the industrialized world contributed to create a new responsiveness on the part of the developed consumer countries. In May 1974, the UN General Assembly held a special session on the problems of raw materials and development and called for the establishment of a 'New International Economic Order', involving a reshaping of the world's trade and financial relations. As a further step, in December of the same year, the General Assembly adopted the Charter of Economic Rights and Duties of States. The Declarations and Action Programmes adopted by members of the G-77 at their pre-UNCTAD Ministerial Meetings presented ideas and proposals with a view to addressing the more difficult and less tractable structural problems related to trade and development.

To face the food crisis situations that had developed in several parts of the world, a major effort was launched within the UN framework. The World Food Conference, held in November 1974, led to the creation of the World Food Council (WFC) in December of the same year, to co-ordinate policies and activities affecting the world food situation, and of the *International Fund for Agricultural Development (IFAD), in June 1976, to mobilize additional financial resources to help developing countries improve their food production and nutrition. The *UN Centre for Human Settlements (UNCHS) – Habitat – was set up by the General Assembly in 1978 to serve as a focal point for reviewing and co-ordinating human settlements activities.

On the institutional plane, a co-ordinated response to the first big escalation in oil prices was launched by most of the West's oil-importing countries in 1974 through the creation of the *International Energy Agency (IEA), aimed at promoting stability in world energy markets as well as security of supplies. To discuss the economic crisis caused by the oil-price shock, the heads of state and government of the six largest industrial democracies (France, Germany, Italy, Japan, the UK and the USA) met at Rambouillet, France, in November 1975. In the following summit, held in June 1976 in Puerto Rico, the Prime Minister of Canada also took part and the *Group of Seven (G-7) officially came into being.

On the pan-European scale, a breakthrough in the process of *détente* was achieved by the signing, in August 1975 in Helsinki, of the Final Act of the Conference on Security and Co-operation in Europe (CSCE) with the participation of 33 European countries, the USA and Canada. Not only did the Conference sanction the political and territorial status quo in Europe, fulfilling a longstanding Soviet aspiration, but also introduced in the East–West relationship a human rights dimension whose practical impact far exceeded Western expectations.

As regards West European co-operation, an event of paramount importance was the accession as full members to the European Communities of Denmark, Ireland and the UK in January 1973.

The *Latin American Economic System (SELA) was set up in 1975 to advance mutual trade and co-operation, while respecting and supporting pre-existing arrangements, and to co-ordinate members' policies *vis-à-vis* non-member countries and international organizations. At the subregional level, the *Amazon Co-operation Treaty (Amazon Pact), concluded in July 1978, provided a multilateral framework for promoting the harmonious socioeconomic development of the respective Amazon territories of the member countries. Other forms of co-operation emerged in specific sectors, such as the *Latin American Energy Organization (OLADE), created in 1973. In the Caribbean, a new body endowed with broader competences and having wider aims –

the *Caribbean Community and Common Market (CARICOM) – replaced CARIFTA in 1973.

In Africa, reorganization efforts resulted in the foundation in 1973 of the West African Economic Community (CEAO), replacing UDEAO, and in 1975 in the establishment of the *Economic Community of West African States (ECOWAS). An *Economic Community of the Great Lakes Countries (CEPGL) was formed in 1976. The first Southern African Development Co-ordination Conference (SADCC) was held in 1979 and laid the foundations for closer co-operation among majority-ruled states in the subregion.

Arab oil-exporting countries decided to use part of their revenue to help developing nations to face the impact of oil price rises by channelling substantial resources for the implementation of infrastructural, industrial and agricultural projects through financial institutions and development agencies: the *Arab Bank for Economic Development in Africa (BADEA), created in 1974, and the Arab Fund for Economic and Social Development (AFESD), which began operations in 1973, were among the most important bodies in the field.

A large body with general competence, the *Organization of the Islamic Conference (OIC), embracing the overwhelming majority of Islamic countries, was set up in 1971 to encourage effective solidarity and mutual assistance in all vital fields.

The South Pacific Bureau for Economic Co-operation (SPEC) was formed in 1973 to promote regional co-operation for development, following a recommendation by the *South Pacific Forum (SPF) created in 1971. On the regional defence side, in 1975 altered conditions prompted the remaining member countries to decide to phase out SEATO, which could no longer fulfil its collective security function in South East Asia.

The Weakening of Multilateralism and the New Generation of Global Problems

With the aggravation and deepening of the world economic crisis, several unfavourable developments emerged in the late 1970s and early 1980s. A steadily deteriorating political environment and the commitment of massive resources to armaments of unparalleled destructive capability compounded the economic difficulties manifested in the sluggish growth of developed and developing countries alike, high unemployment, and the widespread resurgence of inflation. In the developed countries, increasing demands for government intervention to protect specific sectors from external competition and to subsidize ailing industries led to the introduction of new trade barriers and extensive use of quotas and 'voluntary' export restraints. The dangerous weakening of the fabric of multilateralism and of the corresponding institutional system adversely affected negotiating processes in virtually every international forum.

The beginnings of an economic recovery from the international recession of the early 1980s first became noticeable in the USA. The accelerated pace of American economic activity in 1983, sustained by rapid expansion of domestic demand, laid a sound basis for stronger output growth and slower inflation rates in other Western countries. By the mid-1980s, although the overall rate of expansion had become less rapid, the recovery was spreading increasingly if unevenly to the developing countries, with beneficial effects on both the external position and domestic economic growth. The predominant themes of international debate revolved around the arms race, world trade and financial flows, and the external debt of developing countries. The Paris Club, although initially slow to respond to the debt crisis, eventually agreed on new 'terms' for official debt reduction, taking into account the special needs of low-income countries.

The fortieth anniversary of the UN in 1985 seemed to offer one more occasion to analyse the complex interrelationships of key policy issues which, although viewed from different perspectives by various countries and groups of countries, were of universal concern. Grave questions were raised about the value of the UN system and the general effectiveness of multilateral co-operation – making all the more arduous the search for a co-ordinated response to the new generation of global problems, in relation to both world peace and the world economy. In 1983 the interrelationship of trade, finance, payments and development, in an international context of sharpened interdependence, was once more emphasized both in the Message for Dialogue and Consensus adopted by the G-77 (including 127 members) in Buenos Aires and in the New Delhi Message and the Economic Declaration of the

Heads of State and Government of NAM countries (numbering 101).

On a global plane, noting the crucial importance of continuing efforts to achieve general and complete disarmament under effective international control, the UN General Assembly, meeting in 1980, declared the 1980s as the Second Disarmament Decade and decided to hold the Second Special Session on Disarmament in 1982. However, it did not prove possible to reach agreement on any specific course of action designed to halt and reverse the arms race throughout the world.

In 1980 the General Assembly adopted the International Development Strategy for the Third Development Decade, setting out general goals and objectives and a series of policy measures. Despite a general perception of the crucial links between commodities and the development process and the adoption in 1976 of the ambitious Integrated Programme for Commodities (IPC), primary commodity markets continued to be volatile, showing a marked increase in certain cases. The need to provide special help for the particularly disadvantaged developing countries (the least developed, land-locked and island countries) led to the convening in Paris in 1981 of the Conference on the Least Developed Countries. The Substantial New Programme of Action (SNPA) for the 1980s, calling for considerable expansion of financial and technical assistance, was approved.

In 1985 the launching of a new GATT round of multilateral trade negotiations appeared to open up prospects of curbing protectionist tendencies and strengthening the trading system. In this context the *Cairns Group was formed in 1986 by 14 countries, developed as well as developing, to bring about reforms in international agricultural trade and to represent members' interests in GATT negotiations.

On the financial side, increased flows of concessional assistance were of the utmost priority to low-income countries, particularly in sub-Saharan Africa. A broad consensus emerged on the need to expand the World Bank's lending programme, with a view to meeting more adequately the demands of borrowing member countries and providing further impulses for generating capital flows from other sources. Substantial financial assistance was provided by the IMF to countries undertaking adjustment programmes, while developed countries were encouraged to enlarge their ODA contributions. The IMF experienced an unprecedented net use of its resources, but by the mid-1980s net drawings began to subside, partly because of an improvement in the payments positions of the developing countries.

Within the UN system, a significant event took place in 1985, when UNIDO eventually became a specialized agency. The long-term trend towards an increase in membership of UN specialized agencies was confirmed in the first half of the 1980s by the admission of several countries. However, unfortunate developments took place in UNESCO, with the withdrawals of the USA, the UK and Singapore.

At regional and subregional level, a number of significant events took place. In Western Europe, the enlargement process of the European Communities continued: Greece became the tenth member of the Communities in January 1981, followed by Portugal and Spain in January 1986.

In Latin America, plans originally aimed at reorganizing LAFTA's mechanism eventually resulted in the creation in 1980 of a new region-wide institution, the *Latin American Integration Association (LAIA), based on a tariff preference and regional and partial scope agreements. In Central America, political and social conflicts, complicated by the economic recession, adversely affected attempts to revive the integration process. In the Caribbean, seven small island countries set up the *Organization of Eastern Caribbean States (OECS) in 1981 to foster economic co-operation and to defend their territorial integrity and independence. The new body was to play a role in the American intervention in Grenada in October 1983.

In the face of growing threats to regional stability, in 1981 the Arab oil-producing countries on the western side of the Gulf created the *Gulf Co-operation Council (GCC) to strengthen mutual political and economic solidarity.

In Africa, two new bodies were formed in the early 1980s: the *Economic Community of Central African States (CEEAC) aiming to foster economic and financial integration; and the Preferential Trade Area for Eastern and Southern Africa (PTA), with the prospect of establishing an Economic Community within the region. In West Africa, little of substance was achieved after the establishment of ECOWAS.

In early 1985, the remaining members of OCAM decided on the dissolution of the organization.

A new organization with wide political and economic objectives was founded by India, Pakistan and five other countries at the end of 1985: the *South Asian Association for Regional Co-operation (SAARC), the first significant experience in a region that had no institutional machinery of its own to promote full-scale co-operation.

In the Pacific, the ANZUS crisis, arising from the sharply diverging views of the USA and New Zealand on the use of nuclear warships, deeply affected the operation of the security pact. In order to foster a mutually beneficial expansion of free trade between them, Australia and New Zealand concluded in 1983 the Australia–New Zealand Closer Economic Relations Trade Agreement (ANZCERTA or CER). The arrangement, despite its bilateral nature, may be viewed as a stepping stone to greater trade liberalization vis-à-vis non-member countries in the wider Asia-Pacific region and beyond.

The Post-Cold-War Era and its Challenges for Old and New International Organizations

The almost abrupt return to the realities of a multi-polar world initiated in 1989 altered deep-rooted patterns that had inspired the theory and practice of international organizations for several decades. In the early years of the post-Cold-War era, the UN seemed bound to assume, for the first time in history, the role for which it was originally conceived, fostering genuine co-operation in an increasingly interdependent world sharing the same fundamental values. The streamlining of the UN Secretariat, undertaken in 1992 by the newly-appointed Secretary-General, appeared to many as the first and encouraging sign of a wholly new period in the life of the world Organization. However, the transformation has turned out to be, against the initial expectations, a lengthy and painful process. The commemoration of the fiftieth anniversary of the UN in 1995 took place amid recurrent calls for reform, notably of the Security Council, and grave financial difficulties, despite the widespread awareness of the need for a world body to face threats and disasters that defy the powers of individual countries.

Among major UN conferences and meetings, mention may be made of the 1990 World Summit for Children held in New York, the Second (1990) Conference on the Least Developed Countries in Paris, the 1992 Conference on Environment and Development (UNCED) in Rio de Janeiro, the 1993 World Conference on Human Rights in Vienna, the 1994 International Conference on Population and Development in Cairo, the 1995 World Summit for Social Development in Copenhagen, the 1995 World Conference on Women in Beijing and the 1996 Conference on Human Settlements in Istanbul.

In 1995, the International Sea-Bed Authority – established under the UN Convention on the Law of the Sea (UNCLOS) signed in December 1982 and coming into force in November 1994 – charged with overseeing all exploring and exploiting activities in the international seabed area was established in Kingston, Jamaica. The International Tribunal on the Law of the Sea and the Commission on the Continental Shelf, also provided for by UNCLOS, began operating in 1996. The decision reached at the UN to extend indefinitely the Treaty on the Non-Proliferation of Nuclear Weapons has represented a major step, followed by the adoption by the General Assembly, in September 1996, of a Comprehensive Nuclear-Test-Ban Treaty. A form of 'economic realignment' spread rapidly from the former socialist countries of Europe to Africa, Asia and Latin America, demanding appropriate policy responses from the whole UN system and especially from international financial institutions. The IMF and the World Bank became, in an incredibly short period of time, the truly universal institutions envisioned by their founders and had to face new tasks calling into question their traditional role. Support was provided to the programme of debt and debt-service reduction; besides the settlement of official debt within the framework of the Paris Club, both the World Bank and the IMF were actively involved in the negotiation of packages between debtors and commercial banks. One major challenge facing the Bretton Woods institutions was, and still is, the daunting task of helping the Central and Eastern European countries as well as the republics of the erstwhile USSR make the massive changes in their institutional and regulatory framework that are necessary to establish open market-based economies in a relatively short time. The transition to a market-orientated system has proved far from easy and dramatic drops in living standards have been encountered in a number of countries.

Integration into the world economy and its institutions has been pursued by transition countries, especially after the conclusion of the Uruguay Round negotiations in Marrakesh in April 1994 and the establishment in January 1995 of the *World Trade Organization (WTO) as a successor to GATT with wider powers and functions. The Cairns Group, which represented a largely successful pressure group of agricultural exporters during the Uruguay Round negotiations, continues its activities. The restoration of globalism with the creation of WTO may seem to clash with the proliferation throughout the world of regional arrangements for co-operation and integration. The view seems to be widely held, in fact, that regional arrangements cannot become a substitute for a strong multilateral trading system.

The commitment of a growing number of countries to a market economy and a pluralistic democracy has had an impact also on the membership of the OECD which is expanding to include countries in Latin America, and Central and Eastern Europe. The developing countries made their voice heard through the traditional channels of the G-77 and NAM. The latter, despite the end of the era of rigid 'alignments', has continued to meet at regular intervals, changing its previous highly confrontational attitude. A major change of attitude has also characterized the G-77, which continues to be active in international forums.

The Commonwealth further expanded its membership with the entry of Namibia in 1990, and Cameroon and Mozambique in 1995; the entry of Mozambique, a non-English-speaking country, is a special case finding its explanation in that country's close association with neighbouring Commonwealth countries during the anti-apartheid struggle. A lusophone commonwealth was born in July 1996, in Lisbon, with the establishment of the *Community of Portuguese Speaking Countries (CPLP) grouping seven nations determined to strengthen their cultural, political and economic links as well as their influence in international institutions and forums.

On the pan-European and transatlantic level, a newly-strengthened CSCE – renamed since January 1995 the *Organization for Security and Co-operation in Europe (OSCE) – has emerged as a very important body for political and security consultation and co-ordination, including long-term missions in troubled areas and supervision of elections and referendums. The basic foundations for future action had already been defined in the 'Charter of Paris for a New Europe', adopted at the November 1990 CSCE summit in Paris to stress the commitment of all parties to democracy based on human rights and fundamental freedoms and prosperity through economic liberty. The challenges of pan-European co-operation require either new institutions, such as the *European Bank for Reconstruction and Development (EBRD) set up in 1991, or the restructuring of existing agencies from NATO to the Council of Europe, from the European Communities to the WEU. The participation of NATO members and of their former adversaries of the Warsaw Pact in the newly-created North Atlantic Co-operation Council (NACC) is just an example of the radical transformations going on in Europe. The Partnership for Peace (PfP) programme, launched in 1994 and based on the wider political dialogue initiated through NACC, provides for extended military co-operation and joint participation in peace-keeping missions between NATO members and former Warsaw Pact signatories and traditionally 'neutral' countries in Europe. The new-found co-operation patterns between East and West also brought to an end the activities of Cocom, the Paris-based Committee attempting to prevent exports of strategic equipment and technology to communist-dominated countries. Cocom, officially dissolved in March 1994, was succeeded in December 1995 by a new agreement on international arms sales – the *Wassenaar Arrangement – targeted principally at exports of weapons and technologies to 'suspect' or 'rogue' countries in areas of tension throughout the world, notably the Middle East and North Africa.

The Council of Europe is on the way to doubling its membership in a relatively short period of time, with a view to creating an area of democratic security throughout the whole of Europe and strengthening standards in a number of fields, such as the protection of minorities.

In Western Europe, the EC completed the single market by the end of 1992, while the Maastricht Treaty, in force since November 1993, has created the *European Union (EU). The Union is founded on the existing European Communities supplemented by a common foreign and security policy and by co-operation in the fields of justice and home affairs. In January 1995, Austria, Finland and Sweden joined the EU, bringing the total membership to 15. With the entry of most of its founders into the EU, EFTA consists nowadays of only four countries: Iceland, Liechtenstein, Norway and Switzerland. The EU has become a source of attraction and inspiration also for the former members of CMEA, officially dissolved in 1991, along with its military counterpart, the Warsaw Pact.

The WEU, frequently described as the European pillar of NATO, has enlarged the number of its associate members, associate partners and observers. The Maastricht Treaty establishing the EU expressly charges the WEU with the responsibility of elaborating and implementing decisions of the EU itself which have defence implications.

While the 'old' organizations are striving to adapt their objectives and functions to the challenges of a fast-changing European architecture, new subregional organizations, focused on specific areas and with loose institutional frameworks, are being established on the 'periphery' of Europe; suffice it to mention the *Black Sea Economic Co-operation (BSEC) set up in 1992, the *Council of the Baltic Sea States (CBSS), also inaugurated in 1992, and the *Barents Euro-Arctic Council, launched in 1993. In Central Europe, the former 'Visegrad countries' have been joined by neighbouring countries to form the *Central European Free Trade Agreement (CEFTA). For its part, the *Central European Initiative (CEI), whose origins date back to the 'Quadrangolare' established in late 1989 by Austria, Hungary, Italy and the then Yugoslavia, has grown to a remarkable extent embracing around 15 countries of the Adriatic, the Danube and the Baltic.

In the Western Hemisphere, significant events have been taking place in both North and South America. In North America, Canada, the USA and Mexico signed in December 1992 the *North American Free Trade Agreement (NAFTA), which came into force in January 1994 and might eventually embrace countries in Central and South America. The declaration adopted in December 1994 in Miami by the Summit of the Americas called for negotiations 'to construct the Free Trade Area of the Americas (FTAA) in which barriers to trade and investment will be progressively eliminated'. Negotiations on FTAA, extending from Anchorage to Tierra del Fuego, should be completed by 2005.

After the serious setbacks suffered in the 1980s by Latin American experiments in economic inte-gration, a new awareness of the benefits of closer co-operation seems to have emerged. In Central America, the members of CACM approved in December 1991 the creation of a new organization, the System of Central American Integration (Sistema de Integración Centroamericana – SICA), to co-ordinate efforts towards political and economic integration. The Andean Group countries, for their part, are in the process of revitalizing their co-operation and integration schemes by signing the Act of Trujillo establishing the *Andean Community. A fresh attempt to launch co-operation among all countries in the Caribbean was undertaken in July 1994 with the founding agreement of the *Association of Caribbean States (ACS) among members of CARICOM, the *Group of Three (G-3), consisting of Colombia, Mexico and Venezuela, and other countries in the region. A permanent mechanism for political consultation created in 1986, the *Group of Rio, has provided a framework for the external relations of the continent, particularly with the EU. The countries of *Mercosur – Argentina, Brazil, Paraguay and Uruguay – have pursued their liberalization efforts and signed in December 1994 the Protocol of Ouro Preto, amending the founding Treaty of Asunción of 1991.

With regard to denuclearization, several amendments to the Tlatelolco Treaty were approved in August 1992, with a view to propitiating the full incorporation of Argentina, Brazil and Chile, which eventually became full members of OPANAL in early 1994.

In Africa, efforts are going on to strengthen institutional mechanisms in the prospect of enhanced co-operation in the southern part of the continent, with the participation of the Republic of South Africa. A treaty for the establishment of an African Economic Community was adopted by the OAU Assembly in 1991; the Community is expected to promote economic integration of the African countries in six phases over a period of 34 years. The SADCC, established to reduce the dependence of the front-line states on South Africa, has met the challenge of a wider co-operation effort incorporating the new democratic South Africa and gave way in 1992 to the *Southern African Development Community (SADC). The *Common Market for Eastern and Southern African States (COMESA) has been the result of the transformation in 1993 of the PTA. A new body was also created in West Africa, the *West African Economic and Monetary Union

(UEMOA). This superseded in 1994 the CEAO, which had been operating in the region since 1974. In Central Africa, the Economic and Monetary Community of Central Africa (CEMAC) replaced – with the same membership – the UDEAC. A revised Treaty for ECOWAS was signed in Cotonou, Benin, in July 1993 and eventually came into force in July 1995.

In 1989, the *Arab Maghreb Union (AMU) was created, in an effort to renew efforts at closer economic co-operation between the countries of the subregion, but diverging appreciations of the Gulf crisis and sanctions against Libya have hindered any significant progress. The members of the GCC, in the aftermath of the successful conclusion of the Gulf War, adopted, with the participation of Egypt and Syria, the *Damascus Declaration, to develop a regional defence framework.

The independence of the five Central Asian republics of the former Soviet Union has encouraged the establishment of closer political and economic links with their southern neighbours. The five republics, Armenia and Afghanistan joined in 1992 the *Economic Co-operation Organization (ECO) which had been set up in 1985 by Iran, Pakistan and Turkey as a successor to the RCD.

The Asia-Pacific region has seen the strengthening of the *Asia-Pacific Economic Co-operation (APEC) process, with liberalization commitments gradually moving from the political to the legal plane. APEC represents the first major attempt at institutionalized intergovernmental collaboration among Pacific Rim nations, building on the experience developed – at the non-governmental level – within the framework of the Pacific Economic Co-operation Conference, renamed in 1992 the *Pacific Economic Co-operation Council but retaining its acronym (PECC).

With regard to development co-operation in the Asia-Pacific region, the announcement by both Canada and the UK in late 1991 of their intention to withdraw from the Colombo Plan has seriously affected the Plan's role and activities.

Of particular importance appears the positive evolution of ASEAN, on its way to greater economic integration with the eventual full participation of all countries of South East Asia. Furthermore, the Association's gradual involvement in security matters materialized in 1993 with the establishment of an *ASEAN Regional Forum (ARF), which is becoming of interest for several countries in the Asia-Pacific. The Asia-Pacific formula of 'open regionalism' has certainly attracted remarkable attention and might provide a pattern for future developments in other areas of the world. The signature, in December 1995, of the South East Asia Nuclear-Weapon-Free Zone Treaty eventually concluded a long-term effort to liberate a densely populated area from nuclear arms. In March 1996, France, the UK and the USA signed the Protocols to the South Pacific Nuclear Free Zone Treaty (Treaty of Rarotouga). The objective of a nuclear-free Southern Hemisphere has now been achieved.

A

African Development Bank (AfDB)

The Bank contributes to the economic and social progress of its member countries, individually and jointly, by financing development projects, promoting public and private investment and stimulating economic co-operation between African countries.

Origin and development

The origins of the Bank date back to the Conference of the Peoples of Africa, held in Tunis in 1960, which passed a resolution concerning the creation of an African investment financing institution. Under the aegis of the UN *Economic Commission for Africa (ECA), an agreement was drawn up between 1962 and 1963 by a Committee of Experts of nine African countries. It was formally adopted by the Conference of African Ministers of Finance in August 1963 in Khartoum. The agreement came into effect in September 1964 and the Bank started operations at its headquarters at Abidjan in July 1966. Unlike other regional development institutions, membership of the Bank was originally limited to independent countries within the region, thereby excluding non-African countries from subscribing to the capital stock. In May 1979 a decision was taken to admit non-regional members in accordance with a set of principles aimed at preserving the African character of the Bank. In December 1982, the capital stock was officially opened to non-African countries. The present membership comprises 51 African countries – including Madagascar and other island states that surround the continent – and 26 non-African countries, including several Western European nations, Brazil, Canada, China, India, Japan, the Republic of Korea, Kuwait, Saudi Arabia and the USA. The agreement makes explicit provision for the withdrawal or suspension of member countries.

Objectives

The Bank's basic aims are: to provide loans directly or indirectly for financing national and multinational projects; to encourage public and private investment; to assist member countries to improve the utilization of their resources; to increase the complementarity of economic systems and to promote the balanced growth of foreign trade; to extend technical assistance with a view to studying, preparing and implementing development programmes and projects; to co-operate with national, regional and subregional economic institutions in Africa, as well as with any other outside agency that aims to support African development efforts.

Structure

The Bank is organized like other international financing institutions and is run by the President, the Board of Governors, and the Board of Directors. Each member country nominates one governor to the Board, usually its Minister of Finance, and one alternate governor. The Board, meeting at least once a year, is the highest policy-making body and is vested with all the powers, many of which have been delegated to the Board of Directors. The Board of Governors usually takes its decisions by a majority of the votes cast. Each member is allotted a predetermined number of votes, plus one additional vote for each share (equal to BUA10 000) of stock held; voting rights are therefore related to the amount of each country's share. Amendments to the agreement, such as the admission of non-regional members, require the approval of two-thirds of members, possessing at least 75 per cent of the total voting power.

The Board of Directors, responsible for the current operations of the Bank, is composed of 18 members (who are neither governors nor alternate governors); 12 members are elected by the governors of the regional members and 6 by the governors of non-regional members, for a three-year term.

The President of the Bank, elected by the Board of Governors, serves for a five-year period and acts as Chairman of the Board of Directors; the five Vice-Presidents are nominated by the Board of Directors for a three-year term on the President's recommendation.

Activities

The Bank uses a unit of account (BUA) equivalent to $1 before the devaluation of 1971 and now expressed on the basis of the special drawing right (SDR). The size of the authorized capital stock, initially set at BUA250 million, has grown substantially. At the end of 1992 the subscribed capital amounted to $21017.3 million (of which the paid-up portion was equivalent to $2523.3 million). Payments of amounts subscribed to the paid-up capital are made in gold or convertible currencies. Loans from ordinary resources are not tied to purchases in any specific country and are repayable over a period ranging from 12 to 20 years, including the grace period.

The Bank Group of development financing institutions comprises, in addition to the Bank itself, the African Development Fund (ADF) and the Nigeria Trust Fund (NTF), both providing concessionary loans. Over the past 25 years, four associated institutions have also been set up to channel further public and private resources for the development of Africa.

The African Development Fund was established, as the Bank's soft window, in July 1972 and began operations in August 1973. The Fund uses its own unit of account (FUA) whose value was aligned to that of the BUA from January 1993. Subscriptions to the Fund were made by the Bank itself and by 22 capital-exporting countries outside Africa – thus ensuring the financial contribution of non-regional members to the development of the continent. Concessional loans granted by the Fund for development projects are repayable over very long periods (50 years, including a 10-year grace period) and usually carry no interest as such but only an annual service charge of around 0.75 per cent. Loans concerning feasibility studies are repayable over ten years, after a three year grace period. The fifth replenishment of the Fund, agreed upon in 1987 by donor countries, amounted to $2700 million for 1988–90; the sixth replenishment amounted to $3340 million for 1991–93. The seventh replenishment was proposed in May 1993 but donor countries refused to commit further resources until the Bank's policies and administrative procedures were reviewed thoroughly and streamlined; an agreement was eventually reached in early 1996.

The Nigeria Trust Fund was established by an agreement signed by the Bank and the government of Nigeria in February 1976 and came into effect the following April. The Fund, which is under the Bank's administration, finances national and multinational projects, mainly in the infrastructural sector, granting loans for long periods

(up to 25 years, including the grace period) and charging interest. The Fund's initial resources amounted to 50 million naira and were subsequently replenished.

The four associated institutions are specifically intended to support the Bank's finance and development efforts. The oldest among these institutions is the Société internationale financière pour les investissements et le développement en Afrique (SIFIDA), with headquarters in Switzerland (22 rue François-Perréard, BP 310, 1225 Chêne-Bourg). It was created in November 1970 as a holding company for promoting the establishment and growth of productive enterprises in Africa. Besides the Bank its shareholders include the *International Finance Corporation (IFC) and several financial, industrial and commercial institutions in Europe, North America, the Caribbean and the Asia-Pacific region. The initially authorized capital stock amounted to $50 million, of which $21.1 million subscribed.

The Africa Reinsurance Corporation (Africa-Re), with headquarters in Nigeria (Reinsurance House, 46 Marina, PMB 12765, Lagos), was established by an agreement signed in February 1976 and entered into force in January 1977. The Corporation – whose authorized capital amounts to $30 million, of which 10 per cent is held by the Bank – aims to stimulate the insurance and reinsurance activities as well as the growth of national and regional underwriting capacities.

The Association of African Development Finance Institutions (AADFI), established in 1975 and based in the Côte d'Ivoire (c/o ADB, B.P. 01-1387, Abidjan), promotes co-operation among the development banks of the region with regard to project design and financing.

Shelter-Afrique (Société pour l'habitat et le logement territorial en Afrique), with headquarters in Kenya (Mamlaka Road, POB 41479, Nairobi), is another associated institution, set up in 1982, whose purpose is to finance housing in the Bank's member countries. Besides the Bank, several African countries, Africa-Re and the Commonwealth Development Corporation participate in its share capital.

The Bank has developed close links with several regional and extraregional political, financial and technical institutions: the *Food and Agriculture Organization of the UN (FAO); the *International Bank for Reconstruction and

Development (IBRD); the *International Labour Organization (ILO); the *Organization of African Unity (OAU); the *UN Educational, Scientific and Cultural Organization (UNESCO); and the *World Health Organization (WHO).

Since the first loan was granted in 1967, the Bank has developed its lending activities progressively, supplemented by the non-commercial loans extended by the ADF. Together with its soft loan affiliates (ADF and NTF), by the end of 1992 the Bank had cumulatively disbursed a total $12.9 billion for the development of the African economies. Loans concerned agricultural projects (especially food production), public utilities, transport, education and health, industry, and multi-sector activities (including structural adjustment). The Bank also provides technical assistance, which is financed to a large extent by bilateral aid funds contributed by developed member countries. Since the late 1980s a major new area of activity for the Bank has been assistance to the private sector by providing advisory services and finance, as well as by encouraging private investment from both within and outside the region. The Bank has contributed to the setting up of the African Export Import Bank (Afreximbank), which began operations in December 1993 in Cairo with an authorized capital of $750 million.

In the early 1990s serious disagreements emerged among the Bank's key shareholders with regard to financial and management issues. Growing dissatisfaction with the Bank's procedures and practices, and the ensuing loss of confidence by major donor countries, made it impossible to plan the recapitalization of the Bank and the streamlining of its operations until the election of a new President in August 1995. Non-African members – especially donors such as France, Germany, Japan and the USA – declared in early 1996 their willingness to increase participation in the Bank's capital (to be accompanied by an increase in their voting power), while the new President has undertaken a restructuring of the Bank's management and lending policies.

President: Omar Kabbaj
Headquarters: P.O. Box 01-1387, Abidjan, Côte d'Ivoire (Telephone: +225 204444; fax: +225 227839)
Publications: *Annual Report*; *ADB Today* (every two months); *African Development Report*

References: R.K.A. Gardner and J. Pickett, *The African Development Bank 1964–1984: An Experiment in Economic Co-coperation and Development* (Abidjan, 1984); K.A. Mingst, *Politics and the African Development Bank* (Lexington, MA, 1990); I. Peprah, *The African Development Bank: Taking Stock and Preparing for the 21st Century* (Ottawa, 1994)

Agency for Cultural and Technical Co-operation

(Agence de coopération culturelle et technique)
(ACCT)

The Agency promotes cultural and technical co-operation among French-speaking countries throughout the world.

Origin and development
Established by a Convention signed in March 1970 at Niamey, Niger, during the Second International Conference of Francophone Countries, the Agency currently consists of 37 member countries, in all continents but particularly in Africa, of which French is the official or habitual language, plus five associate members and two participating governments representing the Canadian Provinces of New Brunswick and Quebec. Practically all major French-speaking countries (with the notable exception of Algeria) belong to the Agency, along with other countries (such as Bulgaria, Cambodia, Romania and Vietnam) where French culture is important, though not dominant.

Objectives
The Agency aims to promote and develop multilateral co-operation among French-speaking countries in the fields of education, culture and science, and to provide technical and financial assistance.

Structure
The General Conference, usually meeting every two years, comprises representatives of all member countries at ministerial level and is the supreme authority of the Agency. The General Conference elects its president and several vice-presidents as well as a secretary-general.

Activities

A Permanent Francophone Council was established in 1991 to co-ordinate the institutional activities of the francophone community and to make 'political decisions' on behalf of francophone countries. Canada and France have long been the major supporters, both politically and financially, of the Agency despite occasional conflict between them over the role and functions of the organization.

Secretary-General: Jean-Louis Roy
Headquarters: 13 quai André Citroën, 75015 Paris, France (Telephone: +33 1 4437 3300; fax: +33 1 4579 1498)
Publication: *Lettre de la Francophonie* (monthly)

Agency for the Prohibition of Nuclear Weapons in Latin America and the Caribbean

(Organismo para la Proscripción de las Armas Nucleares en la América Latina y el Caribe)
(OPANAL)

The Agency provides the institutional framework for the fulfilment of the obligations set out in the Treaty for the Prohibition of Nuclear Weapons in Latin America (Tlatelolco Treaty).

Origin and development

The signing of the Tlatelolco Treaty in February 1967 by 14 countries followed a number of preparatory meetings on the denuclearization of Latin America relevant to resolutions of the UN General Assembly. The original contracting parties were joined subsequently by other Latin American and Caribbean nations which decided to apply the Treaty among them, thereby waiving the provision which requires that all regional countries must join before the Treaty enters into effect. Several amendments to the Treaty were approved in August 1992 with a view to facilitating the full incorporation of Argentina, Brazil and Chile. The three countries became full OPANAL members in the first half of 1994. Full contracting parties now total 28; other countries have signed but not ratified the Treaty. The Tlatelolco Treaty remains open for signature by all other sovereign states situated in their entirety south of latitude 35° North in the Western Hemisphere.

The Treaty contains two Additional Protocols: Protocol I, open to the signature of countries which, *de jure* or *de facto*, are responsible internationally for territories lying within the geographical zone defined in the Treaty, and Protocol II, open to the signature of countries possessing nuclear weapons. Protocol I has been signed and ratified by France, the Netherlands, the UK and the USA; Protocol II has been signed and ratified by China, France, Russia, the UK and the USA.

Objectives

To attain the objectives of the Treaty, the Agency aims to ensure the absence of all nuclear weapons in the area under the jurisdiction of the contracting parties, without prejudice to peaceful uses of atomic energy; to prohibit all testing, use, production, deployment and any form of possession of nuclear weapons; and to provide protection against possible nuclear attacks.

Structure

The principal organs of the Agency are the General Conference, the Council, and the Secretariat. The General Conference, consisting of representatives of all member countries, meets in ordinary sessions every two years to lay down policy guidelines and to approve the budget; extraordinary sessions have been held to deal with urgent problems. The Council is the executive body and is composed of five members elected for a four-year term by the General Conference, taking into account the necessity of an equitable geographic representation. The Secretariat is headed by a Secretary General elected by the General Conference for a maximum of two four-year terms.

Activities

The Agency keeps the UN and the *Organization of American States (OAS) informed about the results of on-site inspections and violations of the Tlatelolco Treaty. A co-operation agreement between OPANAL and the *International Atomic Energy Agency (IAEA) was concluded in September 1972.

The Agency has made an important contribution by restraining the proliferation of nuclear weapons and by establishing Latin America as a denuclearized zone under the guarantee of the nuclear powers which signed and ratified Protocol II to the Tlatelolco Treaty. As well as furthering the objectives of the Treaty, the Agency has promoted the development of the peaceful uses of atomic energy through research and fellowship programmes.

Secretary-General: Enrique Román-Morey
Headquarters: Temístocles 78, Col. Polanco, CP 011560, México, D.F., Mexico (Telephone: +52 5 280 4923; fax: +52 5 280 2965)

Amazon Co-operation Treaty (Amazon Pact)

The Treaty fosters co-operation among the Amazon Basin countries with a view to accelerating the harmonious socioeconomic development of their respective Amazon territories.

Origin and development
The Amazon Co-operation Treaty, originally proposed by Brazil in 1977, was concluded in July 1978 in Brasília by all the countries in the Amazon Basin – Bolivia, Brazil, Colombia, Ecuador, Guyana, Peru, Suriname and Venezuela. The first Meeting of Ministers of Foreign Affairs took place in Belém, Brazil, in October 1980. The Declaration of Belém, approved unanimously at the end of the session, restated the basic principles of the Treaty and entrusted the Council with responsibility for the preparation of detailed studies and programmes on the main areas of co-operation.

Objectives
The aims of the Treaty are: to raise standards of living, paying special regard to the interests and needs of the Amazonian peoples; to encourage the development of productive facilities and resources in selected areas; to protect animal and vegetable life through the creation of national parks and other conservation units; to organize joint research and training activities and exchange information and expertise; to establish a fund for financing pre-investment and feasibility studies with the help of international specialized institutions; to develop renewable conventional and non-conventional energy sources; to expand inland and overseas navigation and develop an adequate intercountry transportation and communications infrastructure; and to stimulate tourism in order to promote mutual understanding among Amazonian peoples. All these aims are to be pursued at the interstate level, fully respecting the sovereign and exclusive rights of the participating countries.

Structure
The main organs created by the Treaty are the Meeting of Ministers of Foreign Affairs, and the Amazon Co-operation Council. The Meeting is the highest decision-making organ, responsible for establishing the basic guidelines, adopting the relevant measures, and directing and supervising the activities of the Amazon Co-operation Council. The Council is the executive body, fulfilling the tasks entrusted to it by the Meeting with the assistance of special Commissions and other subsidiary bodies.

Activities
The second Meeting took place in Santiago de Cali, Colombia, in December 1983, and ended with the signature of a Final Act and a Declaration. The Declaration emphasized the commitment of member countries to furthering Amazonian co-operation through improved contacts among national bodies and administrations, the exchange of technical information and know-how, the establishment of a system concerning hydrological and meteorological services, and the adoption of an action plan in the field of applied science and technology.

The third Meeting took place in Quito in March 1989 and was followed in May by a meeting of the Heads of State of the member countries in Manaus, Brazil.

The fifth Meeting was held in Lima in December 1995 and ended with the signature of the Lima Declaration on sustainable development, providing, *inter alia*, for the setting up of a permanent secretariat in Brasília.

Andean Community (formerly Andean Group).

The Community consists of Bolivia, Colombia, Ecuador, Peru and Venezuela, and of the organs and institutions of the Andean Integration System established by the Protocol Modifying the Andean Subregional Agreement (Cartagena Agreement).

Origin and development

The Protocol – adopted on 10 March 1996 at Trujillo, Peru, by the representatives of the five countries participating in the Andean Group – is an Annex to the 'Act of Trujillo' signed on the same day by the Heads of State of Bolivia, Colombia, Ecuador and Peru, the Personal Representative of the President of Venezuela, and the President of Panama acting as an observer. The Protocol is described by the signatories of the Act as a 'new legal framework' to meet the challenges resulting for Andean subregional integration from changes in the world economy.

The Agreement on Subregional Integration creating the Andean Group had formally been signed on 26 May 1969 in Bogotá by the representatives of Bolivia, Chile, Colombia, Ecuador and Peru. While being signed in Bogotá, the instrument establishing the Group was officially designated as the Cartagena Agreement in honour of the city where the conclusive negotiations had taken place. Before the Trujillo Protocol, the text of the Cartagena Agreement had already been revised and supplemented on several occasions, notably by the Quito Protocol of 1987.

In spite of its active involvement at the initial stage of the negotiations, Venezuela did not join the Andean Group until February 1973. Chile withdrew in October 1976 after a dispute on the common rules governing foreign investment. Peru requested a suspension of its active participation in August 1992 and resumed full membership in January 1995. The future participation of Panama in the newly-created Andean Community is expressly welcomed by the Act of Trujillo.

Objectives

The Community's basic aims are to foster closer ties among member countries through the strengthening of democracy, the elimination of poverty, the promotion of sustainable development and environmental protection, market liberalization, and co-ordination of national policies in multilateral negotiating forums.

Structure

According to the Trujillo Protocol, the principal organs through which the Community accomplishes its purposes are: the Andean Presidential Council; the Council of Ministers of Foreign Affairs; the Commission; the General Secretariat; the Court of Justice; and the Andean Parliament. Consultative institutions are envisaged to ensure representation of employers and workers respectively. The two financial institutions already existing – the Andean Development Corporation (Corporación Andina de Fomento) and the Latin American Reserve Fund (Fondo Latinoamericano de Reservas) – are incorporated into the newly-created Andean Integration System through coordination with the General Secretariat of the Community.

The Andean Presidential Council, consisting of the Heads of State of the member countries, is the highest decision-making body, issuing directives concerning the various aspects of Andean subregional integration. Ordinary sessions are held once a year under a rotating presidency lasting one calendar year. The Council of Ministers of Foreign Affairs meets twice a year to implement the directives of the Presidential Council, to co-ordinate the process of integration, and to formulate a common external policy; it issues declarations and decisions adopted by consensus.

The Commission, consisting of a plenipotentiary representative from each country, is empowered: to establish major policies concerning trade and investment and adopt such measures as may be deemed necessary for the attainment of the Community's objectives; to set the essential rules for the co-ordination of economic policies; to supervise the fulfilment by participating countries of obligations arising from the Cartagena Agreement and its Protocols; to approve the annual budget and determine the amount of the contribution to be paid by each country; to give special consideration to the situation of Bolivia and Ecuador in view of the preferential treatment accorded to these countries. Regular sessions of the Commission are held three times a year, generally at the seat of the General Secretariat, with the participation of the absolute majority of the member countries; non-participation is equivalent to abstention. The presidency of the Commission is assured by the representative of the country responsible for the presidency of the Presidential Council. As a rule, the Commission adopts its decisions by absolute majority. Decisions on proposals concerning highly sensitive matters may be made by absolute majority only if the remaining countries have abstained. If any negative vote has been cast, the proposal is brought back to the General Secretariat for further consideration; the revised version of the proposal must be submitted by the General Secretariat within two to six months for approval by the Commission by absolute majority without any negative vote.

The General Secretariat (replacing the former 'Junta' of the Andean Group), whose seat is in Lima, is an executive and technical body acting in the general interest of the Andean subregion under the direction of the Secretary-General assisted by Directors-General and the necessary staff. The Secretary-General is appointed by consensus, for a five-year term renewable only once, by the Council of Ministers of Foreign Affairs enlarged to include members of the Commission. In the discharge of his duties, the Secretary-General is required to refrain from any action incompatible with the character of his/her functions and may not seek or take instructions from any government or from any other national or international body.

The Andean Judicial Tribunal was established as a principal organ in May 1979 by the members of the then Andean Group. The Tribunal, which began operating in January 1984, is located in Quito. It consists of five judges, one from each member country appointed for a renewable six-year term; the Presidency is assumed annually by each judge in turn by alphabetical order of country. The Tribunal is competent to deal with cases relating to the alleged illegality of actions taken by the Commission or the General Secretariat and the infringement by a member country of its obligations under the Cartagena Agreement and the subsequent Protocols. It also has jurisdiction to give preliminary rulings concerning the interpretation of the Cartagena Agreement. Matters may be brought before the Tribunal by any member country, the Commission, the General Secretariat and any natural or legal resident in the Andean subregion.

The Andean Parliament, whose permanent seat is in Santa Fé de Bogotá, Colombia, represents the peoples of the Community; pending the adoption of the Additional Protocol regulating direct election, the Parliament consists of representatives of the national parliaments of member countries. The Parliament fulfils an essentially consultative role through the formulation of proposals and recommendations to the various organs; a gradual extension of the Parliament's influence may develop with the strengthening of the Community.

Activities

The future of the newly-established Community will be affected both by the political will of the participating countries and by the prevailing political and economic situation in the whole of Latin America, including the evolution of the other subregional integration groupings. Also important for the Community's prospects will be the relationship with extraregional integration groupings, notably the *European Union (EU). A five-year agreement had been signed in December 1983 by the Andean Group with the then European Economic Community (EEC) to eliminate obstacles to trade and to foster co-operation programmes; a new agreement with the EEC was signed in April 1993 with a view to strengthening and diversifying co-operation links as well as promoting social development projects. A joint declaration on the political dialogue between the newly-created Community and the EU was adopted in June 1996.

Headquarters: Paseo de la República 3895, San Isidro, Lima 27; P.O. Box 18-1177, Lima 18, Peru (Telephone: +551 1221 2222; fax: +551 1221 3329)
Internet address: http://www.rcb.net.pe/JUNAC/

ANZUS Pact (ANZUS Security Treaty)

The Pact, which is no longer in full operation, was devised to co-ordinate the defence of the three contracting parties in order to preserve peace and security in the Pacific.

Origin and development

The Security Treaty between Australia, New Zealand and the USA (usually known as the ANZUS Pact from the initials of its signatory countries) was signed in San Francisco in September 1951 and entered into force in April 1952. It was intended to be the first step towards the development of a comprehensive system of regional security in the Pacific, within the framework of the defensive alliance systems of the Western world. This system was further developed by the creation of the South-East Asia Treaty Organization (SEATO) under the Manila Treaty of September 1954, which aimed also to protect non-member countries belonging to the region, such as South Vietnam.

Objectives

The parties to the Pact uphold the principles set forth in the UN Charter and affirm their desire to live in peace with all peoples and all governments. The purposes of the parties are to strengthen the fabric of peace in the Pacific; to declare publicly and formally their sense of unity against any potential aggressor; to further their efforts for collective defence; and to co-ordinate their policies. Threats to the territorial integrity, political independence or security of any of the parties in the Pacific give rise to the obligation to consult together. In case of aggression by means of armed attack, each party is bound to act according to its constitutional processes, since attack against any party constitutes a danger to the peace and safety of the others. According to the Pact, an armed attack includes aggression on the metropolitan territory of any of the parties or on the island territories under its jurisdiction in the Pacific, or on its forces, vessels or aircraft in the Pacific. The UN Security Council is to be informed immediately of any armed attack and of all measures adopted to resist it. Such measures are to be terminated when the Security Council has taken appropriate action to restore and maintain peace and security. On the whole, the functions and powers arising out of the Pact are dealt with in general terms, in accordance with the largely declaratory character of the document. The duration of the Pact is unlimited, although any party may withdraw upon one year's notice.

Co-operation to be carried out under the Pact embraces the exchange of strategic intelligence; scientific and technical assistance in defence matters; supply of defence equipment; training programmes; combined ground, air and naval exercises; and visits by military aircraft and naval vessels.

Structure

The main consultative organ of the Pact is the Council, which consists of Foreign Ministers or their deputies. Closed meetings were held annually, rotating between the capitals of the three contracting parties, until the mid-1980s. Decisions were taken unanimously. The Council meetings were also attended by military representatives giving advice on matters related to military co-operation; these representatives also met separately, between sessions of the Council. Officials involved in other forms of practical co-operation held meetings whenever the governments deemed it necessary. The Pact is not endowed with any permanent staff or secretariat; costs are borne by the government in whose territory the meeting takes place.

Activities

The Pact has no formal or informal relationship with the *North Atlantic Treaty Organization (NATO), although both are intended to provide for collective self-defence. The activities carried out under the Pact are limited, as its weak organizational structure suggests. Moreover, the obligation to assist the attacked party is subordinated to compliance with 'constitutional processes' and is therefore not automatic, as in NATO. The influence of the Pact decreased as SEATO developed its activities in South-East Asia and Australasia. After the dissolution of SEATO, the Pact regained importance. Major issues of common concern to contracting parties have been reviewed at the annual sessions of the Council, such as events in Afghanistan and Cambodia and the spread of nuclear weapons on a world scale.

Following the election of a Labour Government in July 1984, New Zealand decided not to allow US warships to enter its ports unless assurance was given that they were not carrying nuclear arms, information that the USA did not disclose as a matter of policy. Because of the New Zealand ban on visits by nuclear warships, joint naval exercises planned for March and October 1985 were cancelled; in August 1986 the USA formally announced the suspension of its security commitment to New Zealand and therefore the Pact ceased to be in full operation. The prospects of the Pact were also affected by the treaty, signed in August 1985 within the framework of the *South Pacific Forum (SPF), providing for the establishment of a South Pacific Nuclear-Free Zone. Instead of the annual trilateral meetings of the Council, bilateral talks are held every year between Australia and the USA. The Pact still governs security relations between Australia and the USA as well as between Australia and New Zealand, since the suspension of obligations affects only the relationship between New Zealand and the USA.

The removal of all nuclear weapons from US vessels decided in the wake of the end of the Cold War prompted in 1992 the government of New Zealand to express an interest in resuming ANZUS co-operation. The continuing importance of the Pact was stressed also by the USA in the early 1990s, and the resumption of high-level contacts between the USA and New Zealand took place in 1994, although no joint military exercises were scheduled.

Headquarters: c/o Department of Foreign Affairs and Trade, Parkes, ACT 2600, Australia (Telephone: +61 6 261 9111; fax: +61 6 273 3577)

References: J. G. Starke, *The ANZUS Treaty Alliance* (London, 1965); J. Bercovitch (ed.), *ANZUS in Crisis. Alliance Management in International Relations* (London, 1987); R. W. Baker (ed.), *The ANZUS States and their Region: Regional Policies of Australia, New Zealand and the United States* (Westport, Conn., 1994)

Arab Bank for Economic Development in Africa

(Banque arabe pour le développement
économique en Afrique) (BADEA)

The Bank contributes to the economic development of Africa by financing infrastructural, industrial and agricultural projects, and by providing technical assistance.

Origin and development

The decision to establish the Bank was taken in November 1973 in Algiers at the Sixth Summit Conference of the *Arab League, and the founding agreement was signed in Cairo in February 1974. The Bank started operations in March 1975 with headquarters in Khartoum, Sudan. Its subscribers include all countries participating in the *League of Arab States, with the exception of Djibouti, Somalia and Yemen. Egypt's membership was suspended in April 1979 and subsequently restored in April 1988. Recipient countries may be all members of the *Organization of African Unity (OAU), except those African countries that belong to the League of Arab States. In total over 40 countries are eligible for the Bank's aid.

Objectives

The Bank's basic aims are: to provide loans to national and regional institutions for financing national and multinational projects; to supply expertise and to promote technical co-operation; and, generally, to co-ordinate aid provided by Arab financial institutions to Africa.

Structure

The structure of the Bank is similar to that of other international financing institutions. The Board of Governors, composed of the finance ministers of the Arab League member countries, is the supreme authority and meets at least once a year to set the general guidelines. The Board of Directors, composed of eleven members and meeting four times a year, performs executive functions and supervises the implementation of decisions adopted by the Board of Governors. The seven countries which are major subscribers to the capital stock have a permanent seat on the Board; appointments to the remaining four seats are made by the Governors for a four-year term. The Chairman is elected by the Board of Directors for a two-year term.

Activities

Loans on concessional terms for development projects may not exceed $15 million, or 50 per cent of the total cost of each project (80 per cent for loans of under $10 million). The Bank also provides technical assistance, mainly in the form of grants for project feasibility studies, and generally stimulates the contribution of Arab capital to African development.

The Bank carries on operations through its ordinary capital resources. These were integrated in November 1976 with the capital stock of the Special Arab Assistance Fund for Africa (SAAFA) which had been created in January 1972, under the name of Arab Loan Fund for Africa, by Arab oil ministers in order to provide urgent aid to African countries. Saudi Arabia was by far the largest subscriber, followed by Libya, Kuwait, Iraq, the United Arab Emirates, Qatar and Algeria. The paid-up capital of the Bank amounted to $1046 million at the end of 1992.

The Bank's links with other Arab and African financial institutions have a special relevance in order to ensure co-ordination in channelling public and private resources for Africa's economic development: particularly close relations exist with the *African Development Bank (AfDB), subregional banks in Central and West Africa, and Arab development agencies.

The Bank has been playing an active, albeit modest, role in promoting Arab investment in Africa and co-ordinating Arab aid for development projects. Among the recipients were nearly all non-Arab members of OAU. In regional terms, West African countries received a very large proportion of total aid. Among the leading recipients of project aid have been Ghana, Senegal, Madagascar, Guinea and Rwanda. The largest share of total lending went to infrastructural projects; agricultural, industrial and energy development projects accounted for the balance. Over the past few years emphasis on agriculture has grown remarkably.

Chairman: Ahmad Abdallah al-Akeil
Headquarters: Sayed Abdar-Rahman el-Mahdi Avenue, P.O. Box 2640, Khartoum, Sudan (Telephone: +249 11 73646; fax: +249 11 70600)
Publications: *Annual Report*; *Co-operation for Development* (quarterly)

Arab Maghreb Union (AMU)

(Union du Maghreb Arabe) (UMA)

The Union represents an attempt at organizing co-operation among Maghreb countries and presenting a common front *vis-à-vis* non-member countries, especially those belonging to the *European Union (EU).

Origin and development

At a meeting at Algiers, in June 1988, the leaders of Algeria, Libya, Mauritania, Morocco and Tunisia decided to prepare a treaty encompassing the 'Greater Arab Maghreb' and strengthening political, economic and cultural bonds. The Treaty establishing the Union was eventually signed in February 1989 at Marrakesh, Morocco, by the Heads of State of the five countries, although membership was left open to other countries 'belonging to the Arab nation or the African group'.

Objectives

The Union's purposes are to create a customs union and later a 'North African Common Market', and to encourage joint ventures and projects in the industrial, agricultural, commercial and social sectors.

Structure

The Presidential Council, comprising the Heads of State of the member countries, is the supreme decision-making body, with a chairmanship rotating annually. Agendas of the Presidential Council are prepared by the Council of Foreign Ministers. A Consultative Council, consisting of 20 representatives from each member country, meets yearly in ordinary sessions to prepare draft resolutions and recommendations to be submitted to the Presidential Council. The Secretary-General supervises the activities of a small staff dealing with mainly administrative tasks.

Activities

Meetings of the Presidential Council – which have suffered several postponements over the past few years – have been unable thus far to chart a definite course for the Union. Initially conceived as a regional response of the Maghreb countries to the then European Economic Community's effort to create a single unified market, the Union soon met with major political and economic difficulties which hampered any significant progress towards the basic goals stated in the founding Treaty and subsequent documents.

Diverging views and conflicts of interest emerged openly on the occasion of the Gulf crisis, when Morocco supplied troops to the US-led coalition to liberate Kuwait while the other member countries firmly opposed an American presence in the Gulf. The imposition in 1992 of UN sanctions against Libya – following that country's refusal to deliver terrorists suspected of involvement in the bombing of an airliner over Lockerbie, Scotland, for trial in the UK or USA – represented another severe setback for co-operation efforts in both political and economic fields. Sanctions against Libya were in fact implemented by the other members of the Union. Despite occasional declarations on continuing commitment to the Union's aims, and the conclusion of a number of agreements in various areas, no major progress seems likely.

Secretary-General: Mohammed Amamou
Headquarters: 27 avenue Okba, Agdal, Rabat, Morocco (Telephone: +212 7 772668; fax: +212 7 772693)

Arab Monetary Fund (AMF)

The Fund assists member countries in coping with balance-of-payments difficulties, and more generally to promote Arab monetary co-operation and integration.

Origin and development
The agreement establishing the Fund was drawn up under the auspices of the Economic Council, operating within the framework of the *League of Arab States, which gave its approval during a meeting held in Rabat, Morocco, in April 1976; it entered into force in February 1977. The present membership includes 16 Arab countries together with the Palestine Liberation Organization (PLO); Iraq, Somalia and Sudan were suspended in February 1993. Egypt's membership was suspended between April 1979 and April 1988.

Objectives
The Fund's basic aims are: to correct disequilibria in the balance of payments of member countries; to promote stability of exchange rates among Arab currencies, the realization of their mutual convertibility and the elimination of restrictions on current payments; to encourage the use of the Arab dinar as a unit of account, thus paving the way for the creation of a unified Arab currency; to co-ordinate policies of member countries with regard to international monetary problems; and to provide a mechanism for the settlement of current payments between members with a view to promoting trade among them.

The Fund, which functions as both a bank and a fund, is empowered: to provide short- and medium-term loans to finance balance-of-payments deficits; to issue guarantees to members with a view to strengthening their borrowing capabilities; to act as intermediary in the issuance of loans in Arab and international markets for the account and under the guarantee of members; to manage funds placed under its charge by members; to consult periodically with members on the situation of their economies; and to extend technical assistance to banking and monetary institutions in member countries.

Structure
The structure of the Fund comprises the Board of Governors, the Board of Executive Directors, and the Director-General. The Board of Governors, composed of one governor and one deputy appointed by each member country for a five-year term, is the supreme policy-making body and meets at least once a year; extraordinary meetings may be convened at the request of half the members or of members possessing at least 50 per cent of the total voting power. The Board of Governors, which has delegated many of its powers to the Board of Executive Directors, takes its decisions by simple majority, with certain exceptions where a larger majority is required. Each member country has a fixed number of votes plus one additional vote for each share of stock held. The Board of Executive Directors, responsible for the general operation of the Fund, consists of eight members, nominated for a renewable three-year term, plus the Director-General of the Fund, who serves as Chairman.

Activities
Operations are carried out by the Fund through its ordinary capital resources. The establishment of a general reserve fund and, if necessary, of special reserve funds, is envisaged by the agreement. The Fund uses its own unit of account – that is, the Arab Accounting Dinar (AAD), which is expressed on the basis of special drawing rights (SDRs); more precisely AAD1 = SDR3. The size of the authorized capital stock of the Fund was initially set at AAD263 million (SDR789 million), comprising 5260 shares, each of them equivalent to AAD50 000. In July 1981, members were obliged to pay the balance of their subscribed

capital. In April 1983, the authorized capital was increased to AAD600 million, comprising 12 000 shares, each having the value of AAD50 000; the increase was to be paid in 5 equal annual instalments. However, only a fraction of the first instalment was in fact paid up, and further payments appeared uncertain.

In 1981 the Fund introduced an Inter-Arab Trade Facility with a view to encouraging trade among member countries. Under this facility, which was discontinued in 1989, a member was allowed to borrow up to 100 per cent of its subscription, paid in convertible currencies, but the amount could not exceed the member's trade deficit with other members. To foster liberalization of trade in goods and services (excluding petroleum) between Arab countries, and to increase the competitive edge of their exporters, Arab financial institutions decided, in March 1989, on the creation of the Arab Trade Financing Program (ATFP), to be based in Abu Dhabi. The first ATPF loan agreement was concluded in early 1992.

The Fund maintains working relations with other economic and financial groupings of Arab countries but appears to be far from achieving its wider political objectives such as the promotion of Arab economic integration and the introduction of a unified Arab currency. The prospects of the Fund will be affected to a very large extent by the continued delay by some member countries in discharging their financial obligations. Ultimately, this might disrupt the revolving nature of the resources of the Fund, making them unavailable to other members needing support for the correction of macroeconomic disequilibria.

Director-General: Jassim al-Mannai
Headquarters: P.O. Box 2818, Abu Dhabi, United Arab Emirates (Telephone: +971 2 215000; fax: +971 2 326454)
Publication: *Annual Report*

Asian Development Bank (AsDB)

The Bank is a development financing institution which fosters economic growth and co-operation in the Asian and Pacific region and contributes to the progress of developing member countries, collectively and individually, by lending funds, promoting investment and providing technical assistance.

Origin and development

The agreement establishing the Bank was drawn up under the auspices of the Economic Commission for Asia and the Far East (ECAFE) – a regional body of the UN later succeeded by the *Economic and Social Commission for Asia and the Pacific (ESCAP). It was formally adopted in Manila at the Ministerial Conference on Economic Co-operation in Asia in December 1965; the agreement entered into effect in August 1966 and the Bank started operations at its headquarters in Manila in December of the same year. Membership of the Bank includes about 40 countries within the ESCAP region, all developing countries except Australia, New Zealand and Japan, plus 16 developed countries outside the region, such as Canada, France, Germany, Italy, the UK and the USA. Among the Bank's developing members are also 'socialist' countries such as the Socialist Republic of Vietnam, which succeeded the former Republic of Vietnam as a regional member in September 1976, and Laos. Cambodia, which had not sent delegations to meetings for several years, resumed participation in 1992. China joined the Bank in March 1986; Taiwan, one of the Bank's founder members, maintained its membership. Three former Soviet republics of Central Asia (Kazakhstan, Kyrgyzstan and Uzbekistan) were granted admission in 1993, subject to payment of capital subscriptions; Kazakhstan and Kyrgyzstan became full members in early 1994.

Objectives

The basic aims of the Bank are: to raise funds from both public and private sources for development purposes, taking into special consideration projects of regional and subregional scope and the needs of the less-developed member countries; to assist members with regard to co-ordination of development, trade and general economic policies; to extend technical assistance, including the formulation of specific proposals and the preparation and implementation of projects; and to co-operate with the UN and its specialized agencies, and with other international and national institutions concerned with investment of development funds in the ESCAP region. Priority must be given to projects and programmes which contribute to the harmonious economic growth of the region as a whole.

Structure

The Bank's structure, which is similar to that of other international financing institutions, consists of the Board of Governors, the Board of Directors, and the President. All the powers are vested in the Board of Governors, which is composed of one governor and one alternate governor appointed by each member country and meets at least once a year. Many of its powers may be and in fact are delegated to the Board of Directors, with important exceptions concerning the admission of new members, changes in the capital stock, amendments of the Charter, and election of Directors and President. The Board of Governors normally adopts its decisions by a majority of the votes cast; the voting power of each country is related to the amount of its quota in the Bank's authorized capital stock. At present, the Board of Directors, responsible for the general direction of the Bank's operations, is composed of twelve members, eight representing countries within the ESCAP region (with about 65 per cent of the voting power) and four representing the remaining countries. Each director serves for a two-year term and may be re-elected. The President of the Bank serves for a five-year period and acts as Chairman of the Board of Directors. The three Vice-Presidents are nominated by the Board of Directors on the President's recommendation.

Activities

The Bank operates with its ordinary capital resources (OCR), composed of subscribed capital, funds raised through borrowings, and reserves, to carry out lending on commercial terms and with the resources of Special Funds to grant concessional (soft) loans. Loans from OCR, which have accounted for over two-thirds of lending since the Bank started operations, are generally made to the more advanced developing member countries, while loans from Special Funds are made almost exclusively to the poorest countries. The size of the capital stock, initially authorized at $1.1 billion, has been growing substantially; at 31 December 1994 the authorized capital amounted to $50.8 billion, of which $30.2 billion had been subscribed. Japan is by far the largest shareholder, holding 21.8 per cent of total voting power, followed by the USA with 11.1 per cent.

The Bank has been borrowing funds from world capital markets since 1969. Loans from OCR (that is, hard loans made on commercial terms) are not tied to the purchase of goods and services in any specific country and are repayable over a period usually ranging from 15 to 25 years, including the grace period. The system of fixed lending rates was abolished in July 1986 and replaced by a system of periodically adjusted rates.

In replacement of the existing Special Funds, a new mechanism, the Asian Development Fund (ADF), was established in June 1974 for the administration of resources available for concessional loans. The initial mobilization of ADF resources (known as ADF I), intended to finance concessional lending up to the end of 1975, was followed by a replenishment (ADF II) of $809 million for 1976–8; a second replenishment (ADF III) of $2150 million for 1979–82; a third replenishment (ADF IV) of $3214 million for 1983–6; a fourth replenishment (ADF V) of $3600 million for 1987–90; and a fifth replenishment (ADF VI) of $4200 million for 1992–5.

The Technical Assistance Special Fund (TASF) extends grants with a view to helping developing member countries improve their capabilities to formulate, design and implement projects. The Japan Special Fund (JSF) was set up in 1988 in order to provide financing, in both public and private sectors, for technical assistance and equity investment.

The Bank acts as executing agency for projects financed by the *UN Development Programme (UNDP) and maintains close working relations with regional and extraregional bodies – from the *Asia-Pacific Economic Co-operation (APEC) forum to the *World Bank group – to co-ordinate technical and financial development assistance efforts within the ESCAP region.

Between 1968 and 1995, the Bank had approved loans from OCR and from the ADF totalling nearly $57 billion for 1295 projects in 34 countries, and an additional $4 billion for 3750 technical assistance projects. Indonesia, Pakistan, the Philippines, Bangladesh, India and the Republic of Korea were among the largest borrowers; China, a member since 1986, has borrowed over $5 billion for about 50 projects. Priority was given to the energy sector and to the agriculture and agro-industry sectors, each accounting for around a quarter of total lending. Transport and communications, and social infrastructure, also took a sizeable share of total loans. A number of recipients in East Asia have graduated from borrower to lender status and are now being urged to contribute to ADF.

The Bank has had a remarkable impact on the progress of its borrowing members, but to meet the fast-growing capital demands of the late 1990s and the new development priorities it needs a substantial increase in its ordinary capital resources and adequate and timely replenishments of its soft window, the ADF. A fourth general capital increase was authorized in May 1994. The demands on the Bank's resources over the next few years will be enormous and only a small proportion of the external financing gap of its developing member countries will be satisfied. Although the Bank's loans were intended to be granted for specific projects, a decision was taken in 1987 to support programmes of sectoral adjustment. A clear trend has emerged to extend the Bank's activities beyond the traditional sectors. Therefore, the Bank is being involved increasingly in assisting the private sector, including direct financial assistance to private enterprises, in supporting financial institutions and capital markets, and in promoting privatization of public-sector enterprises; social and environmental projects are also receiving growing attention. The sixth replenishment of ADF currently represents one of the major challenges for the Bank. In fact, financial difficulties in some lending countries and the prevailing 'donor fatigue' have caused substantial arrears in payments to the Bank.

President: Mitsuo Sato
Headquarters: 6 ADB Avenue, Mandaluyong, (P.O. Box 789), 1099 Metro Manila, Philippines (Telephone: +63 2 711 3851; fax: +63 2 741 7961)
Internet address: http://www.asiandevbank.org
Publications: *Annual Report*; *ADB Review* (six times a year); *Asian Development Outlook* (every two years); *Asian Development Review* (twice a year)
Reference: D. Wilson, *A Bank for Half the World. The Story of the Asian Development Bank 1966–1986* (Manila, 1987)

Asia-Pacific Economic Co-operation (APEC)

APEC has evolved rapidly from an informal dialogue group with limited participation to become the leading intergovernmental forum for promoting open trade and investment, and economic co-operation, in the Asia-Pacific region.

Origin and development

A remarkable part was played by Australia in developing the concept of a regional economic consultative forum after the speech made by the then Prime Minister Bob Hawke in Seoul in January 1989 suggesting the formation of an Asian version of the *Organization for Economic Co-operation and Development (OECD). At the meeting held in Canberra, Australia, in November 1989, an Asia-Pacific Economic Co-operation forum was set up with the participation of the five Pacific industrial powers (Australia, Canada, Japan, New Zealand and the USA), the members of the *Association of South East Asian Nations (ASEAN), and South Korea. The forum was originally conceived as an informal and unstructured arrangement for 'dialogue' among participating countries, partly because of the unwillingness of ASEAN members to commit themselves to another and more powerful regional organization.

The consultation process further developed at the subsequent meeting, which took place in Singapore in July 1990, and made a qualitative step forward at the ministerial session held in Seoul in November 1991. The admission of the 'three Chinas' – that is, China, Hong Kong and Taiwan (under the name of Chinese Taipei) – and the adoption of the 'Seoul Declaration' setting out aims and methods of operation marked a new stage in intergovernmental co-operation in the Asia-Pacific region.

APEC currently includes 18 countries as full members, accounting for about half the world's total annual output and representing over 40 per cent of the world's total merchandise trade.

Objectives

According to the 'Seoul Declaration', the objectives of APEC were defined as follows: (a) to sustain the growth and development of the region; (b) to enhance the positive gains resulting from increasing economic interdependence, including by encouraging the flow of goods, services, capital and technology; (c) to develop and strengthen an open multilateral trading system; and (d) to reduce barriers to trade in goods, services and investment among participants and without detriment to other economies. APEC was to encourage private-sector participation and to support 'open regionalism', promoting trade liberalization throughout the world economy as well as among its members.

Structure

The direction and nature of APEC activities are determined at the highest level by meetings of the leaders which have taken place since 1993 at the end of each year. Meetings of foreign and economic ministers are held annually, hosted by the rotating APEC Chair; every alternate ministerial meeting is held in an ASEAN country. The next ministerial meetings will be held in the Philippines in 1996, Canada in 1997 and Malaysia in 1998. Responsibility for developing the APEC process in accord with the decisions of the ministerial meetings lies with Senior Officials representing each participating country (usually at the head or deputy head of government department level). Senior Officials oversee and co-ordinate the activities of the Committees and Working Groups. Besides the CTI, which has undertaken initiatives to improve the flow of goods, services and technology in the region, there are a Budget and Administrative Committee and an Ad Hoc Group on Economic Trends and Issues. Working Groups promote practical co-operation and are currently active in trade promotion, trade and investment data review, investment and industrial science and technology, human resources development, regional energy co-operation, marine resource conservation, telecommunications, transportation, tourism, and fisheries. The Executive Director of the Secretariat, who is seconded from the member country in the APEC Chair, serves for one year. The Deputy Executive Director is appointed by the country designated to assume the chair the following year.

Activities

At the September 1992 ministerial meeting, held in Bangkok, the decision was adopted to establish a permanent APEC Secretariat in Singapore; it was also decided to set up an eleven-member non-governmental Eminent Persons Group (EPG) responsible for the assessment of trade patterns within the region and the presentation of proposals. The first EPG report (*A Vision for APEC: Towards an Asia Pacific Economic Community*), offering suggestions on ways to expand regional co-operation, was discussed at the ministerial meeting held in Seattle, USA, in November 1993. The EPG – whose mandate was extended – was invited to prepare a second report with specific recommendations for regional trade and investment liberalization. Ministers also decided on the creation of a Committee on Trade and Investment (CTI) to liberalize trade and provide for a more open environment for investment. The enlargement of APEC continued with the admission of Mexico and Papua New Guinea. After the ministerial session, a meeting of leaders (the first at the level of Heads of State) was convened at Blake Island, near Seattle, to conduct informal discussions on the future of APEC; several initiatives were agreed upon, including the establishment of a Pacific Business Forum (PBF), the convocation of ministerial meetings on financial issues and on small and medium business enterprises, and the development of policy dialogue and action plans for energy security, economic growth and environmental protection.

The second EPG report (*Achieving the APEC Vision: Free and Open Trade and Investment in the Asia Pacific Region*) in August 1994 comprised a timetable for trade liberalization throughout the region, taking into due account the differing levels of development of member countries. The leaders meeting in Bogor, Indonesia, in November 1994 adopted the Bogor Declaration of Common Resolve 'on the basis of equal partnership, shared responsibility, mutual respect, common interest and common benefit'. The leaders approved a timetable for the achievement of free trade and investment (no later than 2010 for the industrialized members and no later than 2020 for developing members) and called for the strengthening of the global trading system through the *World Trade Organization (WTO). The activities of the EPG were extended for a further year and the body was entrusted with the preparation of a third report. The PBF was asked to continue its work assessing the progress of APEC and providing further recommendations for increasing co-operation. Agreement was reached on ten 'non-binding investment principles', with a view to strengthening the crucial role played by investment in the economic dynamics of the region. The possibility of establishing a voluntary consultative dispute mediation service to supplement the WTO dispute settlement mechanism was considered in the light of the intensification of trade disputes in the region; the focus was to be on mediation rather than arbitration. Chile was admitted as an APEC member in November 1994, but a moratorium was decided for a three-year period on any further membership application.

The third and last report of the EPG (*Implementing the APEC Vision*), issued in August 1995, advocated, *inter alia*, an acceleration of trade liberalization measures and the establishment of an APEC Dispute Mediation Service. The PBF presented its report (*The Osaka Action Plan: Roadmap to Realising the APEC Vision*) in September 1995 recommending the establishment of timelines and progress reviews for trade and investment liberalization as well as concrete proposals for the integration of the business sector in the APEC work programme.

APEC Leaders met again at Osaka, Japan, in November 1995, and set out a detailed 'Action Agenda' incorporating national 'action plans' for trade liberalization, and decided that liberalization measures were to be implemented from January 1997 instead of January 2000, as had originally been agreed. An APEC Business Advisory Council, made up of private-sector representatives, was to start work in early 1996 as a successor to the PBF, whose term had expired.

APEC draws upon research, analysis and policy ideas contributed by participants as well as by other relevant organizations. The ASEAN Secretariat, the *South Pacific Forum (SPF) and the *Pacific Economic Co-operation Council (PECC) enjoy observer status at APEC Ministerial and Senior Officials' Meetings. The relationship with PECC is of special importance because of PECC's less formal character and wider membership, allowing for the discussion of specific issues and proposals without committing governments to specific actions. On the other hand, the maturing of APEC will stimulate PECC's work programmes. Substantial input for APEC also comes from private-sector bodies, notably the *Pacific Basin Economic Council (PBEC).

The institutionalization of economic co-operation among APEC countries represents a major trend that is likely to continue throughout and beyond the 1990s. Important negotiations have already been carried out and the pledge to liberalize has moved gradually from the political to the legal plane, despite repeated references to 'voluntary' and 'non-binding' commitments. Increased openness to trade and investment in the Asia-Pacific will not only contribute to the economic growth of the region but also strengthen the multilateral trading system. On the other hand, the different political and cultural traditions of the member countries, recurrent trade tensions between major partners, the serious difficulties of implementing a free-trade area among countries with uneven tariff levels, the risks of Mexico-type financial crises, and the delicate interrelationships between APEC and the existing subregional trading arrangements, could represent significant obstacles to the development of the overall APEC process.

Headquarters: 438 Alexandra Road, 19th floor, Alexandra Point, Singapore 0511 (Telephone: +65 276 1880; fax: +65 276 1775)
Internet address: http://www.apecsec.org.sg
Publications: Reports, proceedings of seminars, statistics and guides on various issues
References: A. Elek, 'The Challenge of Asian-Pacific Economic Cooperation', *Pacific Review*, 4 (1991), 322–32; Chia Siow Yue (ed.), *APEC: Challenges and Opportunities* (Singapore, 1994); W. Bodde Jr, *View from the 19th Floor: Reflections of the First APEC Executive Director* (Singapore, 1994)

Asia-Pacific Fishery Commission (APFIC)

The Commission was founded in 1948 by an international Agreement concluded under the aegis of the *Food and Agriculture Organization of the UN (FAO); the founding Agreement was amended in 1952, 1955, 1958, 1961, 1977 and 1993. The present title of the Commission was adopted in 1993; it was originally known as the Indo-Pacific Fisheries Council, and later, as the Indo-Pacific Fishery Commission (IPFC). The Asia-Pacific area, including inland waters, falls within the competence of the Commission. Membership includes some 20 countries, among them France, the UK and the USA. The Commission promotes the full and proper utilization of living aquatic resources by the development and management of fishing and culture operations, and by the development of related processing and marketing activities. Priority is currently being given by the Commission to marine fishery resources in the South China Sea and adjacent waters, and to inland fisheries and aquaculture in mainland Asia.

Headquarters: Maliwan Mansion, Phra Atit Road, Bangkok, Thailand (Telephone: +66 2 281 7844; fax: +66 2 280 0445)
Publications: Proceedings and occasional papers

Association of Caribbean States (ACS)

The Association represents the latest attempt at organizing co-operation among all countries in the Caribbean.

Origin and development
The Association's founding agreement was signed in Cartagena de Indias, Colombia in July 1994, by the representatives of 25 countries, including the then 13 members of the *Caribbean Community (CARICOM), the members of the *Group of Three (G-3) and nine other countries in the region – that is, Costa Rica, Cuba, the Dominican Republic, El Salvador, Guatemala, Haiti, Honduras, Nicaragua and Suriname. Associate membership is envisaged for a dozen dependent territories in the Caribbean but Puerto Rico and the US Virgin Islands refused to join because of Cuba's participation in the Association.

Objectives
The Association aims to promote economic co-operation and integration in the region, to co-ordinate participation in multilateral forums, to undertake concerted action to protect the environment, especially the Caribbean Sea, and to co-operate in the fields of energy, transport, science and technology, and education and culture.

Structure
The annual meeting of the Heads of State and Government is the supreme body setting the general guidelines which are defined by the Council of Ministers; the Secretariat is charged with carrying out administrative tasks. A special fund is to be established to support technical co-operation and research programmes.

Activities
The first summit of the Heads of State and Government of the Association took place in Port of Spain, Trinidad, in August 1995 and was mainly concerned with trade, transport and tourism issues in the regional context; the negative effects of the US economic blockade on Cuba were also discussed.

Secretary General: Simón Molina Duarte
Headquarters: Port of Spain, Trinidad

Association of South East Asian Nations (ASEAN)

The Association, although it does not yet comprise all the countries of the region, is the major body organizing co-operation in South East Asia, and plays a leading role in facilitating economic, social and cultural development, promoting active co-ordination and mutual assistance in matters of common interest, and ensuring regional peace and stability.

Origin and development
The Association originated in August 1967 in Bangkok when a solemn document, known as the Bangkok Declaration, was signed by representatives of Indonesia, Malaysia, the Philippines, Singapore and Thailand. The Declaration set out the aims and features of the new organization, which was intended to replace the Association of South East Asia (ASA), formed by Malaysia, the Philippines and Thailand in the early 1960s to deal with political and economic matters. In January 1984 Brunei joined the five founder members of the Association. Vietnam, formerly an observer, became a full member in July 1995. Laos and Cambodia enjoy observer status; Myanmar (formerly Burma) became an observer in July 1996. The eventual extension of ASEAN membership to include the whole of South East Asia now appears to be a realistic prospect. Papua New Guinea was also accorded observer status but its close affiliation to South Pacific

bodies seems to prevent a future full-scale participation in ASEAN.

Objectives

The basic goals of the Association are phrased rather loosely in the founding Declaration. They include: acceleration of economic growth, social progress and cultural development through joint efforts in the spirit of equality and partnership; provision of mutual assistance in training and research facilities in the educational, professional, technical and administrative fields; promotion of political stability in South East Asia; and the development of close links with other international and regional organizations with similar aims. Within the framework of economic co-operation and development, provision is made for greater utilization of the agriculture and industries of member countries, intensification of trade within the region and with the rest of the world, including the study of the problems of international commodity trade, improvement of transportation and communications, and adoption of joint research and technological programmes and projects.

The functions and powers of the Association, in accord with its basic features, are rather limited in scope, and subject to the principle of consensus with regard to decision-making. Recurring crises in the region have placed severe strains on the internal cohesion of the Association whose powers have been mostly confined to the promotion of voluntary co-ordination of efforts.

Structure

The present institutional framework comprises – besides the meeting of the Heads of Government – the ASEAN Ministerial Meeting (AMM); the ASEAN Economic Ministers (AEM); the Sectoral Ministers' Meeting; the Joint Ministerial Meeting (JMM); the ASEAN Standing Committee (ASC); and the Secretariat.

Summits of the Heads of Government of the member countries, previously taking place irregularly, are since 1992 being held at three-year intervals, with informal meetings every year; the Summit meeting has thus emerged as an important component of the Association's institutional machinery. The AMM consists of the Foreign Ministers of member countries meeting annually in each member country in turn; other relevant Ministers may be included as and when necessary. It is the supreme decision-making and political authority, with the exception of the ASEAN Summits, and is empowered to establish major policies and to set the guidelines for the development of regional co-ordination and co-operation in specific areas of common interest. Annual ministerial sessions are followed by 'post-ministerial conferences' where the Association's foreign ministers meet their counterparts from the 'dialogue partners'. The AEM meets about once a year to discuss major issues of economic co-operation, while other ministers meet as necessary. Ministers for specific sectors of economic co-operation meet as necessary to provide guidance on ASEAN co-operation.

The JMM, comprising the Foreign and Economic Ministers, meets whenever necessary, under the joint chairmanship of the AMM and AEM chairmen, to facilitate the cross-sectoral co-ordination of the Association's activities. The ASC is the policy arm and organ of co-ordination between the AMM; as an advisory body to the Permanent Committees, the ASC reviews the work of the Committees with a view to implementing the policy guidelines defined by the AMM. A permanent central Secretariat was established in 1976 in Jakarta, Indonesia, to perform administrative functions and keep contact with member countries through specially-appointed National Secretariats. The Secretariat was restructured and strengthened in 1992, with staff recruited openly and no longer appointed on the basis of national nomination. The Secretary-General has been vested with an expanded mandate and responsibilities. The post of Secretary-General revolves among member countries in alphabetical order at five-year intervals. The Association's principal organs are assisted by Committees, expert groups, working parties and other technical bodies meeting a broadening range of requirements. Special committees, composed of heads of diplomatic missions of member countries, have been set up in a number of foreign capitals in order to promote policy co-ordination. These ASEAN committees operate at present in Australia, Belgium, Canada, France, Germany, India, Japan, Korea, New Zealand, Switzerland, the UK and the USA.

Activities

A promising area of co-operation is represented by the Association's ties with the *European

Union (EU). A renewable five-year co-operation agreement, strengthening trade relations and increasing joint action in scientific and agricultural spheres, was signed between the Association and the then European Economic Community (EEC) in March 1980 and came into force the following October. A joint co-operation committee meets at yearly intervals. Several initiatives have been launched by the two organizations in order, *inter alia*, to encourage European investment in South East Asia, to identify joint industrial projects and to facilitate access to ASEAN markets. Since the early 1990s the Association and the EU have undertaken efforts to increase trade and investment, to co-operate against drug trafficking and to promote greater participation of the private sector. A joint declaration on human rights was adopted in October 1992 as the European side attempted to establish a link between trade and economic agreements, and social and human rights issues. The Association has developed relations with major countries, especially the 'dialogue partners' whose Foreign Ministers participate in ASEAN's post-ministerial conferences. Besides the EU, these partners currently include Australia, Canada, Japan, Korea, New Zealand and the USA. In 1993 ASEAN initiated a consultative relationship with China and with two 'sectoral partners' (India and Pakistan) to discuss matters of mutual concern in several areas; the three countries became full partners in July 1996. The Association is striving to define its specific role within the context of the efforts for furthering economic co-operation currently going on in the Asia-Pacific region, especially through the *Pacific Economic Co-operation Council (PECC) and the *Asia Pacific Economic Co-operation (APEC) process. ASEAN has also provided the framework for debating the proposals for the establishment of an East Asia Economic Grouping, later renamed East Asia Economic Caucus (EAEC), although little progress has been made so far.

Besides fostering co-operation in basic economic and non-economic sectors, the Association has succeeded in forging an 'ASEAN identity', taking common stands on regional as well as global issues, from Cambodia to Afghanistan. In fact, the ASEAN experience started with a legacy of tense and volatile relations among its founder members, and in the early stages the peaceful resolution of intra-ASEAN conflicts as well as the

resistance to a perceived communist threat were the overriding concerns. Only in the late 1970s did economic issues become a key aspect of ASEAN co-operation, both among members and with regard to non-member countries and international organizations.

ASEAN's first Summit meeting was held at Denpasar, Bali, Indonesia, in February 1976, where two important documents were signed. The Treaty of Amity and Co-operation established the principles of mutual respect for the independence and sovereignty of all nations; noninterference in internal affairs; peaceful settlement of disputes; and effective co-operation. The Treaty was amended in 1987 by a Protocol allowing the accession of other countries within and outside South East Asia. Laos and Vietnam became signatories to the Treaty in July 1992, followed by Myanmar in July 1995. The Declaration of Concord – the second document adopted at the Bali summit – provided guidelines with regard to economic, social and cultural relations, and reaffirmed the commitment of the signatories to the creation of a Zone of Peace, Freedom and Neutrality (ZOPFAN) in South East Asia; the Declaration on ZOPFAN had been approved in Kuala Lumpur in 1971.

Another Summit meeting was held in Kuala Lumpur, Malaysia, in August 1977. The intention to develop peaceful relations with other countries of South East Asia was solemnly reaffirmed; in particular, ASEAN supported the right of the people of Cambodia to self-determination.

A Basic Agreement on the Establishment of Preferential Trading Arrangements (PTA) concluded in January 1977 provided the framework for gradual tariff cuts and other concessions on a wide range of items. However, only a fraction of the value of intra-ASEAN trade was in fact accounted for by preferentially-traded items. The need to enhance economic co-operation programmes was addressed by the third Summit of Heads of Government, which took place in Manila in December 1987 and adopted a new set of priorities for national and regional development.

At the beginning of the 1990s, the end of the East–West confrontation and the eventual solution of the Cambodian crisis offered ASEAN countries a major opportunity to move forward with economic co-operation programmes in an environment no longer characterized by severe security threats.

The fourth Summit was held in Singapore in January 1992; participants decided to allow their foreign ministers to discuss security issues at future meetings, although without giving the Association competences in the military sphere, and recommended the establishment of ZOPFAN and of a South East Asia Nuclear Weapon-Free Zone (SEANWFZ). One of the major decisions of the Summit was the creation of an ASEAN Free Trade Area (AFTA) within 15 years. A 'Framework Agreement on Enhancing ASEAN Economic Co-operation' was adopted, with a view to promoting the conclusion of more detailed implementing arrangements, and a Common Effective Preferential Tariff (CEPT) scheme came into effect in January 1993. Subsequent meetings of economic and trade ministers between 1993 and 1995 enlarged the number of products to be affected by the tariff-reduction process and accelerated the implementation of AFTA setting new deadlines.

The fifth Summit took place in Bangkok in December 1995; the Bangkok Declaration outlines an agenda for greater economic integration within the region and the further expansion of the Association.

ASEAN Regional Forum

The Association's gradual involvement in security matters made a substantive step forward in July 1993 when the ministers of foreign affairs decided on the establishment of an ASEAN Regional Forum (ARF). The first formal meeting of the ARF took place in July 1994, following the ASEAN ministerial session held in Bangkok, and comprised, in addition to ASEAN members, the dialogue partners (Australia, Canada, the EU, Japan, Korea, New Zealand and the USA) plus China, Laos, Papua New Guinea, Russia and Vietnam. Several matters were discussed concerning regional peace-keeping, nuclear non-proliferation, confidence-building measures, and conflicting claims by several countries to the Spratly Islands in the South China Sea. It was decided that ARF meetings would be held every year after the Association's ministerial session. The next ARF meeting took place in Brunei in August 1995 and included Cambodia for the first time. The participating ministers institutionalized the ARF Senior Officials Meeting (ARF-SOM) to provide support and follow-up actions; the ARF itself was to evolve in three stages: promotion of confidence-building, development of preventive diplomacy, and elaboration of approaches to conflicts. Several countries, including India, France and the UK, have expressed interest in joining the ARF. Another ARF meeting was held in July 1996 to consider several issues, some with only marginal relevance to South East Asia.

Secretary-General: Dato' Ajit Singh
Headquarters: Jalan Sisingamangaraja 70A, Jakarta 12110, Indonesia (Telephone: +62 21 7262991; fax: +62 21 7243504)
Internet address: http://www.asean.sec.org
Publications: *Annual Report of the ASEAN Standing Committee*; *ASEAN Update* (every two months); *ASEAN Journal on Science and Technology for Development* (twice a year)
References: J. Wong, *ASEAN Economies in Perspective* (London, 1979); R. H. Fifield, *National and Regional Interests in ASEAN* (Singapore, 1979); M. T. Skully, *ASEAN Financial Cooperation* (London, 1984); M. Rajendran, *ASEAN's Foreign Relations. The Shift to Collective Action* (Kuala Lumpur, 1985); G. Schiavone (ed.), *Western Europe and South-East Asia: Co-operation or Competition?* (London, 1989); H. C. Rieger, 'Regional Economic Co-operation in the Asia-Pacific Region', *Asia-Pacific Economic Literature*, 2 (1989), 5–33

B

Bank for International Settlements (BIS)

The Bank, established to promote co-operation among central banks, is one of the oldest multilateral financial institutions in the world.

Origin and development

Although the first proposals to institutionalize co-operation among central banks date back to the late nineteenth century, the creation of the Bank resulted from conferences held in The Hague, The Netherlands, in 1929 and 1930 to settle the question of German reparations. Negotiations over the revision of the Dawes Plan led to the signing of an international agreement on the Young Plan in January 1930 in The Hague. As a result, the burdens of reparations and war debts were eased considerably and a Bank for International Settlements was established and empowered, *inter alia*, to act as trustee. Another agreement was signed between the governments of Belgium, France, Germany, Italy, Japan and the UK, and the government of Switzerland, for the constitution of the Bank as a limited company with its seat at Basle, Switzerland. The Bank was granted immunities from taxation as well as guarantees against expropriation.

The Charter of the Bank was signed formally in February 1930, in Rome, by the governors of the central banks of the founding countries joined by the representatives of a group of American banks. The Bank started operations at its Basle headquarters the following May. The central banks of other European countries, such as Austria, Denmark, Hungary, The Netherlands, Sweden and Switzerland, joined the founder members shortly afterwards. The aggravation of the economic crisis in Europe prevented other prospective members from participating in the newly-created institution. The Bank's membership increased substantially after the Second World War. The central banks of nearly all European countries have become members. Japan, which had withdrawn in 1953, resumed participation in 1969. Canada, Australia and South Africa have also joined, thereby increasing the importance of non-European members. The Bank's assets are currently owned by 33 central banks.

Objectives

The Bank aims to promote co-operation among national central banks, to provide additional facilities for international financial operations, and to act as trustee or agent in connection with international financial settlements entrusted to it. In order to fulfil its basic aims, the Bank is empowered to: buy and sell gold coin or bullion for its own account or for central banks; hold gold for its own account under earmark in central banks, and accept the custody of gold for these banks; make advances to, or borrow from, central banks against gold and short-term obligations of prime liquidity or other approved securities; discount, rediscount, purchase or sell short-term obligations of prime liquidity, including Treasury bills and other government short-term securities; buy and sell exchange and negotiable securities other than shares; open current or deposit accounts with central banks and accept deposits from them as well as deposits in connection with trustee agreements; act as trustee or agent with regard to international settlements; conclude special agreements with central banks to facilitate the settlement of international transactions.

Structure

The organizational structure of the Bank includes the General Meeting, the Board of Directors, and the President. The General Meeting, attended by representatives of the central banks voting in proportion to the number of shares subscribed, normally takes place every year to approve the budget and the annual report, to decide the distribution of the net income, and to set down the general guidelines for the Bank's activities.

Administration is carried out by the Board of Directors, which at present consists of the governors of the central banks of Belgium, France, Germany, Italy, the UK and the USA, each of whom appoints another member of the same nationality. As a founder member, the USA had been entitled to two seats since the beginning of the Bank's activities, but took them only in September 1994. According to the Charter, the governors of not more than nine other central banks may be elected to the Board; the governors of the central banks of The Netherlands, Sweden and Switzerland, already serving, were joined, in September 1994, by the governors of Canada and Japan. Therefore the number of countries currently represented on the Board is eleven. The Chairman of the Board may also act as President, as is currently the case. The President conducts the ordinary business of the Bank and is assisted by a General Manager, several executive officers and the necessary staff. The Bank has developed close co-operative links with economic and financial institutions within the UN system and with regional or national bodies.

Activities

The Bank is obliged to maintain its liquidity and therefore has to retain assets appropriate to the maturity and character of its liabilities. The Bank's short-term liquid assets may include banknotes, cheques payable on sight drawn on first-class banks, claims in course of collection, deposits at sight or at short notice, and prime bills of exchange. All operations undertaken by the Bank must conform to the monetary policy of the central banks of the countries concerned.

The Bank uses as unit of account the gold franc equivalent to 0.290322 gram of fine gold. The size of the authorized capital stock, initially set at 500 million gold francs, was raised in June 1969 to 1500 million gold francs, divided into 600 000 shares of 2500 gold francs each. The major shareholders are the central banks, which enjoy the corresponding voting rights; private shareholders are not entitled to vote.

Since its establishment, the Bank has performed a significant role in a variety of fields and has effectively succeeded in maintaining its liquidity. At the very beginning of its operations, the Bank had to face the consequences of the Great Depression in almost all the countries of Europe, with the ensuing suspension, in July 1931, of the implementation of the Young Plan and of its activities as trustee. The Bank's role was further reduced when many countries modified or went off the gold standard in the first half of the 1930s. Its difficulties were aggravated by the outbreak of the Second World War. Nearly all the participating banks represented belligerent countries. The Bank decided to pursue a policy of strict neutrality and therefore to abstain from any operation amounting to a breach of such neutrality. The UN Monetary and Financial Conference held at Bretton Woods in 1944 recommended the liquidation of the Bank because of the alleged illegitimacy of its custody of gold for the account of the Reichsbank. Moreover, the functions of the Bank appeared to a very large extent to overlap those of the *International Monetary Fund (IMF) and the *International Bank for Reconstruction and Development (IBRD). However, the peculiar role performed by the Bank through the provision of a framework for co-operation of central banks was eventually recognized, and operations were fully resumed. Since the 1950s the Bank has substantially developed its activities on international financial markets, acted as an important forum for consultation and collaboration among central banks, and provided a helpful and informative analysis of the major features of the world economy through its annual reports.

The Bank provides the secretariat for several committees and groups of experts, such as the Committee on Banking Regulations and Supervisory Practices, established in 1974 by the governors of the central banks of the Group of Ten (G-10) and Switzerland, and responsible for co-ordinating banking supervisory regulations and surveillance systems at the international level.

The Bank acted as a clearing agency for the Organization for European Economic Co-operation (OEEC) in connection with the agreements on intra-European payments and compensation, and the European Payments Union (EPU), replaced by the European Monetary Agreement (EMA) in December 1958. The EMA system was retained in the *Organization for Economic Co-operation and Development (OECD), which succeeded the OEEC in 1960. The Bank acted as depositary under an Act of Pledge concluded with the European Coal and Steel Community (ECSC), and as agent, between June 1973 and December 1993, for the European Monetary Co-operation Fund (EMCF), set up by the member countries of the then European Economic Community (EEC). In early 1994 the Bank's staff supported the European Monetary Institute (EMI) which had been established according to the provisions of the Maastricht Treaty creating the *European Union (EU).

President: W. F. Duisenberg
Headquarters: Centralbahnplatz 2, 4002 Basle,
   Switzerland (Telephone: +41 61 280 8080;
   fax: +41 61 280 9100)
Publication: *Annual Report*

Barents Euro-Arctic Council

The Council, also referred to as the Council of the Euro-Arctic Region, was launched in January 1993 to promote trade and co-operation and the clean-up of pollution and radiation contamination in the area around the Barents Sea. Members currently include Denmark, Finland, Iceland, Norway, Russia and Sweden.

Benelux Economic Union

The economic union between Belgium, Luxembourg and The Netherlands represents a successful example of co-ordination among the member countries in forging closer and more effective economic links.

Origin and development

The Treaty establishing the Union was signed in The Hague, The Netherlands, in February 1958, and came into force in November 1960. It represented the result of several moves initiated in the early 1930s towards closer economic co-operation between the three Benelux countries. An economic union had been formed between Belgium and Luxembourg by the convention concluded in Brussels in July 1921 and came into force the following year. Dissolved in August 1940, the union was re-established in May 1945. After an unsuccessful attempt through the Ouchy Agreement (1932), the governments in exile of the Benelux countries made a fresh effort to advance mutual economic co-operation by signing a Customs Convention in September 1944 in London. This Convention was further defined and interpreted in a Protocol for the establishment of a customs union; it was signed in The Hague in March 1947 and came into force in January 1948. The customs tariffs of the Belgium–Luxembourg Economic Union and of The Netherlands were thus superseded by the joint external tariff of the Benelux customs union. Further protocols (1947, 1950, 1953, 1954) gradually expanded the scope of economic co-operation between the Benelux countries.

In November 1955, a Convention for the establishment of a Benelux Inter-parliamentary Consultative Council, consisting of members of the three national parliaments, was signed in Brussels. In 1958, the Benelux countries decided to set up a full economic union (as envisaged by the Customs Convention of 1944 and the Protocol of 1947), and concluded the present Treaty. In the Preamble to the Treaty, the signatory countries expressly noted that the Rome Treaties of 1957 do not prevent particular member countries from creating an economic union *inter se*. In March 1965, in Brussels, the Benelux countries signed a Treaty creating a Court of Justice with both contentious and advisory jurisdiction.

Objectives

With respect to their relations with non-member countries, the member countries: (a) accept and pursue a joint policy in the field of foreign trade and of payments related thereto; (b) jointly conclude treaties and conventions regarding foreign trade and the customs tariff; and (c) conclude, either jointly or concurrently, treaties and conventions relating to payments in connection with foreign trade. The provisions of the Treaty do not affect the existence and development of the economic union between Belgium and Luxembourg in so far as the objectives of such union are not attained by the application of the Treaty itself.

Structure

The organizational structure of the Union is elaborate and consists of the following institutions: the Committee of Ministers; the Interparliamentary Consultative Council; the Council of the Economic Union; the Committees and the Special Committees; the Secretariat-General; Joint Services; the College of Arbitrators; the Court of Justice; and the Economic and Social Consultative Council.

The real executive power lies with the Committee of Ministers which meets about twice a year, in a formal meeting, in order to supervise the application of the Treaty and ensure the realization of its aims. Each member country appoints at least three government members (generally from among the Ministers of Foreign Affairs, Foreign Trade, Economic Affairs, Agriculture,

Finance and Social Affairs). All decisions are taken unanimously, each country having one vote, but the abstention of one country does not prevent a decision being taken.

The Interparliamentary Consultative Council, created by the Convention of 1955, is entrusted with advisory functions. This 'Benelux Parliament' – consisting of 49 members, 21 each from The Netherlands States-General and the Belgian Parliament, and 7 from the Luxembourg Chamber of Deputies – holds three plenary sessions per year.

The Council of the Economic Union, consisting of one chairman from each member country and of the presidents of the Committees, is responsible for: (a) co-ordinating the activities of the Committees and Special Committees; (b) putting into effect the relevant decisions of the Committee of Ministers; and (c) submitting proposals to the Committee of Ministers.

The numerous Committees and the Special Committees, each within the limits of its competence, implement the relevant decisions of the Committee of Ministers, submit proposals, and monitor the execution by national administrations of resolutions adopted.

The General-Secretariat, located in Brussels, is headed by a Secretary-General of Dutch nationality assisted by two deputies, one from Belgium and one from Luxembourg; all three are appointed and dismissed by the Committee of Ministers. The General-Secretariat services the Committee of Ministers, the Council of the Economic Union and the Committees; since 1985 it has also serviced the Schengen Agreement.

Joint Services have executive powers and may be set up by the Committee of Ministers.

The College of Arbitrators is entrusted with the task of settling any disputes that may arise between member countries from the working of the Union. It consists of six members (two from each member country) appointed by the Committee of Ministers.

The Court of Justice, composed of senior judges from the member countries, is designed to ensure uniformity in the interpretation of the legal rules common to the three members which are specified either in conventions or decisions of the Committee of Ministers. The College of Arbitrators suspends its function in any case where a matter of interpretation of such rules arises, pending a decision of the Court of Justice.

The Economic and Social Consultative Council consists of 27 members and 27 deputy members from representative economic and social organizations, each country supplying one-third of the number. It offers advice on its own initiative, or upon specific request of the Committee of Ministers.

Activities

According to the basic provisions of the Treaty establishing the Union, the nationals of each member country may enter and leave the territory of any other member country freely, and are entitled to the same treatment as nationals of that country with regard to: freedom of movement, sojourn and settlement; freedom to carry on a trade or occupation; capital transactions; conditions of employment; social security benefits; taxes and charges of any kind; and exercise of civil rights, as well as legal and judicial protection of their person, individual rights and interests.

Importation or exportation of goods between the territories of the member countries, irrespective of origin or destination, are free of import, excise and any other duties, charges or dues of any kind, as well as of prohibitions or restrictions of an economic or financial nature, such as quotas or currency restrictions. A common tariff with identical rates applies to goods coming from or destined for non-member countries. Restrictions concerning transfers of capital between the member countries are abolished; the rendering of services is also free of taxes and charges of any kind. The member countries are bound to pursue a co-ordinated policy in the economic, financial and social fields.

The Union entails the free movement of persons, goods, capital and services between Belgium, Luxembourg and The Netherlands, and implies the co-ordination of economic, financial and social policies as well as the pursuit of a joint policy in economic and financial relations with non-member countries. The Benelux countries are therefore in a position to play a stronger role in the furthering of the process of wider European integration as pursued by the *European Union (EU). The Union has brought substantial benefits to the economies of the member countries, and enhanced their full participation in broader European institutions and initiatives.

The Committee of Ministers, meeting in November 1995, has decided to focus the future activities of the Union – besides political co-operation and concertation on European issues – on five major topics: trans-frontier co-operation; internal market and economic co-operation; culture, research, training and education; free movement of persons and co-operation within the framework of the Schengen agreement; and information, publications and statistics.

Secretary-General: B. M. J. Hennekam

General-Secretariat: 39 rue de la Régence, 1000 Brussels, Belgium (Telephone: +32 2 519 3811; fax: +32 2 513 4206)

Interparliamentary Consultative Council: Palais de la Nation, Place de la Nation, 1008 Brussels, Belgium (Telephone: +32 2 519 8552; fax: +32 2 519 8520)

Publications: *Benelux Newsletter* (monthly); *Benelux Review* (quarterly); *Bulletin Benelux*

Reference: J. Meade, *Negotiations for Benelux* (Princeton, NJ, 1957)

Black Sea Economic Co-operation (BSEC)

The organization fosters economic and technological co-operation, both bilaterally and multilaterally, among countries belonging to the Black Sea region.

Origin and development

The creation of an economic grouping of the countries of the Black Sea region was proposed originally by the then President of Turkey, Turgut Özal, in the late 1980s as a subregional framework to promote peace, stability and prosperity in a dramatically changing environment. Following several preparatory meetings in 1990 and 1991, the representatives of Armenia, Azerbaijan, Bulgaria, Georgia, Moldova, Romania, Russia, Turkey and Ukraine adopted a declaration outlining the basic objectives of the grouping in February 1992. The Heads of State and Government of these countries, joined by Albania and Greece, on 25 June 1992 in Istanbul signed the Declaration on Black Sea Economic Co-operation, to contribute to political stability and economic development. Several countries have been granted observer status: Poland became the first observer in December 1992, followed by Egypt, Israel, Slovakia and Tunisia in 1993, and by Austria and Italy in 1995.

The organization is considered to be complementary to the *Organization for Security and Co-operation in Europe (OSCE), the *Central European Initiative (CEI), the *European Union (EU), and other regional economic groupings.

Objectives

Comprehensive multilateral and bilateral co-operation is to be developed 'in the fields of economics, including trade and industrial co-operation, of science and technology and of the environment'. The signatory countries, with the participation of their competent organizations, enterprises and firms, are to implement projects of common interest in fields such as transport and communications, mining, energy, agriculture and the agro-industries, health care and pharmaceutics, tourism, informatics, and science and technology. Special emphasis is given to environmental issues as well as to the promotion of individual and collective initiative of the enterprises and firms directly involved in the co-operation process.

Structure

The institutional structure of the organization is very flexible; the eventual elaboration of a document strengthening the organization's legal and institutional basis is to be considered in concert with the process of developing concrete projects. Besides meetings of the Heads of State and Government, the meeting of the Ministers of Foreign Affairs (MMFA) is the major policy-making body, which is convened twice a year under a six-month chairmanship rotating in alphabetical order. The MMFA is preceded by the Meeting of Senior Officials (MSO). The bulk of the organization's activities is carried on by its subsidiary bodies; there are Working Groups on Trade and Industrial Co-operation, Agriculture and Agro-industry, Transport, Energy, Environmental Protection, Health Care and Pharmaceutics, Communications, Co-operation in Tourism, and an *ad hoc* Working Group on Organizational Matters. A Parliamentary Assembly of BSEC (PABSEC) performs functions of a consultative nature. The Permanent International Secretariat, headed by a Director assisted by the necessary staff, is based in Istanbul.

The scale of contributions to the budget of the International Secretariat is based on the division of the members into three main groups. The countries of Group I (Greece, Russia, Turkey and

Ukraine) pay 16 per cent each; the countries of Group II (Bulgaria and Romania), 8 per cent each; and the remaining five countries of Group III, 4 per cent each.

Activities

The creation of a Black Sea Trade and Development Bank, to be based at Thessaloniki, Greece, was decided in December 1993. The Bank will finance and promote regional projects, and provide other banking services to public and private projects in the member countries. The initial authorized capital stock amounts to SDR1 billion. Increasing emphasis is being devoted to a broader and more efficient involvement of the business circles in the implementation of various concrete projects.

Director: Evgeni G. Kutovoy

Headquarters: I. Hareket Köskü – Dolmabahce Saray Besiktas, 80680 Istanbul, Turkey (Telephone: +90 212 227 7300; fax: +90 212 227 7306)

C

Cairns Group

The Group originated from the attempt of a number of agricultural exporters to create an effective instrument to promote the liberalization of international agricultural trade.

Origin and development

The Group was set up in 1986 with a varied membership currently including Argentina, Australia, Brazil, Canada, Chile, Colombia, Fiji, Hungary, Indonesia, Malaysia, New Zealand, the Philippines, Thailand and Uruguay. The need to present a common front of agricultural exporters in the Uruguay Round of negotiations held under the auspices of the General Agreement on Tariffs and Trade (GATT) – succeeded by the *World Trade Organization (WTO) – led a number of countries to join a group named after the Australian town of Cairns, where the representatives of the interested countries held their first meeting.

Objectives

The purposes of the Group are to bring about reforms in international agricultural trade, including reductions in export subsidies and other support measures, and to represent members' interests in multilateral negotiations. Since its beginning, the Group has included developed, developing and Central European countries brought together by a similarity of trade interests and objectives rather than a regional identity.

Activities

The successful conclusion of the Uruguay Round and the effectiveness of the joint action carried on by the Group have induced participating countries to continue and strengthen their co-operation in the field of agricultural trade.

Contact address: c/o Department of Foreign Affairs and Trade, Bag 8, Queen Victoria Terrace, Canberra, ACT 2600, Australia

Caribbean Community and Common Market (CARICOM)

The main areas of activity of the Community are: economic integration by means of the Caribbean Common Market, which replaced the former Caribbean Free Trade Association (CARIFTA); functional co-operation in specific sectors and operation of certain common services; and co-ordination of foreign policies.

Origin and development

The basic legal instrument of the Community is the Treaty signed in July 1973 at Chaguaramas, Trinidad, by the Prime Ministers of Barbados, Guyana, Jamaica, and Trinidad and Tobago, which came into effect the following August. Eight other Commonwealth Caribbean countries (Antigua and Barbuda, Belize, Dominica, Grenada, Montserrat, Saint Kitts and Nevis, Saint Lucia and Saint Vincent and the Grenadines) acceded to full membership during 1974. The Treaty was amended in 1976 to facilitate the prospective admission of the Bahamas as a member of the Community without participating in the Common Market; the formal admission of the Bahamas took place in July 1983. Suriname, hitherto an observer, became a full member in February 1995, the first non-English speaking country to join the Community. The British Virgin Islands, and the Turks and Caicos Islands, were granted associate membership in 1991. A number of Caribbean islands, Colombia, Mexico and Venezuela have observer status.

Membership in the Community does not necessarily imply membership in the Common Market; the Bahamas were included in the list of countries which might be admitted to the Community but omitted from a similar list regarding the Common Market. Provisions for associate membership are contained in both the Chaguaramas Treaty and its Common Market Annex.

During the 1950s efforts had been made to promote Commonwealth Caribbean regionalism, resulting in the establishment of the short-lived Federation of the West Indies (January 1958); proposals for a customs union were also put forward. An agreement establishing a regional institution, the Caribbean Organization, was signed in June 1960 in Washington. During the 1960s self-government was introduced and/or gradually extended until many of the former British colonies acquired full independence within the Commonwealth. The West Indies Federation was dissolved in February 1962 after the withdrawal of Jamaica, and Trinidad and Tobago. This substantially weakened the Caribbean Organization, and its founding agreement was ended formally in 1965. Under the West Indies Act 1967, new constitutional arrangements raised Antigua, Dominica, Grenada, Saint Kitts–Nevis–Anguilla, Saint Lucia and Saint Vincent to the rank of Associated States of the UK.

In the second half of the 1960s, new initiatives for freeing trade among Commonwealth Caribbean countries led to the signing in April 1968, at St John's, Antigua, of the agreement establishing CARIFTA, following the patterns of the *European Free Trade Association (EFTA) and the Latin American Free Trade Association (LAFTA). The four original signatories (Antigua, Barbados, Guyana, and Trinidad and Tobago) were joined, between May and August 1968, by Jamaica, Grenada, Dominica, Saint Lucia, Saint Vincent, Saint Kitts–Nevis–Anguilla, Montserrat and, in May 1971, by Belize. In June 1968, seven small, less developed countries of the subregion, initially reluctant to join CARIFTA, had formed their own customs union, the *East Caribbean Common Market (ECCM). An autonomous financial institution, the *Caribbean Development Bank (CDB; Caribank), was set up in 1969 with the participation of both regional and non-regional members. A generalized consensus over the need to deepen and improve the integration process and the ensuing negotiations made it possible to replace CARIFTA with the broader and more advanced CARICOM.

Objectives

The basic aim of the Community is to foster unity among peoples of the Caribbean through common or co-ordinated regional actions, in spheres ranging from foreign policy to health, education, labour matters, transport, and economic, financial and trade relations. However, no future merger into a single political unit is envisaged. Foreign policy co-ordination is dealt with by the Ministers of Foreign Affairs of the independent member countries. Functional co-operation involves several sectors which are expressly mentioned, though the list may be expanded.

The Common Market was established by an Annex to the Chaguaramas Treaty with a view to achieving the Community's objectives in the field of economic integration. It is founded on: the erection of a common external tariff, a common protective policy, and the gradual co-ordination of commercial policies; the harmonization of fiscal incentives to industry; the elimination of double taxation; the co-ordination of economic policies and development planning; and, last but not least, the setting up of a special regime for the less developed members. Adequate recognition has been given to differences in levels of economic development in the Commonwealth Caribbean context; Barbados, Guyana, Jamaica, and Trinidad and Tobago have been designated as more developed countries (MDCs) and the remaining members as less developed countries (LDCs). Measures specifically intended to meet the needs of the LDCs are included in the Common Market Annex to the Chaguaramas Treaty to ensure an equitable distribution of benefits from integration. The steady development of the ECCM, composed of seven LDCs, had to take place within the wider framework of the Caribbean Common Market.

Structure

Caribbean political and functional co-operation and economic integration take place within a rather complex institutional structure. The Conference of Heads of Government (whose meetings have been held annually since 1983) is the supreme organ responsible for the determination of basic policies, including relations with non-member countries and international organizations, and the establishment of financial arrangements to meet the Community's expenses. At a special meeting, held in Trinidad and Tobago in October 1992, the Conference decided to establish the Bureau of Heads of Government, a four-member body with competence to initiate proposals, update consensus, mobilize action and secure the implementation of Community decisions. The Bureau, in operation since January 1993, consists of the current Chairman of the Conference, rotating on a six-monthly basis, his/her immediate predecessor and his/her scheduled successor, plus the Secretary-General as chief executive officer.

The Community's second highest organ is the Caribbean Community Council of Ministers, which replaced the Common Market Council of Ministers following the decision taken at the October 1992 meeting of the Conference of Heads of Government. The Council, consisting of a minister of government from each country, deals with operational aspects. It undertakes annual reviews of the Common Market mechanisms, taking into consideration the special needs of the less developed members and submitting reports to the Conference; the latter may issue directives to the Council to this effect. The Council convenes whenever necessary, in particular before meetings of the Conference.

The Assembly of Caribbean Community Parliamentarians, a consultative body designed as a forum to discuss regional issues and increase public and private awareness, was established by an agreement which came into force in August 1994.

The Secretariat (successor to the Commonwealth Caribbean Regional Secretariat) is located in Georgetown, Guyana. It performs technical and administrative functions concerning both the Community and the Common Market, takes appropriate action on decisions of the various organs, initiates and carries out studies on regional co-operation and integration and provides services requested by member countries in order to achieve the Community's objectives. The Secretary-General is appointed by the Conference on the recommendation of the Council for a term not exceeding five years, and may be re-appointed.

The Community's functions and decision-making powers bear no supranational features and are limited by the unanimity principle, applicable in any delicate case. As regards the Common Market, its objectives are often loosely phrased, leaving ample room for further negotiations on specific issues and areas of activity.

Decisions, recommendations and directives are generally adopted unanimously, each member having one vote; non-participation is equivalent to abstention. Decisions that may involve constitutional problems are to be submitted for consideration to member countries before they become legally binding.

There are also specialized institutions in charge of the advancement of co-operation in specific sectors. These institutions include the Conference of Ministers responsible for Health and the Standing Committees of Ministers responsible for Education; Labour; Foreign Affairs; Finance; Agriculture; Industry; Transport; Legal Affairs; Energy, Mines and Natural Resources; Science and Technology; Tourism; and Environment.

The Treaty recognizes as Associate Institutions of the Community a number of regional bodies having their own constitutive documents and enjoying legal autonomy. Besides the already-cited Caribbean Development Bank, among these bodies are: the Caribbean Examinations Council (CEC); the Caribbean Council of Legal Education (CLE); the University of Guyana (UG); the University of the West Indies (UWI); the Caribbean Meteorological Organization (CMO); and the West Indies Shipping Corporation (WISCO).

As regards the co-ordination of foreign policy, the Standing Committee of Ministers responsible for Foreign Affairs aims at developing the Community's relations with non-member countries and international organizations, and preparing joint diplomatic action on matters of particular relevance to the Caribbean.

Activities

The Community has enjoyed observer status at the UN General Assembly since 1992 and has established close ties with UN bodies and regional agencies. The Community's member countries have a special relationship – belonging to the group of African, Caribbean and Pacific (ACP) states – with the *European Union (EU) under the Lomé Convention.

In spite of serious economic and financial constraints and strong nationalistic tendencies, the Community has played a significant role in promoting broader understanding and increased trade and economic relations in the Commonwealth Caribbean. As regards trade liberalization, the Community inherited from its predecessor CARIFTA a free-trade pattern with numerous exceptions whose complete elimination has proved extremely difficult. The first step towards the erection of a common external tariff was taken in August 1973 by the four MDCs, while longer and more flexible schedules were envisaged for the LDCs. As well as through the acceleration of intra-area trade, integration is promoted through the harmonization of economic policies and the establishment and operation of regional industrial and agricultural projects. This implies, *inter alia*, some form of control over foreign investments in key sectors.

Agreements have been concluded to harmonize fiscal incentives to industry and to avoid double taxation among MDCs and among LDCs.

In the last half of the 1970s, most of the countries of the Community (particularly Jamaica and Guyana) were adversely affected by severe economic disturbances, which in some cases led to the introduction of stabilization programmes and the tightening of import restrictions. Moreover, the LDCs showed a growing dissatisfaction and claimed a greater and more equitable share of the benefits of integration. In order to co-ordinate financial and technical assistance, the Caribbean Group for Co-operation in Economic Development was formed in late 1977 by Caribbean countries, donor countries and international development institutions, under the chairmanship of the *International Bank for Reconstruction and Development (IBRD).

The Community has made intensive efforts to formulate long-term solutions to the severe energy problems faced by most member countries. In order to ease serious balance-of-payments difficulties, the Multilateral Clearing Facility (MCF), envisaged by the Common Market Annex to the Chaguaramas Treaty, came into effect in June 1977, while other funds were made available for emergency payments.

In June 1981, the seven less developed members participating in the ECCM established the *Organization of Eastern Caribbean States (OECS). Severe difficulties hindered the development of Caribbean trade and integration during the first half of the 1980s. A group of experts, set up in 1980, drew up a strategy for the decade with respect to production, export, productivity, marketing, energy policy and air transport. Other meetings of experts were held to review the key components of Caribbean economy.

In July 1984, the Conference of Heads of Government, meeting in Nassau, Bahamas, called for structural adjustment in the economies of the member countries with a view to expanding production and reducing imports, and set new target dates for the implementation of the common external tariff. An unsuccessful attempt was also made at relaunching the activities of the MCF, which had collapsed in 1983 after having exceeded its credit limit. In July 1986 the Conference agreed to replace the MCF with a Caribbean Export Bank but the plan was ultimately shelved because of the lack of adequate financing. The Conference held in 1989 adopted a series of measures intended to remove by the early 1990s the remaining barriers to the establishment of a single Caribbean market and set new detailed deadlines which, however, were repeatedly postponed. In 1989 it was also decided to set up a 15-member West Indian Commission to explore new avenues to regional political and economic integration. Between July 1990 and July 1992 the Commission prepared a report recommending the strengthening of the integration process of the Community and the setting up of a larger body, the *Association of Caribbean States (ACS) which was established in July 1994. The Community held in February 1995 a joint meeting with representatives of the OECS to expand region-wide co-operation and prepare for the new challenges of globalization. A dialogue has also been going on since 1993 between the Community and Cuba. The Community has observer status in the *Group of Rio, set up in 1987 to provide a permanent mechanism for joint political action of Latin American countries.

Secretary-General: Edwin W. Carrington
Headquarters: Bank of Guyana Building, P.O. Box 10827, Georgetown, Guyana (Telephone: +592 2 69281; fax: +592 2 66091)
Publications: *Secretary-General's Report* (annual); *CARICOM Perspective* (twice a year)
References: H. J. Geiser, P. Alleyne and C. Gajraj, *Legal Problems of Caribbean Integration* (Leyden, 1976); A. R. Carnegie, 'Commonwealth Caribbean Regionalism: Legal Aspects', *Year Book of World Affairs*, 33 (1979), 180–200; A. W. Axline, *Caribbean Integration. The Politics of Regionalism* (London, 1979); A. J. Payne, *The Politics of the Caribbean Community 1961–79* (Manchester, 1980)

Caribbean Development Bank (CDB; Caribank)

The Bank contributes to the harmonious economic growth and development of member countries in the Caribbean and fosters co-operation and integration by financing investment projects and programmes with due regard to the special needs of its less developed members.

Origin and development

The agreement establishing the Bank was signed in October 1969 and entered into effect in January 1970, when the Bank started operations in Barbados. The creation of an autonomous financial body was part of the efforts towards Commonwealth Caribbean co-operation as shown by the establishment of the Caribbean Free Trade Association (CARIFTA) in 1968. In the early 1970s CARIFTA was succeeded by the *Caribbean Community (CARICOM). The Bank's membership includes the countries participating in CARICOM and other Commonwealth Caribbean countries (Anguilla, British Virgin Islands, Cayman Islands, Turks and Caicos Islands) plus Canada, Colombia, France, Germany, Italy, Mexico, the UK and Venezuela. Among non-member contributors to the resources of the Bank have been The Netherlands, New Zealand, Nigeria, Sweden and the USA.

Objectives

The Bank helps to finance capital infrastructure and investment projects, both large and small, public and private, in the productive sectors of the economy, particularly in the less developed countries (LDCs), as well as regional integration projects in agriculture, and air and sea transportation. The main areas covered by Bank lending are: agriculture and rural development (credits to private farmers and loans to governments for infrastructural projects); manufacturing industries (loans to industrialists, development corporations and other agencies); tourism promotion (loans to hotel operators and governments); and education (loans to governments for the development of higher education, teacher training, and technical and vocational training).

Structure

The Bank's highest decision-making organ is the Board of Governors, appointed by governments and meeting annually. Voting power is roughly proportional to shares subscribed, with a slight weighting in favour of the smaller members. The Directors, currently numbering 17 (twelve representing the regional members and five the non-regional members), are selected by the Board of Governors for a renewable two-year period. The President is elected by the Board ot Governors for a term not exceeding five years.

Activities

The Bank operates with its ordinary capital resources. In addition, a Special Development Fund and other Special Funds have been set up for specific purposes, such as development of small farming, livestock production, technical assistance and housing. The initially authorized capital stock amounted to $192 million, of which over $155 million had been subscribed; the authorized capital has now reached $693.7 million. The subscribed capital amounts to $648.4 million, of which $143.4 million is paid-up and $505.0 million callable.

Financial support has been secured from various governments and institutions, both regional and extraregional. Credits have been granted to the Bank by the *International Bank for Reconstruction and Development (IBRD), the *International Development Association (IDA), the *Inter-American Development Bank (IDB), and the *European Union (EU). Lending from the Bank's ordinary capital resources is subject to stringent criteria which are unlikely to be fully met by applicants from LDCs. In such cases, the Bank may grant loans on non-commercial terms through a soft window provided by its Special Funds resources earmarked for the benefit of less developed members. In 1990 the decision was adopted to create a Special Development Fund of $124 million to make or guarantee loans of high developmental priority calling for longer maturities and lower interest rates than those adopted for ordinary operations; the Fund's resources had reached $432.1 million at the end of 1994. The Basic Needs Trust Fund finances small infrastructure projects for the alleviation of poverty in the less developed borrowing member countries.

The Bank has played a significant role in the process of Commonwealth Caribbean integration and in several cases has effectively operated as a corrective mechanism in favour of the less industrialized and less competitive member countries. The Bank's operations have been considerably smoothed by its close working relations with CARICOM and several financial institutions within and outside the Caribbean.

President: Neville Vernon Nicholls
Headquarters: P.O. Box 408, Wildey, St Michael, Barbados (Telephone: +854 431 1600; fax: +854 426 7269)
Publications: *Annual Report*; *CDB News* (quarterly).

Central American Bank for Economic Integration (CABEI)

(Banco Centroamericano de Integración Económica) (BCIE)

The Bank stimulates and supports efforts towards Central American economic integration by financing public and private investment projects, particularly related to industrialization, infrastructure and the promotion of reciprocal trade.

Origin and development

The agreement establishing the Bank was signed in December 1960 in Managua, Nicaragua, by El Salvador, Guatemala, Honduras and Nicaragua. These countries were also contracting parties to the General Treaty of Central American Economic Integration which laid the foundations for the *Central American Common Market (CACM). Although created as a separate and autonomous body, the Bank was intended to act within the framework of CACM. The founding agreement entered into effect in May 1961 and the Bank started operations in Tegucigalpa, Honduras. Costa Rica decided to join the Bank in 1962. A modified founding agreement entered into force in January 1992. Mexico, Taiwan and Venezuela have a special relationship with the Bank.

Objectives

The Bank is intended to finance: infrastructural projects for the completion of existing regional systems and the reduction of disparities in basic sectors, excluding undertakings of merely local or national scope; long-term investment projects in industries of a regional character; co-ordinated projects related to specialization in agriculture and livestock; enterprises wishing to improve their efficiency and adjust to growing competition; other productive projects concerning economic complementation and the development of Central American trade. Special provisions were introduced subsequently to grant preferential treatment to Honduras.

Structure

The Bank's structure consists of the Board of Governors (composed of the Ministers of Economy and the Presidents of the Central Banks of member countries meeting annually) and five Executive Directors (including the President).

Activities

The Bank operates with its ordinary capital resources; funds for special operations have been set up. The capital stock initially amounting to $20 million was gradually increased to $600 million. Financial support has been secured from several public and private sources and international and national financial institutions operating within and outside Latin America.

The Bank has authorized loans for about $3 billion, mainly destined to infrastructural projects and housing. A Central American Common Market Fund was set up by the Bank's Board of Governors in May 1981. The Bank's future role will largely remain dependent on concrete results achieved by continuing effort towards Central American integration.

Executive President: José Manuel Pacas
Headquarters: P.O. Box 772, Tegucigalpa, Honduras (Telephone: +504 372230; fax: +504 370793)
Publications: *Annual Report*; *Revista de la integración*

Central American Common Market (CACM)

(Mercado Común Centroamericano)

The Common Market originally aimed to establish a customs union and to achieve full liberalization of trade between the five participating countries (Costa Rica, El Salvador, Guatemala, Honduras and Nicaragua). Panama has been incorporated gradually into the Common Market since the early 1990s.

Origin and development

From a legal standpoint, the main formal instrument of CACM remains the General Treaty of Central American Economic Integration, signed in Managua in 1960 for a 20-year period which expired in June 1981. However, in July 1980 the contracting parties declared that the Treaty would continue in operation until agreement was reached on a new integration scheme.

Since the early 1950s, attempts to establish a Central American common market as a means of transcending national frontiers, stimulating foreign trade and reducing heavy economic and financial dependence on outside powers, have been encouraged and supported by the UN *Economic Commission for Latin America and the Caribbean (ECLAC).

The move towards closer economic co-operation received additional impetus from the failure by the Organization of Central American States (ODECA) to make headway on the political plane. A Multilateral Treaty on Free Trade and Central American Economic Integration was signed in Tegucigalpa, Honduras, in June 1958 by all ODECA members, with the exception of Costa Rica, which joined in 1962. A Convention on Integration Industries was also adopted at the same meeting. In 1959 another Central American Convention on Equalization of Import Duties and Charges laid the foundation for the setting-up of a common external tariff. Additional agreements concerning specific sectors were reached during the ensuing years. Further negotiations led to the signing of a Treaty of Economic Association in February 1960 by El Salvador, Guatemala and Honduras. These countries plus Nicaragua concluded the General Treaty of Central American Economic Integration, establishing the Central American Common Market, in Managua, Nicaragua, in December 1960. Costa Rica acceded in July 1962. During their meeting of December 1960, the contracting parties to the General Treaty also set up, under a separate agreement, the *Central American Bank for Economic Integration (CABEI) as an autonomous body.

Objectives

According to the General Treaty, the abolition of barriers to free trade among contracting parties was to be completed within five years. Provision was also made for the erection of a uniform external tariff. Industrial integration and the gradual alignment of foreign economic policies in selected areas were envisaged (within the framework of the Common Market) in several other Central American conventions and protocols. The basic objectives of the General Treaty with regard to

trade liberalization and the creation of a common external tariff were largely achieved by 1969, but the integration process virtually came to a halt, mainly because of the Honduran disengagement.

Structure

The General Treaty provided for the establishment of three main organs: the Central American Economic Council (composed of the five Ministers of Economy and charged with the direction and co-ordination of the integration process), the Executive Council (consisting of one representative and one alternate from each member country), and the Permanent Secretariat (SIECA) based in Guatemala City. No provision was adopted concerning the formal relationship between these bodies and the corresponding organs of ODECA. Following the disruption caused in Central American relations by the outbreak of hostilities between El Salvador and Honduras in July 1969, the Economic Council and the Executive Council were no longer convened. Both Councils were replaced by a Ministerial Commission composed of Ministers and Deputy Ministers of Central American Integration. The already limited functions and powers of the Common Market's institutions were further weakened by disputes between member countries.

Activities

Efforts to carry out the liberalization and co-operation programme on an emergency basis led to the creation of *ad hoc* bodies, while SIECA was charged with studying a new integration scheme and preparing the relevant proposals. A Normalization Commission was set up in 1971 but it made little or no headway and was dissolved in 1972. SIECA drew up a set of proposals for submission to the High Level Committee (CAN) established in December 1972. This body, consisting of officials appointed by the governments of member countries, was originally created to examine SIECA's plans. In February 1975 it was entrusted with the responsibility for preparing a draft Treaty for a Central American Economic and Social Community. CAN was dissolved in March 1976 on completion of a draft establishing new organs, regional institutions, and common economic, financial and social policies. However, recurrent political crises caused by social and economic factors, long-standing rivalries and conflicts of interest made it impossible to convert the draft into a formally-binding instrument.

Since the resumption of diplomatic relations between Costa Rica and Nicaragua, and the conclusion of the General Peace Treaty between El Salvador and Honduras in October 1980, there seemed to be brighter prospects for alleviating tensions and unrest with a view to fully reactivating Central American co-operation and integration in both the economic and political spheres. Several top-level meetings involving Ministers of Foreign Affairs and Ministers and Deputy Ministers responsible for Central American Integration took place, in an effort to translate the widespread consensus over the urgent need to restructure the Common Market into an operational strategy, based on the implementation of specific projects, rather than on the adoption of a comprehensive plan for market integration.

However, political and social conflicts, aggravated by the severe economic recession and the sharp decrease in intra-regional trade in the first half of the 1980s reduced dramatically the possibilities of reviving the Central American integration process. In an effort to find a solution to the crisis, the Ministers responsible for Central American Integration, meeting in Guatemala in July 1984, expressed the intention to re-establish the Economic Council and the Executive Council of the Common Market and to adapt the legal and institutional mechanism of the integration process to 'the new economic realities existing in Central America and the exigencies of economic development of the subregion'. Within this framework, the Central American Tariff and Customs Agreement was signed in December 1984 by Costa Rica, El Salvador, Guatemala and Nicaragua, in the presence of Honduran observers; the instrument came into effect in January 1986, but Honduras insisted on bilateral agreements.

The conclusion of an agreement with the then *European Economic Community (EC) in November 1985 provided CACM with badly-needed support to pursue regional integration plans. Although regional meetings at the ministerial level took place regularly, any significant progress continued to be hindered by heavy external and intraregional debts, protectionist measures by major trade partners, and a number of other economic and non-economic factors.

In May 1986 the Presidents of the five CACM countries approved the creation of a Central American Parliament (Parlamento Centroamericano – Parlacén) whose founding agreement was concluded in 1987 in Guatemala; a Protocol was signed in September 1990 in order to allow the establishment of the Parliament with the participation of representatives from only three countries. In fact, when Parlacén first met, in October 1991, only the representatives of El Salvador, Guatemala and Honduras were present. Costa Rica and Nicaragua had observer status. Panama was subsequently invited to join Parlacén, and in October 1993 signed a Protocol to that effect.

In June 1990, CACM members stressed their renewed willingness to implement a free trade agreement by 1992, and the following December started the drafting of a framework agreement to set up a regional common market. In July 1991, with the participation of Panama, member countries agreed formally on a timetable for trade liberalization for most agricultural products by the end of 1991, and for substantial tariff cuts on most non-agricultural products by the end of 1992. In December 1991, the presidents of the CACM countries and Panama signed the Protocol of Tegucigalpa to the Charter of ODECA for the creation of a new body, the System of Central American Integration (Sistema de la Integración Centroamericana – SICA) with its headquarters in El Salvador, to organize efforts at political and economic co-ordination. In October 1993, the presidents of CACM countries and Panama, meeting at Guatemala City, signed a Protocol to the 1960 General Treaty with a view to attaining full economic integration; however, no firm schedules were set for the implementation of the various commitments. A Treaty on Democratic Security in Central America was signed by the Presidents of the six countries of the region at San Pedro Sula, Honduras in December 1995, with a view to achieving a proper 'balance of forces', intensifying the fight against trafficking of drugs and arms, and reintegrating refugees and displaced persons.

A new framework co-operation agreement with the EC was signed by the CACM countries plus Panama in February 1993. The signature took place on the occasion of the annual ministerial conference held within the framework of the dialogue – launched at San José, Costa Rica in 1984 – between the EC and its members and the countries of Central America, with Colombia, Mexico and Venezuela as co-operating countries.

Secretary-General: Haroldo Rodas Nelgar
Headquarters: 4a Avenida 10–25, Zona 14, P.O. Box 1237, 01901 Guatemala City, Guatemala (Telephone: +502 2 682151; fax: +502 2 681071).
Publications: *Carta informativa* (monthly); several economic and statistical surveys.
References: S. Dell, *A Latin American Common Market?* (London, 1966); J. Cochrane; *The Politics of Regional Integration: The Central American Case* (New Orleans, 1969); F. Parkinson; 'International Economic Integration in Latin America and the Caribbean: A Survey', *Year Book of World Affairs*, 31 (1977) 236–56.

Central Commission for the Navigation of the Rhine

The Commission is among the oldest existing international organizations in Europe.

Origin and development
The Commission, which includes as members Belgium, France, Germany, Luxembourg, The Netherlands and Switzerland, was created by the Congress of Vienna in 1815.

Objectives
The purposes of the Commission are to ensure freedom and security of navigation and equality of treatment to ships of all nations, to draw up navigational rules, to standardize customs regulations, to arbitrate in disputes involving river traffic, and to approve plans for river maintenance work.

Activities
The opening of the Rhine–Main–Danube Canal – a German artificial waterway in operation since September 1992 for which charges are levied – has brought about a substantial expansion of traffic and increased benefits for the shipping companies. This has resulted in the need for an intensification of the co-operation between the Commission and the *Danube Commission on harmonization of the shipping regimes and other priority technical, commercial and legal issues.

Secretary-General: R. Doerflinger
Headquarters: Palais du Rhin, Place de la République, 67000 Strasbourg, France (Telephone: +333 8852 2010; fax: +333 8832 1072)
Publication: *Annual Report*.

Central European Free Trade Agreement (CEFTA)

The Agreement consists of five members gradually implementing trade liberalization among themselves and co-ordinating policies towards major European and international economic organizations.

Origin and development
The agreement was signed in December 1992 by the then Czechoslovakia, Hungary and Poland to undertake concerted trade liberation efforts in view of their prospective entry into the *European Union (EU) and to contribute to the establishment of a new democratic order in Central and Eastern Europe. After the division of Czechoslovakia and the entry in 1995 of Slovenia, CEFTA comprises five member countries.

The origins of the Agreement are to be found in the attempts at institutionalizing triangular co-operation which were undertaken at the Bratislava Summit meeting of April 1990 convened to discuss the 'return to Europe' of Czechoslovakia, Hungary and Poland. The accession of Czechoslovakia the following May to the grouping, which then became known as the 'Pentagonal' (already including Hungary as well as Austria, Italy and Yugoslavia) seemed to jeopardize efforts to establish a genuine Central European grouping. None the less, the Heads of State of Czechoslovakia, Hungary and Poland, meeting in mid-February 1991 in Visegrad, Hungary, adopted a Declaration on the co-operation of the three countries 'on the road to European integration'. Slovenia became the fifth member of CEFTA, in December 1995. Bulgaria and Romania are expected to join in 1996, to be followed somewhat later by the Baltic countries.

Objectives

The Visegrad Declaration emphasized the goal of 'total integration into the European political, economic, security and legislative order', and set up a new mechanism for the co-ordination of policies of the participating countries. The so-called Visegrad Group was created to enhance co-operation with the European Communities and develop a free-trade zone among its members.

Activities

Poland's entry in June 1991 into the 'Hexagonal' – renamed in 1992 the *Central European Initiative (CEI) dropping any reference to the actual number of members – did not affect the prospects of the Visegrad group, which held another summit in Kraków in October 1991. The Declaration adopted at Kraków identified a number of areas for possible co-operation and stressed once more the aspiration of the signatory countries to an association with the European Communities and to the extension of relations with the *North Atlantic Treaty Organization (NATO).

The three countries signed in 1992 the agreement leading to the establishment of a free-trade zone, which was to include four countries after the division of Czechoslovakia in January 1993. The agreement came into effect in March 1993. The 'Protocols of Budapest' in 1994 represented a substantial step towards trade liberalization, while at the Brno Summit in September 1995 the decision was taken to complete the free-trade zone by the year 2000 (2002 in the case of Poland).

Central European Initiative (CEI)

The Initiative represents one of the most significant attempts at facilitating the integration of Central and Eastern countries into Western European structures.

Origin and development

The Initiative originated with the 'Quadrangolare', a four-nation grouping established, as a result of an Italian proposal, in November 1989 in Budapest by the Foreign Ministers of Austria, Hungary, Italy and the then Socialist Federal Republic of Yugoslavia. According to the founding declaration, the four countries intended to encourage 'quadrilateral co-operation in different spheres of social and economic life', with special emphasis on economic and scientific-technical relations and on co-operation in the fields of energy, industry, environmental protection, transport, tourism, culture and education. The subregional approach was originally conceived as an additional institutional mechanism to advance co-operation within Central Europe involving, on an equal footing, a neutral country belonging to the *European Free Trade Association (EFTA) (such as Austria), a member of the Warsaw Pact and the Council for Mutual Economic Assistance (CMEA/Comecon) (such as Hungary), a member of the *North Atlantic Treaty Organization (NATO) and the *European Communities (such as Italy), and a member of the *Non-Aligned Movement (NAM) (such as Yugoslavia). The post-1989 events in the region, including the disintegration of Yugoslavia and the division of Czechoslovakia, set the stage for a reorientation of the grouping with a greatly enlarged membership and new tasks involving the political, security and human rights spheres.

Following the accession of the then Czechoslovakia in May 1990 the Quadrangular grouping became known as the 'Pentagonal' and, after the entry of Poland in June 1991, as the 'Hexagonal'. The Belgrade government had assumed the rotating one-year presidency of the Hexagonal grouping in July 1991, but Yugoslavia was formally suspended the following November, while a number of its former constituent republics applied for full membership. Austria then took on the presidency for the calendar year 1992. The grouping was formally renamed the Central European Initiative, abandoning any numerical designation, by the Conference of Heads of Government held in Vienna in July 1992, when Bosnia and Herzegovina, Croatia, and Slovenia were admitted as full members. The Czech Republic and Slovakia joined the Initiative as independent countries in January 1993, followed by Macedonia in July, thus bringing the total membership to ten. Several other countries have shown interest in establishing close links with the Initiative. Albania, Belarus, Bulgaria, Romania and Ukraine – previously associate members – became full members in 1996. The geographical scope of the Initiative includes the Adriatic, the Danube and the Baltic.

Objectives

The Initiative provides a general framework for co-operation between ten countries in Central Europe, with a view to fostering the co-ordinated implementation of joint projects in the fields where additional advantages can be obtained from the regional harmonization of policies.

Structure

The Conference of Heads of Government and the Conference of Foreign Ministers are the organs which determine guidelines for co-operation in the selected areas. The meetings of Heads of Government are organized, at yearly intervals, by the country holding the rotating chairmanship; Foreign Ministers meet every six months. Meetings of the parliamentarians from the member countries take place regularly.

The Committee of National Co-ordinators, meeting quarterly, is entrusted with the responsibility of ensuring liaison between Working Groups and the national administrations; it also prepares the agendas for the meetings of the Heads of Government and the Foreign Ministers. A Contact Committee of Senior Officials maintains relations with interested non-member countries and various permanent or *ad hoc* bodies.

Working Groups, currently numbering 14, supervise projects in different fields: agriculture, energy, small and medium-sized enterprises, transport, telecommunications, science and technology, tourism, media, culture and education, environment, disaster relief, migration, and national minority questions. Meetings of the Working Groups are also held at ministerial level; project groups are established in co-operation with enterprises, banks and international agencies.

Activities

Finance for the projects undertaken within the framework of the Initiative is provided by the member countries and by several international organizations, in particular the *World Bank, the *European Bank for Reconstruction and Development (EBRD), the *European Investment Bank (EIB) and the PHARE Programme of the *European Union (EU). A Steering Committee supervises the activities of the Project Secretariat that has been created within the EBRD. As regards the preparation and implementation of projects, specific forms of co-operation are being developed with the UN *Economic Commission for Europe (ECE). Opportunities for co-operation are to be found by the Initiative with other newly-created subregional groupings, especially the *Black Sea Economic Co-operation (BSEC) and the *Council of the Baltic Sea States (CBSS). As regards human rights and democracy issues in Europe, the Initiative has close relations with the *Council of Europe and the *Organization for Security and Co-operation in Europe (OSCE). Links have also been established with regional organizations for transborder co-operation.

The first summit of the Heads of Government of the then Pentagonal grouping took place in Venice in July–August 1990. The following summits were held, usually in July, in Yugoslavia (1991); Austria (1992); Hungary (1993); Italy (1994); and Poland (1995).

Besides the results achieved in specific sectors which are the responsibility of the Working Groups, the Initiative has acted as an important forum for dealing with very delicate and controversial issues in the political and humanitarian areas, and facilitating the transition to democracy of Central European countries. The situation in the former Yugoslavia, especially Bosnia and Herzegovina, represented a major concern for the grouping, which requested international assistance to cope with the increasing flow of refugees and to defend the integrity of Bosnian territory. The status of the ethnic Hungarian minority in Slovakia and similar problems in other countries led the Initiative to deal with minority rights, and eventually to draw up, in 1994, an international legal instrument for their protection.

Colombo Plan, The

The Plan links advanced and developing economies in Asia and the Pacific and a number of non-regional members. The geographical scope of the Plan is described by its full official title: the Colombo Plan for Co-operative Economic and Social Development in Asia and the Pacific.

Origin and development

The Plan was founded at a meeting of the Foreign Ministers of the *Commonwealth in Colombo, in

January 1950. It was established formally in 1951 to promote co-operative economic development in South and South East Asia. Following a proposal by Australia for the adoption of a programme of economic assistance to South and South East Asia, a Consultative Committee was set up to draft a Commonwealth Technical Assistance Scheme, administered by a Council for Technical Co-operation, meeting at regular intervals, and assisted by a small permanent bureau located in Colombo. The founder members were Australia, Canada, Ceylon (renamed Sri Lanka in 1972), India, New Zealand, the UK, and the Union of South Africa (which subsequently withdrew). They were joined over the years by many other countries within and outside the Commonwealth. The Plan's role and activities suffered a major setback in October 1991 when Canada and the UK announced their withdrawal, voicing sharp criticism of the organization. Its present membership includes 20 developing countries (all within Asia and the Pacific) and 4 developed countries (Australia, Japan, New Zealand and the USA).

Objectives

The Plan is intended primarily to improve the living standards of the peoples of the region by reviewing aid projects, co-ordinating development assistance, and providing training and research facilities. The objectives and principles of the Plan are broadly formulated, and its functions and powers are essentially confined to consultation and voluntary co-ordination of efforts. Within the multilateral framework provided by the Plan, aid to developing member countries is negotiated and supplied on a bilateral basis. The withdrawal of Canada and the UK has led to greater emphasis on South–South co-operation and technical assistance programmes.

Structure

The organizational structure of the Plan comprises: the Consultative Committee, consisting of Ministers of member countries, which meets every two years to review progress within the region and to consider the general principles of economic and social co-operation; the Colombo Plan Council, composed of the heads of member countries' diplomatic missions in Colombo, meets several times a year to identify issues of interest

for consideration by the Consultative Committee and to give overall guidance; the Colombo Plan Bureau which performs various administrative tasks, represents the Plan, and disseminates information on its activities. The Director of the Bureau is appointed by the Council. Subsidiary bodies, consisting of officials of member countries, hold periodic meetings to review issues for submission to Ministers.

Activities

The Plan has a regular liaison with the relevant UN bodies as well as other international and regional agencies concerned with development assistance. Although basically providing a forum for consultation and co-ordination with no authority to produce a centralized plan for channelling capital aid and technical assistance, the Plan succeeded to a remarkable extent in harmonizing development assistance policies and assuring a substantial flow of resources to developing countries in Asia and the Pacific. Capital aid to developing member countries (in the form of grants and loans for national economic and social development projects) mainly concerned agriculture, industry, communications, energy and education. Technical co-operation programmes provided experts and volunteers, training fellowships and equipment for training and research.

The Drug Advisory Programme was launched in 1973, funded by voluntary contributions from various members; its tasks are to supplement national campaigns concerning drug abuse prevention and to provide assistance to member countries in establishing control offices, improving legislation, and training narcotics officials.

The Colombo Plan Staff College for Technician Education, transferred from Singapore to the Philippines in 1987, was established in 1975 as a specialized institution involving all member countries for the development of training facilities; it is separately financed by most member countries and is supervised by its own Governing Board.

Bureau Director: Hak Su Kim
Headquarters: 12 Melbourne Avenue, P.O. Box 596, Colombo 4, Sri Lanka (Telephone: +94 1 581813; fax: +94 1 580721)
Publications: *Annual Report of the Colombo Plan Council*; *Proceedings and Conclusions of the Consultative Committee* (every two years)

Commission for the Conservation of Antarctic Marine Living Resources (CCAMLR)

The Commission protects all forms of living organisms within its area of competence.

Origin and development
The Commission was established by an international Convention, signed in 1980 and entered into force in 1982; the Convention applies to all species of living organisms, including birds, found south of the Antarctic Convergence. Membership currently includes some 20 countries, plus the *European Community (EC).

Objectives
The Commission aims to ensure that all harvesting and research activities are conducted in accordance with predetermined objectives; to formulate, adopt and revise conservation measures; to compile, analyse and disseminate information on the status of resources; and to facilitate research activities.

Activities
Major concerns of the Commission are the assessment and avoidance of incidental mortality of Antarctic marine living resources, the improvement of the system of observation and inspection, the development of an appropriate conservation strategy, and the compliance with Conservation Measures presently in force. The Conservation Measures refer to fishing regulations, data reporting and research requirements, prevention of incidental mortality of seabirds, and protection of sites for conducting ecosystem monitoring studies. Precautionary catch limits have been adopted with regard to the krill fishery which is the largest in the area within the competence of the Commission.

Headquarters: 25 Old Wharf, Hobart, Tasmania, Australia 7000 (Telephone: +61 2 310366; fax: +61 2 232714)

Commission on Narcotic Drugs (CND)

The Commission is one of the functional commissions operating within the framework of the UN Economic and Social Council.

Origin and development
The Commission was set up in 1946 to review matters pertaining to the relevant international drug treaties and the implementation of their provisions; it is empowered to make recommendations to the Economic and Social Council on the control of narcotic drugs and psychotropic substances.

Objectives
The Commission has primary responsibility for amending the schedules annexed to international treaties in order to bring substances under international control, delete them from control, or change the regime of control to which they are subject.

Structure
Membership of the Commission, originally 15, has been increased repeatedly, eventually reaching 53 in number. Members are elected for a four-year term: (a) from among the members of the UN and members of the specialized agencies and the parties to the Single Convention on Narcotic Drugs, 1961; (b) with due regard to the adequate representation of countries which are important producers of opium or coca leaves, of countries which are important in the field of manufacture of narcotic drugs, and of countries in which drug addiction or the illicit traffic in narcotic drugs constitutes an important problem; and (c) taking into account the principle of equitable geographic distribution. The Council elects, at two-year intervals, 20 and 33 members respectively.

In 1973 the Economic and Social Council established a Subcommission on Illicit Drug Traffic and Related Matters in the Near and Middle East, whose membership has been enlarged gradually and currently includes 20 countries.

Since the mid-1970s a number of additional regional subsidiary bodies of the Commission have been set up under the name of Heads of National Drug Law Enforcement Agencies (HONLEAs). They currently include: HONLEA, Asia and the Pacific; HONLEA, Africa; HONLEA, Latin America and the Caribbean; and HONLEA, Europe. Regional HONLEAs meet annually, except for years in which an interregional HONLEA meeting is held.

The Division of Narcotic Drugs of the UN Secretariat acted as secretariat to the Commission and carried out various functions entrusted to the Secretary-General under international drug-control treaties. Following the General

Assembly resolution of December 1990 establishing a single body responsible for concerted international actions for drug abuse control, the structures and functions of the Division of Narcotic Drugs have been integrated in the newly-created *UN International Drug Control Programme (UNDCP).

Activities

During the session held in early 1991, the Commission focused on ways and means of improving its functioning as a policy-making body pursuant to the direction given by the General Assembly resolution. The need was stressed for the Commission to hold regular annual sessions, instead of meeting biennially, as had previously been the case, in order to fulfil more effectively its responsibilities in keeping with the new functions and mandates of the UN in the field of international control of narcotic drugs and psychotropic substances. At the following (early 1992) session, the Commission, in view of the UN Conference on Environment and Development (UNCED) taking place the following June, adopted a resolution stressing the link that exists between illicit drug cultivation and manufacture, and environmental damage. The implementation of General Assembly resolution of 28 October 1993 on measures to strengthen international co-operation against the illicit production, sale, demand, traffic and distribution of narcotic drugs and psychotropic substances currently represents one of the major tasks of the Commission.

Headquarters: Vienna International Centre, P.O. Box 500, 1400 Vienna, Austria (Telephone: +43 1 21345-0; fax: +43 1 232156)

COMMODITIES

African Groundnut Council

(Conseil africain de l'arachide)

Formed: 1964. Purpose: to ensure remunerative prices for groundnuts and their by-products, to promote consumption, and to organize the exchange of information concerning the production, marketing and possible uses of groundnuts. Members: Gambia, Mali, Niger, Nigeria, Senegal, Sudan.

Executive Secretary: Mour Mamadou Samb
Headquarters: Trade Fair Complex, Badagry Expressway Km 15, P.O. Box 3025, Lagos, Nigeria (Telephone and fax: +234 1 880982)
Publications: Groundnut Review; Newsletter

African Petroleum Producers' Association

Formed: 1986. Purpose: to strengthen co-operation among African petroleum-producing countries and to stabilize prices. Members: Algeria, Angola, Benin, Cameroon, Congo, Côte d'Ivoire, Egypt, Gabon, Libya, Nigeria, Zaire.

President: Belkacem Nabi.
Headquarters: P.O. Box 1097, Brazzaville, Congo (Telephone: +242   836438;   fax: +242 836799)
Publication: Technical Bulletin (quarterly)

African Timber Organization

(Organisation africaine du bois)

Formed: 1976. Purpose: to study and coordinate ways of influencing prices of wood and wood products, to harmonize commercial policies, and to conduct industrial and technical research with a view to ensuring the optimum utilization and conservation of forests. Members: Angola, Cameroon, Central African Republic, Congo, Côte d'Ivoire, Equatorial Guinea, Gabon, Ghana, Liberia, Nigeria, São Tomé and Príncipe, Tanzania, Zaire.

Secretary-General: Mohammed Lawal Garba
Headquarters: P.O. Box 1077, Libreville, Gabon (Telephone: +241   732928;   fax: +241 734030)
Publications: Annual Report; ATO-Information (every two months).

Asian and Pacific Coconut Community (APCC)

Formed: 1969. Purpose: to promote, coordinate and harmonize all activities of the coconut industry towards better production, processing, marketing and research. Members:

Fiji, India, Indonesia, Malaysia, Federated States of Micronesia, Papua New Guinea, the Philippines, Solomon Islands, Sri Lanka, Thailand, Vanuatu, Vietnam, Western Samoa; Associate member: Palau.

Executive Director: P. G. Punchihewa
Headquarters: P.O. Box 1343, Wisma Bakrie Bldg, Jalan H.R. Rasuna Said Kav. Bl., Kuningan, Jakarta 10002, Indonesia (Telephone: +62 21 5250073; fax: +62 21 5205160). Publications: *Annual Report*; *The Cocomunity* (bimonthly newsletter); *Statistical Yearbook*

Association of Iron Ore Exporting Countries

(Association des pays exportateurs de minerai de fer) (APEF)

Formed: 1975. Purpose: to co-ordinate policies of the exporting countries to secure fair and remunerative returns from the exploitation, processing and marketing of iron ore. Members: Algeria, Australia, India, Liberia, Mauritania, Peru, Sierra Leone, Sweden, Venezuela.

Secretary-General: L. Roigart Headquarters: Le Château, 14 chemin Auguste Vilbert, 1218 Grand Saconnex, Geneva, Switzerland (Telephone: +41 22 982955)

Association of Natural Rubber Producing Countries (ANRPC)

Formed: 1970. Purpose: to co-ordinate the production and marketing of natural rubber, to ensure fair and stable prices, and to promote technical co-operation among member countries. Members: India, Indonesia, Malaysia, Papua New Guinea, Singapore, Sri Lanka, Thailand.

Secretary-General: Sucharit Promdej
Headquarters: Natural Rubber Building, 148 Jalan Ampang, 50450 Kuala Lumpur, Malaysia (Telephone: +60 3 261 1900; fax: +60 3 261 3014)
Publications: *ANRPC News; Quarterly Statistical Bulletin*

Association of Tin Producing Countries (ATPC)

Formed: 1983 to administer the International Tin Agreement. Purpose: to promote co-operation in marketing of tin, to gather data and support research. Members: Australia, Bolivia, China, Indonesia, Malaysia, Nigeria, Thailand, Zaire (members account for about 45 per cent of world production). Observers: Brazil and China

Executive Secretary: Jumrus Atikul
Headquarters: Menara Dayabumi, 4th Floor, Jalan Sultan Hishamuddin, 50050 Kuala Lumpur, Malaysia (Telephone: +60 3 274 7620; fax: +60 3 274 0669)

Cocoa Producers' Alliance (COPAL)

Formed: 1962. Purpose: to examine problems of mutual concern to producers, to ensure adequate supplies at remunerative prices, to promote consumption, and to exchange technical and scientific information. Members: Brazil, Cameroon, Clôte d'Ivoire, Dominican Republic, Ecuador, Gabon, Ghana, Malaysia, Mexico, Nigeria, São Tomé and Príncipe, Togo, Trinidad and Tobago.
Secretary-General: Djeumo Silas Kamga

Headquarters: Western House, 8–10 Broad Street, P.O. Box 1718, Lagos, Nigeria (Telephone: +234 1 2635506; fax: +234 1 2635684)

Group of Latin American and Caribbean Sugar Exporting Countries

(Grupo de Países Latinoamericanos y del Caribe Exportadores de Azúcar) (GEPLACEA)

Formed: 1974. Purpose: to serve as a forum of consultation on the production and sale of sugar, and to co-ordinate policies in order to achieve fair and remunerative prices. Members: 22 countries in Latin America and the Caribbean, and the Philippines (representing about 45 per cent of world exports).

Executive Secretary: José Antonio Cerro.
Headquarters: Ejército Nacional 373, 11520 México DF, Mexico (Telephone: +52 5 250 7566; fax: +52 5 250 7591).

Inter-African Coffee Organization (IACO)

Formed: 1960. Purpose: to further the study of common problems concerning African coffee, including production, processing and marketing, in order to ensure the smooth disposal of production and the optimum level of selling prices. Members: 25 coffee-producing countries in Africa.

Secretary-General: Arega Worku
Headquarters: BP V210, Abidjan, Côte d'Ivoire (Telephone: +225 216131)
Publications: *African Coffee* (quarterly); *Directory of African Exporters* (every two years)

International Bauxite Association (IBA)

Formed: 1974. Purpose: to co-ordinate policies of the producing countries in order to secure fair and reasonable profits in the processing and marketing of bauxite, bearing in mind the interests of consumer countries. Members: Ghana, Guinea, Guyana, Indonesia, Jamaica, Sierra Leone, Surinam, Yugoslavia.

Secretary-General: Nenad Altman
Headquarters: 36 Trafalgar Road, P.O. Box 551, Kingston 5, Jamaica (Telephone: +854 926 4535; fax: +854 929 4020)
Publication: *IBA Review*

International Cocoa Organization (ICCO)

Formed: 1973 under the first International Cocoa Agreement, 1972, renegotiated in 1975, 1980, 1986 and 1994. Purpose: to supervise the implementation of the agreement and to provide member countries with conference facilities and up-to-date information on the world cocoa economy and the operation of the agreement. Members: 13 exporting countries in Africa, Latin America and the Caribbean, and the Pacific (which together account for about three-quarters of world cocoa exports), and 14 importing countries (with the important exception of the USA), which account for over half of world cocoa imports.

Executive Director: Edouard Kouamé

Headquarters: 22 Berners Street, London W1P 3DB, England (Telephone: +44 171 637 3211; fax: +44 171 631 0114)
Publications: *Annual Report*; *Quarterly Bulletin of Cocoa Statistics*; *Cocoa Newsletter*

International Coffee Organization (ICO)

Formed: 1963 under the International Coffee Agreement, 1962, renegotiated in 1968, 1976, 1983 and 1994. Purpose: to achieve a reasonable balance between supply and demand on a basis which assures adequate supplies at fair prices to consumers and expanding markets at remunerative prices to producers. Members: 43 exporting countries, which account for over 95 per cent of world coffee exports, Brazil being by far the largest supplier; and 18 importing countries, which account for about 60 per cent of world imports.

Executive Director: Celsius A. Lodder
Headquarters: 22 Berners Street, London W1P 4DD, England (Telephone: +44 171 580 8591; fax: +44 171 580 6129)
Publication: *Quarterly Statistical Bulletin*

International Cotton Advisory Committee (ICAC)

Formed: 1939. Purpose: to review developments affecting the world cotton situation, to collect and disseminate statistics, and to recommend any measures for the furtherance of international collaboration with a view to maintaining and developing a sound world cotton economy. Members: 42 countries in all continents.

Executive Director: L. H. Shaw.
Headquarters: 1629 K Street NW, Suite 702, Washington, DC 20006, USA (Telephone: +1 202 463 6660; fax: +1 202 463 6950)
Publications: *Cotton: Review of the World Situation* (every two months); *Cotton: World Statistics*

International Jute Organization (IJO)

Formed: 1984 (International agreement on jute extended in April 1995 for a further two years). Purpose: to improve and enlarge the global jute market by enhancing the competitiveness of jute and jute products, and encouraging diversified uses of jute, through agricultural and industrial research and development projects and promotional activities. Members: five exporting countries (Bangladesh, China, India, Nepal, Thailand) and 23 importing countries (including the EC).

Executive Director: K. M. Rabbani
Headquarters: 95A Road No. 4, Banani, Dhaka, Bangladesh (Telephone: +880 2 603745; fax: +880 2 883641)

International Lead and Zinc Study Group (ILZSG)

Formed: 1959. Purpose: to provide opportunities for regular consultation on international trade in lead and zinc, to conduct studies, and to consider possible solutions to any special problems or difficulties. Members: 30 countries in all continents.

Secretary-General: Francis Labro
Headquarters: Metro House, 58 St James's Street, London SW1A 1LD, England (Telephone: +44 171 839 8550; fax: +44 171 930 4635)
Publication: *Lead and Zinc Statistics* (monthly)

International Natural Rubber Organization (INRO)

Formed: 1980, under the International Natural Rubber Agreement, 1979, subsequently extended and renegotiated several times (most recent agreement concluded in 1995). Purpose: to achieve a balanced growth between the supply of and demand for natural rubber, thereby helping to alleviate difficulties arising from surpluses or shortages. Members: six exporting countries (Côte d'Ivoire, Indonesia, Malaysia, Nigeria, Sri Lanka, Thailand), and 21 importing countries (including the EC).

Executive Director: Pong Sono
Headquarters: P.O. Box 10374, 50712 Kuala Lumpur, Malaysia (Telephone: +60 3 248 6466; fax: +60 3 248 6485)

International Olive Oil Council (IOOC)

Formed: 1959. Purpose: To co-ordinate policies of member countries in order to ensure fair competition in the olive oil trade, to put into operation, or to facilitate the application of, measures designed to expand the production and consumption of olive oil, to reduce the disadvantages arising from the fluctuations of supplies on the market and generally to foster international co-operation concerning world olive oil problems. Members: five mainly producing countries, one mainly importing country, and the European Community (EC) as parties to the International Olive Oil Agreement (Fourth Agreement) signed in 1986.

Director: Fausto Luchetti.
Headquarters: Juan Bravo 10, Madrid 28006, Spain (Telephone: +34 1 577 4735; fax: +34 1 431 6127)
Publications: *Information Sheet* (fortnightly); *National Policies for Olive Products* (annual)

International Pepper Community (IPC)

Formed: 1972. Purpose: to promote increased consumption and enlargement of markets and to co-ordinate research on the technical and economic aspects of pepper production. Members: Brazil, India, Indonesia, Malaysia.

Executive Director: Mohamed Ismail.
Headquarters: 3rd Floor, Wisma Bakrie, Jalan H. R. Rasuna Said, Kav. B1, Kuningan, Jakarta 12920, Indonesia (Telephone: +62 21 520 5496; fax: +62 21 520 0401).
Publications: *Pepper News* (quarterly); *Pepper Statistical Yearbook*

International Sugar Organization (ISO)

Formed: 1987. Purpose: to administer the International Sugar Agreement, 1992, in force since January 1993, with a view to ensuring enhanced international co-operation, providing a forum for consultation and exchange of information, and encouraging increased demand for sugar. Members: 46 countries.

Executive Director: Dr Peter Baron
Headquarters: 1 Canada Square, Canary Wharf, London E14 5AA, England (Telephone: +44 171 513 1144; fax: +44 171 513 1146)
Publications: *Sugar Year Book*; *Monthly Statistical Bulletin*

International Tea Committee

Formed: 1933. Purpose: originally to administer the International Tea Agreement and subsequently transformed into statistical and information centre. Members: Producer countries (Bangladesh, India, Indonesia, Kenya, Malawi, Sri Lanka, Zimbabwe) and consumer countries.

Chief Executive Secretary: Peter Abel
Headquarters: Sir John Lyon House, 5 High Timber Street, London EC4V 3NH, England (Telephone: +44 171 248 4672; fax: +44 171 248 3011)

International Tropical Timber Organization (ITTO)

Formed: 1985 under the International Tropical Timber Agreement, 1983; Second Agreement concluded in 1994. Purpose: to assist timber-producing countries in sustainable forest management, processing and trade, to collect information and to promote research. Members: 52 producing and consuming countries.

Executive Director: Freezailah Bin Che Yeom
Headquarters: International Organizations Centre, 5th floor, 1-1-1 Minato Mirai, Nishi-ku, Yokohama 220, Japan (Telephone: +81 45 223 1110; fax: +81 45 223 1111)

International Vine and Wine Office

(Office international de la vigne et du vin) (OIV)

Formed: 1924. Purpose: to study the scientific, technical, economic and human problems concerning the vine and its products (wine, grapes, raisins, grape juice) and to spread the relevant knowledge by means of publications, to formulate a rational world policy with respect to viticulture and to address recommendations. Members: 45 countries, mostly in Europe.

Director: Robert Tinlot
Headquarters: 18 rue d'Aguesseau, 75008 Paris, France (Telephone: +33 1 4494 8080; fax: +33 1 4266 9063)
Publications: *Bulletin de l'OIV* (every two months); *Codex oenologique international*

Union of Banana Exporting Countries

(Unión de Países Exportadores de Banano) (UPEB)

Formed: 1974. Purpose: to determine a coordinated policy in order to protect the interests of member countries, to promote the technical and economic development of the banana industry and to further international co-operation in connection with world banana problems. Members: Colombia, Costa Rica, Dominican Republic, Guatemala, Honduras, Nicaragua, Panama, Venezuela.

Executive Director: J. Enrique Betancourt
Headquarters: P.O. Box 4273, Panama City 5, Panama (Telephone: +507 636266; fax: +507 648355)
Publications: *Informe UPEB*; *Estadísticas Bananeras*

West Africa Rice Development Association (WARDA)

Formed: 1970. Purpose: to increase the quantity and quality of rice produced in West Africa with a view to making the area self-sufficient. The Association maintains research stations in certain member countries and provides training and consulting services. Members: 17 countries.

Director-General: Dr Eugene Robert Terry
Headquarters: 01 BP 2551, Bouaké 01, Côte d'Ivoire (Telephone: +225 634514; fax: +225 634714)
Publication: *Annual Report*

Common Market for Eastern and Southern Africa (COMESA)

The organization, grouping 20 countries of Eastern and Southern Africa (with the exception of South Africa), succeeded in 1993 the Preferential Trade Area for Eastern and Southern African States (PTA).

Origin and development

The proposal to establish an international organization aimed at fostering economic co-operation among the countries of Eastern and Southern Africa had been originally launched by the UN *Economic Commission for Africa (ECA) in the mid-1970s and subsequently endorsed by the *Organization of African Unity (OUA) in the 1980 Lagos Plan of Action. The PTA was eventually established by a treaty signed at Lusaka, Zambia in December 1981 by the representatives of nine countries – Comoros, Djibouti, Ethiopia, Kenya, Malawi, Mauritius, Somalia, Uganda and Zambia. They were joined by Lesotho, Swaziland and Zimbabwe in 1982, Burundi and Rwanda in 1984, Tanzania in 1985, Mozambique and Sudan in 1988, and Angola in 1990. At the meeting of the Heads of State of the member countries in January 1992, the proposal was put forward of a merger of PTA – whose results had been far from satisfactory – with the *Southern African Development Community (SADC), which was to be established as a successor body to the Southern African Development Co-ordination Conference (SADCC). In 1993, Eritrea, Madagascar, Namibia and the Seychelles had also joined the PTA. Since the proposed merger with SADC proved impossible, the treaty establishing COMESA was signed during the summit of the member countries of PTA held in November 1993 at Kampala, Uganda. Djibouti, Seychelles, Somalia and Zimbabwe did not participate in the establishment of COMESA; however, Zimbabwe, after some hesitation, signed the treaty the following December. Zaire joined COMESA in 1994, bringing the total membership to 20.

Objectives

The main purposes of COMESA are to improve commercial and economic co-operation within the region and to facilitate financial transactions between member countries with a view to establishing a Common Market and eventually an Economic Community.

Activities

The treaty establishing COMESA came into being formally in December 1994, with the aim of creating a full free-trade area by the year 2000, and a customs union by 2004. However, divisions continue to exist among member countries as regards the still unresolved issue of the relationship with SADC which poses serious risks of overlapping membership and duplication of efforts.

Secretary-General: Bingu Wa Mutharika
Headquarters: Lotti House, Cairo Road, P.O. Box 30051, 10101 Lusaka, Zambia (Telephone: +260 1 229725; fax: +260 1 225107)

Commonwealth, The

The Commonwealth is a voluntary association of 53 sovereign countries – comprising about a quarter of the world's population – that meet and consult on a regular basis to foster common links, to co-ordinate mutual assistance for economic and social development, and to contribute to the restructuring of international economic relations.

Origin and development

The Commonwealth originated from the efforts undertaken after the First World War to reorganize the British Empire on the basis of the union of Britain and the Dominions as autonomous countries enjoying equal rights. The significant contribution of the Dominions to the conduct of the conflict, their participation at the peace conference with separate delegations and signatures, and their individual membership in the League of Nations, were among the events that paved the way to the establishment of a free association of independent countries linked with Britain on an equal footing. After the Imperial Conferences of 1921 and 1923, devoted respectively to the discussion of major foreign policy issues, and the definition of the rights of the Dominions to conclude international treaties independently, the Imperial Conference of 1926 adopted the Balfour Formula on the status of the Dominions, including at the time six countries – Australia, Canada, Eire (Ireland), Newfoundland, New Zealand and the Union of South Africa. Britain and the Dominions were defined as 'autonomous communities within the British Empire, equal in status, in no way subordinate one to another in any aspect of their domestic or foreign affairs, though united by a common allegiance to the Crown, and freely associated as members of the British Commonwealth of Nations.'

The Imperial Conference of 1930 confirmed the Balfour Formula and recognized the full legislative autonomy of the Dominions. The basic principles governing relations within the Commonwealth were embodied in the Statute of Westminster of 1931. The Ottawa Imperial Conference, held in 1932, established a preferential system, based on the concession, on a bilateral basis, of preferential tariffs in the trade between Britain and the other members of the British Commonwealth of Nations.

A new Commonwealth, reflecting the changed needs and roles of its member countries, gradually emerged from the Second World War with the spread of decolonization and the consequent attainment of independence by territories formerly under British jurisdiction or mandate. The requirement of common allegiance to the Crown was dropped, while egalitarianism became a more prominent feature of the association, whose membership began to expand. The countries of the Indian subcontinent were the first to achieve full independence and join the Commonwealth: India and Pakistan became members in 1947, while Ceylon (now Sri Lanka) did so in 1948. A substantial change was brought about in the association in 1949, when India announced its intention to become a republic while retaining full membership. At the London Conference of Commonwealth Prime Ministers in April 1949, unanimous agreement was reached, allowing India to continue 'her full membership of the Commonwealth of Nations and her acceptance of the King as the symbol of the free association of its independent member nations and, as such, the Head of the Commonwealth'. Ghana and the Federation of Malaya (now Malaysia) joined in 1957, followed by Nigeria in 1960.

During the 1960s a steady expansion in membership took place with the entry of Cyprus, Sierra Leone and Tanganyika (now Tanzania) in 1961; Jamaica, Trinidad and Tobago, and Uganda in 1962; Kenya in 1963; Malawi, Malta and Zambia in 1964; The Gambia and Singapore, which had seceded from Malaysia, in 1965;

Guyana, Botswana, Lesotho and Barbados in 1966; Mauritius and Swaziland in 1968; Tonga, Western Samoa and Fiji in 1970. Membership grew at a slower pace during the 1970s and 1980s with the entry of Bangladesh, which had seceded from Pakistan, in 1972; the Bahamas in 1973; Grenada in 1974; Papua New Guinea in 1975; the Seychelles in 1976; the Solomon Islands and Dominica in 1978; Saint Lucia and Kiribati in 1979; Zimbabwe and Vanuatu in 1980; Belize, Antigua and Barbuda in 1981; Saint Kitts and Nevis (1983); and Brunei (1984). Since Brunei's admission, no other country joined the Commonwealth until the entry of Namibia in 1990; Cameroon and Mozambique were admitted in 1995. Nauru (since 1968) and Tuvalu (since 1978) enjoy the status of 'special' members, which entitles them to participate in all functional activities but not to attend meetings of Heads of Government. Saint Vincent and the Grenadines (since 1979) and the Maldives (since 1982) were also special members, but their status was subsequently upgraded to full membership. More than half of the present members of the Commonwealth are republics, while five countries have their own monarchs. The Commonwealth also encompasses dependencies of the UK, Australia and New Zealand.

Membership of the Commonwealth is based on the voluntary acceptance of the Queen's status as symbolic Head by independent countries that have previously been a part of the British Empire; Mozambique is a special case because of its long and close association with neighbouring Commonwealth countries during the anti-apartheid struggle.

The final decision on admission requires the unanimous consent of member countries. There is no incompatibility between membership in the Commonwealth and participation in other international organizations of a political and/or economic nature. Governments of member countries are represented in other Commonwealth countries by High Commissioners, whose rank is equivalent to that of Ambassadors.

Upon attainment of independence, a number of territories did not join the Commonwealth, for various reasons. Among these territories were Egypt, Iraq, Transjordan, Burma (now Myanmar), Palestine, Sudan, British Somaliland, Southern Cameroons, and Southern Yemen. The Maldives and Western Samoa joined some years after independence. Of the seven original members of the Commonwealth, two no longer belong to the association: Eire withdrew in 1949; Newfoundland changed its status from Dominion to crown colony, and eventually became the tenth province of Canada in 1949. The Republic of South Africa, whose white minority government had withdrawn in 1961 after declaring a republic, rejoined in June 1994, following its first multiracial elections held in April. Pakistan, which had left in 1972 when its former Eastern province was recognized by the UK and other Commonwealth member countries as an independent state under the name of Bangladesh, rejoined the Commonwealth in October 1989. The membership of Fiji was declared lapsed in October 1987 after the constitutional changes that followed the military coup. Nigeria was suspended from the Commonwealth in November 1995, the execution by the military government of human rights activists having been considered a grave violation of the principles set out in the 1991 Harare Declaration.

Objectives

Although the objectives of the contemporary Commonwealth are not defined in a formal constitution or founding treaty but are rather to be found in consultation, co-ordination and co-operation procedures, two documents may be considered as embodying its basic principles and ideals: the Declaration of Commonwealth Principles, unanimously adopted in Singapore in 1971, and the Harare Commonwealth Declaration of 1991 which reaffirmed the commitment of the member countries to the 1971 principles and placed special emphasis on the promotion of democracy and respect for human rights. Commonwealth Heads of Government have agreed a number of other declarations and statements to which Commonwealth member countries are committed: the statement (Gleneagles Agreement) on apartheid in sport (1977); the Lusaka Declaration on Racism and Racial Prejudice (1979); the Melbourne Declaration on relations between developed and developing countries (1981); the Goa Declaration on International Security (1983); the New Delhi Statement on Economic Action (1983); the Nassau Declaration on World Order (1985); the

Commonwealth Accord on Southern Africa (1985); the Vancouver Declaration on World Trade (1987); the Okanagan Statement and Programme of Action on Southern Africa (1987); the Langkawi Declaration on the Environment (1989); the Kuala Lumpur Statement on Southern Africa (1989); the Ottawa Declaration on Women and Structural Adjustment (1991); the Limassol Statement on the Uruguay Round of Multilateral Trade Negotiations (1993); the Commonwealth Statement on Disarmament (1995); and the Millbrook Commonwealth Action Programme on the Harare Commonwealth Declaration (1995).

Structure

The basic guidelines of Commonwealth activities are laid down at the meetings of the Heads of Government which take place regularly at biennial intervals. In alternate years, senior government officials hold meetings to review policies and consider important matters of common concern. Finance Ministers meet annually in the week prior to the annual meeting of the *World Bank and the *International Monetary Fund (IMF). Regular meetings are also held by Ministers of Education, Labour, Health and others as appropriate. Several other meetings take place at different levels, on a regular or *ad hoc* basis, to ensure close co-ordination on specific issues. Meetings are open to all member countries and are held in different cities and regions within the Commonwealth in conformity with the multilateral character of the association; votes are not taken.

The central organization for joint consultation and co-operation is provided by the Commonwealth Secretariat, which was established in 1965 at the decision of the Heads of Government. The Secretariat is headed by a Secretary-General, elected by the Heads of Government and assisted by three Deputy Secretaries-General. The Secretariat, located in London and restructured in 1993, organizes and services meetings and conferences, co-ordinates a broad range of activities, and disseminates information on questions of common concern. It is organized in divisions which reflect the main areas of operation: political affairs, legal and constitutional affairs, information and public affairs, administration, economic affairs, human resource development, women's and youth affairs, science and technology, economic and legal advisory services, export and industrial development, management and training services, general technical assistance services, and strategic planning and evaluation. The expenses of the Secretariat are apportioned among member countries according to a scale related to UN contributions. Canada, Australia, India and the UK are among the largest contributors; smaller amounts are contributed by the overwhelming majority of the other members.

Multilateral technical assistance for economic and social development is provided through the Commonwealth Fund for Technical Co-operation (CFTC), established in 1971 and subsequently integrated into the Secretariat for administration. The CFTC, which is supported by the voluntary contributions of member countries, particularly the most developed, provides specialist advice in a wide variety of fields, offers training facilities, and sends out experts. Government and private funds are channelled to meet the special needs of the association's smaller countries: about 30 members have populations of under one million, and about half of these have fewer than 200 000 people. A Commonwealth Small States Office, managed by the Commonwealth Secretariat, is based in New York to ensure that the voices of smaller members of the association are heard in the UN. Several special programmes and other minor undertakings are carried out with a view to improving socioeconomic conditions of the poorest members and/or strengthening the extensive network of co-operation links existing between members at both the intergovernmental and non-governmental level.

Activities

The peculiar nature of the association, characterized by full equality and consensus of members, and freedom from rigid patterns, has improved remarkably its ability to survive through swift and effective adjustment to changed circumstances in the political, economic, financial, technical and social fields.

Besides supporting the UN efforts for international peace and security, the Commonwealth is an active advocate of regional co-operation and has helped to strengthen regional groupings in Africa, the Caribbean, Asia and the Pacific. The Commonwealth maintains close links with many international institutions both within and outside the UN system; observer status was granted to the Commonwealth by the UN General Assembly

in October 1976. Special co-operative relations have developed with the international agencies concerned with development work, such as the World Bank, the IMF, the *Food and Agriculture Organization of the UN (FAO), the *UN Conference on Trade and Development (UNCTAD), the *World Trade Organization (WTO), and the *Organization for Economic Co-operation and Development (OECD). Important relationships are developing with regional economic bodies in Europe, especially the *European Union (EU), Africa, Latin America, the Caribbean and the South Pacific. The contemporary Commonwealth generally provides an effective and flexible framework for consultation and co-operation between countries characterized by wide disparities in political and economic power, interests and ideological views. Major adaptations and adjustments have been necessary in order to help the association maintain and enhance its unique character and role on the world scene.

Severe political strains have been suffered by the association on a number of occasions, such as armed conflicts between members (India and Pakistan) or within the boundaries of a member (Nigeria). The situation in the countries of Southern Africa and the concrete steps to be taken were, for a substantial period of time, one of the Commonwealth's most important concerns. The Commonwealth played an active role in achieving majority rule in Zimbabwe, provided humanitarian technical assistance and support in international forums to Namibia, and opposed apartheid in South Africa. It took a lead in the international efforts to isolate the then white-minority-dominated South Africa in sport through its 1977 Gleneagles Agreement; it also supported the efforts of majority-ruled countries in the region to reduce their economic dependence on South Africa. Attempts have been made consistently by representatives of Commonwealth countries to establish a common position on sensitive matters discussed by major international organizations, especially the UN. The Commonwealth plays a growing role in the fields of economic and financial co-operation and technical assistance, especially since the creation of the CFTC.

The Commonwealth has contributed to international thought on North–South economic disparities through a number of expert group reports, such as those proposing measures to reduce protectionism, reform the Bretton Woods institutions, relieve the debt problems of developing countries and increase the security of small countries. Emphasis on privatization of state-owned enterprises and overall support for the free market have recently characterized the Commonwealth attitudes.

The development of human resources and the promotion of human rights throughout the Commonwealth are areas on which increasing emphasis is being placed at different levels within the framework of the association. The Commonwealth is now concentrating on issues of democratization and good governance; the establishment of a Ministerial Action Group to foster adherence by member countries to the fundamental principles of democracy and human rights as envisaged by the 1991 Harare Declaration was decided in late 1995.

Several Commonwealth organizations, most of them based in the UK, are active in a variety of fields such as agriculture and forestry, health, education and culture, communications, information and the media, legal professions, parliamentary affairs, science and technology, parliamentary affairs, sport, and Commonwealth studies.

Secretary-General: Chief Emeka Anyaoku
Headquarters: Marlborough House, Pall Mall, London SW1Y 5HX, England (Telephone: +44 171 839 3411; fax: +44 171 930 0827)
Publications: *The Commonwealth Today*; *The Commonwealth Factbook*; *The Commonwealth Yearbook*; *Report of the Commonwealth Secretary-General* (every two years); *Commonwealth Currents* (every three months)
References: H. D. Hall, *Commonwealth: A History of the British Commonwealth* (London and New York, 1971); A. Walker, *The Modern Commonwealth* (London, 1976); D. Judd and P. Slinn, *The Evolution of the Modern Commonwealth 1902–80* (London, 1982); A. Smith and C. Sanger, *Stitches in Time. The Commonwealth in World Politics* (New York, 1983); A. J. R. Groom and P. Taylor (eds), *The Commonwealth in the 1980s. Challenges and Opportunities* (London, 1984); R. J. Moore, *Making the New Commonwealth* (Oxford, 1987); D. Austin, *The Commonwealth and Britain* (London, 1988); W. D. McIntyre, *The Significance of the Commonwealth 1965–90* (London, 1991); S. Chan, *Twelve Years of Commonwealth Diplomatic History*: *Commonwealth Summit Meetings 1979–91* (Lampeter, 1992)

Community of Portuguese Speaking (Countries (CPLP)

(Comunidade de Países de Lingua Portuguesa)

The Community groups the seven lusophone countries in the world to organize co-operation and concertation in a variety of fields.

Origin and development
The Community was established by a conference held in July 1996 in Lisbon by the heads of state and government of Angola, Brazil, Cape Verde, Guinea-Bissau, Mozambique, Portugal and São Tomé and Principe. The granting of observer status to specific movements or groups will be decided at a later stage.

Objectives
The Community is intended as a means of strengthening co-operation between members in the pursuit of common interests in the cultural, economic, social, scientific and legal-institutional fields. The lusophone commonwealth should also help member countries expand their influence in international institutions and forums.

Structure
The Conference of the heads of state and government is the supreme decision-making organ whose next session will be held in Cape Verde in 1998. The Council of Ministers is charged with the implementation of the decisions of the Conference. An Executive Secretary is responsible for administrative tasks.

Activities
Besides implementing its first commitment with regard to the Portuguese language, the Community will undertake a thorough examination of the main political and economic issues of direct relevance to its members. The situation in East Timor is likely to be one of the major issues to be considered within the framework of the newly-created Community.

Executive Secretary: Dr Marcolino Moço

Co-operation Council for the Arab States of the Gulf

The Council – generally known as the Gulf Co-operation Council (GCC) – promotes political and economic co-operation and greater solidarity between the Arab oil-producing countries on the western side of the Gulf, in view of the recurring threats to the region's stability.

Origin and development

The need to co-ordinate efforts for the solution of common problems through the establishment of a regional organization of comprehensive aims was emphasized by the Ministers of Foreign Affairs of Saudi Arabia, Bahrain, Kuwait, Oman, Qatar and the United Arab Emirates, at a meeting held in Riyadh, Saudi Arabia, in February 1981. The decision to create the Council was announced by the Foreign Ministers of the six countries meeting at Muscat, Oman, the following March; finally, at Abu Dhabi, in May, the Heads of State of the countries concerned solemnly approved the establishment of the new body.

Objectives

According to the founding document, the member countries of the Council intend to establish between them a community whose scope of activity embraces economic and financial spheres, as well as education and culture, social affairs, health, transportation and communications, trade, customs and legislation. In a Declaration adopted by the Heads of State at Abu Dhabi, emphasis was also placed on the commitment of the member countries to join in efforts to preserve their sovereignty, territorial integrity and independence, and to ensure the stability of the Gulf region, which should remain 'outside the sphere of international conflicts'.

Structure

The institutional structure of the Council reflects the development of co-operation among member countries. The Supreme Council consists of the Heads of State of member countries meeting in ordinary session once a year to decide the general policy and action of the Organization. A special body, the Commission for Settlement of Disputes, is attached to the Supreme Council. The Ministerial Council consists of the Foreign Ministers meeting in ordinary session at quarterly intervals, and in emergency session at the request of at least two members. It is the responsibility of the Ministerial Council to prepare for the sessions of the Supreme Council and to draw up policies, recommendations and projects for the improvement of co-operation and co-ordination between member countries. Periodic meetings are also held by Ministers of Agriculture, Industry, Energy, Transport, Defence, Finance and Economy, assisted by specialized committees. The Secretariat-General assists member countries in the implementation of the recommendations adopted by the Supreme and Ministerial Councils. The Secretary-General, appointed by the Supreme Council on the recommendation of the Ministerial Council for a renewable three-year term, performs administrative and technical functions, in collaboration with two Assistant Secretaries-General, for Political Affairs and for Economic Affairs, respectively. The seat of the Secretariat is in Riyadh.

Activities

The Council has been developing a relationship with other international organizations, especially regional groupings. An agreement was concluded by the Council with the then European Economic Community (EEC) in June 1988 and came into effect in January 1990. Discussions on a free-trade agreement between the two organizations met with several difficulties, aggravated by the European proposals for the introduction of a 'carbon tax' in order to reduce pollution. An improvement in relations between the Council and the *European Union (EU) was expected by the mid-1990s when fresh attempts were made to intensify the political dialogue, strengthen economic co-operation and promote investment in both directions. The prerequisites would then be established for the eventual conclusion of a free-trade agreement.

During its initial period, the Council laid out the strategy for co-operation activities in several fields – in particular the liberalization of the movement of goods, capital, and people between member countries. In June 1981 the Finance Ministers prepared an economic co-operation agreement dealing with petroleum, the abolition of customs duties, and financial and monetary co-ordination. The Ministers of Petroleum met in Riyadh at the beginning of 1982 with a view to drawing up a joint comprehensive strategy on oil matters to be carried out *vis-à-vis* non-member countries and international organizations, including the *Organization of the Petroleum Exporting Countries (OPEC) and the *Organization of Arab

Petroleum Exporting Countries (OAPEC). A unified policy on the acquisition of technology was also adopted. In December 1987, a plan was approved by the Supreme Council in order to allow a member whose production had been disrupted to 'borrow' petroleum from other members and fulfil its export obligations.

As regards the movement of goods, certain customs duties on domestic products of the member countries were abolished in early 1983, while a common minimum tariff on foreign imports was established in 1986. The imposition of higher tariffs on imports representing a threat to manufacturing industries of the Council's member countries has been under consideration for a number of years.

In February 1987 the governors of the central banks reached an agreement, subsequently approved by the Supreme Council, for the co-ordination of exchange rates. To finance specific projects, mainly in the energy and transport sectors, the Gulf Investment Corporation, having an initial capital of $2100 million, and based in Kuwait, was established in 1983. At the beginning of 1990, paid-up capital amounted to $540 million, and a dozen investment projects had been approved.

In the late 1980s a number of measures were adopted within the framework of a common industrial strategy for the protection of industrial products of the Council's member countries, the co-ordination of industrial projects, and the unification of legislation on foreign investment. Progress has also been made for the adoption of a unified agricultural policy. The establishment of a joint telecommunications network has been decided since the mid-1980s.

Co-operation on military and security issues, not expressly mentioned in the founding agreement, was formally included among the Council's activities by a decision of the Supreme Council at the end of 1981. At their meeting in February 1982, the Foreign Ministers stressed that an attack against any member country will be considered an attack against all member countries. In May 1982 the Ministers of Foreign Affairs held an emergency meeting to discuss the issues arising from the conflict between Iraq (supported by the Council's member countries acting individually) and Iran; a peace plan was proposed in May 1983. To foster mutual defence co-ordination, joint military exercises were held in 1983 and 1984. In November 1984 it was decided to set up the 'Peninsula Shield Force' for rapid deployment, under a central command, against external aggression. Repeated offers by the Council to mediate between Iraq and Iran failed to materialize and no joint policy could be adopted vis-à-vis Iran following the cease-fire between that country and Iraq in August 1988.

Immediately after Iraq's invasion of Kuwait in August 1990, the Ministerial Council formally demanded the withdrawal of Iraqi troops; the Defence Ministers, for their part, decided to put on alert the Peninsula Shield Force to prevent an invasion of Saudi Arabia by Iraq. The Supreme Council, meeting in December 1990 in Qatar, demanded Iraq's total and unconditional withdrawal from Kuwait, and recognized that military action might be necessary to expel Iraq from Kuwait. The Peninsula Shield Force subsequently took part in the US-led anti-Iraq alliance, which also saw the development of close links between the Council's member countries on the one hand and Egypt and Syria on the other. The six members of the Council, plus Egypt and Syria, in March 1991 issued the 'Declaration of Damascus', announcing plans to establish a regional peace-keeping force, which failed to materialize because of persisting disagreements concerning its composition; however, meetings of the 'six plus two' *Damascus Declaration States have continued.

In the face of the urgent need to provide conditions for greater political and economic stability in the region, the Council announced in April 1991 the creation of a multimillion-dollar development fund, mainly to assist friendly countries, notably Egypt and Syria, that had played a major role in the Gulf War. The December 1992 Supreme Council meeting, held after the reconciliation between Qatar and Saudi Arabia over a border dispute, strongly criticized Iraq for failing to comply with UN resolutions. The Military Committee was inaugurated in April 1994 to co-ordinate more effectively military activities. The Council's members have taken a favourable attitude concerning the Middle East peace process and the establishment of relations with Israel, ending the boycott that had been adopted within the framework of the *League of Arab States. New tensions arose between Saudi Arabia and Qatar at the meeting of the Heads of State in December 1995 in Oman over the appointment of a Saudi national as the new Secretary-General; grave concern was also expressed over Iraq's failure to conform fully to UN demands.

Secretary-General: Jamil al-Hujaylan
Headquarters: P.O. Box 7153, Riyadh 11462,
  Saudi Arabia (Telephone: +966 1 482 7777;
  fax: +966 1 482 9089)
References: M. Rumaihi, *Beyond Oil: Unity and
  Development in the Gulf* (London, 1986); J. W.
  Twinam, *The Gulf, Co-operation and the Council:
  An American Perspective* (Washington DC, 1992)

Council of Europe, The

The Council is a regional organization aiming to
achieve a greater unity between its member
countries, in order to safeguard and realize the
ideals and principles that represent their common
heritage and to facilitate their economic and
social progress. It has represented over the past
few years the European political organization best
suited to accept, on an equal footing, the former
socialist countries of Eastern Europe and republics of the former USSR.

Origin and development

The Council was created in 1949, following protracted negotiations between the representatives
of several Western European nations. After 1945,
the idea of the political unification of Europe had
gained considerable impetus and led to the creation of numerous movements, at both international and national levels, sponsoring the project
of a European Union. In May 1948, the
International Committee of the Movements for
European Unity organized the Congress of
Europe in The Hague, The Netherlands, bringing
together in a private capacity nearly 1000
influential Europeans, including many prominent
statesmen. One of the resolutions adopted by
the Congress called for the establishment of a
European Assembly and a European Court of
Human Rights. The proposal concerning the
Assembly was considered with the Consultative
Council of the Brussels Treaty Organization, an
institution set up in March 1948 by Belgium,
France, Luxembourg, The Netherlands, and the
UK. In January 1949, the Ministers of Foreign
Affairs of these countries agreed in principle to
establish a Council of Europe, consisting of a
ministerial committee and a consultative assem-
bly. Proposals concerning the basic features of
the new organization were subsequently submitted to a conference of ambassadors includ-

ing, besides the five Brussels Treaty countries,
representatives of Denmark, Ireland, Italy,
Norway and Sweden who had been invited to
participate.

The Statute of the Council was signed by the
representatives of the ten countries on 5 May
1949, in London, and came into effect formally
two months later; subsequently, it has been
amended on a number of occasions. The founder
members were joined by Greece and Turkey later
in 1949; Iceland in 1950; the Federal Republic of
Germany in 1951 (having been an associate
member since 1950); Austria in 1956; Cyprus in
1961; Switzerland in 1963; Malta in 1965;
Portugal in 1976; Spain in 1977; Liechtenstein in
1978; San Marino in 1988; Finland in 1989;
Hungary in 1990; Czechoslovakia and Poland in
1991 and Bulgaria in 1992. After the dissolution
of Czechoslovakia at the end of 1992, both successor states (the Czech Republic and Slovakia)
were granted special guest status and later admitted to full membership. Estonia, Lithuania,
Romania and Slovenia became full members in
1993. Andorra joined in 1994, followed by
Albania, Latvia, Macedonia, Moldova and Ukraine
in 1995, and Russia and Croatia in 1996. Other
countries – Belarus and Bosnia-Herzegovina –
currently enjoying 'special guest' status have
applied for full membership, and accession procedures are under way. The possibility of membership is open to the other republics of the
former Yugoslavia as soon as they are freed from
UN sanctions and are prepared to ensure full
compliance with the commitments accepted by
other members of the Council. Armenia,
Azerbaijan and Georgia may also qualify for membership – provided they expressly indicate their
willingness to be considered as part of Europe –
while the former Soviet republics of Central Asia
might co-operate with the Council on the basis of
flexible and practical arrangements. All member
countries are committed to pluralist democracy,
the indivisibility and universality of human rights,
and the rule of law. Israel has long been a permanent observer. Observer status was also granted
to the USA in December 1995, while Japan's
request is under consideration.

The end of the division of Europe and the resulting need for the creation of an area of democratic
security throughout the whole of Europe led the
Council to reconsider its role and its organizational
mechanism at a Summit Conference of the Heads

of State and Government (the first such meeting in the organization's history) held in Vienna in October 1993. The resulting Vienna Declaration gave new impetus to the definition and implementation of legal standards in a number of fields, such as the protection of minorities, and reinforced and streamlined the judicial control mechanism of the European Convention on Human Rights through the creation of a single European Court, the functions of the former European Commission of Human Rights being assumed by the European Court of Human Rights.

Every member country is bound to accept 'the principles of the rule of law and of the enjoyment by all persons within its jurisdiction of human rights and fundamental freedoms' and must collaborate 'sincerely and effectively' in the realization of the Council's objectives. Ability to provide adequate protection of national minorities by candidates to membership has become a special concern of the Council. According to the 1993 Vienna Declaration, an undertaking by new members to sign the European Convention on Human Rights and accept the Convention's supervisory machinery in its entirety within a short period is also fundamental. Invitations to join the Council are issued by the Committee of Ministers after consultation with the Parliamentary Assembly. While a full member is entitled to participation in both the principal organs of the Council, an associate member is entitled only to representation in the Parliamentary Assembly. The right of withdrawal may be exercised upon giving formal notice and generally takes effect at the end of the financial year in which it is notified. Any country that seriously violates the fundamental obligations arising from membership in the Council may be suspended from its rights of representation and formally requested to withdraw; if such country does not comply with the request, the other member countries may decide its expulsion from the Council.

Objectives

The desire for a united Europe expressed by the representatives of the various movements who met at The Hague Congress of 1948 was fulfilled only to a certain extent by the creation of the Council, which is based upon the principle of voluntary co-operation of the member countries, which retain their full sovereign powers. According to the Statute, the basic aims of the Council are to be pursued by discussion of questions of common concern and by agreements and common action in economic, social, cultural, scientific, legal and administrative matters, and in the maintenance and further realization of human rights and fundamental freedoms. It is worth noting that matters relating to national defence are specifically excluded from the competence of the Council. Although the scope of the Council embraces a very wide range of subjects, defence being the only notable exception, the powers entrusted to the principal organs are fairly limited and substantially confined to the promotion of voluntary co-ordination of efforts, the adoption of recommendations and the drawing-up of conventions and agreements.

Structure

The organs of the Council are the Committee of Ministers and the Parliamentary Assembly, both of which are serviced by the Secretariat. The Committee of Ministers consists of the Ministers of Foreign Affairs of all member countries, each country being entitled to one representative and one vote. When a Minister of Foreign Affairs is unable to attend, an alternative may be appointed, possibly from among members of the government. Members of the Committee take the chair in rotation. The Committee is responsible for taking decisions with binding effect on all matters of internal organization, making recommendations to governments, and drawing up conventions and agreements; it also discusses matters of political concern. The Committee usually meets in private twice yearly, in April/May and November, at the seat of the Council in Strasbourg, France. From 1952 onwards, Ministers' Deputies were appointed to deal with most of the routine work at monthly meetings; they are entitled to take decisions having the same force and effect as those adopted by the Ministers themselves, provided that important policy matters are not involved. Deputies are usually senior diplomats accredited to the Council as permanent representatives of member countries. Decisions of the Committee normally require the unanimity of the representatives casting a vote and must include a majority of all members sitting on the Committee. Questions arising under the rules of procedure or under financial and administrative regulations may be decided by simple majority. A number of matters, concerning, *inter alia*, admission of members, adoption of the budget, rules of procedure, financial and administrative regulations, and amendment of the Statute, require a two-thirds majority of the votes cast and a majority of the representatives entitled to sit on the Committee.

The Parliamentary Assembly is empowered to discuss any matter within the aim and scope of the Council, and to present conclusions, in the form of recommendations, to the Committee of Ministers. It consists of 234 parliamentarians elected or appointed by national parliaments; political parties are represented in each national delegation according to the proportion of their strength in the respective parliament. Each member country is represented by a number of parliamentarians corresponding to its population size, ranging from two seats for countries with the smallest populations to eighteen for those with the largest.

Representatives sit in the Assembly in alphabetical order, not in national delegations, and vote in their individual capacity. Five major groups have been formed according to common political views: the Socialist Group; the Group of the European People's Party (Christian Democrats); the European Democratic (Conservative) Group; the Liberal Democratic and Reformers' Group; and the United European Left Group. The Assembly meets in ordinary session once a year for not more than a month, in public at the seat of the Council. It elects its own President, who controls its proceedings; the session is usually divided into three parts (held in January–February; April–May; and September–October), each part lasting approximately one week. Annual joint meetings with the European Parliament are generally held for one day only. The Assembly may address recommendations to the Committee of Ministers by a two-thirds majority of the representatives casting a vote; resolutions on matters relating to internal procedure and opinions generally require simple majority. Committees have been set up by the Assembly to consider and report on various matters, to examine and prepare questions on the agenda, and to advise on procedural matters. An additional channel of contact between the Committee of Ministers and the Parliamentary Assembly was provided in 1950 by the creation of a Joint Committee, including representatives of both the principal organs of the Council, and acting essentially as a co-ordinating and liaison body.

The establishment in April 1991 of a parliamentary assembly of the then Conference on Security and Co-operation in Europe (CSCE), later renamed the *Organization for Security and Co-operation in Europe (OSCE), originated the problem of a 'division of labour' among the new body and existing parliamentary institutions such as the North Atlantic Assembly, operating within the framework of the *North Atlantic Treaty Organization (NATO), and the Parliamentary Assembly of the Council of Europe. A formula is being devised whereby the Assembly of the Council of Europe will contribute to the work of the OSCE assembly on human rights matters, putting its expertise at the service of the newly-created pan-European body.

The Secretariat is headed by a Secretary-General, responsible to the Committee of Ministers. The Secretary-General and Deputy Secretary-General are appointed by the Assembly for renewable five-year terms on the recommendation of the Committee of Ministers.

The budget of the Council is submitted annually by the Secretary-General for adoption by the Committee of Ministers. The expenses of the Secretariat, as well as all other common expenses, are shared between members according to proportions determined by the Committee of Ministers. France, Germany, Italy and the UK together account for about two-thirds of the Council's ordinary budget.

Activities

The Council has concluded agreements with the UN and several of its specialized agencies in order to exchange observers and documents, and to co-ordinate mutual relations. The 1993 Vienna Declaration stressed the need for fuller co-ordination of the Council's activities with those of other European organizations. Co-operation in the human dimension sphere has been increasing with the relevant bodies of the OSCE, especially the Office for Democratic Institutions and Human Rights and the High Commissioner on National Minorities. Relationships are also close with the *Organization for Economic Co-operation and Development (OECD) and especially with the *European Union (EU), in order to arrange reciprocal communication on matters of important European interest, provide for consultation and co-ordination with a view to avoiding duplication and waste of efforts, and develop joint projects. It is worth mentioning that the Assembly of the *Western European Union (WEU) is composed of representatives of the Union's member countries to the Parliamentary Assembly of the Council. Observers from non-governmental organizations take part in many activities of the Council.

Despite the fluctuating relationship between its principal organs and its fairly limited powers, the Council has succeeded in furthering regional co-operation in several key areas, lowering barriers between European countries, harmonizing legislation or introducing common European laws, eliminating discrimination on grounds of nationality, and undertaking a number of ventures on a joint European basis.

Of paramount importance is the building-up by the Council of a common law of Europe through multilateral conventions and agreements. The European Convention for the Protection of Human Rights and Fundamental Freedoms represents a major achievement; its object is to guarantee internationally fundamental rights and freedoms, and special machinery is provided for the observance and enforcement of the basic standards. The Convention, prepared under the auspices of the Council, was signed in Rome in November 1950 and came into effect in September 1953; several additional protocols have been drawn up subsequently and have entered gradually into force. Unlike the UN Universal Declaration of Human Rights of 1948, whose value essentially lies in the moral sphere, the European Convention is a binding treaty, though important reservations and denunciation are expressly permitted.

Until 1994 a European Commission of Human Rights investigated alleged violations of the Convention submitted to it either by signatory countries or, in certain cases, by individuals; the function of the Commission was basically one of conciliation. Since April 1994 all cases are referred to the European Court of Human Rights, which decides whether or not a violation has taken place. The Court was established in 1959 and consists of a number of judges equal to that of the member countries of the Council. The judgment of the Court is final, but acceptance of its jurisdiction is optional for the signatory countries.

The Council's Steering Committee for Human Rights is in charge of promoting intergovernmental co-operation in human rights and fundamental freedoms; it prepared, *inter alia*, the European Ministerial Conference on Human Rights, which took place in 1985, and the European Convention for the Prevention of Torture, which entered into force in February 1989.

Following the adoption by the 1993 Vienna Summit Conference of a Plan of Action in the Fight against Racism, Xenophobia, Antisemitism and Intolerance, the European Commission against Racism and Intolerance, composed of government experts, was created in 1994.

In an effort to harmonize national laws, to put the citizens of member countries on an equal footing and to pool certain resources and facilities, about 140 conventions and agreements have been concluded within the framework of the Council to cover a variety of aspects: social security; extradition; patents; medical treatment; training of nurses; equivalence of degrees and diplomas; hotel-keepers' liability; compulsory motor insurance; protection of television broadcasts; adoption of children; transportation of animals; movement of persons; and archaeological heritage. A European Social Charter came into force in 1965, setting out the social and economic rights which the signatory countries agree to guarantee to their citizens and complementing to a certain extent the European Convention on Human Rights; in May 1988 the Charter was completed by an Additional Protocol. Two important conventions adopted in 1977 concern the suppression of terrorism, and the legal status of migrant workers. Additional protocols have been adopted to amend and supplement the provisions contained in certain conventions.

In the economic and social fields, particular attention is given to the protection of the socio-economic rights of the individual. The work of the Council ranges from consumer education and participation, to specific aspects of social policy, welfare and labour law. The European Convention on the Legal Status of Migrant Workers has been in force since 1983.

With regard to health, the Council aims to increase the exchange between member countries of medical techniques and equipment, to encourage study projects, and to draw up common standards on the proper use of pharmaceuticals and on the medical and functional treatment of disabled persons. Many member countries co-operate within the framework of the 'Pompidou

Group' to combat drug abuse and illicit drug trafficking. The Convention on Laundering, Search, Seizure and Confiscation of Proceeds from Crime came into force in September 1993.

A Committee for Population Studies, set up in 1973, observes population trends and their implications. In 1956, the Council's Social Development Fund was set up, called the Resettlement Fund for National Refugees and Over-Population, with a view to giving financial aid, particularly in the spheres of housing, vocational training, regional planning, and development. By 1989, total loans granted by the Fund amounted to about $7500 million.

In 1970, the Council set up a European Youth Centre, equipped with audio-visual workshops, reading and conference rooms; about 1500 people can be accommodated annually. In order to provide financial assistance to European activities of non-governmental youth organizations, the Council created the European Youth Foundation, which began operations in 1973.

On the legal plane, the European Committee on Legal Co-operation supervises the Council's work programme for international, administrative, civil and commercial law, and has prepared numerous conventions. The European Committee on Crime Problems has also prepared conventions on matters falling within its competence, such as mutual assistance in procedural matters, international validity of criminal judgments, and transfer of proceedings. The Council for Cultural Co-operation (CCC) carries out the educational and cultural activities of the Council, based on the concepts of permanent education and cultural development. The CCC, which includes the members of the Council plus other signatories of the Cultural Convention, administers the Cultural Fund for the promotion and financing of educational and cultural activities. Several committees and expert groups assist the CCC. The Committee for the Development of Sport has the same membership as the CCC and administers the Sports Fund. Its activities concentrate on the implementation of the European Sport for All Charter of 1975 and related issues.

The Steering Committee on the Mass Media covers all aspects of mass communication, with special reference to broadcasting; it prepared a European Convention on transfrontier television, which was adopted in 1989.

The Steering Committee for the Conservation and Management of the Environment and Natural Habitats, established in 1962, draws up policy recommendations and promotes co-operation on all environmental questions. It introduced a European Water Charter in 1968, a Soil Charter in 1974, and a Charter on Invertebrates in 1986. The Congress of Local and Regional Authorities of Europe was established in 1994 as an advisory organ representing local and regional interests; two chambers have been created within the Congress, one for the local authorities and one for the regions. The Cultural Heritage Committee promotes contacts between authorities in charge of historic buildings and encourages public interest. A Convention for the Conservation of the Architectural Heritage of Europe entered into force in 1987.

Under an agreement concluded in 1990 by several member countries of the Council, the European Commission for Democracy through Law (Venice Commission), composed of independent experts, has been established to handle the legal aspects of democratization in the countries of Central and Eastern Europe.

Secretary-General: Daniel Tarschys

Headquarters: Palais de l'Europe, 67006 Strasbourg, France (Telephone: +333 8841 2000; fax: +333 8841 2781)

Publications: *Forum* (quarterly); *European Yearbook*; *Yearbook on the European Convention on Human Rights*; *Bulletin on Constitutional Case-Law* (three times a year)

References: A. H. Robertson, *The Council of Europe. Its Structure, Functions and Achievements* (London) rev. 2/1961; A. H. Robertson, *European Institutions* (London) rev. 3/1973

Council of the Baltic Sea States (CBSS)

The Council represents a significant attempt at re-establishing and strengthening links among Baltic countries in the post-Cold War era.

Origin and development
The proposal to create the Council was launched in 1991 at a meeting of the German and Danish Foreign Ministers, with a view to providing an institutional framework for economic assistance by the Nordic countries and Germany to the three

Baltic republics (Estonia, Latvia and Lithuania), Poland and Russia. At the inaugural meeting of the Council, held in Copenhagen in March 1992, the Foreign Ministers of Denmark, Estonia, Finland, Germany, Latvia, Lithuania, Norway, Poland, Russia and Sweden broadened considerably the original proposal to include additional areas of co-operation such as the environment, transportation and education.

Objectives

The Council intends to foster co-operation among all countries bordering on the Baltic Sea or its main links to the open sea with a view to helping the establishment of new democratic institutions and co-ordinating policies in the fields of trade and economic development, humanitarian aid, the environment, energy, transport and communications, culture and education. Military and security matters are expressly excluded from the sphere of competence of the Council.

Structure

The Council is endowed – like other newly-created subregional organizations in Europe – with a flexible structure avoiding overly bureaucratic mechanisms; no permanent secretariat has been established thus far. The Council of Ministers meets annually, under a rotating chairmanship, to set basic guidelines, while a Committee of Senior Officials, deciding by consensus, is in charge of the day-to-day operation.

Activities

A number of Working Groups have been created to deal with specific areas such as economic co-operation, nuclear and radiation safety, and human rights. With regard to economic co-operation, the group dealt with a simplification of customs procedures and border crossings as well as with regional transportation and energy projects. The work of the human rights group has paved the way to the appointment in 1994 of a Commissioner on Democratic Institutions and Human Rights, Including the Rights of Persons Belonging to Minorities, within the framework of the Council.

Customs Co-operation Council (CCC)

The Council currently carries out world-wide co-operation in customs matters.

Origin and development

The Convention establishing the Council was signed in December 1950 by the representatives of the 13 countries participating in the Committee for European Economic Co-operation; the Council started operations in January 1953. The original goal in 1947 had been the study of the feasibility of a customs union in Europe, but subsequent difficulties led to a more modest attempt at standardizing customs definitions and procedures. The signatory countries of the Convention for the creation of the Council also adopted the Brussels Definition of Value and the Brussels Nomenclature. Membership currently includes around 140 countries or territories.

Objectives

The Council's aims are to study questions relating to co-operation in customs matters with a view to attaining harmony and uniformity, to prepare draft conventions and recommendations, to ensure uniform interpretation and application of customs conventions, and to circulate information on customs regulations and procedures.

Structure

The institutional structure comprises the Council, where all members participate, while a Policy Commission – in operation since 1979 and including a representative group of the Council's members – acts as a steering committee. The Secretariat performs administrative tasks. A number of subsidiary committees deal with the more technical aspects overseeing implementation of the relevant agreements. The Customs Co-operation Fund was created in 1984 to help the training of national customs officers.

Activities

The radical modification of economic and trade structures in Central and Eastern Europe and the former republics of the USSR has opened up new opportunities for the Council, from simplification and standardization of customs declarations and procedures to technical assistance in the field of training. Fight against widespread commercial fraud, smuggling and drug trafficking as well as protection of intellectual property rights are among the new challenges facing the Council in the late 1990s.

Secretary-General: James W. Shaver

Headquarters: 26–38 rue de l'Industrie, 1040 Brussels, Belgium (Telephone: +32 2 508 4211; fax: +32 2 508 4240)

Publications: *Bulletin* (annual); *CCC News* (periodical);   technical   handbooks   and brochures

D

Damascus Declaration States

The signatories intend to develop co-operation between the Arab countries of the Gulf and Egypt and Syria.

Origin and development
The 'Damascus Declaration for Co-ordination and Co-operation among the Arab States' was signed in the Syrian capital, on 6 March 1991, by Bahrain, Kuwait, Oman, Qatar, Saudi Arabia and the United Arab Emirates – members of the *Co-operation Council for the Arab States of the Gulf, generally known as Gulf Co-operation Council (GCC) – plus Egypt and Syria. Since the beginning of military operations to liberate Kuwait, the GCC members had been considering the prospect of setting up a new regional defence framework with Egypt and Syria, which were also taking part in the US-led anti-Iraq coalition. In the aftermath of the successful conclusion of the Gulf War, the Ministers of Foreign Affairs of the eight countries meeting in Damascus adopted the 'Declaration' as a means of preserving Gulf security from future threats. However, the reluctance of some GCC members to have an Arab peace-keeping force – consisting mainly of Egyptian and Syrian troops – stationed in the Gulf led to the shelving of plans for a permanent military presence in the region, involving non-GCC members.

Objectives
The 'Declaration' aims at establishing and strengthening co-ordination and co-operation: in the political and security fields, recognizing the right of every GCC member country to ask for the support of Egyptian and Syrian forces and their presence in their territories; in the economic and cultural fields, in order to achieve balanced economic and social development, as a prelude to the establishment of an Arab economic grouping, and to encourage the private sector in Arab countries; in the field of joint Arab action, with a view to supporting and strengthening the *League of Arab States.

Structure
The objectives stated in the 'Declaration' are pursued through meetings at the level of Foreign Ministers hosted in turn by each participating country. The assistance of experts and specialists is sought to define the various aspects of co-operation.

Activities
Despite their diverse interests and views, the signatories of the 'Declaration' continued to meet to discuss issues concerning peace and security in the Gulf, while the GCC members inaugurated their own Military Committee in April 1994. The relationship with Iran, including the dispute between that country and the United Arab Emirates over a number of islands in the Gulf, and the 1994 civil war in Yemen emerged as important topics for the 'Declaration' countries. Despite the development of relations with the Jewish state, a firm stand was adopted in early 1995 in view of Israel's refusal to sign the 1968 Nuclear Non-Proliferation Treaty (NPT) and to place its facilities under the safeguard system of the *International Atomic Energy Agency (IAEA).

Danube Commission

The Commission regulates navigation on the Danube in its various aspects, ensuring the application of uniform rules and providing the related services.

Origin and development
The Commission was constituted in 1949 according to the Convention on the regulation of shipping on the Danube, which was signed in Belgrade, Yugoslavia, in August 1948. Recent events, including the break-up of countries which were original signatories of the Convention, and the emergence of newly-independent states with justified interests in the Danube region, will require a new multilateral agreement on the management of the river. The scope of the original Convention should also be broadened to include new areas such as energy production and environmental protection. The preparatory process for a diplomatic conference on questions of Danube co-operation began in 1993.

The need to provide uniform navigation rules on international rivers in Europe led to the establishment of international river commissions under the Peace Treaties of Paris (1814) and Vienna (1815). A European Danube Commission was established on a temporary basis under the Peace Treaty of Paris in 1856, and reconstituted as a permanent institution in 1865. The problems concerning navigation on the Danube were again dealt with in the Peace Treaties with Austria, Bulgaria, Germany and Hungary between 1919 and 1921, and a Convention regarding the 'definitive statute' of the Danube was signed in July 1921. A European Commission of the Danube was set up with jurisdiction over the maritime portion of the river, while an International Commission exercised jurisdiction over the international waterway. After the Second World War, the navigation rules of the Danube were reconsidered in the Peace Treaties with Bulgaria, Hungary and Romania of February 1947, and subsequently became the specific object of the Belgrade Convention providing for the establishment of the present Commission.

Objectives

The Belgrade Convention solemnly declares that navigation on the Danube from Ulm, in Germany, to the Black Sea (with access to the sea through the Sulina arm and the Sulina Canal) is equally free and open to the nationals, merchant shipping and merchandise of all countries as to harbour and navigation fees as well as conditions of merchant navigation. The Commission, which enjoys legal status and has its own seal and flag, is empowered to: supervise the implementation of the provisions of the Belgrade Convention; establish the basic regulations for navigation on the river; ensure facilities for shipping; approve projects for maintenance of navigability and supervise technical services; establish a uniform buoying system on all navigable waterways; co-ordinate the regulations for customs, sanitation control, and the hydrometeorological service; collect relevant statistical data.

Structure

The Commission holds annual sessions and is composed of one representative from each of its member countries; that is, Austria, Bulgaria, Hungary, Romania, Russia, Slovakia, Ukraine and the 'Federal Republic of Yugoslavia' (Serbia and Montenegro). Croatia, Germany (whose represen-

tatives have been attending the meetings of the Commission since 1957 as guests of the Secretariat), and Moldova have declared their interest in full membership and currently enjoy observer status. Ukraine, a founding member of the Commission, resumed membership in 1991. The Russian Federation obtained the former Soviet seat, despite the fact that Russia itself does not border on the Danube, as originally required by the Convention.

Administrative and technical functions are performed by the Secretariat, comprising a technical section, an administrative section and an accounts department. Members of the Commission and elected officers are granted diplomatic immunity. All member countries of the Commission contribute the same annual amount to the budget.

Activities

The hindrances to navigation on the Danube as a result of hostilities in parts of former Yugoslavia, and of international sanctions adopted against Serbia and Montenegro, have deeply affected the activities of the Commission. After a virtual standstill in early 1993, transit traffic not subject to sanctions has been resumed, although with several difficulties. The Commission has developed close contacts regarding the application of sanctions on the Danube with the *European Union (EU), the *Organization for Security and Co-operation in Europe (OSCE), and the *Western European Union (WEU).

The opening of the Rhine–Main–Danube Canal – a German artificial waterway in operation since September 1992, for which charges are levied – has brought about a substantial increase of traffic on the upper Danube. This has resulted in an intensification of the co-operation between the Commission and the *Central Commission for the Navigation of the Rhine on harmonization of the shipping regimes and other priority technical, commercial and legal issues.

Director-General: Hellmuth Strasser
Headquarters: Benczúr utca 25, 1068 Budapest, Hungary (Telephone: +36 1 268 1971; fax: +36 1 268 1980)
Publications: *Basic Regulations for Navigation on the Danube*; *Hydrological Yearbook*; *Statistical Yearbook*

References: R. W. Johnson, 'The Danube since 1948', *Year Book of World Affairs*, 17 (1963); S. Gorove, *Law and Politics of the Danube* (1964)

Desert Locust Control Organization for Eastern Africa (DLCO-EA)

Established in 1962, the Organization aims to promote the effective control of the desert locust in East Africa and to conduct operational research and training programmes; it also assists member countries in the monitoring and extermination of other migratory pests. Members include Djibouti, Ethiopia, Kenya, Somalia, Sudan, Tanzania and Uganda.

Director-General: Prof. Hosea Y. Kayumbo
Headquarters: P.O. Box 30023, Nairobi, Kenya (Telephone: +254 2 501704; fax: +254 2 505137)
Publications: *Annual Report*; *Desert Locust Situation Report* (monthly)

E

Eastern Caribbean Central Bank (ECCB)

The Bank was established in 1983 to maintain a common currency (Eastern Caribbean dollar) between members of the *Organization of Eastern Caribbean States (OECS), to establish a central body with powers to issue and manage the common currency, and to promote monetary stability and a sound financial structure. The Bank also performs an advisory function concerning the economic development of its member countries: Antigua and Barbuda, Dominica, Grenada, Montserrat, Saint Kitts and Nevis, Saint Lucia, Saint Vincent and the Grenadines.

Governor: Dwight Venner
Headquarters: P.O. Box 89, Basseterre, Saint Kitts and Nevis (Telephone: +854 465 2537; fax: +854 465 5614)
Publication: *Annual Report*

Economic and Monetary Community of Central Africa

(Communauté économique et monétaire de l'Afrique centrale) (CEMAC)

The Community was established by a treaty signed in 1994 by the representatives of Cameroon, Central African Republic, Chad, Congo, Equatorial Guinea, and Gabon. The new organization replaced – with the same membership – the Customs and Economic Union of Central Africa (Union douanière et économique de l'Afrique centrale) (UDEAC), which had been operating in the region since 1966. At the summit meeting of UDEAC held in March 1994 in N'Djaména, Chad, the decision was taken to create the Community.

All member countries of the Community use a common currency pegged to the French franc; that is, the franc of the Coopération financière en Afrique centrale (CFA franc) whose issuing bank is the Banque des états de l'Afrique centrale (BEAC) established in 1955 and based in Yaoundé, Cameroon. In response to repeated calls from the *International Monetary Fund (IMF) and the French government, the countries using the CFA franc –

which include all members of the Community plus seven other French-speaking countries in West Africa – devalued the currency by 50 per cent against the French franc in January 1994. The new exchange rate was intended to alleviate balance-of-payments difficulties and restore the competitiveness of the countries involved in the devaluation.

Economic and Social Commission for Asia and the Pacific (ESCAP)

The Commission provides the only intergovernmental forum for the whole of Asia and the Pacific, and fulfils a wide range of functions. It is a regional economic commission operating within the UN system under the authority of the Economic and Social Council, like the *Economic Commission for Africa (ECA), the *Economic Commission for Europe (ECE), the *Economic Commission for Latin America and the Caribbean (ECLAC) and the *Economic and Social Commission for Western Asia (ESCWA).

Origin and development
The Commission was founded in March 1947 upon the adoption of a resolution by the Economic and Social Council. Its members include the countries of Asia and the Pacific (except the Arab countries of South Western Asia pertaining to ESCWA, Israel pertaining to ECE, and Taiwan, which remains outside the UN system), together with four non-regional members – France, The Netherlands, the UK and the USA. Following the dissolution of the USSR, former Soviet republics in Central Asia and the Caucasus have joined the Commission; the Russian Federation became a regional member in 1995. About ten non-self-governing Asian and Pacific territories enjoy associate membership. Previously known as the Economic Commission for Asia and the Far East (ECAFE), the Commission was reorganized and renamed by the Economic and Social Council in 1974.

Objectives
The Commission assists in the formulation and implementation of co-ordinated policies for promoting economic and technological development in the region, and fosters the expansion of trade and economic links among member countries

and with other countries of the world. Besides furthering regional co-operation on economic issues and extending assistance to individual governments to formulate and implement balanced development programmes, the Commission gives increasing attention to the social aspects of economic development and the relationship between economic and social factors, with special emphasis on alleviating poverty in the least-developed areas of the region and promoting sustainable development. Initially involved in the urgent economic problems following the Second World War, the Commission subsequently took into consideration a wider range of objectives in an increasing effort to cover new areas and needs, as well as to intensify practical action for the benefit of the least-developed, land-locked and island countries of the region. Under the terms of reference laid down by the Economic and Social Council, the Commission is also responsible for undertaking or sponsoring investigations and studies of economic and technological problems and developments within the region, and for evaluating and disseminating economic, technological and statistical information originating from this work.

The Commission enjoys considerable autonomy with regard to the fulfilment of its functions, since the corresponding terms of reference are rather broadly formulated. These functions are related to the basic task of initiating and participating in measures with a view to facilitating concerted action for economic and social progress in Asia and the Pacific. The Commission is entitled to make recommendations to both the Economic and Social Council and the governments of member countries. Other powers conferred on the Commission include the adoption of the relevant rules of procedure, the appointment of the Chairman, and the establishment of any necessary subsidiary bodies. The Commission must submit an annual report on its activities and plans to the Economic and Social Council; the budget is sent for approval to the UN General Assembly.

Structure

The Commission ordinarily holds sessions at ministerial level once a year, with participation by the representatives of all member countries, to consider basic policies, set priorities and review projects and programmes that are being carried out. Decisions and resolutions are customarily adopted by consensus, without casting votes. Under no condition is the Commission allowed to take action against any member country without the latter's consent.

Committees, *ad hoc* conferences, working groups and other minor subsidiary bodies have been created by the Commission to provide adequate technical support for its activities. At present there are three thematic committees on regional economic co-operation, on the environment and sustainable development, and on poverty alleviation through economic growth and social development, all of them meeting annually; two other committees – on statistics, and transport and communications, meeting every two years; and two special bodies on least-developed and land-locked developing countries and on Pacific island developing countries, meeting every two years. The Advisory Committee of Permanent Representatives and Other Representatives designated by member countries of the Commission performs consultative and liaison tasks.

The Secretariat, located in Bangkok, provides the technical and administrative services for the meetings of the Commission and its subsidiary bodies and is responsible for a wide range of general and specialized publications. The Executive Secretary is designated by the UN Secretary General and acts on his behalf. An ESCAP Pacific Operations Centre (ESCAP/POC) was set up in Port Vila, Vanuatu, in 1984, to provide assistance at a subregional level and to identify the needs of island countries.

Activities

Close relations exist between the Commission and the relevant UN specialized agencies and bodies in operation in Asia and the Pacific, as well as with the other regional economic commissions. Co-operative links with the economic, technical and financial institutions in the region have been growing steadily, with a view to co-ordinating and implementing programmes and projects of both regional and subregional scope. The Commission is responsible for the following associated bodies: Regional Co-ordination Centre for Research and Development of Coarse Grains, Pulses, Roots and Tuber Crops in the Humid Tropics of Asia and the Pacific (CGPRT Centre) in Bogor, Indonesia; Asian and Pacific Centre for Transfer of Technology (APCTT) in New Delhi;

Statistical Institute for Asia and the Pacific (SIAP) in Tokyo.

Since its inception, the Commission has adapted its work programmes and priorities gradually to meet the changing political, economic and social conditions in the region, as well as extending co-operation to new fields. The vastness of the area concerned and the huge disparities in levels of development and available resources of member countries, as well as the persistence of ideological cleavages have made it difficult to establish effective region-wide multilateral organizations. The Commission has therefore acted, within the UN framework, as a truly Asian–Pacific centre for furthering subregional, regional and interregional co-operation.

In recent years the Commission has made considerable efforts to implement projects of regional or subregional scope; it acts as executing agency for several programmes and projects. Since the mid-1980s, it has concentrated its efforts in the following main areas: food and agriculture; energy; raw materials and commodities; transfer of technology; international trade, transnational corporations and external financial resources transfers; integrated rural development; environmental policies, management and laws; and preferential treatment in favour of the least-developed, land-locked and island countries in Asia and the Pacific. A number of specialized bodies have been set up under the aegis of the Commission or with its assistance; they are located in several Asian cities and their membership varies according to their field of action.

As regards development planning, the Commission has been investigating issues relating to external debt, trade in primary commodities, and foreign investment. An important function has been carried out by the Commission in the creation and subsequent improvement of the Generalized System of Preferences (GSP). Assistance from the Commission was extended for the establishment of groupings dealing with commodities such as the *Asian and Pacific Coconut Community (APCC), the *International Pepper Community (IPC), the *International Jute Organization (IJO) and the *International Natural Rubber Organization (INRO). The *Asian Development Bank (AsDB) was set up under the Commission's auspices and has been in operation since the mid-1960s; in July 1993 a memorandum was signed between the Commission and the Bank identifying priority areas for co-operation. Several agencies have been created to assist member countries in the discovery and use of natural resources, such as the Regional Mineral Resources Development Centre, the South East Asia Tin Research and Development Centre, the Committee for Co-ordination of Joint Prospecting for Mineral Resources in Asian Offshore Areas and the Committee for Co-ordination of Joint Prospecting for Mineral Resources in South Pacific Offshore Areas. In this connection the Commission increasingly stresses the relevance of the environmental impact of the exploitation of natural resources. A new regional training and research institution, the Asian and Pacific Development Centre was established in 1980 to provide assistance and facilities to member countries. Other bodies have been set up in the fields of technology transfer, transport and communications, and typhoon, cyclone and flood warning systems. The Programme on Marine Affairs was set up in 1986 to advise member countries with regard to the 'exclusive economic zones' established under the 1982 UN Convention on the Law of the Sea.

In agriculture the Commission helps to formulate regional and national policies that lead to increased agricultural production; a close co-operation has been developed with the *Food and Agriculture Organization of the UN (FAO) and the *International Labour Organization (ILO). Investigation is being carried out concerning new and renewable energy sources in the region, with special reference to solar, wind and biomass energy. The high rate of population growth in the region has prompted studies on demography and the efficiency of national family-planning programmes, mostly funded by the *UN Population Fund (UNFPA). The Commission is also involved in health programmes covering basic community services, and in health planning, as part of overall development schemes.

Executive Secretary: Adrianus Mooy
Headquarters: United Nations Building, Rajadamnern Avenue, Bangkok 10200, Thailand (Telephone: +66 2 288 1234; fax: +66 2 288 1000)
Publications: *Economic and Social Survey of Asia and the Pacific* (annual); *Economic Bulletin* (twice a year); *Statistical Yearbook for Asia and*

the Pacific; *Quarterly Bulletin of Statistics for Asia and the Pacific*

References: B. G. Ramcharan, 'Equality and Discrimination in International Economic Law (VIII): The United Nations Regional Economic Commissions', *Year Book of World Affairs*, 32 (1978), 268–85; P. W. Newman, Jr, 'Regionalism in Developing Areas: UN Regional Economic Commissions and their Relations with Regional Organizations', in B. Andemicael (ed.), *Regionalism and the United Nations*, (New York, Dobbs Ferry, 1979)

Economic and Social Commission for Western Asia (ESCWA)

The Commission is one of the five regional economic commissions of the UN – the *Economic Commission for Africa (ECA), the *Economic Commission for Europe (ECE), the *Economic Commission for Latin America and the Caribbean (ECLAC), and the *Economic and Social Commission for Asia and the Pacific (ESCAP).

Origin and development

Initially, attempts to set up an economic commission specifically responsible for the Middle East met with considerable difficulties, of a political rather than an economic nature. For a time, the countries of the region had to be served by an *ad hoc* body, the UN Economic and Social Office in Beirut (UNESOB). In 1974, it finally proved feasible to establish a Commission in charge of the region, and a resolution was adopted by the Economic and Social Council. The region included Egypt and the Arab countries of South West Asia and excluded the remaining countries of the Middle East; that is, Iran, Israel, and Turkey. In fact, Israel and Turkey belong to ECE while Iran belongs to ESCAP. In response to the Egypt–Israel peace treaty concluded in Washington in March 1979, the Commission had recommended unsuccessfully to the Economic and Social Council the suspension of Egypt's membership.

At a special session which took place in September 1974, Beirut was chosen as the seat of the Commission until 1979. The sixth session, held in 1979, decided to move the Commission to Baghdad, where permanent headquarters were established in 1982. Temporary headquarters were established in 1991 in Amman; the decision to relocate the permanent headquarters in Beirut was adopted in 1994 but was not immediately implemented.

Objectives

The Commission acts within the UN framework under the authority of the Economic and Social Council; its purposes are primarily the formulation, co-ordination and implementation of policies for the promotion of economic and social development at regional level, and the improvement, through individual and collective actions, of commercial and economic relations among member countries and with the rest of the world. As a body that is specifically in charge of a developing region, the Commission – under the terms of reference laid down by the Economic and Social Council – must deal as appropriate with the social aspects of economic development and the relationship between economic and social factors. It has a broad mandate to consider any action that may be necessary for the attainment of its basic objectives. Besides its primary task of furthering through practical action the development of member countries, the Commission is responsible for promoting investigations and studies of economic and technological problems and developments within Western Asia, as well as for collecting, evaluating and disseminating the resultant economic, technological and statistical information.

The Commission is entitled to address recommendations on any matter falling within its competence, not only to the Economic and Social Council but also directly to governments of member countries. Among the other powers conferred on the Commission are the following: drawing up its own rules of procedure; appointment of the Chairman of its session; and establishment of subsidiary bodies appropriate for the fulfilment of its functions.

Structure

The Commission holds ordinary sessions every two years with the participation of representatives of all member countries. Decisions and resolutions are adopted customarily by consensus, without formal voting. The Commission may act only with the agreement of the governments of the countries concerned. Subsidiary bodies, consisting of government officials and experts have been set up by the Commission to consider specific issues of interest to countries of the region. The Secretariat is headed by an Executive Secretary, nominated by the UN Secretary General and acting on the latter's behalf. An annual report on its activities and plans is submitted to the Economic and Social Council; the budget is subject to formal approval by the UN General Assembly.

Activities

The Commission participates in the work of UN specialized agencies and other bodies operating in Western Asia, and maintains close contacts with the other four regional economic commissions. Co-operation links have been established with Arab economic and financial institutions in the region.

Since its creation, the Commission has made efforts with a view to fostering intersectoral co-ordination and co-operation at the regional level, despite the serious and long-standing problems represented by marked imbalances in economic structures, and large income disparities existing between and within its member countries. Because of limits on recruitment imposed during the latter half of the 1980s, the Commission's programme of activities has had to be reduced substantially.

In 1994, as a consequence of a fundamental reappraisal and restructuring of its programmes, the Commission adopted a 'thematic structure', allowing an interdisciplinary approach and greater mobility in the allocation of resources. Therefore, the Commission is currently at work on five thematic subprogrammes, concerning: Management of Natural Resources and Environment; Improvement of the Quality of Life; Economic Development and Co-operation; Regional Developments and Global Changes; and Special Issues, including as focal points Palestine, the Middle East peace process and the least developed member countries.

Executive Secretary: Hazem El-Beblawi
Postal address: P.O. Box 927115, Amman, Jordan (Telephone: +962 6 669 4351; fax: +962 6 669 4980)
Publications: *Survey of Economic and Social Developments in the ESCWA Region* (annual); *Agriculture and Development in Western Asia* (annual); *Statistical Abstract* (annual)

References: B. G. Ramcharan, 'Equality and Discrimination in International Economic Law (VIII): The United Nations Regional Economic Commissions', *Year Book of World Affairs*, 32 (1978), 268–85

Economic Commission for Africa (ECA)

The Commission is one of five regional economic commissions operating within the UN system: the *Economic Commission for Europe (ECE), the *Economic Commission for Latin America and the Caribbean (ECLAC), the *Economic and Social Commission for Western Asia (ESCWA) and the *Economic and Social Commission for Asia and the Pacific (ESCAP).

Origin and development

The Commission was created in 1958 by resolution of the Economic and Social Council as a subsidiary organ of the UN. Its membership has varied considerably over the years. At the beginning six European nations (Belgium, France, Italy, Portugal, Spain and the UK), with special interests in the region, participated as full members alongside ten independent African countries; nine African countries which were not yet independent were associate members. Subsequently, Italy and Belgium withdrew, France, Spain and the UK became associate members, and Portugal was excluded. As they gained independence, all other African countries joined the Commission as full members; the Republic of South Africa, suspended in 1965, resumed participation in 1994. The Commission's present membership includes all African states and is the same as that of the *Organization of African Unity (OAU) plus Morocco, which no longer belongs to the OAU.

Objectives

The Commission is called upon, under the authority of the UN Economic and Social Council, to initiate and participate in measures for facilitating concerted action for economic development, to maintain and strengthen the economic relations of member countries among themselves and with other countries of the world, and to produce and disseminate economic, technological and statistical information. The Commission was involved from the start in the problems of Africa's economic and social development; as a body specifically intended to serve a developing region and according to the terms of reference laid down by the Economic and Social Council, the Commission was also endowed with rather wide functions concerning technical co-operation and other forms of operational activity. In addition, appropriate consideration should be given to the social aspects of economic development and the relationship between economic and social factors. The basic goals of promoting self-sustaining processes of development at both regional and subregional level, alleviating unemployment and mass poverty, protecting the environment, and establishing equitable and mutually beneficial relations between the continent and the rest of the world, are to be achieved, *inter alia*, through: development of self-sufficiency in food; foundation and strengthening of a sound industrial base; improvement of the physical infrastructure, especially transport and communications; development of natural resources, technology and services; co-ordinated planning of economic growth; and the advancement of economic co-operation and integration within subregional groupings.

The functions of the Commission are of an operational rather than deliberative nature and are closely connected with the fundamental task of promoting sound economic and social progress in the African continent. In accordance with its terms of reference, the Commission may address recommendations on any matter falling within its competence directly to its member countries as well as to the Economic and Social Council. It is empowered to draw up its own rules of procedure, to elect the Chairman of its sessions and to create the necessary subsidiary bodies.

Structure

Until 1965 the Commission customarily held annual sessions, with participation by representatives of all member countries. Biennial sessions were subsequently held until a resolution was adopted in 1969 that these ordinary biennial sessions should be held at ministerial level; they became known as meetings of the Conference of Ministers. At the fourteenth session of the Commission and fifth meeting of the Conference of Ministers in March 1979, it was decided that the Conference of Ministers, as the Commission's highest decision-making organ, should meet

annually. It is the responsibility of the Conference, customarily attended by Ministers of economic or financial affairs, to consider the Commission's basic policies, to set priorities, and to review the course of programmes and projects being implemented, together with international economic issues of interest to Africa. Decisions and resolutions are normally adopted by consensus without any formal vote being cast. Under no circumstances is it possible to take action against any country without the Conference's consent. A number of technical committees and other *ad-hoc* subsidiary bodies, composed of specialists and government officials have been created over the years by the Commission according to its needs.

The Secretariat has its headquarters in Addis Ababa, Ethiopia. It services the meetings of the Conference of Ministers and the various subsidiary bodies, and performs a wide range of technical and administrative functions. It is organized into Divisions responsible for: food and agriculture, jointly with the *Food and Agriculture Organization of the UN (FAO); industry and human settlements; natural resources; trade and development finance; transport, communications and tourism; socioeconomic research and planning; public administration, human resources and social development; statistics; population; administration and conference services. The Commission's Executive Secretary is designated by the UN Secretary General.

The Commission must submit a full annual report on its activities and plans to the Economic and Social Council; the UN General Assembly is responsible for the formal approval of the Commission's budget.

A number of Multinational Programming and Operational Centres (MULPOCs), located in different African cities and serving different subregions, act as field agents for the implementation of development programmes, thus replacing the former UN Multidisciplinary Development Advisory Teams (UNDATs). The African Institute for Economic Development and Planning, operating within the framework of the Commission, is located in Addis Ababa.

Activities

The Commission works in close collaboration with the relevant UN specialized agencies operating in Africa, and with the other four regional economic commissions. Effective co-operation links exist in particular with African international organizations, notably the OAU, subregional integration bodies such as the *Economic Community of West African States (ECOWAS) and financial institutions such as the *African Development Bank (AfDB) and the Association of African Central Banks (AACB). Technical support has been provided by the Commission in the establishment of several of these bodies. Ties between the Commission and Arab countries outside Africa have been growing since the late 1970s within the framework of the Declaration of Afro-Arab Economic and Financial Co-operation adopted at the first Afro-Arab Summit Conference held in March 1977. Regarding development assistance financing in particular, projects are being submitted for consideration to the *Arab Bank for Economic Development in Africa (BADEA). On the whole, the Commission has been playing a role in fostering intraregional co-ordination and co-operation, as well as establishing mutually beneficial and equitable relations between African countries and the rest of the world.

The work programmes of the Commission include a wide range of objectives covering several fields. A strong emphasis is being laid on agricultural problems in order to expand activities in the field of food development and to co-ordinate guidelines for drawing up additional programmes and projects concerning food, livestock, fishery and forestry products. Industrial policies and strategies are especially aimed at improving co-operation between African countries for the mutual supply of raw materials, exchange of technical expertise and implementation of joint projects. Training of personnel for research and development programmes, improvement of indigenous technologies, and import of adequate foreign technologies represent other major fields of action. Assistance is provided by the Commission to enable member countries to inventory mineral, land and water resources and to develop further both conventional and non-conventional sources of energy (including solar, geothermal and biogas energy). The African Regional Centre for Solar Energy began operations in 1989 in Bujumbura, Burundi. Substantial efforts are being made to expand road, rail, sea and air links between member countries and to improve the Pan-African Telecommunication network (PANAFTEL). Efforts at facilitating devel-opment of transport and communications are carried out within the framework of the Second United Nations Transport and Communications Decade for Africa. The promotion of intraregional trade and financial relations is carried forward, *inter alia*, through the negotiation of several protocols after the completion of background technical studies on imports and exports and related production capacities.

Recently, the Commission stressed the commitment of member countries to undertaking the necessary reforms to attract private investment in the continent, and again emphasized the need to promote food security and self-sufficiency. While supporting the implementation of the Abuja Treaty establishing the African Economic Community, the Commission has been studying ways and means to rationalize and harmonize regional integration groupings in West and Central Africa within the context of the newly-established *West African Economic and Monetary Union (UEMOA) and *Economic and Monetary Community of Central Africa (CEMAC).

Executive Secretary: K. Y. Amoako
Headquarters: Africa Hall, P.O. Box 3001, Addis Ababa, Ethiopia (Telephone: +251 1 517200; fax: +251 1 514416)
Publications: *Annual Report*; *Survey of Economic and Social Conditions in Africa* (annual); *African Socio-Economic Indicators* (annual); *African Statistical Yearbook*; *African Trade Bulletin* (twice a year)
References: UN, *ECA Today: Its Terms of Reference, Past Activities and Potential Role in the Socio-Economic Development of Africa* (Addis Ababa, 1979); I. V. Gruhn, *Regionalism Reconsidered: The Economic Commission for Africa* (Boulder, Col., 1979); OAU, *ECA and Africa's Development: 1983–2008. A Preliminary Prospective Study* (Addis Ababa, 1983); T. M. Shaw, 'The UN Economic Commission for Africa: Continental Development and Self-reliance', in D. P. Forsythe (ed.), *The United Nations in the World Political Economy* (London, 1989)

Economic Commission for Europe (ECE)

The Commission operates within the UN framework, under the authority of the Economic and

Social Council, like the other four regional economic commissions; that is, the *Economic Commission for Africa (ECA), the *Economic Commission for Latin America and the Caribbean (ECLAC), the *Economic and Social Commission for Western Asia (ESCWA) and the *Economic and Social Commission for Asia and the Pacific (ESCAP).

Origin and development

The Commission was established in March 1947 by a resolution of the Economic and Social Council as an operational body to deal with the urgent economic problems arising from the Second World War. Its full members included several European countries plus the USA, while a number of non-UN members in Europe, such as Switzerland, were for a time granted consultative status. Subsequently membership increased considerably, despite various obstacles of a mainly political nature that delayed the effective participation of some countries; Switzerland gained full admission in 1972. Another country outside Europe (Canada), joined the Commission in 1973 as a full member, followed at the beginning of the 1990s by Israel, which had never before participated in a regional economic commission. The dissolution of the USSR and the subsequent entry into the Commission of former Soviet republics in Europe, Trans-Caucasia and Central Asia have affected the nature of the body and its activities profoundly. Newly-independent republics belonging to former Yugoslavia have also joined the Commission, whose total membership now includes 55 countries, almost half of which are in transition from centrally-planned to market economies.- The Holy See, which is not a UN member, participates in a consultative capacity.

Objectives

The Commission is charged with the promotion of concerted action for raising the levels of economic activity, expanding trade and economic relations among member countries as well as with other countries, and carrying out investigations of economic and technological developments within the region. Particular emphasis is placed on assisting the countries of Central and Eastern Europe and the former USSR in the transition from centrally-planned to market economies. The Commission is also responsible for undertaking the collection and evaluation and, if appropriate, the publication of economic and statistical information.

Originally devoted to the primary task of post-war reconstruction in Europe, in its early years the Commission had to face the tensions originating from the Cold War. Only gradually could the Commission take on the role of fostering economic co-operation between countries with different economic and social systems, as well as between subregional economic groupings, and forging a partnership between the two halves of the continent in a truly pan-European context. In response to the radical change that had begun in the region in 1989, the Commission has undertaken a process of restructuring and adjustment to the changing needs and realities.

The Commission's functions and powers, according to the rather broad terms of reference laid down by the Economic and Social Council, are essentially related to the initiation of and participation in measures for facilitating concerted action for economic progress in Europe.

Structure

The Commission normally holds an annual session in Geneva, with the participation of the representatives of all member countries, while meetings of subsidiary bodies are convened throughout the year. Decisions and resolutions (both classes of actions having identical legal effects) are customarily adopted by consensus without any formal vote being cast; abstentions are not recorded. Under no circumstances is the Commission allowed to take action against any country without the latter's consent.

Over the years, a number of Principal Subsidiary Bodies have been established by the Commission with the approval of the Economic and Social Council, and after discussion with the specialized agencies operating in the same fields. At present there are several bodies performing tasks of a mainly technical nature in specific sectors, or charged with the study of intersectoral problems. These bodies include the Committees on: Agriculture, Timber, Environmental Policy, Human Settlements, Development of Trade, Energy and Inland Transport; the Senior Economic Advisers to ECE Governments; and the Senior Advisers to ECE Governments on Science and Technology. The work of these organs is supplemented by several minor specialized bodies and *ad-hoc* groups.

The Secretariat is located in Geneva and provides the services necessary for the meetings of the Commission and its subsidiary bodies. It is responsible, *inter alia*, for the publication of general and specialized periodic surveys and reviews, including statistical bulletins. The Commission's Executive Secretary is nominated by the UN Secretary-General and acts on his behalf, but enjoys considerable autonomy in practice. A well-known Swedish economist, Gunnar Myrdal, served as Executive Secretary from the beginning until 1957 and left a remarkable imprint on the Commission's activities and diplomatic initiatives. The Commission, which is entitled to draw up its rules of procedure, is empowered to address recommendations on any matter within its competence directly to its member countries as well as to the Economic and Social Council. A detailed annual report on its activities and plans has to be submitted by the Commission to the Economic and Social Council; the budget is incorporated into the overall UN budget and is subject to formal approval by the General Assembly.

Activities

The Commission co-operates with the relevant UN specialized agencies and other international organizations as well as with the other four regional economic commissions. Effective co-operation has existed since the mid–1960s between the Commission and the *UN Conference on Trade and Development (UNCTAD); there are also close ties with the *UN Environment Programme (UNEP) and the *UN Development Programme (UNDP). The Commission serves as executing agency for the latter. The *European Community (EC) and the *Danube Commission were granted consultative status within the Commission in 1975. The Commission is also linked with the *Organization for Security and Co-operation in Europe (OSCE).

Since its foundation, the Commission has been deeply involved in a wide variety of activities, ranging from early reconstruction problems following the Second World War through to East–West economic co-operation issues. Although inevitably affected by the overall political climate prevailing during four decades in East–West relations, the Commission made substantive efforts to use the available opportunities and to adopt a realistic and essentially pragmatic approach to the most controversial issues, ultimately acting as a bridge between the two halves of the continent. Within the context of the profound changes of the late 1980s and early 1990s, the specific needs and priorities of the countries in transition – some of which are clearly at the stage of developing countries – are currently among the central issues addressed by the Commission attempting to develop intra-European co-operation to the fullest extent practicable within its competence and resources.

The Commission's continuing search for solutions to problems of common concern to member countries has concentrated on the areas covered by its Principal Subsidiary Bodies. A strong emphasis has been placed for several decades on the expansion of trade between centrally-planned and market-economy countries on mutually favourable terms and the correlative elimination of restrictive and discriminatory practices. Facilities were provided with regard to arbitration, insurance, standardization of general conditions of sale of goods, payment arrangements, and compensation procedures and consultations. The Commission has rendered valuable technical assistance in the field of industrial co-operation; long-term agreements rose from 100 to 1000 within a decade, thereby contributing to the growth of specialization between East and West. Major studies have been completed by the Commission in the fields of industrial co-operation, compensation trade and inventory of obstacles to trade. Continuing attention has been given to various branches of industrial activity, particularly steel, chemicals, engineering and automation. The Commission's work has also proved fruitful with regard to problems arising from mechanization and rationalization in agriculture, and market conditions of agricultural products.

Selected problems of economic policy are considered at regular intervals by high-level governmental experts, and medium- and long-term projections, joint research projects and other studies are carried out with a view to facilitating the harmonization of economic policies of member countries. Scientific and technological developments and their related problems are kept under close review and proposals have been put forward towards further international co-operation.

With regard to energy problems, including energy resources and national policies, special attention has been devoted by the Commission to the economic and technical aspects of energy supplies in the face of growing demand and complex conservation and substitution problems. Rising demand for water has led the Commission to undertake a review of major trends and policies concerning use and development of water resources. With regard to environmental questions, the Commission surveys and assesses the state of the environment in the region and considers national policies, institutions and laws, as well as the international implications of environmental policies.

A number of international agreements covering aspects of road, rail and inland water transport are in force following their adoption through the Commission; increased attention is devoted to transport policy and infrastructure, while operational projects are being carried out in conjunction with UNDP. Improvement of national statistics in various fields, exchange of technical information and publication of general and specialized reports have also helped strengthen links between the countries of the region.

In 1990 a number of landmark decisions were adopted designating environment, trade facilitation, transport, economic analysis and statistics as the five priority areas of the Commission's activity, with a view to helping countries in transition to integrate into the European and world economy. The ongoing reform and streamlining of the Commission are taking place in the context of the restructuring of the UN as a whole, and of the strengthening of the role of the regional economic commissions in particular.

Most industrial countries of the world are members of the Commission, which has therefore been actively engaged in working out concessions from developed to developing countries. Steps have been taken by the Commission to develop activities of special interest to its less privileged member countries, particularly in the fields of trade statistics, electric power, transport, agriculture and co-operation in the Mediterranean basin.

Executive Secretary: Yves Berthelot
Headquarters: Palais des Nations, 1211 Geneva 10, Switzerland (Telephone: +41 22 907 4444; fax: +41 22 917 0036)

Internet address: http://www.unicc.org/unece
Publications: *Economic Survey of Europe* (annually); *Economic Bulletin for Europe*; *Annual Report*; separate annual and quarterly bulletins of statistics covering agriculture, timber, coal, general energy, electric energy, gas, chemicals, steel, housing and building, transport and engineering products
References: J. Siotis, 'The United Nations Economic Commission for Europe and the Emerging European System', *International Conciliation*, 561 (1967) 5–72; UN, ECE: *Three Decades of the UN ECE* (New York, 1978); F. Parkinson, 'The Role of the UN Economic Commission for Europe', in G. Schiavone (ed.), *East–West Relations. Prospects for the 1980s* (London, 1982), 111–32

Economic Commission for Latin America and the Caribbean (ECLAC)

The Commission is one of the five regional economic commissions of the UN operating under the authority of the Economic and Social Council – the *Economic Commission for Africa (ECA), the *Economic Commission for Europe (ECE), the *Economic and Social Commission for Western Asia (ESCWA) and the *Economic and Social Commission for Asia and the Pacific (ESCAP).

Origin and development
The Commission came into being in February 1948 by resolution of the Economic and Social Council as a subsidiary organ of the UN under the name Economic Commission for Latin America. The reference to the Caribbean was added to the title in 1984. Besides the countries of the region, the Commission includes as full members: Canada, France, Italy, the Netherlands, Portugal, Spain, the UK and the USA. There are six associate members: Aruba, the British Virgin Islands, Montserrat, The Netherlands Antilles, Puerto Rico, and the US Virgin Islands.

Objectives
The Commission is responsible for facilitating and stimulating concerted action by member countries with regard to regional and national development problems, the expansion of mutual trade,

and economic integration. Established under pressure from several Latin American countries concerned about the urgency and magnitude of their economic difficulties and dissatisfied with the policies of the USA towards its southern neighbours, the Commission initially considered measures for dealing with the basic problems of the period following the Second World War, and for raising the levels of economic activity in the region. Subsequently, considerable emphasis has been given to a wide range of objectives, including: systematic preparation of indicators of economic and social development at national, subregional and regional levels; improvement of planning machinery and techniques and the training of officials and experts; management of the environment and water resources; and the promotion and strengthening of economic integration within subregional and regional groupings, and between these groupings and other organizations of the inter-American and world systems.

The Commission's functions and powers, according to the terms of reference laid down by the Economic and Social Council, are essentially related to the primary task of promoting economic development through concerted measures including technical co-operation and other forms of operational activities. The Commission is also responsible for dealing with the social aspects of economic development and the relationship between economic and social factors.

Structure

The Commission normally holds biennial sessions, with participation of the representatives of all member countries, in one of the Latin American capitals; a Committee of the Whole meets between sessions. Permanent subsidiary bodies have been created by the Commission such as the Central American Economic Co-operation Committee, the Caribbean Development and Co-operation Committee, the Committee of High-Level Government Experts, and many specialized subcommittees. The Secretariat is located in Santiago, Chile, with a subregional office in Mexico City, a subregional headquarters for the Caribbean in Port of Spain, and offices in Bogotá, Brasília, Buenos Aires, Montevideo and Washington. A significant role was played in the early years of the Commission by the Argentine economist Raúl Prebisch, who served as its first Executive Secretary.

The Latin American and Caribbean Institute for Economic and Social Planning (ILPES) was set up in June 1962 under the aegis of the Commission, with financial support from the UN, the *Inter-American Development Bank (IDB), and several Latin American governments, and with the co-operation of the *Organization of American States (OAS), the *International Labour Organization (ILO), the *UN Children's Fund (UNICEF) and other international agencies. The Institute, whose headquarters are located in Santiago, Chile, provides training services, with international and national courses and advisory assistance mainly concerning long-term strategies and medium-term plans, and fosters co-operation among national planning bodies.

The Latin American Demographic Centre (CELADE), set up in 1957 and located in Santiago, Chile, became an integral part of the Commission in 1975. The Centre, with financial assistance from the *UN Development Programme (UNDP) and the *UN Population Fund (UNFPA), investigates the determining factors and consequences of population dynamics, prepares population estimates and projections, carries out advisory activities through numerous technical assistance missions to different countries of the region, and conducts postgraduate courses and seminars.

The annual report of the Commission is submitted to the Economic and Social Council; the budget is subject to the approval of the UN General Assembly.

Activities

The Commission works in close collaboration with UN Headquarters and with specialized agencies and other organizations. Since its establishment, the Commission has played a very active role in fostering intraregional co-operation and integration, assisting in the creation of the Latin American Free Trade Association (LAFTA), the *Central American Common Market (CACM) and the *Latin American Economic System (SELA), and co-operating with the *Andean Community and the *Caribbean Community and Common Market (CARICOM). Intraregional co-operation has been improved and extended to cover a growing number of areas. Substantive steps have been taken to define different degrees of preferential treatment among Latin American countries according to their respective level of economic development. In 1980 this concept was embodied in the treaty establishing the *Latin American Integration Association (LAIA) as an area of economic preferences.

While retaining the specific economic and social needs of Latin America as its basic priority, in recent years the Commission has approached regional issues within the broader framework of North–South relations, with the aim of gradually reducing inequality between developed and developing countries. A major contribution has been made by the Commission in order to establish and improve the Generalized System of Preferences (GSP). Other fields of action are represented by the transfer of resources, international monetary reform, science and technology, industrialization, food and agriculture.

In collaboration with SELA, the Commission organized the Latin American Economic Conference held in Quito, Ecuador, in January 1984, to discuss, in particular, the problems of renegotiation and service of the foreign debt. A special conference to examine national and international strategies for the region's economic recovery was held in January 1987; a regional conference on poverty took place in August 1988. The deterioration of the economic and social situation in the region throughout the 1980s prompted the Commission in May 1990 to advance proposals for overcoming the most serious obstacles to growth, such as the heavy external debt, high interest rates, barriers against Latin American exports, and low commodity prices. The strategies of Latin America and the Caribbean for the 1990s are being considered by the Commission in the prospect of the eventual transformation of the productive structures of the region within a context of increased democracy, progressively greater social equity and overall improvement in the quality of life.

Executive Secretary: Gert Rosenthal
Headquarters: Avenida Vitacura 3030, P.O. Box 179 D, Santiago, Chile (Telephone: +56 2 210 2000; fax: +56 2 208 0252)
Publications: *Economic Survey of Latin America and the Caribbean* (annually); *Statistical Yearbook for Latin America and the Caribbean*; *Social Panorama of Latin America*; *The Economy in Latin America-CEPAL Review* (quarterly)
References: B. G. Ramcharan, 'Equality and Discrimination in International Economic Law

(VIII): The United Nations Regional Economic Commissions', *Year Book of World Affairs*, 32 (1978), 268–85; F. H. Cardoso, *The Originality of the Copy: ECLA and the Idea of Development* (Cambridge, 1977)

Economic Community of Central African States

(Communauté économique des états de l'Afrique centrale) (CEEAC)

The Community was created by a treaty signed in 1983 by Burundi, Cameroon, Central African Republic, Chad, Congo, Equatorial Guinea, Gabon, Rwanda, São Tomé and Príncipe, and Zaire, and which entered into force in 1985. Angola has observer status. A protocol annexed to the treaty provided for the setting up of a clearing house in order to save on the use of convertible foreign exchange in settling payments among member countries. However, the clearing house arrangement that has been operating in the Community is that between the members of the Banque des états de l'Afrique centrale (BEAC) and Zaire, in effect since 1981.

The Community promotes economic co-operation, particularly with regard to free movement of citizens, removal of trade barriers and establishment of a common external tariff, standardization of trade documents, and establishment of a development fund.

Secretary General: Kasasa Mutati Chinyanta
Headquarters: P.O. Box 2112, Libreville, Gabon (Telephone: +241 733547)

Economic Community of the Great Lakes Countries

(Communauté économique des pays des Grands Lacs) (CEPGL)

The Community was intended to foster economic and political co-operation between Burundi, Rwanda and Zaire.

Origin and development

From the mid-1960s onwards several meetings were held and attended by Heads of State and

Foreign Ministers; the Community was formally established in September 1976.

Objectives

The general aims were to protect the security of member countries and their peoples by maintaining order and tranquillity at the respective borders, to promote and expand the free movement of persons and goods, and to undertake concerted efforts with respect to economic and political matters.

Structure

The Community's supreme organ is the Conference of the Heads of State, which ordinarily meets once a year and issues directives to be implemented by its executive organ, the Council of Ministers of Foreign Affairs. The Permanent Executive Secretariat, based in Rwanda, provides administrative services. There are also a Consultative Commission and three Specialized Technical Commissions.

Activities

Four specialized agencies have been set up: the Development Bank of the Great Lakes Countries (BDEGL), based in Goma, Zaire; the Organization of CEPGL for Energy, based in Bujumbura, Burundi; the Institute of Agronomic and Zoological Research, based in Gitega, Burundi; and a regional electricity company (SINELAC), based in Bukavu, Zaire.

The deterioration of the situation in the member countries since the early 1990s, and especially the Hutu–Tutsi conflict in Burundi and Rwanda with the subsequent flow of refugees have had a profoundly negative impact on the actual possibilities and prospects for co-operation which is unlikely to resume until the region returns to a relative stability.

Executive Secretary: Antoine Nouwayo
Headquarters: P.O. Box 58, Gisenyi, Rwanda
   (Telephone: +250 40228; fax: +250 40785).

Economic Community of West African States (ECOWAS)

The Community involves 16 English-, French-, Portuguese- and Arab-speaking West African countries in a wide-ranging integration scheme aimed at establishing a common market and a single currency as well as developing co-operation in the political and security fields.

Origin and development

The original legal instrument of the Community was the Treaty signed in Lagos, Nigeria in May 1975 by the Heads of State and Government of Benin, Burkina Faso (then known as Upper Volta), Côte d'Ivoire, the Gambia, Ghana, Guinea, Guinea-Bissau, Liberia, Mali, Mauritania, Niger, Nigeria, Senegal, Sierra Leone and Togo. The implementation of several basic provisions of the Treaty required the subsequent adoption of five Protocols, which were ratified in November 1976. Cape Verde joined the Community in 1977. A revised treaty for the Community was drawn up in 1991–2 and eventually signed in Cotonou, Benin in July 1993. The Treaty of Cotonou entered into force in July 1995.

Objectives

The Treaty of Cotonou provides for the gradual establishment of a common market – ensuring the free movement of goods, people, services and capital – and of a monetary union and for the prevention and settlement of regional conflicts through 'solidarity and collective self-reliance'. The Treaty also envisages the creation of a regional parliament, an Economic and Social Council and a Court of Justice to replace the existing Tribunal. The protocol for the setting up of the ECOWAS Parliament as a consultative body consisting of representatives from national parliaments was adopted in August 1994.

Structure

The principal organs through which the Community accomplishes its purposes are the Conference of Heads of State and Government, the Council of Ministers, and the Executive Secretariat, assisted by Technical and Specialized Commissions and Committees. Provision has also been made by the Treaty of Cotonou for the establishment of other organs whose powers have not, as yet, been set out in detail.

Activities

The Community has been based from the very beginning on the recognition of the 'realities' prevailing in the different member countries and of the existence of other intergovernmental bodies and economic groupings within the subregion. However, it is the openly declared goal of the Community to be considered the primary regional organization of West Africa and a component of the African Economic Community prognosticated by the *Organization of African Unity (OAU). Delicate problems have arisen in the Community's relationship with other economic and political groupings in West Africa, especially with the West African Economic Community (CEAO) until its demise in 1994 and the newly-created *West African Economic and Monetary Union (Union économique et monétaire ouest-africaine) (UEMOA). A promising area of co-operation is represented by the Community's growing ties with non-African institutions, especially the *European Union (EU).

The problems of political co-operation and security which had not been envisaged by the Treaty of Lagos are now being considered within the framework of the Treaty of Cotonou. However, even before the signature of the Treaty of Cotonou, security agreements had been reached. A protocol on non-aggression was signed in April 1978 by the Heads of State and Government and was followed in May 1981 by a pact on mutual defence agreed upon by 13 members. An attempt at mediating in the civil war in Liberia was made in 1990 and an ECOWAS Monitoring Group (ECOMOG) was sent to that country in order to prevent further conflict and to establish an interim government until elections could be held. Despite the increase in the number of troops participating in the peace-keeping operations, fighting continued throughout the early 1990s among rival groups. The civil war in Liberia has therefore represented a dominant issue on the agenda of the Community, whose repeated calls for the conclusion of a 'workable compromise' among the warring factions for restoring peace have remained unanswered.

The implementation of the basic goals of the Community has met with several obstacles, the major one being the lack of commitment on the part of the governments of the member countries which has materialized, *inter alia*, in the failure to pay contributions on a regular basis, and in the unwillingness to translate into effective national policies the Community's decisions.

Executive Secretary: Dr Abbas Bundu
Headquarters: ECOWAS Secretariat Building, Asokoro, Abuja, Nigeria (Telephone: +234 9 5231858)

Economic Co-operation Organization (ECO)

The Organization provides a framework for co-operation between its three original founders and the newly-independent countries of Central Asia.

Origin and development
The Organization was established in 1985 by Iran, Pakistan and Turkey to replace a former body, the Regional Co-operation for Development (RCD), which had been set up in 1964 to expand economic links between the three countries. The disintegration of the USSR and the independence achieved by the republics of Central Asia made it possible to include in the Organization as full members Kazakhstan, Kyrgyzstan, Tajikistan, Turkmenistan and Uzbekistan, another former Soviet republic in the Caucasus, Azerbaijan, and Afghanistan; the new members formally signed the Organization's founding document in November 1992. The 'Turkish Republic of Northern Cyprus' was granted associate status in early 1992.

Objectives
The aims of the Organization are to encourage and strengthen economic, technical and cultural co-operation, with a view to the eventual creation of a common market, and to promote the economic advancement and welfare of the peoples of the region.

Structure
The meeting of the Heads of State and Government of the member countries is the supreme organ whose decisions are implemented by the meetings of the Foreign ministers.

Activities

The three original members of the Organization had established a joint postal organization (the South and West Asia Postal Union) in 1988, and a joint Chamber of Commerce and Industry in 1990. The meeting of the Heads of State and Government which took place in February 1992 in Teheran endorsed the enlargement of the Organization; agreement was also reached on a preferential trading arrangement and the creation of an investment and development bank. The second summit, held in July 1993 in Istanbul, adopted the 'Istanbul Declaration', and was followed by a meeting of the Foreign Ministers in January 1994 to discuss co-operation in specific sectors. The third summit, held in Islamabad, Pakistan, in March 1995, approved the 'Islamabad Declaration', emphasizing the need to improve the functioning of the Organization and selecting four areas for co-operation: transport and communications; trade and investment; energy; and environmental protection. The future prospects of the Organization will depend to a considerable extent on the internal situation of the member countries and the evolution of their mutual political and security relations in the wider context of the region.

Secretary-General: Shamshad Ahmad
Headquarters: 5 Hejab Avenue, Blvd Keshavarz, P.O. Box 14155–6176, Teheran, Iran (Telephone: +98 21 658045; fax: +98 21 658046)
Publication: *Annual Report*

Entente Council

(Conseil de l'Entente)

The Council develops co-operation among French-speaking countries of West Africa.

Origin and development

The Council was founded in May 1959 in Abidjan, Côte d'Ivoire, by the representatives of Côte d'Ivoire, Dahomey (renamed Benin in 1975), Niger, and Upper Volta (renamed Burkina Faso in 1984), which were at that time autonomous republics within the French Community after having been territories of French West Africa from 1904; the four countries attained full independence in August 1960. Togo, independent from April 1960, joined the Council in June 1966.

Objectives

The Council is an association pledged to promote harmonization of mutual relations among member countries in political and economic matters. According to the founding document, the Council has no·supranational features and its co-ordination activities are based on the principles of friendship, fraternity and solidarity among members. The Council's functions and powers are broadly defined in conformity with the loose character of the association; all decisions are to be taken by unanimous consent.

Structure

The main organ of the Council – originally conceived as the deliberating and executive body of the Union of Sahel-Benin – is the Conference of the Heads of State of member countries, assisted by those ministers who are responsible for the matters on the agenda of each particular meeting. Ordinary sessions are held annually, the venue rotating each year between members, and are chaired by the Head of State of the host country; extraordinary sessions may be convened at the request of at least two members. The Conference of the Heads of State held in March 1960 decided to set up a Secretariat charged with limited administrative functions and headed by an Administrative Secretary appointed annually by the Chairman of the Conference. However, secretaries were nominated only for the first three years. In 1963, Dahomey experienced a major political crisis and abstained from participating in the Council's activities until January 1965. In May 1970 the Conference of the Heads of State decided to establish a Council of Ministers in order to improve the activities of the Council and to increase efficiency.

Activities

To foster economic and financial co-operation, the Council's founding document provided for the creation of a Solidarity Fund whose resources, mainly contributed by the Côte d'Ivoire, had to be redistributed for the benefit of the least-developed members. The comparative ineffectiveness of the

Solidarity Fund led to its transformation in June 1966 into a stronger body, the Mutual Aid and Loan Guarantee Fund (Fonds d'entraide et de garantie des emprunts). The new financial institution aimed to promote economic growth in the region, to assist in the preparation of specific projects and to mobilize funds from other sources, acting as a guarantee fund for loans granted to member countries for profitable agricultural, industrial and infrastructural projects and encouraging trade and investment between member countries.

In December 1973 another agreement was signed in order to empower the Fund to finance the reduction of interest rates and the extension of maturity periods of foreign loans to member countries. The resources of the Fund consist of annual contributions from member countries, subsidies and grants, as well as investment returns and commissions from guarantee operations. The Fund's budget for 1992 amounted to 1.75 billion francs CFA. The Fund has supported projects for the improvement of crops, breeding of livestock, assistance to small and medium-sized enterprises, standardization, vocational training, production of geological maps, and improvement of transport and telecommunications network. Financial aid for the projects was also provided by external donors, mainly France and the USA.

The Executive Board of the Fund holds annual sessions and is vested with all governing powers which have been to a large extent delegated to the Management Committee, comprising three representatives from each member country and meeting twice a year. The Executive Board is composed of the Heads of State of member countries and therefore has the same membership as the Entente Council. The Secretariat of the Fund is headed by an Administrative Secretary. It also provides technical and administrative services to the Council, which in practice has gradually been absorbed by the Fund. Economic and financial co-ordination among member countries has in fact gained priority over issues related to political co-operation.

An associated Economic Community of Livestock and Meat (Communauté économique du bétail et de la viande du Conseil de l'Entente) was created in 1970 to provide technical and financial support with a view to promoting the production, processing and marketing of livestock and meat and co-ordinating policies to combat drought and cattle disease.

Administrative Secretary: Paul Kaya
Headquarters: Mutual Aid and Loan Guarantee Fund, 01 BP 3734, Abidjan, Côte d'Ivoire (Telephone: +225   332835;   fax: +225 331149)
Publications: *Rapport d'activité* (annual); *Entente Africaine* (quarterly)

European Bank for Reconstruction and Development (EBRD)

The Bank provides multilateral financing of projects and investment programmes in the countries of Central and Eastern Europe and the former USSR.

Origin and development

The Bank was established by a treaty signed in May 1990 by countries of Western and Eastern Europe, along with major industrial countries outside Europe, to contribute to the progress and economic reconstruction of the former socialist countries willing to respect and put into practice the principles of multiparty democracy and a market economy. Shareholders of the Bank include 58 countries plus the *European Community (EC) and the *European Investment Bank (EIB). The Bank started operations at its headquarters in London in April 1991.

Objectives

The Bank's objectives are to provide advice, loans and equity investment, and debt guarantees to qualified applicants with a view to fostering the transition towards democracy and open market-orientated economies, and to promoting private and entrepreneurial initiative. The Bank lends and invests exclusively in 'countries of operations'; that is, the nations of Central and Eastern Europe, including the republics of the former USSR and the former Yugoslavia. The Bank's mandate gives it a special concern for the promotion of democratic institutions and human rights as well as of environmentally sound and sustainable development in its countries of operations.

Structure

The organization of the Bank, which is largely similar to that of other international financial institutions, comprises the Board of Governors, vested with full management powers, the 23-member Board of Directors, responsible for current operations, and the President.

Activities

The Bank's resources include the subscribed capital stock and the funds borrowed in capital markets to supplement the equity capital. The initially subscribed capital of the Bank amounted to ECU10 billion, of which ECU3 billion to be paid in. The EC members together with the European Commission and EIB contributed 51 per cent, Central and Eastern European countries 13.5 per cent, the USA (which is the largest single shareholder) 10 per cent, Japan 8.5 per cent. At the annual meeting held in Sofia in April 1996, the decision was taken to double the Bank's subscribed capital to ECU20 billion (about $25 billion); the injection of new capital will take place over a period of 12 years between 1998 and 2009. Cash and promissory notes will account for 22.5 per cent of the total, the rest being represented by 'callable shares'.

The Bank is a unique combination of merchant bank and development bank. Not less than 60 per cent of the Bank's funding will be directed to private-sector enterprises or state-owned enterprises implementing a programme to achieve private ownership and control; not more than 40 per cent will be directed to public infrastructure or other projects.

Funds are granted in accordance with sound banking and investment principles and within commercial decision-making time frames. More precisely, funding is offered on a market rather than on a subsidized or concessionary basis, including: loans with a maximum final maturity of 10 years for commercial enterprises and of 15 years for infrastructure projects; equity; guarantees and underwriting. Loans are usually denominated in convertible currencies or currency units; as a matter of policy, the Bank does not accept currency risk on repayment. The Bank does not issue guarantees for export credits nor undertake insurance activities. It is important to stress that loans to commercial enterprises, including those made to state-owned enterprises implementing a programme to achieve private ownership and control, are granted without government guarantees and require a full commercial return. The Bank limits its financing normally to 35 per cent of the total cost of a borrower's total capital on a pro forma, market-value basis. The Bank does not take controlling interests nor assume direct responsibility for the management of enterprises. In a number of cases, the Bank may offer financial advice and training and technical assistance on the basis of funds specifically provided by certain of its member governments.

The Bank co-operates with other international financial organizations and with a range of public and private financial institutions through co-financing arrangements.

Between 1991, when it started operations, and 1995, the Bank financed nearly 300 projects for a total amount of ECU8.94 billion. The EC has actively supported the operations of the Bank providing substantial amounts from the PHARE and TACIS budgets for financing technical assistance projects. The activities of the Bank had remarkably expanded and diversified by the mid-1990s, with the private sector accounting for a greater proportion of commitments (particularly with a view to financing small and medium-sized enterprises) and special emphasis on the development of the countries relatively less advanced in the process of transition to a market economy. The decision to double the subscribed capital of the Bank taken in 1996 will allow a substantial increase in lending before the end of the century, helping to prepare the recipient countries for entry into the *European Union (EU). On the other hand, the Bank is expected to shift its focus gradually from the relatively advanced Central and Eastern European countries to the republics of the former USSR.

President: Jacques de Larosière

Headquarters: One Exchange Square, London EC2A 2EH, England (Telephone: +44 171 338 6000; fax: +44 171 338 6100)

References: P. A. Menkveld. Origin and Role of the European Bank for Reconstruction and Development (London, 1991)

European Conference of Ministers of Transport (ECMT)

(Conférence européenne des ministres des transports) (CEMT)

Established in 1953 following an initiative of the then Organization for European Economic Co-operation (OEEC) – succeeded in 1960 by the *Organization for Economic Co-operation and Development (OECD) – the Conference currently includes 23 member countries of Western Europe; Australia, Canada, Japan and the USA enjoy associate status. The Conference aims to achieve, at general or regional level, the maximum use and most rational development of European inland transport of international importance. Ministers meet twice a year to deal with economic, technical and administrative issues related to road transport, railways and inland waterways and to draw up resolutions and conventions. The Secretariat is responsible for the preparation and dissemination of statistics in the field of transport.

Secretary-General: J. C. Terlouw
Headquarters: 19 rue de Franqueville, 75116 Paris, France (Telephone: +33 1 4524 9710; fax: +33 1 4524 9742)
Publication: *Annual Report*

European Conference of Postal and Telecommunications Administrations

(Conférence européenne des administrations des postes et des télécommunications) (CEPT)

Established in 1959 within the framework of the *Universal Postal Union (UPU), the Conference groups the postal and telecommunications administrations of over 30 countries in Western Europe with a view to strengthening relations between members, and harmonizing and improving administrative and technical services. The Conference has a managing administration rotating among members; the Liaison Office provides permanent administrative and secretariat service to the Managing Administration.

Liaison Office: Seilerstrasse 22, P.O. Box 1283, 3001 Bern, Switzerland (Telephone: +41 31 338 2081; fax: +41 31 338 2078)

European Free Trade Association (EFTA)

With the achievement of free-trade among members and the entry of most of its founders into the *European Union (EU), the Association consists at present of only four countries: Iceland, Liechtenstein, Norway and Switzerland.

Origin and development

EFTA was set up in 1960 by those countries of Western and Northern Europe that wished to create a larger market for their manufactured goods through the liberalization of mutual trade but were not prepared to accept the far-reaching political and economic obligations inherent in membership of the then European Economic Community (EEC). After the failure of the free-trade-area negotiations within the framework of the Organization for European Economic Co-operation (OEEC) at the end of 1958, the suggestion was put forward to establish a free-trade zone between the countries that remained outside the EEC. Government officials of Austria, Denmark, Norway, Portugal, Sweden, Switzerland and the UK met at Saltsjobaden, Stockholm in June 1959 to draft a plan with a view to establishing a European Free Trade Association. The Convention setting up the Association was signed in Stockholm in January 1960 and went into effect the following May. In March 1961 an Agreement creating an association between the 'Seven' and Finland was signed in Helsinki; the Agreement lapsed in January 1986 when Finland became a full member. Iceland became a member in March 1970 and was immediately granted duty-free entry for exports of industrial goods while being allowed a ten-year period in order to eliminate its own import duties. Two founder members, the UK and Denmark, left the Association in 1972 to join the European Communities; they were followed by Portugal in 1985, and by Austria, Finland and Sweden in 1994. Liechtenstein, formerly associated through its customs union with Switzerland, applied for full membership in March 1991 and was admitted the following September.

Objectives

According to the Convention, the basic objectives of the Association were: (a) to promote a sustained expansion of economic activity, full employment, increased productivity and the rational use of resources, financial stability and continuous improvement in living standards; (b) to secure that trade between member countries takes place in conditions of fair competition; (c) to avoid significant disparity between member countries in the conditions of supply of raw materials produced within the area of the Association; and (d) to contribute to the harmonious development and liberalization of world trade.

The Association is based essentially on a free-trade zone progressively achieved through the reduction, and ultimately the elimination, of customs duties, charges with equivalent effect and quantitative restrictions imposed on industrial goods wholly or partly produced within the territory of the Association. Unlike a customs union, a free-trade area does not require the establishment by participants of a common external tariff on goods entering from non-member countries. Agricultural goods are generally excluded from the free-trade area provisions but may be the object of specific agreements between any two or more member countries in order to increase trade and to provide reasonable reciprocity to those members whose economies depend to a great extent on exports of such goods. As regards fish and other marine products, which are also excluded from the free-trade area, the objective of the Association is to promote an increase in trade in order to compensate the member countries exporting those products for the loss of tariffs on imported industrial goods.

Structure

The institutional structure of the Association is extremely simple and reflects the peculiar origin and nature of the organization. The Council is the supreme organ responsible for the supervision and application of the Convention, and consists of one representative with one vote for each member country. It has a broad mandate to consider any action that may be necessary in order to promote the attainment of the objectives of the Association and to facilitate the establishment of closer links with non-member countries, unions of states or international organizations. The Council is empowered to take

decisions which are binding on all members and to address recommendations. In principle, decisions and recommendations to members are to be made unanimously, but abstentions are permitted and not considered as negative votes. A majority vote, however, is sufficient on certain issues, such as decisions and recommendations adopted under the general consultations and complaints procedure or under the special procedures envisaged to attenuate or compensate for the effect of restrictions introduced by a member because of balance of payments difficulties.

In the exercise of its powers to set up any subsidiary organs it considered necessary, the Council created a number of Standing Committees, including a Consultative Committee acting as a forum for an exchange of views and information between the organs of the Association and representatives of the main sectors of economic life in the member countries. The Committee of Members of Parliament of the EFTA Countries held its first meeting in November 1977; it is convened at least once a year, acting as a consultative and liaison body between the Association and the parliaments of the member countries.

Administrative functions are carried out by a small permanent Secretariat in Geneva headed by a Secretary-General. The Association has an office in Brussels which keeps in regular contact with the EU.The Council has full responsibility for establishing the financial arrangements and the budget of the Association as well as for apportioning the expenses between the member countries.

Activities

Close relations have been established with the *Organization for Economic Co-operation and Development (OECD), successor to the OEEC, and with several European bodies. Reports ar submitted by EFTA to the Parliamentary Assembly of the *Council of Europe. Formal relations also exist with the *Nordic Council. The Association has formal ties with countries of Central and Eastern Europe, the Baltic countries, Albania, Slovenia and Turkey, as well as with countries outside Europe, including Israel and the *Gulf Co-operation Council (GCC).

The Association has substantially achieved its basic goals. Import duties on industrial goods within the territory of the founder members of the Association were removed in eight stages up to the end of 1966, three years ahead of schedule; Finland removed her remaining tariffs a year later, in December 1967. Iceland had completely eliminated import duties by December 1979. All import quotas were abolished by the end of 1966, and export quotas had been eliminated by the end of 1961. Tariffs or import duties have been removed on all products except farm products, although a number of goods manufactured from agricultural products are duty-free. Free trade in fish and other marine products came into effect in July 1990.

At a meeting held in Vienna in May 1977, the Heads of Government of member countries adopted a Declaration setting out the guidelines for the future activities of the Association. After the completion of the free-trade system covering all members of the Association and the then EEC, attention was given to non-tariff barriers such as differences in compulsory technical requirements for electrical and other products, and rules for obtaining patent protection for new products. The broadening and deepening of co-operation in several areas with the European Community led to the EFTA–EC Luxembourg Declaration of April 1984, which stressed the common goal of creating an open economic space comprising the whole of Western Europe. In March 1989 the Heads of Government restressed their commitment to establish a homogeneous and dynamic European Economic Area (EEA) embracing all the members of EFTA and the EEC. The EEA Agreement was signed by all members of the EEC and EFTA in May 1992; an Adjustment Protocol, taking into account Switzerland's withdrawal after the negative result of the referendum of December 1992, was signed in March 1993. The Agreement eventually came into force in January 1994, covering free movement of goods (with special arrangements for a number of products), persons, capital and services throughout the Area.

Secretary-General: Kjartan Jóhansson
Headquarters: 9–11 rue de Varembé, 1211 Geneva 20, Switzerland (Telephone: +41 22 749 1111; fax: +41 22 733 9291)

Brussels Office: 78 rue de Trèves, 1040 Brussels, Belgium (Telephone: +32 2 286 1711)
Publication: *Annual Report*
Reference: J. S. Lambrinidis, *The Structure, Function and Law of a Free Trade Area* (London, 1965); H. Wallace, *The Wider Western Europe. Reshaping the EC/EFTA Relationship* (London, 1992)

European Investment Bank (EIB)

The Bank is the financial institution of the *European Union (EU).

Origin and development
The Bank was created in 1958 under the Treaty of Rome, to which its statute is annexed. It is endowed with its own legal personality and has an administrative structure separate from that of the other Community institutions. In 1994 the Bank, in partnership with the European Commission and over 60 banks from member countries, set up a new guarantee instrument, the European Investment Fund (EIF). The members of the Bank are the countries participating in the EU that have subscribed to its capital.

Objectives
The Bank's activity is aimed at furthering the EU's economic objectives, both within the Union and in an increasing range of countries outside, by providing long-term finance for specific capital projects, in keeping with strict banking practice.

Structure
The Bank's governing body is the Board of Governors consisting, generally, of the Finance Ministers of the member countries. It lays down general directives on credit policy, approves the balance sheet and annual report, decides on capital increases, and appoints members of the Board of Directors, the Management Committee and the Audit Committee. The Board of Directors, responsible for the general management of the Bank, consists of 24 Directors and 12 Alternates nominated by member countries, plus one Director and one Alternate nominated by the European Commission. Following nominations, members of the Board of Directors are

appointed by the Governors for a renewable five-year term. The Management Committee, consisting of eight members, controls all current operations, recommends decisions to Directors, and is responsible for carrying them out. The Bank's President, or in his absence one of the seven Vice-Presidents, chairs the meetings of the Board of Directors.

Activities

The initial subscribed capital, contributed by the then six member countries, amounted to ECU1000 million. The capital has been increased repeatedly, also in connection with the entry of new member countries. As at January 1995, the subscribed capital amounted to ECU62 013 million, of which ECU4652 million was paid in and to be paid in. The Bank's Statute stipulates that aggregate loans and guarantees outstanding may not exceed 250 per cent of subscribed capital; this ceiling has been raised to ECU155 billion. The aggregate amount outstanding in respect of loans from own resources and guarantees was approximately ECU115 billion at the end of 1995, leaving the Bank substantial headroom for future activity.

The Bank's lending activity is financed mainly from the proceeds of borrowings launched on the national and international capital markets, which constitute the resources of the Bank together with its own funds. Loans may be granted to public or private sector borrowers for financing projects in all sectors, from communications, environmental and energy infrastructure to industry, services and agriculture. The 1992 Maastricht Treaty restressed that the main task of the Bank is to contribute to the balanced and steady development of the common market, providing funding for economically worthwhile investment in EU regions lagging most seriously behind in their development, as well as for projects of common interest to several member countries. The Bank facilitates the financing of investment programmes in conjunction with assistance from the Community's Structural Funds and other financial instruments. Moreover, the Maastricht Treaty calls for a common policy in areas in which the Bank is already committed, such as the creation of trans-European transport, telecommunications and energy supply networks, the increase of industrial competitiveness, environmental protection and development co-operation with non-member countries.

The Bank's operations outside the EU currently include some 130 countries in the following geographical areas: (a) Central and Eastern Europe (including the Baltic countries and Slovenia), with special regard to cross-border industrial and infrastructure projects supporting the process of economic conversion; (b) the Mediterranean basin (including the Gaza Strip and the West Bank) with a view to implementing the financial component of the EU's Mediterranean policy; (c) Africa, the Caribbean and the Pacific for the ACP states signatories to the Lomé Convention, plus the Overseas Countries and Territories (OCT) where the Bank has long participated in development aid policy, with special focus on the growth of the industrial sector; and (d) Asia and Latin America, where operations conducted since 1993 have developed substantially after the conclusion of framework agreements with a number of countries.

Large-scale projects are financed by means of individual loans (upwards of ECU25 million) concluded directly or through various financial intermediaries. Small and medium-scale ventures are funded indirectly through global loans. In all cases, the Bank finances only part of the investment costs, supplementing the borrower's own funds and other sources. Loans, as a rule, do not exceed 50 per cent of investment costs. The maturity of medium- and long-term loans granted by the Bank depends on the project concerned; it may be extended to 20 years or more for infrastructural schemes, with the possibility of a grace period. Loans may be disbursed at par in a single currency or in several currencies. The method adopted for setting interest rates is the same for all countries and sectors. The Bank does not grant interest subsidies, although these may be provided by third parties. Special arrangements apply to financing made available outside the EU in accordance with the various financial co-operation agreements.

Total financing provided by the Bank from 1959 to 1995 amounted to a total of over ECU190 billion, of which over ECU170 billion was within the EU and the rest outside.

The Bank participates in several international co-operation programmes involving other multilateral financing institutions such as the *World Bank and the *European Bank for Reconstruction and Development (EBRD) as well as the *United Nations Development Programme (UNDP).

Over nearly four decades, the Bank has adjusted to far-reaching changes in EU policies and has broadened the range and nature of its operations gradually, to the extent that, in terms of lending volume, it is now the world's largest multilateral credit institution. Within the EU, the Bank is stepping up its support for structural development by providing substantial additional funding, particularly directed towards trans-European networks, and small and medium-sized enterprises. Outside the EU, the Bank has been associated closely since the 1960s with the implementation of co-operation and development aid policies vis-à-vis an increasing number of non-member countries, and since 1990 with the mobilization of financial resources for priority projects in Central and Eastern Europe to help those countries in their transition towards a market economy.

President: Sir Brian Unwin
Headquarters: 100 boulevard Konrad Adenauer, 2950 Luxembourg (Telephone: +352 4379-1; fax: +352 437704)
Publications: *Annual Report; EIB Information*

European Organization for Nuclear Research

(Organisation européenne pour la recherche nucléaire) (CERN).

The Organization provides for collaboration among European countries in nuclear research of a purely scientific and fundamental character, having no concern with work for military requirements.

Origin and development

The Convention for the establishment of the Organization was signed in July 1953 under the sponsorship of the *UN Educational, Scientific and Cultural Organization (UNESCO). The present membership includes about 20 countries from Western and (since the early 1990s) Eastern Europe (among them France, Germany, Hungary, Italy, Poland and the UK); three countries (Israel, Russia and Turkey) enjoy observer status, along with the *European Union and UNESCO.

Yugoslavia's affiliation was suspended in June 1992. The Organization co-operates with non-member countries such as China, Japan and the USA.

Objectives

According to the Convention, the work of CERN is for peaceful purposes only and deals with sub-nuclear, high-energy and elementary particle physics; it is not concerned with the development of nuclear reactors or fusion devices. Moreover, the results of experimental and theoretical work must be published or otherwise made generally available.

Structure

The Council is the highest policy-making body, composed of two representatives of each member country and headed by a President assisted by two Vice-Presidents. The structure of the Organization also comprises a Committee of the Council, and Committees on Scientific Policy and Finance. The staff is headed by a Director-General.

Activities

Among the experimental facilities operated by the Organization are the following: the Synchro-Cyclotron (SC) of 600 MeV, in operation since 1957; the Proton Synchrotron (PS) of 28 GeV, in operation since 1959; the Super Proton Synchrotron (SPS) of 450 GeV. The Intersecting Storage Rings (ISR), which began operating in 1971 and closed down in 1984.

A Large Electron-Positron Collider (LEP) of 27 km circumference (of 50 GeV per beam) was commissioned in July 1989. In December 1991, the Organization recognized the importance of developing the Large Hadron Collider (LHC) for research in the field of high-energy physics; the building of the LHC is expected to start in 1997.

Director-General: Prof. Christopher Llewellyn Smith
Headquarters: 1211 Geneva 23, Switzerland (Telephone: +41 22 767 6111; fax: +41 22 767 6555)
Publications: *CERN Courier* (monthly); *Annual Report*

European Organization for the Exploitation of Meteorological Satellites

(Organisation européenne pour l'exploitation de satellites météorologiques) (EUMETSAT)

The Organization is intended to operate European weather satellites.

Origin and development
Established in 1986, the Organization includes as members 17 Western European countries: Austria, Belgium, Denmark, Finland, France, Germany, Greece, Ireland, Italy, Netherlands, Norway, Portugal, Spain, Sweden, Switzerland, Turkey and the UK.

Objectives
The prime objective of the Organization is to establish, maintain and operate a European system of meteorological satellites.

Activities
The Organization currently operates Meteosat-5, a geostationary satellite orbiting above the equator. Plans are being prepared to build Europe's first polar satellites orbiting the earth from pole to pole.

Director: John Morgan
Headquarters: Am Elfengrund 45, 64242 Darmstadt, Germany (Telephone: +49 6151 5392-0; fax: +49 6151 950125)

European Organization for the Safety of Air Navigation (EUROCONTROL)

The Organization, originally intended to strengthen co-operation in its specific area of competence between Western European countries, is gradually expanding to include countries in Central and Eastern Europe.

Origin and development
The Organization was established by a Convention signed in Brussels in December 1960 and entered into force in March 1963. Since the late 1950s several meetings had been held by representatives of civil and military aviation of Western European countries to discuss plans for the formulation of an appropriate air traffic control procedure in order to provide maximum freedom consistent with the required level of safety. The Convention was eventually signed in Brussels by Belgium, France, Germany, Luxembourg, The Netherlands and the UK; the founder countries were joined by Ireland in 1965, Portugal in 1986 (after a period as an associate member), Greece in 1988, Malta and Turkey in 1989, Cyprus in 1991, Hungary and Switzerland in 1992, Austria in 1993, and Denmark and Norway in 1994. Other European countries are expected to accede to the Organization over the next few years.

Objectives
The Organization aims at strengthening co-operation in matters of air navigation, making due allowance for defence needs, and in particular at providing for the common organization of air traffic services in the upper airspace.

Structure
The Permanent Commission for the Safety of Air Navigation is the governing body, consisting of delegates from each member country representing both civil aviation and national defence. The executive body is the Agency for the Safety of Air Navigation administered by a Committee of Management comprising two delegates from each country.

Activities
Air traffic control services are provided by the Organization from its centre at Maastricht in The Netherlands. Despite the reluctance of member countries to surrender prerogatives such as the control of military airspace, the activities of the Organization have been expanding rapidly since the late 1980s, also in connection with the forms of co-operation being developed with the countries of Eastern Europe.

Director-General: Yves Lambert
Headquarters: 96 rue de la Fusée, 1130 Brussels, Belgium (Telephone: +32 2 729 9011; fax: +32 2 729 9044)

European Space Agency (ESA)

The Agency promotes co-operation among European countries in space research and technology, and their application for exclusively peaceful purposes.

Origin and development

The Agency was established by an agreement signed at a meeting of the European Space Conference in Brussels in July 1973 and entered into effect in May 1975. The Agency, based in Paris, replaced the European Space Research Organization (ESRO) and the European Organization for the Development and Construction of Space Vehicle Launchers (ELDO). The present membership includes about 15 countries of Western Europe (among them are France, Germany, Italy and the UK). Greece and some Central and Eastern European countries signed co-operation agreements in the early 1990s, while Canada has been a 'co-operating state' for several projects since 1979.

Objectives

The Agency was formally entrusted with all the functions previously assigned to its forerunners as well as with new tasks, particularly in the field of space applications. More precisely, the Agency: elaborates a long-term space policy and recommends space objectives to member countries; implements activities and programmes in the field of space; co-ordinates the European space programme and national programmes, integrating the latter as completely as possible into the European space programme.

Structure

The Council, composed of the representatives of all member countries and headed by a Chairman, is the highest policy-making organ of the Agency. The Director General, appointed by the Council, performs executive functions. The Agency runs three centres: the European Space Research and Technology Centre (ESTEC) at Noordwijk, The Netherlands; the European Space Operations Centre (ESOC) at Darmstadt, Germany; and the Space Documentation Centre (ESRIN) at Frascati, Italy.

Contributions to the general and scientific budgets of the Agency are made by member countries, on the basis of a percentage of their GNP; contributions to specific programmes are also made on an *ad hoc* basis by 'co-operating' non-member countries.

Activities

The Agency has entered into co-operation agreements with a number of international and national bodies in order to co-ordinate research and carry out joint efforts. A joint project has been undertaken with the *European Communities. Close ties have been established with the National Aeronautics and Space Administration (NASA) of the USA, Russia and Japan.

The activities of the Agency have covered a wide range of programmes in several major areas, especially with regard to scientific and applications satellites. Meteorological satellites have been put into orbit and are providing valuable data for meteorological research and weather forecasts. The European satellites for maritime communications provide links between ships and shore stations. The Ariane launcher has been developed to give Europe a launching capability for its own applications and scientific satellites. Mention has to be made of the Spacelab, a manned and reusable space laboratory, and of the European Retrievable Carrier, a reusable payload carrier. In July 1991 the Agency launched the first European Remote Sensing (ERS-1) satellite, with a view to providing weather and sea-state forecasting. In the early 1990s the Agency has further reinforced its co-operation with European organizations and non-member countries following the end of the East–West confrontation.

Director General: Jean-Marie Luton
Headquarters: 8–10 rue Mario Nikis, 75738 Paris Cedex 15, France (Telephone: +33 1 5369 7654; fax: +33 1 5369 7560).
Publications: *Annual Report; ESA Bulletin; ESA Journal*
Reference: G. Collins, *Europe in Space* (London, 1990)

European Telecommunications Satellite Organization (EUTELSAT)

The purposes of the Organization, formed in 1977, are to design, construct, establish, operate and maintain space segments of telecommunications satellite systems with a view to providing international public telecommunications. The membership currently comprises 26 national telecommunications administrations in Western Europe.

Headquarters: Tour Maine Montparnasse, 33 avenue du Maine, 75015 Paris, France (Telephone: +33 1 4538 4747; fax: +33 1 4538 3700)

European Union (EU)

The Union is founded on the existing European Communities, supplemented by the policies and forms of co-operation established by the Treaty on European Union, signed in Maastricht on 7 February 1992 and entered into force on 1 November 1993. The Union currently consists of 15 members: the six founder countries (Belgium, France, Germany, Italy, Luxembourg and The Netherlands) having been joined, between 1973 and 1995, by Austria, Denmark, Finland, Greece, Ireland, Portugal, Spain, Sweden and the UK.

Origin and development

In order to establish co-operation between the old war-enemies, France and Germany, in May 1950 the French Minister of Foreign Affairs, M. Robert Schuman, proposed a plan to place the entire coal and steel production of France and Germany under the control of an independent High Authority, within the framework of an organization open to the participation of other European countries. Belgium, Italy, Luxembourg, The Netherlands and the Federal Republic of Germany accepted the French invitation to take part in a conference to consider the Schuman Plan. Negotiations between the six countries culminated with the signing in Paris, in April 1951, of the Treaty setting up the European Coal and Steel Community (ECSC). The Treaty of Paris, effective from July 1952 for a 50-year period, provided for the pooling of coal and steel production of the member countries and was regarded as a first step towards a united Europe. However, attempts to establish a political union met with overwhelming difficulties between 1952 and 1953, while

plans for the establishment of a European Defence Community (EDC) eventually collapsed after rejection by the French National Assembly in August 1954.

The success of the sectoral integration scheme put into effect by the ECSC encouraged efforts to expand the common market to other major areas. At the Conference of Foreign Ministers of the ECSC member countries held in Messina, Italy, in June 1955, plans were laid down for the creation of two more communities aimed at gradually integrating the economies of the Six as well as paving the way towards closer political co-ordination. After extensive negotiations, the European Economic Community (EEC) and the European Atomic Energy Community (Euratom) were set up under separate treaties signed in Rome in March 1957 and entered into effect in January 1958. The Treaties of Rome contained provisions for the establishment by stages, over a transitional period, of a common market, including at its core a customs union, and the approximation of economic policies, as well as the promotion of growth in nuclear industries for peaceful purposes. Although the three Communities were established as distinct organizations, based on separate constituent treaties, their institutional structure was similar. Each Community was endowed with its own executive organ (called Commission in both the EEC and Euratom, and High Authority in the ECSC) composed of individuals acting only in the Community's interest, and with an organ responsible for policy-making representing the governments (called Council in both the EEC and Euratom, and Special Council of Ministers in the ECSC).

Simultaneous with the signing of the Treaties of Rome, a 'Convention on certain institutions common to the European Communities' was concluded, providing a single Court of Justice and a single Assembly for all three Communities. Subsequently, a 'Treaty establishing a single Council and a single Commission of the European Communities' was signed in Brussels in April 1965 and entered into effect in July 1967, transferring the various powers of the corresponding bodies of the ECSC, the EEC and Euratom to the new institutions.

The first unsuccessful negotiations over British entry into the Communities took place between 1961 and 1963. In June 1970, membership negotiations began between the Six and Denmark, Ireland, Norway and the UK; these four countries signed the Treaty of Accession to the EEC and Euratom in January 1972. The accession of the new members to the ECSC was enacted, in accordance with the Treaty of Paris, by a decision of the Council of the European Communities. Ireland, Denmark, and the UK became full members of the Communities in January 1973, when the instruments concerning the accession entered into effect. Norway held a popular referendum in September 1972 which rejected entry into the Communities and eventually decided not to accede. The Treaty concerning the accession of Greece was signed in May 1979 and came into force in January 1981. At the end of a process which had begun in May 1979 with the introduction of home rule and the gradual transfer of certain powers from Denmark to the local government, Greenland left the Community in February 1985 and became an overseas territory associated with the Community.

Negotiations for the entry of Portugal and Spain having largely been completed by early 1985, the instruments of accession were signed in Lisbon and Madrid in June 1985, and became effective in January 1986. The enlargement of the Community was accompanied by renewed efforts to promote European integration and by a wide-ranging debate about the Community's political and institutional future which culminated in the signing, in February 1986, of the Single European Act (SEA). The SEA, which represented the first major revision of the Treaty of Rome, came into force in July 1987. Not only did the SEA constitute an expression of the willingness of the member countries to implement basic objectives – completion of the unified internal market by the end of 1992 and strengthening of economic and social cohesion – but also modified the institutional system by rehabilitating majority voting in the Council of Ministers, providing for greater involvement of the European Parliament in the decision-making process, and strengthening European co-operation in the sphere of foreign policy.

Following the unification of Germany in October 1990, the former German Democratic Republic became part of the Communities, although a transitional period was envisaged before certain Community legislation was fully applied.

Meeting in December 1989, the European Council decided to convene an intergovernmental conference on economic and monetary union; in June 1990 the decision was taken to hold a second intergovernmental conference on political union. As a result, two conferences opened in December 1990 in Rome and continued to work in parallel throughout 1991. The conferences ended, at the Maastricht European Council of December 1991, with an agreement on the draft Treaty on European Union. After legal editing and harmonization of the texts, the Treaty – including a large number of protocols – was signed in February 1992 and submitted for ratification by the parliaments of all member countries. Before ratification, the Maastricht Treaty was submitted to popular referendum in some countries. The first referendum, held in Denmark in June 1992, obtained a negative response from voters; a second referendum, held in May 1993, reversed the previous decision, and approved the Treaty. In 1992 favourable referendums were also held in Ireland in July and in France in September (in the French case with a very narrow majority). In Germany, the Treaty was declared compatible with the German Constitution by the Federal Constitutional Court in October 1993.

With the preparations for the coming into force of the Maastricht treaty still going on, criteria were drawn up in 1992 to prepare an enlargement of the Community which had become the focus of the aspirations of most other European countries. According to Article 0 of the Maastricht Treaty, 'any European State may apply to become a member of the Union'. Besides satisfying the three prerequisites of European identity, democratic status, and respect for human rights, candidates for accession were requested to accept – and be able to implement – the *acquis communautaire* in its entirety, subject to transitional and temporary arrangements, as well as the provisions on the common foreign and security policy, and on co-operation in the fields of justice and home affairs. Official negotiations for accession, however, could start only after the Maastricht Treaty had been ratified.

In February 1993 accession negotiations began with Austria, Finland and Sweden, followed by Norway in April. The Treaties of Accession and related Final Acts were signed in June 1994 by the representatives of the 12 member countries and of the four applicants. The Austrians, the Finns and the Swedes voted in favour of their respective accessions in popular referendums held between June and November 1994, while the Norwegians rejected accession, with the result that, as of January 1995, the Union comprised 15 member countries.

Future enlargements are likely to require a redefinition of the priorities of the Union in the light of all its members' interests, and this will affect the structure of the Union and the balance of power between its institutions to a very great extent. The present structures, developed over four decades to arrange for six and now 15, countries, cannot be stretched to accommodate 25 or even 30 members. As envisaged by the Maastricht Treaty, the reform of the institutions, including the weighting of votes and the threshold for the qualified majority in the Council, and the revision of policies and mechanisms of co-operation, are being dealt with at the Inter-governmental Conference which opened in March 1996 in Turin, Italy and is likely to be concluded in 1997. The need for efficient operation should be reconciled with further democratic development of the institutions, putting the citizen back at the heart of the Union.

Objectives

The Maastricht Treaty has marked the beginning of a decisive stage 'in the process of creating an ever closer union among the peoples of Europe' through: (i) the expansion of the scope of responsibilities of the European Communities, that is the European Economic Community (EEC), renamed the European Community (EC), the European Coal and Steel Community (ECSC) and the European Atomic Energy Community (Euratom); (ii) the implementation of a common foreign and security policy; and (iii) the development of close co-operation in the fields of justice and home affairs.

The basic objectives of the Union are to promote economic and social progress through the creation of an area without internal frontiers, the strengthening of economic and social cohesion, and the establishment of economic and monetary union, ultimately including a single currency, to ensure the consistency of its external activities in the context of foreign relations, economic and development policies, and to protect the rights and interests of the nationals of its member countries through the introduction of a citizenship of the Union.

Structure

The Union is served by a single institutional framework ensuring the consistency and continuity of the activities carried out in order to attain its objectives, while respecting and building upon the *acquis communautaire*. Besides the European Council setting the Union's basic guidelines, the European Parliament, the Council of the European Union, the European Commission, the Court of Justice of the European Communities, and the European Court of Auditors exercise their powers according to the provisions of the Treaties establishing the European Communities and subsequent instruments modifying them, and to the other provisions of the Maastricht Treaty. In addition, there are a number of advisory bodies representing economic, social and regional interests.

The European Council   The European Council – providing the Union with the necessary impetus for its development, and defining the general political guidelines – consists of the Heads of State or Government of the member countries and of the President of the Commission and is assisted by the Foreign Ministers and a member of the Commission. It meets at least twice a year – generally in the country which exercises the rotating presidency of the Council of the European Union – and submits to the European Parliament a yearly report on the progress achieved by the Union.

The European Parliament   Parliament participates in the process leading to the adoption of Community acts by exercising its powers under the procedures laid down in the Treaties and by giving its assent or delivering advisory opinions. The SEA established a 'co-operation procedure' giving Parliament a bigger say in a significant range of policy areas. Since the coming into force of the Maastricht Treaty, the involvement of Parliament in the decision-making process has resulted, *inter alia*, in the adoption, together with the Council, of a number of instruments covered by the 'co-decision procedure'. A Conciliation

Committee, composed of the members of the Council and of an equal number of representatives of the Parliament, is entrusted with the task of reaching agreement on the joint text of an act by a qualified majority of the Council and a majority of the representatives of Parliament. The Commission takes part in the proceedings of the Conciliation Committee with a view to reconciling the positions of Parliament and the Council. Difficulties have arisen in Parliament's relations with the Council and have been overcome temporarily through the adoption of an agreement on a *modus vivendi* between Parliament, the Council and the Commission, to apply until the revision of the Treaties, to be carried out by the 1996–7 Intergovernmental Conference.

Together, Parliament and the Council form the budgetary authority, with Parliament voting on the adoption of the Union's annual budget and overseeing its implementation.

Elected by direct universal suffrage since 1979, members of the European Parliament (MEPs) currently represent 370 million people; the most recent elections were held in June 1994, for a five-year mandate. The 626 MEPs are apportioned as follows: Germany, 99; France, Italy and the UK, 87 each; Spain, 64; The Netherlands, 31; Belgium, Greece and Portugal, 25 each; Sweden, 22; Austria, 21; Denmark and Finland, 16 each; Ireland, 15; and Luxembourg, 6. Members sit in Parliament in political, not national, groups.

Political parties at European level are expressly recognized by the Maastricht Treaty as an important factor for integration within the Union, contributing to the formation of a European awareness and to the expression of the political will of the citizens. Party representation in Parliament (as of January 1996) was as follows: Party of European Socialists (PES), 217; European People's Party (EPP), 173; Union for Europe (UFE), 54; European Liberal, Democratic and Reformist Party (ELDR), 52; Confederal Group of the European United Left (EUL), 33; Greens, 27; European Radical Alliance (ERA), 20; Europe of the Nations (EN), 19; Non-affiliated (NI), 31.

Parliament holds an annual session, divided into about 12 one-week part-sessions, taking place in Strasbourg with additional sittings in Brussels. Committee meetings are held in Brussels while the Secretariat is based in Luxembourg. Parliament is run by a Bureau including the President and 14 Vice-Presidents elected by secret ballot. Specialized committees deliberate on proposals for legislation put forward by the Commission before Parliament's final opinion is delivered by a resolution in plenary session.

Parliament has adopted resolutions on its own initiative, not only on Community matters but also on a variety of international issues of major concern to European public opinion. It also conducts an active diplomacy through exchange visits with the parliaments of many countries.

The Council of the European Union The Council of the European Union – composed of ministers from the member countries with responsibility for the policy area under discussion at a given meeting – is the main decision-making institution representing the national as opposed to the Community interest. The Council is responsible for co-ordinating the general economic policies of the member countries and adopting, on proposals from the Commission, the main decisions relating to the common policies, in accordance with procedures that involve Parliament in varying degrees. It plays a predominant role in the two areas based on intergovernmental co-operation; that is, the common foreign and security policy, and justice and home affairs. It also adopts international agreements negotiated by the Commission.

The office of President is exercised for a six-month term by each member of the Council according to the following order, beginning in January 1995: France, Spain, Italy, Ireland, the Netherlands, Luxembourg, UK, Austria, Germany, Finland, Portugal, France, Sweden, Belgium, Spain, Denmark and Greece. This order may be altered by a unanimous decision of the Council. Meetings of the Council are convened by the President acting on his own initiative, or at the request of one of its members or of the Commission. The Council is assisted by a General Secretariat based in Brussels. Nearly 80 meetings were held by the Council in 1995.

The voting procedure of the Council depends upon the Treaty under which it acts and on the specific procedure required for the particular action to be taken. There are three types of voting: simple majority; qualified majority; and unanimity. Where conclusions require a qualified majority, the total votes (87) of the Council's members are distributed as follows: France, Germany, Italy and the UK, 10 votes each; Spain, 8; Belgium, Greece, the Netherlands and Portugal, 5 each; Austria and Sweden, 4 each; Denmark, Finland and Ireland, 3 each; and Luxembourg, 2. A minimum of 62 votes is required for decisions by qualified majority; in a few specific cases, the 62 votes must be cast by at least 10 members. Abstentions do not prevent the taking by the Council of conclusions requiring unanimity. The right of 'veto' in several areas was substantially restricted by the SEA. In accordance with the Maastricht Treaty, the range of decisions that can be taken by qualified majority now embraces a substantial proportion of the Community's new powers, as well as many environmental decisions. Unanimity is generally required for action under the common foreign and security policy or in justice and home affairs co-operation. Publicity arrangements have been adopted by the Council regarding the outcome of voting and statements of explanation of votes; results of voting on legislation are routinely announced, unless a simple majority decides otherwise.

Preparation and co-ordination of the Council's work are entrusted to a Committee of Permanent Representatives, meeting in Brussels and commonly known as Coreper, which consists of the ambassadors of the member countries assisted by working groups.

The European Commission The European Commission – consisting of 20 members chosen on the grounds of their general competence and appointed for a renewable five-year term – acts independently in the general interest of the Community. Its basic task is the implementation of the Treaties, and in this it has the right of both initiative and execution. The governments of member countries nominate by common accord, after consulting the European Parliament, the person they intend to appoint as President, and – in consultation with the nominee for President – nominate the other Commissioners. The President and the other Commissioners are subject, as a body, to a vote of approval by Parliament. The Commission may be forced to resign by a vote of censure of Parliament adopted by a two-thirds majority.

The Commission works on the principle of collegiate responsibility, but each member is in charge of one or more policy areas. It may not include more than two members having the same nationality. At present, France, Germany, Italy, Spain and the UK have two members each; the other countries have one member each. The number of members of the Commission may be altered by a unanimous vote of the Council. One or two Vice-Presidents may be appointed by the Commission. In carrying out their tasks, the members of the Commission may not seek or accept instructions from any government or other body. Any Commissioner who no longer fulfils the conditions required for the performance of his duties, or commits a serious offence, may be declared, at the request of the Council or of the Commission itself, removed from office by the Court of Justice.

The Commission acts by majority vote and performs the following functions: (a) to ensure application of the provisions of the Treaties and the provisions enacted by the institutions of the Communities; (b) to formulate recommendations or opinions regarding matters which are the subject of the Treaties; (c) to dispose of a power of decision of its own and to participate in the preparation of acts of the Council and of the European Parliament; and (d) to exercise the competence conferred on it by the Council for the implementation of the rules laid down by the latter. The Commission can initiate infringement proceedings against any member country and may, if necessary, refer matters to the Court of Justice. In the areas of intergovernmental co-operation, the Commission enjoys the same rights as the individual member countries with regard to making proposals. The Commission, whose headquarters are in Brussels, operates through 23 Directorates-General plus other similar departments, employing approximately 15 000 officials.

The Court of Justice of the European Communities The Court, composed of 15 judges assisted by 9 advocates-general and sitting in Luxembourg, bears prime responsibility for ensuring the observance of law and justice in the interpretation and application of the Treaties. The judges and advocates-general are appointed for renewable six-year terms by common accord between the governments of the member countries; they are chosen from persons whose independence can be fully relied upon and who fulfil the conditions required for the exercise of the highest judicial functions in their respective countries, or are legal experts of universally recognized ability. A partial renewal of the Court takes place every three years, affecting both judges and advocates-general. The President of the Court is appointed by the judges from among themselves for a renewable three-year term. The Court sits in plenary session but may set up within itself Chambers, each consisting of three, five or seven judges, either to undertake certain preparatory inquiries or to judge particular classes of cases.

A Court of First Instance, currently comprising 15 judges and also sitting in Luxembourg, was created in 1989, following a decision of the Council, with jurisdiction to hear and determine certain categories of cases which had hitherto been dealt with by the Court of Justice. These categories include cases arising under the competition rules of the EC Treaty, cases brought under the ECSC Treaty, and cases brought by Community officials. The judges of the Court of First Instance are appointed by common accord of the governments of member countries for renewable six-year terms; a partial renewal takes place every three years.

The Court of Justice has jurisdiction to settle disputes within the Communities and may impose a lump sum or penalty payment to be paid by the member countries concerned. It may review the legal validity of acts adopted jointly by the European Parliament and the Council, of acts of the Council and of the Commission (other than recommendations and opinions), and of acts of Parliament intended to produce legal effects *vis-à-vis* third parties. The Court is competent to give judgment on actions by a member country, the Commission or the Council on grounds of incompetence, infringement of the Treaties or of any legal provision relating to their application, or misuse of powers. Any natural or legal person may, under the same conditions, institute proceedings against a decision directed to that person, or against a decision which, although in the form of a regulation or decision addressed to another person, is of direct and specific concern to that person. After the creation of the Court of First Instance, the Court is also empowered to hear cases concerning compensation for damage, disputes between the Communities and their employees, fulfilment by member countries of obligations arising from the Statute of the *European Investment Bank (EIB), arbitration clauses contained in any contract concluded by or on behalf of the Communities, and disputes between member countries in connection with the objects of the Treaties, where such disputes are submitted to the Court under a special agreement. Preliminary rulings are given by the Court, at the request of national courts, on the interpretation of the Treaties, the validity and interpretation of acts of Community institutions, and the interpretation of the statutes of bodies set up by the Council, where those statutes so provide. Between 1952 and 1995 about 9000 actions were brought before the Court whose judgments and interpretations have contributed to creating a substantial body of European law, thereby furthering the process of European integration.

The European Court of Auditors   The Court of Auditors is composed of 15 members appointed for a renewable six-year term by the Council acting unanimously, after consultation with the European Parliament. The President is elected by members for a renewable three-year term. The Court – based in Luxembourg – examines the accounts of all revenue and expenditure of the Communities and of all bodies created by the Communities, and assists the Parliament and the Council in exercising powers of control over the implementation of the budget. The Court cooperates closely with the national audit bodies that supervise the national authorities responsible for enforcing Community law.

The consultative bodies   There are three major consultative bodies whose members are appointed in a personal capacity and are not bound by any mandatory instructions.

The Economic and Social Committee   is composed of members representing economic and social fields (employers, workers and other interests) appointed for a renewable four-year term by the unanimous vote of the Council. The 222 members of the Committee are apportioned as follows: France, Germany, Italy and the UK, 24 each; Spain, 21; Austria, Belgium, Greece, The

Netherlands, Portugal and Sweden, 12 each; Denmark, Finland and Ireland, 9 each; and Luxembourg, 6. The Committee, meeting in Brussels, performs advisory functions and is consulted by the Council or the Commission, particularly with regard to agriculture, free movement of workers, harmonization of laws, and transport.

The ECSC Consultative Committee, consisting of 108 members representing producers, workers, consumers and traders in the coal and steel industries, and appointed by the Council for a two-year term, is attached to the Commission and performs an advisory role with regard to the coal and steel sectors.

The Committee of the Regions is a new advisory body set up under the Maastricht Treaty and consists of 222 full members and an equal number of alternate members, appointed by the Council for a four-year term, representing regional and local authorities. The number of members from each country is the same as for the Economic and Social Committee. The Committee must be consulted on matters regarding education, culture, public health, trans-European networks, and economic and social cohesion. It is informed of all requests for an opinion addressed to the Economic and Social Committee, and may issue opinions on its own initiative.

The European Monetary Institute (EMI) was established in January 1994 in Frankfurt in accordance with the Maastricht Treaty, to coincide with the start of the second stage of economic and monetary union. It is consulted by the Council on any proposal for a Community instrument in its fields of competence; it may also formulate opinions or recommendations on the general direction of monetary policy. The EMI, the members of its Council and its staff enjoy the privileges and immunities granted to the Community institutions.

Besides the bodies already mentioned, there are several hundred specialized groups, representing a wide variety of interests within the Communities, which hold unofficial talks with the Commission.

Legal instruments Under the provisions of the EC and Euratom Treaties, the European Parliament, acting jointly with the Council, the Council itself and the Commission, in order to carry out their tasks, are empowered to make 'regulations', issue 'directives', take 'decisions', make 'recommendations' or deliver 'opinions'. Regulations have a general application and are binding in every respect and directly applicable in each member country. Directives bind, as to the result to be achieved, any member country to which they are addressed, while leaving to national authorities the choice of form and methods. Decisions are binding in their entirety upon those to whom they are addressed. Recommendations and opinions have no binding force. Under the ECSC Treaty, a different system is used: 'decisions' are binding in every respect; 'recommendations' are binding only with respect to the objectives, while leaving to the addressee the choice of the appropriate methods; 'opinions' are deprived of binding force.

Budget The general budget of the Union includes 'compulsory' expenditure items, arising from the European Treaties or acts adopted under the Treaties, which account for about half of the total commitments. The ECSC's financial activities are being scaled down gradually in view of the expiry of the ECSC Treaty in July 2002. One of the distinctive features of the budget is the very high level of expenditure on agriculture; structural, social and regional expenditure takes second place. Research and technological development and the other internal policies – transport, education, culture, energy, environment, consumer protection, the internal market and industry – represent a significant percentage of the total financial commitments of the Union. The general budget and the European Development Fund (EDF), which does not come under the Union budget, provide substantial sums for co-operation with the developing world and the new democracies in Central and Eastern Europe. Expenditure for the needs of the European institutions accounts for about 5 per cent of the budget.

Expenditure under the general budget is financed by automatic payments made by the member countries from the revenue they collect in agricultural levies and customs duties, from a percentage of the revenue from value-added tax (VAT) on goods and services, and on the basis of a levy on the GNP of each country. The provision of the Community's 'own resources' started in 1975 when the six original member countries began to pay a growing proportion of their contributions through the new system of automatic payments. The general budget reflects the priorities set out in the Maastricht Treaty: the strengthening of economic and social cohesion, the creation of an environment favourable to the improvement of the competitiveness of European industry and the stepping up of external action. The introduction of the principle of subsidiarity in the EC Treaty and the changes made to institutional arrangements (increasing the role played by the Court of Auditors and establishing the Committee of the Regions) also had a significant impact. A new Interinstitutional Agreement on budgetary discipline and procedures for the period 1993–9 was concluded in October 1993. This involves, in particular, a procedure for an interinstitutional 'trialogue' (Parliament, Council and Commission) to discuss possible priorities for the budget of the coming year. Under the new financial framework, the 'own resources' ceiling is planned to rise gradually from 1.20 per cent of GNP in 1993, to 1.27 per cent in 1999, and the structure of these resources will be modified. Between 1995 and 1999 the call-in rate for the VAT resource will drop gradually from 1.4 per cent to 1 per cent of the common base (the base to be taken into account for the VAT resource will be reduced gradually).

The protection of the Community's financial interests is a major issue calling for closer partnership with the national authorities of the member countries; fraud prevention, which is crucial to the effectiveness of policies, has been given a new impetus as well as a new institutional framework by the provisions of the Maastricht Treaty. Several cases of large-scale fraud and irregularities have shown the existence of well-organized smuggling networks.

Activities

The single internal market   The single internal market, representing the core of the process of economic integration, is characterized by the four fundamental freedoms with the abolition, as between member countries, of obstacles to the free movement of goods, persons, services and capital.

A complete customs union between the six original member countries of the then EEC was achieved in July 1968, covering the exchange of all goods, the removal of customs duties, charges having equivalent effect and quantitative restrictions on imports and exports between member countries, and the adoption of a common external tariff in relations with non-member countries. The common customs duties have been modified several times to adjust to the concessions resulting from bilateral and multilateral negotiations, mainly conducted within the framework of the General Agreement on Tariffs and Trade (GATT), succeeded in 1995 by the *World Trade Organization (WTO). Special transitional periods have been adopted over the years as new member countries have joined the Community. However, the movement of goods between member countries remained restricted by a number of national non-tariff barriers, such as health and safety regulations and technical standards. Under the SEA, all remaining barriers to free movement of goods, persons, services and capital had to be removed by December 1992. National tax barriers on the movement of goods still persist in a number of cases but will be removed gradually, and VAT will be levied in the country where the goods originate.

The free movement of workers between member countries, except those employed in the public service, became effective in July 1968. Nationals of member countries are granted equal treatment in every important field relating to employment, including matters relating to taxation, social insurance and dependants. Individuals, companies and firms from one member country may establish themselves in another member country for the purposes of pursuing an economic activity under the same conditions applied to nationals of that country. Social security benefits are guaranteed to employees and the self-employed – as well as their families – throughout the Community. In 1990, the right of residence, originally granted only to workers and those seeking work, was extended to students, the non-employed and pensioners.

The principle of equal treatment for all citizens of the Union also applies to people taking up and pursuing independent occupations, such as doctors and lawyers, and those involved in technical, artistic, and craft activities. Moreover, the freedom of establishment covers the establishment and running of businesses, companies, agencies, branches and subsidiaries. The freedom to provide services regards activities which are limited in time and covers the providers as well as the recipients of services, such as tourists, students and patients undergoing medical treatment.

The first steps towards an effective liberalization of capital movements were taken only in the late 1980s; since January 1993, member countries have fully liberalized capital markets and financial services, and restrictions may be introduced only in exceptional circumstances. As regards competition, the provisions embodied in the Treaties for action against practices which restrict or distort competition in the common market have been implemented to a significant degree. The Community has made extensive use of its powers to control cross-frontier amalgamations, take-overs, and other arrangements between firms likely to create abuse of market power. Conflicts between national and Community authorities have arisen in this area. In September 1990 new regulations came into force concerning mergers of large companies that might create unfair competition.

The economic and monetary union The establishment of the single market provides the essential foundation for the next phase of integration; that is, the economic and monetary union. Before the Maastricht Treaty several unsuccessful attempts had been made in that direction. Efforts undertaken between 1969 and 1972, on the basis of the Werner Report, failed for a number of reasons, notably the lack of determination of the member countries in the field of economic policy co-ordination. Plans providing for a common central bank system, invariable exchange-rate parities, and Community decisions on important economic questions were shelved after the crisis of the Bretton Woods international monetary system and the first oil shock of 1973. Another major attempt to promote a convergence of economic policies of member countries was made with the establishment of the European monetary system

(EMS), which began operations formally in March 1979. Unlike its predecessor, the 'snake', which had been introduced in 1972 and was merely a common exchange-rate system, the EMS was intended to keep the cross rates of exchange of the currencies of the participating countries within specific fluctuation margins, to co-ordinate intervention on the foreign exchange markets, and to grant credit facilities. Following the introduction of the EMS, the European Currency Unit (ECU) was created on the basis of a 'basket' of national currencies, 'weighted' according to the economic strength of each country. The EMS aimed to create close monetary co-operation, leading to a zone of monetary stability in Europe, chiefly by means of an exchange-rate mechanism (ERM) supervised by the ministries of finance and the central banks of member countries. Under the ERM, a central rate was fixed for each currency in ECUs, with established fluctuation margins. However, several currencies either remain outside the ERM or are allowed to fluctuate within fairly wide bands.

A new effort to be implemented through a number of stages leading to economic and monetary union was undertaken in the late 1980s. In July 1990 the first stage began through the setting up of convergence programmes aimed at achieving convergence as well as improving economic performance of the member countries. Under the Maastricht Treaty, the second stage began in January 1994 with the establishment of the EMI in order to create the necessary conditions for transition to the third stage, to oversee the functioning of the European Monetary System (EMS), and to prepare the introduction of a European System of Central Banks (ECSB), the implementation of a single monetary policy and the establishment of a single currency. The resources of the EMI consist of contributions from the central banks based on a key (50 per cent population; 50 per cent gross domestic product) identical to that of the future European Central Bank (ECB). The ECB will take over the tasks of the EMI and will be endowed with the exclusive right to authorize the issue of banknotes within the Union.

Each participating country must meet a number of convergence criteria in order to be allowed to proceed to the third stage. The criteria relate to: the inflation rate (within 2.5 percentage points of the average rate of the three countries with the lowest inflation); the nominal long-term interest rate (within 2 percentage points of the average rate of the three countries with the lowest interest rates); the national budget deficit (not exceeding 3 per cent of GDP); the national debt (not exceeding 60 per cent of GDP); the national currency (must not have been devalued for the last two years, remaining within the 2.25 per cent fluctuation margin provided for by the EMS).

The countries meeting the convergence criteria will introduce in the third and final stage – scheduled to begin in January 1999 – a single currency. The ECB, to be set up during the third stage and six months before the adoption of the single currency (to be called the 'Euro'), will manage the monetary policies of the participating countries in full independence *vis-à-vis* national governments. The UK has reserved the right to opt out of the third stage, while Denmark may exercise its right to hold a referendum on the matter.

The common agricultural policy With respect to agriculture, a common policy was developed step by step from the early 1960s in order: (a) to increase agricultural productivity through technical progress and the rational development of agricultural production, and the optimum utilization of the factors of production, particularly labour; (b) to ensure a fair standard of living for the agricultural population; (c) to stabilize markets; and (d) to assure regular supplies as well as reasonable consumer prices. The Common Agricultural Policy (CAP) was established on the following main elements: a single market, calling for common prices, stable currency parities and the harmonization of administrative, health and veterinary legislation; Community preference, for the protection of the Community market from imports and world market fluctuations; and common financing of the European Agricultural Guidance and Guarantee Fund supporting, through its Guarantee Section, all public expenditure intervention, storage costs, marketing subsidies and export rebates. In several cases, the CAP has encouraged excess production and the consequent formation of costly surpluses, causing strong public criticism. Moreover, the operation of the CAP has been characterized by

serious fraud, mainly in the form of false claims for subsidies and intervention payments.

Several efforts have been undertaken over the past few years with a view to reforming the CAP and reducing its burden on the Community budget (over 63 per cent in 1988). Eventually, in June 1992, a wide-ranging reform of the CAP was adopted by the Council; the bulk of legislation for implementing CAP reform was adopted in 1993. The main aim of the long-overdue reform is to make the agricultural sector more responsive to the level of supply and demand, and to reduce agricultural subsidies, particularly in the context of the commitments resulting from the Uruguay Round of multilateral trade negotiations conducted within the framework of GATT. Agriculture and regional policy were issues of primary importance in the 1993–4 negotiations relating to the enlargement of the Union, since all three applicant countries used agricultural policy as an instrument of regional policy. A study has been made by the Commission of alternative development strategies for the future integration into the CAP of the agriculture sectors in the Central and Eastern European countries.

Fisheries Although the need for a common policy for fisheries is acknowledged by all member countries, agreement on the main elements of such a policy has not proved easy to achieve. In principle, the common fisheries policy (CFP), in effect since January 1983, gives all EC fishermen equal access to the waters of member countries. From 1977 the Community has reserved a zone extending up to 200 nautical miles (370 km) from the shore around all its coastlines, within which all member countries have access to fishing and other economic uses of the sea. According to the CFP, the total allowable catch for each species in each region will be set and then shared out between member countries according to pre-established quotas; special rules apply in order to conserve fish stocks, and financial support is granted to help fleets adjust capacity and equipment to the new circumstances. The CFP includes measures in favour of the preservation of marine biodiversity and the pursuit of fishing on a sustainable basis. In 1994 common arrangements were established for the conservation and management of fishery resources in the Mediterranean also taking into account the specific socioeconomic role of fisheries in some coastal regions. As with agricultural produce, export subsidies are paid to enable the export of fish, and import levies are imposed. Agreements have been signed with several countries allowing reciprocal fishing rights and other advantages.

The industrial policy   The promotion of the conditions necessary for the competitiveness of the Community's industry is one of the key objectives of the Maastricht Treaty. Within a framework of open and competitive markets, the Community's industrial policy is aimed at speeding up adjustment to structural changes, creating a favourable environment for the growth of businesses, particularly small and medium-sized enterprises, and promoting innovation, research and technological development. In its White Paper on growth, competitiveness and employment presented to the European Council in December 1993, the Commission recommended practical measures to gear up European businesses for competition on world markets. Action is being taken with a view to relieving businesses of unnecessary burdens, safeguarding competition, and strengthening co-operation with non-member countries. Industrial policy is also being targeted on such growth areas as the markets in information and culture.

Research and technological development
Since the early 1980s 'framework programmes' have been adopted by the Community to foster research and technological development (R&TD) activities. A shift is gradually taking place towards better co-ordination of the European research effort and a more effective focusing of R&TD activity on social problems. The Fourth Framework Programme for R&TD for the period 1994–8 was adopted by Parliament and the Council in April 1994. The European Science and Technology Assembly (ESTA), consisting of 100 scientists and representatives of the world of industrial research, was created in 1994 in order to assist the Commission in implementing all aspects of the R&TD policy. The Community promotes research: (a) through the Joint Research Centre (JRC) comprising eight institutes based at Ispra, Italy; Geel, Belgium; Karlsruhe, Germany; and Petten, The Netherlands; (b) by contracting specific tasks to national centres or firms, and by 'association contracts' through the contribution of finance and personnel; and (c) by joining international projects.

Transport and trans-European networks
Progress towards a common transport policy had been remarkably slow until the mid-1980s, when the Court of Justice ruled that firms anywhere in the Community should be free to provide goods and passenger services in the member countries irrespective of nationality or place of establishment. The SEA envisaged transport as an essential element of the single market, and listed measures to be adopted in order to develop a common policy in the area. The new overall approach to transport policy goes beyond the mere elimination of artificial barriers to the provision of services through the promotion of an integrated transport system which is environmentally and socially acceptable and provides a high level of safety. Under the Maastricht Treaty, the Community must contribute to the establishment and development of trans-European networks in the areas of transport, telecommunications and energy infrastructures. An action programme has been adopted by the Commission, setting the guidelines for a common approach to transport for the period 1995–2000. The Union's goal of an information society, based on advanced information and communications technologies and services, will require changes in the regulatory frameworks to encourage expansion of the market and ensure interconnection of networks and inter-operability of services.

Energy   Many difficulties have to be overcome in order to establish an effective energy policy at Community level and beyond in the light of recent institutional and geopolitical changes in Europe. The completion of the internal energy market and the development of trans-European gas and electricity networks are among the Community's major tasks, along with the integration of energy policy and environment policy. The European Communities were among the signatories, in December 1994, of the European Energy Charter Treaty and the Protocol on energy efficiency and related environmental aspects.

Citizens' rights and the social dimension

One of the major goals of the Maastricht Treaty is to build a Union closer to its citizens, more democratic and more open. The principle of subsidiarity ensures that anything carried out at Community level is justified by the fact that the objectives pursued cannot be achieved sufficiently by the member countries and can be better achieved by the Community as a whole. In light of the subsidiarity principle, existing legislation has been reviewed and a number of instruments have been recast, simplified or repealed. Measures to improve transparency have been adopted to strengthen democratic control over European institutions. The European citizenship, supplementary to national citizenship, is a new concept introduced by the Maastricht Treaty, according to which every person holding the nationality of a member country becomes a citizen of the Union and enjoys the relevant rights. These include the right to move and settle freely in any member country, and to vote and stand as a candidate at municipal elections in the country of residence. Any resident also has the right – exercised for the first time in the June 1994 European elections – to vote and stand as a candidate for the European Parliament in the country of residence. In the territory of a foreign country in which his own country is not represented, any citizen of the Union enjoys the protection of the diplomatic or consular authorities of any other member country.

Any citizen of the Union has the right to address a petition to Parliament on a matter coming within the Community's fields of activity and which affects him directly. This rule also applies to any natural or legal person residing in a member country. An Ombudsman, appointed by Parliament, is empowered to receive complaints from any citizen of the Union or any natural or legal person, residing or having its office in a member country, concerning instances of maladministration in the activities of the Community institutions or bodies. In July 1995 Jacob Söderman became the first Ombudsman of the Union.

The promotion of close co-operation between member countries in the social field was from the very beginning among the Community's basic aims, particularly in matters relating to employment, labour legislation and working conditions, occupational and continuation training, social security, and protection against occupational accidents and diseases. The SEA emphasized the need for 'economic and social cohesion', and granted the Community extensive powers in the social field. A Charter of the Fundamental Social Rights of Workers – covering freedom of movement, fair remuneration, improvement of working conditions, right to social security, freedom of association and collective wage agreements, and development of participation by workers in management – was adopted in December 1989 by eleven Community members, with the only exception being the UK. Subsequently, the same eleven countries adopted the Protocol and the Agreement on Social Policy annexed to the Maastricht Treaty covering workers' health and safety, information and consultation, fair pay, better working and living conditions, proper social protection, freedom of association and collective bargaining, vocational training, equal opportunities for men and women in the labour market, industrial democracy, and the protection of children, the elderly and the disabled.

Economic and social cohesion The strengthening of economic and social cohesion – with a view to narrowing the gap between the levels of development of the different regions, promoting job creation and helping workers to adjust to industrial change – was reaffirmed as a major goal of the Community by the Maastricht Treaty. The policy is no longer defined in financial terms but on the basis of five priority objectives regarding regions and subregions lagging behind or affected by industrial decline, long-term unemployment and the integration of young people into working life, the adjustment of farm structures and the development of rural areas. The main instruments are the 'structural funds' – the Guidance Section of the European Agricultural Guidance and Guarantee Fund (EAGGF), the European Regional Development Fund (ERDF), and the European Social Fund (ESF) – and the EIB. In 1988 the Council of Ministers approved a reform of the structural funds with a view to selecting priority targets and concentrating action in the least-favoured regions. In the second phase of the implementation of the reform (1994–9), the rules and operating provisions governing the structural funds have been improved, Community support frameworks and single programming documents have been adopted, and the financial allocation and geographical coverage of the eligible areas have been increased.

The EAGGF was established in 1962 under the administration of the Commission; the Guidance Section contributes credits for structural reforms in the agricultural sector. The ERDF, in operation since the mid-1970s, is responsible for encouraging investment and improving infrastructure in depressed regions as a means of compensating the unequal rate of development in different areas of the Community. In 1993, the scope for assistance was extended to take better account of the specific needs of the regions involved, including investment in education and health, and stressing the importance of certain priority areas. The ESF was originally set up in 1960 under the EEC Treaty with a view to improving opportunities for employment within the Community by assisting training and workers' mobility; the scope of ESF was subsequently modified several times. The objectives of ESF were redefined in 1993, in order to facilitate the integration of young people, to assist the adaptation of workers to industrial changes and to boost human potential in research, science and technology. Also in 1993, a Financial instrument for fisheries guidance (FIFG) was created with a view to bringing together the resources allocated to structural measures in the fisheries sector. The structural funds co-ordinate their activities between themselves and with the operations of the EIB and the other existing financial instruments.

According to the provisions of the Maastricht Treaty, a new Cohesion Fund was established in May 1994 to help finance projects in the fields of transport infrastructures and environmental protection; the beneficiary member countries (currently Greece, Ireland, Portugal and Spain) must have a per capita GNP of less than 90 per cent of the Community average.

Following the decision of the European Council of December 1992, the European Investment Fund (EIF) eventually started operations in 1994 in Luxembourg with a view to financing investment projects associated with the trans-European networks, and funding small and medium-sized enterprises. The major shareholders of the EIF – which operates on a commercial basis – include the EIB (40 per cent of the capital) and the EC (30 per cent). At the end of 1995, the subscribed capital of the EIF stood at ECU1.8 billion (out of a total authorized capital of ECU2 billion).

Environment, consumer and education policies The Community's environment and consumer protection policy was launched in 1972. The SEA gave environmental policy its proper place with a view to making the protection of the environment an integral part of economic and social policies. The Community aims at preventing pollution (prevention principle), rectifying pollution at source wherever possible, and imposing the costs of prevention, cleaning up and compensation upon the polluters themselves (polluter-pays principle). The European Environment Agency was officially inaugurated in Copenhagen in October 1994 in order to help base the Community's environment policy on reliable scientific data.

Consumer protection policy is expressly envisaged by the Maastricht Treaty and is aimed at protecting the health, safety and economic interests of consumers and providing them with adequate information; any member country is allowed to maintain or introduce protective measures which are more stringent than the ones adopted at Community level. Community action in the area of public health is mainly directed towards the prevention of major diseases, including drug addiction, and by promoting health information and education as well as research.

General education and vocational training policies are also dealt with by the Maastricht Treaty. Although member countries retain full responsibility for the content of teaching and the organization of education and vocational training systems, the Community develops the European dimension, encouraging mobility of students and teachers (including the academic recognition of diplomas and periods of study), improving initial and continuing vocational training and encouraging mobility of instructors and trainees, and stimulating co-operation and exchanges of information and experience.

External relations

International relations are maintained by the Communities – each having a distinct international personality of its own – with non-member countries and other international organizations. Over 160 countries have accredited permanent missions to the Communities in Brussels, while the Commission has been steadily opening new delegations abroad, currently numbering about 130. Representations of international organizations and bodies to the Commission now number around 20.

As regards its European neighbours, the Community has established very close economic and political ties with the member countries of the *European Free Trade Association (EFTA) through the creation of a European Economic Area (EEA), in operation since January 1994, involving the free movement of goods, services, people and capital, as well as participation in several Community programmes. However, the EEA basically appears to be a transitional arrangement, since most of its former member countries have joined the Union, and Switzerland has refused to take part in the Area. The dramatic changes in political and economic systems in Central and Eastern European countries have led to ever-closer forms of association between these countries and the Community. 'Europe Agreements' covering economic, financial and cultural co-operation as well as political dialogue have been signed by the Community with Bulgaria, the Czech Republic, Hungary, Poland, Romania and Slovakia, and with the Baltic countries (Estonia, Latvia and Lithuania). Full membership of the Union will become possible for these associated countries – all of which have already submitted formal accession applications – as soon as they satisfy the appropriate economic and political conditions. Partnership and co-operation agreements (PCAs) have been concluded in June 1994 between the Union and Russia and Ukraine; more PCAs are being concluded with other members of the Commonwealth of Independent States (CIS). The Union is gradually developing its relations with Yugoslavia's successor republics, by extending financial support and humanitarian aid.

The Commission co-ordinates assistance from the Group of Twenty-four (G-24) to countries in Central and Eastern Europe (including Albania and some former Yugoslav republics) through the PHARE programme, while the TACIS programme is in operation for the countries of the erstwhile USSR.

A Euro-Mediterranean partnership based on a global approach involving political and economic co-operation and an eventual free-trade area, as well as substantial financial assistance and technical co-operation, was launched by the Union in the early 1990s. A Euro-Mediterranean ministerial conference took place in Barcelona in November 1995 with the participation of the Union and its 12 Mediterranean partners. The three key components of the partnership are: reinforced and regular political dialogue; enhanced economic and financial co-operation with a view to creating a free-trade area; and further strengthening of the social, cultural and human dimension. Association agreements leading to customs union have been signed with Cyprus, Malta and Turkey. The customs union between the Community and Turkey eventually came into effect in January 1996.

Co-operation agreements are currently in force with the Maghreb countries (Algeria, Morocco and Tunisia), the Mashreq countries (Egypt, Jordan, Lebanon and Syria) and Israel. An agreement will be concluded in due course with the Palestinian Authority. As the biggest donor to the Palestinian Territories, the Union is making a strong contribution to the development of the Middle East peace process.

The strengthening of the multilateral trade system – largely achieved through the creation of the WTO as an outcome of the successful conclusion of the Uruguay Round – and the challenges of job creation, growth and competitiveness are the major issues that characterize the Union's relationship with other industrial countries. These issues are debated regularly at the Western Economic Summits held by the *Group of Seven (G-7).

In 1976 the Community signed its first Framework Agreement for Commercial and Economic Co-operation with an advanced industrial country, Canada, covering not only trade promotion but also wide-ranging collaboration in the economic sphere; a Declaration on EC–Canada Relations was adopted in 1990.

The economic relationship between the Community and the USA is currently the most important in the world and a system of consultations between the two sides has come into existence since the adoption, in November 1990, of the EC–US Transatlantic Declaration. Over the years EU–US summits held within the context of the Transatlantic Declaration have become more effective and wide-ranging. A breakthrough took place with the adoption, at the EU–US summit held in December 1995, of an important statement of political commitment, the New Transatlantic Agenda, and a comprehensive EU–US Action Plan identifying over 150 specific actions where the parties will work together, both bilaterally and multilaterally.

In July 1991 a first summit meeting was held between the Community and Japan, and a Joint Declaration was adopted calling for greater co-operation and dialogue. Annual high-level consultations between the EU and Japan deal with bilateral economic relations, including the disputes connected with access to the Japanese market.

Relations with the countries of Asia were redefined by the Union in the early 1990s in the light of the increasing economic and political importance of the Asia-Pacific region. Besides strengthening bilateral and regional relations, backing co-operation schemes for the safeguard of peace and security, and improving co-ordination in the management of development aid, the Union aims to ameliorate Europe's image in Asia and to create a climate conducive to the development of trade and investment.

The Union has improved remarkably the political and economic dialogue with the Latin American countries, strengthening existing ties and developing financial and technical co-operation as well as promoting democratization and respect for human rights.

ACP countries Relations between the Community and sub-Saharan Africa date back to the late 1950s, when most countries in the region had not yet attained sovereign status. At present, 70 African, Caribbean and Pacific (ACP) countries, mainly former colonies of the Community's members, participate in the Lomé Convention, first signed in 1975 and renewed in October 1979, December 1984 and December 1989. The Fourth Convention (Lomé IV), running for the ten

years starting in March 1990, includes innovations such as the provision of assistance for structural adjustment programmes, increased support for the private sector, environmental protection, and measures to avoid a further increase in the recipient countries' indebtedness. The ACP–EU institutions comprise: the Council of Ministers, consisting of one minister from each signatory country and meeting annually; the Committee of Ambassadors, composed of one ambassador from each signatory country and meeting at least every six months; the Joint Assembly, attended by delegates from each of the 70 ACP countries and an equal number of members of the European Parliament and meeting twice a year. The mid-term review of Lomé IV began in May 1994 with the objectives of promoting human rights, democracy and the rule of law, establishing an open political dialogue with the ACP countries, and improving programming and co-operation instruments and procedures. An agreement was reached by mid-1995 on the amount of the financial allocations for the period 1995–2000, the revision of the country-of-origin rules for manufactured goods, the sustainable management of forest resources, and the support of the banana industry. The revised Convention was signed in November 1995; however, the crisis situation prevailing in some ACP countries has made the dialogue extremely difficult.

Humanitarian aid to ACP and other developing countries has been provided through the European Community Humanitarian Office (ECHO), set up in 1992 to assist victims of conflicts and natural disasters worldwide.

Development co-operation The objectives of the Community's development co-operation policy have been set by the Maastricht Treaty: sustainable economic and social development of the developing countries, particularly the most disadvantaged among them; the smooth and gradual integration of developing countries into the world economy; and the campaign against poverty. Community policy in this area pursues the broad aim of contributing to the progress and consolidation of democracy and the rule of law, and to the respect for human rights and fundamental freedoms. The development policies of the member countries should complement one another and be co-ordinated with the Community's policy, both in international forums and in individual countries.

To assist the trade of developing countries, in July 1971 the Community introduced a Generalized System of Preferences (GSP) to over 90 developing nations, which was later extended to include additional countries. The scheme was subsequently revised with a view to granting varying preferential advantages according to the degree of competitiveness of the beneficiary countries. Since 1977 the Community has progressively liberalized GSP access for the least-developed countries by according duty-free entry on all products as well as exemption from virtually all preferential limits. Since the late 1980s the GSP has been extended gradually to countries in Central and Eastern Europe and to republics of the former USSR; South Africa became a beneficiary country in 1994. A new GSP strategy for 1995–2004 was launched in 1994, with a view to introducing, in addition to the standard scheme, special incentive arrangements granting further tariff reductions if more enlightened social and environmental practices were adopted by the beneficiary countries. Sectors and/or countries having already achieved a certain level of development are excluded gradually from preferential treatment.

Relations with international organizations
The Community maintains relations with several UN organs and specialized agencies; it has observer status at the UN and was made a full member of the *Food and Agriculture Organization of the UN (FAO) in November 1991. Thus the EC became the first regional economic integration organization to join a UN specialized agency.

Close links, expressly envisaged by the Treaties, have been established between the Community and the *Council of Europe, the *Organization for Economic Co-operation and Development (OECD), and the *Western European Union (WEU). The Community co-operates closely with other European regional organizations such as the *European Bank for Reconstruction and Development (EBRD) and the *Organization for Security and Co-operation in Europe (OSCE).

As regards relations with non-European international organizations specifically concerned with economic co-operation and integration, the Community has developed close relations with regional groupings in Asia (notably the *Association of South East Asian Nations (ASEAN) and the *South Asian Association for Regional Co-operation (SAARC)), Latin America (from the *Andean Community and the five countries of Central America and Panama to the *Group of Rio and *Mercosur), the Middle East (the *Gulf Co-operation Council (GCC)) and Africa (especially the *Southern African Development Community (SADC)).

Common foreign policy and defence
European political co-operation – involving regular consultation and co-ordination efforts on major external relations issues among foreign ministers of the member countries – has been in place since the early 1970s and obtained full recognition in the SEA. The Maastricht Treaty, laying the foundation for political union, established a common foreign and security policy with the following objectives: to safeguard the common values, fundamental interests and independence of the Union; to strengthen the security of the Union and its member countries; to maintain peace and international security according to the principles of the Charter of the UN as well as the principles and aims of the OSCE; to advance international co-operation; to develop and consolidate democracy and the rule of law, and to ensure respect for human rights and fundamentals freedoms. Most decisions in the area of common foreign and security policy are taken at the intergovernmental level, although they may be closely related to specific Community instruments such as economic co-operation and financial assistance. After the European Council has provided the general guidelines, the Council decides on joint actions to be taken – laying down objectives and procedures for implementation – and defines the matters on which joint action may be carried on by qualified majority voting instead of unanimity.

Within this framework, the Union has carried out several joint actions in respect of the former Yugoslavia, the peace process in the Middle East, Russia, South Africa, the pact on stability in Central and Eastern Europe, nuclear non-proliferation, and control of exports to non-member countries of goods which can be used for both civil and military purposes.

The common foreign and security policy might in time 'lead to a common defence', to be elaborated and implemented by the WEU which would then become the military arm of the European Union. However, the WEU Treaty is due to expire in 1998 and only 10 out of the 15 members of the Union participate fully in the WEU, the remaining members, plus the countries of Central and Eastern Europe, having established a more limited form of partnership. The objective of common defence should also be reconciled with the obligations arising for eleven countries of the Union from their participation in the *North Atlantic Treaty Organization (NATO); the role and functions of the 53-member OSCE should also be taken into account. The Maastricht Treaty expressly envisages a revision of the rules dealing with security and defence policy at the 1996 Intergovernmental Conference.

Justice and home affairs   The achievement of the objectives of the Union requires the extension of co-operation to the fields of justice and home affairs which, however, are basically dealt with at the intergovernmental level – as is the case for the common foreign and security policy – by the Council deciding unanimously. The primary area of co-operation in the field of home affairs is represented by policy towards non-member countries concerning immigration and asylum. The Schengen Agreement – although it applies to a limited number of member countries – has represented a substantial step towards the standardization of procedures and more effective controls at the external borders of the Union. In the field of justice, co-operation mainly focuses on preventing and combating terrorism and drug-trafficking, money-laundering and large-scale international fraud and other serious forms of international crime.

A European Police Office (Europol) will organize a Union-wide system for exchanging information and drawing up strategies for preventing and combating serious forms of international organized crime.

Addresses: European Parliament, General Secretariat: Centre Européen, Plateau du Kirchberg, 2929 Luxembourg (Telephone: +352 43001); Council of the European Union, General Secretariat: 175 rue de la Loi, 1048 Brussels (Telephone: +32 2 285 6111; fax: +32 2 285 7397/7381); European Commission: 200 rue de la Loi, 1049 Brussels, Belgium (Telephone: +32 2 299 1111); Court of Justice of the European Communities: Boulevard Konrad Adenauer, 2925 Luxembourg (Telephone: +352 43031; fax: +352 4303 2600); European Court of Auditors: 12 rue Alcide de Gasperi, 1615 Luxembourg (Telephone: +352 43981; fax: +352 439342); Economic and Social Committee: 2 rue Ravenstein, 1000 Brussels (Telephone: +32 2 546 9011; fax: +32 2 513 4893); Committee of the Regions: 79 rue Belliard, 1040 Brussels (Telephone: +32 2 282 2211; fax: +32 2 282 2896); ECSC Consultative Committee: Bâtiment Jean Monnet, rue Alcide de Gasperi, 2920 Luxembourg (Telephone: +352 43011); European Monetary Institute: Postfach 10 20 31, 60020 Frankfurt am Main, Germany (Telephone: +49 69 2400 0691); ACP Secretariat: ACP House, 451 avenue Georges Henri, 1200 Brussels (Telephone: +32 2 733 9600).

Internet address of the European Commission: http://www.cec.lu

Members of the Commission with their responsibilities: President: Jacques Santer (Luxembourg),   Secretariat-General, Legal Service, Security Office, Forward Studies Unit, Inspectorate-General, Joint Interpreting and Conference Service, Spokesman's Service, Monetary matters (with Mr de Silguy), Common foreign and security policy and human rights (with Mr Van den Broek), Institutional matters and Intergovernmental Conference (with Mr Oreja).

Vice-President: Sir Leon Brittan (UK), External relations with North America, Australia, New Zealand, Japan, China, Korea, Hong Kong, Macao and Taiwan, Common commercial policy, Relations with OECD and WTO.

Vice-President: Manuel Marín González (Spain), External relations with southern Mediterranean countries, the Middle East, Latin America and Asia (except Japan, China, Korea, Hong Kong, Macao and Taiwan), including development aid.

Martin Bangemann (Germany), Industrial affairs, Information and telecommunications technologies.

Karel Van Miert (Belgium), Competition.

Hans van den Broek (The Netherlands), External relations with the countries of Central and Eastern Europe, the former Soviet Union, Mongolia, Turkey, Cyprus, Malta and other European countries, Common foreign and security policy and human rights (in agreement with the President), External missions.

João de Deus Pinheiro (Portugal), External relations with African, Caribbean and Pacific countries and South Africa, including development aid, the Lomé Convention.

Padraig Flynn (Ireland), Employment and social affairs, Relations with the Economic and Social Committee.

Marcelino Oreja Aguirre (Spain), Relations with the European Parliament, Relations with Member States (transparency, communication and information), Culture and audio-visual policy, Office for Official Publications, Institutional matters and Intergovernmental Conference (in agreement with the President).

Anita Gradin (Sweden), Immigration, home affairs and justice, Relations with the Ombudsman, Financial Control, Fraud prevention.

Edith Cresson (France), Science, research and development, Joint Research Centre, Human resources, education, training and youth.

Ritt Bjerregaard (Denmark), Environment, Nuclear safety.

Monika Wulf-Mathies (Germany), Regional policies, Relations with the Committee of the Regions, Cohesion Fund (in agreement with Mr Kinnock and Mrs Bjerregaard).

Neil Kinnock (UK), Transport (including trans-European networks).

Mario Monti (Italy), Internal market, Financial services and financial integration, Customs, Taxation.

Franz Fischler (Austria), Agriculture and rural development.

Emma Bonino (Italy), Fisheries, Consumer policy, European Community Humanitarian Office (ECHO).

Yves-Thibault de Silguy (France), Economic and financial affairs, Monetary matters (in agreement with the President), Credit and investments, Statistical Office.

Erkki Antero Liikanen (Finland), Budget, Personnel and administration, Translation and in-house computer services.

Christos Papoutsis (Greece), Energy and Euratom Supply Agency, Small business, Tourism.

Publications: *Bulletin of the European Union* (eleven issues a year plus supplements); *General Report on the Activities of the European Union* (annual); *The Agricultural Situation in the European Union* (annual); *Report on Competition Policy* (annual); *Report on the Application of Community Law* (annual); *European Economy* (quarterly); *The Courier EEC–ACP* (every two months); *Official Journal of the European Communities* (in three series: Legislation; Information and notices; Supplement on public works and supply contracts); *Reports of Cases before the Court of Justice and the Court of First Instance of the European Communities*; *Energy Statistics* (monthly); *Eurostatistics: Data for Short-term Economic Analysis* (eleven issues a year); *Monthly External Trade Bulletin*

References: W. Hallstein, *Europe in the Making* (London, 1973); C. Cook and M. Francis, *The First European Elections* (London, 1979); D. A. C. Freestone and J. S. Davidson, *The Institutional Framework of the European Communities* (London and New York, 1988); J. Lodge (ed.), *The European Community and the Challenge of the Future* (London, 1989); J. Lodge (ed.), *The 1989 Election of the European Parliament* (London, 1990); P. S. Mathijsen, *A Guide to European Community Law* (London) rev 5/1990; A. G. Toth, *The Oxford Encyclopedia of European Community Law*, vol. I, Institutional Law (Oxford, 1990); J. Pinder, *European Community: The Building of a Union* (Oxford and New York, 1991); C. Archer and F. Butler, *The European Community: Structure and Process* (London, 1992); J. Delors, *Our Europe: The Community and National Development* (London, 1993); E. R. Grilli, *The European Community and the Developing Countries* (Cambridge, 1993); L. N. Brown and T. Kennedy, *The Court of Justice of the European Communities* (London, 1994); N. Nugent, *The Government and Politics of the European Union* (London) 3rd edn 1994; W. Rawlinson and M. P. Cornwell-Kelly, *European Community Law* (London, 1994); W. Carlsnaes and S. Smith (eds), *European*

Foreign Policy. The EC and Changing Foreign Policy Perspectives in Europe (London, 1994); P.-H. Laurent (ed.), The European Community: To Maastricht and Beyond (London, 1994); A. M. Williams, The European Community: The Contradictions of Integration (Oxford) 2nd edn 1994; D. Dinan, Ever Closer Union? An Introduction to the European Community (London, 1994)

F

Fishery Committee for the Eastern Central Atlantic (CECAF)

Set up following a resolution of the Council of the *Food and Agriculture Organization of the UN (FAO) adopted in 1967 and amended in 1992, the Committee includes around 30 member countries of West Africa, Europe (including the European Community (EC)), and Asia, plus Cuba and the USA. The Committee aims to promote programmes of development for the rational utilization of fishery resources, to help establish a basis for regulatory measures, and to encourage training; the area of competence is that of the Eastern Central Atlantic between Cape Spartel and the Congo River. Among the Committee's concerns are the development of industrial fisheries in the region, the characteristics and development prospects of intraregional fish trade, the problems of technical assistance, and the adverse effects of the high degree of illegal fishing on the economies of several developing coastal countries concerned.

Secretariat: P.O. Box 1628, Accra, Ghana (Telephone: +233 21 666 851-4; fax: +233 21 668 427)

Food and Agriculture Organization of the UN (FAO)

The Organization is the UN specialized agency in charge of all matters relating to food and agriculture; the term 'agriculture' and its derivatives include fisheries, marine products, forestry and primary forestry products.

Origin and development

The creation of the FAO was recommended by the UN Conference on Food and Agriculture held at Hot Springs, Virginia, USA in May and June 1943; an Interim Commission was set up to plan the new international agency and draw up its Constitution. In October 1945, delegates of 42 countries met in Quebec, Canada, and formally adopted the Constitution establishing the Organization. The Constitution has subsequently been amended on a number of occasions. Headquarters of the Organization were first in Washington, DC and moved to Rome, Italy in 1951. Under a Protocol signed in March 1946, the International Institute of Agriculture, founded in Rome in 1905, was dissolved and its functions and assets were transferred to the new Organization. A relationship agreement was concluded with the UN and came into force in December 1946. The present membership of the Organization includes over 170 countries and the *European Community (EC), which was granted full membership in November 1991. Puerto Rico is an associate member.

Any nation submitting an application for membership as well as a formal declaration that it will accept the obligations of the Constitution may be admitted to the Organization by a two-thirds majority vote of the Conference. The Twenty-Sixth Conference approved amendments to the Basic Texts allowing regional economic integration organizations to become members of the Organization. Thus the EC was made a member and became the first regional organization to join a UN specialized agency. Territories or groups of territories not responsible for the conduct of their international relations may be granted associate membership, again by a two-thirds majority vote, upon application made on their behalf by the full member having responsibility for their international relations, which must also submit a formal declaration of acceptance of the relevant obligations. The right to withdraw is allowed upon submission of notice to the Director-General; withdrawal takes effect one year thereafter.

Objectives

The Organization aims to raise levels of nutrition and standards of living of the peoples of member countries; secure improvement of production and distribution of all food and agricultural products; better the conditions of rural populations; contribute to an expanding world economy, ensuring humanity's freedom from hunger; and act as a co-ordinating agency for development programmes in the whole range of food and agriculture, including forestry and fisheries.

The Organization is empowered to promote and, where appropriate, recommend national and international action with respect to: (a) scientific, technological, social and economic research relating to nutrition, food and agriculture; (b) the improvement of education and administration, and the spread of public knowledge of nutritional and agricultural science and practice; (c) the conservation of natural resources and the adoption of improved methods of agricultural production; (d) the improvement of the processing, marketing and distribution of food and agricultural products; (e) the adoption of policies for the provision of adequate agricultural credit, national and international; and (f) the adoption of international policies with respect to agricultural commodity arrangements.

Other functions of the Organization include the extension of such technical assistance that governments may request as well as the organization, in co-operation with the governments concerned, of expert missions. The Organization is also entrusted with the task of collecting, interpreting and disseminating information relating to nutrition, food and agriculture.

Structure

The work of the Organization is carried out by three principal organs: the Conference, the Council, and the Secretariat. The Conference, composed of one representative from each member, normally meets biennially to formulate overall policies, determine the programme of work, and approve the budget. It also elects the Director-General of the Secretariat and the Independent Chair of the Council. The Conference may, by a two-thirds majority of the votes cast, make recommendations to members, either full or associate, concerning questions relating to food and agriculture, for consideration by them with a view to implementation by national action. The Conference is also empowered to review any decision taken by the Council or by any commission or committee of the Conference or Council or by any other subsidiary body.

The Council, consisting of representatives of 49 member countries elected by the Conference for staggered three-year terms, meets at least once a year under an Independent Chair and serves as the interim governing body of the Organization between sessions of the Conference. The Council has three small elected committees: the Programme Committee, the Finance Committee, and the Committee on Constitutional and Legal Matters.

The Council has also five major committees which are non-elective and open to all members: the Committee on Commodity Problems (CCP), with several specialized intergovernmental groups; the Committee on Fisheries (COFI); the Committee on Forestry (COFO); the Committee on Agriculture (COAG); and the Committee on World Food Security (CFS), keeping under continuous review supplies and stocks of basic foodstuffs.

The Director-General enjoys full power and authority to direct the work of the Organization under the general supervision of the Conference and the Council.

The basic Regular Programme budget of the Organization is voted by the Conference and paid by all member countries in shares relating to their GNP. Additional funds come from a variety of sources, the most important being the *UN Development Programme (UNDP). Other funds are received from several agencies to cover the cost of specialist services provided by the Organization.

Activities

The Organization has entered into formal agreements with the specialized agencies of the UN and with other international institutions, both intergovernmental and non-governmental. Close relations exist with the relevant UN bodies; in particular, the Organization acts as an executing agency of the UNDP.

The action of FAO over five decades has covered several areas of paramount importance and has in many ways helped to increase the productivity of agriculture, fisheries and forestry, and improved the conditions of that very large part of the world population whose livelihoods come from these basic activities. However, long-standing problems and difficulties continue to beset food production and agriculture, particularly in the developing countries where production increases have been offset by growing population, thereby aggravating dependence on world markets. Moreover, abnormal food shortages, mainly caused by drought and bad weather in some major grain-producing and exporting countries, have adversely affected the perspectives of world food and agriculture since the beginning of the 1980s. On the other hand, the remarkable increase in the value of world exports of agricultural, forestry and fishery products has been predominantly price-based rather than caused by an increased volume of products.

In its action to improve the quality of life and the economic returns of rural populations, FAO has attacked the problem of widespread hunger, not as a mere result of inadequate food production but as the most critical element of an overall situation of poverty. In carrying out its aims, the Organization encourages the development of basic soil and water resources, improved production and protection of crops and livestock, and the transfer of technology to agriculture, fisheries and forestry in developing countries, as well as the promotion of agricultural research. It also promotes the preservation of plant genetic resources and the rational use of fertilizers and pesticides; combats epidemics of animal diseases; promotes effective utilization of resources of the seas and inland waters; provides technical assistance in such fields as nutrition, food management and processing, soil erosion control and irrigation engineering; and encourages co-operation among developed and developing countries to achieve stable commodity markets and improve the export earnings of the poorest nations.

The Organization responds to the urgent need for capital for agricultural development by helping developing countries to identify and prepare investment projects that will attract external financing. To this end, it works closely with a number of international and national financing institutions, such as the *World Bank, regional development banks, Arab funds and national development banks. Joint activities with regional development banks increased during the 1980s. In conformity with the strategy currently followed by many investment financing institutions, increasing emphasis is being placed on projects directly affecting the lives of the poorer farmers in developing nations. A special watch is kept on the food situation of the countries experiencing food shortages, through an Early Warning System on areas where famine situations are likely to develop.

In the early 1970s, the Organization put forward proposals to maintain minimum world food security, under an internationally coordinated plan, by building up national food reserves to be used in the event of crop failure or high prices. The World Food Conference, held in Rome in November 1974, endorsed the pro-

posals and requested the Organization to act accordingly. The Food Security Assistance Scheme, set up in 1976, is intended to help developing countries strengthen their food security by creating food reserves as well as by developing national and regional early warning systems. The Organization is also actively engaged in an action programme for the Prevention of Food Losses, launched in 1977. It also attempts to ensure that national nutrition strategies are incorporated by developing countries into their national development plans.

The first global International Conference on Nutrition (ICN), jointly organized by FAO and the *World Health Organization (WHO) in December 1992 in Rome, unanimously adopted a World Declaration on Nutrition, stressing the 'determination to eliminate hunger and to reduce all forms of malnutrition' and recognizing that 'access to nutritionally adequate and safe food is a right of each individual'. The ICN also adopted a Plan of Action for Nutrition and affirmed a determination to revise or prepare national plans of action.

The FAO is a sponsor, together with the UN, of the *World Food Programme (WFP) which became operational in January 1963 and uses food commodities, cash and services (particularly shipping) contributed on a voluntary basis by member countries to back programmes of economic and social development as well as for emergency relief for victims of natural and man-made disasters.

The governing bodies of the Organization and of the WHO established in 1962 the FAO/WHO Codex Alimentarius Commission to protect the health of consumers and to ensure fair practices in the food trade by guiding the preparation and revision of international food standards and by promoting the co-ordination of all the relevant work undertaken by international organizations. Over 150 countries currently participate in the Commission.

World Food Day (WFD) was established by the Organization in November 1979 with the goal that 'food for all' should become a human right for present and future generations; the date chosen – 16 October – is the anniversary of FAO. It has since been observed every year throughout the world, providing a reminder of the Organization's constant search for a long-term solution to the problems of hunger and poverty. On 16 October

1995, the 'Declaration of Québec' was solemnly adopted, to mark the fiftieth anniversary of the founding of the Organization.

The Organization collects the latest information on food, agriculture, forestry and fisheries from all over the world and makes it available to all member countries; statistical yearbooks, surveys and scientific monographs cover a very wide range of agricultural questions. Every ten years the Organization co-ordinates and publishes the results of a census of world agricultural resources.

Director-General: Jacques Diouf

Headquarters: Viale delle Terme di Caracalla, 00100 Rome, Italy (Telephone: +39 6 52251; fax: +39 6 5225 3152)

Publications: *The State of Food and Agriculture* (annual); *Production Yearbook*; *Trade Yearbook*; *Yearbook of Fishery Statistics*; *Yearbook of Forest Products*; *Commodity Review and Outlook*

Reference: S. Marchisio and A. Di Blase, *The Food and Agriculture Organization* (Dordrecht, Boston and London, 1991)

G

Gambia River Development Organization

(Organisation de mise en valeur du fleuve Gambie) (OMVG)

The Organization groups four countries with a view to developing the resources of the river Gambia.

Origin and development
The Organization was set up by Senegal and the Gambia in 1978; the founder countries were joined by Guinea in 1981 and Guinea-Bissau in 1983.

Objectives
The basic aims of the Organization are the co-ordination of the development of the Gambia basin and the preparation of plans for common projects, with special regard to irrigation and hydroelectricity.

Activities
Current activities include projects for the construction of a bridge over the River Gambia and the agricultural development of the Kayanga/Geba and Koliba/Corubal river basins. Studies are under way concerning the integration of energy production and transmission among member countries.

Executive Secretary: Nassirou Diallo
Headquarters: P.O. Box 2353, 13 passage Le Blanc, Dakar, Senegal (Telephone: +221 223159; fax: +221 225926)

General Fisheries Council for the Mediterranean (GFCM)

Established by an international Agreement signed in 1949 under the aegis of the *Food and Agriculture Organization of the UN (FAO), the Council includes some 20 countries bordering the Mediterranean and the Black Sea. Currently, the countries bordering the Black Sea are negotiating a convention regarding the Black Sea fisheries. The purposes of the Council are to promote, in the Mediterranean and the Black Sea, the development, conservation, rational management and best utilization of living marine resources, and to encourage training in co-operative projects. Activities of the Council concentrate on fishery statistics, resource assessments, management measures, and the utilization of small pelagic species, as well as the structures and technologies designed to boost coastal production. Since 1990 the Council has held regular expert consultations on stocks of large pelagic fishes in the Mediterranean with the *International Commission for the Conservation of Atlantic Tuna (ICCAT).

Headquarters: FAO, Room NF-411, Via delle Terme di Caracalla, 00100 Rome, Italy (Telephone: +39 6 5225 6435; fax: +39 6 5225 6500)
Publications: *GFCM Session Reports*; studies and reviews.

Group of Rio

The Group represents an important forum for consultation and policy co-ordination among Latin-American countries.

Origin and development
The Group was founded in Acapulco, Mexico, in 1987 – as the 'Group of Eight' (G-8 Debtor Countries) – to present a joint response of member countries (Argentina, Brazil, Colombia, Mexico, Panama, Peru, Uruguay and Venezuela) to international creditors regarding debt issues; in particular, the participating countries called for a reduction in interest rates and a limit on debt-service payments. Panama was suspended from the Group in 1988 and expelled in March 1990, but later readmitted after the return of a democratic government. Other countries have joined the eight founder members: Bolivia, Chile, Ecuador and Paraguay. Central America is currently represented by Nicaragua; the *Caribbean Community (CARICOM) by Trinidad and Tobago.

Objectives
The Group aims to provide a permanent mechanism for joint political action through consultation and co-ordination in order to liberalize regional trade and expedite the process of Latin-American integration.

Structure

The Group has no legal status and no permanent headquarters. The annual summits of the Heads of State and regular meetings of the Foreign Ministers share the decision-making power.

Activities

The political and economic dialogue between the Group and the *European Union (EU), institutionalized in December 1990 through regular meetings, is based on the tightening of political ties, the stepping-up of economic integration and free trade, and the focusing of co-operation on priority areas. Co-operation is also being developed in the areas of social reform; consolidation of civil society; support for the private sector, and culture, education, science and technology. Increased investment and technology transfers and trade liberalization on the part of EU members have been repeatedly urged by the Group. The sixth Ministerial Conference between the Group and the EU took place in April 1996 in Cochabamba, Bolivia, and focused on four main areas: sustainable development; trade and investment; drug-trafficking; and the fight against corruption and terrorism.

The ninth summit of the Heads of State of the Group was held in Quito, Ecuador, in September 1995 and adopted a 24-point 'Declaration of Quito' including commitments to fight official corruption, drug abuse, drug traffic and drug-related money laundering, and all forms of terrorism. An agreement was reached on the creation of a regional free trade zone by 2005.

The further development and effectiveness of the activities of the Group will depend on closer co-ordination with other regional bodies such as the *Latin American Economic System (SELA) and the *Latin American Integration Association (ALADI).

Group of Seven (G-7)

The Group represents a forum for consultation and policy co-ordination at the highest level among the largest industrial economies.

Origin and development

The first summit took place at Rambouillet, France in November 1975 on the initiative of the French President, Valéry Giscard d'Estaing, German Chancellor, Helmut Schmidt, to discuss the economic crisis following the oil-price shock of 1973–4. Four other Heads of State and Government, from Italy, Japan, the UK and the USA attended the meeting, which concentrated on the world economic situation, on the human, social and political implications of economic problems and on plans for resolving them.

Less than a year later, in June 1976, the Six met again at San Juan, Puerto Rico, and were joined by the Prime Minister of Canada; the G-7 then officially came into existence. The third summit was held at Downing Street, London, in May 1977, by the Seven, with the participation of the President of the Commission of the European Communities. The final Declaration announced measures to maintain the momentum of economic recovery and was supplemented by an Appendix dealing with world economic prospects, balance of payments financing, the international trading system, energy, and North–South relations.

The meeting in Bonn in July 1978 produced an agreement on economic and trade policy co-ordination as well as a statement on air-hijacking.

The Declaration adopted at the conclusion of the Tokyo summit, in June 1979, contained, *inter alia*, figures indicating the ceilings on oil imports agreed upon by the participating countries; statements on Indo-Chinese refugees, and on hijacking supplemented the Declaration.

The June 1980 summit, held in Venice, focused on the price and supply of energy and their implications for the level of economic activity, but other topics were also considered, such as the situation in Afghanistan, hijacking, the taking of diplomatic hostages, and the ever-increasing number of refugees. The following summits held in July 1981 in Ottawa, June 1982 in Versailles, May 1983 in Williamsburg (Virginia), June 1984 in London, May 1985 in Bonn, May 1986 in Tokyo, and June 1987 in Venice were largely devoted to monetary and financial problems, but contained several references to non-economic issues covering terrorism, drugs, arms control issues, and refugees.

International economic policy co-ordination was again discussed by the summit held in Toronto in June 1988, which considered the issue from the standpoint of macroeconomic and exchange-rate policies and also from the angle of structural reform. As to the developing countries' problems with foreign debt, the summit called on the *Paris Club to work out a formula for comparing the different options available for reducing the debt service burden on the poorest countries. An economic declaration and political declarations on East–West relations, China, human rights and terrorism were the outcome of the summit held in Paris in July 1989; a renewed debt strategy applied on a case-by-case basis, and environmental problems were given prominence. The EC Commission was asked to co-ordinate aid for economic restructuring in Poland and Hungary.

Objectives

The Group aims at holding regular and relatively informal discussions on major economic and political international issues and at intensifying efforts for closer co-operation within existing institutions and other international fora. The Group has become closely involved with international financial issues and the work of the relevant multilateral institutions, notably the *International Monetary Fund (IMF). Non-economic issues of paramount importance and urgency gradually came to be considered by the Heads of State and Government in following summits, which therefore lost their strictly economic character.

Structure

The Group, although lacking a formal structure, represents a significant opportunity for the Heads of State and Government of the participating countries, and for the representatives of the *European Union (EU) to discuss major international economic and political issues. At the 1979 Tokyo summit, the Heads of State and Government of the Seven were joined by two representatives of the European Community (EC), that is, the President of the European Commission and the President of the European Council, for discussion of matters within the EC's competence. The participation of the Head of Government holding the six-month rotating presidency of the European Council – in cases when that Head of Government does not belong to a member country of the Group – ensures the representation of other EU members.

The 1986 Tokyo summit decided to form a new Group of Seven Finance Ministers (consisting of the Group of Five Finance Ministers plus Canada and Italy) to work in the periods between the annual summit meetings and to report progress to such meetings. The 1987 Venice summit again asked the Finance Ministers and the governors of the central banks to improve the effectiveness of the co-ordination process with regard to economic policies.

Senior officials (the so-called 'sherpas') and experts from economic and foreign affairs ministries prepare the agenda for the Group's meetings with the aim of working out more detailed commitments.

Activities

The 1990 summit, held in Houston, Texas, in July, discussed the continuation of aid to Central and Eastern European countries and the possibility of granting aid to the USSR, the still-unresolved Uruguay Round issues, and several political matters such as terrorism and the non-proliferation of nuclear, chemical and biological weapons. An economic declaration, a political declaration on the international order, and a declaration on sales of conventional weapons and the non-proliferation of nuclear, chemical and biological weapons resulted from the summit held in London in July 1991. A decision was also adopted to hold an annual high-level meeting with the USSR.

The summit held in Munich in July 1992 was aimed at defining, *inter alia*, a new economic and political partnership with the rest of Europe and the rest of the world, and discussing the measures needed to ensure stronger, sustainable, non-inflationary growth based on sound monetary and financial policies.

At the summit which took place in July 1993 in Tokyo measures were agreed upon in order to bring about a rapid reduction in European interest rates, to ensure a reduction in the US budget deficit, and to achieve growth led by strong domestic demand in Japan. Special measures were adopted to support the privatization and restructuring programme in Russia.

The twentieth summit took place in Naples in July 1994 with the participation of the Russian President in political discussions. The Heads of State and Government considered measures to maintain the momentum of liberalization of international trade, to strengthen international co-operation on environmental matters, to fight transnational crime and money-laundering, and to intensify assistance to developing and transition economies.

The twenty-first summit was held in Halifax (Canada) in June 1995, with the Russian President participating in political discussions on the role of the UN, arms control and the extension of the Nuclear Non-Proliferation Treaty, and the fight against terrorism and organized crime. With regard to economic matters, the summit stressed the importance of the role of international economic organizations, recommending improvements to the early warning and surveillance system for economic policies and financial markets of the IMF, the strengthening of the role of the newly-created *World Trade Organization (WTO), and the development of activities by multilateral agencies to promote sustainable development, combat poverty and provide humanitarian and emergency aid.

Many of the issues of the preceding summit were again considered by the twenty-second summit, held in Lyons, France, in June 1996. The economic declaration dealt, *inter alia*, with trade and investment issues, stating the commitment of the Seven to the rules of WTO and the 'codes' of the *Organization for Economic Co-operation and Development (OECD). The political declaration, adopted with the participation of Russia, stressed the commitment of the parties to support the peace process in Bosnia and Herzegovina, recognized the gravity of the financial crisis of the UN and the necessity to review the scale of individual contributions, and reaffirmed the willingness of the G-7+1 to conclude negotiations in Geneva on a Comprehensive Test Ban Treaty (CTBT) in the nuclear field. A G-7+1 summit specially devoted to nuclear safety and security had been held in April 1996 in Moscow adopting a declaration, two statements and a programme for preventing and combating illicit trafficking in nuclear material.

The Group has been playing an effective role in policy co-ordination among its member countries on several major international issues, paying an increasing attention to political matters and gradually involving Russia in the decision-making process. On the other hand, the lack of a proper institutional framework has hindered to a certain extent the effective supervision over the implementation of the commitments undertaken by the various members. In the longer term, the composition of the Group itself may be called into question and eventually lead to the entry of large and fast growing non-European economies in replacement of some current members.

Group of Seventy-seven (G-77)

The Group is the main forum for consultation and policy co-ordination on major international economic issues among the developing countries.

Origin and development

The emergence of the Group took place at the first session of the *UN Conference on Trade and Development (UNCTAD), held in 1964 in Geneva. The unity of the then 77 developing countries at UNCTAD I originated from the common interest in a new international trade and development policy to be articulated through a permanent instrument. Although lacking a proper institutional machinery, the Group managed to take advantage of the existing regional groups which had already established permanent co-ordination links between themselves.

Being focused mainly on economic and commercial matters – without taking a stand on highly controversial political issues – the Group has been able to enlarge its membership to include nearly all the developing countries in the world, unlike the *Non-Aligned Movement (NAM), whose often 'aligned' positions have sometimes discouraged moderate pro-Western developing nations from participation. The Group currently includes some 130 countries, of which over a third are in Africa and the rest almost equally distributed between two regions, Latin America and the Caribbean, and the Asia-Pacific, with only a few members in Europe; China enjoys associate membership.

Objectives

The Group's main goal is the elaboration and implementation of common strategies on trade and development issues in international forums, with a view to enhancing the bargaining power of developing countries *vis-à-vis* the industrialized nations of the West.

Structure

The annual meeting of the Ministers for Foreign Affairs of the member countries represents the most important decision-making body. The Office of the Chairman of the Group is based in New York. The Joint Co-ordinating Committee (JCC), established in New York in partnership with NAM, operates under the chairmanship of the presidents of the two movements and plays a significant role in harmonizing their respective positions on North–South as well as in South–South issues.

Activities

Over the past three decades the Group's policies have been dictated at different times by the 'moderates' or by the 'radicals', depending on the prevailing balance of power within the '77'. Unity of intent has often been achieved at the highest level of demand *vis-à-vis* the developed world, which made it extremely difficult to achieve concrete results. The Group, then consisting of nearly 90 countries, met in 1967 in Algiers to prepare for UNCTAD II to be held in New Delhi in 1968; as a result of the meeting, the 'Charter of Algiers' was approved, expressing the Group's position before UNCTAD II.

Attempts to work out a common and realistic approach *vis-à-vis* the developed nations were made in 1971 in Lima, Peru, by the 77 (which numbered at that time nearly 100) in preparation for UNCTAD III scheduled for 1972 in Santiago, Chile. Many divisions emerged within the Group on major issues, the only significant result of UNCTAD III being the proposal for a 'Charter of Economic Rights and Duties of States', later approved by the UN General Assembly. However, the implementation of a 'New International Economic Order' proved impossible during the second half of the 1970s, while the South–South gap widened, with a number of developing countries attaining remarkable rates of growth and other developing countries dramatically affected by the sudden rise in oil prices. The fragmentation of the developed world and the diverging interests of major regions – Africa, Asia and Latin America – made it difficult to articulate clearly-defined goals concerning international debt of developing countries and the lowering of tariff barriers of developed nations. The Cancen meeting of 22 Heads of State in October 1981 failed to achieve institutionalization as a permanent forum for North–South dialogue and new sources of dissensions arose within the Group.

The growing difficulties surrounding a meaningful North–South dialogue in the 1980s called into question the bloc-to-bloc approach to international trade and development issues, while the continuation of the activities of UNCTAD itself seemed in jeopardy. The emergence of regional and subregional integration goupings with their own specific interests and goals and the end of the Cold War and the anti-colonial struggle seemed to deprive the Group of its original raison d'être.

Although the Group has managed to maintain its unity and still has a role to play in international for, the present international climate calls for a major change of attitude going far beyond the traditional approach which had characterized the Group's early experience.

Office of the Chairman of the Group of 77:   c/o UN Secretariat, Room S-3959, New York, NY 10017, USA (Telephone: +1 212 963 4777; fax: +1 212 963 3515)

Publication: *Group of 77 Journal* (monthly newsletter)

Group of Three (G-3)

The Group aims to liberalize trade among its member countries.

Origin and development

The Groups is formed by Colombia, Mexico and Venezuela, which in December 1993 concluded a trade pact dealing with access to markets, rules of origin, trade in services, intellectual property, and government purchases. A free-trade agreement was signed by the Heads of State of the member countries in June 1994 and came into effect in January 1995; it envisages the gradual elimination of most tariff and non-tariff barriers and the setting up of a dispute resolution body.

Objectives

The Group aims to foster economic cooperation among member countries, initially by removing restrictions on trade. Co-operation is also envisaged with regard to employment, health and energy body.

Activities

A framework trade agreement was concluded by the Group with El Salvador, Guatemala and Honduras in February 1993. At an important meeting of the Group with the *Caribbean Community and Common Market (CARICOM) and Suriname in October 1993 joint agreements were concluded to combat drug-trafficking and to promote environmental protection activities. In July 1994 members of the Group were among the signatories of the founding agreement of the *Association of Caribbean States (ACS).

Contact address: Grupo de los Tres, Torre Ministerio de Relaciones Exteriores, Conde à Carmelitas, Código 1010, 2° Piso, Dirección General, Caracas, Venexula (Telephone: +58 2 881847 8610909; fax: +58 2 861 1528)

I

Indian Ocean Commission (IOC)

The Commission fosters economic co-operation among Indian Ocean island countries.

Origin and development

The establishment of the Commission was announced in July 1982 by Madagascar, Mauritius and the Seychelles; in December 1982 the Foreign Ministers of the three countries agreed on the basic features of the new body. A general agreement on regional co-operation was signed in January 1984. France (representing Réunion) and the Comoro Islands joined the Commission as full members in January 1986.

Objectives

The purpose of the Commission is to promote regional co-operation in all sectors, with special emphasis on economic development.

Structure

Annual ministerial sessions, under a rotating chairmanship, represent the policy-making body. The first meeting of Heads of State or Government of the member countries took place in 1991. The Secretary-General, elected for a four-year term by the ministerial session, is charged with the implementation of projects. Permanent committees cover the main areas of co-operation. The Committee of Permanent Liaison Officers (OPL) prepares the ministerial sessions and implements the relevant decisions.

Activities

Projects currently under consideration regard research on new and renewable energy systems, the development of tuna fishing, the encouragement of regional tourism, the promotion of industrial co-operation, the protection and management of environmental resources, and the strengthening of meteorological services. Substantial financial assistance is being provided by the European Community (EC). Attempts are also being made to stimulate and intensify trade links among member countries.

Secretary-General: J. Bonnelame
Headquarters: 4 avenue Sir Guy Forget, P.O. Box 7, Quatre Bornes, Mauritius (Telephone: +230 425 9564; fax: +230 425 1209)
Publication: *Guide Import/Export*

Indian Ocean Fishery Commission (IOFC)

Established by a resolution of the Council of the *Food and Agriculture Organization (FAO) in 1967, the Commission has a membership of 45 countries; its competence covers all living marine resources of the Indian Ocean and the adjacent seas, with exclusion of the Antarctic area. The Commission promotes research activities and programmes for fishery development and conservation and examines management problems, with particular reference to offshore resources.

As a consequence of the entry into force in March 1996 of the Agreement establishing the *Indian Ocean Tuna Commission (IOTC), the activities of the Commission will be limited to species other than tuna; since these species are geographically localized, the three remaining subsidiary bodies of the Commission appear to be well placed to manage the relevant fishery resources at the subregional level.

Headquarters: FAO, Room NF-412, Via delle Terme di Caracalla, 00100 Rome, Italy (Telephone: +39 6 5225 3637; fax: +39 6 5225 6500)

Indian Ocean Tuna Commission (IOTC)

The Commission promotes the conservation and management of stocks of tuna in the Indian Ocean.

Origin and development

The Commission was established in 1994 by an Agreement concluded – after a long negotiating process initiated in early 1989 – under the aegis of the *Food and Agriculture Organization of the UN (FAO); the Agreement came into force in March 1996. As a consequence of the establishment of the Commission, the competences of the already existing *Indian Ocean Fishery Commission (IOFC) have been substantially reduced and confined to species other than tuna. Members of the Commission are countries belonging to the Indian Ocean region as well as countries whose vessels engage in fishing in the area. The European Community (EC) is also a member in its own right as a regional economic integration organization contemplated by the Commission's founding Agreement.

Objectives
The Commission aims to keep under review the conditions and trends of the stocks, and to gather and disseminate the relevant scientific and statistical information; to co-ordinate research and development activities, including the transfer of technology; and to adopt conservation and management measures, bearing in mind, in particular, the interests of developing coastal countries.

Activities
The area of competence of the Commission is defined as the Indian Ocean and adjacent seas, north of the Antarctic convergence, in so far as it is necessary to cover such seas for the purpose of conserving and managing stocks migrating into or out of the Indian Ocean.

Headquarters (temporary):   FAO, Room NF-412, Via delle Terme di Caracalla, 00100 Rome, Italy (Telephone: +39 6 5225 3637; fax: +39 6 5225 6500)

Inter-American Development Bank (IDB)

The Bank is the oldest regional institution in the world in the field of development financing, and its volume of operations is second only to the *International Bank for Reconstruction and Development (IBRD).

Origin and development
Recurring Latin American proposals to the USA for the creation of an inter-American agency contributing capital resources and technical assistance on flexible terms and conditions were eventually accepted in 1958 within the framework of an overall plan (Operation Pan-America) to further economic co-operation in the Western hemisphere. The agreement establishing the Bank was signed in April 1959 in Washington DC by the representatives of the member countries of the *Organization of American States (OAS), at that time the USA and 20 Latin American republics; it came into effect in December 1959. The Bank began operations in Washington DC in October 1960. Membership of the Bank was substantially increased in the latter half of the 1970s to include nations outside the Western hemisphere, and now totals 46 countries. Most countries in North and South America and the Caribbean (except Cuba) belong to the Bank, along with 16 countries in Europe, Israel and Japan.

Objectives
According to the Charter, the Bank's basic goal is to contribute to the acceleration of development of member countries, individually and collectively, through financing economic and social development projects and provision of technical assistance. To achieve its aims, the Bank promotes public and private investment for development purposes, uses its own capital, the funds borrowed in the world capital markets, and other resources to finance the development of its members, extends financial assistance to encourage private investment in cases where private capital is not available at reasonable terms, and provides technical co-operation with regard to resource surveys, feasibility studies and professional training. Loans are usually granted for specific development projects to governments, public agencies, and private enterprises, without requiring a guarantee from the government concerned; since 1990 loans are also granted for the implementation of economic adjustment programmes.

Structure
The Bank's structure includes the Board of Governors, the Executive Directors, and the President. All the powers are vested in the Board of Governors, which consists of one governor and one alternate governor for each member country and meets once a year, usually in a Latin American capital. Each member has 135 votes, plus one vote for each share of capital stock held. Most powers are delegated by the Board of Governors to the Executive Directors, permanently residing in Washington DC, who conduct the Bank's general operations. There are at present twelve Executive Directors, eight elected

by Latin American countries, two by member countries outside the region, one appointed by the USA and one by Canada. The President of the Bank is elected by the Board of Governors and acts as Chairman of the Executive Directors; the Executive Vice-President is nominated by the Executive Directors. Felipe Herrera of Chile served as President from the foundation of the Bank until 1970; he was succeeded by Antonio Ortiz Mena of Mexico. The current President is Enrique Iglesias of Uruguay.

Activities

The Bank operates with its ordinary capital resources and a Fund for Special Operations, both contributed by all member countries. In addition to its own resources, the Bank administers other funds entrusted to it by several donor countries (both member and non-member) for financial assistance to Latin America. The ordinary resources of the Bank are made up of the subscribed capital stock and retained earnings, and, to a very large extent, of the funds raised in the capital markets through the issue of securities and the sale of short-term bonds to central banks. The resources are also replenished through the flow of repayments. The capital stock initially authorized by the Charter amounted to $850 million, divided into 85 000 shares having a par value of $10 000 each. The shares originally subscribed by the USA amounted to $350 million. Because of repeated general increases in the shares and the doubling of the Bank's members, the size of the capital stock has grown substantially. At the end of 1993, the subscribed ordinary capital stock, including interregional capital, amounted to $54.2 million, of which $3.2 million had been paid in. The remainder was subject to call if required to meet the obligations assumed by the Bank in order to increase its lendable ordinary resources.

Replenishments are made every four years. In 1983, agreement was reached on the Sixth Replenishment, raising the authorized capital to $35 000 million. Agreement on the Seventh Replenishment was finally reached in April 1989. Further increases in the Bank's capital were announced in April 1994. Lending from the Bank's ordinary capital resources (that is, hard loans made on commercial terms) may not exceed the net amount of subscribed capital. Loans are not tied to the purchase of goods and services in any specific

country and are repayable in the currencies loaned over a period ranging from 15 to 40 years.

In cases where lending of the more traditional type cannot be effective, the Bank makes concessional (non-commercial) loans through the Fund for Special Operations whose resources are made up of the contributions of all members. Concessional loans are granted under terms and conditions which take into account the particular practical constraints arising in specific countries, or with respect to specific projects. Lower interest rates are charged and longer repayment terms are allowed than those applied to loans from the ordinary resources. In most cases, loans may be repaid in whole or in part in the currency of the borrower.

A Multilateral Investment Fund, aimed at providing technical assistance and facilitating private investment in the region, was established in 1993 by 21 Bank members pledging to contribute $1.2 billion.

Besides the ordinary and special operations resources, a number of funds placed under its administration enable the Bank to extend additional financial assistance to developing member countries. A role of outstanding importance has been played by the Social Progress Trust Fund, established by the USA under the ten-year programme of the Alliance for Progress in 1961 in the sum of $394 million; an additional $131 million contribution in 1964 raised the total amount to $525 million. In spite of repeated Latin American requests to the USA, no further replenishments of the Social Progress Trust Fund have been provided. Several Western European countries, Japan, Canada and Argentina have been providing aid through the agency of special funds entrusted to the Bank. A fund was established by the UK in 1966, and additional contributions were made in 1971 and 1972. The Vatican set up a $1 million fund in 1969, in connection with the encyclical Populorum Progressio. Another fund, equivalent to $500 million, was established in 1975 by the Venezuelan Investment Fund. A technical Co-operation Fund Programme was established in 1991. Loans from these special funds are extended under terms mutually agreed between the Bank and the countries providing the funds.

The Bank maintains close working relations with the World Bank and other international and regional agencies in order to assure the coordination of technical and financial development assistance activities. Since approval of the

Seventh Replenishment, the Bank has initiated programmes of sector-adjustment and structural-adjustment lending and several operations have been cofinanced with the World Bank.

At 31 December 1993, cumulative lending by the Bank amounted to $45 975 million, of which $34 635 million was from the ordinary and inter-regional capital; $9775 million from the Fund for Special Operations; and $1565 million from the other funds. Almost all the developing member countries of the region have obtained the Bank's loans: Brazil and Mexico have been the largest recipients, followed by Argentina, Colombia and Chile. The sectoral distribution of loans has covered all major areas: agricultural projects, industry, energy and non-fuel minerals, water and sewerage facilities, low-cost housing, transportation and communications, electric power, education and tourism, pre-investment funds, and export financing. Technical co-operation has been provided in conjunction with specific development loans, or arranged independently.

The Bank's attention is being focused increasingly on integrating the poorest sections of population in the development process through an expansion of productive work opportunities and an effort to manage the continuing rapid shift from rural to urban areas. After the capital increase agreed upon in 1989, the Bank has started lending for sectoral reforms in order to allow developing member countries to introduce policy changes and improve institutions. On the whole, the Bank has had a remarkable impact on Latin American economic and social development, despite the inadequacy of its resources in relation to the magnitude of the problems that face the poorer developing countries of Latin America and the Caribbean.

The Institute for Latin American and Caribbean Integration (INTAL) was created in 1964 as an international agency for the Bank, with headquarters in Buenos Aires (Esmeralda 130, 1035 Buenos Aires). The Institute has provided technical co-operation services concerning the various aspects of the integration process to the Bank units, individual developing member countries, organizations for regional co-operation, and other public and private institutions; a new and more focused strategy was adopted in 1996.

In March 1986, the Charter of the Inter-American Investment Corporation (IIC), an institu-tion affiliated to the Bank, came into force, with a view to encouraging private investment, especially in small- and medium-sized enterprises. The initial capital stock of IIC amounted to $200 million, of which 55 per cent was contributed by developing member countries, 25.5 per cent by the USA, and the remainder by members outside the region.

President: Enrique V. Iglesias
Headquarters: 1300 New York Avenue, N.W., Washington DC 20577, USA (Telephone: +1 202 623 1000; fax: +1 202 623 3096)
Internet address: http: //www.adb.org
Publications: *Annual Report*; *Economic and Social Progress in Latin America* (annual survey)

Inter-American Tropical Tuna Commission (I-ATTC)

Established by an international Convention signed in 1949 and entering into force in 1950, the Commission has the Eastern Pacific Ocean as its area of competence; membership currently includes Costa Rica, France, Japan, Nicaragua, Panama, the USA, Vanuatu and Venezuela. The purposes of the Commission are to study the biology, ecology and population dynamics of the tropical tuna and related species of the eastern Pacific Ocean with a view to determining the effects of fishing and natural factors on stocks and to recommend joint action for appropriate conservation measures. In 1992, the countries participating in the surface fishery for tunas in the Eastern Pacific Ocean reached agreement on an International Dolphin Conservation Programme (IDCP) intended to reduce gradually the mortality of dolphins from around 19 500 in 1993 to less than 5000 in 1999.

Headquarters: c/o Scripps Institution of Oceanography, 8604 La Jolla Shores Drive, La Jolla, California 92037, USA (Telephone: +1 619 546 7100; fax: +1 619 546 7133)
Publications: *Annual Report*; *Bulletin* (irregular)

Intergovernmental Authority on Drought and Development (IGADD)

The Authority groups seven countries of Eastern Africa in their fight against drought.

Origin and development

As a response to the severe drought that had affected their respective countries, the Heads of State and Government of Djibouti, Ethiopia, Kenya, Somalia, Sudan and Uganda decided to create the Authority at a conference held in January 1986 in Djibouti. Organizational and financial rules were established the following April at a meeting of the Council of Ministers of the member countries, with a view to attracting the interest of potential international donors. Eritrea became the seventh member of the Authority in September 1993, shortly after having achieved independence.

Objectives

The purposes of the Authority are to co-ordinate measures with a view to combating the effects of drought and desertification and to promote regional policies and projects on short- and medium-term economic development.

Structure

The principal organs of the Authority comprise the Assembly of the Heads of State and Government, which is the highest policy-making body, the Council of Ministers, in charge of implementing decisions, and the Secretariat. In 1992 proposals were put forward to streamline the institutional mechanism and to establish links with the *Arab Maghreb Union (UMA) and the *Permanent Inter-State Committee on Drought Control in the Sahel (CILSS).

Activities

Implementation of projects concerning the creation of an early-warning system for drought, proper storage and distribution of food, and promotion of agricultural research and water resources management has been hindered by widespread domestic unrest, including rebel activity and, in countries such as Ethiopia, Somalia and Sudan, large-scale civil wars. Difficulties were further exacerbated by the existence of substantial arrears in the contributions of members. Peace initiatives have been undertaken by the Authority in some member countries to end civil wars, but results have been limited. At a special meeting of the Heads of State held in April 1995 in Addis Ababa, Ethiopia, the relaunching and ex-

pansion of the goals of the Authority were considered in order to improve the co-ordination of development and trade policies and food security strategies, as well as to create favourable conditions for foreign investment.

Executive Secretary: David Stephen Muduuli
Headquarters: P.O. Box 2653, Djibouti (Telephone: +253 354050; fax: +253 356994)
Publications: *Annual Report*; *Food Situation Report* (quarterly)

International Atomic Energy Agency (IAEA)

The Agency seeks to accelerate and enlarge the contribution of atomic energy to peace, health and prosperity throughout the world, and to ensure that the assistance provided to that effect is not used for the furtherance of military purposes.

Origin and development

The text of the Statute of the Agency was adopted unanimously in October 1956 by a UN International Conference on the Peaceful Uses of Atomic Energy, held in New York, and entered into force in July 1957. A relationship agreement linking the Agency with the UN entered into effect in November 1957. According to the agreement, the Agency has a special status *vis-à-vis* the UN: it is 'under the aegis of the UN' and functions 'as an autonomous international organization' reporting annually to the UN General Assembly and, as appropriate, to the Security Council and the Economic and Social Council. The Agency is not, therefore, a 'specialized agency' according to the UN Charter, though administratively it is part of the UN system. The present membership of the Agency includes over 120 countries. All countries with significant nuclear programmes and activities participate in the Agency.

Any sovereign country, whether or not a member of the UN or of any of the specialized agencies, may be admitted to participation in the Agency, provided that approval has been secured by the General Conference upon the recommendation of the Board of Governors. Any member may withdraw from the Agency by giving written notice to that effect. Provision is made for the suspension from the exercise of the privileges and rights of membership of any country which has persistently violated the Statute.

Each member should make available such information as it judges to be helpful to the Agency. Any member or group of members wishing to set up research projects for peaceful purposes may request the assistance of the Agency in securing special fissionable and other materials.

With respect to any of its projects or other arrangement where it is requested by the parties concerned to apply safeguards, the Agency has the right to examine and approve the design of specialized equipment and facilities, including nuclear reactors, to require the observance of health and safety measures as well as the maintenance and production of operating records, to call for and receive progress reports, to approve the means for the chemical processing of irradiated materials, and to send into the territory of the recipient country inspectors having access at all times to all places and data, and to any relevant person. In the event of non-compliance and failure by the recipient to take corrective steps within a reasonable time, the Agency is authorized to suspend or terminate assistance and withdraw any materials and equipment made available.

Objectives

According to the Statute, the Agency is authorized: (a) to encourage and assist research on, and development and practical application of, atomic energy for peaceful purposes; (b) to make provision for materials, services, equipment and facilities to meet the needs of research and practical application; (c) to foster the exchange of scientific and technical information on peaceful uses of atomic energy; (d) to encourage the exchange and training of scientists and experts; (e) to establish and administer safeguards designed to ensure that special fissionable and other materials, services, equipment, facilities and information made available are not diverted to military use; (f) to establish, in consultation or collaboration with the competent organs of the UN and the specialized agencies concerned, standards of safety for protection of health and minimization of danger to life and property; and (g) to acquire or establish

facilities, plant and equipment which are deemed useful for the implementation of its tasks.

The Agency is also authorized to provide for the application of safeguards and standards, at the request of the parties, to operations under any bilateral or multilateral arrangement or, at the request of any country, to any of that country's activities in the field of atomic energy. Activities are to be conducted by the Agency in conformity with UN policies furthering the establishment of 'safeguarded worldwide disarmament'. Moreover, resources must be allocated in such a manner as to secure efficient utilization and the greatest possible general benefit in all areas of the world, bearing in mind the special needs of the developing nations.

Structure

The Agency's structure is made up of three principal organs: the General Conference, the Board of Governors, and the Secretariat. The General Conference, consisting of representatives of all member countries, meets in regular annual sessions and in such special sessions as may be necessary. It is empowered to discuss any questions within the scope of the Statute and may make recommendations to the membership of the Agency and/or the Board of Governors. The General Conference establishes the Agency's policies and programmes, approves the budget, considers the annual report of the Board of Governors, decides on applications for membership and suspends member countries from the privileges and rights of membership, elects members of the Board of Governors and approves the appointment of the Director-General. Decisions of the General Conference on financial questions, amendments to the Statute and suspension from membership require a two-thirds majority of the members present and voting; decision on other questions is made by simple majority.

The Board of Governors consists of the representatives of 35 member countries. It meets about four times a year and carries out the executive functions. The General Conference elects 22 of the Board members, and 13 are designated by the Board itself. The designation criteria, such as the level of advancement in nuclear technology and equitable geographical distribution, ensure adequate representation and continuity of membership. Under its own authority, the Board approves all safeguards agreements, important projects and safety standards. Decisions of the Board are made by a majority of the members present and voting, with the exception of decisions on the Agency's budget which require a two-thirds majority.

The Secretariat is headed by the Director-General who is appointed by the Board of Governors for a renewable four-year term and is responsible for the administration and implementation of the Agency's programme.

Annual budget estimates for the expenses of the Agency are prepared by the Director-General and submitted for approval, through the Board of Governors, to the General Conference. Administrative expenses are apportioned by the Board of Governors among member countries, in accordance with a scale fixed by the General Conference. The Board of Governors is responsible for establishing periodically a scale of charges, including storage and handling charges, for materials, services, equipment and facilities furnished to member countries by the Agency.

Activities

Since the very beginning of its activities, the Agency has entered into co-operation agreements with many specialized UN institutions such as the *UN Educational, Scientific and Cultural Organization (UNESCO), the *International Labour Organization (ILO), the *World Health Organization (WHO), the *World Meteorological Organization (WMO), the *International Civil Aviation Organization (ICAO) and the *Food and Agriculture Organization of the UN (FAO). In 1964, the Agency and the FAO combined forces in a Joint Division of Atomic Energy in Food and Agriculture. An International Consultative Group on Food Irradiation (ICGFI), currently consisting of 43 countries, has been operating since 1984. Technical assistance programmes are carried out within the framework of the *UN Development Programme (UNDP) and many large-scale projects are in operation. Several projects are also being implemented jointly with the *UN Environment Programme (UNEP). The work of the Agency is carried out in co-operation with dozens of other bodies, both non-governmental and intergovernmental, such as the *Organization for Economic Co-operation and Development (OECD).

The Agency has made a substantial contribution to the development of the peaceful uses of atomic energy on a world-wide scale. It has formulated basic safety standards for radiation protection, and issued regulations and codes of practice on specific types of operation, including the safe transport of radioactive materials. A system has been established by the Agency to facilitate emergency assistance to member countries in the event of radiation accidents. Codes of practice and safety guides have been prepared in the areas of governmental organization, siting, design, operation and quality assurance with regard to nuclear power reactors. In 1961, the Agency adopted a safeguards system for small research reactors. Subsequent amendments have expanded the system to cover all types and sizes of nuclear plants. In 1982, with a view to providing member countries with advice on the safe operation of nuclear power plants, the Agency set up operational safety review teams which visit power plants on request. After the accident to the nuclear power plant at Chernobyl, Ukraine, in April 1986, proposals were put forward in order to reinforce the Agency's role in developing safer plants and preventing nuclear terrorism. Two conventions were drawn up in 1986 under the auspices of the Agency: the first commits parties to provide early notification and information about nuclear accidents with possible trans-boundary effects; the second commits parties to endeavour to provide assistance in the event of a nuclear accident or radiological emergency.

Assistance is also provided to member countries on technical, safety, environmental and economic aspects of nuclear fuel cycle technology, including uranium prospecting and radioactive waste management. In co-operation with OECD, every two years the Agency prepares estimates of world uranium resources, demand and production. The Waste Management Advisory Programme (WAMAP) was created in 1987. A code of practice to prevent the illegal dumping of radioactive waste was drawn up in 1989, and a further code on the international trans-boundary movement of waste was drawn up in 1990.

In March 1970 the Treaty on the Non-Proliferation of Nuclear Weapons (NPT) came into force. It requires the 'non-nuclear-weapon' countries to conclude safeguards agreements with the Agency, covering all nuclear materials in all their peaceful nuclear activities. Between 1978 and 1981, three nuclear-weapon countries (the UK, the USA and France) concluded safeguards agreements with the Agency. Another nuclear-weapon country, the then USSR, had concluded an agreement with the Agency in 1985 on the application of safeguards to certain Soviet peaceful nuclear installations. A safeguards agreement with China was signed in 1988. The Agency also administers full applications of safeguards in relation to the 1967 Treaty for the Prohibition of Nuclear Weapons in Latin America (Tlatelolco Treaty) on the basis of a co-operation agreement concluded in 1972 with the *Agency for the Prohibition of Nuclear Weapons in Latin America and the Caribbean (OPANAL).

A significant role has been played by Agency's teams in inspecting Iraq's nuclear research facilities according to the terms of the UN cease-fire in the Gulf War of 1991. Since May 1994 inspectors of the Agency have been monitoring the freeze of the graphite moderated reactor programme in the Democratic People's Republic of Korea. The Agency also verified the abandonment by South Africa, in 1993, of its nuclear weapon capacity, the first such instance in the world.

A Convention on Nuclear Safety was adopted under the auspices of the Agency in 1994; the Agency administers the Convention on Physical Protection of Nuclear Material of 1987 and the Vienna Convention on Civil Liability for Nuclear Damage of 1977.

The Agency's safeguards system is primarily based on nuclear material accountancy, with containment and surveillance being important complementary measures. About 850 nuclear installations and other locations are currently under the Agency's safeguards, representing around 95 per cent of the world's nuclear facilities and materials outside the five nuclear-weapon countries.

In 1970, the Agency established the International Nuclear Information System (INIS), which covers virtually every aspect of the peaceful uses of nuclear science and technology, and employs a technique of decentralized input preparation combined with centralized processing of information. The Agency co-operates with FAO in an information system for agriculture (AGRIS). Over the years, a large number of international conferences and symposia, as well as smaller panel and group meetings, have been organized by the Agency to enable scientists and experts to discuss new ideas and developments.

A remarkable contribution of the Agency in the field of pure science was the establishment in 1964 of the International Centre for Theoretical Physics in Trieste, Italy – now operated jointly with UNESCO. The Centre offers seminars followed by a research workshop, as well as short topical seminars, training courses, symposia and panels.

The Agency's programme in physical sciences is concentrated on practical problems arising from the use of atomic energy, radiations and isotopes, particularly in developing countries. With regard to life sciences, the Agency co-operates with WHO in the fields of medical applications of radioisotopes and instrumentation, dosimetry for intentional radiation applications, and radiation biology.

In its technical assistance programme, the Agency seeks to promote the transfer of skills and knowledge relating to the peaceful uses of atomic energy to enable the recipient developing countries to carry out their atomic energy activities safely and more efficiently. Since 1958, the Agency has provided technical assistance to developing countries in the form of services of advisers, fellowships, training opportunities and equipment. In collaboration with FAO, the Agency conducts programmes of applied research on the use of radiation and isotopes.

Director-General: Hans Blix
Headquarters: Vienna International Centre, Wagramerstrasse 5, P.O. Box 100, 1400 Vienna, Austria (Telephone: +43 1 2060-0; fax: +43 1 20607)
Publications: *Annual Report*; *Nuclear Safety Review* (annual); *IAEA Newsbriefs* (monthly); *IAEA Bulletin* (quarterly); *Nuclear Fusion* (monthly); *Meetings on Atomic Energy* (quarterly); *INIS Atomindex* (fortnightly)

International Baltic Sea Fishery Commission (IBSFC)

Established by an international Convention signed in 1973 and entering into force in 1974, the Commission includes as members the three

Baltic countries, Poland, Russia and the *European Community (EC). The Commission aims to co-ordinate scientific research and to recommend regulatory measures, including catch quotas and enforcement schemes, for the Baltic Sea and the Belts, as well as to take other steps toward rational and effective exploitation of the living resources. The Commission examines in yearly sessions the actual state and expected future changes in stocks of cod, herring, sprat and salmon. Whenever feasible, the Commission sets total allowable catches as well as their allocation among member countries.

Headquarters: Hoza 20, 00-528 Warsaw, Poland (Telephone: +48 2 628 8647; fax: +48 2 625 3372)

International Bank for Reconstruction and Development (IBRD)

The Bank, a specialized agency of the UN, is the leading organization in the field of multilateral financing of investment and technical assistance and, because of the recent increase in its membership, has become a truly global institution.

Origin and development
Together with the *International Monetary Fund (IMF), the Bank originated from the UN Monetary and Financial Conference held at Bretton Woods, New Hampshire (USA), in July 1944, with the participation of 44 countries. According to the 'division of labour' between the two institutions envisaged at Bretton Woods, the Bank was to be concerned essentially with long-term project and economic development finance, while the Fund's activities were primarily intended to provide temporary balance-of-payments assistance. The Bank, whose Articles of Agreement came into force in December 1945, began operations in Washington DC in June 1946. Although initially concerned with the reconstruction of Europe after the Second World War, the Bank has essentially been providing funds and technical assistance to developing nations and underdeveloped areas of the industrialized world. Only members of the IMF are eligible for membership in the Bank; in turn, the latter is a prerequisite for membership of the *International Development Association (IDA), the *International Finance Corporation (IFC) and

the *Multilateral Investment Guarantee Agency (MIGA). The Bank and IDA, although legally and financially distinct, are from an operational standpoint a closely integrated unit, sharing the same staff.

The 'World Bank', as it is commonly known, comprises the IBRD and IDA; these two institutions, together with the IFC, MIGA and the *International Centre for Settlement of Investment Disputes (ICSID) form the 'World Bank Group', whose common objective is to meet the entire range of the financial and technical requirements of development by channelling financial resources from industrial countries to the developing world. ICSID operates, as a distinct international organization, at the Bank's headquarters. Membership of the Bank totals about 180 countries of the industrial and developing world in widely different stages of economic development and representing a variety of economic systems, from centrally planned to market economies. Among non-members mention must be made of Cuba, North Korea, and Taiwan, the latter having been replaced as a member by the People's Republic of China in 1980. Russia and the other former Soviet republics joined in early 1992.

The first operations of the Bank included the lending of $497 million to West European countries to facilitate the importation of essential goods. After the launching of the Marshall Plan and the assumption by the Organization for European Economic Co-operation (OEEC) of the task of economic recovery in Western Europe, the Bank has concentrated essentially on assisting the economic development of its member nations.

Objectives
The Bank extends financial assistance in cases where private capital is not available at reasonable terms; promotes private investment loans through guarantees or participations; and provides technical assistance in the field of overall development plans and specific investment projects. Project loans may include funds earmarked for resource surveys, feasibility studies and training.

Structure
The organization of the Bank, which is similar to that of the IMF, comprises the Board of Governors, the Executive Directors, and the

President.The Board of Governors is vested with full management powers and consists of one governor and one alternate governor appointed by each member country. The Board of Governors normally holds an annual meeting to consider the Bank's operations and set down the basic guidelines to be implemented by the Executive Directors, to whom the Board delegates many of its powers. The powers that cannot be delegated by the governors concern, inter alia, the admission of new members, changes in the capital stock and the distribution of the net income of the Bank. The Board's decisions are adopted by a majority of the votes cast, except as otherwise specifically provided. Each member has 250 votes, plus one additional vote for each share of stock held; voting rights are therefore related to the amount of each country's quota in the Bank's capital stock. As of 30 June 1995, the largest shareholder was the USA, which subscribed 17.48 per cent of the capital stock and held 16.98 per cent of the total voting power. Japan subscribed 6.41 per cent and held 6.24 per cent of the voting power. The respective percentages were 4.95 and 4.82 for Germany; and 4.74 and 4.62 each for France and the UK.

There are at present 24 Executive Directors, who permanently reside in Washington DC, meet as often as required and are responsible for the Bank's general operations under the powers delegated to them by the Board of Governors. Each of the five largest shareholders (that is the USA, Japan, Germany, France and the UK) appoints a single Executive Director who casts the votes to which each country is entitled. The remaining Directors are elected for a two-year term by the other member countries, grouped according to geographic and other criteria. Each Director casts all the votes of the countries which contributed to his election. It should be noted, however, that the present practice is that most decisions are taken on the basis of consensus, rather than votes cast formally.

The President of the Bank serves as Chairman of the Executive Directors by whom he is elected, conducts the ordinary business of the Bank and is responsible for the organization, appointment and dismissal of the officers and staff. According to a consolidated tradition, the President of the Bank is a US citizen. Robert S. McNamara served as President from 1969 until June 1981, when he was succeeded by A. W. Clausen. The latter was succeeded by Barber Conable, who remained in charge until mid-1991. Lewis T. Preston held his post from mid-1991 until his death in June 1995. The current President is James D. Wolfensohn.

Activities

The Bank, using its own capital and funds raised through borrowing in the world capital markets, lends only for productive projects within the territories of its members and pays due regard to the prospects of repayment. Since July 1982, loans have been made at variable interest rates; before then, they were made at fixed rates.

The Bank's resources include the subscribed capital stock and its retained earnings and, primarily, the funds borrowed in capital markets. The resources are replenished through the flow of repayments and the sale of portions of outstanding loans, mainly without the Bank guarantee. The capital stock initially authorized by the Articles of Agreement amounted to $10 billion, divided into 100 000 shares with a par value of $100 000 each and available for subscription only by members. The shares subscribed by the original members amounted to $9100 million, the balance of $900 million having been left available for further subscriptions by the founders and by new member countries. Since 1959, because of repeated general increases in the shares and the admission of new members, the Bank's capital stock has been substantially increased. In April 1988 the Board of Governors approved a further increase of about 80 per cent in the Bank's authorized capital to $171 billion. At 30 June 1995, the subscribed capital amounted to $176.4 billion, or 96 per cent of authorized capital of $184 billion; of subscribed capital, less than 10 per cent ($10.9 billion) was in fact paid in, partly in gold or dollars, and partly in national currencies. The remainder is subject to call if required to meet the Bank's obligations.

The Bank makes its loans at terms which are fair but sufficient to earn a profit in the form of interest and commission fees. The principal amounts of loans are repayable in the currencies loaned. The Bank has not suffered any losses on loans receivable, although from time to time certain borrowers have found it difficult to make timely payments for protracted periods, resulting in their loans being placed in non-accrual status. In any case, the Bank maintains a provision for loan losses. Since 1964, it has been the Bank's policy to transfer to IDA part of the year's income that was not needed for allocation to reserves. No dividends are distributed by the Bank to member countries.

The Bank's largest resource is made up by its borrowing operations, including public issues or private placements throughout the world. As at 30 June 1995, the Bank's outstanding medium- and long-term borrowings, denominated in 25 different currencies, amounted to $104 507 million. The Bank's securities have been placed with investors in more than 100 countries. This diversity allows the Bank flexibility in selecting the markets that will allow optimum borrowing conditions; the same diversity lessens its dependence on any specific market.

The Bank's lending is limited to member countries; the total amount of loans outstanding may not exceed the net amount of subscribed capital stock plus reserves. Each loan must be guaranteed by the government concerned, thus limiting the eligibility for loans to governments and to public bodies and corporations, and virtually excluding private companies. The Bank's decision to lend should be based only on economic considerations. The general requirements concern the borrower's ability to meet its obligations and the profitability of the projects to be financed, priority being given to those that appear to be most useful. Loans had to be made in principle only for specific development projects which could not be financed from other sources at reasonable terms. The Bank usually finances part of the investment required for each project, and specifically the expenditure in foreign currencies on purchases from other countries of goods and services required for the project, the borrower being required to cover the expenditures in local currency. Each project is closely followed and audited by the Bank in all stages of its implementation. As Bank loans are not tied, borrowers are not required to purchase goods and services in any particular member country. The Bank makes medium- and long-term loans, usually 10–20 years, with repayments generally beginning after a grace period of five years. The Bank may make, participate in, or guarantee loans to the IFC for use in its lending operations.

The breadth of the Bank's functions and the multiplicity of the organizations operating in the field of technical and financial development assistance require close interagency co-ordination to prevent overlapping and waste of resources. Guidelines for collaboration between the Bank and its sister Bretton Woods institution, the IMF, have been in place since 1966 and have been reviewed periodically in order to make procedures and practices more effective and systematic. Both organizations share the basic objective of promoting sustained growth and development of member countries and fulfil differing but complementary roles in the pursuit of that objective. The Bank has primary responsibility for development strategies, structural adjustment programmes and efficient allocation of resources, whereas the Fund is mainly concerned with the aggregate aspects of macroeconomic policies. Positive results have so far been achieved in a number of areas, including that of debt strategy and arrears.

Long-standing relations are maintained by the Bank with UN agencies and programmes concerned with various aspects of development work. Activities have focused increasingly on strengthening the capacity of developing countries to implement and sustain policy reform. The Bank currently acts as executing agency for a growing number of projects financed by the *UN Development Programme (UNDP).

Increasing interagency co-operation involves environmental issues reflecting the widespread concern with the link between environment and development. The UNDP, the *UN Environment Programme (UNEP) and the Bank jointly manage a Global Environment Facility (GEF) to channel scientific and financial resources to middle-income and lower-income countries to help finance programmes and projects affecting the global environment. The facility is intended to cover four main areas: (a) protection of the ozone layer; (b) limitation of greenhouse-gas emissions; (c) protection of biodiversity; and (d) protection against degradation of international water resources. The GEF was established in 1991 as a pilot programme; it was subsequently restructured with a new and replenished Trust Fund. As at July 1996, 156 countries were participating. Funds committed amounted to $2 billion for the period June 1994 – June 1997. The Bank administers the facility, the UNDP is responsible for technical assistance, and UNEP provides environmental expertise. Through the end of fiscal 1995, some 150 projects worth $869 million had been endorsed by the GEF participants.

Co-operation has been expanding rapidly between the Bank and the *UN Centre for Human Settlements (Habitat) with a view to supporting developing countries in the improvement of urban management and disaster preparedness.

The Bank also maintains close working relations with major regional development institutions, such as the *African Development Bank (AfDB), the *Asian Development Bank (AsDB) and the *Inter-American Development Bank (IDB), and with the *European Union (EU) to assure co-ordination of development assistance activities. The Bank is closely collaborating with other international agencies, including the *Organization for Economic Co-operation and Development (OECD) and the *European Bank for Reconstruction and Development (EBRD), to help Central and Eastern European countries meet fundamental challenges such as transformation of the economic system, social protection, and environmental clean-up.

Together with the *Food and Agriculture Organization of the UN (FAO) and UNDP, the Bank sponsors the Consultative Group on International Agricultural Research (CGIAR), an informal association of 43 public- and private-sector donors supporting a network of international agricultural-research centres. An invitation has been extended to UNEP to become the fourth sponsoring member of CGIAR. The Bank continues to promote co-operation with non-governmental organizations (NGOs) to ensure that grassroots insights and expertise are taken into account at both policy and project levels.

The Bank is engaged in providing training for government officials at the middle and upper levels of responsibility who are involved in development programmes and projects through the Economic Development Institute (EDI), founded in 1955. Courses and seminars are held at headquarters in Washington DC, or in developing countries. In keeping with the Bank's increased focus on a growth process promoting both equity, and financial and environmental sustainability, the Institute concentrates on the issues concerning poverty reduction, human resource development, protection of the environment, debt and adjustment, public sector management and private sector development. The Institute sup-

ports training institutions overseas through teaching, advice, course planning and the supply of material. It is also supporting countries making the transition from centrally-planned systems and works closely with policy-makers on issues such as project management, civil service reform, and privatization. The Joint Vienna Institute (JVI), co-sponsored by the Bank and four other international agencies, conducts courses for key officials in charge of implementing reforms, and manages four regional centres, in Kiev, Moscow, Prague and Tashkent.

The Bank traditionally has financed a large number of projects, especially in the field of capital infrastructure, such as roads and railways, airports, ports and power facilities, and telecommunications. In response to the deteriorating prospects for the developing countries, a programme of structural-adjustment lending was inaugurated by the Bank in 1980. The lending supports programmes of specific policy changes and institutional reforms in developing countries designed to achieve a more rational use of resources and thereby: (a) to contribute to a more sustainable balance of payments in the medium and long term and to the maintenance of growth in the face of severe constraints; and (b) to provide the basis for regaining momentum for future growth. In 1987 the Bank renewed its efforts to alleviate poverty and to mitigate the unfavourable social effects of economic adjustment programmes. A 'Special Programme of Assistance' for sub-Saharan Africa has increased concessional lending to heavily-indebted and impoverished African countries. In the late 1980s special emphasis was also placed on assisting heavily-indebted middle-income countries, most of them in Latin America. In the past few years the Bank has also been making a sustained effort to provide advice and capital to the countries of Central and Eastern Europe making the transition from command-driven economies to those that are market-orientated. The Gulf crisis initiated by the invasion of Kuwait affected a large number of developing countries, both inside and outside the Middle East, and the Bank, along with the IMF, played a significant role in the mobilization of resources in support of the affected countries.

The present developmental strategy of the Bank places a greater emphasis on the financing of projects likely to bring immediate benefits to the poor people in developing countries. The new strategy is particularly directed at operations which promote productive employment and give the poor greater access to social services – health care, basic education, family planning and nutrition; the full integration of women in the development process is another major objective. The traditional emphasis on the public sector has given way gradually to a development strategy increasingly focused on the role of the private sector, the creation of viable enterprises, and the development of domestic capital markets.

The protection of the environment is being accorded growing importance – also in the context of the UN Conference on Environment and Development (UNCED) of June 1992 – and the impact of projects (especially in agriculture and energy) on the environment is assessed and monitored. All relevant sectors and all types of project with potential for major environmental effects are addressed, although the question of the sustainability of economic growth and of the viability of alternative development strategies is still open to considerable debate. In any case, there seems to be little doubt that major adjustments are urgently needed in technologies, policies and institutions.

Continuing support is provided to the programme of debt and debt-service reduction; both the Bank and the IMF are actively involved in the negotiation of packages between debtors and commercial banks. Within the context of efforts to encourage private-sector development, a strategy and work programme are being adopted by the Bank in close co-operation with IFC and MIGA. The Bank has undertaken a programme of expanded co-financing with a view to supporting borrowers' access to private capital markets within the context of the Bank's country-assistance strategies. A 'core poverty programme' for the direct alleviation of poverty among specific groups has been introduced. A comprehensive long-term strategy to address the challenge of poverty (which increased in many countries during the 1980s), has emerged gradually and will characterize all assistance programmes undertaken by the Bank in the current decade.

Most Bank activities involve various forms of technical assistance to meet gaps in project preparation and for institution building. Project loans and credits may include funds specifically earmarked for feasibility studies, resource surveys, management and planning advice, and training. Technical assistance, usually reimbursable, is also extended to countries which do not need financial support, notably for training and transfer of technology and for the preparation of overall and sectoral development strategies.

The record of the development experience over the past 50 years seems to be both encouraging and sobering. A positive role has certainly been performed by the Bank in helping towards a solution of the problems of underdevelopment in the area of both financial and technical assistance. The Bank – through its support for over 6000 operations in some 140 countries, with more than $300 billion in financing – has made a substantial contribution. Yet, despite progress in the growth rates of the developing countries, the living standards of the poor in some of the slower-growing countries have not improved, or have even deteriorated.

The Bank is currently making an effort to enhance, primarily at the country level, its two basic roles: financial, through the mobilization and investment of sizeable resources for development; and advisory, through the dissemination of its own cross-country experience. Five major challenges have been identified by the Bank as being crucial to future progress: the pursuit of economic reforms promoting broad-based growth and reducing poverty; the investment in people, enabling the poor to take advantage of the opportunities created by growth; the protection of the environment to ensure lasting growth, benefiting tomorrow's generations as well as today's; the stimulation of the private sector; the reorientation of government to complement private-sector activity, and carry out essential tasks efficiently.

President: James D. Wolfensohn
Headquarters: 1818 H Street, N.W., Washington DC 20433, USA (Telephone: +1 202 477 1234; fax: +1 202 477 6391)
Internet address: http://www.worldbank.org
European Office: 66 Avenue d'Iéna, 75116 Paris, France (Telephone: +33 1 4069 3000; fax: +33 1 4069 3066)
Tokyo Office: Kokusai Building, 1-1 Marunouchi 3-chome, Chiyoda-ku, Tokyo 100, Japan (Telephone: +81 3 3214 5001; fax: +81 3 3214 3657)

Publications: *Annual Report*; *The World Bank Atlas* (annual); *World Development Report* (annual)

References: A. J. M van de Laar, *The World Bank and the World's Poor* (The Hague, 1976); E. H. Rotberg, *The World Bank: A Financial Appraisal* (Washington, 1976); R. T. Libby, T*he Ideology and Power of the World Bank* (Ann Arbor, Michigan, 1977); C. Payer, *The World Bank: A Critical Analysis* (London, 1972); I. Shihata, *The World Bank in a Changing World. Selected Essays* (Dordecht, 1991); R. W. Richardson and J. H. Haralz, *Moving to the Market: The World Bank in Transition* (New York, 1994); J. M. Boughton and K. S. Lateef (eds), *Fifty Years after Bretton Woods: The Future of the IMF and the World Bank* (Washington DC, 1995)

International Centre for Settlement of Investment Disputes (ICSID)

The Centre provides conciliation and arbitration procedures to settle disputes arising between foreign investors and host governments.

Origin and development

The Centre has been established under the Convention on the Settlement of Investment Disputes between States and Nationals of Other States, opened for signature in 1965 and entered into effect in October 1966. The Centre has therefore been added to the 'World Bank Group' which comprises, besides the 'World Bank' as such – including both the *International Bank for Reconstruction and Development (IBRD) and the *International Development Association (IDA) – other two institutions, the *International Finance Corporation (IFC) and the *Multilateral Investment Guarantee Agency (MIGA). The common objective of the 'World Bank Group' is to meet the entire range of financial and technical requirements of development by channelling financial resources from industrial countries to the developing world. The Centre operates, as a distinct international organization, at the World Bank's headquarters in Washington DC. Around 120 countries have completed the process of joining the Centre; other 15 countries have signed but not yet ratified the Convention.

Objectives

The purpose of the Centre is to provide conciliation and arbitration services for disputes between foreign investors and host governments which arise directly out of an investment. Subject to the consent of both parties, a Contracting State and a foreign investor who is a national of another Contracting State may therefore settle any legal dispute that might arise out of such an investment by conciliation and/or arbitration before an impartial international forum.

Structure

The governing body of the Centre is the Administrative Council, consisting of one representative of each Contracting State, each of whom has equal voting power. The President of the IBRD is ex officio the non-voting Chairman of the Administrative Council.

Activities

Besides its basic tasks, the Centre has also pursued its investment promotion objectives by carrying out a range of research and publications activities in the field of foreign-investment law.

Chairman: James D. Wolfensohn

Headquarters: 1818   H   Street,   N.W., Washington DC 20433, USA (Telephone: +1 202 477 1234; fax: +1 202 477 6391)

Publications: *ICSID Review – Foreign Investment Law Journal* (every six months); *Investment Laws of the World; Investment Treaties*

International Civil Aviation Organization (ICAO)

The Organization develops the principles and techniques of international air navigation and assists in the planning and improvement of international air transport throughout the world.

Origin and development

The Organization was established under the Chicago Convention on International Civil Aviation, adopted in December 1944 at the conclusion of the International Civil Aviation Conference, and came into force in April 1947. For about two years, pending the formal establishment of the permanent organization, an interim organization was in operation – the Provisional International Civil Aviation Organization (PICAO). A relationship agreement with the UN was concluded by PICAO and subsequently ratified by the permanent organization in 1947.

As between contracting parties, the Chicago Convention superseded the provisions of the

Convention relating to the Regulation of Aerial Navigation, signed in Paris in October 1919, which established the International Commission for Air Navigation (ICAN), and the Convention on Commercial Aviation concluded at Havana in February 1928. The Chicago Convention is supplemented by a number of Annexes containing specifications concerning international standards and recommended practices and procedures, with which member countries are to comply in order to ensure the safety and regularity of international air navigation. Specifications are under constant review and revised periodically in keeping with technological developments and changing requirements. The present membership of the Organization includes over 180 countries.

According to the Convention, the expression 'international air service' means any scheduled air service, performed by aircraft for the public transport of passengers, mail or cargo, which passes through the air space over the territory of more than one country.

Members of the UN may accede to the Organization, according to current provisions. Any sovereign country that is not a member of the UN, may be admitted to the Organization by means of a four-fifths vote of the Assembly. Withdrawal is permitted upon submission of notice of denunciation; and takes effect after one year.

Objectives

The objectives of the Organization are basically the following: to ensure safe and orderly growth of international civil aviation; to encourage skills in aircraft design and operation for peaceful purposes; to improve airways, airports and air navigation facilities; to meet the needs of the peoples of the world for safe, regular, efficient and economical air transport; to prevent the waste of resources caused by unreasonable competition; to safeguard the rights of member countries to operate international airlines; to prevent discriminatory practices; to promote safety of flight in international air navigation; to foster the development of all aspects of international civil aeronautics. The most significant functions of the Organization include: establishing international standards and recommended practices and procedures; promoting simpler formalities at international borders; developing regional plans for ground facilities and services; collecting and publishing air-transport statistics;

preparing studies on the economic aspects of aviation; and fostering the development of air law conventions.

Structure

The Organization's structure is made up of an Assembly, a Council with various subordinate bodies, and a Secretariat. The Assembly, composed of representatives of all member countries, is the legislative body and meets at least once every three years. It lays down basic policies; examines and takes appropriate action on the reports of the Council, and decides on any matter referred to it by the Council; approves the budget; considers proposals for the modification or amendment of the Convention; and deals with any matter within the sphere of action of the Organization not specifically assigned to the Council. Decisions of the Assembly are taken by a majority of the votes cast, unless expressly provided otherwise.

The Council is the permanent governing body, composed of the representatives of 33 countries elected by the Assembly for a three-year term; it holds three 12-week sessions a year, thus providing continuing direction to the work of the Organization. Members of the Council are appointed under three headings: countries of chief importance in air transport; countries making the largest contribution to the provision of facilities for international civil air navigation; and countries whose designation will ensure that all major geographical areas are represented. The Council carries out Assembly directives; administers the Organization's finance; adopts international standards and recommended practices, incorporates them as Annexes to the Convention and notifies all member countries to that effect; takes whatever steps are necessary to maintain safety and regularity of operation of international air transport; provides technical assistance; compiles, examines and publishes information on air navigation; and may act, if requested by the member countries concerned, as a tribunal for the settlement of any dispute relating to international civil aviation. The Council elects its President, appoints the chief executive officer, who is called the Secretary-General, and makes provision for the appointment of the necessary staff. Decisions by the Council normally require approval by a majority of its members.

The Council is assisted by an important subsidiary body, the Air Navigation Commission, composed of 15 people with suitable qualifications and experience, and appointed by the Council from among nominations submitted by member countries. The Commission is responsible for considering and recommending to the Council the adoption or amendment of the Annexes to the Convention; establishing technical sub-commissions; and advising the Council about the collection and communication to member countries of all information that is considered necessary and useful for the advancement of air navigation. Other subsidiary bodies include standing Committees on Air Transport; Joint Support of Air Navigation Services; Finance; Legal Problems; Technical Co-operation; Personnel; and Unlawful Interference.

The Secretariat operates under the Secretary-General. Besides its headquarters in Canada, the Organization has regional offices for Western and Central Africa (Dakar); Eastern and Southern Africa (Nairobi); Asia and Pacific (Bangkok); Europe (Neuilly-sur-Seine, France); Middle East (Cairo); North America, Central America and the Caribbean (Mexico City); and South America (Lima). These offices assist, expedite and follow up the implementation of the Air Navigation Plans and maintain their currency. Annual budgets, annual statements of account and estimates of all receipts and expenditures are submitted to the Assembly by the Council. The expenses of the Organization are apportioned among member countries on a basis determined by the Assembly.

Activities

The Organization works in close co-operation with other agencies of the UN such as the *World Meteorological Organization (WMO), the *International Telecommunication Union (ITU), the *Universal Postal Union (UPU), the *World Health Organization (WHO), and the *International Maritime Organization (IMO). Technical assistance is extended to developing countries under the *UN Development Programme (UNDP) and other specific programmes. Non-governmental institutions which participate in the Organization's work include the International Air Transport Association (IATA), the International Federation of Air Line Pilots Associations, and the International Council of Aircraft Owner and Pilot Associations.

From its inception, the Organization has provided efficient machinery for the achievement of international co-operation in the air, improving

safety and regularity and promoting the use of new technical methods and equipment. Among the Organization's activities special mention should be made of standardization; that is, the establishment and amendment of international standards and recommended practices and procedures in the technical sphere: licensing of personnel; rules of the air; aeronautical meteorology; aeronautical charts; units of measurement; operation of aircraft; nationality and registration marks; airworthiness; aeronautical telecommunications; air traffic services; search and rescue; aircraft accident inquiry; aerodromes; aeronautical information services; and aircraft noise. Extensive work has been undertaken by the Organization in the areas of automatic reporting of data on aircraft accidents, all-weather operations, automation of air traffic services, and the application of computers in meteorological services. The Organization has become increasingly concerned with questions regarding aviation and the protection of the environment. Efforts have also been made towards simplification of government customs, immigration, public health and other regulations relating to international air transport. The Organization has been responsible for drafting several international air law conventions, involving such varied subjects as the international recognition of property rights in aircraft, damage done by aircraft to parties on the surface, the liability of the air carrier to its passengers, crimes committed on board, and unlawful interference with civil aviation. Through technical assistance, the Organization has helped developing countries to build up air transport services and to train personnel; most of the work has been directed towards the development of ground services and the creation of large civil aviation training centres at regional level.

Secretary-General: Dr Philippe Rochat
Headquarters: 1000   Sherbrooke   St   West, Montréal, Quebec, Canada H3A 2R2 (Telephone: +1 514 285 8221; fax: +1 514 288 4772)
Publications: *Annual Report*; *ICAO Journal* (monthly)

International Commission for the Conservation of Atlantic Tuna (ICCAT)

Established by an international Convention signed in 1966, entered into force in 1969 and amended in 1984 and 1992, the Commission has as its area of competence all waters of the Atlantic Ocean, including the adjacent seas, in which tuna are likely to be found. The Commission currently has 23 member countries. The aim of the Commission is to maintain the populations of tuna and tuna-like fish in the Atlantic Ocean at levels that will permit the maximum sustainable catch for food and other purposes.

The Commission has regulatory powers and has thus far recommend several measures concerning catch quotas, minimum weight of fish, and limitation of incidental catches.

Headquarters: Calle Principe de Vergara 17-7°, 28001 Madrid, Spain (Telephone: +34 1 431 0329; fax: +34 1 576 1968)
Publications: *Statistical Bulletin*;   scientific papers; data records

International Committee of the Red Cross (ICRC)

The Committee is a private institution acting as a neutral and independent intermediary in humanitarian matters during international conflicts, civil wars and other internal disturbances.

Origin and development
The Committee was founded in 1863 in Geneva, Switzerland, where it still has its headquarters; it is a private Swiss organization, independent of any government. The Committee is the founding organ of the International Red Cross and Red Crescent Movement, which consists of three components: the Committee itself; the National Red Cross and Red Crescent Societies officially recognized by their countries' governments; and the *International Federation of Red Cross and Red Crescent Societies.

The Committee's role during conflicts is defined in the four Geneva Conventions of August 1949 and their two Additional Protocols of June 1977. The First Geneva Convention deals with the amelioration of the condition of the wounded and sick in armed forces in the field; the Second with the amelioration of the condition of wounded, sick and shipwrecked members of armed forces at sea (including forced landing at sea by or from aircraft); the Third with the treatment of prisoners of war; and the Fourth with the protection of civilian persons in time of war. The First Protocol

extends the Conventions, taking into consideration modern means of warfare and transport, and aiming to provide additional protection to civilians. The Second Protocol provides a code of minimum protection for the combatants and the civilian population during internal conflicts.

Objectives
Assistance is provided to military as well as civilian victims – to prisoners of war and civilian detainees, to the war wounded and to civilian populations in occupied or enemy territory. The seven Red Cross principles – humanity, impartiality, neutrality, independence, voluntary service, unity, and universality – serve as the Committee's guidelines.

Structure
The Committee is composed of a maximum of 25 Swiss citizens meeting about ten times a year as the Assembly. The Assembly is the supreme policy-making body, which lays down principles and basic guidelines and supervises all the Committee's activities. The Executive Board comprises the President, the permanent Vice-President, two other members of the Assembly, the Director-General, the Director of Operations, and the Director for Principles, Law and Relations with the Movement.

As a private body with no capital endowment and no income of its own, the Committee is financed by voluntary contributions from governments, National Red Cross and Red Crescent Societies, and private donors.

Activities
The Committee's operations are undertaken throughout the world, providing impartial support for all victims of conflicts. Recent large-scale operations were conducted in Rwanda, Angola, the former Yugoslavia, Afghanistan, Israel and the Palestinian territories, and Sudan. The Committee visits political detainees to examine the material and psychological conditions of detention and the treatment accorded to detainees following their arrest. The Committee's tracing agency pursues the objective of restoring family ties severed during situations of armed conflict or internal violence, especially through the family message, whereby one-page open notes are exchanged between family members who otherwise have no way of communicating.

President: Cornelio Sommaruga

Headquarters: 19, avenue de la Paix, 1202 Geneva 11, Switzerland (Telephone: +41 22 734 6001; fax: +41 22 730 8280)

Publications: *ICRC Annual Report*; *Panorama* (photographic review); *International Review of the Red Cross* (six times a year); *Red Cross, Red Crescent* (joint magazine of the ICRC and the International Federation of Red Cross and Red Crescent Societies, three issues a year)

International Council for the Exploration of the Sea (ICES)

Formed in 1902 by an international Convention as the Permanent International Council for Exploration of the Sea, the Council adopted its present title in 1964. Membership includes 17 European countries plus Canada and the USA. The Council's purposes are to promote and encourage research and investigation, particularly related to living resources; to draw up relevant programmes; and to publish or otherwise disseminate the result of research and investigation. The Council's area of competence includes the Atlantic Ocean and its adjacent seas, with particular reference to the North Atlantic. The Secretariat of the Council serves as the data centre for several fisheries, oceanographic, and marine pollution data bases. In 1992, the Council restructured its Advisory Committee on Marine Pollution and renamed it the Advisory Committee on the Marine Environment, in order to address a wider range of problems. The Advisory Committee on Fishery Management (ACFM) provides scientific information and advice, including recommendations for management measures such as total allowable catches, to several international bodies dealing with fisheries in the North Atlantic Ocean.

Headquarters: Palaegade   2-4,   1261 Copenhagen K, Denmark (Telephone: +45 3315 4225; fax: +45 3393 4215)

Publications: *ICES Journal of Marine Science*; *ICES Marine Science Symposia*; *ICES Fisheries Statistics*

International Development Association (IDA)

The Association is a lending agency intended to finance development projects in the poorer developing member countries. The Association and the *International Bank for Reconstruction and Development (IBRD) are commonly referred to as the 'World Bank'.

Origin and development

The Association was established as an affiliate of the IBRD by Articles of Agreement which were opened for signature in February 1960 and came into force in September of the same year. The agreement was drawn up by the Executive Directors of the IBRD, pursuant to a resolution of the Board of Governors of October 1959. Membership is open to all members of the IBRD, and about 160 of them have joined to date. Although legally and financially distinct from the IBRD, the Association is administered by the same staff. These two institutions, together with the *International Finance Corporation (IFC), the *Multilateral Investment Guarantee Agency (MIGA) and the *International Centre for Settlement of Investment Disputes (ICSID), form the 'World Bank Group', whose common objective is to help raise standards of living in the developing countries by conveying financial resources from the developed world.

Objectives

The Association finances development projects for the same general purposes as the IBRD, but on terms that are more flexible and bear less heavily on the balance of payments than those of conventional loans – thereby furthering the objectives of the IBRD and supplementing its activities. The Association concentrates its assistance on very poor countries – those with an annual per capita GNP of less than $696 (in 1993 dollars). About 60 developing countries are eligible under this criterion.

Structure

The Association comprises the Board of Governors, the Executive Directors, the President and the necessary operating staff. All the powers of the Association are vested in the Board of Governors – consisting of one governor and one alternate from each member country – which delegates to the Executive Directors (at present 24) authority to exercise many of its powers. Governors and Directors of the IBRD serve ex officio in the Association; the President of the

IBRD (at present James D. Wolfensohn of the USA) is ex-officio President of the Association and Chairman of the Executive Directors. Officers and staff of the IBRD serve concurrently as officers and staff of the Association.

All matters before the Association are decided by a majority of the votes cast, except as specifically provided otherwise. Voting rights are related, at least in part, to the amount of each country's contribution to the Association's resources. As of 30 June 1995, the USA held 15.34 per cent of the total voting power, followed by Japan with 10.51 and Germany with 6.90.

Activities

The funds used by the Association, called 'credits' to distinguish them from IBRD loans, come mainly from subscriptions, general replenishments from the more industrialized and developed members, and special contributions by richer members, as well as transfers from the net earnings of the IBRD. Membership is divided into two categories. Part I countries pay all subscriptions and supplementary resources in convertible currencies (Australia, Austria, Belgium, Canada, Denmark, Finland, France, Germany, Iceland, Ireland, Italy, Japan, Kuwait, Luxembourg, The Netherlands, New Zealand, Norway, Portugal, Russia, South Africa, Spain, Sweden, Switzerland, United Arab Emirates, the UK, and the USA). Part II countries (including over 130 developing nations) pay 10 per cent of their initial subscriptions in freely convertible currencies and the remaining 90 per cent of their initial subscriptions, all additional subscriptions and any supplementary resources in their own currencies. The currency of any Part II member may not be used for projects located outside the territory of the member except by agreement between the member and the Association. Operations are conducted in the currencies of all member countries. As at 30 June 1995, total subscriptions and contributions committed (through the various replenishments) amounted to $92 891 million, of which $89 926 million were contributed by Part I members. Resources are replenished periodically by contributions from the more affluent member countries. The ninth replenishment became effective in January 1991. Fiscal years 1994–6 covered the period of the tenth replenishment, the agreed size of which amounted to SDR13 billion. Meetings on the eleventh replenishment began in October 1994 and continued the following year, in an environment of budgetary pressure for a number of donors.

The Association's lending is limited to member countries, normally only for specific projects, and is based on principles similar to those of the IBRD. Each credit must be guaranteed by the government concerned. The decision to lend must be based only on economic considerations in light of the needs of the area or areas concerned. Funds are made available to the recipient only to meet expenses in connection with the project as they are actually incurred; the use of credits cannot be restricted to the purchase of goods and services in any particular member country. Each project is closely followed in all stages of its implementation, with attention being paid to considerations of economy, efficiency and competitive international trade. Credits are usually extended for a period of 35 or 40 years, with a ten-year initial grace period, and carry a service charge of 0.75 per cent.

The Association co-operates with several organizations within and outside the UN system. Although co-operative relationships are in some cases spelt out in formal agreements, more often they evolve as informal consultations on specific problems and from joint missions and parallel undertakings, especially as regards assistance to low-income countries whose development prospects have been severely impaired by external factors.

While the Association traditionally has financed all kinds of capital infrastructure, its present developmental strategy is focused on projects that directly affect the well-being of the poorest segments of society in the developing countries by mobilizing domestic resources to achieve faster growth. This strategy is increasingly evident in agriculture and rural development projects as well as in projects concerning education, population, health and nutrition. Besides poverty alleviation, the Association is increasingly focusing on debt and debt-service reduction, private-sector development, the reform of socialist economies, and the role of women in development.

President: James D. Wolfensohn
Headquarters: 1818 H Street, N. W., Washington DC 20433, USA (Telephone: +1 202 477 1234; fax: +1 202 477 6391)

Internet address: http://www. worldbank. org

European Office: 66 Avenue d'Iéna, 75116 Paris, France (Telephone: +33 1 4069 3000; fax: +33 1 4069 3066)

Tokyo Office: Kokusai Building, 1-1 Marunouchi 3-chome, Chiyoda-ku, Tokyo 100, Japan (Telephone: +81 3 3214 5001; fax: +81 3 3214 3657)

Publications: *World Bank Annual Report*; *World Development Report* (annual)

International Energy Agency (IEA)

The Agency operates within the framework of the *Organization for Economic Co-operation and Development (OECD).

Origin and development

The Agency was established by the Council of the OECD in the mid-1970s when the energy problems of Western countries had become acute because of the dramatic increase in oil prices by the members of the *Organization of the Petroleum Exporting Countries (OPEC).

The Agreement on an International Energy Programme was signed in November 1974 in Paris and came into force in January 1976. Under the Programme, countries participating in the Agency agree to share oil in emergencies, to strengthen long-term co-operation with a view to reducing dependence on oil imports, to increase the availability of information on the oil markets, and to establish closer ties with the oil-producing and other oil-consuming countries. The Long-Term Co-operation Programme envisages co-ordinated efforts to conserve energy, to accelerate the development of alternative sources through specific and general measures, to encourage research and development of new technologies, and to remove legislative and administrative obstacles to increased supplies. Members of the Agency currently include 23 countries (all OECD members except Iceland, Mexico and the Czech Republic). The European Commission is also represented.

Objectives

The Agency aims to foster co-operation among major oil importing nations; to promote stability in world energy markets and to ensure the security of energy supplies, to reduce detrimental environmental effects at all stages of energy production, conversion and use; and to step up co-operation and dialogue with energy market participants in view of the globalization of markets.

Structure

The decision-making power in the Agency rests with the Governing Board, composed of ministers or senior officials of member countries. Decisions are taken by unanimous vote only if member countries are to be charged with additional obligations not already specified in the founding Agreement. On all other questions, the rule of weighted majority is in use. A qualified majority is required on a number of important questions, such as aspects of stockpiling, oil-sharing contingency plans, and relations with the oil companies. A simple majority suffices with regard to routine matters. The Governing Board is assisted by four Standing Groups which are responsible for: Emergency questions; Long-term co-operation; Oil market; and Relations with producers and other consumer countries. There are also a High-Level Committee on Energy Research and Development, and a Coal and Oil Industry Advisory Board; the latter body is composed of industrial executives. Administrative functions are performed by the Secretariat headed by a Chairman assisted by an Executive Director and a Deputy Executive Director.

Activities

The Agency has adopted an emergency oil-sharing plan to be put into operation in the event of a reduction in oil supplies to member countries. An extensive system providing information and consultation on the oil market and its prospects is in force. A contingency plan with a view to ensuring 'security of supply' and keeping prices stable was activated in early 1991 during the Gulf War. Regular reviews are conducted to assess the effectiveness of national programmes of member countries in the fields of energy conservation and the use of alternative sources. Since the early 1990s the Agency's attention has been focused on nuclear energy issues, particularly the risks concerned with the operation of power-generating nuclear reactors in the former USSR and Eastern Europe.

Executive Director: Robert Priddle

Headquarters: 2 rue André Pascal, 75775 Paris Cedex 16, France (Telephone: +33 1 4524 8200; fax: +33 1 4524 7911)

Publications: *Oil Market Report* (monthly); *World Energy Outlook* (annually); *Energy Policies of IEA Countries* (annually); *Energy Statistics of OECD Countries* (annually); *Energy Balances of OECD Countries* (annually); *Energy Statistics of Non-OECD Countries* (annually)

Reference: R. Scott, *The History of the IEA: Volume I – Origins and Structures* (Paris, 1994); *Volume II – Major Policies and Actions* (Paris, 1995)

International Federation of Red Cross and Red Crescent Societies

The Federation is a non-governmental organization alleviating human suffering through the activities of National Red Cross and Red Crescent Societies.

Origin and development

The Federation was founded in 1919 in Paris as the 'League of Red Cross Societies', with a view to complementing, through an international federation, the entirely Swiss *International Committee of the Red Cross (ICRC); founder member societies were those of the USA, France, Italy, Japan and the UK. The 'League', which changed its name to 'International Federation' in 1991, is one of the components of the International Red Cross and Red Crescent Movement, the others being the ICRC and recognized National Societies. In many Islamic countries, the Red Crescent replaces the Red Cross. The Federation is the permanent liaison body of National Societies and acts as their spokesman and representative internationally.

Objectives

The Federation encourages the creation and development of National Societies in countries throughout the world; advises and assists National Societies in the development of their community services focusing on vulnerable people; organizes and co-ordinates relief operations for victims of natural disasters and epidemics, often launching worldwide appeals for aid; and promotes the adoption of national preparedness plans.

Structure

The governing body of the Federation is the General Assembly, meeting every two years and consisting of representatives of all member National Societies. The Executive Council meets every six months to carry out the decisions of the Assembly and exercise emergency powers if necessary. The Federation's financial resources consist of annual dues from member National societies and voluntary contributions for relief and development.

Activities

The involvement of the Federation in long-term operations has shown a tendency to increase, although donors often stipulate the use and destination of their contributions, thus creating difficulties for some operations. The Federation is participating in the UN International Decade for Natural Disaster Reduction (1990–9).

Secretary-General: George Weber

Headquarters: 17 chemin des Crêts, P.O. Box 372, 1211 Geneva 19, Switzerland (Telephone: +41 22 730 4222; fax: +41 22 733 0395)

Publications: *Weekly News*; *Review* (annual); *Red Cross, Red Crescent* (joint magazine of the Federation and the ICRC, three issues a year)

International Finance Corporation (IFC)

The Corporation fosters growth in the private sector in developing countries. The Corporation co-ordinates its activities with the other institutions of the 'World Bank Group' – the *International Bank for Reconstruction and Development (IBRD), the *International Development Association (IDA) and the *Multilateral Investment Guarantee Agency (MIGA), whose common aim is to facilitate economic development in the poorer member countries by providing funds and technical assistance.

Origin and development

The Corporation was established by Articles of Agreement drawn up within the framework of the IBRD and opened for signature in April 1955. The agreement came into force in July 1956 and has subsequently been amended. Membership of the

IBRD is a prerequisite for membership in the Corporation, which now totals 165 countries. Legally and financially, the Corporation and the IBRD are separate entities. The Corporation has its own operating and legal staff, but draws upon the IBRD for administrative and other services.

Objectives

The Corporation aims to assist developing countries by promoting growth in the private sector of their economies and helping to mobilize domestic and foreign capital; it finances private-sector ventures and projects in partnership with private investors and, through its advisory work, helps governments to create conditions that stimulate the flow of both domestic and foreign private savings and investment. The Corporation combines the characteristics of a multilateral development bank and a private financial institution. The basic functions of the Corporation are: (a) to provide – in association with private investors and without government guarantee – risk capital for productive private enterprises of economic priority in developing member countries, in cases where sufficient private capital is not available on reasonable terms; (b) to stimulate and to help create conditions conducive to the flow of domestic and foreign private capital into productive investment; (c) to encourage the development of local capital markets; (d) to provide financial and technical assistance to privately controlled development finance companies; (e) to support joint ventures which provide opportunities to combine domestic sponsorship and knowledge of market and other conditions with the technical and managerial experience available in the industrial countries; and (f) to revolve its portfolio and to undertake new commitments by selling parts of its investments to other investors. The Corporation also provides businesses and governments with advisory services and technical assistance on a wide range of topics. The Corporation does not engage in operations intended primarily for refunding, direct financing of exports or imports, or land development.

Structure

The Board of Governors, in which all powers of the Corporation are vested, consists of the governors and alternates of the IBRD who represent countries which are also members of the Corporation. Most powers are delegated to the Board of Directors, composed ex officio of the Executive Directors of the IBRD who represent countries which are also members of the Corporation; project financing operations are approved by the Board of Directors. The voting power of each member country is related to its contribution to the capital stock. As at 30 June 1995, the USA had paid 22.43 per cent of the capital stock and held 21.96 per cent of the total voting power. Japan had paid 7.53 per cent and had 7.38 of the voting power, followed by Germany whose percentages were respectively 5.68 and 5.57; France and the UK had paid 5.33 per cent each of the capital stock and held 5.23 per cent of the voting power. The President of the IBRD serves ex officio as Chairman of the Board of Directors and is President of the Corporation. The President is assisted by an Executive Vice-President, responsible for overall management and day-to-day decision-making, and by six Vice Presidents. Besides its headquarters in Washington DC, the Corporation has Special Representatives in Frankfurt, London, Paris and Tokyo, as well as Regional and Resident Missions in several developing countries.

Activities

The Corporation's resources come from subscriptions by its member countries and from accumulated earnings; however, most of the funds for lending activities are raised through bond issues in the international financial markets. The Corporation also borrows from the World Bank, with which it has a Master Loan Agreement (MLA) governing terms of annual Corporation's borrowings from IBRD; the MLA was amended in March 1988 to reflect the growing market orientation of the Corporation and the complex range of funding options provided by the Corporation itself to its borrowers.

An increase in the authorized capital of the Corporation from $110 million to $650 million was approved in 1977; following the authorization, in 1985, of new shares in the amount of $650 million, the capital rose to $1300 million. In May 1992, the authorized capital was increased to $2300 million; in December 1992 a selective increase of $150 million brought the authorized capital to $2450 million, in order to provide sufficient shares for the full entitlement of the former Soviet republics and to provide adequate shares for additional requests for existing or prospective members. As at 30 June 1995, paid-in capital amounted to $1875 million.

The Corporation provides financing by subscribing to shares, usually in conjunction with a long-term loan; loan capital without equity or an equity feature is provided only in exceptional cases. The proportion of equity-to-loan capital and the interest rate on loan funds are determined in relation to a number of factors such as the risk involved and the prospective overall return on the investment. The Corporation invests in shares which are denominated in the currency of the country in which the enterprise is located; loans may be denominated in any major international currency, but most of them are usually expressed in terms of US dollars. The Corporation has gradually been transforming its role from that of a fixed-rate lender of long-term funds and direct equity investor to a provider of a range of variable-rate loans, and both equity and quasi-equity instruments; risk-management instruments have also been introduced.

As the Corporation seeks to supplement and not to compete with private capital, it looks to other investors to provide a substantial part of the capital required for a project. The Corporation generally mobilizes substantial project financing from other sources, either indirectly, in the form of co-financing, or directly, through loan syndications, and underwriting of debt and equity issues in domestic and international markets. It expects its investment partners to provide management and does not seek representation on the board of directors. Annual financial statements, audited by independent public accountants, are required by the Corporation from the companies in which it invests.

The Foreign Investment Advisory Service (FIAS), established by the Corporation in 1986 and now jointly operated with the World Bank, helps governments to meet long-term development needs by obtaining the greatest possible benefit from foreign investment – not only in terms of capital but also from the transfer of technology and managerial expertise. FIAS has worked in about 85 developing countries, advising governments on laws, policies, regulations, programmes and procedures necessary for the creation of an attractive investment climate and the increase of inflows of productive foreign direct investment. The operations of FIAS are financed by the Corporation, the World Bank, the FIAS Trust Fund, the *UN Development Programme (UNDP) and other multilateral and bilateral agencies and donors.

The Corporation co-operates closely with other international agencies involved in development assistance activities and the promotion of investment opportunities. Between 1956 (the date of its founding) and 1995, the Corporation had provided nearly $17 billion in financing for about 1600 companies in over 110 developing member countries.

The Corporation has established itself as the largest source of direct financing for private-sector projects in developing countries. According to the strategy followed at present by the World Bank Group in order to adjust to the new economic environment, the Corporation's operations have been redirected towards becoming more responsive to the evolving needs of its poorer member countries. Private-sector development is widely recognized as a major tool for the stimulation of economic growth and the alleviation of poverty in developing countries. Supported by its most recent capital increase, the Corporation will be expanding the amount and number of investments and adding to the number of countries in which it is active. The catalytic role of the Corporation, through the mobilization of large amounts of capital from private sources, retains its paramount importance; new mobilization techniques, such as securitized loan sales, are being developed.

Priority will be given to assisting governments with privatization programmes, and direct financial and non-financial assistance to small and medium-sized enterprises will be increased. All projects with a potential impact on the environment will be reviewed during the appraisal process and monitored after implementation to ensure conformity with World Bank and international guidelines and host-country rules. Financial and technical assistance is especially needed in Central and Eastern European countries making their transition to a market-based economy and building their private sectors. It is to be expected that in the near future the Corporation will play a leading part in developing private-sector strategies, while the World Bank will retain its primary role in policy dialogue with governments.

President: James D. Wolfensohn
Headquarters: 1850 I Street, N. W., Washington
    DC   20433,   USA   (Telephone:
    +1 202 477 1234; fax: +1 202 676 0365)
Publication: *Annual Report*

International Fund for Agricultural Development (IFAD)

The Fund mobilizes financial resources for agricultural development in the developing countries.

Origin and development

Following one of the proposals put forward by the 1974 World Food Conference, the agreement establishing the Fund was adopted in June 1976 by the representatives of 91 countries at a UN Conference of Plenipotentiaries. After the attainment of initial pledges of $1 billion, the agreement was opened for signature in December 1976; it came into force in November 1977 and the Fund began its operations the following month. The present membership includes 160 countries divided into three main groups: Category I consists of 22 developed countries, all of which are members of the *Organization for Economic Cooperation and Development (OECD); Category II is composed of 12 oil-exporting developing countries, all of which are members of the *Organization of the Petroleum Exporting Countries (OPEC); Category III is made up of 126 other developing countries. Members of Category I and II (donor countries) contribute to the resources of the Fund, while members of Category III (recipient countries) may do so. The present classification of countries will be abolished and a new voting system will be introduced upon completion of the fourth replenishment of the Fund's resources.

Objectives

The purpose of the Fund is to mobilize additional financial resources for agricultural and rural development in developing countries through projects and programmes specifically designed to improve food production systems, the nutritional level of the poorest populations and the conditions of their lives. The Fund makes loans or grants to developing member countries or to intergovernmental organizations in which such members participate, for financing projects which introduce or improve methods of food production and strengthen related national policies and institutions. In line with the Fund's focus on the rural poor, priority is given to projects that meet three interrelated objectives: to increase food production, particularly on small farms; to generate employment and additional income for poor and landless farmers; and to improve nutritional levels and food distribution systems.

Structure

All the powers of the Fund are vested in the Governing Council, in which each member country is represented by a governor and an alternate governor. The Governing Council holds ordinary sessions at yearly intervals and may delegate certain powers to the Executive Board. The 18 members and 17 alternates of the Executive Board are elected for a three-year term by the Governing Council, one third by each category. The Executive Board, meeting three or four times a year, is responsible for the general operation of the Fund and for the approval of loans and grants. The Governing Council elects the President of the Fund by a two-thirds majority for a four-year term, renewable only once. The President also acts as Chairman of the Executive Board. In January 1995, the Governing Council decided to abolish the three original categories of membership and to give member countries two types of vote – the original membership vote and votes related, to the amount of each country's contribution. The entry into force of these amendments is subject to the completion of the fourth replenishment.

Activities

Financing by the Fund is provided through loans or grants made to member countries or to intergovernmental organizations in which such countries participate. Loans are of three kinds: highly concessional loans, repayable over very long periods (40 years, including a 10-year grace period), carrying no interest but only an annual service charge of 0.75 per cent; intermediate term loans, repayable over 20 years (including a 5-year grace period), bearing an interest rate equivalent to 50 per cent of the variable reference interest rate; and ordinary term loans, repayable over 15 to 18 years (including a 3-year grace period), carrying an interest rate equivalent to 100 per cent of the variable reference interest rate.

The reference interest rate is determined annually by the Fund's Executive Board.

The administration of loans is usually entrusted by the Fund to competent international financial institutions in order to avoid duplication of work. The Fund has succeeded in attracting other external donors and beneficiary governments for the co-financing of projects, thereby stretching the impact of its own resources.

The Fund's total initial resources amounted to a little over $1 billion. Of the total amount pledged, 55.5 per cent was contributed by members of Category I; 42.5 per cent by Category II; and 2 per cent by Category III. Periodical reviews are conducted to appraise the adequacy of available resources. In January 1980 a resolution was adopted recommending replenishment of the Fund's resources at a level sufficient to provide an increase in real terms in the level of its operations. A final agreement on the level of the first replenishment (amounting to $1045 million for the period 1981–4) was reached in early 1982. Negotiations took place between 1983 and 1985 on the second replenishment, and a compromise was finally reached in January 1986 on a replenishment of $460 million; this was supplemented by an extra $300 million for a Special Programme for Sub-Saharan African Countries Affected by Drought and Desertification (SPA). The third replenishment was agreed upon in June 1989 for an amount of $523 million. A Second Phase of the Special Programme for Africa (SPA II), emphasizing the need to develop a long-term drought contingency plan for the countries of the region, was approved in May 1991 and became effective in January 1993. The two phases of the SPA were terminated in December 1995 and integrated into the Fund's resources in January 1996.

The target level of the fourth replenishment was established, in January 1995, at $600 million, to be contributed in freely-convertible currencies.

The Fund co-operates closely with other international institutions, notably its sister food agencies in Rome; that is, the *Food and Agriculture Organization (FAO) and the *World Food Programme (WFP). Co-operative relations exist with the *World Bank and the *International Monetary Fund (IMF), regional development banks, and many other UN agencies and bodies such as the *UN Development Programme (UNDP), the *UN Children's Fund (UNICEF) and the *UN Population Fund (UNFPA).

Between 1978 and 1995, loans and grants extended by the Fund under the Regular Programme and the Special Programme for Africa amounted to $4775.7 million, of which $4548.3 million were represented by loans and $227.4 million by technical assistance grants. During this period about two-thirds of the loans were in the highly concessional category. The size of the Fund's operations had decreased between 1982 and 1986 because payments by some member countries were much slower than expected; the Fund's financing levels have fully recovered since that period.

Besides its regular efforts to identify projects and programmes, the Fund organizes programming missions to selected countries to undertake a comprehensive review of the constraints affecting IFAD-type projects among the rural poor, and to help countries to design strategies for the removal of these constraints. Projects recommended by programming missions generally focus on institutional improvements at national and local level, with a view to directing inputs and services to small farmers and the landless rural poor. Since the late 1980s increased emphasis has been placed on environmental conservation in an attempt to alleviate poverty resulting from the deterioration of natural resources. A particularly significant initiative was a Conference on Hunger and Poverty organized by the Fund in November 1995 in Brussels, in association with the *European Union (EU), the World Bank, FAO, WFP and several European countries. The Conference focused on civil society institutions and non-governmental organizations, and adopted a Programme of Action in order to build an effective 'coalition to combat hunger and poverty'.

President: Fawzi H. Al-Sultan
Headquarters: Via del Serafico 107, 00142 Rome, Italy (Telephone: +39 6 54591; fax: +39 6 504 3463)
E-mail: IFAD@IFAD. ORG
Publication: *Annual Report*

International Institute for the Unification of Private Law

(Unidroit)

The Institute provides for the harmonization and co-ordination of the private law of its member countries.

Origin and development

Originally set up in 1926 as an auxiliary organ of the League of Nations, the Institute was re-established in 1940 on the basis of a multilateral agreement. Membership, which currently includes around 60 countries in all continents, is restricted to states that have acceded to the Unidroit Statute.

Objectives

The aims of the Institute are to study methods for harmonizing and co-ordinating the private law of states and groups of states, to prepare drafts of laws and conventions with the object of establishing uniform internal law, and to prepare drafts of agreements for the improvement of international relations in the field of private law.

Structure

The General Assembly, composed of one representative from each member country and meeting at least once a year, is the supreme decision-making body, It adopts the Institute's budget every year, approves the Work Programme every three years, and elects the members of the Governing Council every five years. The 25-member Governing Council is responsible for the preparation of the Work Programme and for the determination of appropriate ways to achieve the aims of the Institute. The President, appointed by the Italian Government, is an ex officio member of the governing Council. The Secretariat performs administrative tasks under the direction of the Secretary-General, who is appointed by the Governing Council on the nomination of the President. The Administrative Tribunal (having jurisdiction over disputes between the Institute and its staff) and the Permanent Committee (overseeing general staff matters) are the other two organs envisaged by the Institute's statute.

Activities

Since its foundation, the Institute has prepared many studies and drafts concerning several branches of law, such as the law of sale and kindred matters, credit law, the law of carriage, the law relating to civil liability, the law of procedure, and tourism law. The work of the Institute has materialized in several international conventions adopted by conferences convened by its member countries or has served as a basis for a number of international instruments signed under the auspices of other international organizations.

Secretary General: Malcolm Evans
Headquarters: Via Panisperna 28, 00184 Rome, Italy (Telephone: +39 6 6994 1372; fax: +39 6 6994 1394)
Publications: *News Bulletin* (every six months); *Uniform Law Review* (every two years).

International Labour Organization (ILO)

The Organization operates for the improvement of working conditions throughout the world.

Origin and development

The Organization was established as an autonomous institution within the system of the League of Nations, its Constitution being embodied in a separate part of the Peace Treaties of 1919 and 1920. The supreme body of the Organization met in 1945 and 1946 and amended the Constitution in order to sever the link with the League of Nations and to anticipate a new relationship with the UN. Other amendments were introduced on several subsequent occasions. The Organization became the first specialized agency associated with the UN, through the conclusion of a formal relationship agreement which entered into effect in December 1946.

As distinct from the automatic membership of the Organization originally provided for all members of the League of Nations, membership is now entirely voluntary. Members of the UN may accede to the Organization in conformity with current provisions. Any sovereign country that is not a member of the UN may be admitted to the Organization by a vote concurred on by two-thirds of the delegates attending the session of the International Labour Conference, including two-thirds of the government delegates present and voting. Unilateral withdrawal is allowed upon submission of written notice to that effect to the Director-General, and takes effect two years thereafter. Withdrawal does not affect the continued validity of obligations arising under any international labour convention ratified by the country which terminates its membership.

The Organization, which originally comprised 45 countries, now numbers about 175 members.

In 1977 the USA exercised its right to withdraw from the Organization, mainly on political grounds, but resumed full participation in February 1980.

Objectives

The principal aim of the Organization is to contribute to the establishment of universal and lasting peace based on social justice by improving, through international action, working and living conditions.

Under the Declaration concerning the Aims and Purposes of the Organization adopted in Philadelphia in May 1944, the fundamental principles which inspire the Organization's work include the following: (a) labour is not a commodity; (b) freedom of expression and freedom of association are essential to sustained progress; (c) poverty anywhere constitutes a danger to prosperity everywhere; and (d) the war against want is to be carried on by continuous and concerted international effort in which the representatives of workers and employers, enjoying equal status with those of governments, join with them in free discussion and democratic decision with a view to promoting common welfare.

The Declaration solemnly affirms the right of all human beings, irrespective of race, creed or sex, to pursue both their material well-being and their spiritual development in conditions of freedom and dignity, economic security and equal opportunity. The attainment of such conditions must constitute the central aim of national and international policies and measures, especially those of an economic and financial character, which should therefore be considered by the Organization in the light of this fundamental objective.

Structure

The Organization's structure is made up of the International Labour Conference, the Governing Body, and the International Labour Office. The Conference is the supreme deliberative organ and meets annually in Geneva, with a session devoted to maritime questions when necessary. National delegations are composed of two government delegates plus one delegate representing employers and one representing workers. As every delegate is entitled to vote individually, non-government delegates can speak and vote independently of the views of their respective governments. The primary function of the Conference is to adopt international labour conventions and recommendations by a two-thirds majority of the votes cast by the delegates present.

The Governing Body (elected by the Conference for a three-year term) is the Organization's executive council. It meets three or four times a year in Geneva, to implement policies and programmes and to supervise the work of the International Labour Office and of the various committees and commissions. The Governing Body has the same tripartite structure as the Conference. It is composed of 56 members, 28 representing governments, 14 representing employers and 14 representing workers. Of the 28 persons representing governments, 10 are appointed by the members of 'chief industrial importance' (at present Brazil, China, France, Germany, India, Italy, Japan, Russia, the UK and the USA), and 18 are appointed by the members selected every three years by the government delegates to the Conference, excluding the delegates of the 10 members mentioned above. Employers' and workers' members are elected as individuals, not as national candidates.

The International Labour Office is headed by a Director-General. It serves as secretariat, operational headquarters, research centre and publishing house. In particular, it collects and distributes information, assists governments upon request in drafting legislation on the basis of decisions of the Conference, administers the technical co-operation programmes, undertakes special investigations, and provides machinery to assist in the effective application of conventions. Operations are decentralized to regional, area and branch offices in about 40 countries. Regional offices are based in Abidjan (for Africa), Lima (for the Americas), Geneva (for Arab States), and Bangkok (for Asia and the Pacific).

Activities

According to the Constitution, the improvement of labour conditions is to be achieved, *inter alia*, by the regulation of the hours of work, including the establishment of a maximum working day and week; the regulation of the labour supply; the prevention of unemployment; the provision of an adequate living wage; the protection of the worker against sickness, disease and injury arising out of his employment; the protection of children, young persons and women; the provision for old age and injury; the protection of the interests of workers when employed in countries other than their own; the recognition of the principle of equal remuneration for work of equal value; the recognition of the principle of freedom of association; and the organization of vocational and technical education. To this end, the Organization brings together government, labour and management to recommend international minimum standards and to draft international labour conventions.

Member countries are required to submit conventions, within a prescribed period of time, to the competent national authorities for the enactment of legislation or other appropriate action. When the competent authorities give their consent, the member is bound to communicate the formal ratification of the convention to the Organization and to take all necessary steps. The member is required to make a periodical report to the Organization on the implementation of the provisions of the convention. The obligation to report periodically the position of national law and practice, with regard to the matters dealt with in a convention, also applies to the non-ratifying member which, moreover, must state the difficulties preventing or delaying ratification. In the case of recommendations, members are required to bring them before the competent national authorities but are under no further obligation other than that of reporting to the Organization, at appropriate intervals, the position of the law and practice in their countries showing the extent to which effect has been given to the provisions of such recommendations with any modifications that have been found necessary. Besides its legislative functions, the Organization provides extensive technical assistance in co-operation with the governments concerned, and carries out research and publication activities on social and labour matters, with a view to promoting democracy and human rights.

The International Institute for Labour Studies was established by the Organization in March 1960 in Geneva. It is an advanced educational and research institution dealing with social and labour policy and bringing together international experts representing employers, management, workers, and government interests and other specialists. Its activities are financed by grants and an Endowment Fund to which governments and other bodies contribute. The International Centre for Advanced Technical and Vocational Training was opened by the Organization in October 1965 in Turin, Italy. It provides programmes for directors in charge of technical and vocational institutions, training officers, senior and middle-level managers in private and public enterprises, trade union leaders, and technicians, primarily from the developing nations.

The Organization maintains working relations and co-operates closely with UN bodies, including the *UN Development Programme (UNDP) and the *UN Population Fund (UNFPA), and with the specialized agencies operating within the UN system. Arrangements for co-operation or consultation have been concluded with many international institutions, both intergovernmental and non-governmental, and national bodies. Arrangements for the approval, allocation and collection of the biennial budget of the Organization are determined by the Conference by a two-thirds majority of the votes cast by the delegates present. Expenses are allocated among member-countries in accordance with a scale which is revised from time to time.

The activities of the Organization have met with many serious difficulties caused by a variety of factors. Some of the difficulties and conflicts of interest originated from the participation of member countries which did not possess independent employers' and workers' organizations, with the result that all their delegates were government-instructed. Since it began operations in 1919 the Organization has adopted a large number of conventions and recommendations, which cover almost every aspect of labour conditions: basic human rights; freedom of association and abolition of forced labour; wages; hours of work; minimum ages for employment; conditions of work for various classes of workers; workmen's compensation; social insurance; vacation with pay; industrial safety; employment services; and labour inspection. Since the establishment of the Organization, the International Labour Conference has adopted well over 350 Conventions and Recommendations, which together form the International Labour Code.

Special emphasis is given to the World Employment Programme, launched by the Organization in 1969 to assist policy-makers in identifying and putting into effect specific measures for promoting employment. Several employment strategy missions have been carried out under the Programme. The work of the missions is complemented by action-orientated research activities covering such major project areas as technology, income distribution, population, education and training, urbanization, trade expansion, and emergency schemes in their relation to employment problems. A World Employment Conference took place in June 1976. Technical co-operation, including expert missions and a fellowship programme, is also a major concern for the Organization. In keeping with the recommendations of the Technical Co-operation Programme, adopted in 1979, the Organization's operational activities are orientated toward a stronger tripartite participation, increasingly involving not only government agencies but also workers' and employers' organizations in project preparation and implementation. A growing number of projects are concerned with the complex problems posed by development, especially to disadvantaged groups such as migrants, refugees, women and uneducated youth.

Assistance is extended in a wide field of social and labour matters such as employment promotion, productivity, human resources development (including vocational and management training), development of social institutions, small-scale industries, rural development, social security, industrial safety, and hygiene. Current operational priorities are represented by the elimination of child labour, the promotion of democracy, the fight against poverty, and the protection of working people.

The Organization was awarded the Nobel Peace Prize in 1969.

Director-General: Michel Hansenne
Headquarters: 4 route des Morillons, 1211 Geneva 22, Switzerland (Telephone   +41 22 799 6111; fax: +41 22 798 8685)
Publications: *International Labour Review* (six a year); *Official Bulletin* (three a year); *Legislative Series* (two a year); *Bulletin of Labour Statistics* (quarterly); *Year Book of Labour Statistics*; *World of Work* (five a year)
References: J. W. Follows, *Antecedents of the International Labour Organization* (Oxford, 1951); G. Foggon, 'The Origin and Development of the ILO and International Labour Organizations', in *International Institutions at Work*, P. Taylor and A. J. R. Groom (eds) (London, 1988), 96–113

International Maritime Organization (IMO)

The Organization fosters co-operation on technical matters regarding merchant shipping.

Origin and development
A provisional Maritime Consultative Council was set up, to act only until the establishment of a permanent intergovernmental agency in the maritime field, by an agreement concluded in October 1946 in Washington DC, and entered into effect in April 1947. The Convention establishing the Intergovernmental Maritime Consultative Organization (IMCO) was adopted in March 1948, at the conclusion of the UN Maritime Conference held in Geneva, but did not enter into force until March 1958 because of the delay in securing ratifications by at least 21 countries, including seven with at least one million gross tons of shipping each.

The Convention has been amended and supplemented on a number of occasions; in May 1982, upon the entry into force of the relevant amendments, the Organization had the words 'Intergovernmental' and 'Consultative' dropped from its name and adopted the present denomination. On the basis of a relationship agreement, the Organization has been recognized since 1959 as the specialized agency of the UN in the field of shipping.

Members of the UN may accede to the Organization in conformity with current provisions. Any sovereign country not belonging to the UN may be admitted to the Organization provided that, upon the recommendation of the Council, the application has been approved by two-thirds of the full members. Territories that do not enjoy full sovereignty, and to which the Convention has been made applicable either by full members responsible for their international relations or by the UN, may be granted associate membership. Any member may withdraw from the Organization by written notification given to the UN Secretary-General; the withdrawal takes effect twelve months thereafter. Membership of the Organization now includes over 150 countries.

Objectives

The Organization facilitates international co-operation on technical matters related to merchant shipping, with a view to achieving safe and efficient navigation and to protecting the marine environment from pollution caused by ships and craft.

The basic purposes of the Organization are to foster co-operation and exchange of information among member countries regarding government regulations and practices relating to technical matters of all kinds that affect shipping engaged in international trade; to encourage the general adoption of the highest practicable standards with regard to maritime safety, efficiency of navigation and the prevention and control of pollution from ships, and to deal with the relevant legal questions; to promote the abolition of discriminatory action and unnecessary restrictions by governments; to consider unfair restrictive practices by shipping concerns; and to deal with any matters concerning shipping that may be referred to it by any organ or specialized agency of the UN.

In order to achieve its purposes, the Organization is endowed with consultative and advisory powers. It considers and makes recommendations about matters submitted by member countries, by any organ or specialized agency of the UN, or by any other intergovernmental institution. It is also responsible for convening international conferences on matters within its competence; drafting international maritime conventions, agreements or other suitable instruments; and recommending these to governments and intergovernmental organizations. Finally, the Organization provides appropriate machinery for consultation and exchange of information. At the request of one of the countries concerned, the Organization may consider any matter related to unfair restrictive practices by shipping concerns, provided that such matter has proved incapable of settlement through the normal processes of international shipping business and has been the subject of direct negotiations between members.

Structure

The Organization's structure consists of an Assembly, a Council, a Maritime Safety Committee, a Secretariat, and several subsidiary bodies in charge of specific questions. The Assembly is the policy-making body and is composed of representatives from all member countries meeting for regular sessions every two years. It elects the members to be represented on the Council and the Maritime Safety Committee, considers the reports of the Council and decides upon any question referred to it by the Council, approves the budget, and refers to the Council for consideration or decision any matters within the scope of the Organization. The Assembly also recommends to member countries measures concerning maritime safety as well as the prevention and control of pollution caused by ships and craft operating in the marine environment.

Between sessions of the Assembly, the Council, elected for a two-year term and normally meeting twice a year, performs all the functions of the Organization but is not empowered to make recommendations on maritime safety and pollution control to member countries, a function expressly reserved for the Assembly. The Council receives the recommendations and reports of the Maritime Safety Committee and transmits them to the Assembly, together with its comments and recommendations. With the approval of the Assembly, it appoints the Secretary-General. It makes a report to the Assembly at each regular session.

The Council consists of 32 members, of which 8 represent countries with the largest interest in providing international shipping services, 8 represent countries with the largest interest in international seaborne trade, and 16 represent other countries which have a special interest in maritime transport or navigation and whose participation ensures representation of all major geographical areas.

The Maritime Safety Committee is open to all members of the Organization and meets at least once a year. It has set up a number of specialized subcommittees to deal with specific problems, such as: bulk chemicals; containers and cargoes; carriage of dangerous goods; fire protection; life-saving appliances and arrangements; search and rescue; radio communications; safety of navigation; standards of training and watchkeeping; and ship design and equipment. The Committee, through the Council, submits proposals to the Assembly on technical matters affecting shipping, including prevention of marine pollution.

Decisions are generally taken by the Assembly, the Council, or the Maritime Safety Committee by a majority of members present and voting; where a two-thirds majority is required, decisions are taken by a two-thirds majority vote of the members who are present.

The Secretariat comprises the Secretary-General, the Secretary of the Maritime Safety Committee and the necessary staff.

The main subsidiary bodies of the Organization are: the Legal Committee, originally created to deal with legal problems resulting from the Torrey Canyon pollution disaster of 1967 and later made a permanent body; the Facilitation Committee, dealing with measures to simplify the documentation and formalities required in international shipping; and the Technical Co-operation Committee, for the evaluation and review of technical assistance programmes and projects. All these bodies were established by the Council between 1967 and 1972. Another important subsidiary body, the Marine Environment Protection Committee, was set up by the Assembly in 1973 to co-ordinate work on the prevention and control of pollution. These Committees are open to full participation by all members of the Organization.

Financial statements for each year and budget estimates on a biennial basis, with estimates for each year shown separately, are prepared by the Secretary-General for consideration by the Council, which submits them to the Assembly with its comments and recommendations. The expenses of the Organization are apportioned among member countries according to a scale which is fixed by the Assembly after consideration of the proposals of the Council.

Activities

The Organization works in close co-operation with UN bodies and specialized agencies as well as with other international institutions, both intergovernmental and non-governmental. Technical assistance in the field of shipping is extended to developing countries under the *UN Development Programme (UNDP) and other specific programmes.

Besides the activities carried out over the years by its various organs in the fields of maritime safety and environmental protection, the Organization has been working in connection with many international instruments, of which it is the depository. These instruments include International Conventions concerning: Prevention of Pollution of the Sea by Oil, 1954 (OILPOL); Safety of Life at Sea, 1960 (SOLAS); Facilitation of International Maritime Traffic, 1965 (FAL); Load Lines, 1966 (LL); Tonnage Measurement of Ships, 1969 (TM); Intervention on the High Seas in Cases of Oil Pollution Casualties, 1969 (CSI); Civil Liability for Oil Pollution Damage, 1969 (CLC); Civil Liability in the Field of Maritime Carriage of Nuclear Material, 1971 (LNM); Establishment of an International Fund for Compensation for Oil Pollution Damage, 1971 (IFC); Special Trade Passenger Ships Agreement, 1971 (STP); Prevention of Marine Pollution by Dumping of Wastes and Other Matter, 1972 (LDC); International Regulations for Preventing Collisions at Sea, 1972 (COLREG); Safe Containers, 1972 (CSC); Prevention of Pollution from Ships, 1973, as modified by the Protocol of 1978 (MARPOL 73/78); Safety of Life at Sea, 1974 (SOLAS); Carriage of Passengers and their Luggage by Sea, Athens, 1974 (PAL); International Maritime Satellite Organization (INMARSAT) and Operating Agreement, 1976; Limitation of Liability for Maritime Claims, 1976 (LLMC); Safety of Fishing Vessels, Torremolinos, 1977 (SFV); Standards of Training, Certification and Watchkeeping for Seafarers, 1978 (STCW); Maritime Search and Rescue, 1979 (SAR); Suppression of Unlawful Acts against the Safety of Maritime Navigation, 1988; and Salvage, 1989. Some conventions have not yet entered into force, pending formal ratification by the prescribed number of countries. In addition to conventions, the Organization has developed numerous codes of practice, such as the International Maritime Dangerous Goods Code. Finally, the Organization has issued hundreds of resolutions and recommendations.

The Organization also works with the Oslo Commission (OSCOM), established by the Convention for the Prevention of Marine Pollution by Dumping from Ships and Aircraft; and the Paris Commission (PARCOM), established by the Convention for the Prevention of Marine Pollution from Land-based Sources.

The Organization provides consultancy and advisory services, arranges for training through its fellowship scheme, and is involved in individual maritime projects in many countries. Most involve training, including the establishment of maritime training academies. The World Maritime University (WMU) opened in July 1983 in Malmö, Sweden, to provide advanced training for administrators, educators and others involved in shipping at a senior level.

Secretary-General: William A. O'Neil

Headquarters: 4 Albert Embankment, London SE1 7SR, England (Telephone: +44 171 735 7611; fax: +44 171 587 3210)

Publications: *IMO News* (quarterly); specialized publications, including international conventions of which IMO is depository

International Maritime Satellite Organization (INMARSAT)

The Organization improves maritime communications by operating a system of satellites.

Origin and development

The convention and operating agreement relating to the Organization were the result of three sessions of a conference held between April 1975 and September 1976 under the auspices of the then Intergovernmental Maritime Consultative Organization (IMCO) – later renamed the *International Maritime Organization (IMO). Both acts entered into force in July 1979 and the Organization began operations in February 1982. The convention was amended in 1985 and 1989 to include aeronautical and global land-mobile communications respectively. Membership includes around 80 countries throughout the world.

Objectives

The purposes of the Organization are, by means of a system of satellites, to improve maritime communications for distress and safety of life at sea, efficiency and management of ships, maritime public correspondence services and radio determination capabilities and to serve the worldwide maritime community exclusively for peaceful purposes.

Structure

The institutional structure consists of the Assembly, the Council and the Directorate. The Assembly, where all member countries are represented on an equal basis, meets every two years to set the basic guidelines. The Council, meeting at least three times a year, comprises 18 signatories or groups of signatories with largest investment shares and four signatories elected by the Assembly paying due regard to equitable geographic distribution and the interests of developing members. Voting power in the Council is related to membership shares based on actual utilization of the system; the US has the largest number of shares (25 per cent), followed by the UK, Norway and Japan. The Directorate is headed by a Director-General and performs administrative and technical functions.

Activities

The Organization, operating a system of several satellites whose capacity is steadily increased and providing emergency transportable communications in cases of natural or man-made disaster, has started in 1993 the commercial operation of a portable mobile satellite telephone system.

Director-General: Olof Lundberg

Headquarters: 40 Melton Street, London NW1 2EQ, England (Telephone: +44 171 387 9089; fax: +44 171 387 2115)

Publications: *Ocean Voice* (quarterly); *Aeronautical Satellite News* (quarterly).

International Monetary Fund (IMF)

The Fund is a specialized agency of the UN established to foster international monetary consultation and co-operation.

Origin and development

Together with the *International Bank for Reconstruction and Development (IBRD), the Fund originated from the Final Act of the UN Monetary and Financial Conference held at Bretton Woods, New Hampshire (USA), in July 1944, with the participation of representatives of 44 countries. According to the 'division of labour' between the two institutions envisaged at Bretton Woods, the Fund's activities were primarily intended to provide temporary balance of payments assistance, while the IBRD was to be essentially concerned with long-term projects and economic development finance.

The Articles of Agreement of the Fund came into force in December 1945, when 35 countries, whose quotas amounted to 80 per cent of the Fund's resources, deposited their ratification of the Bretton Woods Agreement. The Fund began operations in Washington in March 1947.

'Original members' of the Fund include the countries participating in the Bretton Woods Conference which accepted the Articles of Agreement within a prescribed time limit; 39 out of 44 countries became original members, the then USSR being the only important exception. 'Other members' are the countries that have joined the Fund subsequently,under the terms and conditions set out in the Fund's resolutions admitting them to membership. A few countries – Czechoslovakia, Indonesia and Poland – withdrew from the Fund but later rejoined.

Membership of the Fund, which is a prerequisite for membership of the IBRD, totals about 180 countries of the industrial and developing world, in widely different stages of economic development and representing a variety of economic systems from centrally-planned to market economies. Among non-members, mention must be made of Cuba, North Korea and Taiwan, the latter having been replaced as a member by the People's Republic of China in 1980. Switzerland is the first member of the Fund that is not a member of the UN. A Special Association agreement was signed between the Fund and the then USSR in October 1991. Following the dissolution of the Soviet Union, all 15 republics applied for membership in the Fund and subsequently joined the Fund and the World Bank.

Objectives

The Fund promotes international co-operation and stabilization of currencies, to facilitate the expansion and balanced growth of world trade, and to help member countries meet temporary difficulties in foreign payments. It is unique among intergovernmental organizations in its combination of consultative, financial and regulatory functions, with a view to ensuring a stable world financial system and sustainable economic growth.

The original purposes of the Fund are: to provide the machinery for consultation and collaboration on international monetary problems; to promote exchange stability, to maintain orderly exchange arrangements among members, and to avoid competitive exchange depreciation; to assist in the establishment of a multilateral system of payments in respect of current transactions between members and in the elimination of foreign exchange restrictions which hamper the growth of international trade; to make resources available to members, under adequate safeguards, to enable them to correct maladjustments in the balance of payments without resorting to measures destructive of national or international prosperity; to shorten the duration and lessen the degree of disequilibrium in the international balances of payments of members.

Structure

The organization of the Fund, which is similar to that of the IBRD, comprises the Board of Governors, the Executive Directors, and the Managing Director; advisory Committees also play a significant role.

The Board of Governors is vested with all powers and consists of one governor and one alternate governor appointed by each member country. It holds an ordinary annual meeting – usually in September and in conjunction with that of the World Bank Group – to consider the Fund's operations and set down the basic guidelines to be implemented by the Executive Directors, to whom the Board has delegated many of its powers; between annual meetings the governors may take votes by mail or other means. Certain fundamental powers cannot be delegated and remain the sole responsibility of the Board of Governors. They concern, *inter alia*, the admission or suspension of members, the adjustment of quotas, the distribution of net income, the liquidation of the Fund, and the election of Executive Directors. In principle, the Board's decisions are to be adopted by a majority of the votes cast, except as otherwise specifically provided. Each member has 250 basic votes, plus one additional vote for each part of its quota equivalent to SDR100 000. Voting rights are therefore proportionate to the amount of each member's quota. The USA remains by far the largest shareholder in the Fund, holding 17.8 per cent of total votes, followed by Germany and Japan, each with 5.6 per cent. France and the UK hold 5.0 per cent each, followed by Saudi Arabia with 3.5.

There are at present 24 Executive Directors, who reside permanently in Washington DC, meet as often as required (usually several days a week) under the chairmanship of the Managing Director, and are responsible for the day-to-day operations under the powers delegated by the Board of Governors. The five members with the largest quotas – the USA, Germany, Japan, France and the UK – each appoint their Executive Directors. The other 19 Directors are elected every two years by the Governors of the remaining member countries, grouped according to geographical and other criteria; each Director casts all the votes of the countries that contributed to his election. Since a member's voting power depends on the size of its quota, quotas also have a bearing on the formation of the constituencies. However, in practice most decisions are taken on the basis of consensus rather than of formally-cast votes.

The Managing Director, elected by the Executive Directors for a five-year term, which may be extended, is ex officio Chairman of the Executive Directors and is assisted by a Deputy. He conducts the ordinary business of the Fund and is responsible for the organization, appointment and dismissal of the officers and staff. According to an established practice, the post of Managing Director of the Fund is reserved to a European citizen, while a US citizen is appointed President of the IBRD.

An Interim Committee of the Board of Governors on the International Monetary System and a Joint Committee of the Boards of Governors of the Fund and the World Bank on the Transfer of Real Resources to Developing Countries (Development Committee) were established with advisory functions and held their initial meetings in January 1975. Since that date both organs have met on a semi-annual basis generally at the same time. The Second Amendment to the Articles of Agreement empowers the Board of Governors to decide, by a large majority of the total voting power, the establishment of a new organ, the Council, which would be similar to the Interim Committee as regards composition and terms of reference but would have decision-making powers.

Activities

Members commit themselves to mutual collaboration to promote orderly exchange arrangements and a system of stable exchange rates, and undertake certain specific obligations relating to domestic and external policies that affect the balance of payments and the exchange rate. Members are bound to furnish such information as the Fund deems necessary for its operations and the effective discharge of its duties, including national data on official holdings, as well as holdings by banking and financial agencies at home and abroad, of gold and foreign exchange; production, exports and imports of gold; total exports and imports of merchandise, according to countries of destination and origin; international balance of payments; international investment position; national income; price indices; buying and selling rates for foreign currencies; and exchange controls.

Each member country is assigned a quota related to its national income, monetary reserves, trade balance and other economic indicators. A member's subscription is equal to its quota and is payable in special drawing rights (SDRs), in other members' currencies or in its own currency. The quota approximately determines a member's voting power, the amount of foreign exchange it may purchase from the Fund, and its allocation of SDRs. In 1978, under the Seventh General Review of Quotas, agreement was reached on a 50 per cent increase in members' quotas, to raise the Fund's resources from SDR39 011.2 million to SDR58 616.3 million. Under the Eighth General Review of Quotas, completed in 1983, a 47 per cent increase was decided, raising the total quota to SDR90 000 million. At the Ninth General Review of Quotas, agreement was reached on a 50 per cent increase in overall quotas, bringing the Fund's general resources to SDR135 214.7 million. The total of members' quotas at 1 May 1995 was SDR144 954 million ($228 018 million).

Each member deals with the Fund only through its Treasury, central bank, stabilization fund, or other similar fiscal agency, and the Fund deals only through the same agencies. The Fund's resources are made available, on an essentially short-term and revolving basis, to members which need temporary assistance for the solution of their payments problems. More precisely, exchange transactions take the form of members' purchases (drawings) from the Fund of the currencies of other members for the equivalent amounts of their own currency. A member is entitled to buy the currency of another member from the Fund, subject to certain conditions, including its likely ability, with the help of resources provided by the Fund, to overcome payments difficulties within a short time. Drawings are limited by provisions governing both the rate of increase and the total amount of the Fund's holdings of a member's currency expressed as a percentage of its quota. Reserve-tranche purchases – that is, purchases that do not bring the Fund's holdings of the member's currency to a level above its quota – are allowed more or less automatically and unconditionally. Further purchases on the part of a member are subject to the principle of 'conditionality' which, although not expressly mentioned in the Fund's Articles of Agreement, is the guiding concept of the various policies and facilities based on the requirement that resources be made available to members 'under adequate safeguards'. In line with this principle, a member must commit itself to sound economic management and agree to adjust its fiscal, monetary, exchange and trade policies as stipulated by the Fund. The revised Guidelines on Conditionality, adopted in 1979, obliged the Fund to take a much broader view of a country's economic requirements, making express reference to the social and political objectives of member countries and to the causes of their balance-of-payments difficulties. Conditionality, therefore, is not based on a rigid set of operational rules but may vary according to individual programmes and the types of policy or facilities that are used.

A member's purchases of currency from the Fund must be repaid by repurchases or by the purchase of that member's currency by another member. As a general rule, members undertake to repay within a period not exceeding three to five years; exceptions are made in the case of extended arrangements. Repurchases are made in SDRs or in usable currencies. Purchases outside the reserve tranche are made in four credit tranches, each equivalent to 25 per cent of the member's quota; repurchases must be made within a specified period of time.

The Fund is expected to depend primarily on its own resources – that is, on its quota-based or subscribed resources – but when members face extraordinary financing requirements it is authorized to supplement its resources by borrowing. Although it can borrow a member's currency, with the concurrence of the member itself, from any source, the Fund has borrowed thus far only from official sources, primarily member countries and their central banks. Since a member's access to Fund financing is no longer strictly limited to the size of its quota, borrowing has enabled the Fund to expand its lending capability, although the exercise has often proved to be costly and time-consuming.

Under the General Arrangements to Borrow (GAB) of 1962, ten industrialized members – the Group of Ten (G-10) including Belgium, Canada, France, the Federal Republic of Germany, Italy, Japan, The Netherlands, Sweden, the UK, and the USA – undertook to lend the Fund up to $6 billion, in their own currencies, should this be necessary to forestall or cope with an impairment of the international monetary system. Switzerland became associated with the GAB in 1964. Since their inception, the Arrangements have been activated on several occasions and have been reviewed periodically and renewed with some modifications. In January 1983, the Group of Ten reached an agreement on major revisions and a substantial enlargement of the GAB from SDR6.4 billion to SDR17.0 billion, with Saudi Arabia contributing SDR1.5 billion. The Swiss National Bank became a full participant in the GAB in April 1984. The decision was adopted in 1995 to double the GAB by means of a parallel arrangement, using in addition the resources of countries other than the ones belonging to the G-10.

Stand-by Arrangements, introduced in 1954, enable members to negotiate credit in advance of actual needs, with a view to forestalling speculative attacks that might aggravate impending difficulties. Under these arrangements, drawings up to specified limits may be made within an agreed period, subject to certain conditions. The usual duration of a stand-by arrangement does not exceed 12 months, with repayment within a period of three to five years.

To further support members facing temporary balance-of-payments problems, the Fund has adopted a number of devices, including the establishment of a compensatory financing facility (February 1963, replaced in 1988); a buffer stock financing facility (1969); an oil facility (June 1974); an extended facility for medium-term assistance to members in special circumstances of balance-of-payments difficulty (September 1974); another oil facility (April 1975); a Trust Fund (May 1976), which was terminated in April 1981; and a supplementary financing facility for members facing serious payments imbalances (1978). In 1981 the Fund inaugurated the policy of 'enlarged access', allowing for a maximum cumulative use of its resources of up to 450 per cent of quota over a period of three years. This policy enabled the Fund to provide assistance to members whose balance-of-payments deficits are large in relation to their quotas, and which need resources in larger amounts and for longer periods than are available under the regular credit tranches.

The Fund established in August 1988 the Compensatory and Contingency Financing Facility (CCFF), which replaced and expanded the former compensatory financing facility of 1963. The CCFF was modified in December 1990, to include a petroleum import financing component in the context of the Middle East crisis, and was subsequently discontinued. A Structural Adjustment Facility (SAF) was set up in March 1986 in order to provide balance of payments assistance to low-income developing countries on concessional terms; loans are granted to support medium-term macroeconomic and structural adjustment programmes. To provide additional assistance to the adjustment efforts of heavily-indebted countries the Enhanced Structural Adjustment Facility (ESAF) was established in December 1987, setting the access limit to 250 per cent of the member's quota (compared with 70 per cent under the SAF). Resources committed under ESAF are provided by the Structural Adjustment Facility of the Special Disbursement Account and by the ESAF Trust Loan Account. At 30 April 1995, ESAF arrangements in effect reached SDR5.1 billion of which SDR3 billion disbursed.

In April 1993 the Fund established the Systemic Transformation Facility (STF) to provide financial assistance to members such as the countries of the former USSR and those of Central and Eastern Europe finding themselves at an early stage of the transition process and unable to use other facilities.

The Articles of Agreement of the Fund have been amended substantially on three occasions, in 1969, 1978 and 1992. The First Amendment entered into force in July 1969 with the introduction of SDRs, created by the Fund to meet a long-term global need to supplement existing international reserves; SDRs have become usable and acceptable reserve assets and a substitute for gold in international payments. Members are allocated SDRs in proportion to their quotas in the Fund and may use them bilaterally to buy back from other members equivalent amounts of their own currencies, or to obtain convertible currency from members designated by the Fund.

Reconstitution provisions setting limits to a member's average holdings of SDRs have been introduced to prevent an excessive reliance on SDRs to finance large or persistent balance-of-payments deficits. Since January 1981, the calculation of SDRs has been reduced from an original basis of 16 leading currencies to a basket including only the currencies of five member countries. The percentage weights in the valuation basket currently in effect are 40 for the US dollar, 21 for the Deutsche mark, 17 for the Japanese yen and 11 each for the French franc and the Pound sterling.

The suspension of the convertibility of the dollar into gold, announced by the USA in August 1971, the modifications of the par values of currencies and other related events in the financial and monetary fields, gave rise to a major crisis in the international monetary order as envisaged by the Bretton Woods Agreement. More than four years of intensive efforts on international monetary reform culminated during 1976, when negotiations were completed, with the approval of the Second Amendment, which entered into effect in April 1978.

The Second Amendment is designed to adapt the Fund and its operations to current needs in six main areas: (a) the promotion of orderly exchange arrangements and a stable system of exchange rates in compliance with certain obligations undertaken by members with regard to domestic and external economic and financial policies; (b) the reduction of the role of gold (including the elimination of its function as the unit of value of the SDR, the abolition of the official price of gold, and the disposition of part of the Fund's own holdings of gold), with a view to making the SDR the principal reserve asset in the international monetary system; (c) the provision for wider uses of the SDR by endowing the Fund with increased powers over the categories of holders of SDRs, the relevant transactions and the rules for the reconstitution of members' holdings of SDRs; (d) the simplification and expansion of the types of financial operations and transactions carried out by the Fund; (e) the possible establishment of the Council as a new organ of the Fund; and (f) the improvement of the organizational and administrative mechanism of the Fund.

The par value of the dollar is no longer defined in terms of the SDR and gold, and the USA is not obliged to establish and maintain a par value for the dollar.

The Third Amendment, which entered into force in 1992, empowers the Fund to suspend the voting and certain related rights of members that fail to fulfil any of their obligations under the Fund's Articles of Agreement, other than obligations with respect to SDRs.

The Fund is actively engaged in the training of officials of member countries and their financial organizations. Courses offered by the Fund's Institute, established in 1964, deal with financial analysis and policy, balance-of-payments methodology, and public finance; assistance is also extended to national and regional training centres. Several departments of the Fund provide training and technical assistance in their areas of special competence.

The Fund may co-operate, within the terms of its Articles of Agreement, with 'any general international organization and with public international organizations having specialized responsibilities in related fields'; a relationship agreement was concluded between the Fund and the UN in November 1947.

Close relations, mainly of a non-financial character, are maintained by the Fund with its sister Bretton Woods institution, the World Bank. Co-operation has become closer in the past few years as both organizations are increasingly concerned with structural adjustment issues; guidelines establishing the policy areas on which each institution must concentrate were first formalized in 1986 and have been reviewed periodically since then. Administrative procedures have been adopted to promote collaboration and more efficient use of staff resources. These procedures are supplemented at the operational level by joint or parallel missions, systematic contacts in the field and co-operation in technical assistance activities.

A co-operative relationship is being developed between the Fund and the newly-created *World Trade Organization (WTO) on trade policy issues and their repercussions in the payments field with a view, *inter alia*, to strengthening the trade reform content of Fund-supported programmes. As regards the provision of technical assistance for the improvement of economic and financial management, the Fund has become, in 1989, an executing agency for the *UN Development Programme (UNDP).

In five decades, the Fund has performed a significant role despite the fundamental political and economic changes that have occurred in many parts of the world, and has maintained an effective presence at the centre of the international monetary and payments system. The amendments to the Articles of Agreement adopted so far represent important stages in the evolution towards a new monetary order whose establishment will, however, ultimately depend on a number of factors largely beyond the powers and scope of the Fund. Disruptions and manipulations of exchange rates have often prevented effective adjustments of the balance of payments of member countries. The recent expansion of facilities and other types of operation should benefit in particular developing member countries.

The total of stand-by and extended arrangements in effect at 30 April 1995 amounted to SDR20 billion, of which nearly SDR12 billion was utilized. The total amount of Fund credit outstanding under its various facilities, including drawings made under earlier arrangements, reached over SDR32 billion at 30 April 1995, of which over SDR29 billion was represented by general resources and the remainder by borrowed resources.

The role of the SDR and the possibility of new SDR allocation have been discussed extensively; in fact, no allocations of SDRs have been made since January 1981. More precisely, SDRs were allocated in 1970–2 and 1979–81 for a cumulative total of SDR21.4 billion. The value of the SDR is calculated daily on the basis of the market exchange rates of the relevant currencies.

A number of central banks, intergovernmental monetary institutions and development institutions have been designated by the Fund as 'prescribed holders' of SDRs. These institutions are therefore entitled to acquire and use SDRs in transactions and operations with participants in the SDR Department (all Fund members) and other prescribed holders under the same terms and conditions as Fund members. In addition to its uses as a medium of exchange and for settlements among participants and prescribed holders, the SDR is the unit of account for Fund transactions and operations, and for its administered accounts. The SDR is also used as a unit of account by a number of international and regional organizations and in capital markets. Several international conventions use the SDR to express monetary magnitudes, notably those expressing liability limits in the international transport of goods and services.

With a view to reducing the role of gold, in the mid-1970s the Fund undertook a gold sales programme: one-sixth of the Fund's gold (25 million troy ounces, or 775 metric tons) was sold directly to member countries and a further one-sixth was sold at public auction for the benefit of developing member countries. On completion of the programme, in the first half of 1980, 24.5 million ounces had been sold directly to 126 members in four annual restitution sales and a further 25 million ounces had been sold at public auction. The profits of the gold auction totalled over $4.6 billion, of which $1.3 billion was transferred directly to 104 developing member countries and the remainder made available for loans by the Trust Fund.

In the late 1990s the Fund is likely to face new as well as traditional challenges; in any case, its role will remain essentially 'catalytic'; that is, mobilizing additional market financing rather than replacing it. One major problem that will remain is that of the heavy indebtedness of some developing countries whose situation has not substantially improved because of inadequate policies and/or insufficient financial support. In the area of debt reduction operations, co-operation with the IBRD and the *International Development Association (IDA) will be crucial, since these operations represent a major element in a country's financial and development strategy. The large and persistent external payments imbalances among major industrial countries represent another concern of paramount importance. Last but not least is the daunting task of helping the Central and Eastern European countries, as well as the republics of the erstwhile USSR, make the massive changes in their institutional and regulatory framework that are necessary to establish open market-based economies in a relatively short time.

Managing Director: Michel Camdessus
Headquarters: 700 19th Street, N. W. , Washington DC 20431, USA (Telephone: +1 202 623 7000; fax: +1 202 623 4661)
Internet address: publications@imf. org
Publications: *Annual Report of the Executive Board*; *Annual Report on Exchange Arrangements and Exchange Restrictions*; *Summary Proceedings* (annual); *International Financial Statistics* (monthly, with yearbook); *Balance of Payments Statistics Yearbook*; *Direction of Trade Statistics* (quarterly, with yearbook); *World Economic Outlook* (twice a year); *International Capital Markets: Developments, Prospects and Policy Issues* (annual); *IMF Survey* (twice a month)

References: S. Horie, *The International Monetary Fund* (London, 1964); H. Aufricht, *The International Monetary Fund. Legal Bases, Structure, Functions* (London, 1964); B. Tew, *International Monetary Co-operation 1945–70* (London, 1970); M. G. de Vries, *The International Monetary Fund 1966–1971* (Washington, 1976); A. Van Dormael, *Bretton Woods: Birth of a Monetary System* (London, 1978); J. Gold, *Legal and Institutional Aspects of the International Monetary System: Selected Essays* (Washington DC, 1979); R. Solomon, *The International Monetary System 1945–1981* (London, 1982); R. W. Edwards, Jr, *International Monetary Collaboration* (Dobbs Ferry, New York, 1985); M. Garritsen De Vries, *The IMF in a Changing World 1945–85* (IMF, Washington DC, 1986); T. Ferguson, *The Third World and Decision Making in the International Monetary Fund: The Quest for Full and Effective Participation* (London, 1988); D. Ghai (ed), *The IMF and the South. The Social Impact of Crisis and Adjustment* (London, 1992); G. Bird, *IMF Lending to Developing Countries: Issues and Evidence* (London, 1995); J. M. Boughton and K. S. Lateef (eds), *Fifty Years after Bretton Woods: The Future of the IMF and the World Bank* (Washington, DC, 1995)

International Narcotics Control Board (INCB)

(Organe international de contrôle des stupéfiants) (OICS)

The Board ensures the continuous evaluation and overall supervision of governmental implementation of drug control treaties as well as the availability of drugs for medical and scientific purposes.

Origin and development

The formal establishment of the Board was envisaged by the Single Convention on Narcotic Drugs (1961) which consolidated earlier

Conventions (February 1925, July 1931) placing natural or synthetic narcotics, cannabis and cocaine under international control. The 1961 Convention came into force in December 1964; the Board, which took over the functions of the Permanent Central Narcotics Board and the Drug Supervisory Body, began operating in March 1968. The growing abuse of several drugs, such as hallucinogens, amphetamines, barbiturates, non-barbiturate sedatives and tranquillizers, not covered by international treaties prompted the *Commission on Narcotic Drugs (CND) to draw up a legal instrument dealing with these substances. As a result, a Convention on Psychotropic Substances was adopted in 1971 in Vienna by a UN Conference and entered into effect in 1976. The 1961 Convention was amended by a Protocol, signed in 1972 in Geneva and entered into force in 1975, which considerably enlarged the functions and membership of the Board and stressed the need for treatment and rehabilitation of drug addicts. The UN Convention against Illicit Traffic in Narcotic Drugs and Psychotropic Substances, adopted in 1988 and in force from 1990, deals with areas not previously regulated by international treaties.

Objectives

The basic objective of these international instruments is to limit the supply of and demand for narcotics and psychotropic substances to medical and scientific needs, through co-ordinated national and international action.

The functions of the Board are to ensure that the aims of the drug control treaties are not endangered because of the failure of any country or territory to implement the relevant provisions; to review and confirm annual estimates of licit narcotic drug requirements submitted by governments and to monitor the licit movement of psychotropic substances; to prevent the illicit cultivation, production and manufacture of, and illicit trafficking in and use of, drugs; to require governments to adopt remedial measures in case of breaches of the treaties and to bring violations to the attention of the parties, the Economic and Social Council and the CND. In order to assist countries that experience difficulties in carrying out the provisions of the treaties, the UN Fund for Drug Abuse Control (UNFDAC), established in March 1971, contributes to projects to replace illicit opium cultivation, treat and rehabilitate drug

addicts, strengthen control measures, or organize information and education programmes.

Structure

The Board consists of 13 members elected for a five-year period by the Economic and Social Council in their individual capacities and not as representatives of governments. Members are elected as follows: (a) three members with medical, pharmacological or pharmaceutical experience from a list of at least five nominated by the *World Health Organization (WHO); and (b) ten members from a list of persons nominated by the members of the UN and by parties to the Single Convention on Narcotic Drugs which are not UN members.

Meetings are held at least twice a year, in closed session, in order to review the drug situation throughout the world and to supervise the implementation of the drug control treaties. The Board is assisted by a permanent secretariat which receives and evaluates information from governments and submits it for the Board's attention.

According to the General Assembly resolution of December 1990, the Board's secretariat has been integrated in the newly-created *UN International Drug Control Programme (UNDCP), which has also taken over the functions of the Division of Narcotic Drugs of the UN Secretariat and assumed responsibility for the financial resources of UNFDAC.

Activities

A significant role has been played by the Board in the supervision of national control over production and distribution of narcotic drugs in accordance with the relevant treaties; the Board is also concerned with the effectiveness of the treaties, highlighting areas in need of strengthening. However, both 'classical' and new drugs are increasingly abused by large numbers of people in most parts of the world, thus making it more and more difficult for the Board to exercise an effective international control.

Headquarters: Vienna International Centre, P.O. Box 500, 1400 Vienna, Austria (Telephone: +43 1 213450; fax: +43 1 232156)

Publications: *Annual Report*; *Estimated World Requirements of Narcotic Drugs (annual)*; *Statistics on Narcotic Drugs and Maximum Levels of Opium Stocks* (annual)

International Organization for Migration (IOM)

The Organization is a humanitarian agency with a predominantly operational mandate, in order to ensure orderly and planned migration.

Origin and development

At the initiative of Belgium and the USA an International Migration Conference was convened in Brussels in 1951, at which the Provisional Intergovernmental Committee for the Movement of Migrants from Europe (PICMME) was founded. The Organization established its headquarters in Geneva and started operations in February 1952 as the Intergovernmental Committee for European Migration (ICEM). The Constitution of ICEM was adopted in 1953 and entered into force the following year. While the early activities of the Organization were confined to population movements from Europe to North America, Latin America and Oceania, international events led gradually to an extension of operations on a world-wide scale. The global role of the Organization was recognized formally in 1980 by member countries, which decided to drop the word 'European' from the agency's name.

The role and mandate of the Intergovernmental Committee for Migration (ICM) were again modified in May 1987 when a special Council session adopted amendments to the Constitution and changed the name to International Organization for Migration. Amendments, which entered into force in November 1989, recognized, *inter alia*, that international migration services may be needed throughout the world and in a variety of circumstances, such as temporary migration, voluntary return migration, intraregional migration, migration of refugees, displaced persons and other individuals. The link between migration and development was emphasized and the need for close co-operation and co-ordination among international organizations was stated explicitly. The Organization's current membership includes about 55 countries plus 46 countries enjoying observer status.

Objectives

The objectives of the Organization include the provision of orderly and planned migration to meet the specific needs of both emigration and immigration countries, and the processing and movement of refugees, displaced persons and other individuals in need of international migration services to countries offering them permanent resettlement opportunities.

To fulfil its basic goals, the Organization carries out the following functions: (a) the handling of orderly and planned migration; (b) the transfer of qualified human resources to foster the economic, social and cultural advancement of the receiving countries; (c) the organized transfer of refugees, displaced persons and other individuals compelled to leave their homeland; and (d) the provision of a forum to states and other partners to discuss experiences, exchange views, devise measures and promote co-operation and co-ordination of efforts on migration issues.

Structure

The decision-making power with regard to policy, programmes and financing of the Organization rests with the Council, composed of representatives of all member countries (including observers) and normally meeting at yearly intervals. The Executive Committee, consisting of ten members annually elected by the Council, meets twice a year to prepare the work of the Council and make recommendations on the basis of reports from the Sub-Committee on Budget and Finance and the Sub-Committee on the Co-ordination of Transport. The Director-General, assisted by a Deputy Director-General and necessary staff, is in charge of administrative functions.

The budget of the Organization has two components: the administrative part funded by assessed contributions from all member countries, according to an agreed percentage scale; and the operational part funded through voluntary contributions from governmental sources and from migrants themselves or their sponsors.

Activities

The Organization co-operates closely with other international organizations working in the field of refugee assistance or dealing with social, economic and demographic aspects of international migration. Refugee activities are co-ordinated with the *UN High Commissioner for Refugees (UNHCR) and with governmental and non-governmental organizations.

Since 1952 the Organization has assisted well over 5 million people (some two-thirds refugees and displaced persons, and one-third national mi-grants), an important proportion of whom were family reunion cases. The Organization's world-wide activities are carried out by some 60 field missions and sub-offices.

For refugees, the Organization provides docu-mentation, processing and medical services to respond to entry requirements in resettlement countries, as well as language and cultural orien-tation courses; for national migrants, the Organization arranges for counselling, recruit-ment, selection and processing in the country of origin, reception, placement and integration in the receiving country, and language courses for migrant workers. Reliable transportation for the movement of migrants is financed by the Organization through its Loan Fund. In order to help developing countries meet their urgent needs for highly skilled people, the Organization has developed specific 'Migration for Development' initiatives which comprise: the Return of Talent programme for Latin America and Africa; the Selective Migration programme in Latin America; the Integrated Experts programme in Latin America and Asia; the Horizontal Co-operation in the Field of Qualified Human Resources programme in Latin America. In August 1993 the Organization initiated the special Emergency Humanitarian Return Programme (EHRP) for former scholarship-holders from Africa, Latin America and Asia, residing in Central and Eastern Europe and the erstwhile USSR and desiring to return home. The Organization pro-vides advisory services and carries out studies to co-operate with member countries in the formula-tion and implementation of their migration policy, legislation and administration. The Centre for Information on Migration in Latin America (CIMAL) was set up in 1983 by the Organization in Santiago, Chile. The Organization also acts as a multilateral forum where key migration issues may be discussed in the course of international seminars.

Director: James N. Purcell
Headquarters: 17 route des Morillons, P.O. Box 100, 1211 Geneva 19, Switzerland (Telephone: +41 22 717 9111; fax: +41 22 798 6150)
E-mail: telex@geneva iom.ch
Publications: *Monthly Dispatch*; *International Migration* (quarterly); *IOM Latin American Journal* (three a year)

International Red Locust Control Organization for Central and Southern Africa (IRLCO-CSA)

The Organization was formed in 1971 as succes-sor to the International Red Locust Control Service (IRLCS) established in 1949. Its purpose is to promote and undertake the most effective control of the significant populations and swarms of red locusts in recognized outbreak areas; as-sistance is also provided in the control of African army-worm and quelea-quelea. Members include Botswana, Kenya, Lesotho, Malawi, Mozambique, Swaziland, Tanzania, Uganda, Zambia, and Zimbabwe.

Director: E. K. Byaruhanga
Headquarters: P.O. Box 240252, Ndola, Zambia (Telephone: +260 2 615684; fax: +260 2 614285)
Publications: *Annual Report*; *Monthly Report*

International Telecommunications Satellite Organization (INTELSAT)

The Organization facilitates the operation of the telecommunications satellite system.

Origin and development
The first world-wide satellite communications system originated in 1964 with the establishment of the interim International Telecommunications Satellite Consortium, open to all member coun-tries of the *International Telecommunication Union (ITU). A steadily expanding membership reflecting the growing importance of the sector led to the creation of the present Organization by means of two international instruments: the Agreement establishing the Organization itself concluded among states; and the Operating Agreement concluded among states and public and private telecommunications bodies desig-nated by the states. Both instruments entered into force in February 1973. Over 130 countries now participate as full members, while another 50 enjoy the status of 'non-signatory users'.

Objectives
The Organization develops, establishes, operates and maintains the space segment of the global commercial telecommunications satellite system.

Structure

The Assembly of Parties meets every two years to establish general guidelines, and consists of representatives of the states. The Meeting of Signatories, dealing mainly with technical, financial and operational matters, also includes the other parties who are signatories to the Agreements. Effective policy co-ordination is in the hand of the Board of Governors with 27 members meeting about four times a year; the Governors are appointed by major contributors or groups of contributors, but due regard is also given to the need of equitable geographic representation of all members. The Director-General oversees the activities of the staff.

Activities

The Organization provides, by means of its satellites, a substantial proportion of the world's international telecommunications services between over 800 earth stations in around 180 countries or territories and is becoming more commercially orientated to satisfy the growing demands of users.

Director-General: Irving Goldstein
Headquarters: 3400 International Drive, N. W., Washington DC 20008-3098, USA (Telephone: +1 202 944 6800; fax: +1 202 944 7860)

International Telecommunication Union (ITU)

The Union, which is the oldest intergovernmental organization in existence, promotes the development and rational use of telecommunications.

Origin and development

The Union was founded in Paris in May 1865, as the International Telegraph Union, by the representatives of 20 countries, with the adoption of the first Telegraph Convention and the relevant Regulations. A Bureau of the Union was set up in Berne, Switzerland, in 1868. The first international Radio Conference was held in Berlin in 1906, with the participation of 27 countries, and a Convention and Radio Regulations were drawn up. The Union's full title was changed to the present one at the Madrid Conferences (1932), when the existing Telegraph and Radiotelegraph Conventions were replaced by the first single International Telecommunication Convention, which came into effect in January 1934. At the Atlantic City Plenipotentiary and Radio Conferences (1947), the Union was reorganized and entered into a relationship agreement with the UN under which it was recognized as the specialized agency for telecommunication; the agreement came into force in January 1949. The seat of the Union was transferred to Geneva in 1948. The concept of 'telecommunications' applies to any transmission, emission or reception of signs, signals, writing, images and sounds or intelligence of any nature by wire, radio, optical or other electromagnetic systems – that is, telegraph, Telephone and radio, and all their applications such as television and telex.

The International Telecommunication Convention, which is the constitutional document of the Union, has been revised radically several times. At present the Union is governed by the Geneva Constitution and Convention adopted by the Additional Plenipotentiary Conference held in Geneva in December 1992, which entered into force in 1994.

Members of the UN may accede to the Union, according to current provisions. Any sovereign country, not a member of the UN, may be admitted to the Union if the request has secured approval by at least two-thirds of member countries. Membership of the Union now includes about 185 countries.

Objectives

The aims of the Union are to maintain and extend co-operation for the improvement and rational use of telecommunications of all kinds; to assist the development of technical facilities and their most efficient operation; to promote the extension of the benefits of the new telecommunications technologies to all the world's inhabitants; and to foster, at the international level, a new approach to the issues of telecommunications in the global information economy and society.

The Union works to fulfil its basic purposes in three main ways: international conferences and meetings; publication of information and organization of world exhibitions; and technical co-operation. Basic functions of the Union include: allocating radio frequencies and recording the assignments; co-ordinating efforts to eliminate harmful interference between stations; establishing the lowest possible rates consistent with efficient service, and taking into account the necessity of maintaining the independent financial administration of telecommunication on a sound basis; promoting the adoption of measures for ensuring the safety of life through telecommunications; making studies and recommendations which also cover space telecommunication techniques and regulations; and collecting and publishing information for the benefit of its members. As regards technical co-operation with developing countries, the Union promotes the development of regional telecommunication networks; helps strengthen technical and administrative services; and develops the human resources required for telecommunications, especially through the training of personnel. Assistance is provided in the specialized fields of telephony, telegraphy, radiocommunications, frequency management, satellite communications, planning, organization, administration, and management.

Structure

According to the 1992 Geneva Constitution, the structure of the Union consists of the Plenipotentiary Conference, the Council, World conferences on international telecommunications, the Radiocommunication sector, the Telecommunication Standardization Sector, the Telecommunication Development Sector, and the General Secretariat.

The Plenipotentiary Conference is composed of representatives of all member countries and normally meets every four years. It is the supreme authority of the Union, laying down general policies, reviewing the Union's work, revising the Convention if necessary, and establishing the basis for the budget. The 46-member Council, acting on behalf of the Plenipotentiary Conference, holds one annual meeting. World conferences on international telecommunications are held at the request of plenipotentiary conferences; radiocommunication conferences are held every two years, along with a Radiocommunication Assembly; telecommunication standardization conferences are held every four years (an additional conference may be held upon the request of one-quarter of the members); development conferences are held at regular intervals. In principle, within the four-year period between plenipotentiary conferences, one world conference and

one conference is convened in each of the regions (Africa, the Americas, the Arab States, Asia-Pacific, and Europe). The Radiocommunication Sector is in charge of world and regional radiocommunication conferences, radiocommunication assemblies and the Radio Regulations Board. The Telecommunication Standardization Sector, including world telecommunication standardization conferences, is in charge of technical, operating and tariff questions and issues recommendations with a view to standardizing telecommunications on a world-wide basis. The Telecommunication Development Sector includes world and regional telecommunication development conferences and the Telecommunication Development Bureau (TDB); the TDB is responsible for presenting to developing countries the range of policy and structural options leading to greater resources for telecommunication development. The First World Telecommunication Development Conference (WTDC 94) was held in Buenos Aires, Argentina, in March 1994 and adopted a Declaration and an Action Plan setting the main orientations and programmes for achieving a balanced telecommunication development. The General Secretariat is directed by a Secretary-General elected by the Plenipotentiary Conference for a renewable term. The Secretary-General is responsible for all the administrative and financial aspects of the Union's activities.

Each meeting of the Plenipotentiary Conference fixes the maximum amount of expenditure the Union may reach before the next meeting. Expenses are borne in common by member countries, which are divided for this purpose into various contribution classes.

Activities

The Union, mainly within the framework of the *UN Development Programme (UNDP), administers a programme through which telecommunications experts are sent to various countries throughout the world to advise on the operation of telegraph, telephone and radio systems, or to help to train technicians. Surveys for modern international telecommunication networks have been conducted in several developing areas. The Union co-operates actively with the *Universal Postal Union (UPU) with a view to preparing and executing joint technical assistance projects, particularly in the vocational training field. Close co-operative contacts are also maintained with other UN specialized agencies, as well as with several intergovernmental and non-governmental institutions.

Since its establishment, the Union has made fundamental contributions to the development and improvement of telecommunication, laying down basic principles and provisions, and adapting itself to new pressing needs. In the field of technical co-operation, mention should be made, *inter alia*, of the Plan Committees (World Committee and Regional Committees for Africa, Latin America, Asia and Oceania, and Europe and the Mediterranean Basin) responsible for preparing plans establishing circuit and routing requirements for international telecommunications. In 1981 the UN General Assembly proclaimed 1983 as World Communications Year, and designated the Union as the leading agency for coordinating activities, with special regard to the development of communications infrastructures.

The Union's 14th Plenipotentiary Conference met in Kyoto, Japan, in 1994 to establish general policies, to adopt an overall strategic plan for the following four years, and to improve the Union's effectiveness in light of the changes that have characterized the world of telecommunications, including enhanced participation of the industry and other organizations in the Union's work and decision-making process; the Conference also decided on measures to strengthen the financial base of the Union.

Secretary-General: Pekka Johannes Tarjanne

Headquarters: Place des Nations, 1211 Geneva 20, Switzerland (Telephone: +41 22 730 5111; fax: +41 22 733 7256)

Publications: *Annual Report*; *International Telecommunication Journal* (monthly); conventions, statistics, technical documents and manuals.

References: G. A. Codding, Jr, *The International Telecommunication Union: An Experiment in International Co-operation* (Leiden, 1952, reprinted 1972); G. A. Codding, Jr and A. M. Rutkowski, *The International Telecommunication Union in a Changing World* (Dedham, Mass., 1982); G. A. Codding Jr, 'The International Telecommunication Union', in P. Taylor and A. J. R. Groom (eds), *International Institutions at Work* (London, 1988), 167–83

International Trade Centre (ITC)

The Centre, operated by the UN and the *World Trade Organization (WTO), promotes the international trade of the developing countries.

Origin and development

The Centre was set up in 1964 under the auspices of the General Agreement on Tariffs and Trade (GATT); in 1968 the *UN Conference on Trade and Development (UNCTAD) joined the GATT as a co-sponsor of the Centre. Since the establishment of the WTO in 1995, the Centre is operated jointly by the WTO and the UN, the latter acting through UNCTAD. In 1984 the Centre became an executing agency of the *UN Development Programme (UNDP), directly responsible for carrying out UNDP-financed projects related to trade promotion.

Objectives

The Centre assists developing countries in the formulation and implementation of export promotion programmes as well as import operations and techniques. It provides advice on marketing techniques and export markets, and helps in establishing export promotion and marketing services and in training the necessary personnel.

Structure

The Joint Advisory Group on the International Trade Centre (JAG) meets annually to review technical co-operation programmes, establish guidelines and make the relevant recommendations.

Activities

Technical co-operation projects, undertaken at the request of governments, are carried out in all developing areas at the national, subregional, regional and interregional levels. Assistance is provided free of charge to the least-developed countries.

The Centre, because of its legal status of joint subsidiary organ, does not have a membership of its own; *de facto* members are the member countries of WTO and of UNCTAD. As an executing agency of the *UN Development Programme (UNDP), the Centre bears direct responsibility for implementing UNDP-financed projects in developing countries related to trade promotion.

Executive Director: J. Denis Bélisle
Headquarters: 54-56 rue de Montbrillant, 1211 Geneva 10, Switzerland (Telephone: +41 22 730 0111; fax: +41 22 733 4439)
Publications: *International Trade Forum* (quarterly); handbooks, market surveys, monographs, directories and training material

International Union for the Protection of New Varieties of Plants (UPOV)

The Union protects the industrial property rights of breeders of new plant varieties.

Origin and development
The Union was established by a Convention signed in Paris in 1961 and came into force in 1968; revisions took place in 1972, 1978 and 1991. Membership currently includes around 30 countries, mainly in Europe and North and South America.

Objectives
The purposes of the Union are to oblige member countries to recognize and secure to breeders of new plant varieties an industrial property right (plant breeder's right), to harmonize such rights, and to encourage co-operation between members in their administration of such rights.

Structure
The Council is the highest decision-making body, meeting at yearly intervals and consisting of representatives of all member countries. The Council is assisted by three Committees – the Consultative Committee, the Administrative and Legal Committee, and the Technical Committee. Administrative and technical tasks are performed by the Secretariat-General, known as the 'Office of the Union'.

Activities
Although it is an independent intergovernmental organization, the Union works in close co-operation with the *World Intellectual Property Organization (WIPO) whose Director-General is the Union's Secretary-General.

Secretary-General: Dr Arpad Bogsch
Headquarters: 34 chemin des Colombettes, 1211 Geneva 20, Switzerland (Telephone: +41 22 730 9111; fax: +41 22 733 5428)

International Whaling Commission (IWC)

The Commission promotes the conservation of whale stocks as well as research concerning whales.

Origin and development
The Commission was established in 1946 and has concentrated its efforts on the limitation of commercial whaling. Member countries are allowed to grant permits for the taking of whales for scientific research purposes; permits have been given in recent years by Iceland, Japan and Norway. The current membership includes about 40 countries in all continents.

Objectives
The purposes of the Commission are to provide for the proper preservation of whale stocks, to encourage research relating to whales and whaling, to collect and analyse statistical information concerning conditions and trend of whale stocks, and to appraise and disseminate information about methods of maintaining and increasing whale stocks.

Structure
The annual meeting of the representatives of all member countries is the policy-making body of the Commission.

Activities
The first moratorium on commercial whaling was declared by the Commission in 1982, with effect from 1985, and was reconfirmed in June 1995, notwithstanding Japan's requests for a limited resumption. Only 'subsistence whaling' was allowed for limited quotas to meet the needs of indigenous communities in Alaska, Greenland, and Saint Vincent and the Grenadines. Norway did not accept the moratorium and despite widespread protest resumed whaling operations in 1993, continuing in 1994 and 1995. Japan, for its

part, has been catching a small amount of whales for 'scientific purposes'. In addition to the safe area in the Indian Ocean, created in 1979 with a ban on commercial whaling, a whale sanctuary is to be established in the Antarctic, thereby ensuring protection to around 80 per cent of the world's whales.

Secretary: Dr Ray Gambell
Headquarters: The Red House, Station Road, Histon, Cambridge CB4 4NP, England (Telephone: +44 1223 233971; fax: +44 1223 232876)
Publication: *Annual Report*

Islamic Development Bank (IsDB)

The Bank is among the biggest Arab development funds financing economic and social development.

Origin and development

The origins of the Bank date back to the Declaration of Intent issued by a Conference of Finance Ministers of Islamic countries, held in Jeddah, Saudi Arabia, in December 1973. The Agreement establishing the Bank was signed under the auspices of the *Organization of the Islamic Conference (OIC) in August 1974 in Jeddah; the Bank began functioning in that town in October 1975, and financial operations started in 1976. Present membership includes about 45 Moslem countries in Africa and Asia, plus Albania, Turkey and the Palestine Liberation Organization (PLO).

Objectives

The Bank aims to finance the economic development and social progress of its member countries and of Moslem communities in non-member countries, in accordance with the principles of the Shari'a, that is Islamic Law. It is, at present, the biggest of Arab development funds.

Structure

The Bank comprises the Board of Governors, the Board of Executive Directors, and the President. The Board of Governors is the supreme body composed of one governor, usually the Minister of Finance, or his alternate, appointed by each member country and meeting at least once a year. Many powers have been delegated by the Board of Governors to the executive organ; that is, the Board of Executive Directors, consisting of eleven members and responsible for the Bank's general operations. Five directors are appointed by the five largest subscribers; the governors of the remaining subscribers are entitled to elect the other six directors for a three-year term. The President of the Bank serves for a five-year period and acts as Chairman of the Board of Executive Directors, by whom he is elected.

Activities

In its activities, the Bank follows the Koranic principle forbidding usury; it does not extend loans or credits for interest, and supports economic and social development by taking up equity participation in public and private enterprises in member countries, financing infrastructural projects, granting funds to Islamic communities in non-member countries, and providing technical assistance. It may establish and operate special funds for specific purposes in order to preserve the value of its assets. In particular, the Bank seeks to develop new financial instruments, in accordance with Islamic principles, for additional resource mobilization.

The Bank uses as a unit of account the Islamic Dinar (IsD) which is equivalent to one special drawing right (SDR). The size of the authorized capital stock was set at IsD2000 million, divided into 200 000 shares, each of them having a value of IsD10 000. At the end of 1992 the authorized capital amounted to IsD6000 million and the subscribed capital to IsD4000 million; paid-up capital was IsD1688 million. The five largest subscribers are Saudi Arabia, Libya, Kuwait, the United Arab Emirates and Turkey.

Co-operative links are maintained by the Bank with various international institutions, both Islamic and non-Islamic. It is a member of the Co-ordination Secretariat of Arab National and Regional Development Institutions.

Under the Bank's Special Assistance Account, emergency aid and other forms of assistance are provided, mainly with a view to promoting education in Islamic communities in non-member countries. A sizeable share of the Bank's concessional financing goes to about 20 members which are among the world's least-developed countries according to the United Nations classification. The Bank also undertakes the distribution of meat sacrificed by Muslim pilgrims.

In 1987 the Bank launched the Islamic Banks' Portfolio for Investment and Development, to finance trade and leasing activities in the private sector. A Longer-Term Trade Financing Scheme was introduced in 1987/8 with a view to promoting trade among member countries, especially in non-traditional commodities. In order to mobilize additional resources from the market, the Bank introduced a Unit Investment Fund, specifically targeted to institutional investors, in December 1989.

An Islamic Research and Training Institute was established in 1982 to promote research on economic, financial and banking activities conforming to Islamic law, and to provide training for staff involved in development activities in the Bank's member countries.

President: Ahmad Muhammad Ali
Headquarters: P.O. Box 5925, Jeddah 21432, Saudi Arabia (Telephone: +966 2 636 1400; fax: +966 2 636 6871)
Publication: *Annual Report*

L

Lake Chad Basin Commission (LCBC)

The Commission was established in 1964 by Cameroon, Chad, Niger and Nigeria with the purpose of co-ordinating the development of the Chad basin, recommending plans for common projects and joint research programmes, and ensuring the most efficient use of the subterranean and surface water resources in relation to agriculture, animal husbandry and fisheries. The Central African Republic became a full member in March 1994 when agreement was also reached on the setting-up of a joint security force and on a plan providing for sound environmental management of the Lake Chad Basin.

Executive Secretary: Abubakar B. Jauro
Headquarers: P.O. Box 727, N'Djaména, Chad (Telephone: +235 514145; fax: +235 514137)

Latin American Economic System

(Sistema Económico Latinoamericano) (SELA)

The System is intended to provide Latin American countries with permanent institutional machinery for joint consultation, co-ordination and co-operation in economic and social matters at both the intraregional and the extraregional levels.

Origin and development

After a relatively brief period of negotiation, with Mexico and Venezuela playing a very active role, the agreement establishing SELA was signed in October 1975 in Panama by the representatives of 25 Latin American and Caribbean countries (including Cuba); Suriname joined in 1979, followed by Belize in 1991. SELA has taken over the functions formerly performed by the Special Latin American Co-ordinating Commission (CECLA), which was created in the first half of the 1960s as a forum for the formulation of common policies on trade and development issues towards international organizations and countries outside Latin America.

Objectives

The basic aims of the System are to advance Latin American trade and co-operation, while respecting and supporting the existing regional arrangements, and to co-ordinate the positions and strategies of individual members regarding external countries and agencies with a view to strengthening the bargaining power of the area.

To achieve its main objectives, the System: (a) promotes the better utilization of regional resources through the creation of Latin American multinational enterprises; (b) defends the prices of raw materials exported from Latin America and encourages the transformation of these materials within the region; (c) formulates measures and policies which ensure that the operations of transnational companies are in accordance with the development goals of the region and the interests of individual members; (d) improves the collective negotiating capacity for acquiring and utilizing capital goods and technology; and (e) furthers the drafting and implementation of economic and social projects of interest to member countries.

Structure

The System's institutional structure includes the Latin American Council, several Action Committees and the Permanent Secretariat. The Latin American Council is the supreme body of the System and consists of one representative from each member country, with one vote. It meets annually at ministerial level; extraordinary meetings may be held whenever necessary. The Council establishes the System's general policies, defines common positions of members concerning non-member countries, groups of countries and international organizations, approves the budget and elects the Permanent Secretary. Decisions concerning basic policies and joint positions must be approved by consensus. Specific agreements and projects are adopted on a fully voluntary basis and therefore need the approval only of those countries choosing to participate in them. Action Committees may be established by the Council or by two or more interested member countries in order to draft and carry out specific programmes and projects, as well as to prepare and adopt joint negotiating positions on issues of interest to member countries in international forums. Each Action Committee, funded by participating member states, establishes its own headquarters and secretariat.

The Permanent Secretariat is charged with the technical and administrative functions of the System. It organizes and carries out preliminary studies on projects of common interest to member countries, implements the decisions of the Latin American Council and co-ordinates the activities of the Action Committees. The Permanent Secretary is appointed by the Latin American Council for a four-year term and may be re-elected once, but not for consecutive periods.

Activities

The System has gradually been developing active co-operative relations with international organizations, especially Latin American regional economic and financial bodies, and with non-member countries. In conformity with its basic purposes and principles, and in spite of the relative weakness of its organizational machinery, the System has been making a notable effort to expedite regional co-operation and to build up Latin American solidarity on international economic issues in regard to external countries and organizations. After its first ordinary meeting in October 1975, the Latin American Council held an extraordinary technical session in January 1976 in order to fund an operating budget (contributed according to the economic development level of each member country) and to formulate a common Latin American position in preparation for the fourth session of the *UN Conference on Trade and Development (UNCTAD). At subsequent meetings, the Latin American Council defined the rules governing the operations of the Action Committees and laid the foundations for setting up Latin American multinational enterprises in specific sectors of vital importance to the region.

The Action Committee for the manufacture of fertilizers inspired the establishment in May 1980 of MULTIFERT, a Latin American multinational enterprise for the marketing of fertilizers, located in Panama City. In addition to MULTIFERT, the following agencies have been set up within SELA: Action Committee for the Support of Economic and Social Development in Central America (CADESCA), based in Panama City; Action Committee for Latin American Co-operation and Concertation on Plant Germplasm (CARFIT), based in Mexico City; Latin American and Caribbean Trade Information and Foreign Trade Support Programme (PLACIEX), based in Lima; Latin American Agency for Specialized Information Services (ALASEI), based in Mexico City; *Latin American Organization for the Development of Fisheries (OLDEPESCA), based in Lima; Latin American Programme for Co-operation on Handicrafts (PLACART), based in Caracas; Latin American Maritime Transport Commission (COLTRAM), based in Caracas; Latin American Commission for Science and Technology (COLCYT), based in Caracas; Latin American Technological Information Network (RITLA), based in Brasília.

At the extraregional level, initiatives to establish and maintain a common policy within an appropriate consultative framework have been a regular feature of meetings of the Latin American Council. Joint positions have been adopted towards the *Group of 77 and UNCTAD, while a remarkable effort has been carried out to develop dialogue and co-operation with the *European Community (EC). In the early 1980s the System concentrated – in collaboration with the *Economic Commission for Latin America and the Caribbean (ECLAC) – on a debt and development strategy, and called for broad debt relief measures. However, the regional approach to debt reduction sponsored by the System met with reluctance from the interested member countries wishing to retain their autonomy in order to negotiate individual packages. The situation was further complicated by the establishment in 1987 of the Group of Eight, subsequently succeeded by the *Group of Rio, also concerned with foreign debt issues.

On the whole, SELA may still play a role in the promotion of economic integration through the creation of a number of Latin American joint ventures, but the formation and implementation of a region-wide economic policy appears to be a distant goal.

Permanent Secretary: Carlos Moneta
Headquaters: Av. Francisco de Miranda, Urb. Campo Alegre, Torre Europa, Piso 4, Caracas 1060, Venezuela (Telephone: +58 2 905 5111; fax: +58 2 951 6953)
Publication: *Capítulos del SELA* (quarterly)

Latin American Energy Organization

(Organización Latinoamericana de Energía)

(OLADE)

The Organization was formed in 1973 to facilitate and promote co-operation and co-ordination among the countries of Latin America with regard to policies concerning the protection, conservation, proper utilization and marketing of the energy resources of the region. Members currently include 26 Latin American and Caribbean countries. Programmes carried out by the Organization are intended to integrate the energy sector into overall economic and development planning in the region.

Executive Secretary: Francisco Gutiérrez
Headquaters: Avenida Occidental, OLADE Building, Sector San Carlos, Casilla 6413 CCI, Quito, Ecuador (Telephone: +593 2 538280; fax: +593 2 539684)
Publication: *Revista Energética*

Latin American Integration Association (LAIA)

(Asociación Latinoamericana de Integración)

(ALADI)

The Association succeeded the Latin American Free Trade Association (LAFTA) in 1980, with a view to establishing a common market among Latin American countries.

Origin and development

The Treaty creating the Association was signed in Montevideo, Uruguay, in August 1980 by the Ministers of Foreign Affairs of the same eleven countries that had founded LAFTA under the Treaty of Montevideo of February 1960, or had subsequently joined it (Argentina, Bolivia, Brazil, Chile, Colombia, Ecuador, Mexico, Paraguay, Peru, Uruguay and Venezuela). At the same time, several resolutions were approved concerning the renegotiation of LAFTA's 'historical heritage', meaning the various commitments arising from LAFTA's Trade Liberalization Programme.

The adoption of a new and more flexible integration scheme for Latin America represented the outcome of complex efforts originally intended to reorganize and update LAFTA's structure and mechanisms. The Montevideo Treaty of 1960 en-visaged the establishment within a 12-year period of a free-trade area through the gradual elimination of tariff and non-tariff barriers. Tariff reductions covering 55 per cent of intrazonal trade were achieved during the first rounds of negotiations. However, further progress proved extremely difficult, and the transition period was extended to 1980 under the Caracas Protocol of 1969. 'Complementation agreements' in particular sectors largely failed to strengthen policies of economic and industrial integration. Financial co-operation largely failed to materialize and no agreement was reached on the creation of a regional financial institution. In 1967, LAFTA had expressly authorized the drawing-up, within its legal framework, of subregional agreements between its members, to encourage the formation of common markets on a more limited scale, with the ultimate goal of a future merger in a single Latin American market. In accordance with this policy, in May 1969, Bolivia, Colombia, Chile, Ecuador and Peru concluded the Cartagena Agreement establishing the Andean Group (succeeded in 1996 by the *Andean Community).

In recognition of the slow progress on basic issues and the widespread disappointment over the lack of concrete perspectives, in December 1979 a detailed agenda was set up for the negotiation of a new Montevideo Treaty. After two preparatory meetings, in June 1980 the Conference of Contracting Parties held an extraordinary session in Acapulco, Mexico, to consider the final draft of the Treaty. It was signed in Montevideo the following August and entered into force in March 1981.

Membership of the Association is open to other Latin American countries but may not be subject to reservations. Members may withdraw from the Association provided one year's notice is given. However, special rules apply to the withdrawal of concessions granted under the regional tariff preference scheme and regional and partial scope agreements.

At present there are permanent observers representing 15 countries from Latin America, Europe and Asia, and five international agencies; that is, the UN *Economic Commission for Latin America and the Caribbean (ECLAC), the *UN Development Programme (UNDP), the *European Union (EU), the *Inter-American Development Bank (IDB) and the *Organization of American States (OAS).

Objectives

The Association pursues the long-term goal of establishing a common market through the creation of an area of economic preferences, based on a regional tariff preference and regional and partial scope agreements. In addition, a support system for less-developed member countries is envisaged.

The Montevideo Treaty of 1980 envisages the gradual and progressive establishment of an economic preferences area and not of a free-trade area, like its predecessor. In addition, no rigid mechanisms, schedules or time limits are set out for the achievement of basic objectives. The exact content and scope of the area of economic preferences depend on the nature of the agreements to be reached, whether regional or partial, and on the depth of the regional preference margin to be applied with reference to tariff levels in force for non-member countries. All members participate in regional agreements; partial scope agreements are applicable only to interested countries but must aim at progressive multilateralization and provide for extension to other members. Partial agreements may be concluded for periods of at least one year in the spheres of trade, economic and industrial complementation, agriculture and livestock, and export promotion.

The Association's objectives are to be pursued while paying due regard to a set of basic principles which involve differential treatments based on the classification of member countries, according to their economic structure, into three main categories: most developed (Argentina, Brazil and Mexico); intermediate (Chile, Colombia, Peru, Uruguay and Venezuela); and least developed (Bolivia, Ecuador and Paraguay). More favourable terms are granted to intermediate countries, while additional, special benefits are provided for the least developed and landlocked members. The functions of the Association, in conformity with the rules and mechanisms of the Treaty, include the promotion of reciprocal trade and economic complementation, and the development of economic co-operation activities directed to the enlargement of markets.

Structure

The Association accomplishes it purposes by means of three 'political' organs (the Council of Ministers of Foreign Affairs; the Evaluation and Convergence Conference; and the Committee of Representatives) plus a technical organ (the General Secretariat). Subsidiary organs performing advisory and technical functions may be set up in order to facilitate the study of specific problems; one such organ is to consist of officials who, in their respective countries, are responsible for integration policies. Other consultative bodies are to include representatives of the various sectors of economic activity of each member country.

The Council, which is the supreme body, has a broad mandate to consider any action that may be necessary for the attainment of the objectives of economic integration. It is empowered to lay down the essential rules for the harmonious development of the integration process; appraise the results of the tasks performed by the Association; adopt corrective measures upon the recommendation of the Conference in order to propitiate convergence; direct the work of the other organs; set basic guidelines concerning relations with other regional organizations and international bodies; revise and adapt the fundamental rules on convergence and co-operation agreements concluded with other developing countries and integration groupings; modify and supplement the Treaty; decide on the admission of new members; and appoint the Secretary-General. The Council is convened by the Committee of Representatives and may not meet and take decisions unless all its members are present.

The Evaluation and Convergence Conference, consisting of plenipotentiaries from member countries, is convened by the Committee of Representatives; the presence of all members is required. The Conference is entrusted with responsibility for appraising the integration process in all its aspects and the convergence of partial scope agreements through their progressive multilateralization, as well as for recommending to the Council the adoption of corrective measures of multilateral scope. The Conference is also responsible for carrying out periodic revisions of differential treatments; assessing the results of the implementation of the system for supporting the relatively less-developed members; effecting multilateral negotiations with regard to the regional tariff preference; and facilitating the negotiation of regional agreements involving all members.

The Committee is the Association's permanent organ, composed of a permanent and a deputy representative from each country plus representatives from the permanent observers. It may not hold meetings and adopt resolutions unless two-thirds of its members are present. Its principal powers are to convene governmental meetings for the negotiation of regional agreements, especially with regard to tariff reductions; to take the necessary steps for the implementation of the Treaty; to undertake the work assigned to it by the Council and the Conference; to approve the Association's annual budget and to fix the contributions of each member; to convene the Council and the Conference; to represent the Association in dealings with non-member countries; to submit proposals and recommendations to the Council and the Conference; to evaluate multilaterally the partial scope agreements reached by the interested members.

The three political organs of the Association may take decisions when affirmative votes are cast by at least two-thirds of the member countries; non-participation is equivalent to abstention. On highly sensitive issues, which are considered to be vital to the integration process, decisions may be adopted by a two-thirds majority, provided that no negative vote is cast.

Several subsidiary bodies have been created: the Council for Financial and Monetary Affairs, composed of the Presidents of member countries' central banks; the Advisory Commission on Financial and Monetary Affairs; the Advisory Commission on Customs Valuation; the Tourism Council; the Entrepreneurial Advisory Council; the Labour Advisory Council; the Nomenclature Advisory Commission; the Advisory Council for Export Financing; the Council on Transport for Trade Facilitation; and the Meeting of Directors of National Customs Administrations.

The General Secretariat is headed by a Secretary-General – elected by the Council for a three-year term and eligible for a further period – who is assisted by two Deputy Secretaries-General. The Secretariat's duties are to prepare proposals for consideration by the political organs; to carry out studies and other activities included in the annual work programme; to represent the Association in dealings with international economic agencies and bodies; to recommend to the Committee the creation of subsidiary organs; to establish an Economic Promotion Unit responsible for the least-developed members;

and to submit to the Committee an annual report on the results of the implementation of the Treaty.

Activities

Special emphasis is given by the Association to co-ordination and co-operation with other countries and integration groupings in Latin America with a view to establishing a Latin American tariff preference and concluding partial scope agreements. Under special circumstances, partial agreements may also be reached with other developing countries (or the relevant integration areas) outside Latin America.

A series of initiatives have been taken, within the Association's framework, for saving and widening the concessions granted under the auspices of LAFTA and for promoting bilateral and multilateral agreements in the economic and financial fields. The multiplicity of ways provided to facilitate agreement on integration actions, together with the effort to propitiate convergence and progressive multilateralization, should lead to the choice of the most feasible means of complying with the ultimate goal of the Montevideo Treaty of 1980. Partial economic complementation agreements with emphasis on the industrial, energy, technological and financial sectors may offer ample possibilities for strengthening co-operation, not only among members but also with non-members in Central America and the Caribbean.

By the end of 1983 the transition from LAFTA to the Association had been completed, with the renegotiation of over 23 000 tariff cuts granted among the partners, from 1962 onwards. Some LAFTA institutions have been retained by the Association, such as the Accord on Reciprocal Payments and Credits (revised in 1982) and the Multilateral Credit Agreement to Alleviate Temporary Shortages of Liquidity (revised and extended in 1981).

The agreement on the Regional Tariff Preference (RTP) for goods originating in the eleven member countries was eventually signed in April 1984 and entered into effect the following July. A new system of tariff nomenclature was adopted from January 1990 to facilitate common trade negotiations and statistics.

Over 120 agreements have entered into force thus far. Seven are 'regional scope' agreements, involving all member countries and dealing, *inter alia*, with regional tariff preferences, market access in favour of the three least-developed members, scientific and technological co-operation, and cultural co-operation. The remaining agreements have a 'partial' scope, concerning two or more countries and facilitating trade and co-operation in particular sectors. The Treaty establishing *Mercosur is one of the most significant 'partial agreements'. The proliferation of subregional arrangements presents a serious challenge for the Association, which should act as an 'umbrella' organization. A further challenge has been represented by the participation of Mexico in the *North American Free Trade Agreement (NAFTA); to make such participation possible, an Interpretative Protocol to the Montevideo Treaty had to be adopted in June 1994 expressly allowing the conclusion of preferential trade agreements between members and developed countries.

Secretary-General: António de Cerqueira Antúnes
Headquaters: Cebollatí 1461, P.O. Box 577, Montevideo, Uruguay (Telephone: +598 495915; fax: +598 490649)
Publication: *Nuestro Perfil* (monthly, in Spanish)

Latin American Organization for the Development of Fisheries (OLDEPESCA)

Founded by an agreement signed in 1982 and entered into force in 1984, the Organization covers the oceans bordering Latin America and groups nine countries: Bolivia, Ecuador, El Salvador, Guatemala, Mexico, Nicaragua, Panama, Peru and Venezuela. The Organization's purpose is to provide adequately for the food needs of Latin America and the Caribbean through the use of the potential of fishery resources for the benefit of the people living in the region.

The Conference of Ministers is the supreme authority setting the guidelines and policies of the Organization through declarations and resolutions, which are generally prepared, in the form of recommendations to the Conference, by the Governing Council. The Organization is involved in research concerning fisheries resources and their exploitation, aquaculture, training and environmental protection.

Headquarters: Calle las Palomas 422, Urbanización Limatambo, Apartado 10168, Lima 34, Peru (Telephone: +51 14 413858; fax: +51 14 429925)

League of Arab States (Arab League)

The League represents the most important attempt that has been made so far to strengthen solidarity and co-ordinate policies among Arab countries.

Origin and development

The foundation of the League as a regional political arrangement for the pursuit of comprehensive goals emerged from an effort to restore the Arab community. However, the existence of many separate states and administrations under mandatory control (as a result of the 1919 peace settlement), and the long-standing tensions and rivalries between conservative and revolutionary groups and movements, as well as between oil-rich and poor countries, led Arab leaders to shelve union or federation plans in favour of a voluntary association of sovereign states. A Pan-Arabic conference was held in the autumn of 1944. It drew up the Alexandria Protocol outlining the basic features of the new organization, which was formally established by the signing of the Pact of the League of Arab States in March 1945 in Cairo.

The Pact establishing the League was concluded in 1945 by the representatives of seven Arab countries that had achieved independence (Egypt, Iraq, Lebanon, Saudi Arabia, Syria, Transjordan, and Yemen). The original members were joined by Libya (1953); Sudan (1956); Tunisia and Morocco (1958); Kuwait (1961); Algeria (1962); Southern Yemen (1967); Bahrain, Qatar, Oman and the United Arab Emirates (1971); Mauritania (1973); Somalia (1974); Djibouti (1977); and the Comoros (1993). Palestine is considered independent *de jure* even though, according to the Pact Annex on Palestine, 'the outward signs of this independence have remained veiled as a result of force majeure' – and therefore a full member of the League since the beginning. In response to the signing in March 1979 of a peace treaty between Israel and Egypt, the latter's membership of the League was suspended and the League's headquarters were transferred from Cairo to Tunis; Egypt's readmission took place in May 1989 and the League moved its headquarters back to Cairo at the end of October 1990.

Each member is bound to respect the form of government existing in other member countries and to refrain from any action tending to change such form. Members are not allowed to use force for the settlement of disputes between them. The League is entitled to mediate in a dispute which may lead to war between two members, or between a member and another country, in order to conciliate them. In case of aggression or threat of aggression by any country against a member, the League may decide, by unanimous vote, upon the necessary measures to repel the aggression. The collective security aspects of the Pact were further developed and specified in the Joint Defence and Economic Co-operation Treaty, which was concluded between members of the League in April 1950 and entered into force in August 1952.

Every independent Arab state has the right to belong to the League, whose Council will decide upon the application presented to this effect. The right of withdrawal is expressly envisaged, provided one year's notice is given; however, a member that does not approve an amendment to the Pact may withdraw before such amendment becomes effective, no minimum period of notice being required. Any member that is not fulfilling its obligations under the Pact may be excluded from the League by a decision taken unanimously.

Objectives

The purposes of the League are to strengthen the ties between Arab countries, to co-ordinate their policies and activities, to safeguard their sovereignty, and to consider in a general way the affairs and interests of the Arab countries; co-operation is to take place paying due regard to the structure of each country and the conditions prevailing therein.

As well as the basic aim of promoting coordination on the political plane, a close co-operation between member countries is envisaged by the Pact in economic and financial affairs, including trade, customs, currency, agriculture, and industry; communications, including railways, roads, aviation, navigation, and postal and telegraphic services; cultural affairs; matters related to nationality, passports, visas, execution of judgments and extradition; social welfare; and health.

Structure

The basic organizational structure of the League is fairly simple, comprising the Council, assisted by a number of Committees, and the permanent General Secretariat. The Council is the highest policy-making body, composed of the representatives of member countries and of Palestine, each member having one vote. Ordinary sessions are held either at the seat of the League or at any other designated place, and are presided over by representatives of member countries in turn. Extraordinary sessions may be convened at the request of at least two member countries whenever the need arises. The Council is entrusted with the functions of realizing the purposes of the League, supervising the implementation of agreements concluded between members on specific matters, and setting the guidelines for co-operation with other international organizations in the political, economic and social spheres. In principle, decisions are taken by the Council unanimously; these decisions are obligatory on all member countries that are bound to act in conformity with their own constitutional rules. Some important questions may, however, be dealt with by majority vote, such as decisions relating to arbitration and mediation, personnel, budget, internal organization, and termination of sessions. Amendments to the Pact require a two-thirds majority.

At present there are 15 special Committees attached to the Council. It is the responsibility of these Committees to establish the basis and scope of co-operation in the form of draft agreements to be submitted to the Council for consideration. As a rule, decisions are taken by the Committees by simple majority. The Political Committee, usually composed of the Foreign Ministers of all member countries, reports to the Council sessions on major political questions and may represent the Council itself in dealing with emergencies. The Cultural Committee is charged with the follow-up of the cultural activities of the various organs of the League and of the relevant bodies of member countries. Other special Committees deal with communications, social affairs, legal problems, information, health, human rights (with special regard to violations by Israel), administrative and financial matters, and meteorology. Reference should also be made to the Committee of Arab Experts on Co-operation, the Arab Women's Committee, the Organization of

Youth Welfare, and the Conference of Liaison Officers; the last-mentioned body is responsible for the co-ordination of activities among Arab commercial attachés abroad. Economic issues have been discussed within the framework of the Economic Council, whose first meeting was held in 1953.

The General Secretariat is composed of the Secretary-General, a number of Assistant Secretaries-General, and necessary staff. It is the central and permanent organ, carrying out the policies and programmes decided upon by the Council and the Political Committee, and providing administrative services. The General Secretariat includes departments which deal with Arab affairs, economic, international, legal, social and cultural affairs, information, Palestine, and administrative and financial affairs. The Secretary-General is elected by the Council by a two-thirds majority for a five-year term. The Assistant Secretaries-General and the principal officials are appointed by the Secretary-General with the approval of the Council.

A significant role within the institutional framework of the League has been played by the periodic meetings of Arab Kings and Presidents – that is, the 'Summit Conference', the first session of which was held in Cairo in January 1964.

The member countries of the League participate in the Specialized Agencies which constitute an integral part of the League and are designed to develop specific aspects of co-operation, or to deal with special technical matters of common interest to Arab states. The Specialized Agencies include: the *Arab Bank for Economic Development in Africa (BADEA); the Arab Administrative Development Organization; the Arab League Educational, Cultural and Scientific Organization (ALECSO); the Arab Organization for Social Defence Against Crime; the Arab Organization for Agricultural Development; the Arab Labour Organization; the Arab Industrial Development and Mining Organization; the Arab Postal Union; the Arab Telecommunications Union; the Arab States Broadcasting Union (ASBU); the Arab Centre for the Study of Arid Zones and Dry Lands (ACSAD); the Arab Maritime Transport Academy; the Arab Satellite Communication Organization (ARABSAT); the Council of Arab Ministers of the Interior; and the Inter-Arab Investment Guarantee Corporation.

The seats of the Specialized Agencies are located in different member countries.

Activities

The League is considered to be a 'regional organization' under Chapter VIII of the UN Charter. Besides its links with the UN, the League co-operates closely with several UN specialized bodies, such as the *UN Educational, Scientific and Cultural Organization (UNESCO), the *International Labour Organization (ILO), the *World Health Organization (WHO), and the *International Civil Aviation Organization (ICAO), and other international and national agencies. Arab League Offices and Information Centres have been set up in New York and Geneva and in many more capitals throughout the world. All members are expected to contribute to the budget of the League according to a scale of quotas determined by the Council.

The activities of the League have developed considerably since its inception, affecting more or less closely a wide range of aspects of inter-Arab co-operation. Although it lacks the indispensable cohesion to make substantial progress towards a permanent integration of the basic policies of its member countries, the League has achieved a remarkable degree of unity on issues vital to Arab foreign policy. The League maintained a general unity on the Palestinian issue and the non-recognition of Israel until President Sadat's visit to that country in 1977; the Camp David agreements and the consequent peace treaty between Egypt and Israel imposed a major strain on inter-Arab relations. The League has been dealing with inter-Arab disputes over boundaries, and with the recurring crises in Lebanon, but obtaining only modest results so far. On the economic plane, a boycott has been carried out against Israel, and public and private establishments throughout the world dealing with Israel. On the cultural and technical plane, rather elaborate structures have been established, and various records of achievements are to be found. In any case, the Palestinian issue and the consequent inter-Arab tensions have long exerted a strong influence on all aspects and forms of co-operation and on the prospects for the achievement of effective Arab unity within the framework of the League.

Efforts to bring about a negotiated settlement of the Iran–Iraq conflict were undertaken by the

League in 1984; unanimous support for Iraq in the defence of its legitimate rights against Iran was expressed in 1987. In May 1990 a Summit Conference held in Baghdad (and boycotted by Syria and Lebanon) criticized the emigration of Soviet Jews to Israel and the efforts of Western governments to prevent Iraq from acquiring advanced weapons technology. In August 1990 an emergency Summit Conference was convened to discuss the invasion and annexation of Kuwait, by Iraq; 12 members approved a resolution condemning Iraq and requesting its withdrawal from Kuwait, while the remaining members condemned the presence of foreign troops in Saudi Arabia. Growing inter-Arab conflicts over the conduct to be followed in the Gulf crisis (especially Western military presence in Saudi Arabia) and the proposed return of the League's headquarters to Cairo led to the resignation of the Secretary-General in September 1990. The divisions in the Arab world made it impossible to convene another meeting of the League until March 1991, when a session took place at ambassadorial, rather than ministerial, level and any discussion of the war in the Gulf was avoided. In May 1991 the Egyptian Minister of Foreign Affairs was unanimously elected as Secretary-General, confirming the return of Egypt to its former position in the Arab world. The Middle East peace process begun in the early 1990s has led to a gradual modification of the economic boycott of the League vis-à-vis Israel and its trading partners, but Arab countries remain divided over a number of issues concerning the relationship with the Jewish state. The refusal of Libya to hand over to the League the two alleged terrorists involved in the Lockerbie air crash of December 1988 has been a further cause of conflict within the pan-Arab body. Unpaid arrears by several members have recently put the League under a severe financial strain.

Secretary-General: Ahmad Esmat Abd al-Meguid
Headquarters: Tahrir Square, Arab League Bldg, Cairo, Egypt (Telephone: +20 2 5750511; fax: +20 2 5775626)
Publications: *Information Bulletin* (daily); separate reports covering specific problems; bulletins of treaties and agreements concluded between member countries; monthly and fortnightly bulletins in several languages issued by Offices and Information Centres abroad especially to present the Palestinian case
References: M. Khalil, *The Arab States and the Arab League* (Beirut, 1962); R. W. Macdonald, *The League of Arab States* (Princeton, NJ, 1965); H. A. Hassouna, *The League of Arab States and Regional Disputes* (Dobbs Ferry, New York, 1975); A. M. Gomaa, *The Foundation of the League of Arab States* (London, 1977); F. A. Clements, *Arab Regional Organizations – Bibliography* (Oxford and New Brunswick, 1992)

M

Mano River Union (MRU)

The Union groups Guinea, Liberia and Sierra Leone to develop joint co-operation with special regard to the potential resources of the Mano River.

Origin and development

Efforts to organize co-operation date back to the Mano River Declaration issued by the Heads of State of Liberia and Sierra Leone in October 1973 and followed by the signature of a number of protocols in 1974. The founder members were joined by Guinea in 1980. After a promising start with the establishment of a customs union in 1981, tensions between Liberia and the other two members brought about a virtual standstill in the Union's activities until 1986. The conclusion of a non-aggression and security treaty in 1986 improved political relations among member countries for a short period of time but without, however, any major improvement in the Union's prospects because of continuing budgetary difficulties.

Objectives

The purpose of the Union is to develop a common policy and co-operation regarding harmonization of tariffs and regulations concerning customs, telecommunications and postal services, forestry and maritime activities, and to promote joint development projects, with special emphasis on the hydroelectric potential of the Mano River.

Activities

Progress on some infrastructural projects in energy, transport and communications was definitively stopped by the outbreak of civil war in Liberia at the beginning of 1990. The situation in the region further deteriorated after the April 1992 military coup in Sierra Leone and the insurrection in the south-eastern section of the country adjoining Liberia. Political instability in Guinea and factional fighting in the other two member countries have prevented the Union from carrying out any effective form of co-operation.

Secretary-General: Dr Abdoulaye Diallo
Headquarters: Private Mail Bag 133, Freetown, Sierra Leone (Telephone: +232 22 226883)

Mekong River Commission

Established in April 1995 in Chiang Rai, Thailand, as a successor to the Committee for Co-ordination of Investigations of the Lower Mekong Basin (created in 1957), the Commission aims to foster co-operation for the sustainable development of the resources of the lower Mekong basin among the four riparian countries – that is, Cambodia, Laos, Thailand and Vietnam. The Commission's purpose is to deal primarily with problems concerning drainage and flood control, hydroelectric power, irrigation, improvement of navigation, and development of agriculture, fisheries and forestry. Freedom of navigation along the river is accorded, regardless of national boundaries; any member country may use the waters, except during the dry season, without having to obtain approval from other members.

Headquarters: Pibultham Villa, Kasatsuk Bridge, Rama I Road, Bangkok 10330, Thailand (Telephone: +66 2 225 0029; fax: +66 2 225 2796).

Mercosur (Mercado Común del Sur)

The grouping represents one of the most significant efforts undertaken so far to promote co-operation between Argentina, Brazil and the smaller countries of the Southern Cone.

Origin and development

After a relatively brief period of negotiation, the 24-article agreement establishing Mercosur (Treaty of Asunción) was signed in March 1991 by representatives of Argentina, Brazil, Paraguay and Uruguay; it came into effect the following November. The signatory countries committed themselves to the progressive reduction of barriers to trade, the establishment of a common external tariff and the harmonization of economic policies. As required by the Treaty of Asunción, before the completion of the Common Market by the end of 1994, an extraordinary meeting had to be held to decide on the permanent institutional structure of Mercosur and the voting procedures. Accordingly, in

December 1994, the member countries signed the Protocol of Ouro Preto, which amends and supplements the founding treaty.

Membership of Mercosur will be open to other member countries of the *Latin American Integration Association (LAIA) five years after the entry into force of the Treaty of Asunción, although exceptions may be made for those LAIA members that do not participate in other sub-regional or extraregional integration schemes.

Close links are being forged with both Chile and Boliva. The former, although it belongs to the Southern Cone countries, has decided not to join Mercosur, since it does not seem to offer, for the time being, any significant advantages for a relatively advanced and open economy. For its part, Bolivia might appear to be a likely candidate to membership despite being part of the *Andean Community.

Objectives

The Group intends to establish a common market providing for the free movement of goods, services, capital and labour among member countries. According to the Treaty of Asunción, the Common Market, which was to be established by January 1995 and was implemented substantially on schedule, implies: (a) the free circulation of goods, services and production factors through the elimination of customs duties and non-tariff barriers; (b) the establishment of a common external tariff and the adoption of a common commercial policy; (c) the co-ordination of macro- economic and sectoral policies concerning foreign trade; agriculture; industry; fiscal, monetary and exchange issues; services; transport; and communications; and (d) the harmonization of individual state legislation in the relevant areas in order to strengthen the integration process. The Common Market is based on the reciprocity of rights and obligations among the contracting parties, although some exceptions are envisaged in favour of Paraguay and Uruguay during the transitional period.

The main instruments for the establishment of the Common Market are: (a) a Trade Liberalization Programme involving the gradual elimination of tariff and non-tariff barriers; (b) the co-ordination by stages of macroeconomic policies; (c) a common external tariff; and (d) the adoption of sectoral agreements with a view to achieving efficient economies of scale. The

schedule for the implementation of the targets envisaged by the Treaty of Asunción was the object of a decision in June 1992 and was revised in July 1993 and in January 1994. Agreement was also reached, between January and December 1994, on the common external tariff. From January 1995 tariffs among member countries were abolished for about 90 per cent of traded goods, while common external tariffs averaging 14 per cent were imposed on 80 per cent of goods entering the Mercosur area. The remaining products are covered by transitional arrangements, which should terminate by the year 2000.

Structure

The institutional structure of Mercosur – as redefined by the Protocol of Ouro Preto – includes three principal organs with decision-making powers: the Council of the Common Market; the Common Market Group; and the Trade Commission.

The Council of the Common Market, which is the supreme body responsible for the formulation and the implementation of the integration process, meets at ministerial level whenever necessary. It consists of the Foreign Affairs and Economic Ministers of the member countries, but other ministers may be invited depending on the issues under consideration. At least every six months the Council holds a meeting with the participation of the Heads of State of the member countries. The presidency of the Council rotates at six-monthly intervals among the member countries, in alphabetical order. The Council adopts, by consensus, decisions that are binding for all member countries.

The Group is the executive organ whose activities are co-ordinated by the ministries of foreign affairs. It is composed of four delegates and four alternates from each member country representing the ministries of foreign affairs and economy (including industry and foreign trade) and the central banks. The Group oversees, within the limits of its competence, the implementation of the Treaty of Asunción and its Protocols, adopts the necessary measures to carry out the decisions of the Council, proposes concrete actions for the co-ordination of macroeconomic policies and the negotiation of agreements with non-member countries, and approves the budget submitted by the Administrative Secretariat.

Resolutions adopted by the Group, by consensus, are binding for all member countries.

The Trade Commission assists the Group and oversees the implementation of the instruments of the common commercial policy agreed upon by member countries, dealing with all issues related to trade between members and with non-member countries. It is composed of four delegates and four alternates from each member country meeting at least once a month under the co-ordination of the ministries of foreign affairs. The Commission adopts directives and proposals, the former having a binding character for all member countries. It is worth noting that the Trade Commission was not envisaged by the Treaty of Asunción; it was established by a decision of the Council in August 1994 and subsequently incorporated by the Protocol of Ouro Preto into the institutional structure.

The Protocol of Ouro Preto also created the Joint Parliamentary Commission, which represents the parliaments of the member countries and may submit recommendations to the Council; and the Economic and Social Consultative Forum, which represents the economic and social sectors and may submit recommendations to the Group.

The Administrative Secretariat, based in Montevideo, has been changed by the Protocol of Ouro Preto from a body servicing the Group to a body servicing the whole Mercosur. The Secretariat is headed by a Director elected by the Group, on a rotating basis, for a non-renewable two-year term.

The procedure to follow in the settlement of disputes was outlined by the Protocol of Brasília adopted in December 1991, in fact the first decision to be taken by the Council of the Common Market.

Activities

Mercosur, which enjoys legal personality, is expected to develop active co-operative relations with other countries and integration groupings both within and outside Latin America. A trade and investment agreement was concluded with the USA in June 1991. An interregional framework Agreement for commercial and economic co-operation was signed with the *European Union (EU) in December 1995 in Madrid by the member countries of Mercosur, thus laying the foundation for the creation of a Mercosur–EU free-trade zone at the beginning of the next century. In June 1996, a free-trade agreement was signed between Mercosur and Chile setting an eight-year timetable to liberalize most mutual trade; sensitive and extra-sensitive products will enjoy a longer period of protection. Bolivia also signed an agreement with Mercosur, although of a more limited scope.

Despite the often sobering record over the past decades of several Latin American attempts at economic integration and the huge differences in the economic potential of its member countries, Mercosur seems to offer prospects of real progress because of its flexible institutional machinery and pragmatic approach. A solid foundation for the success of the initiative may also lie in the fact that it draws to some extent on the basically positive experience of the Argentina–Brazil integration treaty of November 1989.

Director: Juan Antonio Remedi
Headquaters: Rincón 575 P.12, Montevideo, Uruguay (Telephone: +598 2 964590; fax: +598 2 964591)

Multilateral Investment Guarantee Agency (MIGA)

The Agency, established as an affiliate of the *International Bank for Reconstruction and Development (IBRD), encourages the flow of investment for productive purposes among its member countries, through the mitigation of non-commercial barriers to investment, notably political risk. The Agency thus complements the developmental efforts of the other members of the World Bank Group: the IBRD, the *International Development Association (IDA), the *International Finance Corporation (IFC) and the *International Centre for Settlement of Investment Disputes (ICSID).

Origin and development

The Convention setting up the Agency entered into effect in April 1988 and has been signed by over 150 countries. Membership of the Agency, currently amounting to about 130 countries, is open to all countries belonging to the IBRD. The Agency is owned by its member countries; as of 30 June 1995, subscribed capital exceeded $1 billion, of which $208 million had been paid in.

Members are divided into capital-exporting and capital-importing countries; the latter contribute 40 per cent of the share capital. Guarantees made available by the Agency can reach a maximum of five times the total capital and reserves. The USA is by far the largest subscriber and holds 17.39 per cent of total voting power, followed by Japan (4.43 per cent), Germany (4.41 per cent) and France and the UK (4.23 per cent each).

Objectives

The basic objective of the Agency is to guarantee eligible investments against losses resulting from non-commercial risks, in four main categories: (a) transfer risk resulting from host government restrictions on currency conversion and transfer; (b) risk of loss resulting from legislative or administrative actions of the host government; (c) repudiation by the host government of contracts with investors in cases in which the investor has no access to a competent forum; and (d) risk of armed conflict and civil unrest.

Structure

The Agency, which is legally and financially separate from the IBRD, is supervised by a 23-member Board of Directors. Five Directors are appointed by the five largest shareholders (the USA, Japan, Germany, France and the UK), and 18 are elected by the other shareholders. The President of the World Bank is President of the Agency and Chairman of the Board of Directors.

Activities

Eligible investments include contributions in cash or in kind in the form of equity, loans made or guaranteed by equity holders, and certain forms of non-equity direct investment. The Agency's standard policy covers investments for 15 years; in exceptional cases, coverage may be extended to 20 years. In addition to new projects, the Agency can insure the expansion of existing ones, including privatizations and financial restructurings. No minimum investment is required to be eligible for insurance. The Agency co-operates with national investment insurance agencies and private insurers to co-insure or re-insure eligible investments.

The Board has recently approved a substantial increase in the Agency's guarantee authority and a streamlining of operational regulations with a view to expediting the issuance of contracts to investors. In its first years of operation, the Agency issued guarantees for several projects in developing countries involving investors from major industrial countries, and provided policy and advisory services. Investment-promotion conferences have also been held under the Agency's sponsorship and as a result several joint ventures have been finalized.

At the end of fiscal year 1995, the Agency had signed 155 contracts of guarantee, facilitating an estimated $8.6 billion in total foreign private investment; the outstanding maximum contingent liability exceeded $1.6 billion. In the field of technical assistance, the Agency promotes the introduction of new management and marketing techniques to help developing member countries maximize the effectiveness of their programmes in attracting foreign direct investment.

President: James D. Wolfensohn

Headquarters: 1818 H Street, N.W., Washington DC 20433, USA (Telephone: +1 202 477 1234; fax: +1 202 477 6391)

Publications: *Annual Report*; *MIGA News* (quarterly).

Reference: I. Shihata, 'Towards a Greater Depoliticization of Investment Disputes: The Roles of ICSID and MIGA', *ICSID Review–Foreign Investment Law Journal*, 1, 1, Spring 1986

N

Niger Basin Authority

(Autorité du bassin du Niger)

The establishment of the Authority dates back to 1964 when the River Niger Commission (Commission du fleuve Niger) (CFN) was created; the present title was adopted in 1980. Members of the Authority comprise Benin, Burkina Faso, Cameroon, Chad, Côte d'Ivoire, Guinea, Mali, Niger and Nigeria. The Authority aims to promote the most effective use and development of the resources of the Niger basin in all fields. Main activities include navigation regulation, environmental control, hydrological forecasting, infrastructure, and agro-pastoral development.

Executive Secretary: A. A. Magaji
Headquarters: P.O. Box 729, Niamey, Niger
  (Telephone: +227 723102)
Publication: *Bulletin*

Non-Aligned Movement (NAM)

The Movement has played an important role for over three decades, emphasizing the political and economic concerns of most developing countries in the world *vis-à-vis* the industrialized nations of the West.

Origin and development
The creation of the Movement dates back to September 1961, when the first Conference of Non-Aligned Heads of State representing 25 countries was held in Belgrade, Yugoslavia to enable Third-World nations to articulate and promote their collective political and economic interests and to enhance their bargaining power in international forums. Non-alignment appeared at that time to be a genuine alternative to the division of the world into two opposing blocs, despite the risk of setting up a new bloc between East and West. The countries participating in the Belgrade meeting were for the most part Asian and African, continuing to a certain extent the co-operation and co-ordination efforts undertaken at the Bandung Conference of 1955 in Indonesia.

The establishment of the *Group of Seventy-seven (G-77) in 1964 – as a forum where developing nations could elaborate and harmonize their negotiating positions on trade and development issues – brought about to some extent a 'division of labour' between NAM and the G-77, the former mainly dealing with broad political matters and the latter with economic and financial aspects.

Under the pressure of a number of 'socialist' developing members, the Movement often sided openly with the USSR and its allies, instead of adopting a balanced and truly 'non-aligned' stance between East and West on major international issues. The effective 'alignment' of the Movement – especially during periods of heightened tension between the two blocs – discouraged moderate pro-Western developing countries from joining; therefore, actual membership of the Movement – currently including over 110 countries – has always been somewhat lower than potential membership. A number of countries and international agencies have been granted 'observer' status. Other countries – among them several European countries, including some members of the *European Union (EU) – and international organizations enjoy 'guest' status.

The end of the East–West polarization and of the Cold War 'alignments' that had been a paramount peculiarity of international relations for decades, has represented a major challenge for the Movement, unexpectedly deprived of its original *raison d'être*. Despite the withdrawal of a few members because of specific reasons, the Movement has continued to meet at regular intervals. Its member countries account for more than half the world's population, about 85 per cent of global oil production, but only 7 per cent of gross world output.

Objectives
Among major goals of the Movement may be mentioned the pursuit of a new world order based on freedom, equality and social justice; the elimination of disparities in the level of global development; the attainment of independence for all peoples living under colonial or alien domination and foreign occupation; the achievement of sustainable and environmentally sound development; and the strengthening of the effectiveness and role of the United Nations (UN).

Structure

The organizational structure of the Movement comprises the Conference of Heads of State meeting at three-year intervals to set the general guidelines, which are implemented by the Conference of Foreign Ministers. A Co-ordinating Bureau, established in 1973 and subsequently expanded, currently consists of 36 members representing the various regions of the world; the Bureau meets at ministerial and senior officials levels to prepare the above-mentioned conferences and fulfil the relevant administrative tasks. The Presidency of the Movement has rotated among the member countries which hosted the meetings of the Conference of Heads of State. The Joint Co-ordinating Committee (JCC), established in New York in partnership with the G-77, operates under the chairmanship of the presidents of the two groups and plays a significant role in harmonizing their respective positions on North–South and South–South issues.

Activities

After Belgrade in 1961, summit meetings, characterized by a growing participation of developing countries, took place in Cairo (1964), Lusaka (1970), Algiers (1973), Colombo (1976), Havana (1979), New Delhi (1983), Harare (1986), Belgrade (1989), and Jakarta (1992); the eleventh meeting took place in Cartegena de Indias, Colombia, in 1995. The 1964 Cairo Conference openly condemned Western colonialism and the retention of foreign military installations in developing nations. The completion of the decolonization process throughout most of the Third World led the Movement in the 1970s to pay increasing attention to economic issues, despite the heavy political pressures of pro-socialist countries at the 1979 Havana Conference. Debt relief and increased aid for development were among the topics debated at the 1983 New Delhi Conference, while the 1986 Harare Conference dealt to a large extent with the measures to be adopted by the international community to fight apartheid in South Africa. Long-standing disputes and deep-rooted divisions among members of the Movement characterized the second half of the 1980s. The 1989 Belgrade Conference saw the emergence of a more balanced and realistic posture on the part of the Movement, also because of the absence from the meeting of decidedly anti-Western countries. The collapse of the socialist bloc and the disintegration of Yugoslavia in 1991 seemed to jeopardize the very existence of the Movement, but a new lease of life was provided in 1992 by the Indonesian chairmanship. Leaving aside the traditional confrontational stance in favour of a pragmatic approach, the 1992 Jakarta Conference called for a constructive relationship between the developing and the developed world, with a view to establishing a more equitable global economy and resolving the debt problem. The 1995 Conference dealt with several issues, demanding, *inter alia*, easier credit and more open trade from the 'neo-protectionist' developed countries, and denouncing human rights abuses in Bosnia and the Palestinian territories, nuclear testing, the responsibilities in drug-trafficking also of developed consuming countries, and terrorism.

Proposals for reform of the United Nations (UN) and other international institutions, to make them genuinely democratic and more responsive to the needs of the developing world, were also discussed.

Nordic Council

The Council provides a forum for consultation and co-operation among Scandinavian countries.

Origin and development

The Council was established in March 1952 and inaugurated in 1953 as an advisory body on economic and social co-operation, consisting of delegates elected from the parliaments of Denmark, Iceland, Norway and Sweden; Finland joined in 1955. In March 1962, the five Scandinavian countries concluded a Treaty of Co-operation (Treaty of Helsinki) concerning economic, social, cultural, legal and communications questions, which has been amended several times (in 1971, 1974, 1983 and 1985). The need to strengthen and institutionalize joint efforts in many areas of mutual concern led the five northern countries to sign a Treaty on cultural co-operation in 1971 (subsequently amended in 1983 and 1985).

Objectives

The Council organizes co-operation on economic, social, cultural, legal, labour and environmental matters; new areas concerning foreign policy and security issues have recently been added to the Council's competence.

Structure

The Nordic Council of Ministers, created in 1971 as a separate body whose composition varies according to the subject under consideration, is advised by the already existing Nordic Council of parliamentary delegates. Formal decisions taken unanimously by Ministers are immediately binding on member countries in all cases where ratification by national parliaments is not required. The Council of Ministers is the highest decision-making organ, meeting for formal or informal sessions attended by Cabinet members responsible for the subjects under discussion.

Annual reports on progress and prospects of co-operation are sent by the Council of Ministers to the Nordic Council. This advisory body holds annual ordinary sessions and is made up of 87 delegates elected annually by and from the respective parliaments of member countries. The various parties are proportionately represented on the basis of their representation in the national parliaments. The Faeroe Islands and Aland Islands were granted representation in 1970, within the Danish and Finnish delegations respectively. Greenland has been entitled to separate representation within the Danish delegation since 1984. Observers from the Sami (Lapp) local parliaments of Finland, Norway and Sweden were admitted in 1994. Recommendations adopted by delegates are submitted to the Council of Ministers for consideration. The delegates are divided into six Standing Committees (Economic; Legal; Communications; Cultural; Social and Environmental; Budget and Control), which are also entitled to discuss the subjects within their competence with the Council of Ministers. Each delegation to the Nordic Council has a secretariat at its national parliament. The work of the Council between sessions is directed by a Presidium composed of eleven parliamentary delegates; the secretariat of the Presidium is based in Stockholm. The Secretariat of the Council of Ministers, located in Copenhagen, performs technical and administrative functions under the direction of the Secretary-General.

The amount of each country's contribution to the ordinary budget of the Council is determined in proportion to the respective national product; many forms of co-operation are financed directly from national budgets.

Activities

Nordic co-operation has been developing over the years through the setting up of a large number of specialized institutions and other permanent bodies, and the implementation of common programmes and projects. The Nordic Investment Bank was established in 1975 to provide finance and guarantees for investments and exports, with special regard to energy, metal and wood-processing industries, and manufacturing; the authorized and subscribed capital amounted to SDR1600 million. Under the Nordic Project Investment Loan Scheme, established in July 1982, loans are also made outside the Nordic region, mainly to developing countries.

Efforts towards closer co-ordination of national policies in economic, financial and trade spheres are being made, despite the full membership of Denmark, Finland and Sweden in the *European Union (EU); of Iceland and Norway in the *European Free Trade Association (EFTA); and of Denmark, Finland, Norway and Sweden in the *Council of the Baltic Sea States (CBSS). All the five countries of the Nordic Council have co-operated closely with Russia since 1993 in the newly-created *Council of the Euro-Arctic Region.

The active promotion of educational, cultural and scientific ties has contributed to improving national standards in the member countries of the Council. Other successful areas of implementation of joint programmes and projects have been transport and communications, social welfare, drug misuse, health and environment.

Secretariat of the Presidium of the Nordic Council: Tyrgatan 7, P.O. Box 19506, 10432 Stockholm, Sweden (Telephone: +46 8 453 4700; fax: +46 8 411 7536)

Publications: *Yearbook of Nordic Statistics*; *Nordisk Kontakt* (periodical)

Secretariat of the Nordic Council of Ministers: Store Strandstraede 18, 1255 Copenhagen, Denmark (Telephone: +45 3396 0200; fax: +45 3396 0202)

References: E. Solem, *The Nordic Council and Scandinavian Integration* (New York, 1977); F. W. Wendt, *Nordisk Rad, 1952–1978: Struktur, Arbejde, Resultater* (Stockholm, 1979)

North American Free Trade Agreement (NAFTA)

The Agreement is designed to remove trade barriers between Canada, Mexico and the USA.

Origin and development

Growing out of the Canada–US Free Trade Agreement (CUFTA) – signed in January 1988 with effect from January of the following year and extending tariff-free treatment to trade between the two countries – NAFTA was agreed upon by the two North American countries and Mexico in August 1992, and formally signed the following December. The 2000-page document containing the trade pact was completed in August 1993 by the signature of labour and environmental 'side agreements'. The two 'side agreements' cover workers' rights and the environment; in case of alleged violation of these rights or environmental damage, a panel will have the power to adjudicate and directly impose fines and trade sanctions on the USA or Mexico, while Canada will enforce compliance through its own legal system.

Despite substantial domestic opposition, NAFTA was approved in November 1993 by the US Congress; Canada and Mexico also approved NAFTA, which came into force in January 1994.

Objectives

Under NAFTA nearly all restrictions on trade and investment between the signatory countries are to be eliminated gradually over a period of 15 years. Besides taking over the basic CUFTA commitments, the USA and Mexico were to remove all tariffs on agricultural trade (the majority upon entry into effect of the agreement, and the remainder over a transitional period). Tariffs on textiles and automobiles were to be abolished over a ten-year period in all three countries. Additional areas of obligation include financial services (with Mexico opening its financial sector to USA and Canadian investment, and eliminating all restrictions by the year 2007); intellectual property protection (including copyrights, patents and trademarks); and government procurement (with Mexico removing preferential treatment for domestic companies over a transition period of ten years). Mexico, on the other hand, is not bound to lower its barriers to foreign investment in the petroleum industry, which will remain a state-run monopoly.

Structure

As regards the settlement of disputes, intergovernmental consultation will be resorted to in the first instance; if a dispute is not solved within 30–40 days, a government may have recourse to a three-member Free Trade Commission which meets at the ministerial level. Should the Commission fail to settle the issue, a panel of experts will be appointed to adjudicate.

Activities

Expansion of NAFTA to include other countries of Latin America, first of all Chile, is to be expected in the near future, in keeping with the goal of gradually extending integration to the whole Western hemisphere.

References: G. C. Hufbauer and J. J. Schott, *NAFTA: An Assessment* (Washington DC, 1993); R. S. Grinspun and M. A. Cameron (eds), *The Political Economy of North American Trade* (New York, 1993); C. D. De Fouloy, *Glossary of NAFTA Terms* (Dordrecht, 1994)

North Atlantic Marine Mammals Commission (NAMMCO)

Established by an Agreement on Co-operation in Research, Conservation and Management of Marine Mammals in the North Atlantic signed in April 1992, the Commission groups the Faeroe Islands, Greenland, Iceland and Norway. Membership is open to other countries in the region.

The purposes of the Commission are to provide a forum for the study and exchange of information on matters concerning marine mammals; to set up management committees and co-ordinate their activities, establishing the relevant guidelines and objective; to establish working arrangements with the *International Council for the Exploration of the Sea (ICES) and other appropriate bodies. The Commission consists of a Council, Management Committees, a Scientific Committee and a Secretariat.

Headquarters: University of Tromsö, 9037 Tromsö,   Norway   (Telephone: +47   77 645908; fax: +47 77 645905)

North Atlantic Salmon Conservation Organization (NASCO)

Established by an international Convention signed in 1982 and coming into force the following year, the Organization groups Denmark (for the Faeroe Islands and Greenland), Iceland, Norway, the European Community (EC), Russia, Canada and the USA.

The Organization aims to foster the analysis and dissemination of scientific information pertaining to salmon stocks in the North Atlantic Ocean, and to promote the conservation, restoration, enhancement and rational management of salmon stocks through international co-operation.

The Organization's area of competence covers the Atlantic Ocean north of 36°N latitude. This area is subdivided into three regions, serviced by the North American Commission, covering all maritime waters off the east coast of North America; the West Greenland Commission, covering all maritime waters off the coast of West Greenland; and the North East Atlantic Commission.

Headquarters: 11 Rutland Square, Edinburgh EH1 2AS, United Kingdom (Telephone: +44 131 228 2551; fax: +44 131 228 4384)

North Atlantic Treaty Organization (NATO)

The Organization groups 16 countries of Western Europe and North America in order to preserve their security through mutual guarantees and stable relations with other countries.

Origin and development

The North Atlantic Treaty was signed in Washington DC, in April 1949 and entered into force the following August. It represented the outcome of initiatives taken on both sides of the Atlantic. In March 1948 widespread concern over the security of Western Europe in the face of the steadily deteriorating political climate led to the

signing of the 50-year Brussels Treaty of economic, social and cultural collaboration and collective self-defence, by the Foreign Ministers of Belgium, France, Luxembourg, The Netherlands, and the UK. The following April, the Canadian Secretary of State for External Affairs suggested that the Brussels Treaty Organization be replaced by an Atlantic defence system that included the countries of North America. The beginning of the Berlin blockade by the USSR and other grave political events on the European continent prompted the American Senate, in June 1948, to adopt the Vandenberg Resolution, calling, *inter alia*, for the 'progressive development of regional and other collective arrangements for individual and collective self-defence' in accordance with the UN Charter, and recommending 'the association of the US with such regional and other collective arrangements'. In October 1948, the Consultative Council of the Brussels Treaty powers announced 'complete agreement on the principle of a defence pact for the North Atlantic and on the next steps to be taken'. The following December, negotiations on the drafting of the North Atlantic Treaty opened in Washington DC, between the countries party to the Brussels Treaty, the USA and Canada. Among European countries, Denmark, Iceland, Italy, Norway and Portugal accepted the invitation to participate in the Atlantic Alliance, while Ireland and Sweden declined. In April 1949, the Foreign Ministers of Belgium, Canada, Denmark, France, Iceland, Italy, Luxembourg, The Netherlands, Norway, Portugal, the UK, and the USA signed the Treaty, establishing an Alliance for the defence of Western Europe and North America. Greece and Turkey acceded to the Treaty in February 1952, followed by the Federal Republic of Germany in May 1955. The accession of Spain was approved by the Organization in December 1981, and took place formally in May 1982, bringing the total membership to 16.

According to the Treaty, any other European country in a position to further the principles of the Alliance and to contribute to the security of the North Atlantic area may be invited to join by unanimous consent of the member countries. The open character of the Organization has recently been reaffirmed, but its enlargement would require the assumption of full responsibility for organizing and managing security on a truly European scale, without jeopardizing its present effectiveness and deterrence capabilities. The right to withdraw is expressly envisaged after the Treaty has been in force for 20 years (that is, from 1969); withdrawal takes effect one year after notice of denunciation has been given.

In March 1966, General de Gaulle announced France's intention to withdraw from the military structure of the Alliance, and as a consequence Allied military forces and military headquarters were removed from France. In December 1995, the French government announced resumption of active participation by France in the military command structure. The military *coup d'état* in Cyprus and the subsequent landing of Turkish troops in July 1974 resulted in the withdrawal of Greek forces from the integrated military structure of the Alliance the following August. Greece agreed to rejoin the military structure in October 1980. It is important to stress that, despite the temporary withdrawal by France and Greece of their military personnel from the integrated commands, neither country ever ceased to be a party to the Treaty, which therefore remained unaffected.

The end of the Cold War and the new balance of power in Europe and the world have brought about a far-reaching process of transformation, involving all those political and military aspects of the Organization that had been built up over past decades. In an increasingly complex security environment – characterized by the demise of the Warsaw Pact and the disintegration of the USSR and Yugoslavia – the new NATO remains first and foremost a means of common defence through collective arrangements. In spite of the fact that changes and innovations are generally introduced in an atmosphere of shared purpose among the member countries, many questions still have to be solved with regard to the Organization's future role and tasks. There seems to be a widespread consensus among the participating countries that if the Organization is needed less for short-term protection, it is needed more for long-term stability.

In light of the challenges and prospects of the new Europe, the role of the present 14 European members is being enhanced and the North American commitment reduced, although it is expected to remain militarily meaningful. Instability and uncertainty in the former Soviet republics, in Central and Eastern Europe, especially the Balkans, and in the 'crisis belt' from the Maghreb to the Middle and Near East seem to call for the continued presence of NATO, which remains the only functioning collective security alliance with binding treaty commitments among its members and common military assets.

Objectives

The Organization was designed in 1949 basically as a military alliance, linking West European countries (at that time numbering ten) with the USA and Canada, to prevent or to repel aggression from the USSR and its Eastern European allies. It was also intended to provide a framework for continuous co-operation and consultation on political, economic and other non-military issues between member countries. Over four decades, the Organization's basic aim has been to maintain sufficient forces to preserve the military balance with the USSR and Eastern Europe (allied since May 1955 in the Warsaw Pact, which was dissolved in 1991) and to provide a credible deterrent against aggression.

The Preamble to the Treaty emphasizes the determination of the signatory countries to safeguard the freedom, common heritage and civilization of their peoples, founded on the principles of democracy, individual liberty and the rule of law, with a view to promoting conditions of stability and well-being in the North Atlantic area. Under the Treaty, the member countries undertake to settle, by peaceful means, international disputes in which they may be involved, and to refrain in their international relations from the threat or use of force in any manner inconsistent with the purposes of the UN. It is the intention of the member countries to contribute towards the further development of peaceful and friendly international relations, to eliminate conflict in their international economic policies, and to encourage economic collaboration between any or all of them. To this end, the member countries, separately and jointly, by means of continuous and effective self-help and mutual aid, agree to maintain and develop their individual and collective capacity to resist armed attack. They are bound to consult together whenever the territorial integrity, political independence or security of any of them is threatened; joint consultation must take place whenever a member country believes that such a threat exists. Of great importance is the provision in which the members agree to consider an armed attack against one or more of them in Europe or North America as an attack against them all, and consequently to assist the member or members so attacked. More precisely, each member is under an obligation to take at once, individually, and in concert with the other members, 'such action as it deems necessary, including the use of armed force, to restore and maintain the security of the North Atlantic area'. Although members are committed to help each other in the event of an armed attack, it is for each individual member to decide on whatever action it considers appropriate. The area in which the provisions of the Treaty apply is the North Atlantic area north of the Tropic of Cancer.

Structure

The Treaty dealt very briefly with the institutional aspects, mentioning only the establishment of a Council empowered to set up subsidiary organs, in particular a defence committee; as a result, the organizational structure has developed in keeping with the growing requirements of co-operation and co-ordination. The highest decision-making body and forum for consultation and negotiation within the Alliance is the North Atlantic Council, composed of representatives of all member countries and 'so organized as to be able to meet promptly at any time'. At ministerial meetings of the Council, held at least twice a year, members are represented by Ministers of Foreign Affairs. The Council also meets on occasion 'at the summit' (that is, at the level of Heads of State and Government). In permanent session, at the level of Permanent Representatives (Ambassadors), the Council meets at least once a week. The Council, which is also empowered to give political guidance to the military authorities, is not bound to follow any voting procedure and, in practice, votes are never cast. Decisions are therefore expressions of the collective will of the members, arrived at by common consent. The Defence Planning Committee (DPC) is composed of the representatives of those countries that partake in the Organization's integrated military structure and includes, at present, all member countries, because France in late 1995 decided to resume full participation; in fact, France had been attending meetings with an agenda relevant to French interests from January 1994. The DPC deals with matters specifically related to defence and is the highest forum for discussion of military policy. Like the Council, the DPC meets both in permanent session at the level of Permanent Representatives and at ministerial level, twice a year, with the participation of Defence Ministers. The Council and the DPC are chaired by the Organization's Secretary-General, regardless of the level of the meeting. Opening sessions of ministerial meetings of the Council are presided over by the President, an honorary position held annually by the Foreign Minister of a member country, following English-language alphabetical order. Nuclear matters are discussed by the Nuclear Planning Group (NPG), in which 14 countries fully participate under the chairmanship of the Secretary-General; France does not attend the meetings, while Iceland participates as an observer. The NPG meets regularly at the level of Permanent Representatives and twice a year at the level of Defence Ministers.

A number of Committees have been established by the Council over the years; the Committee on the Challenges of Modern Society (CCMS), founded in 1969, examines the methods of improving co-operation in creating a better environment, and undertakes pilot studies of relevance to member countries. All Committees perform advisory functions and are supported by an International Staff, made up of personnel drawn from all member countries, and responsible to the Secretary-General. The Secretary-General promotes and directs the process of consultation within the Alliance. He may propose items for discussion and is empowered to use his good offices at any time in cases of dispute between members and, with their consent, to initiate enquiries or mediation, conciliation or arbitration procedures. The Deputy Secretary-General assists the Secretary-General in his functions.

Besides the civil structure, the Organization has a military structure which also operates under the authority of the Council. The Military Committee (MC), the highest military body in the Alliance, is responsible for addressing recommendations to the Council and the DPC on military matters, and for providing guidance on military questions to Allied Commanders and subordinate military authorities. The MC, composed of the Chiefs-of-Staff of all members, except France and Iceland (which has no military forces), meets at Chiefs-of-Staff level, normally three times a year, but functions in permanent session, with effective powers of decision, at the level of Permanent Military Representatives. Liaison between the MC and the French High Command is effected through the Chief of the French Military Mission. The Presidency of the MC rotates annually in alphabetical order of countries; the Chairman, elected for a period of two to three years, represents the MC on the Council. The MC is assisted by an integrated International Military Staff (IMS), headed by a Director; the IMS is responsible for the implementation of the policies and decisions of the MC, the preparation of plans, the carrying out of studies, and the formulation of recommendations on military matters.

The strategic area covered by the Treaty has been divided since July 1994 into two Commands, the European and the Atlantic, which replaced the original three Commands responsible for the Atlantic Ocean, Europe and the Channel respectively. Plans for the defence of the North American area are drawn up by the Canada–United States Regional Planning Group which meets alternately in Washington DC, and Ottawa, and makes recommendations to the MC. Several civilian and military agencies have been created and charged with specific tasks; generally, civilian agencies are under the authority of the Council, while military agencies are responsible to the MC.

A parliamentary body 'unofficially' operates within the framework of the Organization. The North Atlantic Assembly – known between 1955 and 1966 as the NATO Parliamentarians' Conference – is basically a forum where members of parliaments from the countries of the Alliance meet regularly with a view to encouraging Atlantic solidarity and co-operation in national parliaments. The Assembly, composed of 188 members delegated by national parliaments (plus associate delegates from former socialist countries), meets in plenary session twice a year, in the spring and autumn, to discuss reports of the Committees and to address recommendations to the Secretary-General of the Organization. Meetings are held in national capitals on a rotation basis at the invitation of national parliaments. Parliamentary delegations from the countries of Central and Eastern Europe and the former USSR began to participate in the North Atlantic Assembly as soon as new parliaments were elected democratically, and have been granted 'associate delegation' status.

Activities

The Organization has always maintained close relations with several international institutions, in particular those operating in Western Europe. In the new Europe, the Organization is involved in the establishment of a security framework in which the Organization itself, the *Organization for Security and Co-operation in Europe (OSCE) which since 1995 has replaced the Conference on Security and Co-operation in Europe (CSCE), the *European Union (EU), the *Western European Union (WEU) and the *Council of Europe complement each other. Appropriate links and consultation procedures are being developed, especially between the EU and the WEU on the one hand, and the Organization on the other, to ensure that the countries not participating in the forging of a European identity in foreign and security policy and defence may be involved effectively in decisions that are likely to affect their own security. The crisis in the former Yugoslavia has brought about a significant opportunity for the Organization to co-operate with the UN, helping to enforce a naval blockade and a 'no-fly' zone.

The Organization was conceived essentially as a defensive coalition maintaining military preparedness in order to prevent war. Its political task was to provide for consultation on all political problems of relevance to members or to the Alliance as a whole, and to give directions to the military side. In peacetime, the Organization was responsible for drawing up joint defence plans, setting up the necessary infrastructure, and arranging for joint training and exercises. Apart from the integrated staffs at the Organization's different military headquarters and certain defence units on constant alert, all national forces have received orders only from national authorities.

The Organization has substantially achieved its primary purpose; that is, the safeguarding of the security of member countries by deterring aggression, through a policy based on the twin principles of defence and *détente*. The dual approach of maintaining credible collective defence while at the same time pursuing a policy of *détente* through improved dialogue with the USSR and its

Warsaw Pact allies provided the foundation for NATO policy for over two decades until the events of late 1989 began to change fundamentally the European and global environment.

The new political and military goals of the Alliance were defined and progressively adjusted to rapidly changing realities through a number of meetings of the Heads of State and Government of the member countries held in July 1990 in London, in November 1991 in Rome, and in January 1994 in Brussels. The end of the Cold War was sanctioned by the 1990 London Summit, which proposed to the former adversaries the conclusion of a non-aggression pact and of a conventional arms agreement. In May 1991 the Organization's Defence Ministers agreed on a sizeable reduction of troop strength (including a cutback of US forces in Europe) and the creation of an Allied Rapid Reaction Corps to confront small-scale crises.

The 1991 Rome Summit marked a watershed in the history of NATO as well as in the history of Europe, by deciding on the establishment of a new relationship with the countries of Central and Eastern Europe; the elaboration of a new military strategy; and the pursuit of the arms control process beyond the Conventional Forces in Europe (CFE) Treaty, with a view to limiting the offensive potential of armed forces to the point at which surprise attack or major aggression would become impossible. Additional reductions were decided in Rome concerning conventional and nuclear forces; on the other hand, multinational formations were expected to play a greater role within the integrated military structure. The new 'strategic concept' of the Alliance – as illustrated by the Declaration adopted by the Rome Summit – maintains the 'core functions' of the Organization while making it possible, within the radically-changed situation in Europe, to realize in full the members' approach to 'stability and security encompassing political, economic, social and environmental aspects, along with the indispensable defence dimension'. Within a broad concept of security, the Alliance retains 'its purely defensive purpose, its collective arrangements based on an integrated military structure as well as co-operation and co-ordination agreements, and for the foreseeable future an appropriate mix of conventional and nuclear forces'.

The relationship between NATO and its former adversaries in Central and Eastern Europe and Central Asia was put on a new basis with the establishment, in December 1991, of the North Atlantic Co-operation Council (NACC) as a forum for consultation and co-operation on security matters and related issues. Several former Warsaw Pact countries had in fact expressed interest in NATO membership, arousing Russian concern.

In November 1992, NATO began to participate in the enforcement of the UN embargo against the 'Federal Republic of Yugoslavia' (Serbia and Montenegro), which represented the first major example of NATO–WEU co-operation. In February 1994, following a request by the UN, NATO aircraft conducted strikes against Serbian targets – the first direct military action in the history of the Alliance – which were repeated several times during 1995.

At the 1994 Brussels Summit, the Partnership for Peace (PfP) programme was launched in order to establish formal ties not only with the former Warsaw Pact adversaries but also with all the other members of the then CSCE. The PfP programme, based on the wider political dialogue fostered by NACC, was accepted in a short period of time by over two dozen countries, including previous Warsaw Pact signatories, former Soviet republics and long-time 'neutral' countries. Individual Partnership Programmes (IPPs) were developed jointly by the Organization and by the partner countries, with the approval of the North Atlantic Council. Although falling short of the full membership requested by several Central and Eastern European countries, the PfP provides extended military co-operation, sharing of defence and security information, and joint participation in peacekeeping missions. Russia signed a PfP agreement but asked for recognition of its special place and role in European and world affairs. The development of a mature relationship between NATO and Russia will be of paramount importance in the construction of the new European security architecture although it should not represent a factor affecting future enlargement of the Atlantic Alliance.

Secretary-General: Javier Solana
Headquarters: 1110   Brussels,   Belgium (Telephone: +32 2 728 4111; fax: +32 2 728 4579)
Internet address: http://www.nato.int
Publications: *NATO Review* (six a year); *NATO Facts and Figures*; *NATO Handbook*

References: P. Hill-Norton, *No Soft Options: The Politico-Military Realities of NATO* (London, 1978); R. S. Jordan, *Political Leadership in NATO: A Study in Multinational Diplomacy* (Boulder, Col., 1979); J. Godson, *Challenges to the Western Alliance* (London, 1986); G. Williams and A. Lee, *The European Defence Initiative* (London, 1986); S. R. Sloan, *NATO's Future: Towards a New Transatlantic Bargain* (London, 1986); D. Cook, *The Forging of an Alliance* (London, 1989); S. R. Sloan, *NATO in the 1990s* (Washington DC, 1989); J. Smith (ed.), *The Origins of NATO* (Exeter University Press, 1990); F. H. Heller and J. R. Gillingham (eds), *NATO: The Founding of the Atlantic Alliance and the Integration of Europe* (London, 1992); P. Williams: *North Atlantic Treaty Organization – Bibliography* (Oxford and New Brunswick, 1994); T. van den Doel, *Central Europe: The New Allies? The Road from Visegrad to Brussels* (Boulder, Col. 1994); M. J. Weger, *The Evolution of NATO: The Brussels Summit and Beyond* (London, 1995)

North-East Atlantic Fisheries Commission (NEAFC)

Established by an international Convention signed in 1980, the Commission covers the North-East Atlantic Ocean and groups Denmark (for the Faeroe Islands and Greenland), Iceland, Norway, the European Community (EC), plus Poland and Russia. The Commission is intended to provide a forum for consultation and exchange of information on the state of fisheries resources in the North-East Atlantic, and on related management policies, to ensure the conservation and optimum utilization of such resources, and to recommend conservation measures in waters outside national jurisdiction.

The Commission is empowered to recommend measures applicable to the high seas concerning the conduct and control of fisheries, and the collection of relevant statistical information. In recent years, the Commission has agreed on a number of measures, including the setting of total allowable catches for certain species, and establishing minimum fish sizes and mesh sizes.

Headquarters: 425 Noble House, 17 Smith Square, London SW1P 3JR, United Kingdom (Telephone: +44 171 238 5923; fax: +44 171 238 5721)

North Pacific Marine Science Organization (PICES)

Established by an international Convention signed in 1990 and entered into force in 1992, the Organization's competence covers all living marine resources within the temperate and sub-Arctic region of the North Pacific Ocean and adjacent seas. Current membership of the Organization includes Canada, China, Japan, Korea, Russia and the USA. The objectives of the Organization are to encourage and co-ordinate marine scientific research in order to advance scientific knowledge of the area concerned and of its living resources, and to promote the collection and exchange of relevant data and information. The activities of the Organization are confined to the scientific field and are intended to cover both areas under national jurisdiction and the high seas under its competence.

Headquarters: Institute of Ocean Sciences, P.O. Box 6000, Sidney, B.C., Canada V8L 4B2 (Telephone: +1 604 363 6366; fax: +1 604 363 6827)

Northwest Atlantic Fisheries Organization (NAFO)

Active since 1979 as successor to the International Commission for the Northwest Atlantic Fisheries (ICNAF) established in 1950, the Organization currently groups ten European countries (including Russia and Denmark, which participates in respect of the Faeroe Islands and Greenland) and the European Community (EC), plus Canada, Cuba, Japan, Korea and the USA. The Organization aims to investigate, protect and conserve fishery resources of the North-West Atlantic Ocean and to encourage international co-operation and consultation.

The General Council, meeting annually, is the principal organ. The organization covers all fishery resources with the exception of salmon, tuna and marlin, cetacean stocks managed by the *International Whaling Commission (IWC), and sedentary species of the continental shelf.

Executive Secretary: J. C. E. Cardoso
Headquarters: P.O. Box 638, Dartmouth, Nova
    Scotia B2Y 3Y9, Canada (Telephone: +1 902
    469 9105; fax: +1 902 469 5729)
Publications: *Annual Report*; *Statistical Bulletin*
    (annual); *List of Fishing Vessels*

Nuclear Energy Agency (NEA)

The Agency promotes, within the framework of
the *Organization for Economic Co-operation and
Development (OECD), the development and application of nuclear power for peaceful uses.

Origin and development

The Agency was originally established as a
Western European body – under the title of
European Nuclear Energy Agency (ENEA) – by a
decision adopted in December 1957 by the
Council of the Organization for European
Economic Co-operation (OEEC); the decision took
effect from February 1958. The Agency represented a response, on a regional scale, to the creation in March 1957 of the *European Atomic
Energy Community (Euratom) by the 'Six' (that is,
Belgium, France, Germany, Italy, Luxembourg,
and The Netherlands). The Council of the OECD,
which succeeded the OEEC in 1960, formally
decided to retain the Agency within the framework
of the new Organization. The Agency dropped the
term 'European' from its official title and adopted
its present name in April 1972. Between May
1972 and October 1976 four of the five OECD
members outside Europe (that is Australia,
Canada, Japan and the USA), plus Finland, were
admitted to full participation. Membership of the
Agency now includes all OECD countries (with the
exception of New Zealand) and Korea.

Objectives

The Agency's basic task is to promote a common
effort between member countries in the peaceful
use of nuclear energy through international research and development projects, as well as the
exchange of scientific and technical experience
and information. It is also concerned with the
safety and regulatory aspects of nuclear energy,
including the adoption of uniform standards governing safety and health protection, and a uniform
legislative regime for nuclear liability and insur-

ance. Conferences and symposia on specific
subjects are held under the sponsorship of the
Agency from time to time.

Structure

The controlling body of the Agency is the OECD
Steering Committee for Nuclear Energy, presided
over by a Chairman assisted by Vice-Chairmen.
The Agency's Secretariat performs administrative
functions under a Director-General, assisted by
the necessary staff.

Activities

The Agency conducts and publishes studies on
world uranium resources, production and demand,
long-term nuclear fuel cycle requirements, and
nuclear legislation, in close co-operation with other
international institutions, in particular the
*International Atomic Energy Agency (IAEA).

Among these studies, two series, updated periodically, give present status and projected trends
in nuclear energy development: the *Nuclear
Energy Data* and the *Projected Costs of
Generating Electricity*. A high priority is given to
the Agency's work on the safety and regulation of
nuclear power, including studies and projects for
the prevention of nuclear accidents and the long-
term safety of radioactive waste disposal
systems.

A Data Bank was set up in January 1978 in
Saclay, France, to allow the participating countries to share larger computer programmes used
in reactor calculations and nuclear data applications; the Data Bank collects and verifies nuclear
data and computing codes, before making them
available to national laboratories, manufacturers
and universities.

Only a few countries, among them France,
Japan and Korea, are likely to expand their existing nuclear capacity. Nuclear power is expected
to maintain an almost constant share of 24 per
cent of total electricity demand. The Agency continues to meet the requests of its member countries facilitating co-operation, especially in the
safety, regulatory, scientific and economic aspects
of nuclear power. The Agency has embarked on a
programme of co-operation with Central and
Eastern European countries and the republics of
the former USSR, notably to transfer knowledge
and provide encouragement and support in the
field of nuclear safety. Nuclear development and
the fuel cycle, nuclear safety and regulation,

radiation protection and public health, radioactive waste management, and the revision of the international nuclear liability regime are at present among the Agency's major areas of interest.

Director-General (*ad interim*):   Samuel Thompson
Headquarters: Le Seine St Germain, 12 Bld des Iles,   92130   Issy-les-Moulineaux,   France

(Telephone: +33 1 4524 1010; fax: +33 1 4524 1110)

Publications: *NEA Activities: Annual Report*; *NEA Newsletter* (every six months); *Nuclear Energy Data* (annually); *Nuclear Law Bulletin* (two issues and supplement annually); *Uranium Resources, Production and Demand*

O

OPEC Fund for International Development (OFID)

The Fund – established by the members of the *Organization of the Petroleum Exporting Countries (OPEC) – assists developing countries that do not produce oil, by the provision of financial support on appropriate terms.

Origin and development

A special Fund to provide loans to finance balance-of-payments deficits and development projects was created by OPEC countries through an agreement signed in Paris in January 1976. In May 1980, OPEC Finance Ministers decided to convert the special Fund into an autonomous development agency for financial co-operation and assistance enjoying legal personality, and renamed it the 'OPEC Fund for International Development'.

Objectives

The Fund is empowered to: (a) provide concessional loans for balance-of-payments support; (b) provide concessional loans for the implementation of development projects and programmes; (c) contribute and provide loans to eligible international agencies; and (d) finance technical assistance and research through grants. Beneficiaries of the assistance may be the developing countries other than OPEC members and international development agencies; countries with the lowest income are given priority. The loans are not tied to procurement from Fund members or any other countries.

Structure

The structure of the Fund is similar to that of other international financing institutions, and comprises: the Ministerial Council, which is the supreme authority and consists of the Ministers of Finance of the member countries; the Governing Board performing executive functions and consisting of one representative and one alternate for each member country; and the Director-General.

Activities

The resources of the Fund, initially set at $800 million, have been replenished repeatedly. Payments of contributions by member countries are made voluntarily upon demand by the Governing Committee with a view to ensuring the timely disbursement of the loans committed.

A variety of loans to about 90 developing countries have been granted, on advantageous terms, since the Fund began operations. The geographic distribution of lending operations is concentrated mainly on African countries south of the Sahara. Most projects financed by the Fund are co-financed by other development agencies. Direct loans are supplemented by grants for technical assistance, food aid and research.

The Fund has played a significant role in the co-ordination of the policies of its member countries in various international forums and *vis-à-vis* international organizations, in particular the *International Fund for Agricultural Development (IFAD).

Director-General: Yesufu Seyyid Abdulai
Headquarters: P.O. Box 995, 1011 Vienna, Austria (Telephone: +43 1 515640; fax: +43 1 513 9238)
Publications: *Annual Report*; *OPEC Fund Newsletter* (three times a year); *OPEC Aid and OPEC Aid Institutions* (annual)
References: I. Shihata, *The OPEC Fund for International Development: The Formative Years* (London, 1983); A. Benamara and S. Ifeagwu (eds), *OPEC Aid and the Challenge of Development* (London, 1987)

Organization for Economic Co-operation and Development (OECD)

The Organization promotes economic growth, employment and improved standards of living in member countries (currently 29 of the world's advanced industrial economies), by assisting them in the formulation and co-ordination of appropriate policies, and stimulates and harmonizes its members' efforts in favour of developing nations.

Origin and development

The Convention establishing the Organization was signed in Paris in December 1960 and came into

effect in September 1961. The Organization succeeded – with a new title, an enlarged membership, and wider aims and functions – the
Organization for European Economic Co-operation (OEEC). The OEEC had been created in April
1948, primarily to administer Marshall Plan aid, in
conjunction with the Economic Co-operation
Administration (ECA) set up by the USA, with the
long-term objective of promoting the achievement
of a sound European economy through the co-
operative efforts of its members. Although participation was formally open to 'any signatory
European country', the OEEC became in fact a
Western European body, since the USSR and the
Eastern European countries refused to join; in
particular, Poland and Czechoslovakia recanted,
under Soviet pressure, their affirmative replies to
the Marshall Plan Conference held in Paris
between July and September 1947. In early 1949,
the USSR and the countries of Eastern Europe ri-
posted on the institutional plane by establishing
the Council for Mutual Economic Assistance
(CMEA; Comecon) with the basic goal of organizing multilateral economic co-operation between
them. Notwithstanding the lack of any reference
to the possibility of associate membership in the
OEEC Convention, Canada, Japan, and the USA
were granted the status of associate members.

At the end of the 1950s, it was felt that the fundamental aims of the OEEC had been largely
fulfilled, with the economic recovery of Western
Europe, and that a new institution, with an emphasis on the promotion of members' economic
growth and development aid to developing
nations and a broadened field of operation,
should be set up, with the accession of Canada
and the USA as full members. A proposal to that
effect was put forward in a communiqué issued in
Paris in December 1959 by the representatives of
France, the Federal Republic of Germany, the UK,
and the USA. Discussions took place throughout
1960, and a Preparatory Committee was entrusted with the task of drafting the Convention
creating the new institution. The reconstitution of
the OEEC as the Organization for Economic Co-
operation and Development (OECD) was eventually accomplished in December 1960, with the
signing of the Convention by the representatives
of 18 Western European countries plus Canada
and the USA. Another European country, Finland,
and three non-European countries – Australia,

Japan and New Zealand – acceded to the
Convention between 1964 and 1973. The
Organization's membership remained stable for
two decades until the accession of Mexico in May
1994. The Czech Republic was the first among
former socialist countries of Eastern Europe to
sign an agreement to join the Organization, in
October 1995, followed by Hungary in March
1996. South Korea was admitted in late 1996.
Other countries in Europe (Poland and Slovakia),
Latin America (Argentina, Brazil and Chile) and
Asia might follow suit in the near future. Both
Asian and Latin American dialogue partners
have expressed their keen interest in a more
structured relationship with the Organization. The
Commission of the *European Union (EU) takes
part in the work of the Organization.

Any sovereign country may be invited, by unanimous decision, to join the Organization; the right
of withdrawal may be exercised by giving twelve
months' notice to that effect. Unlike the OEEC
Convention, there is no provision concerning the
expulsion of members.

Objectives

According to the Convention, the Organization is
responsible for promoting policies designed: (a) to
achieve the highest sustainable economic growth
and employment, and a rising standard of living in
member countries, while maintaining financial stability, and thus to contribute to the development
of the world economy; (b) to contribute to sound
economic expansion in member as well as non-
member countries in the process of economic
development; and (c) to contribute to the
expansion of world trade on a multilateral, non-
discriminatory basis in accordance with international obligations.

To this end, the member countries undertake,
both individually and jointly, obligations with
regard to the efficient use of economic resources;
the promotion of research and vocational training
and the development of resources in the scientific
and technological field; the pursuit of policies for
the achievement of economic growth and internal
and external financial stability, without endangering the economies of other countries; the reduction or abolition of obstacles to the exchange of
goods and services and current payments, and
the maintenance and extension of the liberalization of capital movements; the economic devel-

opment of both member and non-member countries in the process of economic development by appropriate means, in particular the flow of capital, taking into account the importance of technical assistance and of securing expanding export markets.

With a view to fulfilling these undertakings, the member countries agree: (a) to keep each other informed and provide the Organization with the information necessary for the accomplishment of its tasks; (b) to consult together on a continuing basis, carry out studies and participate in agreed projects; and (c) to co-operate closely and, where appropriate, take co-ordinated action.

The Organization is empowered to adopt decisions which, except as otherwise provided, are binding on all members, to address recommendations to members and to enter into agreements with members, non-members and international institutions. Decisions and recommendations are adopted by mutual consent of all members, each having one vote; in special cases, a majority vote may suffice, if the Organization agrees unanimously to that effect. Abstentions do not impair the vote, and abstaining members are not bound by any act adopted without their consent. Moreover, no decision is binding on any member until it has complied with the requirements of its own constitutional procedures. Although the legal personality possessed by the OEEC continues in its successor, it is expressly provided that all decisions, recommendations and resolutions adopted by the OEEC require the approval of the new Organization to remain effective.

Structure

The Council, from which 'all acts of the Organization derive', is the supreme governing body, composed of one representative for each member country. It meets either at the level of permanent representatives (that is, the heads of national delegations with rank of ambassador), about twice a month, under the chairmanship of the Secretary-General, or at ministerial level, usually once a year, under the chairmanship of a minister elected annually. The Council is responsible for all questions of general policy and is empowered to establish an Executive Committee and such subsidiary bodies as may be required to achieve the aims of the Organization. Each year the Council designates 14 of its members to form

the Executive Committee, which is called upon to prepare the work of the Council itself and, where appropriate, to carry out specific tasks. The Executive Committee has power of decision only upon express delegation by the Council.

The Secretariat, performing technical and administrative functions, is headed by a Secretary-General appointed by, and responsible to, the Council. The Secretary-General assists the Council in all appropriate ways and has the of submitting his own proposals to the Council or any other body of the Organization. Three Deputy Secretaries-General, as well as special counsellors and advisers, assist the Secretary-General.

Each year the Secretary-General presents to the Council for approval an annual budget, accounts and such subsidiary budgets as may be necessary. The general expenses of the Organization are apportioned among member countries according to a scale fixed by the Council; other expeditures are financed on such basis as the Council may decide.

The Council has made ample use of its authority to set up subsidiary organs for the performance of the Organization's functions. The largest part of the work is prepared and carried out by specialized committees and working parties, currently numbering more than 200. Among the main subsidiary bodies are: the Economic Policy Committee, composed of governments' senior officials with a major responsibility for the formulation of general economic policies, which is chiefly concerned with economic growth and the related policy measures; the Economic and Development Review Committee, in charge of the preparation of the annual economic surveys of individual member countries, whose results are regularly published; the Development Assistance Committee (DAC) – consisting of the representatives of major OECD capital-exporting nations – which aims to expand the aggregate volume of resources made available to developing countries, to improve their effectiveness, and to conduct periodical reviews of the amount and nature of its members' contributions to aid programmes, both bilateral and multilateral; the Trade Committee, dealing with commercial policies and practices, and specific trade problems; and the Committee on International Investment and Multinational Enterprises, which prepared a voluntary code of conduct for multinational corporations adopted by the OECD in 1976.

Other important Committees are responsible for: Environment; Invisible Transactions; Financial Markets; Fiscal Affairs; Tourism; Maritime Transport; Consumer Policies; Agriculture; Scientific and Technological Policy; Education; Industry; Energy; Manpower and Social Affairs. In addition, there is a High-Level Group on Commodities, and a Group on North–South Economic Issues. A working group on biotechnology was created in 1994.

The variety of functions assigned to the Organization has involved the establishment of a number of operating agencies, related in varying degrees to the Organization's machinery, which enjoy autonomous or semi-autonomous status. These bodies, each one of them with its own governing committee, comprise – besides the *International Energy Agency (IEA) and the *Nuclear Energy Agency (NEA) – the Development Centre, created in 1962 for the analysis of development and aid problems and policies, as well as for the training of specialists; and the Centre for Educational Research and Innovation (CERI), established in 1968 to facilitate the introduction of reforms in the educational systems of member countries. The Centre for Co-operation with European Economies in Transition (CCET) was set up in 1990 to help Central and Eastern European countries move towards democratic and market-orientated systems.

Activities

The Organization has gradually developed a complex network of co-operative relations with many international agencies, including those belonging to the UN system. Particularly close relations exist with international economic and social institutions, both intergovernmental and non-governmental, operating in Europe, in order to achieve an effective co-ordination of policies and efforts.

The Organization has been engaged actively over more than three decades in a wide range of activities that have represented, to a certain extent, a continuation of the work of the OEEC within an expanded framework, and with revised purposes to reflect the changes in the world and European contexts. In spite of the purely voluntary character of co-operation, since the ultimate implementation

of the Organization's decisions rests with each member country, co-ordinated action has been carried out in a number of areas of major importance, such as international trade rules, capital movements, export credits, and aid to developing countries. The publication of regular surveys, specialized reports and monographs, and statistics on economic and social subjects, has contributed to a deeper understanding of the state of the economies of both member and non-member countries. Conferences, seminars and other meetings at different levels have provided in-depth analyses of many problems affecting the growth prospects of industrial countries and their relations with developing nations. Periods of low growth in developed countries, inflation, high interest rates and unemployment have encouraged protectionist trading and industrial policies, and consequently involved reductions in the level of concessional aid. On the other hand, conflicts of economic interests between the European countries and the USA, as well as long-standing tensions between all of them and Japan – as illustrated in the early 1990s in the Uruguay Round of multilateral trade negotiations – have repeatedly affected co-operation between members. New tasks have emerged for the Organization in order to assist and sustain the reform process in Eastern Europe and the former USSR; a co-operation agreement was signed with Russia in June 1994 to help that country integrate into the world economy. The expected growth in membership over the next few years and the higher profile of recent suggestions and recommendations to confront specific problems, from unemployment to bribery practices, might gradually lead to an increase in the Organization's role and responsibilities during the rest of the present decade.

Secretary-General: Donald Johnston

Headquarters: 2 rue André Pascal, 75775 Paris, France (Telephone: +33 1 4524 8200; fax: +33 1 4524 8500)

Publications: *Activities of OECD* (annual report); *News from OECD* (monthly); *The OECD Observer* (every two months); *Main Economic Indicators* (monthly); *Economic Survey* (annually for each member country); *Development Co-operation Report* (annual)

References: H. G. Aubrey, *Atlantic Economic Co-operation: The Case of OECD* (New York, 1967); M. J. Esman and D. S. Cheever, *The*

Common Aid Effort. The Development Assistance Activities of the OECD (Columbus, Ohio, 1967); D. J. Blair, *Trade Negotiations in the OECD: Structures, Institutions and States* (London, 1993)

Organization for Security and Co-operation in Europe (OSCE)

The Organization – called the Conference on Security and Co-operation in Europe (CSCE) until December 1994 – is the most important pan-European body for political and security consultation and co-ordination.

Origin and development

The origins of the Organization date back to the proposals put forward in the 1960s by the USSR with a view to sanctioning the political and territorial status quo in Europe resulting from the Second World War. After considerable diplomatic efforts, an invitation by the Finnish government was accepted by over 30 European countries, Canada and the USA, and multilateral preparatory talks began in Helsinki in November 1972. The talks developed over three stages, the first and last taking place in Helsinki and the second in Geneva. At the end of the first stage, in July 1973, the foreign ministers of the 35 participating countries approved the Final Recommendations, which were to constitute the scheme for the Final Act of the CSCE. Negotiations continued intermittently in Geneva from September 1973 to late July 1975. From 30 July to 1 August 1975 the Conference was held in Helsinki, with the participation of leaders from 35 countries and the *European Community (EC).

The Final Act was signed in Helsinki on 1 August 1975 and represented a major achievement in the process of détente. The Final Act consisted of three main 'baskets': methods to prevent accidental confrontations between opposing military blocs; proposals for economic, scientific and technological co-operation respecting the two different economic and social systems; and an understanding on closer contacts between peoples of the two different systems, together with a reaffirmation of respect for human rights.

It is important to stress that 'Basket IV' of the Final Act envisaged a series of follow-up conferences and experts' meetings, thus giving birth to the CSCE 'process'. Follow-up meetings were held in 1977–8 in Belgrade, in 1980–3 in Madrid, and in 1986–9 in Vienna. The Vienna meeting, taking place when Cold War confrontation was already giving way to a new era of East–West détente, brought about a new understanding on human rights, and agreements on mandates for two new sets of negotiations on conventional armed forces, among the members of the *North Atlantic Treaty Organization (NATO) and the Warsaw Pact, and on Confidence and Security-Building Measures (CSBMs) among all CSCE members.

A summit meeting of CSCE heads of government took place in November 1990 in Paris, ending with the signature of the 'Charter of Paris for a New Europe', pledging steadfast commitment to democracy based on human rights and fundamental freedoms, prosperity through economic liberty, and equal security for all countries. Moreover, a far-reaching Treaty on the Reduction of Conventional Forces in Europe (CFE) was signed by 22 countries, that is the 16 members of NATO and the 6 members of the Warsaw Pact. Also in 1990, the CSCE adopted a comprehensive document on CSBMs and a Declaration on the Open Skies Treaty.

The fourth follow-up meeting of the CSCE, held in Helsinki, started in March 1992 and was concluded the following July with the summit of the heads of state or government. The CSCE Helsinki Document 1992 consists of the Helsinki Summit Declaration and the Helsinki Decisions entitled 'The Challenges of Change'. The Helsinki Document formally proclaimed the Conference a 'regional organization' under Chapter VIII of the UN Charter, with a view to strengthening its role in conflict prevention and crisis management.

After the signing of the Open Skies Treaty in 1992, a special Declaration was adopted by the CSCE, whose Secretariat currently services the weekly meetings in Vienna of the Open Skies Consultative Commission, following compliance with the provisions of the Treaty.

The first CSCE Implementation Meeting on the Human Dimension took place in late 1993 in Warsaw, to review the situation in member countries with respect to democracy, the rule of law, minorities, migration, torture and the death penalty.

A new role and a new name for the then CSCE resulted from the review conference held in Budapest from 10 October to 2 December 1994, and the following summit of the heads of state or government (5–6 December) which adopted a Document entitled 'Towards a Genuine Partnership in a New Era'. Major differences emerged between participating countries on a number of issues, but agreement was eventually reached in several key areas. The Organization was established as a primary instrument for early warning, conflict prevention and crisis management, and the institutional structure was strengthened accordingly. A 'Code of Conduct' was adopted concerning the political and military aspects of security, including the democratic control of armed forces and their use in internal situations.

The Organization currently groups over 50 countries (all European states, including republics of the former USSR and the former Yugoslavia, plus Canada and the USA). Japan and Korea are the Organization's 'Partners for Co-operation', while Algeria, Egypt, Israel, Morocco and Tunisia are the 'Mediterranean Partners'.

Objectives

The Organization was originally devoted to the promotion of co-operation in three main areas (military security, economic and trade relations, and observance of human rights), and was later strengthened and extended to cover other aspects of pan-European relations such as conflict prevention and crisis management. All participating countries have equal status and decide on the basis of consensus.

The upgrading from CSCE to OSCE is clear evidence of the determination of the participating countries, from a 'region' stretching from Vancouver to Vladivostok, to create an umbrella organization with wide-ranging objectives and competences in economic and security issues.

Structure

The institutionalization of the CSCE and then of the OSCE has been a lengthy and somewhat complicated process. The Western countries participating in the diplomatic exercise of the Conference were reluctant initially to adopt measures to create a permanent institutional framework. Only by gradual steps did the organizational structure develop and become stronger.

The inclusion of a section on 'New Structures and Institutions of the CSCE Process' in the 'Charter of Paris for a New Europe' in November 1990 was a major step towards institutionalization. Besides the intensification of consultations at all levels, the heads of government meeting in Paris decided to establish a Conflict Prevention Centre (CPC) in Vienna, and an Election Observation Office in Warsaw. Moreover, a permanent CSCE Secretariat was to be established in Prague. The Charter also set up three political consultative bodies: the Council of Ministers, consisting of foreign ministers of the participating countries, meeting at least once a year; the Committee of Senior Officials to assist the Council; and regular summit meetings of heads of state or government every two years, starting in 1992. The creation of a CSCE parliamentary assembly 'involving members of parliaments from all participating states' was called for as a recognition of the 'parliamentary dimension' still missing from the Helsinki process.

In response to the increasing violations of ethnic rights in some countries, the CSCE Helsinki Document 1992 called for the establishment of a CSCE High Commissioner on National Minorities. The July 1992 Helsinki meeting decided the creation of the Forum for Security Co-operation, which laid the foundation for a new approach to military aspects of security within Europe and beyond, and confirmed the arrangement whereby the Chairman-in-Office of the Council of Foreign Ministers was to carry out his tasks with the assistance of his immediate predecessor and designated successor.

The constituent meeting of the CSCE Parliamentary Assembly was held in July 1992 in Budapest, with the participation of over 300 members of national parliaments from all member countries; the Assembly meets once a year and is supported by a Secretariat in Copenhagen. The first High Commissioner on National Minorities, whose office is based in The Hague, was appointed in December 1992.

In May 1993 the first Secretary-General of the CSCE was appointed for a three-year term in order to provide support for the Chairman-in-Office and supervise the organizational structure. The former Secretariat in Prague, and the

Executive Secretariat and the Secretariat of the CPC, both based in Vienna, were merged to form, under the newly-appointed Secretary-General, an integrated CSCE Secretariat, which was opened in Vienna in late 1993. Also in 1993, a new body, the Permanent Committee, was established in Vienna to carry out political consultation and decision-making on a weekly basis. The Committee of Senior Officials, still meeting in Prague, was to assume overall responsibility for all decisions to be taken between the annual meetings of the Council of Foreign Ministers. The Warsaw-based Office for Free Elections was assigned a broader mandate and renamed the Office for Democratic Institutions and Human Rights.

Following decisions taken in Budapest in December 1994, the Organization's institutional mechanism now consists of: annual meetings of the Ministerial Council (composed of the foreign ministers) as the central decision-making and governing body; half-yearly meetings of the Senior Council (replacing the Committee of Senior Officials) in Prague and yearly meetings of the same Council as the Economic Forum; and weekly meetings of the Permanent Council (formerly Permanent Committee) in Vienna for the day-to-day operational work. The Chairman-in-Office, whose term lasts one year, is the foreign minister of the country that organizes the current Ministerial Council session. Priorities and orientations at the highest political level are provided by the summit of heads of state or government whose next meeting, scheduled to take place in Lisbon in late 1996, will decide on the frequency of future sessions. The Economic Forum is essentially concerned with questions of economic transition in Central and Eastern Europe, while the Forum for Security Co-operation – a permanent body meeting weekly in Vienna – concentrates ·mainly on regional problems, especially in South-Eastern Europe, and the implementation of CSBMs.

In December 1994 the Convention on Conciliation and Arbitration within the OSCE, establishing a Court to be based in Geneva, came into effect; the Court will settle disputes submitted to it by OSCE members that have signed the Convention.

Activities

The gradual institutionalization of the Organization has favoured the establishment of links with other international agencies. Since 1993 the Organization has enjoyed observer status at the General Assembly of the UN; agreement was reached in 1994 on a division of responsibilities between the Organization and the UN for operations in Eastern Europe and the Caucasus. Close co-operation links have been developed with the *Council of Europe, especially with the regard to the Human Dimension. As regards security and peacekeeping questions, contacts are maintained with NATO, the *Western European Union (WEU) and the *North Atlantic Co-operation Council (NACC).

Since the early 1990s, the Organization has carried out a series of initiatives intended to reduce dangerous tensions and prevent the outbreak of armed conflicts, ranging from long-term missions in regions of the former Yugoslavia and the Caucasus and sanction assistance missions to support UN sanctions against the Federal Republic of Yugoslavia (Serbia and Montenegro), to the supervision of parliamentary and presidential elections and referendums in several Central and Eastern European countries. At the December 1995 Ministerial Meeting in Budapest, the Organization accepted the request of the signatory parties to the Dayton Peace Agreement to play a key role in building peace, democracy and stability in Bosnia and Herzegovina; the Organization is therefore called to face a huge challenge supervising elections, monitoring the respecting of human rights, and assisting the parties in negotiations on arms control and confidence-building measures. Conflicting political interests and views among major powers, and long-standing ethnic rivalries – often degenerating into open conflicts – will represent a crucial test of the ability of the Organization to settle disputes by peaceful means and to inaugurate the 'new era of democracy, peace and unity' announced by the Charter of Paris.

Secretary-General: Giancarlo Aragona

Secretariat: Kärntner Ring 5–7, 1010 Vienna, Austria (Telephone: +43 1 514 3650; fax: +43 1 514 3699)

References: L. V. Ferraris (ed.), *Report on a Negotiation: Helsinki–Geneva–Helsinki 1972–1975* (Leiden, 1979); S. Lehne, *The Vienna Meeting of the Conference on Security and Co-operation in Europe, 1986–89: A Turning Point in East–West Relations* (Oxford,

1991); J. Freeman, *Security and the CSCE Process: the Stockholm Conference and Beyond* (London, 1991); V. Mastny, *The Helsinki Process and the Reintegration of Europe, 1986–1991: Analysis and Documentation* (London, 1992); A. Heraclides, *Security and Co-operation in Europe: The Human Dimension 1972–1992* (London, 1992); A. Bloed (ed.), *The Conference on Security and Cooperation in Europe*: *Analysis and Basic Documents, 1972–1993* (Dordrecht, 1993); M. R. Lucas (ed.), *The CSCE in the 1990s: Constructing European Security and Co-operation* (Baden-Baden, 1993)

Organization for the Development of the Senegal River

(Organisation pour la mise en valeur du fleuve Sénégal) (OMVS)

The Organization groups four countries to exploit the resources of the Senegal basin.

Origin and development
The founder members of the Organization in 1972 were Mali, Mauritania and Senegal; after following the activities of the Organization as an observer since 1987, Guinea became a full member in 1995.

Objectives
The Organization's purpose is to develop, by means of a close co-operation among member countries, the resources of the Senegal basin (agricultural, industrial and mining projects, hydroelectric dams, ports).

Structure
The Heads of State of the member countries represent the highest decision-making body.

Activities
The Djama dam in Senegal was completed in 1986 and the Manantali dam in Mali was completed in 1988. In 1991 it was decided to set up a special company – the Agence de gestion pour les ouvrages communs (AGOC) – with the responsibility of managing joint projects; initiatives have been undertaken to facilitate co-operation with foreign entrepreneurs and the Organization's development partners. The founding treaty has been amended in 1995 with a view to developing co-operation with foreign private entrepreneurs.

Secretary General: K. Dembele
Headquarters: 46 rue Carnot, P.O. Box 3152, Dakar, Senegal (Telephone: +221 223679; fax: +221 234762)

Organization for the Management and Development of the Kagera River Basin

(Organisation pour l'aménagement et le développement du bassin de la rivière Kagera)

The Organization groups four countries for the exploitation of the Kagera basin.

Origin and development
The Organization was formed in 1978 but recurring tensions and inter-state and intra-state conflicts have hindered any substantial progress. Burundi, Rwanda, Tanzania and Uganda are full members.

Objectives
The Organization aims to achieve the integrated development of the water and land resources of the Kagera River Basin.

Activities
Projects have been envisaged in the fields of agricultural development, river transport, and construction of a hydroelectric dam and of a railway network linking member countries. Severe political instability in the region accompanied by factional fighting and civil wars have been negatively affecting any attempt at effective co-operation over the past several years.

Executive Secretary: Jean-Bosco Balinda
Headquarters: P.O. Box 297, Kigali, Rwanda (Telephone: +250 84665; fax: +250 82172)

Organization of African Unity (OAU)

The Organization groups all countries of the continent to foster unity and solidarity among them.

Origin and development
The Organization's Charter was signed in May 1963 in Addis Ababa, by the Heads of State and

Government of 30 countries of Africa and Madagascar. The present membership of the Organization comprises over 50 African countries, including Madagascar and other islands surrounding Africa. Eritrea joined in 1993, upon achieving independence; South Africa was admitted in June 1994, upon termination of white minority rule. Any 'independent sovereign African state' is eligible for membership; decision on admission requires a simple majority of the member countries.

The Sahrawi Arab Democratic Republic (SADR), proclaimed by Polisario, was eventually recognized by 26 member countries which called for its admission to the Organization. Admission took place in February 1982 but was disputed by Morocco and other countries, which claimed that a two-thirds majority was needed to admit a state whose very existence was in question. Morocco declared its intention to withdraw from the Organization, with effect from November 1985, when a delegation from the SADR took part in the works of the Assembly in November 1984.

The existence of substantial budgetary arrears, caused by delays in the payment of national contributions, has led the Organization into serious problems that threaten its ability to address the continent's pressing economic and social needs. After repeated warnings, the Organization announced in November 1995 that ten countries (Angola, the Central African Republic, Chad, Comoros, Equatorial Guinea, Guinea-Bissau, Niger, São Tomé and Príncipe, Sierra Leone and the Seychelles) had lost their right to vote or to speak at any meeting because they had failed to pay their contributions in full or in part during the previous eleven years.

Objectives

The Organization operates to promote unity and solidarity among African countries, through the co-ordination of efforts in the fields of politics and diplomacy, economy, science and technology, education and health, defence and security; to eliminate all forms of colonialism in the continent; and to foster international co-operation, having due regard to the Charter of the UN and the Universal Declaration of Human Rights.

The Organization's basic principles are the equality of members, non-interference in internal affairs, respect for territorial integrity, peaceful set-

tlement of disputes, unconditional condemnation of political subversion, and dedication to the goal of the complete emancipation of dependent African territories.

The Organization's functions and powers are very briefly described by the Charter; this reflects the proper nature of the body, designed to promote a rather loose co-operation, not bound by rigid patterns which, in any case, would hardly be applicable in practice.

Structure

The main organs are the Assembly of the Heads of State and Government, the Council of Ministers, the General Secretariat, and the Commission of Mediation, Conciliation and Arbitration. The Assembly, which is the supreme organ, meets in ordinary sessions once a year to consider matters of common concern to Africa; to co-ordinate and harmonize the Organization's general policy; and, when required, to change the structure, functions and activities of the organs and specialized institutions formed in accordance with the Charter. The Assembly's resolutions are taken by a two-thirds majority, each member having one vote, with the exception of procedural matters, for which a simple majority is sufficient. The Council of Ministers, formed in principle by the Foreign Ministers of the member countries, is the executive body responsible for the implementation, in conformity with the policies laid down by the Assembly, of inter-African co-operation; it meets at least twice a year and decides by simple majority. The General Secretariat, headed by a Secretary-General appointed by the Assembly for a four-year term, performs administrative duties. The Commission of Mediation, Conciliation and Arbitration was established by a special protocol signed in Cairo in 1964 to promote the peaceful settlement of disputes between member countries. It consists of 21 members elected by the Assembly for a five-year term; no country may have more than one member.

The subsidiary bodies include specialized commissions for economic, social, transport and communications affairs; education, science, culture and health; defence; human rights; and labour. In May 1963 the Co-ordinating Committee for Liberation Movements in Africa was established, with the participation of a certain number of the Organization's member countries. The African Liberation

Committee, with headquarters in Dar-es-Salaam, Tanzania, which had provided financial and military assistance to nationalist liberation movements, was eventually disbanded in August 1994 following the end of apartheid in South Africa.

Member countries contribute to the budget of the Organization in accordance with their UN assessment; no country may be assessed for an amount exceeding 20 per cent of the regular budget.

Activities

The Organization has traditionally been geared towards fighting colonialism and apartheid and has contributed only to a limited extent to lowering intra-African tensions, mediating in African conflicts and fostering regional unity. Strongly diverging views among major member countries on several important issues have considerably weakened the Organization, making the promotion of African solidarity an extremely hard task. Despite the solemn declaration adopted by the Assembly of Heads of State and Government in 1964 on the inviolability of the colonial boundaries existing at the time of gaining independence by the member countries, the Organization has proved unable to mediate effectively in territorial and other disputes, and to stop civil wars and secession attempts. Many important issues, such as the Western Sahara, have highlighted opposing attitudes, bringing about a polarization into 'moderate' and 'progressive' countries.

Throughout the second half of the 1980s and the early 1990s various meetings of the Assembly called for the imposition of comprehensive economic sanctions against South Africa, denouncing white minority rule and condemning the links still maintained with that country by some Western and African countries.

Repeated requests by the Assembly to convene an international conference of creditors and borrowers in order to seek a solution to the problem of Africa's heavy external debt proved unsuccessful. The political and socioeconomic changes taking place in Central and Eastern Europe have led the Assembly to review the implications of such changes for the African continent. A treaty on the creation of the African Economic Community was adopted by the Assembly in June 1991 and was to enter into force after ratification by two-thirds of the Organization's member countries.

In the early 1990s mediation efforts between the warring factions in several African countries proved largely unsuccessful while the Organization's financial crisis gradually worsened. The establishment of a Central Mechanism for Preventing, Managing and Resolving African Crises, which had been proposed several times, was eventually approved in June 1993 by the Assembly of Heads of State and Government. Final arrangements on the Mechanism were completed by the Foreign Ministers in November 1993. In June 1994, nine countries were nominated to serve on the Bureau of Conflict Resolution, the central organ of the Mechanism; the Assembly also adopted a Code of Conduct on Inter-African Relations with the aim of fostering 'political consultation and co-operation'. Proposals for the setting up of a rapid reaction force failed to be approved at the June 1995 Assembly, while sanctions were announced on countries in substantial arrears with their membership dues.

Secretary-General: Salim Ahmed Salim

Headquarters: P.O. Box 3243, Addis Ababa, Ethiopia (Telephone: +251 1 517700; fax: +251 1 513036)

References: M. Wolfers, *Politics in the Organization of African Unity* (London, 1976); A. Sesay, O. Ojo and O. Fasehun, *The OAU after Twenty Years* (Boulder, Col., 1985); Y. El-Ayouty (ed.), *The Organization of African Unity after Thirty Years* (New York, 1994); G. Harris, *The Organization of African Unity – Bibliography* (Oxford and New Brunswick, 1994)

Organization of American States

(OAS)

The Organization, which is the oldest international regional agency in the world, promotes security and economic and social development in the Western Hemisphere.

Origin and development

The Organization's Charter was signed in April 1948 in Bogotá, Colombia, by the representatives of 20 Latin-American countries and the USA, to consolidate the principles, purposes and policies that had been evolving since 1890 within the framework of the inter-American system. The original members were joined subsequently by several Commonwealth Caribbean countries, Surinam, Belize and Guyana. Although Cuba as a national entity is still considered to be a member, its 'present government' has been excluded from participation in the inter-American system since 1962. Several European, African and Asian countries enjoy the status of permanent observers. Canada, a long-time permanent observer, eventually requested to join the Organization in October 1989 and acquired full membership in January 1990. Member countries of the Organization now total 35, but Cuba's participation remains suspended despite recent calls from some members for its unconditional return.

The first move towards a coalition of the American republics dates back to the signing by Colombia, Central America, Peru and Mexico in 1826 of the Treaty of Perpetual Union, League and Confederation at the Amphictyonic Congress of Panama convoked by Simón Bolívar. The bases for the inter-American system were laid formally at the First International Conference of American States (held in Washington DC, from October 1889 to April 1890), with the establishment of the International Union of American Republics served by a central office – the Commercial Bureau located in Washington – for the promotion of trade and the exchange of commercial information among the member states. The 1890 agreement was signed on 14 April, a date that has ever since been celebrated as Pan American Day. The conferences held in 1901 and 1906 extended the scope of inter-American co-operation, approved conventions on international law and arbitration and developed the role of the Commercial Bureau. At the Fourth International Conference of American States in 1910, the name of the organization was changed to Union of American Republics, and the Commercial Bureau was renamed the Pan American Union. The four conferences that followed, in 1923, 1928, 1933 and 1938, laid the foundation for closer economic, social, cultural and juridical co-operation within the Union; established 'non-intervention' as a basic principle of the inter-American system; and proclaimed the solidarity of the member countries against all foreign intervention or aggression. Substantial headway towards the consolidation and strengthening of inter-American peace and security was made through the adoption in 1945 of the Act of Chapultepec on Reciprocal Assistance and American Solidarity.

The provisions of the Act were embodied in the Inter-American Treaty of Reciprocal Assistance (Rio Treaty) of 1947, which represented the first comprehensive convention on collective security to which all the American states became parties.

Finally, in 1948, at the Ninth International Conference of American States at Bogotá, a Charter was adopted and the Union of American Republics changed its name to the Organization of American States, while the General Secretariat of the Organization continued to be called the Pan American Union until 1970. The Ninth Conference also approved the American Treaty on Pacific Settlement (Pact of Bogotá) which was intended to replace the existing agreements for the prevention and peaceful solution of disputes. The Organization's Charter was revised substantially by the Protocol approved at the Third Special Inter-American Conference held in Buenos Aires in 1967; the amendments, setting new standards for co-operation and establishing the General Assembly as the supreme organ in place of the Inter-American Conference, entered into effect in February 1970. Other amendments to the Charter are contained in the Protocol of Cartagena, approved in 1985 and coming into force in November 1988; these amendments increased the powers of the Secretary-General and of the Permanent Council. The Protocol of Washington, adopted in December 1992, also amended the Charter, incorporating a provision for the suspension of any member whose democratic government had been overthrown by force. Further amendments were introduced in June 1993 through the Protocol of Managua, creating an Inter-American Council for Integral Development to replace two existing Councils, and strengthening the Organization's activities in the field of technical co-operation.

Any independent American state wishing to join the Organization may be admitted, upon recommendation of the Permanent Council, by decision of the General Assembly; both the recommendation and the decision require a two-thirds majority. The status of permanent observer was officially created in 1971, to enable co-operating non-member countries to participate in the Organization's meetings.

Objectives

The Organization is devoted to the strengthening of the security of the Western hemisphere, the settlement of inter-American disputes by pacific means, and the promotion, through co-operative efforts, of its members' economic, social and cultural development. The Organization has a formal relationship with the UN as a regional arrangement for the maintenance of peace and security.

The basic goals of the Organization are to achieve an order of peace and justice, foster mutual solidarity and co-operation, and defend the sovereignty, territorial integrity and independence of the member states. The Charter reaffirms the principle that 'an act of aggression against one American state is an act of aggression against all the other American states' and solemnly proclaims the fundamental rights of the individual regardless of race, nationality, creed or sex, and the equal rights and duties of states. The duty to abstain from intervention in the internal or external affairs of any other state is meant to imply proscription not only of armed force but also of 'any other form of interference or attempted threat against the personality of the state or against its political, economic and cultural elements'. Besides the submission of inter-American disputes to peaceful procedures and the safeguard of collective security, the Charter provides for a wide range of mechanisms to improve economic, social, educational, scientific and cultural standards and to support regional economic integration. The eradication of extreme poverty was included among the Organization's basic goals by the 1992 Protocol of Washington.

Structure

The highly complex structure of the Organization includes the following principal organs: the General Assembly; the Meeting of Consultation of Ministers of Foreign Affairs; the three Councils; the Inter-American Juridical Committee; the Inter-American Commission on Human Rights; the Inter-American Court of Human Rights; and the General Secretariat. Subsidiary organs may be established whenever necessary.

The General Assembly consists of the representatives of all members, each state having one vote, and holds its regular sessions during the second quarter of the year, either in one of the member countries or at headquarters; special sessions may be convoked by the Permanent Council with the approval of two-thirds of the member states. It is the responsibility of the General Assembly to determine the basic policies and functions of the Organization and to consider any matter of common interest to the member states; decisions are taken by absolute majority, except in those cases such as budgetary questions that require a two-thirds vote. The Meeting of Consultation of Ministers of Foreign Affairs may be held to consider urgent problems of common interest to the American states under the Organization's Charter, or to serve as Organ of Consultation under the Rio Treaty of 1947 in cases of armed attack or other threats to peace and security.

The three Councils, where all member states are equally represented, are directly responsible to the General Assembly and make proposals and recommendations on matters within their respective competence. The Permanent Council, meeting regularly at the Organization's headquarters in Washington DC, oversees the maintenance of friendly relations among members, assisting them in the peaceful settlement of their disputes and serving as a provisional Organ of Consultation in case of an armed attack. According to the Protocol of Cartagena, the Permanent Council is now allowed to try to resolve a dispute among members regardless of the fact that all the parties concerned (as previously stipulated) agree to take the matter before the Organization. A subsidiary body, the Inter-American Committee on Peaceful Settlement, assists the Permanent Council in its peacekeeping function. The Permanent Council is also responsible for supervising the operation of the General Secretariat, improving the functioning of the Organization and developing co-operation with the UN and other American agencies.

The Inter-American Economic and Social Council (CIES), created in 1945 and incorporated into the Organization's Charter in 1948, has for its principal purpose the furthering of inter-American co-operation for economic and social development, through the recommendation of programmes and courses of action and the co-ordination of all economic and social activities. The objectives of the Inter-American Council for Education, Science and Culture (CIECC) are to foster not only inter-American cultural relations but also education and cultural advancement in individual countries. Both CIES and CIECC – according to the 1993 Protocol of Managua – are to be replaced by a new body, the Inter-American Council for Integral Development.

The Inter-American Juridical Committee, consisting of eleven jurists from different member states and functioning in Rio de Janeiro, advises the Organization on legal matters, promotes the development and codification of international law, and investigates the problems related to the integration of the developing members and the possibility of achieving uniformity in their legislation. The Inter-American Commission on Human Rights (IACHR) – a consultative organ set up in 1960 and composed of seven members chosen from panels presented by governments – seeks to promote the observance and protection of human rights and recommends measures and legislation conforming to the rules of the American Convention on Human Rights (Pact of San José) signed in 1969. The Inter-American Court of Human Rights, based in San José, Costa Rica, was established in 1978 as an autonomous judicial institution, composed of seven members, responsible for the application and interpretation of the American Convention on Human Rights.

The General Secretariat, located in Washington DC, is the central and permanent organ carrying out the policies and programmes decided upon by the General Assembly, the Meeting of Consultation of Ministers of Foreign Affairs and the Councils, and performing several functions assigned to it in other inter-American treaties and agreements. The Protocol of Cartagena has strengthened the role of the Secretary-General, who is now empowered to bring to the attention of the Permanent Council matters that 'might threaten the peace and security of the hemisphere or the development of the member states'. Both the Secretary-General and the Assistant Secretary-General are elected by the General Assembly for a five-year term and may not be re-elected more than once or succeeded by a person of the same nationality. The Assistant Secretary-General, who serves as adviser to the Secretary-General and may act as his delegate, is also Secretary of the Permanent Council.

A significant role is played by the Specialized Organizations, which are intergovernmental agencies established by multilateral agreements, with specific functions concerning technical matters. While preserving their status as integral parts of the Organization and complying with the recommendations of the General Assembly and the Councils, these agencies enjoy full technical autonomy and maintain close relations with international bodies working in similar fields. At present there are six Specialized Organizations, dealing respectively with the promotion of health, the protection of children, the extension of women's rights, geographical and historical studies, the welfare of American Indians, and agricultural cooperation. The headquarters of the organizations are located in different member countries on the basis of geographical representation. The Pan American Health Organization (PAHO), whose seat is in Washington, is the oldest international health agency in the world, serving also as the regional office for the Americas of the *World Health Organization (WHO).

In addition to the Specialized Organizations, a number of agencies co-operate with various bodies of the Organization for the achievement of specific objectives within fields of common interest to all American states. These agencies, all of which are based in Washington DC, include the Inter-American Defence Board (IADB) for military co-operation; the Inter-American Statistical Institute (IASI) for the advancement of science and the administration of statistics; the Inter-American Nuclear Energy Commission (IANEC) for the peaceful use of nuclear energy; the Inter-American Emergency Aid Fund (FONDEM) for the supply and co-ordination of assistance in the event of natural disasters; and the Administrative Tribunal, competent to pass judgment on applications alleging non-observance of conditions established in appointments or contracts regarding staff members of the Organization's General Secretariat.

Activities

Besides the formal link with the UN as a regional arrangement, the Organization co-operates more or less closely with UN specialized agencies and with many inter-American economic, technical and financial institutions. All member states are supposed to contribute to the regular budget of the Organization according to a scale of quotas determined by the General Assembly on the basis of several elements; however, substantial arrears in payment of contributions caused a financial crisis by the end of the 1980s. Specific projects are financed by voluntary contributions to special multinational funds.

The Organization's status and role have changed remarkably over recent decades as a result of a number of critical issues emanating from within the inter-American system and not always conducive to the strengthening of an association embracing the USA, Latin American and later also Caribbean countries. In addition, the evolution of the inter-American system itself has been affected strongly by crucial extra-hemispheric events, and world-wide problems and pressures. The fundamental questions of peace and security have increasingly been linked to economic and social development, the effective exercise of representative democracy, and the respect for human rights. As regards the maintenance of international peace within the hemisphere, the Organization has been dealing with inter-American disputes (mainly occurring in the Caribbean and Central American region) and with threats of subversion and extracontinental intervention. Apart from the crises in Guatemala (1954) and the Dominican Republic (1965), and several boundary disputes, the Cuban issue imposed a major strain on inter-American relations. Despite the suspension of Cuba in 1962 and the repeated condemnation of Cuban sponsorship of subversive activities and acts of terrorism, the Organization proved unable to adopt a common policy towards the Castro regime. A resolution leaving the parties to the Rio Treaty free to normalize relations with Cuba was eventually approved in 1975. The continued troubles and tensions in Central America pose other major challenges to the Organization's functions in the sphere of peace-keeping.

With regard to the long-standing dispute between Argentina and the UK over the Falkland (Malvinas) Islands, the Ministers of Foreign Affairs called on both parties to negotiate a peaceful settlement of the conflict, taking into account Argentina's 'rights of sovereignty' as well as the interests of the islanders.

Inter-American co-operation in the economic and social fields has attracted growing attention since the 1960s in an effort to reconcile the primary concern of the USA for hemispheric security with Latin American economic interests and rising expectations. The foundation in 1959 of a regional development bank, the *Inter-American Development Bank (IDB), as an autonomous agency designed to finance loans to governments and public and private enterprises, represented a significant step towards more effective financial co-operation. A vast co-operative plan (the Alliance for Progress) to stimulate economic and social development in Latin America during the 1960s was launched officially at a Special Meeting of the Inter-American Economic and Social Council held in Punta del Este, Uruguay, in August 1961. However, despite the strong initial commitment of the USA, only modest results were attained. The Organization has effectively been operating through comprehensive development programmes and specific projects in the field of technical assistance and co-operation, while in the main leaving to the UN *Economic Commission for Latin America and the Caribbean (ECLAC) the task of encouraging and supporting the establishment of regional integration groups and 'common markets', largely patterned on the Western European models. The protectionist practices and trade restrictions that are frequently used as instruments of 'economic aggression' against Latin American countries, and problems connected with unemployment, food shortages, strong inflationary pressures and the energy crisis, constitute matters of concern for the Inter-American Economic and Social Council and its Special Committee for Consultation and Negotiation (CECON). Various records of achievement are to be found in other areas of inter-American co-operation – tourism, educational services, statistics, the protection of the historical and archaeological heritage, and the improvement of traditional handicrafts.

The Organization – through its highly controversial organ, the Inter-American Commission on Human Rights – has become deeply involved with the alleged violations of human rights by some of its members. Several resolutions on the subject have been adopted by the General Assembly, recommending *inter alia* the creation of the Inter-American Court of Human Rights subsequently installed in Costa Rica. The questions related to the consolidation of democracy and to the observance of human rights and their full legal recognition in the juridical as well as economic, social and cultural spheres, exert considerable influence on inter-American relations and on the prospects for the integral development of the Latin American countries. Electoral assistance and observer missions have been sent by the Organization to a number of member countries. In June 1991 a resolution on representative democracy was adopted, providing for an emergency meeting of the Permanent Council in the case of the abandonment of democratic procedures or the overthrow of a democratically elected government in a member country; the resolution was subsequently incorporated into the Protocol of Washington. Constitutional crises in Haiti, Peru and Guatemala were closely followed by the Organization in the early 1990s through *ad-hoc* meetings of the Ministers of Foreign Affairs. As regards the recent Peru–Ecuador border dispute, the Organization has been making attempts at working out a definite solution. Besides political and security issues, organized crime, drug trafficking and poverty are currently perceived by the Organization as major challenges to its efforts to establish a hemispheric order.

Secretary-General: César Gaviria Trujillo

Headquarters: 17th Street and Constitution Avenue, N.W., Washington DC 20006, USA (Telephone: +1 202 458 3000; fax: +1 202 458 3967)

Publications: *Américas* (six times a year); *Annual Report*

References: G. Connell-Smith, *The Inter-American System* (London, 1966); M. M. Ball, *The OAS in Transition* (Durham, North Carolina, 1969); Galo Plaza, *The Organization of American States: Instrument for Hemispheric Development* (Washington DC, 1969); L. J. LeBlanc, *The OAS and the Promotion and Protection of Human Rights* (The Hague, 1977); V. P. Vaty and H. Muñoz: *The Future of the Organization of American States* (New York, 1993); O. C. Stoetzer, *The Organization of American States* (2nd edn) (New York, 1993)

Organization of Arab Petroleum Exporting Countries (OAPEC)

The Organization groups Arab oil-exporting countries in the Middle East and Africa.

Origin and development

Established in January 1968 by the governments of Saudi Arabia, Kuwait and Libya, the Organization was subsequently joined by other Arab oil-exporting countries in Africa (Algeria, Egypt and Tunisia) and Asia (Bahrain, Iraq, Qatar, Syria and the United Arab Emirates). Tunisia withdrew at the end of 1986 since its status had changed from net exporter to net importer of energy. Egypt's membership, suspended in April 1979 after the signing of the bilateral peace treaty with Israel, was restored in May 1989.

Objectives

The basic aim of the Organization is to safeguard the interests of member countries and to determine ways and means to implement mutual co-operation and co-ordination in various forms of economic activity in the petroleum industry. Besides the establishment of close co-operative links and the protection of the legitimate interests, individual as well as collective, of member countries, the Organization is entrusted with the tasks of securing the supply of petroleum to consumer countries at equitable and reasonable prices, and creating favourable conditions for capital and technological investments in the oil industry.

Structure

The basic institutional structure of the Organization includes the Ministerial Council, the Executive Bureau and the Secretariat. The Council, which is the supreme authority meeting at least twice a year, consists of the representatives of all members, normally the Ministers of Petroleum, each with one vote. The Council formulates the general policy of the Organization, directs its activities and lays down its governing rules; it is chaired for one-year terms by the representative of each country in turn. The Bureau, whose members are senior officials appointed by each country, is the principal executive organ, normally meeting before the sessions of the Council and responsible for the management of the Organization's affairs, the implementation of resolutions and recommendations, and the drawing up of the Council's agenda. The Secretariat, headed by the Secretary-General, performs administrative functions. Within the framework of the Secretariat are four Departments (Finance and Administrative Affairs; Information and Library; Economics; and Technical Affairs). There is also a Tribunal consisting of nine judges whose task is to settle differences in the interpretation and application of the Organization's Charter.

Activities

A number of joint undertakings have been set up in order to supplement the Organization's activities in several specialized fields, and thus to promote and strengthen Arab participation. These undertakings, based in different member countries, include: the Arab Maritime Petroleum Transport Company (AMPTC) and the Arab Shipbuilding and Repair Yard Company (ASRY), both created in the early 1970s to increase Arab participation in the transport of hydrocarbons; the Arab Petroleum Services Company (APSC), providing various services and training specialized personnel; the Arab Petroleum Training Institute; and the Arab Petroleum Investments Corporation (APICORP), with an authorized capital of $1200 million (of which $400 million subscribed), granting funds for a wide range of projects related to the oil industry, with priority being given to Arab joint ventures.

The Organization maintains close working relations with the *League of Arab States and its specialized institutions. It also co-operates with several UN organs and agencies, such as the *UN Conference on Trade and Development (UNCTAD), the *UN Industrial Development Organization (UNIDO), and the *International Maritime Organization (IMO), and other national and international bodies.

The Organization has played a significant role in its efforts to improve inter-Arab co-operation on vital petroleum issues and to co-ordinate, as far as possible, Arab policies within the broader framework of the *Organization of the Petroleum Exporting Countries (OPEC). Several conferences and seminars, as well as training and research programmes, have been carried out under the auspices of the Organization. Special emphasis was placed on the promotion of inter-Arab trade in petroleum products and petrochemicals. However, the invasion of Kuwait by Iraq in August 1990 and the subsequent Gulf War severely affected the Organization's activities and prospects. In December 1990 headquarters were temporarily moved to Cairo; the reopening of the Kuwaiti headquarters took place in 1994. Fluctuating oil prices and tension among member countries over OPEC production quotas have hampered the Organization's efforts to foster effective co-operation and co-ordination.

Secretary-General: Abd al-Aziz al-Turki
Headquarters: P.O. Box 22525, Safat, 13086 Kuwait (Telephone: +965 4844500: fax   +965 4815747); Cairo Office: P.O. Box 108, Maglis Al Shaab 11516, Cairo, Egypt (Telephone: +20 2 354 2660; fax: +20 2 354 2601)
Publications: *Secretary-General's Annual Report; OAPEC Monthly Bulletin*

Organization of Eastern Caribbean States (OECS)

The Organization groups the smaller countries of the Eastern Caribbean in order to strengthen their security and foster their development.

Origin and development

The Organization's current members (Antigua and Barbuda, Dominica, Grenada, Montserrat, Saint Kitts and Nevis, Saint Lucia, Saint Vincent and the Grenadines) were participants in a pre-independence grouping – the West Indies Associated States – created in 1966. In June 1968, these same countries, initially reluctant to join the newly-created Caribbean Free Trade Association (CARIFTA), formed their own customs union, the East Caribbean Common Market (ECCM).

The attainment of independence led the seven countries belonging to the least-developed group of the *Caribbean Community and Common Market (CARICOM), which had succeeded CARIFTA, to join forces and to establish the Organization; the relevant treaty was signed at Basseterre, Saint Kitts and Nevis, in June 1981 and entered into force the following month. The Central Secretariat was to be located in Saint Lucia, while the Economic Affairs Secretariat was to be based in Antigua. The British Virgin Islands enjoy the status of associate member.

Objectives

The aims of the Organization are to promote co-operation and economic integration among member countries, to defend their sovereignty, territorial integrity and independence, and to establish, as far as possible, common positions on international issues.

Structure

The Authority of Heads of Government is the supreme policy-making body meeting biannually. The Foreign Affairs Committee and the Defence and Security Committee are responsible for the co-ordination of external relations and the preparation of a common position of the Organization in multilateral forums. The Economic Affairs Committee, assisted by the Economic Affairs Secretariat, supervises the operation of the Eastern Caribbean Common Market (ECCM). The Central Secretariat performs technical and administrative functions and oversees the general functioning of the Organization.

Activities

The Organization formally requested the intervention of troops from the USA following serious political unrest in Grenada in October 1983; troops from the Organization's member countries and other Caribbean islands also participated in the operations. Proposals for the formation of a political union among the member countries have been put forward several times, the Windward countries (Dominica, Grenada, Saint Lucia and Saint Vincent) having been the most active, but domestic difficulties have caused plans to be shelved temporarily. A deepening and strengthening of the Organization's founding treaty was called for in February 1995, on the occasion of a joint meeting with CARICOM. The establishment of a single market has also met with considerable difficulties because of continuing protectionist attitudes of member countries. The Eastern Caribbean States Export Development Agency, based in Dominica, was set up in 1989 with the support of the then European Economic Community (EEC).

Director-General: Dr Vaughan A. Lewis
Headquarters: P.O. Box 179, The Morne, Castries, Saint Lucia (Telephone: +854 452 2537; fax: +854 453 1628)
Economic Affairs Secretariat: P.O. Box 822, St John's, Antigua

Organization of the Islamic Conference (OIC)

The Organization fosters solidarity and policy co-ordination on major international issues among Islamic countries.

Origin and development

The Organization was established formally in May 1971, following a summit meeting of the Heads of State of 24 Islamic countries held in Rabat, Morocco, in September 1969 and conferences of the Foreign Ministers held in Jeddah, Saudi Arabia, in March 1970, and Karachi, Pakistan, in December 1970. The Charter of the Organization was adopted by the Foreign Ministers in 1972. Heads of State meetings took place in Lahore, Pakistan, in 1974, and at Mecca, Saudi Arabia, in 1981, when a plan of action strengthening economic co-operation was adopted and the Organization, with an increased membership, began to play a more significant role. Membership grew further in the early 1990s, after the fall of the Communist regimes, when Albania, Mozambique and four republics of the former Soviet Central Asia (Kazakhstan, Kyrgyzstan, Tajikistan and Turkmenistan) joined the Organization; Bosnia–Herzegovina enjoys observer status. The present membership includes about 50 Moslem countries in Africa and Asia, plus Albania and Turkey; Palestine is a full member. Observer status has been granted to the Moslem community of the 'Turkish Federated State of Cyprus' and to the Moslem Moro National Liberation Front of the southern Philippines. Egypt's membership was suspended in May 1979 after it signed a peace treaty with Israel; it was restored in March 1984. The suspension of Afghanistan took place in January 1980 as a consequence of the Soviet invasion; in March 1989 Afghanistan was readmitted, represented by the government formed by the Mujaheddin after the withdrawal of Soviet troops. Nigeria withdrew in May 1991, while Zanzibar renounced in 1993 an application that had been presented; it is unclear, however, whether the Organization has recognized the withdrawal of these two countries.

Objectives

The purpose of the Organization is to promote effective solidarity and to strengthen co-operation among Islamic countries in the economic, social and political fields. Besides the general promotion of Islamic solidarity, the Organization's basic aims are: to improve co-operation in the economic, social, cultural, scientific and other vital fields; to arrange consultations among members participating in international institutions; to endeavour to eliminate racial segregation and discrimination as well as colonialism in all its forms; to take the necessary measures to support the establishment of international peace and security based on justice; to co-ordinate all efforts for the safeguard of the Moslem Holy Places and to help the Palestinian people; to help Moslem peoples preserve their dignity, independence and national rights; and to create a suitable atmosphere for the development of co-operation and mutual understanding between members and other countries.

Structure

The basic institutional structure of the Organization is fairly simple and comprises the Conference of the Heads of State, the Conference of Foreign Ministers and the Secretariat; several subsidiary bodies have been created since the 1970s. The Heads of State had met at irregular and fairly long intervals until the session held in 1981, where it was decided that summit meetings should be held every three years; issues of paramount importance to Islamic countries are usually discussed, on the basis of reports prepared by the Conference of Foreign Ministers. This latter organ holds ordinary sessions once a year, in the capital or other important town of a member country, and is entrusted with the functions of fulfilling the Organization's tasks and setting the guidelines for relations with non-member countries. General and administrative services are provided by the General Secretariat, based in Jeddah, which is composed of a Secretary-General (elected by the Conference of Foreign Ministers for a non-renewable four-year term), four Assistant Secretaries-General, and the necessary staff.

Among the specialized bodies there are the Islamic Commission for economic, cultural and social affairs, established in 1976, and three Standing Committees established in 1981, responsible for Economic and Commercial Co-operation; Information and Cultural Affairs; and Scientific and Technological Co-operation. The Al-Quds (Jerusalem) Committee was set up in 1975 to carry out the resolutions concerning the status of the Holy City and has met at the level of Foreign Ministers since 1979.

A number of other bodies have been established to supplement the Organization's activities in selected fields, such as: the Statistical, Economic and Social Research and Training Centre for the Islamic Countries (located in Ankara); the Islamic Institute of Technology (Dhaka); the Islamic Foundation for Science, Technology and Development – IFSTAD (Jeddah); the Islamic Chamber of Commerce and Industry (Karachi); the Islamic Educational, Scientific and Cultural Organization – ISESCO (Rabat); the International Islamic News Agency and the Islamic States Broadcasting Organization (both in Jeddah). Two specialized bodies are responsible for monetary and financial co-operation: the Islamic Solidarity Fund, founded in 1974 to accord emergency aid and to support Islamic hospitals, schools, cultural centres and universities; and the *Islamic Development Bank (IsDB) which started its financial operations in 1976. The Islamic Centre for the Development of Trade began operations in 1983 in Casablanca.

Activities

The Organization, which was granted observer status by the UN General Assembly in 1975, has taken part in UN efforts to reduce tensions in Islamic countries such as Afghanistan, Somalia and Tajikistan. In order to promote understanding and co-operation between Islamic and non-Islamic countries in the relevant areas, links are maintained with several international bodies, such as the *UN Educational, Scientific and Cultural Organization (UNESCO), the *Food and Agriculture Organization of the UN (FAO), the *World Health Organization (WHO) and the *UN Children's Fund (UNICEF).

The effective pursuit of the Organization's goals has been affected adversely by recurring tensions and disputes between member countries which hold widely differing views on many fundamental issues. A general unity on the Palestinian question and the status of Jerusalem was maintained until Egypt's recognition of Israel. With regard to Afghanistan, the Conference of Foreign Ministers held an extraordinary session in January 1980 and called for the immediate and unconditional withdrawal of Soviet troops. Resolutions were also adopted opposing foreign pressures exerted on Islamic countries in general, and Iran in particular, and condemning armed aggression against Somalia. The third session of the Conference of the Heads of State of member countries took place in January 1981, in Saudi Arabia, to consider broad political, economic and financial issues. The problems in Afghanistan and Iran, and the armed conflict between Iran and Iraq, continued to be major topics of discussion within the framework of the Organization. The fourth Summit Conference, held in January 1984 in Casablanca, agreed to restore the full membership of Egypt, despite the opposition of seven member countries. The fifth Summit Conference took place in Kuwait in January 1987 and debated issues related to the Iran–Iraq war as well as to conflicts in Chad and Lebanon. In August 1990 a majority of Ministers of Foreign Affairs condemned Iraq's invasion of Kuwait and demanded the withdrawal of the occupation forces. The situation in the Gulf led to the deferment of the sixth Summit Conference, which was held in Dakar in December 1991 with limited participation by Heads of State; Iraq did not participate and was condemned for its failure to comply with UN resolutions. In the following months the Foreign Ministers discussed the problems arising from the critical situation of the Moslem communities in Bosnia and Herzegovina and from increased fundamentalist militancy in several Islamic countries. The peace agreement negotiated between the Palestine Liberation Organization (PLO) and Israel was welcomed by the Conference in late 1993. A contact group was set up by Foreign Ministers in 1994 to deal with 'human rights violations' in Jammu and Kashmir and to promote the Kashmiri cause.

The seventh Conference of Heads of State, which took place in Casablanca in December 1994, established a fund to provide further humanitarian and economic assistance to Bosnian Moslems and declared that the UN arms embargo on Bosnia–Herzegovina could not be applied. The Casablanca summit adopted a Code of Conduct for Combating International Terrorism in an effort to repress the activities of Moslem extremist groups and to build up Islamic solidarity against fundamentalism. The Organization's meeting in Conakry, Guinea, in December 1995 urged the return of Jerusalem to Palestinian control and expressed support for the Dayton peace accord on Bosnia-Herzegovina.

Secretary-General: Hamid Algabid

Headquarters: Kilo 6, Mecca Road, P.O. Box 178, Jeddah 21411, Saudi Arabia (Telephone: +966 2 680 0800; fax: +966 2 687 3568)

Reference: H. Moinuddin, *The Charter of the Islamic Conference. The Legal and Economic Framework* (Oxford, 1987)

Organization of the Petroleum Exporting Countries (OPEC)

The Organization groups most oil-exporting countries in the world and acts to safeguard their interests *vis-à-vis* major oil-importing countries.

Origin and development

Established in September 1960 at a conference held in Baghdad with the participation of Saudi Arabia, Iran, Iraq, Kuwait and Venezuela, the Organization was joined subsequently by several other oil-exporting countries: Qatar in 1961; Indonesia and Libya in 1962; Abu Dhabi in 1967 (membership afterwards transferred to the United Arab Emirates); Algeria in 1969; Nigeria in 1971; Ecuador in 1973 (after a few months as an associate member); the United Arab Emirates in 1974; and Gabon in 1975 (an associate member from 1973). In September 1992 Ecuador announced its intention to withdraw from the Organization, the first member to do so in more than 30 years; withdrawal became effective in January 1993.

Initially established to consider measures for coping with cuts in the posted price for crude oil introduced by oil companies in the late 1950s, the Organization gained increasing importance as a result of the admission of new countries and of the development of a strategy using oil supplies as an instrument of political as well as economic pressure. The Organization's members currently produce about a third of the world's oil (compared with 45 per cent in 1980 and over 55 per cent in 1973) and possess over three-quarters of the total known reserves.

Membership of the Organization is open to any country which is a substantial net exporter of crude and has fundamentally similar interests to those of other member countries. Admission requires acceptance by a majority of three-quarters of the full members, including the concurrent vote of the five founders. A country which does not meet all the requirements for full membership may be admitted as an associate member.

The Organization's Statute, adopted by the conference held in January 1961 in Caracas, has been extensively amended on several occasions.

Objectives

The basic aim of the Organization is the co-ordination and unification of the petroleum policies of member countries and the protection of their individual and collective interests. To achieve its basic aim, the Organization devises methods to ensure the stability of prices in international oil markets with a view to eliminating harmful fluctuations. Under the Statute, this goal is to be attained giving due regard to the necessity of securing a steady income to the producing countries, an efficient, economical and regular supply to the consuming countries, and a fair return on their capital to those investing in the oil industry.

Structure

The main organs are the Conference, the Board of Governors, and the Secretariat. The Conference, which is the supreme authority meeting at least twice a year, consists of the representatives of all members, each with one vote. All decisions, other than those concerning procedural matters, must be adopted unanimously. The Conference formulates the general policy of the Organization and determines the ways and means for its implementation; confirms the appointments of the members of the Board of Governors, whose activities it directs; considers or decides upon the reports and recommendations submitted by the Board of Governors; and approves the budget. The Conference's resolutions become effective 30 days after the conclusion of the meeting at which they were adopted, unless in the meantime one or more members have given to the Secretariat notification of their opposition.

The Board of Governors, whose members are appointed for a two-year term by each country and confirmed by the Conference which appoints the Chairman, is responsible for the management of the affairs of the Organization and for the implementation of the decisions of the Conference. The Board of Governors, each of whom has one vote, meets no less than twice a year and adopts its decisions by a simple majority of attending members.

The Secretariat, consisting of the Secretary-General, the Deputy Secretary-General and such staff as may be required, performs the executive functions under the direction of the Board of Governors.

In 1964 the Economic Commission was established as a specialized body, operating within the framework of the Secretariat, in order to assist the Organization in promoting stability of international oil prices at equitable levels; it meets at least twice a year.

Activities

The Organization has maintained formal relations with the UN Economic and Social Council, and with a number of bodies such as the *UN Conference on Trade and Development (UNCTAD).

Despite frequent disagreements between the 'moderates', led by Saudi Arabia, and the 'radicals', such as Algeria, Libya and Iraq, over the policies to be followed on pricing, production, export capacity and royalties, the Organization showed during the 1970s a remarkable degree of cohesion *vis-à-vis* the major industrial countries, especially Western Europe and Japan (which are more or less heavily dependent on oil imports). On the other hand, the setting and maintenance of a single level of prices throughout the Organization proved to be an extremely difficult goal.

For a long period, almost from the end of the Second World War to 1973, oil prices had been decreasing appreciably in both monetary and real terms, thus contributing to the establishment in the industrial countries of a development pattern based on the extensive use of low-cost energy sources. Following the Teheran agreement of 1971 between the producing countries of the Gulf and the major oil companies, the situation began to change radically. The failure of subsequent negotiations with oil companies to revise the Teheran agreement and to adjust prices induced the Organization's members to increase prices unilaterally. The posted price of crude oil (which at the beginning of the 1970s was less than $2 per barrel) was raised to $11.65 per barrel in December 1973. Subsequent meetings of the Organization decided on further increases, some of them to take place in several stages, but not all members agreed or observed these stages. After the Iranian revolution and the further deterioration of the overall climate in the Middle East, including the armed conflict between Iran and Iraq, agreement on a long-term pricing and production strategy applicable by all member countries became even harder to reach.

In order to defend an OPEC-wide price structure, it was decided in March 1982 (for the first time in the Organization's history) to impose an overall production ceiling of 18 million barrels per day (bpd). No agreement, however, was reached on individual production quotas. Despite continuing efforts over the following years, it proved very difficult to establish and maintain an official marker price and production ceiling effectively applicable to all members of the Organization. Differences over the Organization's strategy, particularly with respect to production quotas, became even more intractable in early 1986 when the collapse in the oil market and the continued decline of the US dollar brought prices, in real terms, to their lowest level since the middle of 1973. A return to production quotas and to a fixed pricing system, decided in late 1986, succeeded in stabilizing prices, despite the fact that a number of members had exceeded the agreed production limit. Increases in production were allowed in 1989, but again some member countries declared that they did not feel bound to respect the limits, thereby further weakening the Organization's credibility. Effective co-operation with non-OPEC members for common production strategies has also proved unfeasible. After Iraq's invasion of Kuwait in August 1990 and the subsequent international embargo on oil exports from the two countries there was a marked increase in the price of oil, which reached a peak of $40 a barrel in early October but subsequently fell to about $25 per barrel. During the last months of 1990 and the beginning of 1991 several members of the Organization produced in excess of their agreed quotas. In September 1991 an agreement was reached to raise the collective production ceiling to 23.6 million bpd. Overproduction and

falling demand led the Organization in February 1992 to reintroduce individual production quotas for the first time since August 1990. New collective quotas were negotiated in 1993 but prices continued to fall, reaching a five-year low at $12.9 per barrel in February 1994. A ministerial meeting in March 1994 decided to maintain the ceiling of 24.5 million bpd effective since late 1993. The ceiling was confirmed in November 1994 for one year and subsequently extended until June 1996. However, overproduction by some members put the quota system under severe strain and increased output from non-OPEC countries continued to hinder the Organization's efforts to raise world oil prices.

Secretary-General: Rilwanu Lukman
Headquarters: Obere Donaustrasse 93, 1020 Vienna, Austria (Telephone: +43 1 211120; fax: +43 1 264320)
Publications: *Annual Report*; *Annual Statistical Bulletin*; OPEC Review (quarterly); *OPEC Bulletin* (monthly)
References: F. Ghadar, *The Evolution of OPEC Strategy* (Lexington, Ky, 1977); T. H. Moran, *Oil Prices and the Future of OPEC: the Political Economy of Tension and Stability in the Organization of Petroleum Exporting Countries* (Washington DC, 1978); I. Seymour, *OPEC, Instrument of Change* (London, 1980); J. Griffin and D. Teece (eds), *OPEC Behaviour and World Oil Prices* (London, 1982); D. Aperjis, *OPEC Oil Policy and Economic Development (Cambridge*, Mass., 1982); S. M. Ghanem, *OPEC: The Rise and Fall of an Exclusive Club* (London, 1986); L. Skeet, *OPEC: 25 Years of Oil and Politics* (Cambridge, 1988); F. Al-Chalabi, *OPEC at the Crossroads* (Oxford, 1989)

P

Pacific Basin Economic Council (PBEC)

The Council is a non-governmental body grouping business leaders of the Pacific Rim countries.

Origin and development

Established in 1967 to provide a forum for business leaders, the Council is made up of Committees in Australia, Canada, Chile, China, Colombia, Fiji, Hong Kong, Indonesia, Japan, Korea, Malaysia, Mexico, New Zealand, Peru, Philippines, Russia, Taiwan, Thailand and the USA.

Objectives

The Council aims at increasing trade and investment flows through open markets in the Pacific and at fostering co-operation with governments and international organizations on key issues affecting the development of the Pacific region.

Activities

The Council has played a significant role in advising governments as well as serving as a liaison between business representatives and government officials. Several business symposia have taken place under the sponsorship of the Council which has also been carrying on a programme of business missions. The Council is an 'institutional member' of the *Pacific Economic Co-operation Council (PECC), participating in all its activities but without voting power.

International General Director: Robert G. Lees
Headquarters: 1001 Bishop Street, Suite 1570, Honolulu, Hawaii 96813, USA (Telephone: +1 808 521 9044; fax: +1 808 599 8690)
Publication: *PBEC International Bulletin* (several issues a year)

Pacific Economic Co-operation Council (PECC)

The Council is a non-governmental organization promoting growth and economic development in the Pacific Rim. In January 1992 the organization changed its original name – Pacific Economic Co-operation Conference – to the present one.

Origin and development

The organization traces its origins to the Pacific Community Seminar held in Canberra, Australia, in September 1980, at the initiative of the Australian and Japanese prime ministers. The Canberra Seminar – convened to explore ways and means for a loosely structured but purposeful approach to region-wide co-operation – was attended by participants from eleven countries: that is, the five Pacific industrial powers (Australia, Canada, Japan, New Zealand and the USA), the then five members of the *Association of South East Asian Nations (ASEAN), and South Korea, plus a delegation representing collectively the Pacific Island Nations. Among the special features of what turned out to be the first PECC general meeting was the tripartite structure of the delegations, comprising representatives from business and industry (mainly members of the *Pacific Basin Economic Council (PBEC)), academics (mainly members of the Pacific Trade and Development Conference (PAFTAD)), and government officials, all of them participating in their private capacities, and deciding on the basis of consensus. Particular emphasis was laid on the need for all members – industrial and developing – to be placed on an equal footing, excluding any form of associate membership for the developing economies of the region. Particular elements of Pacific regional co-operation were identified in the exclusion of military and security issues – so as 'to create a sense of community without creating a sense of threat' – and the furtherance of the 'economic aims and interests' of the countries belonging to ASEAN and to the SPF.

At present PECC consists of 22 member committees representing 14 economies in the Asia-Pacific (Australia, Brunei, China, Hong Kong, Indonesia, Japan, Korea, Malaysia, New Zealand, the Philippines, Singapore, Taiwan, Thailand and Vietnam); two in North America (Canada and the USA); four in Latin America (Chile, Colombia, Mexico and Peru); plus Russia, and the Pacific Island Nations, which are collectively represented by the *South Pacific Forum (SPF). Taiwan participates under the name of Chinese Taipei. Two international non-governmental organizations – the PBEC and PAFTAD, the latter being a region-wide body grouping academic economists – are 'institutional members', participating in all activities but without voting power. Other countries have expressed interest in full membership.

Objectives

The Council is a tripartite non-governmental organization bringing together academics, business people and government officials to discuss co-operation and policy co-ordination in areas that would promote economic growth and development in the Pacific Rim. It has become a clearing house for policy and business research, and serves as a catalyst for new initiatives in policy change.

Besides its main work on trade and investment policy development and forecasts of economic trends, the organization is also committed to promoting opportunities for sectoral programmes of development and co-operation in infrastructure and key market areas. By virtue of its peculiar tripartite structure reflecting the concerns of a wide constituency of interests, and its accumulated experience, PECC appears to be in a position to complement and support the APEC process, laying the foundations for stronger economic links among Pacific Rim countries as well as promoting the further strengthening of openness in the region and in the global economic system.

Structure

At PECC II, the first measures were adopted with regard to the institutional mechanism; it was decided to set up a Standing Committee, made up of representatives of the national member committees, as the highest decision-making body responsible for the evolution of the PECC process. It was also decided to establish a number of task forces to report on specific issues.

At PECC III, institutional arrangements were considered, identifying five components: the Conference (holding periodic general meetings); the Standing Committee; the Task Forces; the Co-ordinating Group (composed of task-force leaders and other experts); and the Member Committees (set up on a national basis).

At PECC VI it was decided to set up a permanent Secretariat in Singapore, with a view to consolidating the institutional capability of PECC.

A major institutional development at PECC VIII was the adoption of the PECC Charter, consisting of eight articles codifying past practice, and including the entire text of the 'Vancouver Statement' as an Appendix.

Activities

After the 1980 Canberra Seminar, a follow-up meeting – under the official name of Pacific Economic Co-operation Conference and now known as PECC II – was held in Bangkok in June 1982 to concentrate on economic issues 'which are neither sufficiently nor effectively dealt with at international and bilateral fora'.

The results of the work of the task forces created at PECC II were discussed at PECC III, in November 1983 in Bali, where the 'task force approach' was confirmed and new topics were selected for further study. At PECC IV, in the spring of 1985, special attention was devoted to trade policy issues in view of the proposed new round of multilateral negotiations within the framework of the then General Agreement on Tariffs and Trade (GATT).

The launching of the Uruguay Round was welcomed by participants in PECC V (Vancouver, November 1986) which included for the first time delegations from both China and Taiwan (the latter under the name of Chinese Taipei) as full members. A remarkable achievement was the endorsement of the 'Vancouver Statement on Pacific Economic Co-operation' enshrining the basic aims, institutional features and practices of PECC as they had been developing since 1980. A framework thus emerged of 'open regionalism', committed on the one hand to achieving greater region-wide economic co-operation and interaction, while recognizing, on the other, 'both the realities of and the benefits accruing from global interdependence and continuing to encourage increased economic co-operation and interaction with other nations and regions'. The 'Vancouver Statement' now forms the basis for the preamble to the PECC Charter and must be considered a prerequisite for joining the organization.

At PECC VI (Osaka, May 1988), the Central Fund was formally set up, with a view to providing financial support for member committees from developing countries; the establishment of the Fund represented, *inter alia*, the first step towards the creation of a permanent PECC Secretariat. The focal point of PECC VII, held in Auckland in November 1989, was the relationship of the organization to the *Asia-Pacific Economic Co-operation (APEC) ministerial meeting, held the previous week in Canberra.

The eighth general meeting (PECC VIII) took place in Singapore in May 1991 and saw a further expansion of the co-operative links with APEC. For the first time, representatives from the member committees of Chile, Hong Kong, Mexico and Peru attended the meeting as full PECC members.

The ninth general meeting of PECC (PECC IX) was held in September 1992 in San Francisco, where a Declaration on 'Open Regionalism: A Model for Global Economic Co-operation' was adopted, restressing the member countries' commitment to a stronger and more open global economic system. The tenth general meeting – with 'Open Regionalism: The Way Ahead' as its theme – was held in Malaysia in the spring of 1994.

Director General: David Parsons

Headquarters: 4 Nassim Road, Singapore 1025 (Telephone: +65 737 9823; fax: +65 737 9824)

Publications: *PECC Newsletter* (quarterly); *Pacific Economic Outlook* (annually)

Reference: L. T. Woods; 'Non-governmental Organizations and Pacific Cooperation: Back to the Future?', *The Pacific Review*, 4 (1991), 312–21

Paris Club

The Club is an informal forum where industrial creditor countries negotiate the settlement of official loans with countries unable to meet their debt servicing obligations.

Origin and development

The Club was established in 1956 to deal with the liquidity problems faced by several debtor countries, most of them from Latin America.

Participants include the *International Monetary Fund (IMF), the *World Bank, the *UN Conference on Trade and Development (UNCTAD), the *European Union (EU) and the creditor and debtor countries concerned. To participate, debtor countries must have concluded a policy arrangement with IMF; co-ordination between the Club and the IMF has been developing in order to define the scale of debt-restructuring negotiations.

Objectives

The Club provides the framework where debtor countries usually negotiate the rescheduling of debt service payments on loans extended or guaranteed by the governments or the official agencies of participating creditor countries. Debts to commercial banks are not renegotiated within the Club, but with committees of the banks involved.

Structure

The Club has not been endowed with a legal basis or with a proper institutional mechanism, and its membership varies from one meeting to another. Meetings are convened at the request of debtor countries and are chaired by a senior official of the French Treasury. The burden of debt relief is evenly divided among the creditor countries, which are usually members of the *Organization for Economic Co-operation and Development (OECD); although OECD countries are the principal members, other creditor countries with similar claims are encouraged to participate.

Activities

The grave debt crisis of the 1980s represented a major challenge for the Club; with the Toronto agreement of 1988, creditor governments recognized the need for debt reduction with regard to non-concessional official debt owed by low-income countries. The 'Toronto terms' were subsequently modified, and other specific 'terms' have been adopted to meet new challenges, such as the 'Trinidad terms', deepening concessionality in existing debt-relief measures, and the 'Naples terms', agreed upon by the *Group of Seven (G-7) at the July 1994 summit meeting. New terms tend to set easier debt relief conditions, including provisions for up to two-thirds of debt falling due to be written off.

Settlements take place in the form of debt consolidation, involving a rescheduling of redemption obligations and interest payments. However, debt relief becomes effective only when bilateral agreements negotiated with individual creditor countries establish the debts covered by the rescheduling and the relevant interest rate.

The Club has adopted an increasingly differentiated treatment of debtors, depending on their situation, and an increased flexibility in the coverage of rescheduling. Over the past few years, negotiations within the framework of the Club have involved substantial debt cancellation, depending on the implementation by the debtor country of an adjustment programme agreed with the IMF.

Reference: D. Sevigny: *The Paris Club: An Inside View* (Ottawa, 1990)

Permanent Inter-State Committee on Drought Control in the Sahel

(Comité permanent interétats de lutte contre la sécheresse dans le Sahel) (CILSS)

The Committee groups Sahel countries in the fight against drought.

Origin and development
The western parts of the Sudano-Sahelian region of Africa were affected by severe droughts in the late 1960s and early 1970s, with disastrous consequences for vegetation and livestock, and threatening to destroy traditional ways of life. The affected countries established the Committee in 1973 with a view to organizing joint efforts to combat drought and alerting the international community to the seriousness of the situation. The UN Sudano-Sahelian Office (UNSO) was set up in the same year to alleviate the impact of future droughts and to help the affected countries achieve food self-sufficiency. UNSO, transferred in 1976 to the *UN Development Programme (UNDP), has played a significant role in the preparation of the International Convention to Combat Desertification in Those Countries Experiencing Serious Drought and/or Desertification, Particularly in Africa, which was signed by 87 countries in October 1994.

The Committee includes as full members Burkina Faso, Cape Verde, Chad, Gambia, Guinea-Bissau, Mali, Mauritania, Niger and Senegal.

Objectives
The prime objective of the Committee is to overcome the effects of chronic drought and to promote co-operative development in the Sahel region by improving grain production and irrigation, halting deforestation and creating regional food reserves.

Structure
The structure of the Committee is relatively simple and flexible, with summit meetings held by the Heads of State to consider major initiatives. Besides the Conference of Heads of State there are periodic meetings of the Council of Ministers, where all members are represented. An Executive Council, created in 1985, is charged with monitoring all the Committee's operations, including the preparation of the budget.

Activities
The Committee has undertaken a major effort in developing an early warning system for food shortages, expanding water supplies, protecting vegetation, promoting alternative energy sources, and raising external aid from donor governments and international organizations such as the *European Community (EC). Co-operative links have also been developed with the *Food and Agriculture Organization of the UN (FAO). In the early 1990s the traditional aims of the Committee were expanded considerably to include economic integration, while the administrative mechanism has been streamlined and made more efficient. However, the Committee has been experiencing severe financial problems, and repeated appeals to members urging them to pay contribution arrears have met with only a partial response.

Executive Secretary: Cisse Mariam K. Sidibe
Headquarters: P.O. Box 7049, Ouagadougou, Burkina Faso (Telephone: +226 306758; fax: +226 306757)

S

South Asian Association for Regional Co-operation (SAARC)

The Association has represented the first significant attempt at organizing co-operation among the countries of South Asia.

Origin and development

The Association originated in December 1985 in Dhaka, Bangladesh, when a solemn document, known as the Dhaka Declaration, and a Charter setting out the objectives and structure of the new organization, were signed at a summit meeting attended by the Heads of State and Government of Bangladesh, Bhutan, India, the Maldives, Nepal, Pakistan and Sri Lanka. The summit meeting was held at the recommendation of the Foreign Ministers of the seven countries grouped in the Committee for South Asia Regional Co-operation (SARC).

The need for closer co-operation among the countries of South Asia had been recognized since the early 1980s. Between 1981 and 1983 several multilateral meetings were convened at foreign secretariat level in order to forge operational and institutional links for the pursuit of common goals. A declaration setting up the SARC Committee was eventually approved in August 1983 in New Delhi, by a ministerial conference which launched an integrated programme of action (IPA) covering agriculture, rural development, health and population, and telecommunications, as well as arts and culture. The tasks of supervising the programme, identifying additional areas of co-operation and mobilizing regional and external resources, were entrusted to the Committee, while a technical body was created to oversee the implementation of the co-ordinated programmes in the various fields. The ministerial meetings held in the Maldives in July 1984, and in Bhutan in May 1985, reviewed the implementation of the action programme and paved the way for the Dhaka summit, which agreed upon the formal establishment of the Association.

Regional co-operation is envisaged by the Dhaka Declaration as a 'logical response' to the dramatic challenges posed to the countries of South Asia by 'poverty, underdevelopment, low levels of production, unemployment and pressure of population compounded by exploitation of the past and other adverse legacies'. Effective co-operation is expected to prepare the ground for optimum use of national and regional strengths, human and natural resources, and economic complementarities.

Objectives

The Association aims basically at increased economic, social, cultural and technical collaboration among the countries of South Asia, with a view to accelerating the pace of economic development and strengthening collective self-reliance.

According to the Charter, the objectives of the Association are: (a) to improve the welfare and quality of life of South Asian peoples; (b) to accelerate economic growth, social progress and cultural development; (c) to promote collective self-reliance among the member countries; (d) to contribute to mutual trust, understanding and appreciation of one another's problems; (e) to promote active collaboration and mutual assistance in the economic, social, cultural, technical and scientific fields; (f) to strengthen co-operation with other developing countries; (g) to strengthen co-operation among member countries in international forums on matters of common interest; and (h) to co-operate with international and regional organizations having similar aims and purposes.

These widely-phrased objectives appear to leave ample room for further negotiations on specific issues and areas of operational activity. Co-operation within the framework of the Association should not interfere with existing bilateral and multilateral obligations, and should be conducted according to the principle of non-interference in internal affairs.

The Association's functions and decision-making powers have no supranational features and are fairly limited by the unanimity principle which is required for all deliberations; 'bilateral and contentious issues' are expressly excluded from the competence of the Association.

Structure

The basic structure of the Association consists of the Summit Meeting of Heads of State or Government taking place annually, the Council of

Ministers meeting at least twice a year, the Standing Committee of Foreign Secretaries, the Technical Committees, and the Secretariat. The Standing Committee meets as often as necessary, usually prior to the meetings of the Council of Ministers, and plays an important operational role. The technical committees are established to study and supervise co-operation programmes in: agriculture and forestry; rural development; health and population; education and culture; environment; communications; science and technology; transport; meteorology; women and development; tourism; and prevention of drug trafficking and drug abuse. Terrorism 'as it affects the stability' of member countries also falls within the competence of technical committees.

Following the decision taken at the Second Summit in Bangalore in November 1986 to establish a Secretariat, a Secretary-General assumed charge in January 1987 and further steps were taken to recruit and establish the Secretariat itself in Kathmandu. It was decided that the Secretary-General would be appointed on the basis of rotation by country, in alphabetical order. The Secretariat is not a policy-making body but coordinates the implementation of the Association's activities and services its meetings.

Activities

The Third Summit of the Association was held in Kathmandu in November 1987 and saw the signing of the Regional Convention on the Suppression of Terrorism, which came into force in August 1988. Proposals were made for a SAARC Audio Visual Exchange Programme and a SAARC Documentation Centre. An agreement was also concluded with a view to establishing a SAARC Food Security Reserve, which began operations in 1988; the Reserve consists of nearly 250 000 metric tons of grain to meet emergency food needs in member countries. The SAARC Agricultural Information Centre was set up in 1988 in Dhaka.

The Fourth Summit was held in Islamabad in December 1988. The Fifth Summit – held in Malé, the Maldives, in November 1990 – saw the signing of the SAARC Convention on Narcotic Drugs and Psychotropic Substances, which entered into force in September 1993. In Malé, member countries also asked for Iraq's withdrawal from Kuwait. The Sixth Summit took place in Colombo in December 1991 and accorded the highest priority to the allevi-

ation of poverty in all South Asian countries. After two postponements, the Seventh Summit was held in Dhaka in April 1993 and approved the Framework Agreement for the liberalization of intraregional trade under the so-called SAARC Preferential Trading Arrangement (SAPTA). The SAARC Documentation Centre (SDC) was set up in New Delhi in May 1994, and the SAARC Meteorological Research Centre (SMRC) was established in Dhaka in January 1995. At the Eighth Summit, which took place in New Delhi in May 1995, the Heads of State or Government declared 1995 the 'SAARC Year of Poverty Eradication'. Calls were made by leaders participating in the Summit for broadening and deepening co-operation 'within a specific and rapid time-frame in the core areas of trade and economic relations in the region', and for the implementation of SAPTA. The Eighth Summit also endorsed the establishment of a three-window South Asian Development Fund (SADF), with the merger of existing funds. The Governing Board of SADF held its first meeting in Dhaka in June 1996.

A number of studies have been completed or are under way on trade, manufactures and services, the causes and consequences of natural disasters, the protection of the environment, and the 'greenhouse effect'. The extension and strengthening of co-operation to vital areas such as trade, industry, financial and monetary issues and energy could gradually bring about the hoped-for increase in 'collective self-reliance', which is one of the basic goals of the Association. As regards external relations, the Association is interested in developing mutually beneficial co-operation with major international organizations, notably the *Association of South East Asian Nations (ASEAN), the *European Union (EU) and the *Asian Development Bank (AsDB). In July 1996, a Memorandum of Understanding an Administrative Co-operation was signed with the EU as a first step in setting up a framework for strengthening mutually beneficial links.

The creation of the seven-member Association has represented no small achievement for South Asia, a region with a total population of around 1 200 million (of which three-quarters are in India), which had not yet set up an institutional machinery of its own to promote full-scale co-operation. Although the Association does not deal with bilateral matters, it may well be that the very existence of a multilateral framework will help South Asian countries concentrate on common problems and solutions, and ultimately lessen tensions arising from crucial issues such as the activities of separatist and terrorist groups. On the commercial side, the intensification of trade negotiations for the implementation of SAPTA – according to the reiterated commitments of member countries – could lead to the launching of the South Asian Free Trade Area (SAFTA) by the year 2000.

Secretary-General: Naeem U. Hasan
Headquarters: P.O. Box 4222, Kathmandu, Nepal (Telephone: +977 1 221785; fax: +977 1 227033)
E-mail address: saarc@mos.com.np
Publication: *SAARC Newsletter* (monthly)
References: F. Ashraf, *South Asian Association for Regional Cooperation* (Islamabad, 1988); B. Pradhan, *SAARC and its Future* (Kathmandu, 1989); K. B. Lall, H. S. Chopra and T. Meyer (eds), *The European Community and SAARC* (New Delhi/London, 1993)

Southern African Development Community (SADC)

The Community – established in 1992 by the then ten member countries of the Southern African Development Co-ordination Conference (SADCC) – promotes economic co-operation and integration among the countries of Southern Africa.

Origin and development
One of the original goals of SADCC, besides the promotion of economic co-operation in all major areas, was to reduce the region's economic dependence on the Republic of South Africa. With the end of the apartheid regime in South Africa, the Council of Ministers of SADCC, meeting in January 1992, approved proposals to convert the Conference into a fully integrated regional Community, ultimately including a democratic non-racial South Africa. The relevant treaty was signed at Windhoek, Namibia, on 17 July 1992, and came into force on 5 October 1993. The ten founder members of the Community were subsequently joined by South Africa in 1994 and Mauritius in 1995.

The SADCC originated in July 1979 when the first Southern African Development Co-ordination Conference took place in Arusha, Tanzania, with the participation of the economic ministers of the Front-Line States (FLS) – Angola, Botswana, Mozambique, Tanzania and Zambia – and of representatives from governments of industrial countries and international agencies that had been promoting closer co-operation among majority-ruled states in the subregion. After a series of contacts at different levels, the Heads of State or Government of the five FLS, joined by Lesotho, Malawi, Swaziland and Zimbabwe, meeting in April 1980, signed the Lusaka Declaration on Economic Liberation and formally brought SADCC into existence. A programme of action was approved, allotting specific studies and tasks to member countries. Namibia became the tenth member of the Conference upon achieving independence in 1990.

All SADCC members were eligible for membership in the Preferential Trade Area for Eastern and Southern African States (PTA), a body that was formally replaced in December 1994 by the newly-created *Common Market for Eastern and Southern Africa (COMESA). The largely overlapping membership, first of SADCC and PTA and later of SADC and COMESA, has always represented a highly controversial issue, with recurring proposals either for a merger of the two organizations or for a clearly defined 'division of labour' between them.

Objectives
The general purpose of the Community is to deepen economic co-operation and integration, with the goal of establishing a regional common market, and to strengthen regional solidarity, peace and security.

Structure
The formal structure of the Community is made up of the Summit Meeting of Heads of State or Government, which takes place annually; the Council of Ministers (meetings of energy ministers, transport ministers, and so on) to approve projects for inclusion in the Community's Programme of Action; the Committee of Officials, who screen projects prepared by 'sectoral co-ordinators' working in specialized units of government departments; and the Secretariat, headed

by an Executive Secretary with administrative duties. Meetings and consultations are also held with donor governments and international agencies, to review projects and financing issues.

Two specialized regional institutions have been established so far: the Southern African Centre for Co-operation in Agricultural Research (SACCAR); and the Southern African Transport and Communications Commission (SATCC).

Activities

During the SADCC experience, close links were developed with several organizations – notably the *European Union (EU) and the *African Development Bank (AfDB). On the whole, EU member countries remain the major contributors, bilaterally and collectively through the Lomé Convention.

The transformation of SADCC into SADC has given new impetus to efforts at close economic co-operation and the eventual establishment of a common market, along with increased political and security co-ordination. Joint infrastructure development, establishment of regional production policies and co-ordination of investment procedures were among the major tasks of the newly-created Community. The entry of South Africa, on the other hand, has significantly changed the balance of power within the organization. The consultative conference of the Heads of State or Government held in Lilongwe, Malawi in February 1995, decided to give South Africa the responsibility for the co-ordination of the economic, financial and monetary policies of the member countries. At the August 1995 meeting of the Heads of State or Government – held for the first time in Johannesburg, South Africa – agreement was reached on the preparation of a treaty, to be considered at the 1996 summit, providing for the setting up of a regional common market with the elimination of all trade barriers by the year 2000.

Executive Secretary: Dr Simbarashe Makoni
Headquarters: SADC Building, Private Bag 0095, Gaborone, Botswana (Telephone: +267 351863; fax: +267 372848)
Publications: *SADC Annual Report*; *SADC Energy Bulletin*
References: D. G. Anglin, 'Economic Liberation and Regional Cooperation in Southern Africa:

SADCC and PTA', *International Organization*, 37 (1983), 681–711; D. G. Anglin, 'SADCC in the Aftermath of the Nkomati Accord', in I. S. R. Msabaha and T. M. Shaw (eds) *Confrontation and Liberation Southern Africa: Regional Directions after the Nkomati Accord*, (London, 1987) 173–97; OECD/SADCC, *Implementing the SADCC Programme of Action* (Paris and Gaborone, 1988)

South Pacific Commission (SPC)

The Commission promotes the economic and social development of the peoples of the South Pacific region.

Origin and development

The Commission was established by an agreement signed in February 1947 in Canberra, Australia, and effective from July 1948. The founder members were six governments with territories in the region: Australia, France, The Netherlands, New Zealand, the UK, and the USA. The Netherlands withdrew in 1962, when it ceased to administer the western part of New Guinea; the UK withdrew at the end of 1995. The original agreement has been supplemented by several documents in order to extend the territorial scope of the Commission and to adapt its functions and powers to the changing needs and aspirations of the peoples of the region.

Under new arrangements adopted in 1983, full membership in the Commission currently includes 26 governments and administrations: the developing islands of the Pacific plus Australia, New Zealand, France and the USA.

Objectives

The Commission, as a consultative and advisory body to the participating governments in matters affecting the economic and social development of the region, has the power to make recommendations in respect of agriculture, communications, transport, fisheries, forestry, industry, labour, marketing, production, trade and finance, public works, education, health, housing and social welfare – having due regard to the necessity of co-ordinating local projects that are of regional significance. In addition, the Commission has the responsibility of facilitating research in scientific, economic and social fields, to ensure the maximum co-operation among research bodies and to provide technical assistance.

Structure

The South Pacific Conference is the supreme organ, which meets ordinarily every year in October to discuss the Commission's basic policies and to adopt the programme of activities and the budget. Since 1974 the Conference has combined into a single meeting; the former Commission Session attended by the delegates of the member governments and the former South Pacific Conference representing the territorial administrations. A representative having one vote is sent by each government and territorial administration.

The Committee of Representatives of Governments and Administrations (CRGA) comprises delegates of the 26 member states and territories, having equal voting rights. It was established in 1983 to replace the former Committee of Representatives of Participating Governments (consisting of only 13 members), and the Planning and Evaluation Committee.

The CRGA, which operates as a Committee of the Whole, meets twice a year to consider and recommend the administrative budget, evaluate the effectiveness of the preceding year's work programme, examine the draft budget and work programme presented by the Secretary-General, and nominate the principal officers of the Commission; the reports of the two meetings of the CRGA are submitted to the annual Conference. The Secretariat, headed by the Secretary-General, who is the chief executive officer of the Commission, has a Management Committee performing supervisory and advisory functions over the activities carried out by the Commission.

Activities

The Commission maintains working relations with other international agencies such as the UN *Economic and Social Commission for Asia and the Pacific (ESCAP) and with many national institutions directly concerned with the region. The member governments and administrations contribute to the regular budget of the Commission on the basis of a formula related to per capita income; voluntary contributions from govern-

ments, international organizations and other sources account for a substantial proportion of the Commission's total budget.

The Commission arranges conferences and training courses and provides assistance to applied research, information services and data analysis. Special attention is given to the needs of the smaller countries not endowed with mineral resources, such as phosphates and nickel, and largely based on subsistence farming and fishing. The Commission's main areas of interest currently include agriculture, plant protection and forestry, fisheries, conservation and environmental management, socioeconomic and statistical services, cultural conservation and exchanges, and community health and education. In particular, the development and sustainable management of marine resources (fish and, less immediately, the mineral riches of the sea bed) represent a very important test for the Commission's ability to organize and foster effective co-operation on a broad regional basis.

The Commission served as the implementing agency for the South Pacific Regional Environment Programme (SPREP) until 1990, when it was decided to establish SPREP as an autonomous and financially independent body. In November 1986 the Commission hosted a Conference which adopted the Convention for the Protection of the Natural Resources and Environment of the South Pacific Region intended to 'prevent, reduce and control pollution'.

Controversy about budgetary and management procedures in the early 1990s and recurrent financial constraints, further exacerbated by the withdrawal of the UK, have induced the Commission to re-examine its basic goals and to consider an expansion of membership to other Pacific Rim countries with a view to broadening funding sources.

Secretary General: Robert Dun
Headquarters: P.O. Box D 5, 98848 Nouméa, New Caledonia (Telephone: +687 26 20 00; fax: +687 26 38 18)
Publications: *Annual Report*; *Report of the South Pacific Conference* (annual)

South Pacific Forum (SPF)

The Forum is the gathering of the Heads of Government of the independent and self-governing countries of the South Pacific.

Origin and development

The Forum's first meeting was held in Wellington, New Zealand, in August 1971 by the Heads of Government of Australia, the Cook Islands, Fiji, Nauru, New Zealand, Tonga, and Western Samoa; the SPF was subsequently joined by Papua New Guinea and several Pacific islands as they gained independent or self-governing status, and at present has 16 members. The Forum's activities, functions and powers are not governed by any formal instrument. A meeting is held every year by the Heads of Government to discuss political and economic issues of common concern. Decisions are arrived at by consensus and no formal vote is taken. Each meeting has been followed since 1989 by 'dialogues' with representatives of major countries influential in the region such as Japan, China, Korea, the USA, Canada, France, the UK and the *European Union (EU). In October 1995, France's dialogue status was suspended because of nuclear tests conducted in French Polynesia.

Objectives

The objectives of the Forum have gradually been extending from regional trade and economic issues to cover all major political and security topics concerning the countries of the South Pacific.

Structure

The Forum Secretariat was established in 1973 as an intergovernmental regional organization – under the name of South Pacific Bureau for Economic Co-operation (SPEC) – by an agreement signed at the third meeting of the Forum held in Apia, Western Samoa.

The Secretariat's executive board is the Committee, consisting of representatives and senior officials from all member countries. The Committee meets twice a year, immediately before the meetings of the SPF, and at the end of the year, to examine the Secretariat's work programme and annual budget. Australia and New Zealand each contribute a third of the annual budget, the remaining third being shared equally among the other members.

The Secretariat – originally headed by a Director, whose status was upgraded to that of Secretary-General in 1988 when SPEC was renamed the Forum Secretariat – performs administrative functions for all Forum-related meetings; it has been responsible for the day-to-day operation of the SPF since 1975, when the then SPEC became the Forum's official secretariat. Since 1981 SPEC had acted also as the secretariat to the Pacific Group Council of African, Caribbean and Pacific (ACP) countries, receiving assistance from the European Union under the Lomé Conventions. An agreement was signed with the EU in late 1994 to implement an agricultural development programme funded under Lomé IV. An important role was also played by the Forum Secretariat in the South Pacific Regional Environment Programme (SPREP) along with the *South Pacific Commission (SPC).

Activities

The initial Forum meetings were mainly concerned with regional trade and economic issues as well as with French nuclear testing in the South Pacific. In the late 1970s attention focused on transport and fisheries, and led to the creation of the Pacific Forum Line – a joint venture to provide shipping services – in 1977, and the Forum Fisheries Agency in 1978. The Association of South Pacific Airlines and the South Pacific Trade Commission were both established in 1979. The Forum has undertaken practical measures for the expansion of regional commercial relations through the removal of tariff and non-tariff barriers, and the promotion of trade in products of particular interest to the smaller countries. The then SPEC had assisted these countries in negotiating, with Australia and New Zealand, the South Pacific Regional Trade and Economic Co-operation Agreement (SPARTECA), in force since January 1981. Under the SPARTECA, Australia and New Zealand allow duty-free and unrestricted access to specified products originating from the developing island members; further liberalization measures have been introduced gradually by Australia and New Zealand.

Political issues, including the decolonization of New Caledonia, acquired major importance in the 1980s. The August 1984 meeting, held in Tuvalu, charged a group of experts to draft a treaty for establishing a South Pacific Nuclear-Free Zone. The treaty was eventually signed in August 1985 in Rarotonga, the Cook Islands, and came into force in December 1986. Major nuclear powers were invited to sign protocols in support of the treaty, but the offer was initially accepted only by the then USSR and China. France, the UK and the USA, in response to increased diplomatic pressure from the Forum members, eventually signed the protocols in March 1996.

In the 1990s, the Forum's interests and activities have been further enlarged, to include the preparation of programmes for the revitalization of specific traditional industries, the protection of the environment with all related issues, the promotion of private-sector development and of tourism, the co-ordination of efforts related to the improvement of intraregional transport and communications, and the provision of advisory services. Since the late 1980s meetings of the Forum have discussed topics of paramount importance to South Pacific islands, such as the threats posed by the predicted rise in sea-level (caused by heating of the atmosphere as a result of the 'greenhouse effect') and by the extensive and indiscriminate use of drift-net fishing. The 1993 Forum stressed the need to establish closer ties with Asia–Pacific bodies, especially the *Asia–Pacific Economic Co-operation (APEC), and to promote the expansion of intraregional trade. The adoption of measures to control the exploitation of forestry resources was considered by the Forum meetings in 1994 and 1995. A treaty to ban the import into the region of radioactive and other hazardous wastes (the Waigani Convention) was adopted at the 1995 meeting, which also protested against the resumption of French nuclear tests, and decided to reactivate the ministerial committee to monitor developments in New Caledonia.

Among regional organizations reporting to the Forum are the Pacific Islands Development Programme, the South Pacific Applied Geoscience Commission and the University of the South Pacific. The Forum has enjoyed observer status at the UN General Assembly since the end of 1994.

Secretary-General: Ieremia T. Tabai
Headquarters: P.O. Box 856, Suva, Fiji (Telephone: +679   312600;   fax: +679 301102)
Publications: *Annual Report*; *Forum News* (quarterly); *Forum Secretariat Directory of Aid Agencies*

South Pacific Permanent Commission (CPPS)

The Commission groups four Latin American countries for the conservation and management of marine resources.

Origin and development

Established by an Agreement signed by Chile, Ecuador and Peru in 1952, and later joined by Colombia, the Commission collaborates closely with the *Food and Agriculture Organization (FAO) and the *Latin America Organization for the Development of Fisheries (OLDEPESCA).

With a view to attaining the general goal of providing food supplies for the peoples of the member countries, and to furnish them with the means of developing their economies, the Commission determines protected species and lays down general regulations for hunting and fishing; studies and proposes measures suitable for the protection, conservation and use of marine resources; encourages scientific and technical study of the biological phenomena in the south Pacific; and prepares general statistics on the industrial use of marine resources.

Headquarters: Casilla 16638, Agencia 6400-9, Santiago 9, Chile (Telephone: +56 2 726652; fax: +56 2 695 1100)
Publications: *Bulletin on Climatic Alert* (monthly); bulletins on fisheries statistics

U

United Nations (UN)

The UN is a voluntary association of sovereign countries which have committed themselves, through signing the Charter, to ensure international peace and security, and to further international co-operation in solving economic, social, cultural and humanitarian problems, and in promoting respect for human rights and fundamental freedoms.

Origin and development

The name 'United Nations' was devised by President Franklin D. Roosevelt, and was first used in the Washington Declaration by the United Nations of 1 January 1942, when representatives of 26 countries pledged their governments to continue fighting together against the Axis Powers. In addition to the original 26 signatories, 21 other countries subscribed to the Declaration. On 30 October 1943, the Moscow Conference of Foreign Ministers of the UK, the USA and the USSR and the Chinese Ambassador to Moscow, recognized the necessity of establishing 'a general international organization, based on the principle of the sovereign equality of all peace-loving states, and open to membership by all such states, large and small, for the maintenance of international peace and security'. The following year, the basic principles of the proposed organization were worked out during the discussions, held at Dumbarton Oaks (near Washington DC), between the UK, the USA, and the USSR from August to September, and between China, the UK, and the USA from September to October. At the Yalta Conference of February 1945, an agreement was reached by Winston Churchill, Roosevelt and Josef Stalin on the voting procedure to be adopted in the Security Council of the UN and the granting of the 'veto power' to the permanent members.

The Charter of the new institution was drawn up by the representatives of 50 countries at the UN Conference on International Organization, held in San Francisco between 25 April and 26 June 1945, and was eventually signed on 26 June. Poland, not represented at the Conference, signed the Charter later and became the fifty-first original member of the Organization. The UN came into existence formally on 24 October 1945, when the Charter became effective following ratification by China, France, the UK, the USA, and the USSR, and by a majority of other signatories; 24 October is now universally celebrated as United Nations Day. In April 1946, the League of Nations – predecessor of the UN – was officially dissolved, following a decision of its Assembly. Amendments to the Charter come into effect when they have been adopted by a two-thirds vote of the members of the General Assembly and ratified by two-thirds of the members of the UN, including all the permanent members of the Security Council. The amendments introduced so far have related to the expansion of two main organs, the Security Council and the Economic and Social Council.

Membership of the UN is open to all peace-loving nations which accept the obligations of the Charter and, in the judgement of the Organization, are able and willing to carry out these obligations. The original members of the UN are those countries which, having participated in the San Francisco Conference of 1945, or having previously signed the Declaration by the United Nations of 1942, have signed and ratified the Charter. Other countries may be admitted to membership by a two-thirds majority vote by the General Assembly upon the recommendation of the Security Council. The Assembly, therefore, may decide to reject the application of a candidate country having the support of the Security Council, but may not admit a country in the absence of a recommendation of the Security Council. Members may be suspended or expelled by the Assembly on the recommendation of the Security Council: they may be suspended if the Security Council is taking enforcement action against them, or expelled if they persistently violate the principles of the Charter. The rights of a suspended member may be restored by the Security Council.

The number of member countries of the UN has risen from the original 51 to 185, including practically all the independent nations in the world; the only notable exceptions are Switzerland, Taiwan (which occupied the Chinese seat from 1945 until 1971, when it was replaced by the People's

Republic of China), and the Vatican City State (Holy See). The Holy See, Switzerland, Nauru and Tonga, although not members of the UN, participate in certain of its activities. After the dissolution of the USSR, its former constituent republics have been granted separate UN membership. The Russian Federation has succeeded the USSR in all organs of the UN, thereby occupying a permanent seat in the Security Council. The Byelorussian SSR (now Belarus) and the Ukrainian SSR (now Ukraine), although being at the time of the signature of the Charter integral parts of the USSR and therefore not independent countries, have enjoyed separate UN membership as 'original members' since 1945.

With the approach of the twenty-first century, new challenges and opportunities have unfolded for the UN, which must address an ever-expanding security, economic and social agenda whose ultimate goal is the improvement of the human condition. The UN is not a world government and is not authorized, in principle, to intervene in the internal affairs of any country; however, the UN has gradually been taking on an unprecedented degree of responsibility for facing global pressures that defy control by individual countries.

Objectives

The primary purpose of the UN, as it was with the League of Nations, is to maintain peace and security throughout the world and to develop friendly relations among nations. In the Charter, the peoples of the UN express their determination to save succeeding generations from the scourge of war. To this end, they pledge themselves to live in peace as good neighbours, to unite their strength in order to maintain peace and security, and to ensure that armed force shall not be used except in the common interest. The UN is based on the sovereign equality of all its member countries, which undertake to fulfil in good faith their Charter obligations; to settle their international disputes by peaceful means and without endangering peace, security and justice; to refrain in their international relations from the threat or use of force against other countries; and to give the UN every assistance in any action it may take in accordance with the Charter, and not to assist countries against which preventive or enforcement action is being taken. The UN is to ensure that non-member countries act in accordance

with these principles in so far as it is necessary for the maintenance of international peace and security. However, the UN as such has no competence in matters 'which are essentially within the domestic jurisdiction' of any country, and its member countries are not required 'to submit such matters to settlement' under the Charter.

Unlike the Covenant of the League of Nations, the UN Charter reflects the awareness of its draftsmen of the close relationship existing between the maintenance of world peace and the promotion of international economic and social stability, including the safeguarding of human rights and fundamental freedoms. The UN must act as 'a centre for harmonizing the actions of nations in attaining these common ends' in both the political and non-political fields, through the furtherance of co-operation and co-ordination.

Structure

There are six principal organs of the UN: the General Assembly, the Security Council, the Economic and Social Council, the Trusteeship Council, the International Court of Justice, and the Secretariat. In fact, both the Economic and Social Council and the Trusteeship Council are auxiliary bodies whose basic task is to assist and advise the General Assembly and the Security Council. The official languages in all these organs, other than in the International Court of Justice, are Chinese, English, French, Russian and Spanish. Working languages are English and French, with the addition of Russian, Chinese and Spanish in the General Assembly and the Security Council, and Spanish in the Economic and Social Council. Arabic has been added as an official language of the General Assembly, the Security Council and the Economic and Social Council. English and French are the working languages of the Secretariat in New York. The official languages in the International Court of Justice are English and French.

The General Assembly The General Assembly is the main deliberative organ and consists of all the members of the UN, each country having one vote and being entitled to be represented at meetings by five delegates and five alternates. Regular sessions are held once a year, commencing on the third Tuesday in September and normally lasting until mid-December; there is a

United Nations – Growth of Membership

Year	No.	Original Member States
1945	51	Argentina, Australia, Belgium, Bolivia, Brazil, Byelorussian Soviet Socialist Republic, Canada, Chile, China, Colombia, Costa Rica, Cuba, Czechoslovakia, Denmark, Dominican Republic, Ecuador, Egypt, El Salvador, Ethiopia, France, Greece, Guatemala, Haiti, Honduras, India, Iran, Iraq, Lebanon, Liberia, Luxembourg, Mexico, Netherlands, New Zealand, Nicaragua, Norway, Panama, Paraguay, Peru, Philippines, Poland, Saudi Arabia, South Africa, Syria, Turkey, Ukrainian Soviet Socialist Republic, Union of Soviet Socialist Republics, United Kingdom, United States, Uruguay, Venezuela, Yugoslavia

Year	No.	New Member States
1946	55	Afghanistan, Iceland, Sweden, Thailand
1947	57	Pakistan, Yemen
1948	58	Burma
1949	59	Israel
1950	60	Indonesia
1955	76	Albania, Austria, Bulgaria, Democratic Kampuchea, Finland, Hungary, Ireland, Italy, Jordan, Lao People's Democratic Republic, Libyan Arab Jamahiriya, Nepal, Portugal, Romania, Spain, Sri Lanka
1956	80	Japan, Morocco, Sudan, Tunisia
1957	82	Ghana, Malaysia
1958	83	Guinea
1960	100	Benin, Burkina Faso, Cameroon, Central African Republic, Chad, Congo, Cyprus, Gabon, Côte d'Ivoire, Madagascar, Mali, Niger, Nigeria, Senegal, Somalia, Togo, Zaire
1961	104	Mauritania, Mongolia, Sierra Leone, United Republic of Tanzania
1962	110	Algeria, Burundi, Jamaica, Rwanda, Trinidad and Tobago, Uganda
1963	112	Kenya, Kuwait
1964	115	Malawi, Malta, Zambia
1965	118	Gambia, Maldives, Singapore
1966	122	Barbados, Botswana, Guyana, Lesotho
1967	123	Democratic Yemen
1968	126	Equatorial Guinea, Mauritius, Swaziland
1970	127	Fiji
1971	132	Bahrain, Bhutan, Oman, Qatar, United Arab Emirates
1973	135	Bahamas, Federal Republic of Germany, German Democratic Republic
1974	138	Bangladesh, Grenada, Guinea-Bissau
1975	144	Cape Verde, Comoros, Mozambique, Papua New Guinea, São Tomé and Príncipe, Suriname
1976	147	Angola, Samoa, Seychelles
1977	149	Djibouti, Vietnam
1978	151	Dominica, Solomon Islands
1979	152	Saint Lucia
1980	154	Saint Vincent and the Grenadines, Zimbabwe
1981	157	Antigua and Barbuda, Belize, Vanuatu
1983	158	Saint Kitts and Nevis
1984	159	Brunei
1990	159*	Liechtenstein, Namibia
1991	166	Democratic People's Republic of Korea, Estonia, Federated States of Micronesia, Latvia, Lithuania, Marshall Islands, Republic of Korea
1992	179	Armenia, Azerbaijan, Bosnia and Herzegovina, Croatia, Georgia, Kazakhstan, Kyrgyzstan, Moldova, San Marino, Slovenia, Tajikistan, Turkmenistan, Uzbekistan
1993	184	Andorra, Czech Republic,** Eritrea, Monaco, Slovakia,** Former Yugoslav Republic of Macedonia
1994	185	Palau

Notes:

*In 1990 the gain of two members was offset by the loss of two members because of the unification of Democratic Yemen and Yemen, and of the two German states.

**The Czech Republic and Slovakia were admitted as successor states to Czechoslovakia.

Membership of the United Nations

Member	Date of Admission		Member	Date of Admission	
Afghanistan	19 Nov.	1946	Federated States of Micronesia	17 Sep.	1991
Albania	14 Dec.	1955	Fiji	13 Oct.	1970
Algeria	8 Oct.	1962	Finland	14 Dec.	1955
Angola	1 Dec.	1976	France	24 Oct.	1945
Andorra	28 July	1993	Gabon	20 Sep.	1960
Antigua and Barbuda	11 Nov.	1981	Gambia	21 Sep.	1965
Argentina	24 Oct.	1945	Georgia	31 July	1992
Armenia	2 Mar.	1992	Germany	18 Sep.	1973
Australia	1 Nov.	1945	Ghana	8 Mar.	1957
Austria	14 Dec.	1955	Greece	25 Oct.	1945
Azerbaijan	2 Mar.	1992	Grenada	17 Sep.	1974
Bahamas	18 Sep.	1973	Guatemala	21 Nov.	1945
Bahrain	21 Sep.	1971	Guinea	12 Dec.	1958
Bangladesh	17 Sep.	1974	Guinea-Bissau	17 Sep.	1974
Barbados	9 Dec.	1966	Guyana	20 Sep.	1966
Belarus	24 Oct.	1945	Haiti	24 Oct.	1945
Belgium	27 Dec.	1945	Honduras	17 Dec.	1945
Belize	25 Sep.	1981	Hungary	14 Dec.	1955
Benin	20 Sep.	1960	Iceland	19 Nov.	1946
Bhutan	21 Sep.	1971	India	30 Oct.	1945
Bolivia	14 Nov.	1945	Indonesia	28 Sep.	1950
Bosnia and Herzegovina	22 May	1992	Iran	24 Oct.	1945
Botswana	17 Oct.	1966	Iraq	21 Dec.	1945
Brazil	24 Oct.	1945	Ireland	14 Dec.	1955
Brunei Darussalam	21 Sep.	1984	Israel	11 May	1949
Bulgaria	14 Dec.	1955	Italy	14 Dec.	1955
Burkina Faso	20 Sep.	1960	Jamaica	18 Sep.	1962
Burundi	18 Sep.	1962	Japan	18 Dec.	1956
Cambodia	14 Dec.	1955	Jordan	14 Dec.	1955
Cameroon	20 Sep.	1960	Kazakhstan	2 Mar.	1992
Canada	9 Nov.	1945	Kenya	16 Dec.	1963
Cape Verde	16 Sep.	1975	Kuwait	14 May	1963
Central African Republic	20 Sep.	1960	Kyrgyzstan	2 Mar.	1992
Chad	20 Sep.	1960	Lao People's Democratic Republic	14 Dec.	1955
Chile	24 Oct.	1945	Latvia	17 Sep.	1991
China	24 Oct.	1945	Lebanon	24 Oct.	1945
Colombia	5 Nov.	1945	Lesotho	17 Oct.	1966
Comoros	12 Nov.	1975	Liberia	2 Nov.	1945
Congo	20 Sep.	1960	Libya	14 Dec.	1955
Costa Rica	2 Nov.	1945	Liechtenstein	18 Sep.	1990
Côte d'Ivoire	20 Sep.	1960	Lithuania	17 Sep.	1991
Croatia	22 May	1992	Luxembourg	24 Oct.	1945
Cuba	24 Oct.	1945	Madagascar	20 Sep.	1960
Cyprus	20 Sep.	1960	Malawi	1 Dec.	1964
Czech Republic	19 Jan.	1993	Malaysia	17 Sep.	1957
Democratic People's Republic of Korea	17 Sep.	1991	Maldives	21 Sep.	1965
Denmark	24 Oct.	1945	Mali	28 Sep.	1960
Djibouti	20 Sep.	1977	Malta	1 Dec.	1964
Dominica	18 Dec.	1978	Marshall Islands	17 Sep.	1991
Dominican Republic	24 Oct.	1945	Mauritania	27 Oct.	1961
Ecuador	21 Dec.	1945	Mauritius	24 Apr.	1968
Egypt	24 Oct.	1945	Mexico	7 Nov.	1945
El Salvador	24 Oct.	1945	Moldova	2 Mar.	1992
Equatorial Guinea	12 Nov.	1968	Monaco	28 May	1993
Eritrea	28 May	1993	Mongolia	27 Oct.	1961
Estonia	17 Sep.	1991	Morocco	12 Nov.	1956
Ethiopia	13 Nov.	1945	Mozambique	16 Sep.	1975

Membership of the United Nations

Member	Date of Admission		Member	Date of Admission	
Myanmar	19 Apr.	1948	Slovakia	19 Jan.	1993
Namibia	23 Apr.	1990	Slovenia	22 May	1992
Nepal	14 Dec.	1955	Solomon Islands	19 Sep.	1978
Sri Lanka	14 Dec.	1955	Somalia	20 Sep.	1960
Netherlands	10 Dec.	1945	South Africa	7 Nov.	1945
New Zealand	24 Oct.	1945	Spain	14 Dec.	1955
Nicaragua	24 Oct.	1945	Sri Lanka	14 Dec.	1955
Niger	20 Sep.	1960	Sudan	12 Nov.	1956
Nigeria	7 Oct.	1960	Suriname	4 Dec.	1975
Norway	27 Nov.	1945	Swaziland	24 Sep.	1968
Oman	7 Oct.	1971	Sweden	19 Nov.	1946
Pakistan	30 Sep.	1947	Syria	24 Oct.	1945
Palau	15 Dec.	1994	Tajikistan	2 Mar.	1992
Panama	13 Nov.	1945	Thailand	16 Dec.	1946
Papua New Guinea	10 Oct.	1975	The Former Yugoslav Rep. of		
Paraguay	24 Oct.	1945	Macedonia	8 Apr.	1993
Peru	31 Oct.	1945	Togo	20 Sep.	1960
Philippines	24 Oct.	1945	Trinidad and Tobago	18 Sep.	1962
Poland	24 Oct.	1945	Tunisia	12 Nov.	1956
Portugal	14 Dec.	1955	Turkey	24 Oct.	1945
Qatar	21 Sep.	1971	Turkmenistan	2 Mar.	1992
Republic of Korea	17 Sep.	1991	Uganda	25 Oct.	1962
Romania	14 Dec.	1955	Ukraine	24 Oct.	1945
Russian Federation	24 Oct.	1945	United Arab Emirates	9 Dec.	1971
Rwanda	18 Sep.	1962	United Kingdom	24 Oct.	1945
Saint Kitts and Nevis	23 Sep.	1983	United Republic of Tanzania	14 Dec.	1961
Saint Lucia	18 Sep.	1979	United States	24 Oct.	1945
Saint Vincent and the			Uruguay	18 Dec.	1945
Grenadines	16 Sep.	1980	Uzbekistan	2 Mar.	1992
Samoa	15 Dec.	1976	Vanuatu	15 Sep.	1981
San Marino	2 Mar.	1992	Venezuela	15 Nov.	1945
São Tomé and Príncipe	16 Sep.	1975	Vietnam	20 Sep.	1977
Saudi Arabia	24 Oct.	1945	Yemen	30 Sep.	1947
Senegal	28 Sep.	1960	Yugoslavia	24 Oct.	1945
Seychelles	21 Sep.	1976	Zaire	20 Sep.	1960
Sierra Leone	27 Sep.	1961	Zambia	1 Dec.	1964
Singapore	21 Sep.	1965	Zimbabwe	25 Aug.	1980

resumption for some weeks in the new year, if necessary. Special sessions may be convened by the Secretary-General at the request of the Security Council, of a majority of the members of the UN, or of one member if the majority of the members concur. An emergency special session may be convoked within 24 hours of a request by the Security Council on the vote of any nine members of the Council itself, or by a majority of the UN members, or by one member concurred with by the majority of the members. The Assembly elects a new President, 21 Vice-Presidents and the Chairmen of its six Main Committees at the start of each regular session.

The General Assembly is empowered to discuss any matter within the scope of the Charter or affecting the powers and functions of any UN organ and, except where a dispute or situation is being discussed by the Security Council, to make recommendations on it. In addition, the following specific competences of the Assembly are envisaged by the Charter: (a) to make recommendations on the principles of co-operation in the maintenance of international peace and security, including the principles governing disarmament and the regulation of armaments; (b) to make recommendations for the peaceful settlement of any situation, regardless of origin, which might impair

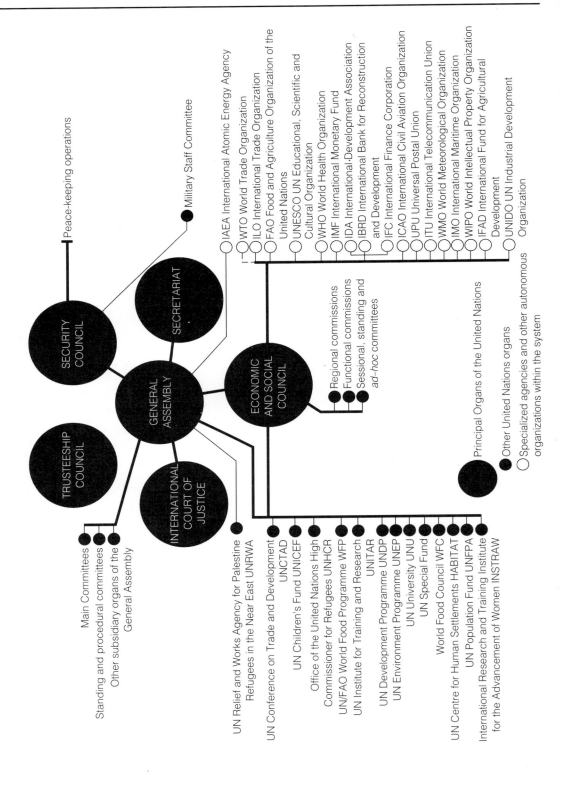

CHART – THE UNITED NATIONS SYSTEM

SECURITY COUNCIL

SECRETARIAT

GENERAL ASSEMBLY

ECONOMIC AND SOCIAL COUNCIL

TRUSTEESHIP COUNCIL

INTERNATIONAL COURT OF JUSTICE

Peace-keeping operations

Military Staff Committee

IAEA International Atomic Energy Agency
WTO World Trade Organization
ILO International Trade Organization
FAO Food and Agriculture Organization of the United Nations
UNESCO UN Educational, Scientific and Cultural Organization
WHO World Health Organization
IMF International Monetary Fund
IDA International-Development Association
IBRD International Bank for Reconstruction and Development
IFC International Finance Corporation
ICAO International Civil Aviation Organization
UPU Universal Postal Union
ITU International Telecommunication Union
WMO World Meteorological Organization
IMO International Maritime Organization
WIPO World Intellectual Property Organization
IFAD International Fund for Agricultural Development
UNIDO UN Industrial Development Organization

Regional commissions
Functional commissions
Sessional, standing and ad-hoc committees

Main Committees
Standing and procedural committees
Other subsidiary organs of the General Assembly

UN Relief and Works Agency for Palestine Refugees in the Near East UNRWA
UN Conference on Trade and Development UNCTAD
UN Children's Fund UNICEF
Office of the United Nations High Commissioner for Refugees UNHCR
UN/FAO World Food Programme WFP
UN Institute for Training and Research UNITAR
UN Development Programme UNDP
UN Environment Programme UNEP
UN University UNU
UN Special Fund
World Food Council WFC
UN Centre for Human Settlements HABITAT
UN Population Fund UNFPA
International Research and Training Institute for the Advancement of Women INSTRAW

Principal Organs of the United Nations

Other United Nations organs

Specialized agencies and other autonomous organizations within the system friendly relations among nations; (c) to initiate studies and make recommendations to promote international political co-operation, the development of international law and its codification, the realization of human rights and fundamental freedoms for all, and international collaboration in economic, social, cultural, educational and health fields; (d) to receive and consider reports from the Security Council, the Secretary-General and other organs; (e) to supervise, through the Trusteeship Council, the execution of the trusteeship agreements for all areas not designated as strategic; (f) to approve the UN budget, to apportion the contributions among members, and to examine the budgets of specialized agencies; (g) to elect the non-permanent members of the Security Council, the members of the Economic and Social Council and those members of the Trusteeship Council which are elected; (h) to take part with the Security Council in the election of judges of the International Court of Justice; and (i) to appoint the Secretary-General upon recommendation of the Security Council.

Under the 'Uniting for Peace' resolution, adopted by the General Assembly in November 1950, the Assembly may take action if the Security Council, because of lack of unanimity of the permanent members, fails to exercise its primary responsibility in any case where there appears to be a threat to the peace, a breach of the peace or an act of aggression. More precisely, the Assembly is empowered to consider the matter immediately, with a view to making recommendations to members for collective measures – including, in the case of a breach of the peace or act of aggression, the use of armed force when necessary to maintain or restore international peace and security. If the Assembly is not in session, an emergency special session may be convened at very short notice.

The General Assembly has a substantive right of decision only with regard to the internal affairs of the UN; as a general rule, recommendations, whatever their political and/or moral force, have no legally binding character and cannot create direct legal obligations for members. All members are entitled to equal voting rights, with decisions on 'important questions' – such as recommendations on peace and security; election of members to organs; admission, suspension and expulsion of members; trusteeship questions; and bud-

getary matters – being taken by a two-thirds majority of the members present and voting, and decisions on 'other questions' by a simple majority. The term 'decision', in relation to the General Assembly and the other organs of the UN, is used in a wide sense and covers all types of action, including 'recommendations', 'resolutions' and so on. The vote can be by 'acclamation', show of hands, roll-call, secret ballot, or 'consensus', this last practice being followed whenever direct confrontation is to be avoided.

An elaborate structure of committees and subsidiary organs is required to enable the General Assembly to carry out its wide range of functions. There are six Main Committees, on each of which every member has the right to be represented by one delegate. They are: First Committee (Disarmament and International Security); Second Committee (Economic and Financial); Third Committee (Social, Humanitarian and Cultural); Fourth Committee (Special Political and Decolonization); Fifth Committee (Administrative and Budgetary); Sixth Committee (Legal). In addition, there is a 28-member General Committee – composed of the President and 21 Vice-Presidents of the Assembly and the Chairmen of the Main Committees – which meets frequently during a session to co-ordinate the proceedings of the Assembly and its Committees and generally to supervise the smooth running of the Assembly's work. The Credentials Committee, consisting of nine members appointed on the proposal of the President at the beginning of each session of the Assembly, is charged with the task of verifying the credentials of representatives. There are also two standing committees – an Advisory Committee on Administrative and Budgetary Questions (ACABQ), consisting of 16 members; and a Committee on Contributions, composed of 18 members, which recommends the scale of members' payments to the UN. Many subsidiary and *ad-hoc* bodies have been set up by the Assembly in order to deal with specific matters.

As a rule, the Assembly refers all questions on the agenda to one of the Main Committees, to a joint committee, or to an *ad-hoc* committee; these bodies, which decide by a simple majority, submit proposals for approval to a plenary meeting of the Assembly. Although regular sessions last about three months each year, the work of the Assembly goes on continuously: in special committees and commissions, such as those dealing with decolonization, peacekeeping operations, disarmament, effects of atomic radiation, peaceful uses of outer space, human rights, economic, social and cultural rights, and international law; in the activities of specialized bodies established by the Assembly itself, such as the *UN Development Programme (UNDP), the *UN Children's Fund (UNICEF), the *UN Environment Programme (UNEP), the *UN Conference on Trade and Development (UNCTAD), and many others; in the work programme of the Secretariat; and at international conferences on specific problems, such as the environment, food, population, status of women, law of the sea, peaceful uses of atomic energy, and outer space.

The Security Council The Security Council has the primary responsibility for maintaining peace and security and consists of 15 members, each of which has one representative and one vote. There are five permanent members: China, France, Russia, the UK and the USA, and ten non-permanent members, each elected for a two-year term by a two-thirds majority of the General Assembly and ineligible for immediate re-election. Any member of the UN not on the Council may participate, without vote, in the discussion of questions especially affecting its interests. Both members and non-members of the UN, if they are parties to a dispute being considered by the Council, are invited to take part, without a vote, in the discussions; the conditions regulating the participation of non-members are laid down by the Council. The Presidency of the Council is held by members in monthly rotation, in the English alphabetical order of their names. The Security Council is so organized as to be able to function continuously, and a representative of each of its members must be present at all times at the seat of the UN. The Council may meet elsewhere than at UN Headquarters if it considers this advisable; in 1972 a session was held in Addis Ababa, Ethiopia, and in the following year another session took place in Panama City.

Besides its basic function relating to the maintenance of international peace and security in accordance with the purposes and principles of the UN, the Security Council is empowered: (a) to investigate any dispute or situation which might lead to international friction and to recommend methods of adjustment or appropriate terms of settlement; (b) to determine the existence of any threat to the peace, breach of the peace, or act of aggression, and to make recommendations or decide what action should be taken; (c) to call on members to apply economic sanctions and other measures not involving the use of force, in order to prevent or stop aggression; (d) to take military action against an aggressor; (e) to formulate plans for the establishment of a system to regulate armaments; (f) to exercise trusteeship functions in 'strategic areas'; (g) to recommend the admission of new members and the terms on which states may become parties to the Statute of the International Court of Justice; and (h) to recommend to the General Assembly the appointment of the Secretary-General and, together with the Assembly, to elect the judges of the International Court of Justice.

The Security Council acts on behalf of all UN members, which 'agree to accept and carry out' its decisions; members also undertake to make available to the Council the 'armed forces, assistance, and facilities' necessary to maintain international peace and security. While other organs of the UN make recommendations to governments, the Council alone has the power to take decisions which members are obligated under the Charter to carry out. Decisions on procedural matters are made by an affirmative vote of at least nine of the 15 members of the Council; decisions on substantive matters also require nine votes, including the concurring votes of all five permanent members. Any of the permanent members may therefore exercise a 'veto right' in relation to all questions, except those of a procedural character, and prevent the taking of a decision, having the support of a majority of the Council; the veto, however, may not be exercised if the permanent member concerned is itself a party to a dispute. All five permanent members have exercised the right of veto at one time or another. The practice of abstention of a permanent member is generally accepted and not regarded as a veto; a valid decision may therefore be taken.

The Committee of Experts on Rules of Procedure, the Committee on Council Meetings away from Headquarters, and the Committee on the Admission of New Members are composed of representatives of all the members of the Council. The Military Staff Committee is composed of the chiefs of staff of the permanent members of the

Council or their representatives; this body, although established since 1946 in order to advise and assist the Council for the application of armed force, has so far performed no real function, despite proposals made from time to time for its 'revitalization'. The *ad-hoc* Committees comprise all Council members and meet in closed session; currently, all these bodies deal with matters regarding sanctions imposed by the UN.

The Economic and Social Council The Economic and Social Council, under the authority of the General Assembly, is the organ responsible for the economic and social work of the UN and the co-ordination of the policies and activities of the specialized agencies and institutions – known as the UN 'family' of organizations. It consists of 54 members, 18 of whom are elected each year by the General Assembly, each for a three-year term; every member has one representative and one vote. Retiring members are eligible for immediate re-election. Since 1992, the Council has held one substantive session annually between May and July, lasting about four to five weeks, alternately in New York and Geneva, plus short organizational sessions in New York. The President is elected for one year and may be re-elected immediately.

The Economic and Social Council is empowered: (a) to make or initiate studies, reports and recommendations on international economic, social, cultural, educational, health and related matters; (b) to make recommendations for the purpose of promoting respect for, and observance of, human rights and fundamental freedoms; (c) to call international conferences and prepare draft conventions for submission to the General Assembly on matters within its competence; (d) to negotiate agreements with the specialized agencies, defining their relationship with the UN; (e) to address recommendations to the specialized agencies, the General Assembly and members of the UN; (f) to perform services, approved by the Assembly, for members of the UN and, upon request, for the specialized agencies; and (g) to make arrangements for consultation with non-governmental organizations concerned with matters falling within its competence. Decisions of the Council are made by a simple majority of members present and voting.

A number of standing committees, commissions and other subsidiary bodies have been set up by the Economic and Social Council. They meet at UN Headquarters or in other locations. There are standing Committees on: Non-governmental Organizations; Programme and Co-ordination; Natural Resources; and Development Planning. The functional commissions include the Statistical Commission, Commission on Population and Development, Commission for Social Development, Commission on the Status of Women, *Commission on Narcotic Drugs (CND), Commission on Science and Technology for Development, Commission on Sustainable Development, Committee on New and Renewable Sources of Energy and on Energy for Development, Commission on Crime Prevention and Criminal Justice, Commission on Human Settlements serviced by the *UN Centre for Human Settlements (Habitat), and the Commission on Human Rights (CHR). The Commission on Human Rights has a Sub-Commission on Prevention of Discrimination and Protection of Minorities within whose framework operates a five-member Working Group on Contemporary Forms of Slavery.

Also under the Economic and Social Council's authority are the regional economic commissions aimed at assisting the development of the major regions of the world and at strengthening economic relations of the countries in each region, both among themselves and with other countries of the world. These are the *Economic Commission for Africa (ECA), based in Addis Ababa; the *Economic and Social Commission for Asia and the Pacific (ESCAP), based in Bangkok; the *Economic Commission for Europe (ECE), based in Geneva; the *Economic Commission for Latin America and the Caribbean (ECLAC), based in Santiago; and the *Economic and Social Commission for Western Asia (ESCWA), based in Amman. The commissions are responsible for studying the problems of their respective regions and recommending courses of action to member countries and specialized agencies.

The Economic and Social Council has made arrangements for consultation with international non-governmental organizations and, after consultation with the member countries, with national organizations. There are over 1500 non-governmental organizations, classified into three categories, having consultative status with the Economic and Social Council; they may send observers to public meetings of the Council and its subsidiary bodies and may submit written statements. They may also consult with the Secretariat of the UN on matters of mutual concern.

The Trusteeship Council The Trusteeship Council bore prime responsibility for supervising the administration of territories placed under the International Trusteeship System established by the UN. The basic goals of the system – that is, the promotion of the advancement of the inhabitants of the trust territories and their progressive development towards self-government or independence – have been fulfilled. The trust territories, mainly in Africa, have attained independence, either as separate states or by joining neighbouring independent countries. The Council acts under the authority of the General Assembly or, in the case of a 'strategic area', under the authority of the Security Council. Membership of the Council is not based on a predetermined number, since the Charter intended to provide for a balance between members that administered trust territories and members that did not. At present, the Council, whose size has decreased progressively, consists of the five permanent members of the Security Council, that is China, France, Russia, the UK and the USA. China, however, did not take part in the work of the Council until May 1989. The Trusteeship Council, having fully accomplished its task, will no longer hold regular meetings; special sessions may be convened whenever necessary. Decisions of the Trusteeship Council are made by a majority of the members present and voting, each member having one vote.

The International Court of Justice The Court is the principal judicial organ of the UN; only states may be parties in cases before it. The Court's governing instrument is the Statute which forms an integral part of the UN Charter and is based on the Statute of the Permanent Court of International Justice of the League of Nations. All members of the UN are *ipso facto* parties to the Statute. A country that is not a member of the UN may become a party to the Statute on conditions determined in each case by the General Assembly upon the recommendation of the Security Council; under this rule, Switzerland has become a party. All countries that are parties to the Statute of the Court can be parties to cases before it; other countries can refer cases to it under conditions laid down by the Security Council. The Security Council may recommend that a legal dispute be referred to the Court. The General Assembly and the Security Council can ask the Court for an advisory opinion on any legal question; other organs of the UN and the specialized agencies, when authorized by the General Assembly, can ask for advisory opinions on legal questions falling within the scope of their activities.

The Court – which has its seat at The Hague, The Netherlands, but may sit elsewhere whenever it considers this desirable – consists of 15 'independent' judges elected with an absolute majority for a renewable nine-year term by the General Assembly and the Security Council voting independently. To safeguard continuity, the terms of office of the judges are staggered so that a third of the seats becomes vacant every three years. The judges are elected, regardless of their nationality, from among persons 'who possess the qualifications required in their respective countries for appointment to the highest judicial offices', or are 'jurisconsults of recognized competence in international law'. Care is taken, however, to see that the principal legal systems of the world are represented in the Court, and it is expressly provided that no two judges can be nationals of the same country. Candidates are chosen from a list of people nominated by the various national groups on the panel of arbitrators of the Permanent Court of Arbitration (established by the Hague Conventions of 1899 and 1907), or by equivalent groups. The Court is permanently in session, except during the judicial vacations. It elects its own President and Vice-Presidents, for three years. The full Court of 15 judges normally sits, but a quorum of nine members is sufficient. The Court may form chambers of three or more judges for dealing with particular categories of cases, and forms annually a chamber of five judges to hear and determine, at the request of the parties, cases by summary procedures. Judgments given by any of these chambers are considered as rendered by the Court.

An important feature of the Court is the inclusion of 'national' judges. In fact, judges of the nationality of the parties continue to sit in cases in which their own countries are involved; if there is no judge on the bench of the nationality of the parties to the dispute, each of the parties may designate an *ad-hoc* judge. Such a judge, who need not possess the nationality of the party that appoints him participates on terms of complete equality with the other judges. All questions are decided by a majority of the judges present; in case of a tie, the President of the Court casts the deciding vote. The judgment is final and without appeal, but a revision may be applied for within ten years from the date of the judgment, on the grounds of a new decisive factor.

The jurisdiction of the Court is twofold, contentious and advisory, and covers all questions that the parties refer to it, and all matters provided for in the UN Charter or in treaties and conventions in force. Disputes concerning the jurisdiction of the Court are settled by the Court itself. States may bind themselves in advance to accept the jurisdiction of the Court in special cases, either by signing a treaty or convention which provides for reference to the Court, or by making a special declaration to this effect. In early 1984, the USA stated that it would not accept the Court's compulsory jurisdiction in cases involving Central America for the following two years.

According to the Statute, the Court may apply in its decisions: (a) international conventions establishing rules recognized by the contesting countries; (b) international custom as evidence of a general practice accepted as law; (c) the general principles of law recognized by nations; and (d) judicial decisions and the teachings of the most highly qualified publicists of the various nations, as a subsidiary means for determining the rules of law. If the parties concerned so agree, the Court may decide *ex aequo et bono*, that is, according to practical fairness rather than strict law. The Court may give an advisory opinion on any legal question to any organ of the UN or its agencies. The Security Council can be called upon by one of the parties in a case to determine measures to be taken to give effect to a judgment of the Court if the other party fails to perform its obligations under that judgment.

The Secretariat The Secretariat services the other organs of the UN and administers the programmes and policies laid down by them. At the head of the Secretariat is the Secretary-General, who is the chief administrative officer of the UN, appointed by the General Assembly, deciding by a simple majority on the recommendation of the Security Council adopted by an affirmative vote of at least nine members, including the concurring votes of the permanent members. The Secretary-General appoints the necessary staff in conformity with the regulations established by the Assembly in order to guarantee the international character, integrity and efficiency of the civil service of the UN. Under the Charter, each member country undertakes to respect the exclusively international character of the responsibilities of the Secretary-General and staff, and not to seek to influence them in the discharge of their duties. Each staff member takes an oath not to seek or receive instructions from any government or outside authority. The Secretary-General performs a number of important political, representative and administrative functions and is required to submit an annual report to the General Assembly. He is empowered to bring to the attention of the Security Council any matter which, in his or her opinion, threatens international peace and security, and to address the Assembly on any question it has under consideration. In his capacity as chief administrative officer, the Secretary-General acts, in person or through deputies, at all meetings of the Assembly, the Security Council, the Economic and Social Council, and the Trusteeship Council, and may be entrusted by these organs with additional functions.

The personal contribution of those who have served successively at the head of the Secretariat has been of paramount importance in several cases. The first Secretary-General was Trygve Lie (of Norway) who was appointed in 1946 and resigned in 1953. Dag Hammarskjöld (of Sweden) succeeded Lie and held office until his death in a plane crash in Africa in September 1961 during a Congo mission. After Hammarskjöld's death, U Thant (of Burma, now Myanmar) was elected acting Secretary-General, and a year later elected to office for a full five-year term, retroactive to 1961. Thant served a second five-year term until December 1971, when Kurt Waldheim (of Austria) was appointed. Waldheim served two full terms, from January 1972 to December 1981, when the Assembly appointed Javier Pérez de Cuéllar (of

Peru) whose second term of office expired in December 1991. Boutros Boutros-Ghali (of Egypt) was appointed for a full term from January 1992 to December 1996. The Secretary-General is assisted by several Under-Secretaries-General and Assistant Secretaries-General.

The whole structure of the Secretariat has been reorganized to make it a more efficient tool in the pursuit of traditional and new tasks of the UN. There are separate staffs serving subsidiary organs established by the General Assembly or the Economic and Social Council, including the *UN Children's Fund (UNICEF); the *UN Development Programme (UNDP); the *UN High Commissioner for Refugees (UNHCR); the *UN Population Fund (UNFPA); the *UN Relief and Works Agency for Palestine Refugees in the Near East (UNRWA); and the *UN Conference on Trade and Development (UNCTAD).

The budget The biennial budget of the UN is submitted initially by the Secretary-General and reviewed by the Advisory Committee on Administrative and Budgetary Questions (ACABQ), which is empowered to recommend modifications to the General Assembly. The programmatic aspects are reviewed by the 34-member Committee for Programme and Co-ordination (CPC). The regular budget covers administrative and other expenses of the central Secretariat and the other principal organs of the UN, both at Headquarters and throughout the world. Many activities of the UN are financed mainly by voluntary contributions outside the regular budget; such activities include the UNDP, WFP, UNICEF, UNHCR, UNRWA, and UNFPA. Additional activities are financed by voluntary contributions to trust funds, or special accounts established for each purpose.

Contributions of member countries are the main source of funds for the regular budget, in accordance with a scale of assessments specified by the General Assembly on the advice of the Committee on Contributions. The amount of the contribution of a member country is determined primarily by the total national income of that country in relation to that of other member countries. The Assembly has fixed a maximum of 25 per cent and a minimum of 0.01 per cent of the budget for any one contributor. As a result of arrears in payments by some members, a

serious financial crisis developed in 1986 and 1987. The USA withheld its contributions and demanded financial reforms and the introduction of 'weighted voting' on budgetary matters. A panel of 18 experts was set up in December 1985 to review UN administration and finance; the resulting report was submitted to the Secretary-General in August 1986 and the recommendations were subsequently approved by the General Assembly. The most significant innovation involved greater control over spending and the adoption of the budget by consensus, giving major contributors substantial power, although the budget itself remained subject to approval by the General Assembly. In the 1990s, the financial crisis of the UN has continued to deepen because of unpaid contributions, both for the regular budget and for peacekeeping operations. By mid-1996, unpaid assessed contributions totalled $3 billion, of which $0.8 billlion was due to the regular budget and $2.2 billion to the peacekeeping budget; only 83 countries had paid their 1996 regular budget obligations in full.

In the scale of assessments for 1995, 1996 and 1997, more than 100 countries, or nearly 60 per cent of the membership of the UN, were each contributing between 0.01 and 0.03 per cent of the budget. In 1995, the seven largest contributors included the USA (25 per cent), followed by Japan (13.95), Germany (8.94), France (6.32), Russia (5.68), the UK (5.27) and Italy (4.79).

The 'specialized agencies' Several intergovernmental bodies are linked to the UN by special agreements which entitle them to work in partnership with the Organization and each other in economic, social, scientific and technical fields. The organizations, which are known as 'specialized agencies', according to the definition used in the Charter of the UN, are: the *International Labour Organization (ILO); the *Food and Agriculture Organization (FAO); the *UN Educational, Scientific and Cultural Organization (UNESCO); the *World Health Organization (WHO); the World Bank Group, consisting of the *International Bank for Reconstruction and Development (IBRD), the *International Development Association (IDA), the *International Finance Corporation (IFC), and the*Multilateral Investment Guarantee Agency (MIGA); the *International Monetary Fund (IMF); the International Civil Aviation Organization (ICAO); the

*Universal Postal Union (UPU); the *International Telecommunication Union (ITU); the *World Meteorological Organization (WMO); the *International Maritime Organization (IMO); the *World Intellectual Property Organization (WIPO); the *International Fund for Agricultural Development (IFAD); and the *UN Industrial Development Organization (UNIDO). They report annually to the Economic and Social Council. The *International Atomic Energy Agency (IAEA), an intergovernmental organization set up 'under the aegis of the UN', reports annually to the General Assembly and, as appropriate, to the Security Council and the Economic and Social Council. Co-operative links between the UN and the newly-created *World Trade Organization (WTO), the successor body to the General Agreement on Tariffs and Trade (GATT), are under discussion. Important international organizations, such as the *European Union (EU), have been granted observer status by the General Assembly.

Activities

Over the past 50 years, the UN has undergone major changes, one such change being the enormous increase in membership. The goal of a peaceful world remains first and foremost in UN theory and practice. Activities related to the maintenance of international peace and security, however, account for only part of the current work. Economic and social co-operation has become increasingly important, while new fields of interest and activity have emerged. As regards human rights, several international instruments have been adopted over the past decades. The UN has assisted countries under colonial rule to exercise their rights of self-determination and gain independence. At present, the progress towards general and nuclear disarmament, the reduction of economic and social disparities in the world, the achievement of sustainable development, and the fight against drug abuse and illicit trafficking are issues of grave concern for UN member countries. The intrinsic limitation of the powers of the UN on matters concerning functional international co-operation and human rights, and the climate of continuing confrontation which characterized for more than four decades the relationship between the two superpowers and their

respective allies account for the varying records of achievement of the world Organization in several important spheres. As in all intergovernmental bodies, the authority and effectiveness of the UN ultimately depend on the political resolve and collective will of the member countries.

International peace and security In the furtherance of the basic objectives of international peace and security, the UN has taken many actions for the settlement of international disputes and the restoration of peaceful conditions. In its early years, the General Assembly condemned warlike propaganda (1947); called on nations to refrain from the threat or use of force contrary to the Charter, and from any threat or act aimed at impairing the independence of any country or at fomenting civil strife (1949); condemned intervention by a country in the internal affairs of another country in order to change its legally established government by the threat or use of force (1950); and called upon all countries to develop friendly and co-operative relations and to settle disputes by peaceful means (1957). Following the 1965 Declaration on the Inadmissibility of Intervention in the Domestic Affairs of States and the Protection of their Independence and Sovereignty, the Assembly adopted in December 1981 another document on the inadmissibility of intervention and interference in the internal affairs of states. Two important declarations were adopted in 1970 on the strengthening of international security and the principles of international law concerning friendly relations and co-operation among states. A difficult task, initiated in 1950, was completed in 1974 with the adoption of a definition of aggression as 'the use of armed force by a state against the sovereignty, territorial integrity or political independence of another state, or in any other manner inconsistent with the Charter of the UN'.

Among the more recent documents, mention should be made of the Declaration on the Prevention of Nuclear Catastrophe, adopted in 1981; the Manila Declaration on the Peaceful Settlement of International Disputes (1982); the Declaration on the Right of Peoples to Peace (1984); the Declaration on the Enhancement of the Effectiveness of the Principle of Refraining from the Threat or Use of Force in International Relations (1987); and the Declaration on the Prevention and the Removal of Disputes and

Situations Which May Threaten International Peace and Security and on the Role of the United Nations in the Field (1988). In 1980, the General Assembly approved the establishment of the University for Peace, based at San José, Costa Rica, and devoted to research on disarmament, mediation, the resolution of conflicts, and the relationship between peace and economic development. The year 1986 was proclaimed the International Year of Peace.

On many occasions the UN, through the Security Council, the General Assembly and the Secretary-General, has been involved directly in efforts to resolve a number of international crises and has developed its capacity as a peace-making and peace-keeping body. In some disputes, the UN has acted through peace-keeping forces, observer or fact-finding missions, plebiscite supervision, good offices missions, conciliation panels, mediators, and special representatives; in other cases, the UN has provided the forum for negotiation and a channel for quiet diplomacy. The Security Council has adopted measures of a military nature, of economic embargo and arms embargo, as well as economic sanctions and use of force. Military observer missions are composed of unarmed officers made available by member countries that are considered to be impartial by the parties concerned. Peace-keeping forces consist of contingents of lightly-armed troops made available by member countries in order to assist in preventing the recurrence of fighting, restoring and maintaining law and order, and promoting a return to normal conditions; the use of force is allowed only as a last resort, for self-defence.

The end of the Cold War has contributed to a significant renewal of interest in UN peacemaking and has brought about an increasing demand for peace-keeping forces. With an escalation of regional conflicts worldwide and their transformation from mainly interstate wars to intrastate struggles, the UN has increasingly used peacekeeping operations as flexible instruments adapted to a variety of uses. Although several recent conflicts, such as those in Africa and the former Yugoslavia, are essentially internal, they have far-reaching implications for the security of the subregions concerned. Large-scale military and civilian contingents have been deployed in several countries throughout the world to promote a peaceful transition to democracy and humanitarian relief efforts. Between 1948 and 1995, about 35 peace-keeping operations have been deployed under Security Council resolutions, involving over 720 000 troops at a cost of around $12.5 billion. The cost of peace-keeping has increased enormously, rising from around $626 million a year in 1986 to around $3.6 billion in 1995. Most operations are financed from their own separate accounts on the basis of legally-binding assessments on all countries; in principle, the costs of peacekeeping are the collective responsibility of all members.

In 1959, the General Assembly declared the question of general and complete disarmament to be 'the most important one facing the world today' and called on governments to make every effort to achieve a constructive solution; however, it soon became clear that such a goal was not attainable within a specific period of time. Since 1962 a multilateral disarmament negotiating forum – now known as the Conference on Disarmament – has been active in Geneva within the context of a close relationship with the UN. As a result of UN efforts, several important multilateral and bilateral arms regulation and disarmament agreements have been concluded; among these agreements, the 1968 Treaty on the Non-Proliferation of Nuclear Weapons deserves special attention. In the wake of the inadequate results of the First Disarmament Decade – in the 1970s – the General Assembly decided to declare the 1980s as the Second Disarmament Decade and held two special sessions (in 1978 and 1982) devoted entirely to disarmament. A third special session on disarmament was held in 1988 but, despite the remarkable improvement in relations between the two superpowers, no substantive final document could be adopted. The fundamental changes in Europe and in the major-power relationship have contributed to a considerable extent to efforts for achieving reductions in both nuclear and conventional armaments, and the UN is likely to play a more active role, either as a negotiating forum or as a catalyst. With regard to nuclear powers, the two major nuclear countries signed two treaties on the reduction of their strategic offensive arms (START I in 1991 and START II in 1993). In 1995, the Conference of parties to the Treaty on the Non-Proliferation of Nuclear Weapons reviewed the operation of the Treaty and decided on its indefinite extension.

Multilateral negotiations began in 1994 and continued in 1995 and 1996, in order to conclude a comprehensive nuclear test ban treaty, and a committee was set up to negotiate an end of the production of fissionable material for weapons purposes. The Chemical Weapons Convention, providing for the destruction of stockpiles and the cessation of the production, use and spread of chemical weapons, was concluded in 1993. The question of anti-personnel landmines is being discussed within the framework of the Convention on Inhumane Weapons. The General Assembly established, in 1992, a Register of Conventional Arms, to which member countries may report transfers of certain categories of weapon.

The UN Institute for Disarmament Research (UNIDIR) – based in Geneva – has been issuing, since the second half of the 1980s, a number of studies on various aspects of arms control and disarmament. It had been set up by the General Assembly in 1980 on a provisional basis, and in 1982 was established as an autonomous institute of the UN to undertake independent research on disarmament and related questions, particularly international security issues; its statute became effective in January 1985. The Institute, besides organizing conferences, publishing papers and conducting research projects, has a fellowship programme for scholars from developing countries.

The question of the peaceful uses of outer space has been on the agenda of the General Assembly since 1958. The UN is concerned not only with the orderly uses of outer space but also seeks to ensure that the benefits yielded by space research and technology are shared by all countries. Several legal instruments have resulted from the activities of the Assembly in this area. Two major conferences on the exploration and peaceful uses of outer space have been held, in 1968 and 1982, under the auspices of the UN. In 1986, the General Assembly adopted Principles relating to remote sensing of the earth from outer space, with a view to ensuring that such activities were conducted for the benefit of all countries and to protect mankind from natural disasters.

The establishment of a law governing the use of the sea in all its aspects represents another major concern of the UN. So far, three conferences have been organized: the First Conference (1958) adopted five conventions but left many basic issues unresolved; the Second Conference (1960) brought no progress; the Third Conference (1973–82) adopted an important Convention which came into force in November 1994. The Convention covers, in 320 articles and nine annexes, the behaviour of states in the world's oceans, establishing rules for drawing up sea boundaries, defining maritime zones, attributing legal rights, duties and responsibilities to states, and providing machinery for the settlement of disputes.

The questions of apartheid, as enforced in the Republic of South Africa, and racial discrimination, were before the UN since the beginning of its activities in 1946. The General Assembly condemned apartheid as a 'crime against humanity' and kept the situation in South Africa under continuous review, adopting a variety of measures to exert pressure on the South African authorities. Taking into account the significant changes occurring in that country, the General Assembly adopted in December 1989, at a special session on apartheid, a Declaration setting out the preconditions for negotiations among all the parties concerned in view of the creation of a united, non-racial and democratic South Africa. In December 1991, the General Assembly unanimously approved a resolution recommending that member countries phase out economic sanctions and drop other sanctions against South Africa. In June 1994, South Africa was readmitted to the General Assembly with voting rights.

Economic and social development The UN's aim of 'social progress and better standards of life in larger freedom' has received growing attention over the past decades. The UN system currently devotes most of its personnel and financial resources to the economic and social development of the poorer member countries, in which two-thirds of the world's people live. A wide-ranging international action was initiated by the UN with the proclamation of the Development Decades, beginning with the 1960s. The need for a world plan or 'strategy' on the necessary measures became evident before the first Decade ended. Intensive work over several years led to the agreement on the International Development Strategy for the Second Decade (the 1970s), intended to cover virtually every area of economic and social development; among other goals, the Strategy stressed the need for fairer economic and commercial policies, and greater financial resources for developing countries. However, no substantial progress was deemed to be possible without a far-reaching modification of the structures and rules governing international economic and financial relations.

In 1974 the General Assembly held its first special session on economic problems and adopted a Declaration and a Programme of Action on the Establishment of a New International Economic Order 'to eliminate the widening gap between the developed and the developing countries and ensure steadily accelerating economic and social development in peace and justice'. In December 1974, a few months after the call for a new international economic order, the Assembly adopted a Charter of Economic Rights and Duties of States with a view to establishing 'generally accepted norms to govern international economic relations systematically and to promote a new international economic order'.

The International Development Strategy for the Third Development Decade was proclaimed by the Assembly in December 1980. Despite modest progress in some areas, the key targets were not met and the overall situation in developing countries in fact worsened, while the proposed global negotiations between North and South failed to materialize. The particularly critical situation in Africa prompted the General Assembly to convene a special session devoted to that region in May 1986; the session adopted the UN Programme of Action for African Economic Recovery and Development (UNPAAERD), 1986–90, seeking to mobilize political and financial support for economic reforms. Also in 1986, the Assembly sought to promote international co-operation for resolving the external debt problems of developing countries. In subsequent sessions, the Assembly broadened the area of agreement on measures to cope with major problems arising from the persistent external indebtedness of developing countries. The International Development Strategy for the Fourth UN Development Decade (1991–2000) was adopted in 1990 by the General Assembly. The relationship between economic growth and human welfare has become the crucial theme of development efforts in the 1990s.

To promote a global consensus on development priorities, the UN has begun a series of international conferences dealing with children (New York, 1990), environment and development (Rio de Janeiro, 1992), population and development (Cairo, 1994), social development (Copenhagen, 1995), the advancement of women (Beijing, 1995), and human settlements (Istanbul, 1996).

An autonomous research institute created in 1963, the United Nations Research Institute for Social Development (UNRISD) based in Geneva, conducts research into problems and policies of social development during different stages of economic growth. Programmes are carried out in collaboration with national research teams drawn from local universities and research institutes, mainly in developing countries.

In its efforts to achieve social development involving very large sectors of the population, the UN has stressed the importance of popular participation in rural areas and has urged agrarian reform. The General Assembly has endorsed the Declaration and Programme of Action approved by the World Conference on Agrarian Reform and Rural Development held in Rome in 1979 under the sponsorship of FAO. The co-operative efforts of the UN and its related agencies in economic and social fields are currently being expanded and streamlined, with priority given to problems having a more direct impact on the development process. Direct field activities are carried out by UNDP in co-operation with UN-related agencies and institutions. UNCTAD was established as a permanent organ of the General Assembly in 1964. UNITAR, created in 1965, carries out training and research programmes with a view to improving the effectiveness of the UN.

The UN University (UNU), which opened the doors of its world headquarters in Tokyo in 1975, operates through global networks of associated institutions and research units. A new kind of academic institution, UNU – which is sponsored jointly by the UN and UNESCO and is not a university in the proper sense, since it does not have students or award degrees – undertakes multidisciplinary research, provides postgraduate fellowships for scholars from developing countries, and conducts several training activities. Research and training centres and programmes (RTC/Ps) have been established by UNU in Finland (for development economics), in The Netherlands (for new technologies), in Macau (for software technology), and in Ghana (for natural resources in Africa).

On the recommendation of the 1975 World Conference on the International Women's Year, the General Assembly decided to establish the International Research and Training Institute for the Advancement of Women (INSTRAW), whose Statute was endorsed in 1985. INSTRAW is an autonomous body of the UN funded by voluntary contributions, with headquarters in Santo Domingo, Dominican Republic. Its objectives are to stimulate and assist, through research, training and the collection and exchange of information, the efforts of intergovernmental, governmental and non-governmental organizations aimed at the advancement of women and their integration in the development process, both as participants and beneficiaries.

With a view to providing a forum for the presentation and discussion of the relevant policies, the General Assembly authorized in 1950 the convening, at five-year intervals, of a UN Congress on the Prevention of Crime and the Treatment of Offenders; such congresses have been held regularly since 1955. The Ninth Congress (Cairo, 1995) focused on four major topics: co-operation and technical assistance for strengthening the role of law; action against national and transnational economic and organized crime; improvement of police and criminal justice systems; and crime prevention strategies. In order to strengthen activities in the relevant fields, in 1992 the Economic and Social Council established a 40-member Commission on Crime Prevention and Criminal Justice as a new functional body, meeting annually in Vienna. A World Ministerial Conference on Transnational Organized Crime was held at Naples, Italy, in 1994.

As regards food problems, in 1974 the General Assembly set up the World Food Council (WFC) and sponsors, jointly with FAO, the *World Food Programme (WFP), in operation since 1963 to stimulate economic and social development through aid in the form of food. The World Food Council's basic aim was to provide overall, integrated and continuing attention to achieve the successful co-ordination and follow-up of policies concerning food production, nutrition, food security, food trade, food aid and other related matters, by all organizations and bodies of the UN system. The headquarters of the Council were located in Rome between 1975 and 1992. Following adoption by the UN General Assembly in December 1992 of the resolution 'strengthening the UN response to world food and hunger problems', the posts of the WFC secretariat were transferred to New York, to the new Department for Policy Co-ordination and Sustainable Development.

In order to seek solutions to the widespread problems of pollution, the Assembly convened a Conference in Stockholm in 1972 on the Human Environment, and subsequently created the *UN Environment Programme (UNEP), to monitor changes in the environment and to encourage and co-ordinate appropriate practices. The urgent need to agree on strategies for sustainable and environmentally sound development in all countries prompted the General Assembly to convene, in June 1992 in Rio de Janeiro, Brazil, the UN Conference on Environment and Development (UNCED), called in popular usage the 'Earth Summit'. More than 150 countries signed the UN Framework Convention on Climate Change and the Convention on Biological Diversity. A non-binding Statement of Principles on the Management, Conservation and Sustainable Development of All Types of Forests was also signed, together with the Rio Declaration on Environment and Development (proclaiming 27 Principles) and the Agenda 21 action plan. The Commission on Sustainable Development was established in 1993 as a subsidiary body of the Economic and Social Council to monitor progress in the implementation of Agenda 21.

The control of narcotic drugs has been a widespread concern since the beginning of this century. A series of treaties have been adopted under the auspices of the UN, requiring signatory countries to exercise control over the production and distribution of narcotic drugs and psychotropic substances, and to combat drug abuse and illicit traffic, duly reporting to international organs.

The *Commission on Narcotic Drugs (CND) was established by the Economic and Social Council in 1946 to advise the Council and prepare draft international agreements on all matters relating to the control of narcotic drugs. The *International Narcotics Control Board (INCB), which started operations in 1968, is composed of members elected by the Economic and

Social Council, with a view to supervising governmental implementation of drug control treaties.

In 1984 the General Assembly adopted a Declaration on the Control of Drug Trafficking and Drug Abuse, calling for renewed efforts and strategies aimed at the eradication of increasingly complex drug problems. The first International Conference on Drug Abuse and Illicit Trafficking was held in June 1987 in Vienna and adopted, *inter alia*, a Comprehensive Multidisciplinary Outline of Future Activities in Drug Abuse Control. The UN Convention against Illicit Traffic in Narcotic Drugs and Psychotropic Substances (adopted in 1988 and entered into force in November 1990) addresses areas not envisaged in pre-existing international drug treaties.

The UN anti-drug-trafficking activities were reviewed in February 1990 by the General Assembly, which concluded a special four-day session with the adoption of a Global Programme of Action. In December 1990, the General Assembly adopted a 40-power resolution giving new impetus to UN efforts in the field of drug abuse control through the establishment of a single programme – the *UN International Drug Control Programme (UNDCP). The newly-created programme integrates and co-ordinates the activities of the existing bodies, providing secretariat services to the CND and the INCB. The Fund of the UN International Drug Control Programme, set up in 1991 as a successor to the UN Fund for Drug Abuse Control, represents the main source for financial and technical assistance and is supported entirely from voluntary contributions.

Humanitarian assistance and human rights
A number of bodies have been set up by the UN in order to assist groups needing 'special help' in emergency conditions. The General Assembly created UNICEF in 1946 and extended its mandate indefinitely in 1953. UNHCR was established by the Assembly with effect from January 1951; UNRWA began work in 1950 as a subsidiary organ of the General Assembly. The UN has provided assistance for emergency relief and longer-term rehabilitation on several occasions. It has assisted in medium- and long-term rehabilitation and development programmes, in particular in the Sudano-Sahelian region, through the establishment of the UN Sudano-Sahelian Office (UNSO) in 1973. Activities are funded through the

UN Trust Fund for Sudano-Sahelian activities, managed by UNSO. In order to strengthen the co-ordination of humanitarian assistance, an Emergency Relief Co-ordinator was appointed in 1992 to provide leadership for rapid and coherent response to natural disasters and other emergencies. The Co-ordinator heads the newly-created UN Department of Humanitarian Affairs (DHA), which consolidates within a single body all UN entities dealing with complex emergencies, including the UN Disaster Relief Office (UNDRO).

In furtherance of the UN purpose to achieve international co-operation in promoting and encouraging respect for human rights and fundamental freedoms for all, regardless of race, sex, language or religion, the General Assembly adopted in December 1948 the Universal Declaration of Human Rights, under which, for the first time in history, responsibility for the protection and pursuit of human rights was assumed by the international community, and was accepted as a permanent obligation. The Universal Declaration covers not only civil and political rights, but also economic, social and cultural rights. Another important accomplishment has been the coming into force in 1976 of legally binding international agreements for the protection and promotion of human rights. These are the International Covenant on Economic, Social and Cultural Rights, and the International Covenant on Civil and Political Rights, the latter including an Optional Protocol, all adopted by the General Assembly in 1966. An additional protocol (Second Optional Protocol) to ban capital punishment, under the International Covenant on Civil and Political Rights, was adopted by the General Assembly in 1989.

The General Assembly established in December 1993 the post of *UN High Commissioner for Human Rights (HCHR) as the official with principal responsibility for the Organization's human rights activities. The High Commissioner for Human Rights, and the Centre for Human Rights as the principal unit of the Secretariat dealing with human rights issues, are to be perceived as being united in action: the High Commissioner setting policy directions and priorities, and the Centre dealing with their implementation.

The principle that the individual is to be held responsible for serious violations of human rights

– recognized in the Charter of the Nuremberg Tribunal for the trial of major Second World War criminals – has led the Security Council to establish international tribunals dealing with serious violations of international humanitarian law. The International Tribunal for the former Yugoslavia was set up in 1993, and the International Tribunal for Rwanda in 1994.

Besides torture and other cruel, inhuman or degrading treatment or punishment, attention is being given by the UN to other human rights questions, such as slavery and the slave trade, genocide, statelessness, religious intolerance, and the treatment of migrant workers. The rights of children have been brought by the UN within an all-encompassing document, the Convention on the Rights of the Child, adopted by the General Assembly in 1989. The rights of the disabled, the elderly and the young, as well as human rights in armed conflicts, have also been considered. Another basic commitment of the UN concerns the achievement of equality of rights for men and women, both in law and in fact.

Decolonization The UN has played a crucial role in the transition of peoples belonging to more than 80 nations from colonial domination to freedom. Decolonization made early significant gains under the International Trusteeship System; the progress was greatly accelerated by the Declaration on the Granting of Independence to Colonial Countries and Peoples, proclaimed by the General Assembly in 1960, and by the work of the Special Committee established by the Assembly in 1961 to examine on a regular basis the application of the Declaration and to make recommendations to help speed its implementation. When the Special Committee started operations in 1962, the non-self-governing territories placed on its list amounted to 64; these have now been reduced to 18, located mainly in the Pacific Ocean and the Caribbean, and with a total population of about 2 million. To observe the thirtieth anniversary of the Declaration in 1990, the Assembly designated the final decade of the twentieth century (1990–2000) as the International Decade for the Eradication of Colonialism. The independence of Namibia and its subsequent entry into the UN in 1990 represented the most recent demonstration of the UN's long-standing commitment to the principle of self-determination.

International law As regards international law, in 1947 the Assembly established the International Law Commission, which held its first session in 1949, with a view to promoting the progressive development of international law and its codification. The Commission – composed of 34 members serving in their individual capacity and meeting annually – has prepared drafts on a number of topics. International conferences of plenipotentiaries – convened by the General Assembly on the basis of such drafts – have adopted conventions opened for states to become parties. Two conferences, held in Vienna in 1961 and 1963 respectively, approved the Vienna Convention on Diplomatic Relations and the Vienna Convention on Consular Relations. A conference which met in Vienna in 1968, and again in 1969, approved a Convention on the Law of Treaties. Another conference, which met in Vienna in April 1977, and again in August 1978, completed and adopted the Vienna Convention on Succession of States in Respect of Treaties. Following a 1984 decision of the General Assembly, a UN Conference met in Vienna in March 1986 and adopted the Vienna Convention on the Law of Treaties between States and International Organizations or between International Organizations.

In response to the need for the UN to play a more active role in reducing legal obstacles to the flow of international trade, the Assembly established in 1966 the UN Commission on International Trade Law (UNCITRAL) for the progressive harmonization and unification of the law of international trade; the 36-member Commission also offers training and assistance in international trade law, taking into account the needs of the developing countries. The Commission's activities have focused chiefly on the preparation of uniform rules concerning the international sale of goods, international payments, international commercial arbitration, and international legislation on shipping.

Future prospects The major changes in the international situation that have taken place since the autumn of 1989 and the general shift towards a new world order have had a significant impact on the UN, its functioning and its prospects, both in the short and the long term. The dissolution of the USSR and of its network of alliances in

Europe and elsewhere has brought to an end the traditional East–West confrontation and opened up new avenues for co-operation unhindered by ideological conflicts. The North–South polarization itself has been affected substantially and to a certain extent softened in consequence of these events. The almost abrupt return to the realities of a multipolar world has altered the deep-rooted balances of power that had inspired UN theory and practice for several decades.

The long-overdue reform of the Organization, both in the sense of a return to the 'original' spirit and in the sense of an adaptation to the challenges of the present times, seems now less far away. The new spirit of co-operation among the 'great powers' and the growing awareness of the interdependence among all countries, large and small, could induce the international community to avail itself of the UN in the most appropriate and effective way. The reorganization and streamlining of the Secretariat began in 1992 and may be viewed as a first and encouraging sign of a new period in the life of the world Organization. The reform of the Secretariat is obviously part of a much larger restructuring effort affecting the inter-governmental mechanism, and requiring the full commitment of all member countries. The General Assembly, the Security Council and the Economic and Social Council need further adjustments and improvements. In particular, questions relating to the size and composition as well as to the working methods and procedures of the Security Council to make it more efficient and democratic have been attracting considerable attention.

Headquarters: United Nations, New York, N.Y. 10017, USA (Telephone: +1 212 963 1234; fax: +1 212 963 4879)

Geneva Office: Palais des Nations, 1211 Geneva 10, Switzerland (Telephone: +41 22 310211 – 346011).

Internet address: http,// www.unsystem.org (This provides easy access to the Web sites of UN programmes, as well as those of specialized agencies, autonomous UN bodies, interagency co-ordination mechanisms and a number of other groups dealing with UN issues).

Members of the Security Council: Permanent members: China, France, Russia, the UK, the USA; Elected members: Chile, Egypt, Guinea-Bissau, Poland, South Korea (until December 1997); Costa Rica, Japan, Kenya, Portugal, Sweden (until December 1998)

Members of the Economic and Social Council: Australia, Belarus, Brazil, Colombia, Congo, Côte d'Ivoire, India, Jamaica, Luxembourg, Malaysia, The Netherlands, the Philippines, Poland, South Africa, Sudan, Thailand, Uganda, USA (until December 1997); Argentina, Bangladesh, Canada, Central African Republic, China, Czech Republic, Finland, Gabon, Guyana, Jordan, Lebanon, Nicaragua, Romania, Russia, Sweden, Togo, Tunisia, UK (until December 1998); Cape Verde, Chile, Cuba, Djibouti, El Salvador, France, Gambia, Germany, Iceland, Japan, Latvia, Mexico, Mozambique, South Korea, Spain, Sri Lanka, Turkey, Zambia (until December 1999)

Members of the Trusteeship Council: China, France, Russia, UK, USA

Members of the International Court of Justice, in order of precedence (terms end on 5 February of the year indicated in parentheses): Mohammed Bedjaoui, Algeria (1997), President; Stephen M. Schwebel, USA (1997), Vice-President; Shigeru Oda, Japan (2003); Luigi Ferrari Bravo, Italy (1997); Rosalyn Higgins, UK (2000); Vladlen Vereshchetin, Russia (2000); Gilbert Guillaume, France (2000); Mohamed Shahabuddeen, Guyana (1997); Gonzalo Parra-Aranguran, Venezuela (2000); Christopher Gregory Weeramantry, Sri Lanka (2000); Raymond Ranjeva, Madagascar (2000); Géza Herczegh, Hungary (2003); Shi Jiuyong, China (2003); Carl-August Fleischhauer, Germany (2003); Abdul G. Koroma, Sierra Leone (2003). The terms of office of Judges Bedjaoui and Schwebel as President and Vice-President respectively expire in 1997

Registrar: Eduardo Valencia-Ospina

Secretary General: Kofi Aman

Publications: UN Chronicle (quarterly); Yearbook of the UN (comprehensive account, organized by subject, of UN activities); Basic Facts About the UN; Everyone's United Nations; The UN Disarmament Yearbook; Monthly Bulletin of Statistics; Statistical

Yearbook; *Yearbook of International Statistics*; *World Economic Survey* (annual)

References: T. Lie, *In the Cause of Peace: Seven Years with the United Nations* (London, 1954); U Thant, *Towards World Peace: Addresses and Public Statements, 1957–1963* (New York, 1964); M. Elmandjra, *The United Nations System: An Analysis* (London, 1973); H. G. Nicholas, *The United Nations as a Political Institution* (5th edn) (Oxford, 1975); T. Meron, *The United Nations Secretariat: The Rules and the Practice* (Lexington, Mass., 1977); U Thant, *View from the United Nations* (Newton Abbott, 1978); M. Hill, *The UN System: Co-ordinating its Economic and Social Work* (Cambridge, 1979); G. R. Berridge and A. Jennings (eds), *Diplomacy at the UN* (London, 1985); T. M. Franck, *Nation Against Nation: What Happened to the U.N. Dream and What the U.S. Can Do about It* (New York, 1985); M. J. Peterson, *The General Assembly in World Politics* (Boston, Mass., 1986); D. Steele, *The Reform of the United Nations* (London, 1987); D. Williams, *The Specialized Agencies and the United Nations. The System in Crisis* (New York, 1987); D. P. Forsythe (ed.), *The United Nations in the World Political Economy* (London, 1989); J. W. Muller, *The Reform of the United Nations: A Report* (Dobbs Ferry, 1992); J. N. Rosenau, *The United Nations in a Turbulent World* (Boulder, Col., 1992); P. Baehr and L. Gordenker, *The United Nations in the 1990s* (New York, 1992); B. Urquhart and E. Childers, *Towards a More Effective United Nations* (Uppsala, 1992); A. Roberts and B. Kingsbury (eds), *United Nations, Divided World: The UN's Roles in International Relations*, (2nd edn) (Oxford, 1993); A. Yoder, *The Evolution of the United Nations System* (2nd edn) (Bristol, PA, 1993); K. C. Wellens (ed.), *Resolutions and Statements of the United Nations Security Council (1946–1992): A Thematic Guide* (2nd edn) (Dordrecht, 1993); Y. Z. Blum, *Eroding the United Nations Charter* (Dordrecht, 1993); S. D. Bailey and S. Daws, *The United Nations: A Concise Political Guide* (3rd edn) (London, 1994); E. Luard, *The United Nations: How it Works and What It Does* (London) rev. 3/1994; S. R. Ratner, *The New UN Peacekeeping: Building Peace in Lands of Conflict after the Cold War* (London, 1995); D. Bourantonis and J. Wiener (eds), *The United Nations in the New World Order: The World Organization at Fifty* (London, 1995); G. Simons, *UN Malaise: Power, Problems and Realpolitik* (London, 1995)

United Nations Centre for Human Settlements (UNCHS) – Habitat

The Centre is intended to serve as a focal point for the co-ordination and evaluation of human settlements activities carried out within the UN system.

Origin and development

The establishment of the Centre in 1978 was the result of the UN's long-standing concern with the problems of human settlements, particularly the deteriorating quality of living conditions and the need to link urban and regional development programmes with national plans. The first international meeting on the subject was convened by the UN in Vancouver, Canada, in May–June 1976, under the title 'Habitat: UN Conference on Human Settlements'.

The adoption by the Conference of the Vancouver Declaration on Human Settlements and the Vancouver Plan of Action represented an important commitment on the part of governments and the international community to improving the quality of life for all people through human settlements development. The Plan of Action contained recommendations for national action regarding settlements policies, settlement planning, provision of shelter, infrastructure and services, land use and land tenure, the role of popular participation, and effective institutions and management.

The Vancouver Conference also recommended the strengthening and consolidation of UN activities in a single body concerned exclusively with human settlements. Acting on this recommendation, in December 1977, the UN General Assembly transformed the Committee on Housing, Building and Planning into the Commission on Human Settlements, and in October 1978 established the present Centre to service the Commission and to implement its resolutions.

Objectives

On the basis of the Vancouver Plan of Action, the Centre's major areas of concern include the provision of technical assistance to government programmes, the organization of expert meetings, workshops and training seminars, the publication of technical documents, and the dissemination of information through the establishment of a global information network.

Technical co-operation projects cover, *inter alia*, national settlement policies and programmes, urban and regional planning, rural and urban housing and infrastructure development, slum upgrading and sites-and-services schemes, low-cost building technology, technologies for urban and rural water supply and sanitation systems, and the establishment or strengthening of government institutions responsible for human settlements.

Structure

The Commission on Human Settlements is the governing body of the Centre. It meets every two years and consists of 58 members (16 from Africa, 13 from Asia, 6 from Eastern Europe, 10 from Latin America and the Caribbean, 13 from Western Europe and other countries), each serving for four-year periods. There are Divisions responsible for technical co-operation, research and development, information, audio-visual and documentation, and administration. The Habitat and Human Settlements Foundation (HHSF) serves as the financial arm of the Centre. The Executive Director is the highest official overseeing the work of the Centre.

Activities

The Centre maintains relations with UN bodies, the specialized agencies and other intergovernmental, as well as non-governmental, organizations. The financial sources of the Centre are represented by allocations from the regular UN budget and voluntary contributions by governments; operational activities are financed by the *UN Development Programme (UNDP) and several multilateral and bilateral donor agencies.

The Work Programme of the Centre is divided into several subprogrammes: global policies and strategies; national policies and instruments; managing human settlement development, including financial and land resources: improving infrastructure and the living environment; managing disaster mitigation, reconstruction and development; housing for all; strengthening local communities; and reducing poverty and promoting equity. Audio-visual and documentary materials are produced by the Centre as an integral part of projects and training programmes.

The Centre is responsible for hundreds of technical co-operation projects in all developing regions of the world. It applies advanced technology through its Urban Data Management System and the Housing Finance Software package which is designed to assist in financial management and reporting for small housing and development schemes.

In 1982, the General Assembly proclaimed 1987 the International Year of Shelter for the Homeless (IYSH) and decided that the objectives of the Year would be to improve the shelter situation of the poor and disadvantaged at both individual and community levels, particularly in developing countries, both before and during 1987, and to demonstrate means of continuing those efforts as ongoing national programmes beyond 1987. The General Assembly designated the Commission on Human Settlements as the UN intergovernmental body responsible for organizing the Year, and the Centre as the secretariat for the Year and as the lead agency for co-ordinating the relevant programmes and activities of other organizations and agencies concerned. In 1988 the Commission on Human Settlements approved a Global Strategy for Shelter to the Year 2000; the Strategy was unanimously adopted by the General Assembly in December 1988 and will continue to provide the basis of the Centre's activities to the year 2000.

Meeting in Istanbul, Turkey, in June 1996, the Second UN Conference on Human Settlements (Habitat II), also known as the 'City Summit', evaluated accomplishments since 1976, when Habitat I was held in Vancouver, and reaffirmed the importance of human settlements in both national and international development policies and strategies.

Executive Director: Wally N'Dow

Headquarters: P.O. Box 30030, Nairobi, Kenya (Telephone: +254 2 621234; fax: +254 2 624266)

Publications: *UNCHS Habitat News* (three times a year); studies and technical reports

United Nations Children's Fund (UNICEF)

The Fund, originally intended to carry out relief in Europe after the Second World War, is mainly concerned with meeting the essential needs of children living in the developing countries and lacking even the most rudimentary medical, nutritional and educational services.

Origin and development

The Fund was created by the UN General Assembly in December 1946, under the name of United Nations International Children's Emergency Fund, in order to extend massive relief to the young victims of the Second World War in Europe and China. In the early 1950s, the emphasis shifted gradually to programmes intended to combat the widespread malnutrition, disease and illiteracy afflicting millions of children throughout the developing world. In 1953 the General Assembly decided to extend the Fund's mandate indefinitely and to drop the words 'International' and 'Emergency' from the official name, but the well-known acronym was retained.

Objectives

In 1976 the Fund adopted the 'basic services' strategy, affirmed by the General Assembly, in order to provide to the under-served areas of developing countries effective assistance in the interrelated fields of primary health care, formal and informal education, applied nutrition, clean water and sanitation, responsible parenthood and family planning, child mental health, and improvement in the lives of women and girls. Assistance is extended by the Fund according to mutually agreed priorities for children, in close co-operation with the governments concerned, with special regard to planning, development and extension of low-cost community-based services. Besides its basic long-term involvement in child health, nutrition and welfare programmes, the Fund may also be called upon to provide emergency relief and supplementary aid for mothers and children whenever necessary because of major natural disasters, civil strife or epidemics. Emergency assistance is generally followed by long-range rehabilitation operations.

Structure

The basic policy directives of the Fund are laid down by its governing body, the Executive Board, composed of representatives of 36 countries elected for a three-year term by the UN Economic and Social Council from among members of the UN, or its specialized agencies, or the *International Atomic Energy Agency (IAEA). Eight seats are reserved for Africa; seven for Asia and the Mediterranean countries; four for Eastern Europe; five for Latin America and the Caribbean; and twelve for Western Europe and other countries. The Executive Board meets annually to review the programmes and make commitments for aid.

The Executive Director is nominated by the UN Secretary-General in consultation with the Executive Board, and is responsible for current administrative tasks and the appointment and direction of staff. The headquarters of the Fund are located in New York; several regional offices and field offices complete the organizational structure. Direct links with the public are maintained by the Fund through 38 National Committees, almost all in the developed countries.

Activities

In emergency relief the Fund co-operates very closely with the *UN Development Programme (UNDP) and other UN agencies such as the *UN Population Fund (UNFPA) and the *World Health Organization (WHO), as well as with numerous non-governmental organizations. Over the past few years, a substantial share of emergency assistance has gone to alleviate drought and famine in Africa.

The activities of the Fund are financed in their entirety through voluntary contributions from governments, private organizations and individuals. Nearly 70 per cent of the Fund's income derives directly from governments and miscellaneous sources, and over 30 per cent from the general public, through various fund-raising campaigns, greetings card sales and individual donations.

The Fund is currently engaged in programmes in about 150 countries in all continents to help protect children from disease, malnutrition and other perils of the growing years, and to prepare them for healthy, productive adult lives. Around 40 per cent of the financial and human resources of the Fund are devoted to sub-Saharan Africa.

The Fund's efforts for the 1980s concentrated on the drastic reduction of infant mortality rates through an attack on the principal causes of preventable death and disease, drawing on a wide variety of national and community organizations for support in mobilizing the necessary human and financial resources. The success of these efforts was linked to a very large extent to the community-based services strategy that had been advocated since the mid-1970s. The General Assembly designated the Fund as the 'lead agency' of the UN system responsible for co-ordinating the activities of the International Year of the Child observed in 1979.

The Fund has participated in drafting the Convention on the Rights of the Child, adopted by the UN General Assembly in November 1989 and entering into force in September of the following year. Also in September 1990, the Fund organized the World Summit for Children, with the participation of the Heads of State and Government of more than 70 countries. By setting the protection and development of children as the focal point of international commitment, the meeting emphasized the importance of education, nutrition, health, family planning, and empowerment of women and girls in building the foundations for the future. A declaration was issued aimed at committing countries to reduce infant mortality and the dangers of childbirth worldwide, and to guarantee that all children will have access to clean water and education by the year 2000. The World Summit for Social Development, held in March 1995 in Copenhagen, Denmark has provided new impetus to the activities of the Fund, setting them within the context of an international effort towards poverty eradication and social development. In co-operation with UNDP and UNFPA, the Fund has actively supported the '20/20' formula – adopted by the Copenhagen World Summit, the formula calls on governments of developing countries to allocate at least 20 per cent of their budget to basic social services, and donor countries to earmark a similar proportion of their official development aid for such services. The Fund was awarded the Nobel Peace Prize in 1965.

Executive Director: Carol Bellamy
Headquarters: 3 United Nations Plaza, New York, N.Y. 10017, USA (Telephone: +1 212 326 7000; fax: +1 212 888 7465)

Publications: *UNICEF Annual Report*; *State of the World's Children* (annual)
Reference: M. Black, *The Children and the Nations. The Story of UNICEF* (New York, 1986)

United Nations Conference on Trade and Development (UNCTAD)

The Conference aims to act as the focal point within the UN for the integrated treatment of development and inter related issues in the areas of trade, finance, technology, investment and sustainable development through greater partnership between developed countries, developing and the least developed countries, and countries in transition.

Origin and development

The establishment of the Conference as a permanent organ of the UN General Assembly dates back to December 1964. The original session of the Conference had been convened earlier that year within the framework of the UN Development Decade of the 1960s, launched by a General Assembly resolution in December 1961. The General Assembly had also approved a resolution on international trade as the primary instrument for promoting economic progress in the less developed countries; the resolution envisaged an international conference on trade problems, which was eventually held in Geneva between March and June 1964. Proposals for continuing the work of the Conference through some kind of institutional arrangement led to its establishment as an autonomous body responsible to the General Assembly. Membership of the Conference now totals nearly 190 countries, including all members of the UN plus the Holy See, Switzerland and Tonga.

The Conference generally meets every four years, in the capital of a member country. After its original meeting in 1964, the Conference held the second session in New Delhi (1968), the third in Santiago, Chile (1972), the fourth in Nairobi (1976), the fifth in Manila (1979), the sixth in Belgrade (1983), the seventh in Geneva (1987), the eighth in Cartagena de Indias, Colombia (1992), and the ninth in Midrand, South Africa (1996). The last two sessions, in Cartagena and in Midrand, took far-reaching decisions with a view to revitalizing the Conference, streamlining its institutional structure and reinforcing and clarifying its mandate.

Objectives

The concern of the Conference covers the entire spectrum of policies, in both industrialized and developing areas, which influence the external trade and payments and related development aspects of developing countries.

According to the provisions set out in the General Assembly resolution adopted in December 1964, the principal functions of the Conference were the following: to promote international trade, especially with a view to accelerating economic development and taking into account the tasks performed by existing international organizations; to formulate principles and policies on international trade and related problems of economic development; to make proposals for putting the said principles and policies into effect, and to take other relevant steps, having regard to differences in economic systems and stages of development; to review and facilitate the co-ordination of activities of other institutions within the UN system; to initiate action, where appropriate, in co-operation with the competent organs of the UN for the negotiation and adoption of multilateral legal instruments; to be available as a centre for harmonizing the trade and related development policies of governments and regional economic groupings.

A clear trend has now emerged for the Conference to focus its work on a few trade and development objectives of central importance with a view to making a substantial impact on people's lives in developing countries. Topics on the current international trade agenda, the adoption of a possible multilateral framework on investment, competition laws of particular relevance to development, environmental policies and measures, and the development of small- and medium-sized domestic enterprises are part of the Conference's new mandate resulting from the 1996 session.

Structure

The 1996 session undertook a restructuring and streamlining of the Conference's machinery. The Trade and Development Board, which all Conference members may join, is the permanent body responsible for ensuring overall consistency in the activities of the Conference.

According to the 1996 reform, the Board meets once a year in regular session, in the autumn, to deal with global economic issues from a trade and development viewpoint. It also reviews progress in the implementation of the Programme of Action for the Least Developed Countries and of the UN New Agenda for the Development of Africa, in order to draw policy lessons from successful development experiences. The Board can meet, in executive sessions, three times a year to deal with policy as well as management and institutional matters.

Three subsidiary bodies of the Board – meeting once a year unless otherwise decided by the Board itself – have been established: (i) the Commission on Trade in Goods and Services and Commodities; (ii) the Commission on Investment, Technology and related financial issues; and (iii) the Commission on Enterprise, Business Facilitation and Development. The Conference has a permanent Secretariat headed by a Secretary-General and located in Geneva. A Liaison Office is maintained at UN Headquarters in New York.

Activities

Despite serious problems of co-ordination, the Conference has made sustained efforts towards the realization of the goals of the UN Development Decades, the redefinition of the international economic agenda and the negotiation of a number of agreements that have represented a significant evolution of governmental policies. The Conference has become more and more involved in the analysis of broad economic issues and financial problems, in a growing effort to move beyond the stage of merely enunciating general principles. In particular, it has recommended measures with a view to expanding and diversifying the exports of goods and services of developing countries; stabilizing and strengthening the international commodity markets on which most developing countries depend for export earnings; enhancing the export capacity of developing countries through the mobilization of domestic and external resources, including development assistance and foreign investment; promoting appropriate national trade and transport policies; alleviating the impact of debt on the economies of the developing countries, and reducing the debt burden; providing special support to the 'least developed countries', a category currrently comprising about 50 of the world's poorest and most vulnerable countries; and fostering the expansion of trade and economic co-operation among developing countries.

One of the major endeavours of the Conference is the Integrated Programme for Commodities (IPC), which aims basically to secure remunerative, equitable and stable prices for the primary commodities on which developing countries depend heavily for export earnings. Negotiations on individual commodity agreements are carried out within this framework. In April 1982 the International Rubber Agreement became the first agreement on a new commodity under the IPC to come into operation, providing for a buffer stock and limitations on price fluctuations. An International Agreement on Jute and Jute Products, aimed at promoting research and development and improving marketing, was adopted in October 1982. An International Tropical Timber Agreement, concentrating on conservation of supplies rather than price stabilization, was concluded in November 1983. New agreements were concluded for natural rubber in 1987, and for cocoa and olive oil in 1986. During the 1990s, the role of the Conference in this area has been strengthened by the conclusion of the International Sugar Agreement (1992); of the Protocol amending and extending the International Agreement on Olive Oil and Table Olives (1993); of the Agreement on Cocoa (1993); and of the Agreement on Tropical Timber (1994).

Also envisaged by IPC are measures intended to increase the demand for natural products facing competition from synthetics and to expand the processing of raw materials in developing countries. A key factor of IPC is a Common Fund, designed primarily to finance buffer stocks of certain commodities in order to reduce or eliminate the wide fluctuations in commodity prices. Articles of agreement for establishing the Common Fund for Commodities were adopted in June 1980, after four years of negotiations, and opened for signature the following October. The agreement came into effect in 1989 after ratification by 90 countries, and accounting for two-thirds of directly contributed capital.

Another major effort of the Conference is directed towards the expansion and diversification of the exports of manufactured and semi-manufactured products of developing countries. An important agreement was reached in 1970 on the introduction, for a ten-year period, of a Generalized System of Preferences (GSP) designed to provide developing countries with wider export opportunities beyond the traditional reciprocity and most-favoured-nation rules. The GSP has subsequently been reviewed and extended.

A Set of Multilaterally Agreed Equitable Principles and Rules for the Control of Restrictive Business Practices, including those of transnational corporations, which adversely affect international trade, especially that of developing countries, was adopted in April 1980. The Conference has also adopted an action programme on policies and measures for structural adjustment related to trade that involves both interindustry and intraindustry specialization so as to enable developing countries to increase their share in world trade of manufactured goods. The relevant bodies of the Conference follow closely the issues that are of particular concern to developing countries after the successful outcome of the Uruguay Round of Multilateral Trade Negotiations and the establishment of the *World Trade Organization (WTO) as a successor, with wider powers and competences, to the General Agreement on Tariffs and Trade (GATT).

With regard to international financial issues, the Conference has sought to improve the terms and conditions of aid, as well as to increase its flow, to reduce the rising burden of debt service, and to establish a reformed international monetary system consistent with the pressing needs of development. A resolution was adopted in 1978 for the retroactive adjustment of terms for the official development assistance debt of low-income countries; guidelines for international action in the area of debt rescheduling were drafted in 1980. At its 1987 session the Conference recognized the need for greater flexibility in the rescheduling of debts, though it proved impossible to reach a consensus on the increase of debt relief or the reduction of interest rates.

Increasing emphasis is placed by the Conference on the promotion of trade expansion, economic co-operation, and integration among developing countries, especially with regard to export credits, transportation, insurance and multinational production enterprises.

A substantial work programme has been undertaken in the field of shipping, ports and international shipping legislation, and several Conventions have been concluded under the auspices of the Conference. The Convention on a Code of Conduct for Liner Conferences, adopted in 1974 and entered into force in 1983, provides for the national shipping lines of developing countries to participate on an equal footing with the shipping lines of developed countries; the Convention on the Carriage of Goods by Sea (Hamburg Rules) was adopted in 1978; the Convention on International Multimodal Transport of Goods, adopted in 1980, establishes a single liability regime for the carrying of goods entailing more than one mode of transport. The Conference investigates the implications of open-registry fleets for the merchant marines of developing countries; its efforts in this area led to the conclusion in 1986 of the Convention on Conditions for Registration of Ships which deals with the safety and working conditions aboard ships flying 'flags of convenience'. A new Convention on Maritime Liens and Mortgages was adopted in May 1993, with a view to improving conditions for ship financing and the development of national merchant fleets, and to promoting international uniformity in the field of maritime liens and mortgages.

Recommendations have been put forward by the Conference to meet the special needs of the least-developed, developing island, and land-locked countries. The Statute of a Special Fund for Land-locked Developing Countries was approved by the General Assembly in December 1976, but total sums pledged were not deemed sufficient to enable the Fund to start operations. In 1981 the Conference serviced the special UN Conference on the Least Developed Countries, which led to the adoption of the Substantial New Programme of Action (SNPA) for the 1980s for the Least Developed Countries. The targets contained in the SNPA were not met and the Second Conference on the Least Developed Countries, held in 1990 in Paris, adopted a new Programme of Action embodying commitments by both the developed and the developing nations. The Conference contributes to the UN New Agenda for the Development of Africa in the 1990s and reviews implementation of the Programme of Action for the Least Developed Countries for the 1990s.

The *International Trade Centre (ITC) in Geneva is operated jointly by the Conference and by WTO. As an executing agency of the *UN Development Programme (UNDP), the Conference is also engaged in several technical assistance projects in developing countries.

The restructuring of the Conference machinery, the adoption of more flexible rules and procedures, and the increasing focus on the identification of appropriate domestic policies and measures for promoting growth rather than on the adoption of international agreement or resolutions should lead to the elaboration of a system progressively more effective in dealing with major development-related issues. On the whole, the Conference remains one of the major global forums in which goverments and, increasingly, other interested parties, especially the private sector, are able to negotiate multilateral agreements on trade and development issues.

Secretary-General: Rubens Ricupero
Headquarters: Palais des Nations, 1211 Geneva 10, Switzerland (Telephone: +41 22 907 1234; fax: +41 22 907 0057)
Publications: *UNCTAD Bulletin* (six a year); *Trade and Development Report* (annual); *The Least Developed Countries Report* (annual); *World Investment Report* (annual)
References: A. K. Koul, *The Legal Framework of UNCTAD in the World Trade* (Leyden, 1977); *UNCTAD: The History of UNCTAD 1964–1984* (New York, 1985); M. Williams, *Third World Cooperation. The Group of 77 in UNCTAD* (London, 1991)

United Nations Development Programme (UNDP)

The Programme is the world's largest organization in the field of multilateral technical assistance.

Origin and development
The establishment of the Programme dates back to November 1965, when the UN General Assembly decided to merge two bodies, which were then responsible for providing multilateral technical assistance – the UN Expanded Programme of Technical Assistance, created in 1949, and the UN Special Fund, set up in 1958. The new Programme entered into force in

January 1966 as the central agency of the UN system for funding economic and social development projects around the world.

Objectives

The Programme is intended to help developing countries to increase the wealth-producing capabilities of their natural and human resources. Special attention is paid to the needs of the least developed countries (LDCs), promoting development that is both people-centred and respects the environment.

As a pragmatic field-oriented agency, the Programme is basically responsive only to clearly identified specific needs. Principal project activities include: locating, assessing and activating latent natural resources and other development assets; support for professional and vocational training; expansion of development-related scientific research and applied technologies; and strengthening of national and regional development planning. The scope of technical assistance has been broadened in order to cover all phases of project lifetime, from earliest preparatory studies to long-range follow-up.

Structure

The Programme's policy-making body is the Executive Board, consisting of the representatives of 36 countries (eight from Africa, seven from Asia, four from Eastern Europe, five from Latin America and the Caribbean, and twelve from Western Europe and other countries), which meets at yearly intervals; elections are for a three-year term. The Administrator is responsible for carrying out the activities of the Programme. A Resident Representative of the Programme is stationed in almost every country receiving technical assistance and is responsible for supervising and co-ordinating field operations. Through a world-wide network of 136 offices, the Programme functions as the primary presence of the UN in most developing countries. The Programme is responsible to the General Assembly, to which it reports through the Economic and Social Council.

Activities

Assistance is rendered by the Programme only at the request of governments and in response to their priority needs, integrated into overall national and regional plans. Almost all projects are carried out by UN-related bodies, including all the specialized agencies and the *International Atomic Energy Agency (IAEA), as well as the *UN Population Fund (UNFPA), the *UN Conference on Trade and Development (UNCTAD), the *UN Children's Fund (UNICEF), the *World Food Programme (WFP), the *UN High Commissioner for Refugees (UNHCR), the *UN Environment Programme (UNEP), the *UN Centre for Human Settlements (UNCHS) – Habitat and other bodies. The Programme, financed by voluntary contributions from UN member countries and participating agencies, has gradually been entrusted with resources for tasks well beyond its original mandate. Despite some serious cash flow crises, it has assumed increasing responsibility for meeting global as well as regional and national priorities in 175 developing countries and territories, offering a variety of services not provided by other bodies, and for co-ordinating the UN development system. The Programme also participates in emergency relief operations.

Large-scale decentralization of operations has increased the Programme's speed and efficiency considerably. Responsibility for project execution is being assigned increasingly to governments and institutions in the developing countries receiving assistance. The Programme administers a number of special purpose funds and programmes such as the UN Capital Development Fund (UNCDF), the UN Volunteers (UNV), and the UN Development Fund for Women (UNIFEM). The UNCDF, established in 1966 and fully operational since 1974, assists the least-developed countries by supplementing existing sources of capital assistance by means of grants and loans on concessionary terms; all projects are designed to minimize external dependence and ensure sustainability. The execution of projects is usually entrusted to local institutions, with a view to promoting grassroots self-help activities.

The UNV programme was established by the General Assembly in 1971 and remains the only volunteer-sending programme in the UN system, supplying at modest cost middle-level skills, particularly in the least-developed countries. The volunteers represent over 115 professional categories and serve in both UNDP and UN-assisted projects, as well as development programmes carried out directly by host countries. Some 4000 volunteers, from both developed and developing countries, serve annually, in over 130 nations.

UNIFEM has continued since 1985, on a regular basis, the activities of the Voluntary Fund for the UN Decade for Women, established by the General Assembly in 1975 on the occasion of the proclamation of the period 1976–85 as the UN Decade for Women. In autonomous association with UNDP, UNIFEM supports innovative and experimental activities benefiting women, such as credit funds, small-scale group enterprises, and training in work-saving and fuel-conserving technologies.

UNDP recently restructured its Bureau for Policy and Programme Support to include four divisions concerned with social development and poverty elimination, management development and governance, sustainable energy and environment, and science and technology. Poverty elimination is the overriding priority in UNDP programmes; the traditional programming system, in effect since the 1970s, has been replaced by a new system with a view to providing greater flexibility in the assignment of resources as well as greater incentives for the formulation of high-impact programmes fostering sustainable human development.

With the *World Bank and UNEP, UNDP is one of the managing partners of the recently restructured *Global Environment Facility (GEF).

Administrator: James Gustave Speth
Headquarters: 1 UN Plaza, New York, N.Y. 10017, USA (Telephone: +1 212 906 5000; fax: +1 212 826 2057)
Publications: *Annual Report*; *Human Development Report* (annually since 1990); *Cooperation South* (quarterly)

United Nations Educational, Scientific and Cultural Organization (UNESCO)

The Organization promotes collaboration among nations through education, science, culture and communication, in order to further respect for justice, for the rule of law, and for human rights and fundamental freedoms.

Origin and development

The Constitution of the Organization, adopted at a Conference convened by the government of the UK in association with the government of France in November 1945 in London, came into force in November 1946, after 20 signatories had deposited their instruments of acceptance; it has been amended on several occasions.

Membership of the UN automatically carries with it the right to membership of the Organization; countries that do not belong to the UN may be admitted to the Organization, upon recommendation of the Executive Board, by a two-thirds majority vote of the General Conference. Territories not responsible for the conduct of international relations are eligible for associate membership, provided an application is made on their behalf by the authority in charge of international relations. Any member, either full or associate, may withdraw from the Organization by notice addressed to that effect to the Director-General; such notice takes effect on 31 December of the year following that during which the notice was given. The present membership includes over 180 countries, plus a few associate members; in the early 1980s, the USA, the UK and Singapore left the Organization.

Objectives

In order to realize its purposes, the Organization collaborates in the work of advancing the mutual knowledge and understanding of peoples through all means of mass communication, and to that end recommends such international agreements as may be necessary; gives fresh impulse to popular education and to the spread of culture by collaborating with member countries, at their request, in the development of educational activities and by suggesting educational methods; maintains, increases and diffuses knowledge by conserving the world's inheritance of books, works of art and monuments of history and science, by encouraging cooperation among nations in all branches of intellectual activity and by initiating methods calculated to give the people of all countries access to the printed and published materials produced by any of them. All action is to be carried out according to the principle of preserving the independence, integrity and fruitful diversity of the cultures and educational systems of the member countries.

Structure

The institutional machinery comprises a General Conference, an Executive Board and a Secretariat. It is for the General Conference, as the supreme governing body, to determine the policies and the main lines of work of the Organization and to decide on programmes submitted to it by the Executive Board. Ordinary sessions of the General Conference are held every two years, with the participation of representatives from each member country. Intergovernmental conferences on education, the sciences and humanities or the dissemination of knowledge may be convened by the General Conference. The Executive Board consists of 52 members elected for a single four-year term by the General Conference and acting under its authority; members of the Executive Board represent their respective governments. The Board meets at least twice a year and is responsible for supervising the execution of the programme of work adopted by the Conference. The chief administrative officer and head of the Secretariat is the Director-General, who is nominated by the Executive Board and appointed by the General Conference for a renewable six-year term; he is empowered to formulate proposals for appropriate action by the Conference and the Board. Liaison Offices and Regional Offices for Education, Science and Technology, Culture and Communication exist in most areas served by the Organization. National Commissions or National Co-operating Bodies have been set up in most member countries to act as agencies of liaison between the Organization and the principal bodies interested in educational, scientific and cultural matters in each country.

The Organization adopts recommendations by a simple majority, and international conventions by a two-thirds majority, each member country being under an obligation to submit these to its competent authorities within one year. Moreover, each member country is bound to report periodically to the Organization on its laws, regulations and statistics in the educational, scientific and cultural field as well as on the action taken with regard to recommendations and conventions.

Among the bodies operating within the Organization's framework, mention should be made of the following: the International Institute for Educational Planning (IIEP), set up in 1963 to serve as a world centre for advanced training and research, which is legally and administratively part of UNESCO and is located in Paris (7–9 rue Eugène Delacroix. Telephone: +33 1 4504 2822; fax: +33 1 4072 8366); the International Bureau of Education (IBE), founded in 1925 and a part of UNESCO since 1969, providing information on developments and innovations in education, and based in Geneva (15 route des Morillons, P.O. Box 199. Telephone: +41 22 798 1455; fax: +41 22 798 1486)

Activities

The activities of the Organization fall into three main categories: international intellectual co-operation; operational assistance; and the promotion of peace. This implies, *inter alia*, expanding and guiding education in order to enable people of every country to take their own development in hand more effectively; help in establishing the scientific and technological foundations through which every country can make better use of its own resources; encouragement of national cultural values and the preservation of cultural heritage so as to derive maximum advantage from modernization without the loss of cultural identity and diversity; development of communication for the balanced flow of information and of information systems for the universal pooling of knowledge; prevention of discrimination in education and improvement of access for women to education; and promotion of studies and research on conflicts and peace, violence and obstacles to disarmament, and the role of international law and organizations in building peace.

The Organization is a separate, autonomous body related to the UN by a special agreement and enjoys the status of specialized agency bound to report annually to the UN Economic and Social Council. Effective working relationships have been established with other specialized intergovernmental organizations and agencies whose interests and activities are related to the Organization's purposes; any formal arrangements with such organizations or agencies are subject to the approval of the Executive Board. Nearly 600 non-governmental organizations maintain 'official' relations with the Organization, and some of them take part in the execution of projects; about 1200 non-governmental organizations co-operate with the Organization on an occasional basis.

The Organization's activities are funded through a regular budget provided by member countries and also through other sources, particularly the *UN Development Programme (UNDP). The education programme is based on an overall policy regarding education as a lifelong process and seeks to promote the progressive application of the right to education for all and to improve the quality of education. Priority is increasingly being given to the rural areas of developing countries. The Organization was given responsibility for organizing the International Literacy Year (1990), proclaimed by the UN as a means of initiating a plan of action for the spread of literacy (based on regional literacy programmes that had already been established in the 1980s). In March 1990, the Organization sponsored with other UN agencies the World Conference on Education for All.

In the field of natural sciences and technology, the Organization is active in fostering international co-operation and has set up over the years a number of programmes, such as the Man and Biosphere Programme (MAB) for the solution of practical problems related to environmental resource management; the International Hydrological Programme (IHP) dealing with the scientific aspects of water resources assessment and management; the International Geological Correlation Programme (IGCP), run jointly with the International Union of Geological Sciences; the Intergovernmental Informatics Programme for the promotion of co-operation between developed and developing countries in the field of computer sciences; and UNISIST, which ensures worldwide co-operation with regard to scientific and technological information for development. The Intergovernmental Oceanographic Commission (IOC) encourages scientific investigation into the nature and resources of the oceans. At the regional and subregional level, ministerial conferences are organized periodically to consider science and technology policy as well as the application of science and technology to development. Assistance is also provided at the national level in order to enable individual member countries to carry out training and research programmes and projects, such as those concerning the use of small-scale energy sources for rural and dispersed populations. The social and human sciences programme intends to encourage the development of the social sciences throughout the world by strengthening national and regional institutions; other two programmes concern activities dealing with human rights and peace.

The World Heritage Programme, launched in 1978, is aimed at protecting landmarks of outstanding universal value, in accordance with the 1972 Convention Concerning the Protection of the World Cultural and Natural Heritage, by providing financial aid for restoration, technical assistance, training and management planning. The 'World Heritage List' currently includes some 400 sites, both cultural and natural, all over the world. The International Fund for the Promotion of Culture, set up in 1974, has provided assistance for a great number of projects including translations, recordings and exhibitions.

In the field of communication, the Organization aims to promote a free flow and a wider and better-balanced exchange of information among individuals, communities and countries, and lays increasing stress upon the role of the mass media in advancing international understanding and peace. Programmes are being implemented at national, subregional and regional level in order to expand and strengthen the information and communication systems of developing countries. At the General Conference in October 1980 a New World Information and Communication Order (NWICO), including plans for an international code of journalist ethics and for the 'licensing' of journalists, was approved, despite strong objections from the USA and the UK. Following the adoption of NWICO, the International Programme for the Development of Communication (IPDC) was set up, and funds were granted for the implementation of regional and international projects.

In late 1983, the USA (which provided around 25 per cent of the Organization's budget) announced its intention to withdraw, alleging political bias against the West; endemic hostility towards the institutions of a free society and decreasing attention to individual human rights; widespread mismanagement; and excessive budget growth. The Organization's Executive Board then appointed a 13-member committee to investigate allegations and recommend reforms. The US withdrawal became effective at the end of 1984; in January 1985 the USA established an Observer Mission at UNESCO. The UK and Singapore gave notice in 1984 and withdrew at the end of 1985. In response, reforms have been undertaken with a view to restructuring the Organization and its activities; however, the reforms are still considered to be insufficient by the governments of the UK and the USA, which do not seem to envisage rejoining the Organization in the near future.

Director-General: Federico Mayor Zaragoza
Headquarters: 7 Place de Fontenoy, 75352 Paris 07–SP, France (Telephone: +33 1 4568 1000; fax: +33 1 4567 1690)
Internet address: http://www. unesco. org
Publications: *The UNESCO Courier* (monthly); *Sources* (monthly); *Copyright Bulletin* (quarterly); *Prospects* (quarterly); *International Social Science Journal* (quarterly); *International Review of Education* (quarterly); *Museum International* (quarterly); *Statistical Yearbook*; *World Education Report* (every two years); *World Science Report* (every two years)
References: D. G. Partan, *Documentary Study of the Politicization of UNESCO* (Boston, Mass., 1975); R. Hoggart, *An Idea and its Servants: UNESCO from Within* (New York, 1978); A.-M. M'Bow, *Building the Future: UNESCO and the Solidarity of Nations* (Paris, 1981); P. J. Hajnal, *Guide to UNESCO* (Dobbs Ferry, New York, 1983); C. Wells, *The UN, UNESCO and the Politics of Knowledge* (London, 1987); V.-Y. Ghebali, *UNESCO Adrift: Crisis and Reform in an International Organization* (London, 1988); W. Preston, Jr, E. S. Herman and H.I. Schiller, *Hope and Folly: The United States and UNESCO, 1945–1985* (Minneapolis, Minn., 1989); F. Valderrama, *A History of UNESCO* (Paris, 1995); M. Conil Lacost, *The Story of a Grand Design: UNESCO 1946–1993* (Paris, 1995)

United Nations Environment Programme (UNEP)

The Programme provides the machinery for international co-operation in matters relating to the human environment.

Origin and development
The Programme was established in 1972 by the UN General Assembly, following the recommendations adopted at the UN Conference on the Human Environment held in Stockholm in June of

that year. The Conference adopted the Declaration on the Human Environment proclaiming the right of human beings to a high-quality environment, and their responsibility to protect and improve the environment for future generations. It also adopted an Action Plan, containing over 100 recommendations for measures to be taken by governments and international organizations to protect life, control contamination from man-made pollutants and improve cities and other human settlements.

Objectives
The Programme monitors significant changes in the environment and encourages and co-ordinates sound environmental practices, enabling nations and peoples to improve their quality of life without compromising that of future generations.

According to the Stockholm Conference Action Plan, the Programme is intended to cover the major environmental issues facing both the developed and the developing areas of the world, such as the ecology of rural and urban settlements, the relationship between environment and development, natural disasters, and the preservation of terrestrial ecosystems. It is also responsible for promoting environmental law and education and training for the management of the environment. A number of specific tasks have been assigned to the Programme by the relevant UN bodies and by UN-sponsored meetings and conferences. The various plans and projects drawn up within the framework of the Programme are usually put into practice by governments and other UN agencies.

Structure
The basic policy guidelines concerning the development and co-ordination of environment activities within the UN system are adopted by the Programme's Governing Council, composed of representatives from 58 countries (16 African; 13 Asian; 10 Latin American and Caribbean; 6 Eastern European; 13 Western European and other countries) elected by the General Assembly for four-year terms; half the membership is elected every two years. Regular sessions of the Council are held only in odd-numbered years.

An important role in the co-ordination of environmental action is played by the Secretariat, whose headquarters are in Nairobi, Kenya, with liaison and regional offices. The Secretariat is headed by an Executive Director elected by the General Assembly on the nomination of the Secretary-General for a four-year term. The Secretariat is also charged with the administration of the Environment Fund, established in 1973 to encourage voluntary additional financing for new initiatives relating to the environment. The Executive Director of the Programme acts as ex officio chairman of the Environment Co-ordination Board, which consists of the heads of all bodies responsible for the implementation of environmental programmes within the UN system.

Activities

The Programme has contributed substantially towards focusing world concern on the growing dangers to the human environment. At a special session in 1982, the Governing Council reviewed the achievements and shortcomings that had occurred in the human environment since the Stockholm Conference and discussed the Programme's guidelines for the 1980s. The Programme played a significant role in the pre paration of the UN Conference on Environment and Development (UNCED), held in Rio de Janeiro in June 1992, with a view to adopting long-term integrated environmental strategies leading to sustainable development.

Under the Stockholm Conference Action Plan, the Programme co-ordinates the Environment Assessment Programme (formerly 'Earthwatch'), an international surveillance network. The Global Environmental Monitoring System (GEMS), which began in 1975, is based on a network of stations providing information on the ecological state of the world and on changes in climate, water pollution and tropical forests; to convert the data collected into usable information, a Global Resource Information Database (GRID) was established in 1985.

The INFOTERRA programme is a computerized referral service to sources in about 170 countries for environmental information and expertise; it is responsible for the annual compilation of a Directory of Sources. The International Register of Potentially Toxic Chemicals (IRPTC) works through a network of national correspondents in about 120 countries to provide scientific and regulatory information on chemicals that may be dangerous to health and the environment. In April

1994, the Code of Ethics on the International Trade in Chemicals was concluded in Geneva after two years of negotiations conducted within the framework of the Programme.

Research is being carried out on the 'outer limits' of tolerance of the biosphere and its subsystems to the demands made on it by human activities; studies have been undertaken to assess the effect of carbon dioxide emission on climate (the 'greenhouse effect'). In 1985 the Programme completed a study on the effects of chlorofluorocarbon (CFC) production on the layer of ozone in the earth's atmosphere, and stressed the need to limit such production. The international Convention for the Protection of the Ozone Layer was adopted at a Conference held in Vienna in 1985, and represented an important stage in the Programme's efforts. A protocol to the Convention – adopted in September 1987 and known as the 'Montreal Protocol' – commits participating countries to reduce production of CFCs by 50 per cent by the year 2000. The London (1990) and Copenhagen (1992) Amendments to the Montreal Protocol seek to reduce further damage to the Earth's ozone layer. In order to prevent the 'dumping' of wastes from industrialized countries in developing countries, the Programme promoted the adoption in 1989 of the Basle Convention on the Control of Transboundary Movements of Hazardous Wastes and their Disposal (which came into force in 1992); the adoption of a protocol to the Basle Convention is being considered. The Programme has been entrusted by the 1977 UN Conference on Desertification with the responsibility for carrying out the Plan of Action drawn up to combat the spread of deserts, particularly in the Sudano-Sahelian region; assistance has been provided for the formation of regional networks of non-governmental agencies engaged in anti-desertification activities in Africa, Latin America, and Asia and the Pacific. The UN Convention to Combat Desertification in Countries Experiencing Serious Drought and/or Desertification, especially in Africa, was adopted in June 1994, under the sponsorship of the Programme. The Programme is also actively co-operating with the *UN Centre for Human Settlements (UNCHS) – Habitat to combat deteriorating environmental standards in towns.

The World Conservation Strategy was launched officially in March 1980. The Programme actively supports wildlife conservation in collaboration with the International Union for the Conservation of

Nature and Natural Resources (IUCN). The Programme administers the 1973 Convention on International Trade in Endangered Species of Wild Fauna and Flora (CITES) which has been ratified by some 130 countries; a ban on international trade in ivory was adopted by a CITES-sponsored conference in October 1989. A protocol is being prepared to supplement the 1979 Convention on the Conservation of Migratory Species of Wild Animals.

Substantial efforts are being made under the auspices of the Programme in the struggle against marine pollution, particularly in the Mediterranean; a convention and two protocols were signed to that effect in Barcelona in 1976. A number of priority programmes as well as a long-term study of the development plans of the Mediterranean governments are under way. A treaty for the control of pollution of inland origin was concluded in May 1980 in Athens under the sponsorship of the Programme by most of the countries bordering the Mediterranean. Another important treaty for the protection of natural resources and the marine environment was signed in April 1982 in Geneva. Several other countries outside the Mediterranean are developing various forms of close co-operation against marine pollution within the framework of the Programme. Action plans have been adopted for: the seas around Kuwait; the Caribbean; the West and Central African region; the East African region; the East Asian region; the Red Sea and the Gulf of Aden; the South Pacific; and the South-East Pacific. As regards the oceans, the Programme collects data on pollution and completed in 1984, jointly with the *Food and Agriculture Organization of the UN (FAO), a global Plan of Action for the Conservation, Management and Utilization of Marine Mammals.

Other major initiatives of the Programme have been the preparation of two international instruments opened for signature at UNCED: the Convention on Biological Diversity (CBD), which entered into effect in 1993, and the UN Framework Convention on Climate Change (UNFCCC), which entered into effect in 1994. Protocols to supplement the rules already in force are being considered by the Conference of Parties to both Conventions.

With the *World Bank and the *UN Development Programme (UNDP), the Programme is one of the managing partners of the recently restructured *Global Environment Facility (GEF).

The international environmental agenda that emerged from UNCED has brought about a need to change the Programme's focus and priorities. The new integrated programme currently in force addresses four basic challenges: sustainable management and use of natural resources; sustainable production and consumption; a better environment for health and well-being; and globalization trends and the environment. However, confusion over the 'division of labour' on environmental issues among UN bodies, and the financial difficulties related to the UN system itself, seem to aggravate the Programme's problems.

Executive Director: Elizabeth Dowdeswell
Headquarters: P.O. Box 30552, Nairobi, Kenya (Telephone: +254 2 621234; fax: +254 2 226886)
Publications: *Annual Report of the Executive Director*; *State of the Environment Report* (annually); *Our Planet* (quarterly); *Environmental Events Record* (monthly); studies, reports and technical guidelines

United Nations High Commissioner for Human Rights (HCHR)

The High Commissioner for Human Rights is the UN official with principal responsibility for the Organization's activities in that field.

Origin and development
The 1993 World Conference on Human Rights had adopted by consensus on 25 June the Vienna Declaration which, besides reaffirming the crucial principles of equal rights and self-determination of peoples, peace, democracy, justice and the rule of law, and stressing the need to fight all forms of discrimination and intolerance, called for the General Assembly to consider, as a matter of priority, the creation of the post of UN High Commissioner for Human Rights. Following these recommendations, the post was established by the General Assembly in December 1993. The first High Commissioner was appointed in February 1994.

Objectives
The High Commissioner promotes and protects the effective enjoyment by all of all civil, cultural,

economic, political and social rights. The High Commissioner acts under the direction and authority of the Secretary-General and within the framework of the overall competence, authority and decisions of the General Assembly, the Economic and Social Council and the Commission on Human Rights.

The High Commissioner's mandate spans the whole range of human rights concerns. In particular, the High Commissioner is charged with promoting the realization of the right to development and enhancing support from the UN system for that purpose; providing, through the Centre for Human Rights and other institutions, advisory services and technical and financial assistance to support human rights programmes; co-ordinating UN education and public information programmes; and preventing the continuation of human rights violations throughout the world. The mandate also includes engaging in dialogue with governments to secure respect for human rights, carrying out the tasks assigned to the High Commissioner by the competent bodies of the UN system and making the relevant recommendations, and providing overall supervision of the Centre for Human Rights.

Structure

A restructuring process is going on in order to improve the performance of the Centre for Human Rights and secure financial resources for, *inter alia*, the field missions in Rwanda, Burundi and the former Yugoslavia, the technical projects for the creation of national human rights institutions in about 40 countries, and the implementation of the UN Decade for Human Rights Education.

Activities

Since his appointment, the High Commissioner has undertaken a wide-ranging programme of activities, including personal visits (to countries such as Rwanda, Burundi, Malawi, Cambodia, Nepal and the Baltic states) to strengthen understanding of and respect for human rights, and the development of close links with UN programmes, the specialized agencies and other international organizations, and national institutions and non-governmental organizations engaged in the protection of human rights. The 1995 Dayton Peace Agreement, *inter alia*, has invited the High

Commissioner and the Commission on Human Rights to take part in human rights activities in Bosnia-Herzegovina. Discussions on priority human rights issues have been held by the High Commissioner and the representatives of major intergovernmental bodies such as the *Organization for Security and Co-operation in Europe (OSCE) and the *Council of Europe.

High Commissioner: José Ayala Lasso
Headquarters: Office of the HCHR – D514, Palais des Nations, 1211 Geneva 10, Switzerland (Telephone: +41 22 917 2122; fax: +41 22 917 0245)
Publication: *HCHR News* (monthly)

United Nations High Commissioner for Refugees (UNHCR)

The Office of the High Commissioner provides international legal protection for refugees; seeks permanent solutions to their problems through voluntary repatriation, resettlement in other countries or integration into the country of present residence; and extends material assistance.

Origin and development

The Office was established by the UN General Assembly in 1950, with effect from January 1951, originally for three years. Since 1954 the mandate has been renewed for successive five-year periods.

According to the Statute of the Office, refugees are persons outside their country of nationality because they have a well-founded fear of persecution by reason of race, religion, nationality or political opinion and, because of such fear, are unable or unwilling to avail themselves of the protection of the government of their nationality. Since 1971 the Office has been empowered to carry out a number of special operations for the benefit of displaced persons who are not refugees according to the above definition but find themselves in similar circumstances and are in need of international aid. Under the terms of the resolutions adopted by the General Assembly and the Economic and Social Council over the past few years, the importance of the 'essential humanitarian task' performed by the Office 'in the context of man-made disasters, in addition to its original functions' has been expressly recognized. It should be noted that until 1989 the countries of

Eastern Europe and the then USSR did not participate in the activities of the Office.

Objectives

The primary function of the Office lies in the provision of legal protection on the basis of the main international instrument in the field – that is, the 1951 UN Convention relating to the Status of Refugees, which defines the rights of refugees and lays down a minimum standard of treatment to which they are entitled with regard to employment, education, residence, freedom of movement and security against 'refoulement' (forcible return to a country where their life or liberty might be in danger). A Protocol extending the scope of the 1951 Convention to new groups of refugees came into effect in 1967. More than 130 countries have acceded to the 1951 Convention and/or the 1967 Protocol. International conventions have been adopted at the regional level to define specific rights and duties of refugees.

Structure

The basic policy guidelines concerning the work of the Office are given by the General Assembly or the Economic and Social Council to the High Commissioner, elected by the General Assembly on the nomination of the Secretary-General, and charged with current operations. The High Commissioner is responsible to the General Assembly, to which he reports through the Economic and Social Council. Guidance and advice with respect to material assistance programmes are provided by the Executive Committee of the High Commissioner's Programme, based in Geneva and composed of the representatives of 50 countries, members and non-members of the UN. Sessions are held at yearly intervals, and informal consultations between sessions are customarily held by the High Commissioner with representatives of UN member countries. The High Commissioner has Representatives and Chargés de Mission in the field, covering over 170 countries.

The basic administrative costs of the Office, as well as legal protection activities, are covered by the regular budget of the UN, while material assistance activities and related programme support costs are financed in their entirety by voluntary contributions from both governmental and non-governmental sources; special operations account for a large percentage of these contributions. The overall financial requirements of the Office are growing steadily as a result of the greatly expanded number of people of concern to the High Commissioner, including returnees and groups of displaced persons in 'refugee-like situations'. Recurrent financial constraints severely curtail the ability of the Office to provide adequate protection and assistance for refugees.

Activities

The total number of people of concern to the Office amounts to over 27 million throughout the world, including 14.5 million refugees, 5.4 million internally displaced persons (that is, displaced people who have not crossed an international border), 3.5 million others of humanitarian concern, and some 4 million returnees requiring assistance for reintegration in their countries of origin. The greatest concentration is in Africa, where refugees and related groups live in camps and settlements administered by the Office. The most severe refugee emergency in recent history has occurred in the Great Lakes region of Africa. The Office is also heavily involved in assistance and protection for refugees in the Caucasus and central Asian republics, and co-operates with governments, and voluntary groups and organizations, in housing and maintaining these persons. Major efforts in Latin America are aimed at finding resettlement opportunities for refugees, or organizing the reinstallation and rehabilitation of the returnees, especially in Central America. Refugee and asylum issues became a major concern in Europe in the early 1990s as a result of the disintegration of the former Yugoslavia and of rising tensions in several Eastern European countries.

The Programme has built partnerships with other UN agencies and national and international bodies, to facilitate assistance and reintegration of refugees and related groups within a context which takes into account the links existing between peace, stability, security, sustainable development and respect for human rights. Therefore the Programme has become increasingly involved with peace-making and peace-keeping initiatives carried out by the UN and with human rights mechanisms, especially the newly-created *UN High Commissioner for Human Rights, at the level of field operations.

The Office was awarded the Nobel Peace Prize in 1954 and 1981.

High Commissioner: Sadako Ogata
Headquarters: 154 rue de Lausanne, 1211 Geneva 10, Switzerland (Telephone: +41 22 739 8111; fax: +41 22 731 9546)
Internet address: http://www.unicc.org/unhcr
Publications: *UNHCR Report* (annual); *Refugees* (monthly); *Refugee Abstracts* (quarterly)
Reference: L. Druke, *Preventive Action for Refugee Producing Situations* (New York) rev. 2/1993

United Nations Industrial Development Organization (UNIDO)

The Organization promotes the industrialization of the developing countries through direct assistance and mobilization of national and international resources, with particular emphasis on the manufacturing sector.

Origin and development

Established as an organ of the UN General Assembly in November 1966, the Organization became operational in January 1967 as an action-oriented body, replacing the Centre for Industrial Development, which had been operating within the UN Secretariat since July 1961. The conflict of views between the developing and the developed countries over the most suitable institutional arrangements for intensifying and concentrating UN efforts for the industrialization of the developing world delayed the establishment of the new Organization for a number of years. A consensus was reached only in the mid-1960s for the creation of an autonomous body within the UN. In 1975, the Second General Conference of the member countries stressed the urgent need to increase and expand the autonomy and functions of the Organization and recommended its conversion to the status of a UN specialized agency. The recommendation was subsequently endorsed by the UN General Assembly, and several sessions were held to draft a Constitution, which was eventually adopted by consensus in April 1979 in Vienna. The Constitution entered into force in June 1985, and in January 1986 the Organization became the 16th specialized agency related to the UN.

Objectives

The Organization is entrusted with the task of co-ordinating all activities undertaken by the UN family of agencies in the field of industrial development. It also provides a forum for consultation and negotiations among developing countries, and between developing and industrialized countries. According to the Constitution of April 1979, the primary aim of the Organization is to promote industrial development in the developing countries.

Structure

The work of the Organization is carried out by the following principal organs: the General Conference; the Industrial Development Board; the Programme and Budget Committee (PBC); and the Secretariat.

The General Conference, composed of one representative from each member country, normally meets once every two years to formulate overall policies, determine the programme of work, and approve the budget. The Industrial Development Board, meeting once a year in the Conference years and twice in the non-Conference years, serves as the governing body of the Organization. It is composed of 53 members (of which 33 are from developing countries, 15 from the developed market economy countries, and 5 from Eastern Europe) elected by the General Conference for a four-year term. The Programme and Budget Committee is made up of 27 members elected by the General Conference for a two-year term. The Secretariat performs administrative functions under a Director-General appointed by the General Conference, upon the Board's recommendation, for a period of four years. The Director-General has overall responsibility for administrative and research tasks as well as for all operational activities, including the activities executed by the Organization as a participating agency of the *UN Development Programme (UNDP). Co-operative arrangements link the Organization with several specialized agencies, the UN regional economic commissions, and a number of intergovernmental and non-governmental bodies outside the UN system.

The Organization's finance originally derived from the UNDP, the UN regular budget, the UN Regular Programme of Technical Assistance, and trust funds and contributions from various sources. As from January 1986 the Organization, in keeping with its new status of specialized agency, has assumed full responsibility for its programme and budget based on assessed contributions of its member countries, currently numbering about 170.

To establish and increase links between potential investors and business people in developed countries and enterprises in developing nations, the Organization has set up Investment Promotion Service offices in Athens, Milan, Paris, Seoul, Tokyo, Warsaw, Washington and Zurich. Centres for International Industrial Co-operation are in Beijing and Moscow. Since the 1970s, technical co-operation projects have benefited about 180 countries and regions.

Activities

Activities cover macroeconomic and microeconomic aspects of industrial development. At the macroeconomic level, questions are considered concerning: the formulation of industrial development policies; application of modern methods of production, programming and planning; building and strengthening of institutions and administration in the matter of industrial technology; co-operation with UN regional economic commissions in assisting regional planning of industrial development within the framework of regional and subregional economic groupings; recommendation of special measures to accelerate the growth of the less advanced among the developing countries. At microeconomic level, assistance is provided with regard to problems of technical and economic feasibility, external financing for specific industrial projects, product development and design, management, marketing, quality and research. The Organization is also responsible for proposing measures for the improvement of the international system of industrial property, with a view to accelerating the transfer of technical knowledge to developing countries and strengthening the role of patents consistent with national interests as an incentive to industrial innovations. Technical assistance usually consists of expert services, but sometimes involves the supply of equipment or fellowships for training, such as in management or production. Studies and research programmes, designed to facilitate and support operational activities, include in particular the

compilation, analysis, publication and dissemination of information concerning various aspects of the process of industrialization, such as industrial technology, investment, financing, production, management techniques, programming and planning. Seminars and other specialist meetings are organized on a wide range of subjects related to industrial and technological development.

Criticism and dissatisfaction with the Organization's practices, especially voiced by developed member countries, have prompted efforts to reshape and restructure activities adapting them to the effective needs of industrial development in developing countries. At the Fifth General Conference, held in Yaoundé, Cameroon, in December 1993, five fundamental objectives were identified as a framework for future programmes: industrial and technical growth and competitiveness; human resource development; equitable development through industrialization; environmentally sustainable industrial development; and international co-operation in industrial investment and technology.

Director-General: Mauricio de María y Campos
Headquarters: Vienna International Centre, P.O. Box 300, 1400 Vienna, Austria (Telephone: +43 1 21131-0; fax: +43 1 232156)
Publications: *Annual Report*; *UNIDO Newsletter* (monthly); *Industry and Development* (annual)

United Nations International Drug Control Programme (UNDCP)

The Programme has become the single UN body responsible for concerted international actions for the control of drug abuse.

Origin and development

The Programme – established by the UN General Assembly in December 1990 – integrated fully the structures and functions of the Division of Narcotic Drugs of the UN Secretariat, the secretariat of the *International Narcotics Control Board (INCB) and the United Nations Fund for Drug Abuse Control (UNFDAC), with the aim of enhancing the effectiveness and efficiency of the UN structure for the control of drug abuse. In the light of the structural changes involved with the creation of the Programme, the functioning of the UN *Commission on Narcotic Drugs (CND) as a policy-making body has been improved.

Objectives

The Programme deals with: (a) treaty implementation, which integrates, with due regard to treaty arrangements, the functions of the secretariat of the INCB and the treaty implementation functions of the Division of Narcotic Drugs, taking into account the independent role of INCB; (b) policy implementation and research, with responsibility for implementing policy decisions of the relevant legislative bodies and conducting analytical work; and (c) operational activities, with responsibility for co-ordinating and carrying out the technical co-operation projects currently executed mainly by the Fund, the Division of Narcotic Drugs and the secretariat of INCB.

Structure

The Programme is headed by an Executive Director, appointed by the Secretary-General. The Executive Director enjoys exclusive responsibility for co-ordinating and providing effective leadership for all UN drug control activities, with a view to ensuring coherence of actions within the Programme as well as co-ordination, complementarity and non-duplication of such activities across the UN system. The Fund is entirely supported from voluntary contributions of member countries and private agencies.

Activities

The Executive Director also has direct responsibility for the financial resources of the Fund of the UN International Drug Control Programme – established by the UN General Assembly in 1991 as a successor to UNFDAC – as the major source for financing operational activities of the Programme, especially in developing countries. Activities are carried out on the basis of a three-tier strategy articulated at country, regional and global levels. The Programme serves as the focal point for promoting the observance of the UN Decade against Drug Abuse (1991–2000).

Executive Director: Giorgio Giacomelli
Address: Vienna International Centre, P.O. Box 500, 1400 Vienna, Austria (Telephone: +43 1 21345-4251; fax: +43 1 230 7002)

United Nations Population Fund (UNFPA)

The Fund – a subsidiary organ of the UN General Assembly – is the largest internationally funded provider of population assistance to developing countries.

Origin and development

The UN has been concerned with population problems since 1946, when the Population Commission of the Economic and Social Council was established with a view to improving demographic statistics. Subsequently, the efforts of the General Assembly to shift the emphasis to action-oriented programmes led to the creation in 1967 of the Trust Fund for Population Activities. The Trust Fund was charged with the promotion of population programmes and the extension of systematic and sustained assistance to developing countries, according to their requests. Renamed in 1969 the UN Fund for Population Activities (UNFPA), it became a Fund of the General Assembly officially in 1972, and was made a subsidiary organ of the General Assembly in 1979. In 1987 the name was changed to UN Population Fund, but the existing acronym was retained.

A World Population Conference was held in Bucharest, Romania, in 1974 (designated as World Population Year) and adopted the World Population Plan of Action by consensus of 136 countries. An International Conference on Population was held in Mexico City in August 1984 to review and appraise the 1974 Plan of Action and to provide new directions for the coming decades on the integration of population with development. In connection with another periodic review of the 1974 Plan of Action, in 1989 the UN approved the convening of an international meeting on population in 1994. The International Conference on Population and Development, held in Cairo, Egypt, in September 1994, dealt with six high-priority issues: population growth and demographic structure; population policies and programmes; population, the environment and development; population distribution and migration; population and women; and family planning, health and family well-being. The 20-year Programme of Action adopted by the Conference, albeit with reservations expressed by some 20 countries, emphasized the inseparability of population and development, and focused on meeting the needs of individuals rather than on demographic targets. Empowering women and providing them with more choices through expanded access to education and health services, and promoting skill development and employment, are the basis of the new approach.

Objectives

The Fund aims to provide resources additional to the UN system for technical co-operation activities in the population field. It is empowered to provide financial support – for periods ranging from three to five years – for national, regional and interregional projects concerning basic population data, population dynamics and policy, family planning, and information and education activities. The major areas covered by the financial assistance granted by the Fund include: (a) collection and analysis of data on population trends and structure; (b) study of the interrelationship between population and food demand, and other aspects of economic and social development; (c) formulation of appropriate population policies within the context of national development objectives; (d) direct support to national family planning programmes and establishment of demonstration and pilot projects; (e) training of personnel for research and operational activities and improvement of communication techniques; and (f) application of existing methods of fertility regulation and promotion of research in human reproduction.

Structure

The basic guidelines concerning the activities of the Fund are adopted by its governing body, the UNDP/UNFPA Executive Board, providing intergovernmental support to, and supervision of, the Fund, in accordance with the overall policy guidance of the General Assembly and the Economic and Social Council. An important role is played by the Fund's Executive Director, based in New York, who is in charge of the general operation and maintains close links with recipient governments, relevant UN agencies and bodies, regional and subregional groups, and non-governmental organizations, to ensure effective co-ordination in population activities. The Executive Director has the rank of Under-Secretary-General of the UN. The Fund Deputy Representatives and Senior

Advisers on Population in the developing countries provide assistance to governments in the formulation of requests for aid in the population field, and are responsible for co-ordinating the work of the executing agencies operating in the geographical area within their competence.

Activities

Assistance is generally extended through the UN Regional Economic Commissions and member organizations of the UN system, although in some cases the Fund avails itself of the services of non-governmental organizations or acts as its own executing agency. About two-thirds of the projects financed by the Fund are implemented by agencies within the UN system, and the remainder by recipient governments or by non-governmental organizations. Among executing agencies are the *UN Development Programme (UNDP), the *UN Children's Fund (UNICEF), the *International Labour Organization (ILO), the *UN Educational, Scientific and Cultural Organization (UNESCO), and the *World Health Organization (WHO).

The Fund has made a significant contribution towards focusing international attention on the different aspects of population problems, and encouraging co-operative efforts to that end in developing countries and territories. Comprehensive country agreements have been negotiated in order to implement national population programmes, while hundreds of projects are being carried out at the regional level. A large number of projects are aimed at supporting national family planning activities; many other important projects are in the areas of collection of basic population data and communication and education.

The Fund aims to enhance the status of women and ensure that their needs are taken into account when development and population programmes are prepared. It also has special programmes on youth, on ageing, and on AIDS, involving national as well as regional seminars and training programmes. The Fund brings together potential donors and developing countries in need of support for population activities through a system of 'multi-bilateral' funding, by aiding a government in developing a project and seeking assistance from a donor to implement it; enlisting the help of donors in the provision of expertise, supplies or funds; creating a trust fund to manage donors' contributions; or jointly financing a project with a donor. About three-quarters of the resources of the Fund are concentrated in 'priority' countries most in need of assistance in the population field, notably the poorest developing countries in sub-Saharan Africa.

Executive Director: Nafis Sadik
Headquarters: 220 East 42nd Street, New York, N.Y. 10017, USA (Telephone: +1 212 297 5000; fax: +1 212 370 0201)
Publications: *Annual Report*; *State of World Population Report* (annual); *Population* (monthly); *Inventory of Population Projects Around the World* (annual)
Reference: R. M. Salas, *International Population Assistance: The First Decade. A Look at the Concepts and Policies Which Have Guided the UNFPA in its First Ten Years* (Oxford, 1979)

United Nations Relief and Works Agency for Palestine Refugees in the Near East (UNRWA)

The Agency carries out relief and works programmes for Palestinian refugees.

Origin and development
Established as a subsidiary organ by a resolution of the UN General Assembly in December 1949, the Agency began operations in May 1950. Assistance was to be provided to those needy persons residing in one of the 'host' countries of the Near East whose normal residence had been in Palestine for a minimum of two years before the 1948 conflict and who, as a result of the Arab–Israeli hostilities, had lost both their homes and their means of livelihood. The children and grandchildren of registered refugees were also, under certain conditions, eligible for assistance. After the renewal of hostilities in the Middle East in June 1967, the Agency was additionally empowered by the General Assembly to provide humanitarian aid, as far as practicable, on an emergency basis and as a temporary measure, for people other than Palestine refugees who were newly displaced and in serious need of continued assistance. Assistance is also extended, at the request and on behalf of the government of Jordan, to displaced persons in eastern Jordan

who are not registered refugees of 1948. Following the signing of the Declaration of Principles by the Palestine Liberation Organization (PLO) and Israel in September 1993, the Agency launched, in October of the same year, a Peace Implementation Programme (PIP) aimed at supporting the peace process through the creation of jobs and the improvement of services and the socioeconomic infrastructure. The first phase of PIP received $83 million in funding for projects in the West Bank, the Gaza Strip and the Jericho area, and $10 million for Jordan, Lebanon and Syria. PIP II consists of about $250 million-worth of projects.

Objectives
The Agency aims to provide direct relief, health, education and welfare services, as well as long-term rehabilitation and vocational training, for Palestine refugees in Jordan, Lebanon, Syria, the West Bank and the Gaza Strip; the mandate of the Agency has been renewed periodically by the UN General Assembly.

Structure
A Commissioner-General is responsible for the Agency's operations (supervision, planning and budgeting), with the assistance of an Advisory Commission consisting of the representatives of 10 countries (Belgium, Egypt, France, Japan, Jordan, Lebanon, Syria, Turkey, the UK, and the USA). The Vienna headquarters have been relocated to the area of operations. Close cooperative links are maintained by the Agency with several UN bodies and specialized institutions such as the *World Health Organization (WHO) and the *UN Educational, Scientific and Cultural Organization (UNESCO).

Activities
The Agency depends to a very great extent on voluntary contributions, almost entirely from governments, the remainder being provided by other sources such as voluntary groups and organizations, and business corporations. Services included in the Agency's regular programmes are provided by a staff of more than 20 000, most of whom are themselves Palestine refugees. By 1995 the Agency provided essential services to over 3 000 000 persons. An estimated third of the total refugee population is living in 59 different

refugee camps, while the remaining refugees have settled in already-existing towns and villages. Relief services concentrate on providing food and other welfare assistance to destitute refugees; this new programme replaces the general distribution of basic food rations that was discontinued in 1982.

The Agency's humanitarian role has grown steadily because of the recurrent conflicts in the Middle East, such as the civil war in Lebanon, the Palestinian uprising and the Gulf crisis. With the peace process, the Agency inaugurated a new era in its relationship with the Palestinian people and developed an effective working relationship with the Palestinian Authority. The Agency's services are now being provided to refugees in areas under the control of the Palestinian Authority.

Commissioner-General: Peter Hansen
Headquarters: Vienna International Centre, P.O. Box 700, 1400 Vienna, Austria (Telephone: +43 1 21345, ext. 4530; fax: +43 1 21345 5877)
Publications: *Annual Report of the Commissioner-General*; *Palestine Refugees Today* (quarterly newsletter); *UNRWA Report* (quarterly); *A Survey of United Nations Assistance to Palestine* (every two years)

Universal Postal Union (UPU)

The Union is among the oldest intergovernmental organizations still in existence and has played a leading role in the field of international postal co-operation for over 120 years.

Origin and development

A Treaty concerning the Establishment of a General Postal Union (Berne Treaty) was signed in October 1874 in Berne, Switzerland, by the representatives of 20 European countries, joined by Egypt and the USA; the Treaty came into force in July 1875. The original name of General Postal Union was replaced by Universal Postal Union in 1878. The Union became a specialized agency in relationship with the UN under the terms of an agreement concluded in July 1947 and entered into effect in July 1948; a supplementary agreement was signed in July 1949.

The Postal Congress held in Vienna in 1964 brought about a major structural change by drawing up for the Union a separate and permanent basic Act (Constitution) not subject to revision at each subsequent Congress. The Constitution containing the organic rules of the Union was adopted in July 1964 and came into force in January 1966. It was amended by the Congresses held in 1969 (Tokyo), 1974 (Lausanne), 1984 (Hamburg), 1989 (Washington), and 1994 (Seoul). The General Regulations embody the provisions ensuring the application of the Constitution and the working of the Union. For their part, the Universal Postal Convention and its Detailed Regulations establish the rules applicable throughout the international postal service and the provisions concerning the letter post services. All these Acts are binding on all member countries; since about 190 countries participate in the Union, the provisions embodied in the Acts affect virtually the entire population of the world. Optional agreements, supplemented by the relevant regulations, govern the operation of postal services as regards the handling of insured valuables, parcels, postal money orders and cheques, account transfers, cash on delivery items, collection of bills, savings and subscriptions to newspapers and periodicals. The provisions of the Constitution authorize member countries to establish Restricted Unions and to conclude special agreements on the postal service. However, conditions for the public must not be less favourable than those laid down in the Acts of the Union.

Members of the UN may accede to the Union, in conformity with current provisions; any sovereign country not belonging to the UN may be admitted to the Union if the request is approved by at least two-thirds of the member countries. Each member country may withdraw from the Union by notice of denunciation of the Constitution given through diplomatic channels to the Swiss Government; withdrawal becomes effective one year thereafter.

Objectives

The aim of the Union is to secure the organization and improvement of the postal services and to promote the development of technical assistance and international collaboration. To this end, member countries are considered to form a single postal territory for the reciprocal exchange of letter post items; freedom of transit is guaranteed throughout the entire territory of the Union. The concept of letter post applies to the following categories of items: letters (including aerogrammes), postcards, printed matter, literature in raised relief for the blind, and small packets. Rates, maximum and minimum weight and size limits, as well as conditions of acceptance, are fixed according to the Universal Postal Convention. The Convention prescribes the methods for calculating and collecting transit charges (for letter post items passing through the territories of one or more countries) and terminal dues (that is, the compensation payments that an administration which receives more letter post items than it sends has the right to collect from the dispatching administration). Regulations are also established with regard to the registered items service and the air conveyance of mail, and of objects such as infectious and radioactive substances, whose transport requires special precautions.

Structure

According to the new structure approved by the 1994 Congress in Seoul, the main organs of the Union are the Universal Postal Congress, the Council of Administration, the Postal Operations Council, and the International Bureau. The Congress, composed of representatives of all member countries, is the supreme authority of the Union, usually meeting every five years to review the Universal Postal Convention and its subsidiary agreements. An Extraordinary Congress may be convened at the request, or with the consent, of at least two-thirds of member countries. The Council of Administration consists of 40 members elected by Congress with due regard for equitable geographical representation, plus one member to represent the host country of the Congress. Meeting each year at the Union's headquarters in Berne, the Council of Administration ensures the continuity of the work of the Union between Congresses, maintains close contact with postal administrations, supervises to some extent the activities of the International Bureau, undertakes studies of administrative, legislative and legal problems of interest to the postal service, draws up proposals, and makes recommendations to the Congress. It is also responsible for encouraging, supervising

and co-ordinating international co-operation in the form of postal technical assistance and vocational training. The Postal Operations Council, composed of 40 members elected by the Congress, deals with operational, commercial, technical and economic questions concerning the postal service.

Since the establishment of the Union, a central office known as the International Bureau has functioned in Berne. Besides serving as the permanent secretariat of the Union, it provides liaison, information, consultation and certain financial services for postal administrations, and acts as a focal point for the co-ordination and execution of technical co-operation of all types in the postal sphere. The International Bureau is headed by a Director-General and placed under the general supervision of the Swiss government.

Each Congress fixes the maximum amount which the ordinary expenditure of the Union may reach for the five succeeding years; the annual budget of the Union is approved by the Council of Administration.

Activities

The Union co-operates closely with the *UN Development Programme (UNDP) and executes country and inter-country projects covering practically all aspects of the postal services; priority is given to the needs of the administrations of the postally least-developed countries.

The Union is in close contact with the *International Telecommunication Union (ITU) for the preparation and implementation of joint technical assistance projects, especially in the field of vocational training. Co-operative relations are also maintained with other UN specialized agencies such as the *International Civil Aviation Organization (ICAO) for the development of air mail traffic, the *International Atomic Energy Agency (IAEA) for the postal conveyance of radioactive substances, and the *World Health Organization (WHO) for the transport of perishable biological substances. In addition, contact committees have been set up with several other intergovernmental and non-governmental institutions.

The establishment of the Union has made it possible to conduct international postal exchanges under principles and practices that are largely standardized. Over the past decades the

Union has managed to adjust to the new requirements of technology and development in the postal field, fostering technical co-operation activities in sectors such as planning, organization, management, operations, training and financial services. To this end, the Union has recruited and despatched experts, consultants or volunteers; granted vocational training or further training fellowships for individual or group courses; and supplied equipment and training and demonstration aids.

Director-General: Thomas E. Leavey

Headquarters: Weltpoststrasse 4, 3000 Bern 15, Switzerland (Telephone: +41 31 350 3111; fax: +41 31 350 3110)

Publications: *Union Postale* (quarterly); *Postal Technical Co-operation* (quarterly)

W

Wassenaar Arrangement

The Arrangement represents a successor regime to the Co-ordinating Committee for Multilateral Export Controls (Cocom), established in 1949 by major Western countries to prevent arms transfers to the USSR and its allies throughout the world.

Origin and development
After the end of the Cold War and the subsequent formal dissolution of Cocom in March 1994, it was felt to be necessary to set up a new international mechanism to control international sales of conventional arms and sensitive dual-use commodities. The Arrangement provides a venue for major weapons suppliers to deal collectively with the implications of arms sales and to define common approaches to trade with regions of potential instability, notably the Middle East and South Asia.

After several rounds of negotiations held at Wassenaar, the diplomatic suburb of The Hague, The Netherlands, the Wassenaar Arrangement on Export Controls for Conventional Arms and Dual-Use Goods and Technologies was agreed upon in December 1995 by the 17 members of the disbanded Cocom and 11 other countries, including some of the West's erstwhile adversaries in Eastern Europe. Participants in the Arrangement currently include all member countries of the *North Atlantic Treaty Organization (NATO) (with the exception of Iceland), plus Australia, Austria, the Czech Republic, Finland, Hungary, Ireland, Japan, New Zealand, Poland, Russia, Slovakia, Sweden and Switzerland. The Arrangement may be joined by other countries willing to commit themselves to the application of effective export policies and controls on arms and arms-related technologies, and to regular consultation and exchange of information and intelligence. Several countries, including Argentina, Bulgaria, Romania, South Korea and Ukraine have expressed interest in joining.

Objectives
Although each participating country remains ultimately responsible for decisions concerning its own arms sales, it must provide notification of transfers or denials of items on a list which at present includes the categories of major weapon systems used for the Conventional Forces in Europe (CFE) Treaty and the UN Arms Register. These comprise conventional armaments as well as advanced technologies such as machine tools, computers and telecommunications systems, which may play an important part in the production of weapons. In particular, all participating countries currently maintain strict controls to prevent transfers of weapons and sensitive technologies to Iran, Iraq, Libya and North Korea. The Arrangement complements other non-proliferation regimes, notably the Nuclear Suppliers Group, the Missile Technology Control Regime, and the Australia Group.

Activities
The first plenary meeting within the framework of the Arrangement took place in April 1996; differences emerged between the USA and other major arms suppliers, especially with regard to prior notification of transfers and the convenience of targeting 'rogue' countries specifically.

West African Economic and Monetary Union

(Union économique et monétaire ouest-africaine)
(UEMOA)

The creation of the new organization almost coincided with the dissolution of the West African Economic Community (Communauté économique de l'Afrique de l'Ouest) (CEAO) which had been operating in the region since 1974.

Origin and development
The Union was established by a treaty signed in January 1994 by the Heads of State and Government of Benin, Burkina Faso, Côte d'Ivoire, Mali, Niger, Senegal and Togo; the treaty entered into effect in August 1994.

Objectives
All member countries of the Union use a common currency pegged to the French franc – that is, the franc of the Communauté financière africaine (CFA franc), whose central issuing bank is the Banque centrale des états de l'Afrique de l'ouest, established in 1955 and based in Dakar. In response to repeated calls from the *International

Monetary Fund (IMF) and the French government, the countries using the CFA franc – which include all members of the Union plus six other French-speaking countries in Central Africa – devalued the currency by 50 per cent against the French franc in January 1994. The new exchange rate was intended to alleviate balance-of-payments difficulties and restore the competitiveness of the countries involved in the devaluation.

Activities

The Union may be viewed as a successor to CEAO, although with more limited scope and competence. The future of the new organization will depend to some extent on the relationship that will develop with a much broader regional organization including also non-francophone countries of West Africa – that is, the *Economic Community of West African States (ECOWAS).

Western Central Atlantic Fishery Commission (WECAFC)

Established by a resolution of the Council of the *Food and Agriculture Organization (FAO) adopted in 1973 and amended in 1978, the Commission covers all marine waters of the Western Central Atlantic Ocean and groups over 30 countries. Its purpose is to assist international co-operation for the conservation, development and utilization of all living marine resources that are of interest to two or more countries.

Headquarters: FAO, Room NF-408, Via delle Terme di Caracalla, 00100 Rome, Italy (Telephone: +39 6 5225 5802; fax: +39 6 5225 6500)

Western European Union (WEU)

The Union has the broad aim of strengthening peace and security, promoting unity and encouraging the progressive integration of Europe through the co-ordination of the defence policies and equipment of member countries, as well as through consultation and co-operation with regard to political and economic matters.

Origin and development

The Union came into being in 1955 as a successor – with an enlarged membership, modified purposes and a different denomination – to the Brussels Treaty Organization. Growing concern over the security of Western Europe had prompted the governments of Belgium, France, Luxembourg, The Netherlands and the UK to sign a 50-year Treaty 'of economic, social and cultural collaboration and collective self-defence', with a view, *inter alia*, to taking 'such steps as may be held necessary in the event of renewal by Germany of a policy of aggression'. The Treaty was signed in Brussels in March 1948 and entered into force the following August.

The realization of the inadequacy of the Brussels Treaty Organization to ensure regional security, and the need to involve the USA in any serious effort to build up an effective machinery for collective self-defence, led to the creation in 1949 of the *North Atlantic Treaty Organization (NATO). In December 1950, the Brussels Treaty Organization transferred its defence functions to the NATO command but retained its competence concerning social and cultural activities, in spite of the creation of the *Council of Europe in 1949. After the collapse of plans for a European Defence Community (EDC) because of French rejection, and the decision of the NATO Council to incorporate the Federal Republic of Germany into the Western system of collective security, a conference was held in London in September–October 1954, with the participation of the signatories to the 1948 Brussels Treaty plus Canada, Germany, Italy and the USA. The decisions of the conference were embodied in a series of Protocols, amending and completing the Brussels Treaty, which were drawn up by a ministerial conference held in Paris in October 1954. The Protocols provided, *inter alia*, for the transformation of the Brussels Treaty Organization into the Western European Union, with the inclusion of Germany and Italy as full members; the ending of the occupation regime in the Federal Republic of Germany and the invitation to the latter to join NATO; and the setting up of an Agency for the Control of Armaments. The Protocols entered into force in May 1955, thus bringing the then seven-member Union formally into existence.

One of the first important tasks of the newly-created Union concerned the establishment of an international regime for the Saar territory. Under a Franco-German agreement of October 1954, the Saar was to be granted a statute, within the framework of the Union, subject to approval by the population. In October 1955, the statute was rejected by referendum in favour of a return to Germany. The full political and economic reintegration of the Saar territory with Germany was achieved between January 1957 and July 1959. Another important sphere of competence of the Union disappeared in June 1960, when its social and cultural activities were handed over to the Council of Europe. After a long period of uncertainty about its basic tasks, the late 1980s saw a remarkable expansion in the Union's membership. Portugal and Spain were admitted in November 1988, and Greece became the tenth member in November 1992. Iceland, Norway and Turkey – three countries that belong to NATO but not to the *European Union (EU) – have acceded as associate members but participate fully in most activities. Austria, Denmark, Finland, Ireland and Sweden – all of them EU members – enjoy observer status. In May 1994, nine Central and Eastern European countries (Bulgaria, the Czech Republic, Estonia, Hungary, Latvia, Lithuania, Poland, Romania, and Slovakia) were granted the newly-created status of associate partners of the Union, followed by Slovenia in June 1996; the associate partnership is linked to the conclusion of 'Europe Agreements' with the EU. In total, 27 countries are involved, to differing degrees and with different responsibilities, in the process of shaping new security conditions in Europe. The revised Brussels Treaty is to remain in force until August 1998; there is no provision for withdrawal before that date.

Objectives

The Union, traditionally described as the European pillar of the Atlantic Alliance and now entrusted with the new task of defence arm of the EU, has become the major forum for consultation on matters relating to European security policy and is a fundamental component of the new European security architecture alongside NATO and the *Organization for Security and Co-operation in Europe (OSCE).

According to the modified Brussels Treaty, if any member country should be 'the object of an armed attack in Europe', the other countries will afford the member so attacked 'all the military and other aid and assistance in their power'. Provision was also made for close co-operation between member countries on economic, social and cultural matters according to the principles forming the basis of the common civilization of

their peoples; however, further developments in European co-operation and integration rendered these tasks largely redundant.

A new *raison d'être* for the Union was found at a meeting of the Foreign and Defence Ministers of the member countries, held in Rome in October 1984, when the decision was taken to 'reactivate' the Union through a restructuring of the organizational mechanism and the holding of more frequent ministerial meetings to harmonize views on defence and security issues. According to the Rome Declaration, the task of the Union was 'not only to contribute to the security of Western Europe but also to improve the common defence of all the countries of the Atlantic Alliance'.

A 'Platform on European Security Interests' was adopted in October 1987 by the Union's Ministerial Council at The Hague. The Platform recalled, *inter alia*, the member countries' commitment 'to build a European Union in accordance with the Single European Act' adopted within the European Community's framework.

The 1992 Maastricht Treaty establishing the EU expressly requests the Union 'to elaborate and implement decisions and actions' of the EU itself which have defence implications; a Declaration on Western European Union by its member countries is attached to the Treaty.

Structure

In order to ensure the achievement of the aims of the Union, and closer co-operation between themselves and with other European organizations, the member countries have established a Council which considers matters concerning the execution of the Treaty, its Protocols and their Annexes. The Council consists of the Foreign and Defence Ministers of member countries and meets twice a year in the capital or other town of the presiding country; the presidency, hitherto rotating annually, has been reduced to a six-month period from July 1994 to coincide with the periods of the EU presidency. The Permanent Council meets regularly at ambassadorial level, under the chairmanship of the Secretary-General, at the seat of the Secretariat-General. At the request of any member country, the Council is convened immediately in order to permit consultations with regard to situations which may constitute a threat to peace, in any area whatsoever, or a danger to economic stability. As a rule, decisions are taken unanimously only on questions for which no other voting procedure has been agreed. In the cases provided for in the relevant Protocols, the Council is to follow the prescribed voting procedures, which vary from unanimity to two-thirds or simple majority.

The Council is responsible for: formulating basic policies and issuing directives to the Secretary-General and the various agencies and commissions; ensuring the closest co-operation with NATO; and making an annual report on its activities, in particular concerning the control of armaments, to the Assembly.

The Assembly is composed of 115 representatives of the Union's member countries to the Parliamentary Assembly of the Council of Europe and meets twice a year, usually in Paris. France, Germany, Italy and the UK have 18 representatives each; Spain has 12; Belgium, Greece, The Netherlands and Portugal each have 7; Luxembourg has 3. The Assembly carries out the parliamentary functions arising from the application of the modified Brussels Treaty. Usually taking decisions by majority vote, it considers defence policy in Europe, besides other matters concerning member countries in common, and is empowered to address recommendations or transmit opinions to the Council, national parliaments, governments and international organizations. The Assembly, which officially recognized political parties, has set up a number of Permanent Committees. It has its own Secretariat and a separate budget.

The Secretariat of the Union is headed by a Secretary-General, assisted by a Deputy Secretary-General. Originally established in London, the Secretariat was transferred to Brussels in January 1993 to ensure close co-operation with the EU and NATO.

The WEU Institute for Security Studies was set up in July 1990 in Paris with the following tasks: to carry out studies for the Union's Council and the Parliamentary Assembly; to make the public aware of European security problems; and to organize meetings with institutes of member countries and of Central and Eastern Europe.

The UK, France, Germany and Italy, each country contributing the same amount, bear the largest part of the expenses of the budget of the Union.

Activities

The Union co-operates closely with other European international organizations in order to co-ordinate activities and avoid overlapping and duplication of efforts. At the 1987 Hague meeting, the Council had adopted the 'Platform on European Security Interests' with a view to developing a 'more cohesive European defence identity', while recognizing at the same time that 'the substantial presence of US conventional and nuclear forces plays an irreplaceable part in the defence of Europe'. The dramatic changes occurring in Eastern Europe and the USSR in 1989 and 1990 were discussed extensively within the framework of the Union, which also played a role in co-ordinating the military response of Western European countries to Iraq's occupation of Kuwait in August 1990. The concept began to emerge of a stronger operational Union, eventually equipped to take immediate action in periods of crisis. The Union's Declarations of Maastricht in December 1991 and Petersberg in June 1992 laid the foundations for a truly operational role of the organization in crisis management, peacekeeping, peace enforcement, and humanitarian as well as search and rescue missions. Member countries of the Union began operations in the Adriatic and the Danube in July 1992, in co-ordination with NATO, to monitor compliance with the UN embargo against the 'Federal Republic of Yugoslavia' (Serbia and Montenegro); a single command and control system was subsequently agreed upon with NATO. The Union also sent police officers to Mostar to supplement the EU Joint Action. The partnership with Central and Eastern European countries established in May 1994 under the Kirchberg Declaration has opened new avenues for co-operation in peace-keeping and humanitarian operations.

The Lisbon Ministerial Council of May 1995 adopted important decisions to enhance the Union's operational mechanism, including the creation of a new Politico-Military Group assisting the Council, a Situation Centre, an Intelligence Section, and strengthening the Secretariat. The Union welcomed in 1995 the creation decided by France, Italy, Portugal and Spain of a land force (EUROFOR) to ensure rapid reaction in the Southern region and of a maritime force (EURO-MARFOR); both forces, like other European multinational forces, will be available to the Union as well as to NATO. The 1996–7 Intergovernmental Conference for the revision of the Maastricht Treaty is expected to provide a much-needed clarification on the future tasks and role of the Union within the framework of the European integration process.

Secretary-General: José Cutileiro
Secretariat-General: 4 rue de la Régence, 1000 Brussels, Belgium (Telephone: +32 2 500 4411; fax: +32 2 511 3270)
WEU Assembly: 43 avenue du Président Wilson, 75775 Paris Cedex 16, France (Telephone: +33 1 5367 2200; fax: +33 1 4720 4543)
Publications: *Annual Report of the Council*; *Assembly of WEU: Texts Adopted and Brief Account of the Session* (two a year)

Western Indian Ocean Tuna Organization (WIOTO)

Established by a Convention signed in 1991 and entered into force in 1994, the Organization has at present four members (Comoros, India, Mauritius and the Seychelles) but is expected to include other independent countries bordering the Western Indian Ocean. Its objectives are the harmonization of policies with respect to fisheries, the development of fisheries surveillance and enforcement, and the access to exclusive economic zones of members.

Headquarters (temporary):   Seychelles Fishing Authority, P.O. Box 449, Fishing Port, Mahé, Seychelles (Telephone: +248 224597; fax: +248 224508)

World Food Programme (WFP)

The Programme, sponsored jointly by the UN and the *Food and Agriculture Organization of the UN (FAO), seeks to stimulate socioeconomic development through aid in the form of food, and to provide emergency relief.

Origin and development
The Programme became operational in January 1963, after parallel resolutions adopted by the UN General Assembly and the FAO Conference in late 1961.

The Programme is among the most important UN assistance sources in terms of actual transfer of resources and is now the largest source of

grant assistance within the UN system to sub-Saharan Africa; the largest provider of grant assistance to environmental protection and improvement; and the largest purchaser of food and services in developing countries. It has also become the main channel for and co-ordinator of food aid for refugees. More than a quarter of the world's food aid is handled by the Programme. Member countries of the UN and the FAO make voluntary contributions to the Programme of commodities, cash, and services (particularly shipping).

The General Regulations of the Programme are being amended in the light of the resolutions adopted by the UN and the FAO in 1992 and 1993.

Objectives
The food is used for economic and social development projects in developing countries, and for emergency relief. Food may also be used in low-income countries as a partial substitute for cash wages paid to workers in labour-intensive projects of many kinds (particularly in the rural economy), or may be provided to families resettled for development purposes until first crops are harvested on the new land. The Programme supports institutional feeding schemes where the main emphasis is on enabling the beneficiaries to have an adequate and balanced diet, via operations such as school feeding programmes and supplementary feeding of vulnerable groups, including young mothers and children. Help is also extended to meet emergency food needs created by earthquakes, typhoons, floods and other natural disasters.

Structure
The Committee on Food Aid Policies and Programmes (CFA), which meets twice a year, is the governing body of the Programme. The Committee is composed of 42 members, half elected by the UN Economic and Social Council and half by the FAO Council, for a renewable three-year term; 27 members are from developing countries and 15 from more economically developed countries. The Committee is responsible for the overall policy direction of the Programme, including food aid policy, administration, operations, funds and finances. It also acts as the international body designated to discuss food aid

issues and concerns, including bilateral and non-governmental food aid programmes.

Activities

The projects to which the Programme commits food aid fall into two broad categories: human resource development for improving the people's nutritional, physical and educational well-being; and agricultural and rural development projects for creating jobs and increasing food production.

Priority is given to low-income, food-deficit countries and to highly vulnerable groups such as pregnant women and children. Some projects are especially intended to alleviate the consequences of structural adjustment programmes undertaken by many developing countries, which frequently involve substantial reductions in public expenditure and subsidies for basic foods. Because of the escalation in the number, scale and duration of emergencies throughout the world, particularly those caused by armed conflict, the Programme allocates about three-quarters of its resources to emergency relief assistance, the remainder going to development projects intended to free people from the need for food aid itself.

The Programme enjoys a wide base of support, and substantial amounts of food are being supplied by the world's biggest exporters and cash resources provided by other high-income countries. These donors include, among others, the USA, the *European Union (EU) and its member countries, Canada, the Scandinavian countries, Australia and Japan. Although the most frequently donated commodities are grains, the Programme also handles substantial quantities of milk powder and high-protein food blends, and smaller quantities of other products such as cooking oil, salt and sugar. It is thus possible to provide beneficiaries with balanced diets and to cater for differing food habits. Usually, food aid is combined with non-food contributions to the recipient country.

The Programme co-operates closely with other UN bodies, private agencies, and governments making bilateral contributions. Non-governmental organizations (NGOs) play an increasingly large role in the delivery and monitoring of food aid and the provision of non-food items. The Programme has taken a leading role in co-ordinating food aid deliveries and/or distribution to recipients in several large-scale relief operations, from Africa and Asia to the former Yugoslavia.

Since the 1960s, the Programme has invested more than $14 billion in its fight against hunger, in promoting economic and social development, and in delivering relief assistance in emergencies. The Programme also administers the International Emergency Food Reserve (IEFR) – established by the UN General Assembly with a target of 500 000 tonnes of cereals – to face emergency needs around the world.

The first global International Conference on Nutrition (ICN), jointly organized by FAO and the *World Health Organization (WHO) in December 1992 in Rome, unanimously adopted a World Declaration on Nutrition, stressing the 'determination to eliminate hunger and to reduce all forms of malnutrition' and recognizing that 'globally there is enough food for all and that inequitable access is the main problem'. The ICN also adopted a Plan of Action for Nutrition containing several references to food aid and calling on the international community to play an important role by providing timely and well-targeted food aid in food-for-work and rehabilitation programmes.

Executive Director: Catherine Bertini
Headquarters: Via Cristoforo Colombo 426, 00145 Rome, Italy (Telephone: +39 6 522821; fax: +39 6 512 7400, 513 3537)
Internet address: http://www.unicc.org/wfp
Publications: *WFP Journal* (quarterly); *World Food Programme Food Aid Review* (annual)

World Health Organization (WHO)

The basic aim of the Organization is the attainment by all peoples of the highest possible level of health.

Origin and development

The International Office of Public Health (Office international de l'hygiène publique – OIHP) was established in Paris in 1903 and can be regarded as a predecessor of the present Organization. Another specialized health body was set up subsequently within the framework of the League of Nations, and based in Geneva. In the Western hemisphere, an International Sanitary Bureau had been established in Washington DC, in 1902; the original name was changed to Pan American Sanitary Bureau in 1923, to Pan American Sanitary

Organization in 1947, and eventually to Pan American Health Organization (PAHO) in 1958.

The need for the early establishment of a single international body dealing with health issues had been stressed in a declaration adopted at the UN San Francisco Conference in 1945. An International Health Conference was convened by the UN in 1946 in New York, to consider the creation of a global institution co-ordinating and directing health activities; it resulted in the adoption, in July 1946, of the Constitution of the present Organization, which came into force in April 1948, when the prescribed number of ratifications had been reached. Amendments to the Constitution have been introduced on a number of occasions. The Organization concluded a relationship agreement with the UN in July 1948. Another agreement was concluded with the then Pan American Sanitary Organization, which began to serve as a regional office for the American continent. The present membership of the Organization includes about 190 countries.

Members of the UN may accede to the Organization, in accordance with the provisions of the Constitution. Any sovereign country not a member of the UN may be admitted to the Organization if the relevant request is approved by a simple majority vote of the World Health Assembly.

Territories, or groups of territories, not responsible for the conduct of their international relations may be granted associate membership by the World Health Assembly upon application made on their behalf by the full member having responsibility for their international relations. The World Health Assembly may suspend from the rights and privileges of membership any country if it fails to meet its financial obligations to the Organization or in any other exceptional circumstances.

Objectives

The Organization acts as the central authority on international health work and establishes and maintains effective collaboration with international agencies and bodies, national health administrations, and professional groups. It assists governments in strengthening health services; stimulating and advancing work to eradicate epidemic, endemic and other diseases; promoting maternal and child health, mental health, medical research and the prevention of accidental injuries; improving standards of teaching and training in the health, medical and related professions; and promoting the improvement of nutrition, housing, sanitation, recreation, economic or working conditions and other aspects of environmental hygiene. The Organization is also empowered to propose conventions, agreements and regulations and to make recommendations about international health matters; to revise the international nomenclatures of diseases, causes of death and public health practices; and to establish and promote international standards concerning food, biological, pharmaceutical and similar products.

Structure

The work of the Organization is carried out by three principal organs: the World Health Assembly, the Executive Board, and the Secretariat. The Assembly is composed of delegates of all member countries, chosen from among people most qualified by their technical competence and preferably representing national health administrations. It meets in regular annual sessions and in such special sessions as may be necessary. Its main functions are to determine basic policies and guidelines; to elect the members entitled to designate a person to serve on the Executive Board; to appoint the Director-General; to review and approve reports and activities of the Executive Board and the Director-General, and to issue instructions to them; to supervise financial policies and to approve the budget; and to promote and conduct research in the field of health. The Assembly may adopt, with respect to any matter within the competence of the Organization and by a two-thirds majority, conventions or agreements which will come into force for each member accepting them, in accordance with its constitutional processes. Members which do not accept a convention or an agreement within the established time limit must state the reasons for non-acceptance. The Assembly has the authority to adopt regulations concerning sanitary and quarantine requirements and other procedures designed to prevent the international spread of disease; nomenclatures of diseases, causes of death and public health practices; standards covering diagnostic procedures for international use; standards with respect to the safety, purity and potency of biological, pharmaceutical and similar products moving in international commerce; and advertising and labelling of these same products. Decisions of the Assembly on important questions such as the adoption of conventions or agreements, the approval of co-operation agreements with other intergovernmental organizations and amendments to the Constitution are made by a two-thirds majority of the members present and voting; a simple majority suffices with respect to other questions.

The Executive Board meets at least twice a year and is composed of 32 health experts designated for a three-year period by, but not representing, as many member countries elected by the World Health Assembly. The Executive Board is empowered to give effect to the decisions and policies of the Assembly, and to submit to it advice or proposals and a general programme of work for a specific period. It is also empowered to take emergency measures in case of epidemics or disasters.

The Secretariat consists of technical and administrative staff, headed by a Director-General assisted by a Deputy Director-General and several Assistant Directors-General. Health activities are carried out through six regional organizations, which have been established for: Africa (Brazzaville); the Americas (Washington DC); Eastern Mediterranean (Alexandria, Egypt); Europe (Copenhagen); South-East Asia (New Delhi); and the Western Pacific (Manila). Each regional organization consists of a regional committee composed of the full and associate members in the area concerned, and a regional office staffed by experts in various fields of health.

The Director-General is responsible for preparing and submitting to the Executive Board the annual budget estimates of the Organization. The Executive Board considers and submits these estimates to the Assembly, together with its recommendations. Expenses are apportioned among members in accordance with a scale fixed by the Assembly. An additional fund for specific projects is provided by voluntary contributions from members and other sources. Other funds are received from UN bodies for particular projects and programmes.

Activities

The Organization has established effective relations and co-operates closely with UN bodies – among them are the *UN Development Programme (UNDP), the *UN Children's Fund (UNICEF) and the *UN Population Fund (UNFPA) – and with other specialized agencies such as the *International Labour Organization (ILO), the *Food and Agriculture Organization of the UN (FAO), the *UN Educational, Scientific and Cultural Organization (UNESCO), and the *International Atomic Energy Agency (IAEA). The governing bodies of the Organization and of FAO established in 1962 the FAO/WHO Codex Alimentarius Commission to protect the health of consumers, and to ensure fair practices in the food trade by guiding the preparation and revision of international food standards and by promoting the co-ordination of all the relevant work undertaken by international organizations. Over 150 countries currently participate in the Commission.

Suitable arrangements for consultation and co-operation have also been made by the Organization with non-governmental international institutions and, subject to the consent of the governments concerned, with national bodies, governmental and non-governmental.

Over five decades, the Organization's work has been directed towards a variety of fields such as disease control, environmental health, family health, mental health, training of health workers, strengthening of national health systems, formulation of health regulations for international travel, establishment of drug policies, promotion of biomedical research, and collection and dissemination of statistical data and analyses. All activities have been reoriented to accord with the Global Strategy adopted by the World Health Assembly in May 1981 – 'Health for all by the year 2000' – that is, the attainment by all citizens of the world of a level of health that will enable them to lead a socially and economically productive life. Water supply and sanitation needs of around 100 countries have been assessed in connection with the International Drinking Water Supply and Sanitation Decade (1981–90), which was launched by the UN. A Priority Programme for the Control of Diarrhoeal Diseases has been under way since 1979. The Global Programme on AIDS (Acquired Immunodeficiency Syndrome) was started in 1987; the aims of the Global Programme are to prevent transmission of the human immunodeficiency virus (HIV), to care for HIV-infected people, and to unify national and international efforts against AIDS. The Global Commission on AIDS, made up of biomedical and social scientists and other experts, began its activities in 1989. The Tobacco or Health Programme aims to reduce the use of tobacco, educating tobacco-users and preventing young people from adopting the habit.

The Expanded Programme on Immunization (EPI), launched in 1974, has provided developing countries with assistance against six childhood diseases – diphtheria, measles, pertussis, poliomyelitis, tetanus and tuberculosis. These diseases constitute a major cause of death and disability in the developing countries. To complement the EPI, a new vaccine development programme was launched in 1984. Six widespread diseases of the tropics – filariasis, leishmaniasis, leprosy, malaria, schistosomiasis and trypanosomiasis – are targets of a Special Programme on research and training.

One of the Organization's major achievements has been the eradication of smallpox, following a massive international campaign of vaccination and surveillance. In May 1980 the World Health Assembly recommended that vaccination against smallpox be discontinued in every country. In 1988 the Assembly declared its commitment to eradicating poliomyelitis by the year 2000; similar commitments were adopted in 1990 with regard to iodine deficiency disorders, and in 1991 with regard to leprosy. Intensive efforts are being undertaken against the recrudescence of malaria in many parts of the world.

With regard to non-communicable diseases, intensified research is being carried out with regard to cardiovascular diseases and cancer.

Under an Action Programme on Essential Drugs and Vaccines, developing countries receive technical assistance in selection, quality control, and production of effective and safe drugs and vaccines essential to their needs. The Organization maintains and regularly revises a Model List of Essential Drugs. In order to survey and combat the global increase in drug abuse, through the reduction of the demand for drugs and the control of the supply of psychoactive substances, the Organization has launched a Programme on Substance Abuse in 1990. Humanitarian health assistance has been provided since July 1992 in the former Yugoslavia and to other war-afflicted areas throughout the world, such as Rwanda.

Director-General: Dr Hiroshi Nakajima
Headquarters: 20 Avenue Appia, 1211 Geneva 27, Switzerland (Telephone: +41 22 791 2111; fax: +41 22 791 0746)
Internet address: http://www.who.ch/
Publications: *World Health Forum. An International Journal of Health Development* (quarterly); *WHO Chronicle* (every two months); *Bulletin of the WHO* (every two months); *International Digest of Health Legislation* (quarterly); *World Health Statistics* (annual)
Reference: F. W. Hoole, *Politics and Budgeting in the WHO* (Bloomington, Ind., 1976)

World Intellectual Property Organization (WIPO)

The Organization promotes the protection of intellectual property throughout the world through co-operation among member countries and in collaboration with any other international institution, and seeks to centralize the administration of the various Unions established by multilateral treaties and dealing with legal and technical aspects of intellectual property.

Origin and development

The Organization was established by a Convention signed in Stockholm in 1967 and entered into force in April 1970. It was intended to succeed the United International Bureau for the Protection of Intellectual Property (Bureau international réuni pour la protection de la propriété intellectuelle – BIRPI), which had been set up in 1893 and represented the combined secretariats of the Paris Union (for the protection of industrial property) and the Berne Union (for the protection of literary and artistic works). Because some countries participating in BIRPI have yet to accede formally to the new Organization, BIRPI is still a legal entity. A relationship agreement was concluded by the Organization with the UN and it became a specialized agency in December 1974. The Organization's present membership includes around 165 countries. About 130 countries currently participate in the Paris Union and about 110 in the Berne Union.

Accession to the Organization is open to any sovereign country which is a member of at least one of the Unions, and to other countries that participate in the organizations of the UN system, are party to the Statute of the International Court of Justice, or are invited to join by the Organization itself through its General Assembly. Membership of the Unions is open to any sovereign country.

The expression 'intellectual property' means the legal rights resulting from intellectual activity in industrial, scientific, literary or artistic fields. Intellectual property comprises two main branches: industrial property (inventions in all fields of human endeavour, scientific discoveries, industrial designs, trademarks, service marks, and commercial names and designations); and copyright and neighbouring rights (literary, musical and artistic works, performances by artists, films, records and broadcasts).

Objectives

The overall objective of the Organization is to maintain and increase respect for intellectual property throughout the world, in order to favour industrial and cultural development by stimulating creative activity and facilitating the dissemination of literary and artistic works and the transfer of technology, especially to and among developing countries. To promote the protection of intellectual property, the Organization encourages the conclusion of new international treaties and the harmonization of national legislations. It gives legal and technical assistance to developing countries to promote their industrialization through the modernization of their industrial property and copyright systems, prepares model laws, provides traineeships, organizes seminars, finances assistance, and encourages the flow of scientific and technical documentation. It also performs the administrative tasks of several international treaties dealing with various subjects of intellectual property, assembles and disseminates information concerning the protection of intellectual property, conducts and promotes studies and publishes their results, and maintains services for international registration or other administrative co-operation among member countries.

Structure

The Organization has a Conference, a General Assembly, a Co-ordination Committee and a secretariat which is called the International Bureau. The Conference, composed of all member countries, establishes the basic policies and the bien-

nial programme of legal–technical assistance, and approves the biennial budget of the Organization. The General Assembly, composed of those member countries which are also members of the Paris or Berne Unions, appoints and gives instructions to the Director-General, reviews and approves his reports, and adopts the biennial budget of expenses common to the Unions. Separate Assemblies and Conferences of Representatives continue to be held by the Paris and Berne Unions pending the formal accession to membership in the Organization of all the countries belonging to BIRPI. The Paris and Berne Unions elect Executive Committees from among their members, and the joint membership of these Committees constitutes the Co-ordination Committee of the Organization.

The International Bureau is headed by a Director-General. It prepares the meetings of the various bodies of the Organization and the Unions, mainly through the provision of reports and working documents, carries out projects for the promotion of international co-operation in the field of intellectual property, and acts as the depository of most of the treaties administered by the Organization. The Organization also administers the WIPO Arbitration Centre for the Resolution of Intellectual Property Disputes between Private Parties, which became operational in late 1994.

Activities

The Organization's activities are basically of two sorts: substantive or programme activities, and administrative activities concerned with the international registration of industrial property rights. In both industrial property and copyright, the role of the Organization consists mainly in providing advice and training, as well as documents and equipment.

The Permanent Committee on Patent Information fosters co-operation between national and regional industrial property offices in all matters concerning patent information. Administrative or registration activities are those required for the receiving and processing of international applications under the Patent Co-operation Treaty (PCT) of June 1970, or for the international registration of trademarks, appellations of origin, or deposit of industrial designs. The Organization performs the administrative functions conferred by the Paris Convention for the Protection of Industrial Property, signed in 1883; by various special agreements concluded within the framework of the Paris Convention; by the Berne Convention for the Protection of Literary and Artistic Works, signed in 1886; and by other conventions concerning the protection of literary and artistic property. Conventions and agreements are kept under review and submitted to revision with a view, *inter alia*, to meeting the needs of developing countries. Since the early 1990s, the Organization has been active in providing assistance to countries in transition to a market economy and wishing to upgrade their intellectual property systems. Co-operation links have been established with the newly-created *World Trade Organization (WTO).

Director-General: Dr Arpad Bogsch
Headquarters: 34 Chemin des Colombettes, 1211 Geneva 20, Switzerland (Telephone: +41 22 730 9111; fax: +41 22 733 5428)
Publications: *WIPO Newsletter*; *PCT Gazette* (weekly); *Industrial Property* (monthly); *Copyright* (monthly); *International Designs Bulletin* (monthly)

World Meteorological Organization (WMO)

The Organization co-ordinates, standardizes and improves world meteorological activities, and encourages an efficient and rapid exchange of weather information between members.

Origin and development
An International Meteorological Organization was set up in 1873 at the International Meteorological Meeting held in Utrecht, The Netherlands, and the relevant statutes were subsequently revised several times. The 12th Conference of Directors of the International Meteorological Organization convened at Washington DC, in September 1947, drew up a Convention creating the World Meteorological Organization to which activities, resources and obligations of the original Organization had to be transferred. The Convention, opened for signature in October 1947, came into effect in March 1950. The new Organization was formally established in March 1951, when the first session of its Congress was convened in Paris. A number

of amendments to the text of the Convention have been introduced over the years. A relationship agreement with the UN was concluded by the Organization and came into force in December 1951. The present membership of the Organization includes around 180 countries.

Any member of the UN with a meteorological service may accede to the Organization, in conformity with current provisions. Sovereign countries with a meteorological service and not belonging to the UN may be admitted to the Organization if their request for membership is approved by two-thirds of the member countries. Any territory or group of territories maintaining its own meteorological service but not responsible for the conduct of its international relations may also be admitted to the Organization, provided that the relevant request is presented by the member responsible for international relations and secures the approval of two-thirds of the member countries. Any member may withdraw from the Organization on 12 months' written notice given to the Secretary-General. Provision is made for the suspension from the exercise of the rights and privileges of membership of any country failing to meet its financial obligations or otherwise violating the Convention.

Objectives
The purposes of the Organization are: (a) to facilitate world-wide co-operation in establishing networks of stations to provide meteorological, hydrological or other geophysical observations related to meteorology, and to promote the establishment and maintenance of centres charged with the provision of meteorological and related services; (b) to promote the establishment and maintenance of systems for the rapid exchange of weather information; (c) to promote standardization of meteorological observations and to ensure the uniform publication of observations and statistics; (d) to further the application of meteorology to aviation, shipping, water problems, agriculture and other activities; (e) to promote activities in operational hydrology and to foster co-operation between meteorological and hydrological services; and (f) to encourage research and training in meteorology and to assist in co-ordinating the international aspects of such activities.

The Organization arranges for the international exchange of weather reports, and assists in establishing meteorological services and improving or increasing the application of meteorology and hydrology to economic development projects.

Structure

The structure of the Organization comprises the World Meteorological Congress, the Executive Council, Regional Meteorological Associations, Technical Commissions, and the Secretariat. The World Meteorological Congress, in which all members are represented by delegations headed by the directors of national meteorological services, is the supreme organ and meets for ordinary sessions at least once every four years. The Congress determines general policies; makes recommendations to members on any matter within the purposes of the Organization; considers the reports and activities of the Executive Council; establishes Regional Associations and Technical Commissions and co-ordinates their activities; and elects members of the Executive Council. Each member of the Congress has one vote. However, only members that are sovereign countries are entitled to vote or to take decisions on a number of sensitive subjects such as amendments to the Convention, requests for membership, relations with the UN and other intergovernmental institutions, and elections of individuals to serve in the Organization. Decisions are taken by a two-thirds majority of the votes cast, with the exception of elections of individuals where a simple majority suffices. The 36-member Executive Council consists of 26 directors of national meteorological or hydrological services acting in an individual capacity, plus the president and the three vice-presidents of the Organization and the six presidents of the Regional Associations. It meets at least once a year to supervise the implementation of Congress resolutions and regulations; to initiate studies and make recommendations on matters requiring international action; and to provide members with technical information, advice and assistance. Decisions of the Executive Council are taken by a two-thirds majority of the votes cast.

The maximum expenditure which may be incurred by the Organization is determined by the Congress on the basis of estimates submitted by the Secretary-General, after prior examination by, and with the recommendation of, the Executive Council. Annual expenditures, within the limitations fixed by the Congress, are approved by the Executive Council upon the delegation of the Congress. Expenditures are apportioned among members on the basis of a scale of assessment determined by the Congress.

Regional Meteorological Associations – which are responsible for Africa, North and Central America, South America, Asia, Europe, and the South West Pacific – meet at least once every four years to promote the execution of the resolutions of Congress and the Executive Council within the region of their competence, to co-ordinate meteorological and associated activities, and to consider matters referred to them by the Executive Council.

Technical Commissions are composed of experts meeting at least once every four years to study the applications of meteorology, and problems and developments in specialized fields. At present there are eight Commissions, responsible for Aeronautical Meteorology; Agricultural Meteorology; Atmospheric Sciences; Basic Systems; Climatology; Hydrology; Instruments and Methods of Observation; and Marine Meteorology. The Secretariat is headed by the Secretary-General, appointed by the Congress, and performs administrative functions, organizes meetings of the various bodies, acts as a link between the meteorological and hydrometeorological services of the world, and provides information for the general public.

Activities

Working arrangements have been concluded by the Organization with the *International Atomic Energy Agency (IAEA) and with many UN specialized agencies such as the *World Health Organization (WHO), the *Food and Agriculture Organization of the UN (FAO), the *International Fund for Agricultural Development (IFAD), the *International Civil Aviation Organization (ICAO), the *International Maritime Organization (IMO) and the *UN Educational, Scientific and Cultural Organization (UNESCO). Technical assistance is extended to developing countries under the *UN Development Programme (UNDP) and other specific programmes; environmental prediction research is conducted in collaboration with the *UN Environment Programme (UNEP).

The activities of the Organization are carried out through eight major programmes. The World Weather Programme deserves special consideration, since it is the Organization's basic programme. It has three major components: the Global Data Processing System; the Global Observation System; and the Global Telecommunications System. Based on four polar-orbiting and five geostationary meteorological satellites, about 10 000 land observation and 7000 ship stations, and 300 moored and drifting buoys carrying automatic weather stations, the World Weather Programme provides all members with adequate information to enable them to operate efficient meteorological services and to make local and specialized forecasts. Among special activities of the Programme are: Data Management; System Support, including the Operational Information Service; the Tropical Cyclone Programme; and the WMO Antarctic Activities.

The World Climate Programme addresses the full range of climate and climate change issues, including research into the economic and social consequences of climate and climate change. The Programme also aims to detect and warn governments and the public of possible future variations and changes in climate, either natural or man-made which may affect critical human activities significantly. The Programme supports the work of the Intergovernmental Panel on Climate Change, the Global Climate Observing System, the implementation of the Framework Convention on Climate Change (coming into effect in March 1994), and the negotiations on the Convention on Desertification and Drought.

The World Climate Research Programme – undertaken by the Organization jointly with the International Oceanographic Commission and the International Council of Scientific Unions – is aimed at developing a better understanding of climate, and predictions of global and regional climate changes.

The Atmospheric Research and Environment Programme co-ordinates and promotes research on the structure and composition of the atmosphere, on the physics and chemistry of clouds, and on tropical meteorology and weather forecasting. Disaster mitigation activities will benefit, particularly from advanced research in short- medium- and long-range predictions and from improved quality of weather forecasts.

The Applications of Meteorology Programme assists members in the application of meteorology and climatology to social and economic development, protection of life and property, and weather-sensitive industries and activities. Applications concern agricultural meteorology, aeronautical meteorology (safety of air transport), marine meteorology and associated oceanographic activities, and public weather services.

The Hydrology and Water Resources Programme concentrates on promoting world-wide co-operation in the evaluation of water resources and the development of hydrological networks and services, including data collection and processing, hydrogeological forecasting and warnings for flood protection, and the supply of meteorological and hydrological data for design purposes.

The Education and Training Programme supports the Organization's scientific and technical programmes and provides assistance for the development of personnel in the national Meteorological and Hydrological Services through special courses, seminars and training materials.

The Technical Co-operation Programme is designed to bridge the gap between developed and developing countries by the systematic transfer of meteorological and hydrological knowledge, technology and methodology.

Secretary-General: Professor G. O. P. Obasi
Headquarters: 41 Avenue Giuseppe Motta, 1211 Geneva 20, Switzerland (Telephone: +41 22 730 8111; fax: +41 22 734 2326)
Publications: *Annual Report*; *WMO Bulletin* (quarterly); technical manuals, guides and reports

World Tourism Organization (WTO)

The Organization promotes travel and tourism, and deals with all aspects of tourism on a worldwide basis.

Origin and development

The Organization was established in 1975 to facilitate and improve travel between and within member countries, and with a view to contributing to economic development, international understanding, peace and prosperity, and universal respect for – and observance of – human rights and fundamental freedoms.

The non-governmental predecessor of the Organization was set up in 1925 as the International Congress of Official Tourist Traffic Associations, renamed in 1934 the International Union of Official Tourist Propaganda Organizations (IUOTPO), and renamed again in 1947 the International Union of Official Travel Organizations (IUOTO). The Statutes of the new intergovernmental Organization were adopted in 1970 in Mexico City and entered into force in 1975.

In 1969, the UN General Assembly decided that an agreement should be concluded with the future World Tourism Organization; in 1977 the General Assembly adopted an agreement on co-operation between the UN and the Organization.

The Organization includes over 120 countries as full members, a number of territories not fully responsible for their external relations as associate members, and, as affiliate members, about 300 intergovernmental and non-governmental bodies, and commercial and non-commercial associations, involved in tourism.

Objectives

The objectives of the Organization, according to the indications of the UN General Assembly, are the following: (a) to emphasize the social and cultural function of tourism in society, its role in international trade and its contribution to bringing peoples closer together and safeguarding world peace; (b) to encourage the adoption of measures to facilitate travel as well as for the protection of tourists; (c) to provide for a technical co-operation machinery to assist all countries, especially developing countries, in the formulation of tourism policies, plans and programmes; (d) to develop human resources in the sector through the preparation of teaching and training programmes; and (e) to promote research and exchange of information on all aspects of international and domestic tourism, including statistical data, legislation and regulations.

Structure

The General Assembly, meeting every two years, is the supreme organ of the Organization; it has established six Regional Commissions: Africa; the Americas; Europe; Middle East; East Asia and the Pacific; and South Asia. The Executive Council, meeting at least twice a year, has one member elected on the basis of equitable geographical representation for every five full members of the Organization. One associate member, selected by the associate members themselves, and a representative of the Committee of Affiliate Members participate in the work of the Council without voting rights. Spain, being the Organization's host country, sits on the Council as an ex officio member. A number of subsidiary organs have been established by the Council: the Technical Committee for Programme and Co-ordination (TCPC); the Committee on Budget and Finance (CBF); the Environment Committee; the Committee on Statistics; and the Committee on Quality of Tourism Services.

The Committee of Affiliate Members carries out its own programmes of activity within the framework of the Organization. The Secretariat performs technical and administrative functions under the responsibility of a Secretary-General.

Activities

The Organization has developed close working relationships with several agencies of the UN and acts as an executing agency of the *UN Development Programme (UNDP). The Organization's activities focus on a number of fields such as international technical co-operation/co-operation for development; education and training; quality of tourism services; environment and planning; statistics and market research.

Secretary-General: Antonio Enriquez Savignac
Headquarters: Calle Capitán Haya 42, 28020 Madrid, Spain (Telephone: +34 1 571 0628; fax: +34 1 571 3733)

World Trade Organization (WTO)

The Organization has replaced the General Agreement on Tariffs and Trade (GATT) as the legal and institutional entity overseeing the multilateral trading system.

Origin and development

The Organization was established in January 1995 to administer, through different councils and committees, some 30 agreements covering a wide variety of matters – from agriculture to textiles, and from services to government procurement, to intellectual property – contained in the

Final Act of the Uruguay Round (UR) negotiations signed in Marrakesh, Morocco, in April 1994; attached to these agreements are a number of additional ministerial declarations and decisions related to further obligations and commitments for member countries. As the embodiment of the UR results, the Organization has succeeded GATT with stronger powers and procedures, and extended liberalization to agriculture, textiles, intellectual property rights and services.

For the most part, all members of the Organization subscribe to all multilateral agreements (the Single Undertaking); however, four agreements, originally negotiated in the Tokyo Round of multilateral trade negotiations and known as 'plurilateral agreements', have a limited number of signatories and are binding only on those countries which accept them. These agreements, whose operation is also monitored by the Organization, deal with trade in civil aircraft, government procurement, dairy products, and bovine meat, respectively.

Since GATT was formally dissolved only at the end of 1995, during that year the two bodies co-existed. The Agreement establishing the WTO envisaged a two-year period – until December 1996 – for the 128 contracting parties to GATT to join the new Organization as original members. Any state or customs territory having full autonomy in the conduct of its trade policies may accede to the Organization. Current membership of the Organization accounts for well over 90 per cent of world trade; developing countries and countries in the process of 'transition' to market-based economies are expected to play an increasingly important role. The *European Union (EU) participates in its own right, as is the case for each of its 15 member countries. China, Taiwan, Russia, Ukraine and Vietnam are among the countries preparing to join as full members during the late 1990s. Any member may withdraw from the WTO Agreement and the multilateral trade agreements by sending a written notice of denunciation to the Director-General; withdrawal from a 'plurilateral agreement' takes place according to the rules contained in that agreement.

The GATT was signed in October 1947 in Geneva by the representatives of 23 countries, to record the concessions granted in a tariff conference, pending the formal acceptance of a comprehensive code governing trade policies and the establishment of the International Trade Organization (ITO), which would have been a specialized agency of the UN. However, the ratification of the final version of the ITO Charter, drawn up in March 1948 and generally known as the Havana Charter, proved impossible. The GATT entered into force in January 1948, and thus assumed the commercial policy role originally assigned to the ITO and became the major international agency dealing with trade problems. Although basically unequipped to fulfil the function of an international organization in the proper sense, the GATT remained for nearly half a century, and until the establishment of the WTO, the only multilateral instrument governing international trade, pragmatically adapting its rules and procedures to ever-evolving circumstances. Between 1947 and 1993, eight major multilateral negotiations were completed under the auspices of the GATT, reducing tariffs from an industrial-country average of 40 per cent in 1947 to less than 5 per cent in the mid-1990s.

It should be noted that the GATT was applied provisionally by all contracting parties, which were bound to follow most of its rules only to an extent not inconsistent with their existing domestic legislation (the 'grandfather clause'). The original text of the General Agreement was amended and supplemented several times after 1947. Major amendments intended to improve the trading conditions for developing countries included the addition of Part IV – stating, inter alia, that developed countries were not to expect reciprocity for concessions made to developing countries in negotiations – and the relaxation of the most-favoured-nation (MFN) clause to accommodate the Generalized System of Preferences (GSP) and to allow an exchange of preferential tariff reductions among developing countries.

The amended and updated version of GATT, incorporating the substantive and institutional changes negotiated in the UR, lives on in the WTO and is known as 'GATT 1994', to distinguish it from the old 'GATT 1947'. As an integral part of the WTO Agreement, it continues to provide the fundamental rules governing international trade in goods. Therefore, the newly-created Organization carries on, in a much stronger form, the code of conduct established by GATT, having as its cornerstone the MFN clause, immediately and unconditionally ensuring non-discrimination and equality of treatment with respect to customs duties, charges of any kind and all rules and formalities in connection with importation and exportation of goods. Equality of treatment is also ensured between imported and domestically-produced goods in internal markets. Tariffs are the only acceptable means for protection, with the exclusion in principle of quotas and import licensing; where tariffs have been bound at levels negotiated among members, no increase is allowed unless compensation is offered by the importing country.

Objectives

The Final Act of the UR redrafted the rules embodied in the original GATT and in the so-called Tokyo Round codes in the following areas: technical barriers to trade; trade-related aspects of investment measures (TRIMS); implementation of Art. VI of the GATT (anti-dumping); implementation of Art. VII of the GATT (customs valuation); pre-shipment inspection; rules of origin; import licensing procedures; import subsidies and countervailing measures; and safeguards. Also included in the Final Act are: the General Agreement on Trade in Services (GATS), representing the first set of multilaterally-agreed and legally enforceable provisions ever negotiated to cover international trade in services; and the Agreement on Trade-Related Aspects of Intellectual Property Rights (TRIPS), including trade in counterfeit goods.

Besides the administration and implementation of the multilateral and 'plurilateral agreements' of the Final Act, the Organization acts as a forum for multilateral trade negotiations among its member countries, seeks to resolve trade disputes, oversees national trade policies, and co-operates with other international organizations involved in global economic policy-making.

Structure

Since it is an international institution in its own right, the Organization, unlike GATT, has its proper structure. The Ministerial Conference, consisting of representatives of all members, meeting at least once every two years, is the highest decision-making body, which can take decisions on all matters under any of the multilateral trade agreements. The day-to-day work of the Organization is carried out principally by the General Council, composed of representatives of all members and meeting as required. Besides conducting its regular work on behalf of the Ministerial Conference, the General Council also convenes in two particular forms – as the Dispute Settlement Body (DSB), to oversee the dispute settlement procedures, and as the Trade Policy Review Body (TPRB), to conduct regular reviews of the trade policies of individual members.

Decisions are generally taken not by voting but by consensus; should a consensus prove unrealizable, decisions are taken by a majority of the votes cast, each country having one vote. Decisions to admit a new member require a two-thirds majority in the Ministerial Conference; the same majority is required to amend provisions of the multilateral agreements, which, however, bind only the countries accepting them. A majority of three-quarters is necessary to adopt an interpretation of any of the multilateral trade agreements or to grant a waiver on an obligation imposed on a member by a multilateral agreement.

The General Council delegates responsibility to three other major bodies: the Councils for Trade in Goods and Trade in Services, and TRIPS. The Council for Trade in Goods oversees the implementation and functioning of all the agreements covering trade in goods, including agriculture and textiles and clothing, though many such agreements have their own specific monitoring bodies. The Council for Trade in Services oversees the GATS, consisting of a framework of general rules and disciplines together with annexes and the national schedules of market access commitments; annexes concern the movement of natural persons, financial services, telecommunications, and air transport services. The Council for TRIPS monitors the operation of the relevant agreement which contains a set of basic principles, and addresses protection for different kinds of intellectual property rights such as copyright, trademarks or service marks, geographical indications, industrial designs, trade secrets and expertise, and patents. All these Councils are open to the participation of all the Organization's members and meet whenever required.

A number of other bodies are established by the Ministerial Conference and report to the General Council. The Committee on Trade and Development deals with issues relating to the developing countries, especially the 'least-developed' among them, and reviews their participation in the multilateral system. The Committee on Balance-of-Payments Restrictions is responsible for consultations between the Organization's members and countries adopting trade-restrictive measures. The Organization's financing and budget issues are dealt with by a Committee on Budget, Finance and Administration.

Each of the four 'plurilateral agreements' establishes its own management body, which reports to the General Council.

The Committee on Trade and Environment (CTE) – formally established by the General Council in early 1995 – is concerned, *inter alia*, with issues relating to the relationship between trade measures of multilateral environmental agreements (MEAs) and provisions of the WTO; the impact of environmental measures on market access, particularly for exports of developing countries; exports of domestically prohibited goods; packaging, eco-labelling and recycling requirements; and the transparency of trade-related environmental measures.

Besides its basic administrative tasks, the Secretariat performs a significant number of functions providing extensive support to the Organization's bodies with respect to negotiations and the implementation of agreements and the interpretation of the Organization's rules and precedents, and generally contributing to the adoption of more liberal commercial policies. Peter Sutherland, an Irishman appointed in June 1993 as the new Director-General of GATT, also served in the transition period as Director-General of the Organization until the appointment of Renato Ruggiero of Italy in early 1995, for a four-year term. The Director-General is assisted by four Deputy Directors-General to ensure an equitable geographic representation.

Contributions to the Organization's budget are calculated on the basis of each member's share of the total trade conducted by WTO members. Part of the budget also goes to the *International Trade Centre (ITC); it was set up in 1964 in Geneva under the auspices of the GATT to promote the exports of developing countries and is now operated jointly by the WTO and the UN, the latter acting through the *UN Conference on Trade and Development (UNCTAD).

Activities

Of outstanding importance for the proper functioning of the Organization is the new dispute settlement system following the Understanding on Rules and Procedures Governing the Settlement of Disputes annexed to the WTO Agreement. The new system – overseen by the General Council sitting as the DSB – consists of a unified set of rules applying to all WTO disputes; to ensure prompt settlement of disputes, the procedures and the timetable are set out in detail. The DSB has the sole authority to establish panels, adopt panel and appellate reports, supervise implementation of recommendations and rulings, and authorize the adoption of retaliatory measures. The adoption of panel reports cannot be blocked by parties to the dispute; appeals of panels' final reports are heard by a standing seven-person Appellate Body established by the DSB.

An arrangement has been concluded by the Organization with the UN; under the arrangement, co-operation between the Secretariats will be improved, including a strengthened working relationship between the WTO and UNCTAD. Besides co-operating with the *International Monetary Fund (IMF) and the *World Bank, as well as with the *World Intellectual Property Organization (WIPO), the WTO works closely with other institutions, particularly those concerned with the problems of international trade, industrial and agricultural development and technical assistance.

The UR agreement has reformed trade in agricultural products, providing the basis for market-orientated policies and encouraging the use of fewer trade-distorting domestic support policies, to maintain the rural economy. The needs of net-food importing developing countries and least-developed economies have been taken into account. A prominent role in the agricultural negotiations of the UR has been played by the *Cairns Group of agricultural exporting countries.

Most of the world's trade in textiles and clothing had been covered for two decades by the Arrangement Regarding International Trade in Textiles (or Multifibre Arrangement (MFA)), which came into force under the auspices of GATT. Restrictions negotiated under the MFA applied to a large proportion of the exports of developing countries and Eastern Europe to developed countries. The safeguard procedures permitted, subject to a number of strict conditions and to multilateral surveillance, the introduction of restraints on textile imports when such imports caused market disruption.

Following the entry into force of the Agreement on Textiles and Clothing, included in the Final Act of the UR, the MFA's complex network of quotas will be phased out. Textiles and clothing products will become subject, over a ten-year period implemented in four stages, to the same rules and disciplines as other industrial products.

A major challenge to the newly-created Organization – as had been the case for GATT – is represented by regional economic groupings. A new Committee on Regional Trading Arrangements has been set up by the General Council. The wide variety of integration treaties submitted for approval and the underlying political implications made it difficult for GATT to ensure full conformity with the complex provisions on customs unions and free trade areas. In practice, a tacit waiver had been granted in all cases, including the crucial test of the 1957 Rome Treaty establishing the then European Economic Community (EEC). Nevertheless, the GATT rules exercised an effective influence on the drafting of several regional arrangements. A number of specific regional initiatives – whose goals, however, appear to go beyond the purely economic and commercial spheres, – are currently under consideration by the WTO which is trying to ensure that regionalism remains open and compatible with multilateralism.

Since the end of the UR, a number of topics have been identified as possible items for inclusion in the WTO agenda, and discussions, often very lively, are continuing. These topics include highly controversial issues such as investment and competition policies, the relationship between the trading system and internationally recognized labour standards, the link between immigration policies and world trade, and the interaction between policies relating to trade and those relating to financial and monetary matters, including debt and commodity markets. The first WTO Ministerial Conference is planned to take place in December 1996 in Singapore.

Director-General: Renato Ruggiero

Headquarters: Centre William Rappard, 154 rue de Lausanne, 1211 Geneva 21, Switzerland (Telephone: +41 22 739 5111; fax: +41 22 731 4206)

Internet address: http://www.unicc.org/wto

Publications: *WTO Focus* (newsletter, ten issues a year); *International Trade* (annual)

References: J. H. Jackson, *Restructuring the GATT System* (London, 1990); C. Raghavan, *Recolonization: GATT, the Uruguay Round & the Third World* (London and New Jersey, 1990); A. Oxley, *The Challenge of Free Trade* (New York, 1990); J. Bhagwati, *The World Trading System at Risk* (New York, 1990); L. A. Haus, *Globalizing the GATT: The Soviet Union, Eastern Europe, and the International Trading System* (Washington DC,1992); P. Low, *Trading Free: The GATT and US Trade Policy* (New York, 1993); T. P. Stewart (ed.); *The GATT Uruguay Round: A Negotiating History 1986–92* (Deventer, 1993); Kohna, 'Dispute Resolution under the World Trade Organization', *Journal of World Trade*, 28, 2, 1994; J. Croome, *Reshaping the World Trading System. A History of the Uruguay Round* (Geneva, 1995); Economist Intelligence Unit (EIU), *The EIU Guide to World Trade under the WTO* (London, 1995); E. McGovern, *International Trade Regulation* (with six-monthly updates) (Globefield Press, Globefield, Exeter, 1995).

International Organizations: Membership Tables

Members of the United Nations and of the specialized agencies

Country	UN	ILO	FAO	UNESCO	ICAO	WHO	IBRD	IFC	IDA	IMF	UPU	ITU	WMO	IMO	WIPO	IFAD	IAEA	UNIDO	WTO
Afghanistan	X	X	X	X	X	X	X	X	X	X	X	X	X			X	X	X	
Albania	X	X	X	X	X	X	X	X	X	X	X	X	X		X	X	X		
Algeria	X	X	X	X	X	X	X	X	X	X	X	X		X	X	X	X	X	
Andorra	X			X								X			X				
Angola	X	X	X	X	X	X	X	X	X	X	X	X	X	X	X	X		X	
Antigua and Barbuda	X	X	X	X	X	X	X	X		X		X	X	X		X		X	X
Argentina	X	X	X	X	X	X	X	X	X	X	X	X	X	X	X	X	X	X	X
Armenia	X	X	X	X	X	X	X			X	X	X	X			X	X	X	X
Australia	X	X	X	X	X	X	X	X	X	X	X	X	X	X	X	X	X	X	X
Austria	X	X	X	X	X	X	X	X	X	X	X	X	X	X	X	X	X	X	X
Azerbaijan	X	X		X	X	X	X		X	X	X	X	X	X		X		X	
Bahamas	X	X	X	X	X	X	X			X	X	X	X	X	X				
Bahrain	X	X	X	X	X	X	X			X	X	X	X	X					X
Bangladesh	X	X	X	X	X	X	X	X	X	X	X	X	X	X	X	X	X	X	X
Barbados	X	X	X	X	X	X	X			X	X	X	X	X	X	X		X	X
Belarus	X	X		X	X	X	X			X	X	X	X			X		X	
Belgium	X	X	X	X	X	X	X	X	X	X	X	X	X	X	X	X	X	X	X
Belize	X	X	X	X	X	X	X			X	X	X	X	X		X		X	X
Benin	X	X	X	X	X	X	X	X	X	X	X	X	X	X	X	X		X	X
Bhutan	X		X	X	X	X	X			X	X	X				X			
Bolivia	X	X	X	X	X	X	X	X	X	X	X	X	X	X		X	X	X	X
Bosnia-Herzegovina	X	X	X	X	X	X	X			X	X	X	X	X	X	X	X	X	
Botswana	X	X	X	X	X	X	X	X	X	X	X	X	X			X		X	
Brazil	X	X	X	X	X	X	X	X	X	X	X	X	X	X	X	X	X	X	X
Brunei	X				X	X				X	X	X	X	X					X
Bulgaria	X	X		X	X	X	X	X		X	X	X	X	X		X		X	
Burkina Faso	X	X	X	X	X	X	X	X	X	X	X	X	X			X	X		X	X
Burundi	X	X	X	X	X	X	X	X	X	X	X	X	X		X	X	X		X	X
Cambodia	X	X	X	X	X	X	X			X	X	X	X	X		X	X			
Cameroon	X	X	X	X	X	X	X	X	X	X	X	X	X	X	X	X	X	X	X
Canada	X	X	X	X	X	X	X	X	X	X	X	X	X	X	X	X	X	X	X
Cape Verde	X	X	X	X	X	X	X	X	X	X	X	X	X	X		X			
Central African Republic	X	X	X	X	X	X	X		X	X	X	X	X			X	X		X	X
Chad	X	X	X	X	X	X	X			X	X	X	X			X	X		X	
Chile	X	X	X	X	X	X	X	X	X	X	X	X	X	X	X	X	X	X	X
China	X	X	X	X	X	X	X	X	X	X	X	X	X	X	X	X	X		
Colombia	X	X	X	X	X	X	X	X	X	X	X	X	X	X	X	X	X	X	X
Comoros	X	X	X	X	X	X	X			X	X	X	X			X			
Congo	X	X	X	X	X	X	X			X	X	X	X	X	X	X	X		X	
Costa Rica	X	X	X	X	X	X	X	X	X	X	X	X	X	X	X	X	X	X	X
Côte d'Ivoire	X	X	X	X	X	X	X	X	X	X	X	X	X	X	X	X	X	X	X
Croatia	X	X	X	X	X	X	X	X	X	X	X	X	X	X	X	X	X	X	
Cuba	X	X	X	X	X	X					X	X	X	X	X	X	X	X	X
Cyprus	X	X	X	X	X	X	X	X	X	X	X	X	X	X	X	X	X	X	X
Czech Republic	X	X		X	X	X	X	X	X	X	X	X	X	X	X		X	X	X
Democratic People's Republic of Korea	X		X	X	X	X					X	X	X		X				
Denmark	X	X	X	X	X	X	X	X	X	X	X	X	X	X	X	X	X	X	X
Djibouti	X	X	X	X	X	X	X	X	X	X	X	X	X	X			X			X
Dominica	X	X	X	X		X	X	X	X	X	X			X	X		X		X
Dominican Republic	X	X	X	X	X	X	X	X	X	X	X	X	X	X		X	X	X	X
Ecuador	X	X	X	X	X	X	X	X	X	X	X	X	X	X		X	X		X
Egypt	X	X	X	X	X	X	X	X	X	X	X	X	X	X	X	X	X	X	X
El Salvador	X	X	X	X	X	X	X	X	X	X	X	X	X	X	X	X	X	X	X
Equatorial Guinea	X	X	X	X	X	X	X	X	X	X	X	X			X		X		
Eritrea	X	X	X	X	X	X	X		X	X	X	X	X	X			X		
Estonia	X	X	X	X	X	X	X	X		X	X	X	X	X	X			X	
Ethiopia	X	X	X	X	X	X	X	X	X	X	X	X	X			X	X	X	

Members of the United Nations and of the specialized agencies *Continued*

Country	UN	ILO	FAO	UNESCO	ICAO	WHO	IBRD	IFC	IDA	IMF	UPU	ITU	WMO	IMO	WIPO	IFAD	IAEA	UNIDO	WTO
Fiji	X	X	X	X	X	X	X	X	X	X	X	X	X	X	X	X		X	X
Finland	X	X	X	X	X	X	X	X	X	X	X	X	X	X	X	X		X	X
France	X	X	X	X	X	X	X	X	X	X	X	X	X	X	X	X	X	X	X
Gabon	X	X	X	X	X	X	X	X	X	X	X	X	X	X	X	X	X	X	X
Gambia	X		X	X	X	X	X		X	X	X	X	X	X	X	X		X	
Georgia	X	X		X	X	X	X		X	X	X	X			X			X	
Germany	X	X		X	X	X	X	X	X	X	X	X	X	X	X	X	X	X	X
Ghana	X	X	X	X	X	X	X	X	X	X	X	X	X	X	X	X	X	X	X
Greece	X	X	X	X	X	X	X	X	X	X	X	X	X	X	X	X	X	X	X
Grenada	X	X	X	X	X	X	X	X	X	X	X	X			X			X	X
Guatemala	X	X	X	X	X	X	X	X	X	X	X	X	X	X	X	X	X	X	X
Guinea	X	X	X	X	X	X	X	X	X	X	X	X	X	X	X	X		X	X
Guinea-Bissau	X	X	X	X	X	X	X	X	X	X	X	X	X	X	X	X		X	X
Guyana	X	X	X	X	X	X	X	X	X	X	X	X	X	X	X	X		X	X
Haiti	X	X	X	X	X	X	X	X	X	X	X	X	X	X	X	X	X	X	X
Holy See											X	X			X		X		
Honduras	X	X	X		X	X	X	X	X	X	X	X	X	X	X	X		X	X
Hungary	X	X	X	X	X	X	X	X	X	X	X	X	X	X	X		X	X	X
Iceland	X	X	X	X	X	X	X	X	X	X	X	X	X	X	X		X	X	X
India	X	X	X	X	X	X	X	X	X	X	X	X	X	X	X	X	X	X	X
Indonesia	X	X	X	X	X	X	X	X	X	X	X	X	X	X	X	X	X	X	X
Iran	X	X	X	X	X	X	X	X	X	X	X	X	X	X	X	X	X	X	
Iraq	X	X	X	X	X	X	X	X	X	X	X	X	X	X	X	X	X	X	
Republic of Ireland	X	X	X	X	X	X	X	X	X	X	X	X	X	X	X	X	X	X	X
Israel	X	X	X	X	X	X	X	X	X	X	X	X	X	X	X	X	X	X	X
Italy	X	X	X	X	X	X	X	X	X	X	X	X	X	X	X	X	X	X	X
Jamaica	X	X	X	X	X	X	X	X		X	X	X	X	X	X	X	X	X	X
Japan	X	X	X	X	X	X	X	X	X	X	X	X	X	X	X	X	X	X	X
Jordan	X	X	X	X	X	X	X		X	X	X	X	X	X	X	X	X	X	
Kazakhstan	X	X		X	X		X		X	X	X	X			X			X	
Kenya	X	X	X	X	X	X	X	X	X	X	X	X	X	X	X	X	X	X	X
Kiribati				X	X	X	X	X	X	X	X	X							
Kuwait	X	X	X	X	X	X	X	X	X	X	X	X	X	X		X	X	X	X
Kyrgyzstan	X	X		X	X	X	X		X	X	X	X				X		X	
Lao People's Democratic Republic	X	X	X	X	X	X	X	X	X	X	X	X	X			X		X	
Latvia	X	X	X	X	X	X	X	X	X	X	X	X	X	X	X	X		X	X
Lebanon	X	X	X	X	X	X	X	X	X	X	X	X	X	X	X	X	X	X	
Lesotho	X	X	X	X	X	X	X	X	X	X	X	X	X		X	X	X	X	X
Liberia	X	X	X	X	X	X	X	X	X	X	X	X	X	X	X	X	X	X	
Libyan Arab Jamahiriya	X	X	X	X	X	X	X	X	X	X	X	X	X	X	X	X	X	X	
Liechtenstein	X										X	X			X		X		
Lithuania	X	X	X	X	X	X	X			X		X		X	X			X	
Luxembourg	X	X	X	X	X	X	X	X	X	X	X	X	X	X	X	X	X	X	X
Madagascar	X	X	X	X	X	X	X	X	X	X	X	X	X	X	X	X	X	X	X
Malawi	X	X	X	X	X	X	X	X	X	X	X	X	X		X	X		X	X
Malaysia	X	X	X	X	X	X	X	X	X	X	X	X	X	X	X	X	X	X	X
Maldives	X		X	X	X	X	X	X	X	X	X	X	X	X	X	X		X	X
Mali	X	X	X	X	X	X	X		X	X	X	X		X	X	X	X	X	X
Malta	X	X	X	X	X	X	X			X	X	X	X	X	X	X		X	X
Marshall Islands	X				X	X	X		X										
Mauritania	X	X	X	X	X	X	X	X	X	X	X	X	X	X	X	X		X	
Mauritius	X	X	X	X	X	X	X	X	X	X	X	X	X	X	X	X	X	X	X
Mexico	X	X	X	X	X	X	X	X	X	X	X	X	X	X	X	X	X	X	X
Micronesia	X				X	X	X	X	X	X		X							
Moldova	X	X		X	X	X	X	X	X	X	X	X	X		X			X	
Monaco	X			X	X	X					X	X		X	X		X		
Mongolia	X	X	X	X	X	X	X	X	X	X	X	X	X		X		X	X	
Morocco	X	X	X	X	X	X	X	X	X	X	X	X	X	X	X	X	X	X	X
Mozambique	X	X	X	X	X	X	X	X	X	X	X	X	X	X		X		X	X
Myanmar	X	X	X	X	X	X	X	X	X	X	X	X	X	X		X	X	X	X
Namibia	X	X	X	X	X	X	X	X	X	X	X	X	X	X	X	X	X	X	X
Nauru					X	X					X	X							

Members of the United Nations and of the specialized agencies *Continued*

Country	UN	ILO	FAO	UNESCO	ICAO	WHO	IBRD	IFC	IDA	IMF	UPU	ITU	WMO	IMO	WIPO	IFAD	IAEA	UNIDO	WTO
Nepal	X	X	X	X	X	X	X	X	X	X	X	X	X	X		X		X	
Netherlands	X	X	X	X	X	X	X	X	X	X	X	X	X	X	X	X	X	X	X
New Zealand	X	X	X	X	X	X	X	X	X	X	X	X	X	X	X	X	X	X	X
Nicaragua	X	X	X	X	X	X	X	X	X	X	X	X	X	X		X	X	X	X
Niger	X	X	X	X	X	X	X	X	X	X	X	X	X			X	X	X	
Nigeria	X	X	X	X	X	X	X	X	X	X	X	X	X	X	X	X	X	X	X
Norway	X	X	X	X	X	X	X	X	X	X	X	X	X	X	X	X	X	X	X
Oman	X	X	X	X	X	X	X	X	X	X	X	X	X	X		X		X	
Pakistan	X	X	X	X	X	X	X	X	X	X	X	X	X	X	X	X	X	X	X
Palau	X																		
Panama	X	X	X	X	X	X	X	X	X	X	X	X	X	X	X	X	X	X	
Papua New Guinea	X	X	X	X	X	X	X	X	X	X	X	X	X	X		X		X	X
Paraguay	X	X	X	X	X	X	X	X	X	X	X	X	X	X	X	X	X	X	X
Peru	X	X	X	X	X	X	X	X	X	X	X	X	X	X	X	X	X	X	X
Philippines	X	X	X	X	X	X	X	X	X	X	X	X	X	X	X	X	X	X	X
Poland	X	X	X	X	X	X	X	X	X	X	X	X	X	X	X		X	X	X
Portugal	X	X	X	X	X	X	X	X	X	X	X	X	X	X	X	X	X	X	X
Qatar	X	X	X	X	X	X	X			X	X	X	X	X	X	X	X	X	
Republic of Korea	X	X	X	X	X	X	X	X	X	X	X	X	X	X	X	X	X	X	X
Romania	X	X	X	X	X	X	X	X		X	X	X	X	X	X	X	X	X	X
Russian Federation	X	X		X	X	X	X	X	X	X	X	X	X		X	X		X	X
Rwanda	X	X	X	X	X	X	X	X	X	X	X	X	X		X	X		X	X
Saint Kitts and Nevis	X		X	X		X	X		X	X	X					X		X	X
Saint Lucia	X	X	X	X	X	X	X	X	X	X		X	X	X	X		X	X	X
Saint Vincent and the Grenadines	X		X	X	X	X	X		X	X	X	X			X		X		X	X
Samoa	X		X	X		X		X	X	X	X					X			
San Marino	X	X		X	X	X				X	X	X	X				X		
São Tomé and Príncipe	X	X	X	X	X	X	X			X	X	X	X	X		X		X	
Saudi Arabia	X	X	X	X	X	X	X	X	X	X	X	X	X	X	X	X	X	X	
Senegal	X	X	X	X	X	X	X	X	X	X	X	X	X	X	X	X	X	X	X
Seychelles	X	X	X	X	X	X	X			X	X	X	X	X	X	X		X	
Sierra Leone	X	X	X	X	X	X	X	X	X	X	X	X	X	X	X	X	X	X	X
Singapore	X	X			X	X	X	X	X	X	X	X	X	X	X			X	X
Slovakia	X	X		X	X	X	X	X	X	X	X	X	X	X	X	X		X	X
Slovenia	X	X		X	X	X	X	X	X	X	X	X	X	X	X	X		X	X
Solomon Islands	X	X	X	X	X	X	X	X	X	X	X	X	X	X		X			X
Somalia	X	X	X	X	X	X	X	X	X	X	X	X	X	X	X	X		X	
South Africa	X	X		X	X	X	X	X	X	X	X	X	X	X	X	X	X	X	X
Spain	X	X	X	X	X	X	X	X	X	X	X	X	X	X	X	X	X	X	X
Sri Lanka	X	X	X	X	X	X	X	X	X	X	X	X	X	X	X	X	X	X	X
Sudan	X	X	X	X	X	X	X	X	X	X	X	X	X	X	X	X	X	X	
Surinam	X	X	X	X	X	X	X			X	X	X	X	X	X	X		X	X
Swaziland	X	X	X	X	X	X	X	X	X	X	X	X	X	X	X	X		X	X
Sweden	X	X	X	X	X	X	X	X	X	X	X	X	X	X	X	X	X	X	X
Switzerland		X	X	X	X	X	X	X	X	X	X	X	X	X	X	X	X	X	X
Syrian Arab Republic	X	X	X	X	X	X	X	X	X	X	X	X	X	X	X	X	X	X	
Tajikistan	X	X		X	X	X	X	X	X	X	X	X	X		X	X		X	
Thailand	X	X	X	X	X	X	X	X	X	X	X	X	X	X	X	X	X	X	X
The Former Yugoslav Rep. of Macedonia	X	X		X	X	X	X	X	X	X	X	X	X	X	X	X	X	X	
Togo	X	X	X	X	X	X	X	X	X	X	X	X	X	X	X	X		X	X
Tonga		X	X	X	X	X	X	X	X	X	X	X				X		X	
Trinidad and Tobago	X	X	X	X	X	X	X	X	X	X	X	X	X	X	X	X		X	X
Tunisia	X	X	X	X	X	X	X	X	X	X	X	X	X	X	X	X	X	X	X

Members of the United Nations and of the specialized agencies *Continued*

Country	UN	ILO	FAO	UNESCO	ICAO	WHO	IBRD	IFC	IDA	IMF	UPU	ITU	WMO	IMO	WIPO	IFAD	IAEA	UNIDO	WTO
Turkey	X	X	X	X	X	X	X	X	X	X	X	X	X	X	X	X	X	X	X
Turkmenistan	X	X		X	X	X	X		X	X	X	X	X	X	X		X	X	
Tuvalu				X		X					X					X	X	X	
Uganda	X	X	X	X	X	X	X	X	X	X	X	X	X		X	X	X	X	X
Ukraine	X	X		X	X	X	X	X	X	X	X	X	X		X		X	X	
United Arab Emirates	X	X	X	X	X	X	X	X	X	X	X	X	X	X	X	X	X	X	X
United Kingdom of Great Britain and Northern Ireland	X	X	X		X	X	X	X	X	X	X	X	X	X	X	X	X	X	X
United Republic of Tanzania	X	X	X	X	X	X	X	X	X	X	X	X	X	X	X	X	X	X	X
United States of America	X	X	X		X	X	X	X	X	X	X	X	X	X	X	X	X	X	X
Uruguay	X	X	X	X	X	X	X	X		X	X	X	X	X	X	X	X	X	X
Uzbekistan	X	X		X	X	X	X	X	X	X	X	X	X		X		X	X	
Vanuatu	X		X	X	X	X	X	X	X	X	X		X	X				X	
Venezuela	X	X	X	X	X	X	X	X		X	X	X	X	X	X	X	X	X	X
Vietnam	X	X	X	X	X	X	X	X	X	X	X	X	X	X	X	X	X	X	
Yemen	X	X	X	X	X	X	X	X	X	X	X	X	X	X	X	X		X	
Zaire	X	X	X	X	X	X	X	X	X	X	X	X	X	X	X	X	X	X	
Zambia	X	X	X	X	X	X	X	X	X	X	X	X	X		X	X	X	X	X
Zimbabwe	X	X	X	X	X	X	X	X	X	X	X	X	X		X	X	X	X	X

Membership of Major Regional Organizations: Africa

	AfDB[1]	CEEAC	CEMAC	COMESA	ECA	ECOWAS	Entente Council	IOC[2]	MRU	OAU[3]	SADCC	UEMOA
Algeria	X				X					X		
Angola	X	O		X	X					X	X	
Benin	X				X	X	X			X		X
Botswana	X				X					X	X	
Burkina Faso	X				X	X	X			X		X
Burundi	X	X		X	X					X		
Cameroon	X	X	X		X					X		
Cape Verde	X				X	X				X		
Central African Republic	X	X	X		X					X		
Chad	X	X	X		X					X		
Comoros	X			X	X			X		X		
Congo	X	X	X		X					X		
Côte d'Ivoire	X				X	X	X			X		X
Djibouti	X				X					X		
Egypt	X				X					X		
Equatorial Guinea	X	X	X		X					X		
Eritrea	X			X	X					X		
Ethiopia	X			X	X					X		
Gabon	X	X	X		X					X		
Gambia	X				X	X				X		
Ghana	X				X	X				X		
Guinea	X				X	X			X	X		
Guinea Bissau	X				X	X				X		
Kenya	X			X	X					X		
Lesotho	X			X	X					X	X	
Liberia	X				X	X			X	X		
Libya	X				X					X		
Madagascar	X			X	X			X		X		
Malawi	X			X	X					X	X	
Mali	X				X	X				X		X
Mauritania	X				X	X				X		
Mauritius	X			X	X			X		X	X	
Morocco	X				X							
Mozambique	X			X	X					X	X	
Namibia	X			X	X					X	X	
Niger	X				X	X	X			X		X
Nigeria	X				X	X				X		
Rwanda	X	X		X	X					X		
São Tomé and Príncipe	X	X			X					X		
Senegal	X				X	X				X		X
Seychelles	X				X			X		X		
Sierra Leone	X				X	X			X	X		
Somalia	X				X					X		
South Africa	X				X					X	X	
Sudan	X			X	X					X		
Swaziland	X			X	X					X	X	
Tanzania	X			X	X					X	X	
Togo	X				X	X	X			X		X
Tunisia	X				X					X		
Uganda	X			X	X					X		
Zaire	X	X		X	X					X		
Zambia	X			X	X					X	X	
Zimbabwe	X			X	X					X	X	

Notes:

O = Observer.

1. Also around 25 non-regional countries.
2. Also France representing Réunion.
3. Sahrawi Arab Democratic Republic admitted in 1982, but membership disputed by Morocco and other countries. Subsequently Morocco withdrew.

Membership of Major Regional Organizations: Asia and The Pacific

	APEC[1]	AsDB[2]	ASEAN	Colombo Plan[3]	ESCAP[4]	PECC[5]	SAARC	SPC[6]	SPF[7]
Afghanistan		X		X	X				
Australia	X	X		X	X	X		X	X
Bangladesh		X		X	X		X		
Bhutan		X		X	X		X		
Brunei	X		X		X	X			
Cambodia		X	O	X	X				
China	X	X			X	X			
Fiji		X		X	X			X	X
Hong Kong	X	X			A	X			
India		X		X	X		X		
Indonesia	X	X	X	X	X	X			
Japan	X	X		X	X	X			
Kiribati		X			X			X	X
Korea, Republic of	X	X		X	X	X			
Laos		X	O	X	X				
Malaysia	X	X	X	X	X	X			
Maldives		X		X	X		X		
Mongolia		X			X				
Myanmar		X	O	X	X				
Nauru		X			X			X	X
Nepal		X		X	X		X		
New Zealand	X	X		X	X	X		X	X
Pakistan		X		X	X		X		
Papua New Guinea	X	X	O	X	X			X	X
Philippines	X	X	X	X	X	X			
Samoa		X			X			X	X
Singapore	X	X	X	X	X	X			
Solomon Islands		X			X			X	X
Sri Lanka		X		X	X		X		
Taiwan	X	X				X			
Thailand	X	X	X	X	X	X			
Tonga		X			X			X	X
Vanuatu		X			X			X	X
Vietnam		X	X		X				

Notes:

O = Observer.
1. Also Canada, USA, Chile, Mexico.
2. Also Cook Islands, Marshall Islands, Micronesia and 16 non-regional countries.
3. Also Iran and the USA.
4. Also Iran, Tuvalu, France, Netherlands, Russia, UK, USA.
5. Also Canada, USA, Chile, Mexico, Peru.
6. Also other regional countries and territories, France, UK, USA.
7. Also other regional countries.

Membership of Major Regional Organizations: Europe

	BSEC[1]	CEI	CERN	Council of Europe[2]	EBRD[3]	EFTA	ESA	European Union	NATO[4]	OSCE[5]	WEU
Albania	X	X		X	X					X	
Austria	O	X	X	X	X			X	X		X	O
Belarus		X			X						
Belgium			X	X	X			X	X	X	X	X
Bosnia-Herzegovina		X			X					X	
Bulgaria	X	X		X	X					X	P
Croatia		X			X					X	
Cyprus				X	X					X	
Czech Republic		X	X	X	X					X	P
Denmark		X		X	X		X	X	X	X	O
Estonia				X	X					X	P
Finland			X	X	X		A	X		X	O
France			X	X	X		X	X	X	X	X
Germany			X	X	X		X	X	X	X	X
Greece	X		X	X	X			X	X	X	X
Hungary		X	X	X	X					X	P
Iceland				X	X	X			X	X	A
Ireland				X	X		X	X		X	O
Italy	O	X	X	X	X		X	X	X	X	X
Latvia				X	X					X	P
Liechtenstein				X	X	X				X	
Lithuania				X	X					X	P
Luxembourg				X	X			X	X	X	X
Macedonia		X		X	X					X	
Malta				X	X					X	
Moldova	X			X	X					X	
Netherlands			X	X	X		X	X	X	X	X
Norway			X	X	X	X	X		X	X	A
Poland	O	X	X	X	X					X	P
Portugal			X	X	X			X	X	X	X
Romania	X	X		X	X					X	P
Russia	X		O	X	X					X	
San Marino				X						X	
Slovakia	O	X	X	X	X					X	P
Slovenia		X		X	X					X	
Spain			X	X	X		X	X	X	X	X
Sweden			X	X	X		X			X	O
Switzerland			X	X	X	X	X			X	
Turkey	X		O	X	X				X	X	A
Ukraine	X	X		X	X					X	
United Kingdom			X	X	X		X	X	X	X	X

Notes:
A = Associated Member.
O = Observer.
P = Partner.
1. Also Armenia, Azerbaijan, Georgia.
2. Also Andorra.
3. Also the EC, the EIB, Canada, USA, Japan, Armenia, Azerbaijan, Georgia, Kazakhstan, Kyrgyzstan, Tajikistan, Turkmenistan, Uzbekistan.
4. Also Canada, USA.
5. Also Canada, USA, Armenia, Azerbaijan, Georgia, Kazakhstan, Krygyzstan, Tajikistan, Turkmenistan, Uzbekistan.

Membership of Major Regional Organizations: Latin America and the Caribbean

	ACS[1]	Amazon Pact	Andean Community	CARICOM[1]	CDB[2]	ECLAC[3]	IDB[2]	LAIA	MERCOSUR	OAS[4]	OECS[1]	Rio Group	SELA
Antigua and Barbuda	X			X	X	X				X	X		
Argentina						X	X	X	X	X		X	X
Bahamas	X			X	X	X	X			X			
Barbados	X			X	X	X	X			X			X
Belize	X			X	X	X				X			X
Bolivia		X	X			X	X	X		X		X	X
Brazil		X				X	X	X	X	X		X	X
Chile						X	X	X		X		X	X
Colombia	X	X	X		X	X	X	X		X		X	X
Costa Rica	X					X	X	O		X			X
Cuba	X					X		O		X			X
Dominica	X			X	X	X				X	X		
Dominican Republic	X					X	X	O		X			X
Ecuador		X	X			X	X	X		X		X	X
El Salvador	X					X	X	O		X			X
Grenada	X			X	X	X				X	X		X
Guatemala	X					X	X	O		X			X
Guyana	X	X		X	X	X	X			X			X
Haiti	X					X	X			X			X
Honduras	X					X	X	O		X			X
Jamaica	X			X	X	X	X			X			X
Mexico	X				X	X	X	X		X		X	X
Nicaragua	X					X	X	O		X			X
Panama						X	X·	O		X			X
Paraguay						X	X	X	X	X		X	X
Peru		X	X			X	X	X		X		X	X
Saint Kitts-Nevis	X			X	X	X				X	X		
Saint Lucia	X			X	X	X				X	X		
Saint Vincent	X			X	X	X				X	X		
Surinam	X	X				X				X			X
Trinidad and Tobago	X			X	X	X	X			X			X
Uruguay						X	X	X	X	X		X	X
Venezuela	X	X	X		X	X	X	X		X		X	X

Notes:
O = Observer
1. Also Montserrat.
2. Also other regional and non-regional countries.
3. Also non-regional countries.
4. Also Canada and the USA.

Membership of Major Regional Organizations: The Middle East and North Africa

	AMU	Arab League[1]	BADEA[1]	Damascus Declaration	ESCWA	GCC	IsDB[2]	OAPEC	OIC[2]
Algeria	X	X	X				X	X	X
Bahrain		X	X	X	X	X	X	X	X
Egypt		X	X	X	X		X	X	X
Iran							X		X
Iraq		X	X		X		X	X	X
Jordan		X	X		X		X		X
Kuwait		X	X	X	X	X	X	X	X
Lebanon		X	X		X		X		X
Libya	X	X	X				X	X	X
Mauritania	X	X	X				X		X
Morocco	X	X	X				X		X
Oman		X	X	X	X	X	X		X
Qatar		X	X	X	X	X	X	X	X
Saudi Arabia		X	X	X	X	X	X	X	X
Syria		X	X	X	X		X	X	X
Tunisia	X	X	X				X		X
United Arab Emirates		X	X	X	X	X	X	X	X
Yemen		X			X		X		X

Notes:
1. Also other Arab countries in Africa.
2. Also other Islamic countries in Africa and Asia.

Classification of
Countries and
Membership of
Major Groups

For analytical and operational purposes, several classification schemes, based on various criteria, are used by international organizations and scholars to arrange the countries of the world into groups and subgroups. Classifications have evolved over time to adjust to new and often unforeseen developments, as has most recently been the case with the 'transition' of centrally-planned economies – where about one-third of the world's population lives – to a market orientation.

The first and most general classification currently adopted divides countries into three major groups: industrial countries, countries in transition, and developing countries. Divisions into subgroups are made within each major group.

Industrial countries include North America (that is, Canada and the USA), Western Europe, Australia, Japan and New Zealand. Most countries belonging to this group may also be defined as high-income economies. The seven largest economies in terms of GDP – which make up the *Group of Seven (G-7) – are collectively referred to as the major industrial countries: the USA, Japan, Germany, France, Italy, the UK and Canada. Highly-developed countries committed to a market economy and a pluralistic democracy are grouped in the *Organization for Economic Co-operation and Development (OECD), whose membership has gradually expanded from Western Europe and North America to Australia, Japan and New Zealand, and most recently to Mexico and countries of Central and Eastern Europe.

Among the European countries an important subgroup is represented by the 15 members of the *European Union (EU): Austria, Belgium, Denmark, Finland, France, Germany, Greece, Ireland, Italy, Luxembourg, The Netherlands, Portugal, Spain, Sweden, the UK. Baltic countries include: Estonia, Latvia, Lithuania. Nordic countries include: Denmark, Finland, Iceland, Norway, Sweden. Southern European countries are: Albania, Greece, Italy, Malta, Portugal, Spain. Northern Mediterranean countries include: Andorra, Cyprus, Malta, San Marino, Turkey, plus the republics of the former Yugoslavia (Bosnia and Herzegovina, Croatia, Macedonia, Slovenia and the newly-created Federal Republic of Yugoslavia, consisting of Serbia and Montenegro). Mediterranean countries' partners of the EU are: Algeria, Cyprus, Egypt, Israel, Jordan, Lebanon, Malta, Morocco, Syria, Tunisia, Turkey and the Palestinian Territories.

Countries in transition include Central and Eastern Europe, the republics of the former USSR, and Mongolia. All of these countries are currently undergoing a transition from central planning to a market-based system.

Central and Eastern Europe comprises Albania, Bulgaria, the Czech Republic, Hungary, Poland, Romania, Slovakia and the republics of the former Yugoslavia. The Baltic countries (Estonia, Latvia and Lithuania) may be included in the Central and Eastern European subgroup. The Visegrad countries are the Czech Republic, Hungary, Poland, and Slovakia.

The republics of the former USSR – also referred to as 'independent states of the former Soviet Union' or 'newly independent states (NIS)' – may be subdivided into European (sometimes including the Baltic states) and non-European. The former comprise Belarus, Moldova, Russia and Ukraine; the latter may be further divided into Transcaucasian countries (Armenia, Azerbaijan and Georgia) and Central Asian countries (Kazakhstan, Kyrgyzstan, Tajikistan, Turkmenistan and Uzbekistan).

Developing countries consist of those countries that are classified neither as industrial nor in transition. In practice, all the countries of Africa, Asia (except Japan), Latin America and the Caribbean, and Oceania (excluding Australia and New Zealand) are classified as developing. Under certain conditions, countries in transition may be considered as 'developing'.

A subdivision of developing countries may be adopted with reference to main geographic regions:

North Africa: Algeria, Egypt, Libya, Morocco, Tunisia.

Sub-Saharan Africa: all developing countries in Africa, except North Africa, Nigeria and South Africa.

Latin America and the Caribbean: all developing countries in the Western Hemisphere.

Western Asia: Bahrain, Iran, Iraq, Jordan, Kuwait, Lebanon, Oman, Qatar, Saudi Arabia,

Syria, United Arab Emirates, Yemen. The countries of Western Asia plus Egypt and Libya may be considered part of the Middle East.

South and East Asia and Oceania: Afghanistan, Bangladesh, Bhutan, Brunei, Cambodia, China, Fiji, Hong Kong, India, Indonesia, Korea, Laos, Malaysia, Maldives, Mongolia, Myanmar (formerly Burma), Nepal, Pakistan, Papua New Guinea, Philippines, Singapore, Sri Lanka, Taiwan, Thailand, Vietnam. Hong Kong, Korea, Singapore, and Taiwan are also identified as newly-industrializing Asian economies.

A further subdivision may be introduced with regard to South and East Asia in order to distinguish between:

South Asia: Bangladesh, Bhutan, India, the Maldives, Nepal, Pakistan and Sri Lanka (in some cases also including Afghanistan and Iran);

South-East Asia: Brunei, Cambodia, Indonesia, Laos, Malaysia, Myanmar, the Philippines, Singapore, Thailand and Vietnam; and

East Asia: China, Hong Kong, Korea, Mongolia, and Taiwan.

Arab countries: include Algeria, Bahrain, Egypt, Iraq, Jordan, Kuwait, Lebanon, Libya, Morocco, Oman, Qatar, Saudi Arabia, Sudan, Syria, Tunisia, United Arab Emirates, Yemen.

In addition to their broad regional classification, developing countries are grouped according to specific criteria, the main ones being those based on export orientation and on the financial situation with respect to external debt; other criteria are used to identify 'miscellaneous groups'.

According to the 'predominant export' criterion, a major distinction is made between fuel exporters and non-fuel exporters. *Fuel-exporting developing countries*, whose average ratio of fuel exports (mainly oil) exceeds 50 per cent of total exports earnings, are: Algeria, Angola, Bahrain, Congo, Gabon, Iran, Iraq, Libya, Nigeria, Oman, Qatar, Saudi Arabia, Trinidad and Tobago, United Arab Emirates and Venezuela. *Non-fuel exporting countries* are those whose total exports of goods and services include a substantial share of: (a) manufactures; (b) primary products; or (c) services, factor income, and private transfers. These

countries are disaggregated into subgroups on the basis of the predominant composition of their exports.

Developing countries *exporters of manufactures*, whose exports of manufactures account for over 50 per cent of total exports earnings, are: China, Hong Kong, Israel, Korea, Lebanon, Singapore and Taiwan. *Exporters of primary products* (43 countries of which two-thirds are in Africa) are further divided into agricultural exporters (29 countries) and mineral exporters (14 countries). The *exporters of services* and recipients of factor income and private transfers number 37 in various continents. Finally, about 30 countries have a *diversified export base*, – that is, their exports are not dominated by any one of the categories mentioned above.

According to financial criteria, a basic distinction is made between *net creditor* and *net debtor* countries. The *net creditors' group* is by far the smallest, and includes: Kuwait, Libya, Oman, Qatar, Saudi Arabia, Taiwan, and the United Arab Emirates. The very large group of *net debtor* countries (around 125 countries) is further disaggregated on the basis of two criteria: (a) the predominant type of source of borrowing (official borrowers, including about 70 countries; market borrowers; and diversified borrowers); and (b) the existence of recent debt-servicing difficulties (about 70 countries have incurred external payments arrears or entered into official or commercial bank debt-rescheduling agreements over the past few years).

Least developed countries, according to the classification of the United Nations, comprise the following: Afghanistan, Bangladesh, Benin, Bhutan, Botswana, Burkina Faso, Burundi, Cambodia, Cape Verde, Central African Republic, Chad, Comoros, Djibouti, Equatorial Guinea, Ethiopia, Gambia, Guinea, Guinea-Bissau, Haiti, Kiribati, Laos, Lesotho, Liberia, Madagascar, Malawi, Maldives, Mali, Mauritania, Mozambique, Myanmar, Nepal, Niger, Rwanda, São Tomé and Príncipe, Sierra Leone, Solomon Islands, Somalia, Sudan, Tanzania, Togo, Tuvalu, Uganda, Vanuatu, Western Samoa, Yemen, Zaire, Zambia.

Low-income countries comprise the developing countries whose per capita gross national product (GNP) did not exceed the equivalent of

$695 in 1993. More precisely, the group includes the least developed countries listed above (except Botswana, Cape Verde, Djibouti, Kiribati, Tuvalu, Vanuatu, and Western Samoa) plus Côte d'Ivoire, Egypt, Ghana, Guyana, Honduras, Kenya, Madagascar, Nicaragua, Nigeria, Pakistan, Sri Lanka, Vietnam, and Zimbabwe.

Land-locked developing countries include: Afghanistan, Armenia, Azerbaijan, Bhutan, Bolivia, Botswana, Burkina Faso, Burundi, Central African Republic, Chad, Ethiopia, Kazakhstan, Kyrgyzstan, Laos, Lesotho, Malawi, Mali, Mongolia, Nepal, Niger, Paraguay, Rwanda, Swaziland, Tajikistan, Turkmenistan, Uganda, Uzbekistan, Zambia, Zimbabwe.

'North' generally refers to the industrial countries located in the Northern Hemisphere and is often used to designate the OECD member countries.

'South' generally refers to the developing countries located mainly in the Southern Hemisphere and has often been used interchangeably with 'Third World'.

Over the years, developing countries have formed a number of groupings based on a convergence of political, ideological and economic interests. The composition of some of these groupings is given below:

Non-Aligned Movement (NAM) includes as full members: Afghanistan, Algeria, Angola, Bahamas, Bahrain, Bangladesh, Barbados, Belize, Benin, Bhutan, Bolivia, Botswana, Brunei, Burkina Faso, Burundi, Cambodia, Cameroon, Cape Verde, Central African Republic, Chad, Chile, Colombia, Comoros, Congo, Côte d'Ivoire, Cuba, Cyprus, Djibouti, Ecuador, Egypt, Equatorial Guinea, Eritrea, Ethiopia, Gabon, Gambia, Ghana, Grenada, Guatemala, Guinea, Guinea-Bissau, Guyana, Honduras, India, Indonesia, Iran, Iraq, Jamaica, Jordan, Kenya, Korea DPR, Kuwait, Laos, Lebanon, Lesotho, Liberia, Libya, Madagascar, Malawi, Malaysia, Maldives, Mali, Malta, Mauritania, Mauritius, Mongolia, Morocco, Mozambique, Myanmar, Namibia, Nepal, Nicaragua, Niger, Nigeria, Oman, Pakistan, Palestine, Panama, Papua New Guinea, Peru, Philippines, Qatar, Rwanda, Saint Lucia, São Tomé and Príncipe, Saudi Arabia, Senegal,

Seychelles, Sierra Leone, Singapore, Somalia, South Africa, Sri Lanka, Sudan, Suriname, Swaziland, Syria, Tanzania, Thailand, Togo, Trinidad and Tobago, Tunisia, Turkmenistan, Uzbekistan, Uganda, United Arab Emirates, Vanuatu, Venezuela, Vietnam, Yemen, Yugoslavia, Zaire, Zambia, Zimbabwe. *Observer status* is enjoyed by: Antigua and Barbuda, Armenia, Brazil, China, Costa Rica, Croatia, Dominica, El Salvador, Mexico, Uruguay. *Guest status* is enjoyed by: Australia, Austria, Bosnia and Herzegovina, Bulgaria, Canada, Dominican Republic, Finland, Germany, Greece, Hungary, The Netherlands, New Zealand, Poland, Portugal, Romania, San Marino, Slovenia, Spain, Sweden.

Group of 77 (G-77) includes: Afghanistan, Algeria, Angola, Antigua and Barbuda, Argentina, Bahamas, Bahrain, Bangladesh, Barbados, Belize, Benin, Bhutan, Bolivia, Bosnia and Herzegovina, Botswana, Brazil, Brunei, Burkina Faso, Burundi, Cambodia, Cameroon, Cape Verde, Central African Republic, Chad, Chile, Colombia, Comoros, Congo, Costa Rica, Côte d'Ivoire, Cuba, Cyprus, Djibouti, Dominica, Dominican Republic, Ecuador, Egypt, El Salvador, Equatorial Guinea, Ethiopia, Fiji, Gabon, Gambia, Ghana, Grenada, Guatemala, Guinea, Guinea-Bissau, Guyana, Haiti, Honduras, India, Indonesia, Iran, Iraq, Jamaica, Jordan, Kenya, Korea DPR, Korea Republic, Kuwait, Laos, Lebanon, Lesotho, Liberia, Libya, Madagascar, Malawi, Malaysia, Maldives, Mali, Malta, Marshall Islands, Mauritania, Mauritius, Micronesia, Mongolia, Morocco, Mozambique, Myanmar, Namibia, Nepal, Nicaragua, Niger, Nigeria, Oman, Pakistan, Palestine, Panama, Papua New Guinea, Paraguay, Peru, Philippines, Qatar, Romania, Rwanda, Saint Kitts and Nevis, Saint Lucia, Saint Vincent and the Grenadines, São Tomé and Príncipe, Saudi Arabia, Senegal, Seychelles, Sierra Leone, Singapore, Solomon Islands, Somalia, South Africa, Sri Lanka, Sudan, Suriname, Swaziland, Syria, Tanzania, Thailand, Togo, Tonga, Trinidad and Tobago, Tunisia, Uganda, United Arab Emirates, Uruguay, Vanuatu, Venezuela, Vietnam, Western Samoa, Yemen, Zaire, Zambia, Zimbabwe. China is an associate member.

Index of Foundation Dates

Organization (NATO); United Nations Relief and Works Agency for Palestine Refugees in the Near East (UNRWA)

1950   Customs Co-operation Council (CCC); Inter-American Tropical Tuna Commission (I-ATTC); Office of the United Nations High Commissioner for Refugees (UNHCR)

1951   ANZUS Pact; Colombo Plan; European Coal and Steel Community (ECSC); Organization of Central American States (Organización de Estados Centroamericanos – ODECA); Provisional Intergovernmental Committee for the Movement of Migrants from Europe (PICMME)

1952   General Fisheries Council for the Mediterranean (GFCM); Intergovernmental Committee for European Migration (ICEM); Nordic Council; South Pacific Permanent Commission (CPPS)

1953   European Conference of Ministers of Transport (ECMT); European Organization for Nuclear Research (Organisation européenne pour la recherche nucléaire – CERN)

1954   South East Asia Treaty Organization (SEATO)

1955   Bank of Central African States (Banque des états de l'Afrique centrale – BEAC); Central Bank of Western African States (Banque centrale des états de l'Afrique de l'ouest – BCEAO); Central Treaty Organization (CENTO); International Finance Corporation (IFC); Warsaw Pact; Western European Union (WEU)

1956   International Atomic Energy Agency (IAEA); Paris Club

1957   Committee for Co-ordination of Investigations of the Lower Mekong Basin; European Atomic Energy Community (Euratom); European Economic Community (EEC); European Nuclear Energy Agency (ENEA)

1958   Benelux Economic Union; UN Economic Commission for Africa (ECA)

1959   Entente Council; Equatorial Customs Union (Union douanière équatoriale – UDE); European Conference of Postal and Telecommunications Administrations (Conférence européenne des administrations des postes et des télécommunications – CEPT); Inter-American Development Bank (IDB); International Lead and Zinc Study Group (ILZSG); International Olive Oil Council (IOOC); West African Customs Union (Union douanière de l'Afrique de l'Ouest – UDAO)

1960   Caribbean Organization; Central American Bank for Economic Integration (CABEI); Central American Common Market (CACM); European Free Trade Association (EFTA); Inter-African Coffee Organization (IACO); International Development Association (IDA); Latin American Free Trade Association (LAFTA); Organization for Economic Co-operation and Development (OECD); Organization of the Petroleum Exporting Countries (OPEC)

1961   African and Malagasy Union (Union africaine et malgache – UAM); Non-Aligned Movement (NAM)

1962   Cocoa Producers' Alliance (COPAL); Desert Locust Control Organization for Eastern Africa (DLCO-EA)

1963   African Development Bank (AfDB); European Organization for the Safety of Air Navigation (EUROCONTROL); International Coffee Organization (ICO); Organization of African Unity (OAU); United Nations Research Institute for Social Development (UNRISD); World Food Programme (WFP)

1964   African and Malagasy Union for Economic Co-operation (Union africaine et malgache de coopération économique – UAMCE); African Groundnut Council (Conseil africain de l'arachide); Central African Customs and Economic Union (Union douanière et économique de l'Afrique centrale – UDEAC); Group of Seventy-seven (G-77); International Telecommunications Satellite Organization (INTELSAT); Lake Chad Basin Commission (LCBC); Maghreb Permanent Consultative Committee (Comité permanent consultatif du Maghreb – CPCM); Regional Co-operation for Development (RCD); River Niger Commission (Commission du fleuve Niger – CFN); United Nations Conference on Trade and Development (UNCTAD)

1965   African and Mauritian Common Organization (Organisation commune africaine et mauricienne – OCAM); Asian Development Bank (AsDB); United Nations Development Programme (UNDP); United Nations Institute for Training and Research (UNITAR)

1966   Customs Union of West African States (Union douanière des états de l'Afrique de l'Ouest – UDEAO); Economic Community of East Africa; International Commission for the Conservation of the Atlantic Tunas (ICCAT); United Nations Industrial Development Organization (UNIDO)

1967   Agency for the Prohibition of Nuclear Weapons in Latin America and the Caribbean (Organismo para la Proscripción de las Armas Nucleares en la América Latina y el Caribe – OPANAL); Association of South-East Asian Nations (ASEAN); Fishery Committee for the Eastern Central Atlantic

(CECAF); Indian Ocean Fishery Commission (IOFC); Pacific Basin Economic Council (PBEC); United Nations Fund for Population Activities (UNFPA); World Intellectual Property Organization (WIPO)

1968 Andean Development Corporation (CAF); Caribbean Free Trade Association (CARIFTA); International Narcotics Control Board (INCB); International Trade Centre (UNCTAD/GATT); International Union for the Protection of New Varieties of Plants (UPOV); Organization of Arab Petroleum Exporting Countries (OAPEC)

1969 Andean Group (Cartagena Agreement); Asian and Pacific Coconut Community (APCC); Caribbean Development Bank (CDB; Caribank); Southern African Customs Union (SACU)

1970 Agency for Cultural and Technical Co-operation (Agence de coopération culturelle et technique – ACCT); Association of Natural Rubber Producing Countries (ANRPC); West Africa Rice Development Association (WARDA)

1971 International Red Locust Control Organization for Central and Southern Africa (IRLCO-CSA); Organization of the Islamic Conference (OIC); South Pacific Forum (SPF)

1972 International Pepper Community (IPC); Organization for the Development of the Senegal River (Organisation pour la mise en valeur du fleuve Senegal – OMVS); United Nations Environment Programme (UNEP)

1973 Caribbean Community and Common Market (CARICOM); International Baltic Sea Fishery Commission (IBSFC); International Cocoa Organization (ICCO); Latin American Energy Organization (Organización Latinoamericana de Energía – OLADE); Mano River Union (MRU); Permanent Inter-State Committee on Drought Control in the Sahel (Comité permanent interétats de lutte contre la sécheresse dans le Sahel – CILSS); South Pacific Bureau for Economic Co-operation (SPEC); West African Economic Community (Communauté économique de l'Afrique de l'Ouest – CEAO); Western Central Atlantic Fishery Commission (WECAFC)

1974 Arab Bank for Economic Development in Africa (Banque arabe pour le développement économique en Afrique – BADEA); UN Economic and Social Commission for Asia and the Pacific (ESCAP); UN Economic and Social Commission for Western Asia (ESCWA); Group of Latin American and Caribbean Sugar Exporting Countries (Grupo de Países Latinoamericanos y del Caribe Exportadores de Azúcar – GEPLACEA); International Bauxite Association (IBA); International

Energy Agency (IEA); Islamic Development Bank; Union of Banana Exporting Countries (Unión de Países Exportadores de Banano – UPEB); World Food Council (WFC)

1975 Association of Iron Ore Exporting Countries (Association des pays exportateurs de minerai de fer – APEF); Conference on Security and Co-operation in Europe (CSCE); Economic Community of West African States (ECOWAS); European Space Agency (ESA); Group of Seven (G-7); Latin American Economic System (Sistema Económico Latinoamericano – SELA); Nordic Investment Bank; World Tourism Organization (WTO)

1976 African Timber Organization (Organisation africaine du bois); Arab Monetary Fund (AMF); Economic Community of the Great Lakes Countries (Communauté économique des pays des Grands Lacs – CEPGL); International Fund for Agricultural Development (IFAD); International Research and Training Institute for the Advancement of Women (INSTRAW)

1977 European Telecommunications Satellite Organization (EUTELSAT)

1978 Amazon Co-operation Treaty (Amazon Pact); Gambia River Development Organization (Organisation de mise en valeur du fleuve Gambie – OMVG); Organization for the Management and Development of the Kagera River Basin (Organisation pour l'aménagement et le développement du bassin de la rivière Kagera); United Nations Centre for Human Settlements (UNCHS) – Habitat

1979 International Maritime Satellite Organization (IN-MARSAT); Northwest Atlantic Fisheries Organization (NAFO); Southern African Development Co-ordination Conference (SADCC)

1980 Commission for the Conservation of Antarctic Marine Living Resources (CCAMLR); Intergovernmental Committee for Migration (ICM); International Natural Rubber Organization (INRO); Latin American Integration Association (LAIA); Northeast Atlantic Fisheries Commission (NEAFC); Niger Basin Authority (Autorité du bassin du Niger); OPEC Fund for International Development (OFID); Pacific Economic Co-operation Council (PECC)

1981 Gulf Co-operation Council (GCC); Organization of Eastern Caribbean States (OECS); Preferential Trade Area for Eastern and Southern Africa (PTA)

1982 Indian Ocean Commission (IOC); Latin American Organization for the Development of Fisheries (OLDEPESCA); North Atlantic Salmon Conservation Organization (NASCO)

1983   Association of Tin Producing Countries (ATPC); Eastern Caribbean Central Bank (ECCB); Economic Community of Central African States (Communauté économique des états d'Afrique centrale – CEEAC)

1984   International Jute Organization (IJO)

1985   Economic Co-operation Organization (ECO); International Tropical Timber Organization (ITTO); South Asian Association for Regional Co-operation (SAARC)

1986   African Petroleum Producers' Association; Cairns Group; European Organization for the Exploitation of Meteorological Satellites (EUMETSAT); Intergovernmental Authority on Drought and Development (IGADD)

1987   Group of Rio; International Organization for Migration (IOM); International Sugar Organization (ISO)

1988   Multilateral Investment Guarantee Agency (MIGA)

1989   Arab Maghreb Union (AMU) (Union du Maghreb Arabe – UMA); Asia-Pacific Economic Co-operation (APEC)

1990   European Bank for Reconstruction and Development (EBRD); North Pacific Marine Science Organization; United Nations International Drug Control Programme (UNDCP)

1991   Damascus Declaration States; International Federation of Red Cross and Red Crescent Societies; Latin American Reserve Fund (Fondo Latinoamericano de Reservas); Mercosur; North Atlantic Co-operation Council (NACC); System of Central American Integration (Sistema de la Integración Centroamericana – SICA); Visegrad Group; Western Indian Ocean Tuna Organization (WIOTO)

1992   Black Sea Economic Co-operation (BSEC); Central European Free Trade Agreement (CEFTA); Central European Initiative (CEI); Council of the Baltic Sea States (CBSS); North American Free Trade Agreement (NAFTA); North Atlantic Marine Mammals Commission (NAMMCO); Southern African Development Community (SADC)

1993   ASEAN Regional Forum (ARF); Barents Euro-Arctic Council; Common Market for Eastern and Southern Africa (COMESA); European Union (EU); Group of Three (G-3); United Nations High Commissioner for Human Rights (HCHR)

1994   Association of Caribbean States (ACS); Economic and Monetary Community of Central Africa (Communauté économique et monétaire de l'Afrique centrale – CEMAC); Indian Ocean Tuna Commission (IOTC); West African Economic and Monetary Union (Union économique et monétaire ouest-africaine – UEMOA)

1995   Mekong River Commission; Organization for Security and Co-operation in Europe (OSCE); Wassenaar Arrangement; World Trade Organization (WTO)

1996   Andean Community; Community of Portuguese Speaking Countries (Comunidade dos Países de Língua Portuguesa – CPLP)

Classified Index

The purpose of this classification of international organizations is to simplify presentation and provide a key to systematic reading of the entries included in the book.

I Universal Organizations

General Competence
United Nations (UN)

UN Specialized Agencies
Food and Agriculture Organization (FAO)
International Atomic Energy Agency (IAEA)
International Civil Aviation Organization (ICAO)
International Fund for Agricultural Development (IFAD)
International Labour Organization (ILO)
International Maritime Organization (IMO)
International Monetary Fund (IMF)
International Telecommunication Union (ITU)
UN Educational, Scientific and Cultural Organization
    (UNESCO)
UN Industrial Development Organization (UNIDO)
Universal Postal Union (UPU)
World Bank Group
International Bank for Reconstruction and Development
    (IBRD)
International Development Association (IDA)
International Finance Corporation (IFC)
Multilateral Investment Guarantee Agency (MIGA)
International Centre for Settlement of Investment Disputes
    (ICSID)
World Health Organization (WHO)
World Intellectual Property Organization (WIPO)
World Meteorological Organization (WMO)
World Trade Organization (WTO)

Other Specialized Agencies
International Maritime Satellite Organization (INMARSAT)
International Organization for Migration (IOM)
International Telecommunications Satellite Organization
    (INTELSAT)
International Union for the Protection of New Varieties of
    Plants (UPOV)
World Tourism Organization (WTO)

Other UN Bodies
Commission on Narcotic Drugs (CND)
International Narcotics Control Board (INCB)
International Trade Centre UNCTAD/WTO
UN Centre for Human Settlements (UNCHS) – Habitat

UN Children's Fund (UNICEF)
UN Conference on Trade and Development (UNCTAD)
UN Development Programme (UNDP)
UN Environment Programme (UNEP)
UN High Commissioner for Human Rights (HCHR)
UN High Commissioner for Refugees (UNHCR)
UN International Drug Control Programme (UNDCP)
UN Population Fund (UNFPA)
UN Relief and Works Agency for Palestine Refugees in the
    Near East (UNRWA)
World Food Programme (WFP)

II Regional Organizations

AFRICA

General Political Competence
Organization of African Unity (OAU)

General Economic Competence
UN Economic Commission for Africa (ECA)

Economic Co-operation and Integration
Common Market for Eastern and Southern Africa
    (COMESA)
Economic and Monetary Community of Central Africa
    (CEMAC)
Economic Community of Central African States
    (CEEAC)
Economic Community of the Great Lakes Countries
    (CEPGL)
Economic Community of West African States (ECOWAS)
Entente Council
Indian Ocean Commission (IOC)
Mano River Union (MRU)
Southern African Development Community (SADC)
West African Economic and Monetary Union (UEMOA)

Agriculture and Forestry
African Timber Organization
Desert Locust Control Organization for Eastern Africa
    (DLCO-EA)
Intergovernmental Authority on Drought and Development
    (IGADD)

International Red Locust Control Organization for Central
    and Southern Africa (IRLCO-CSA)
Permanent Inter-State Committee on Drought Control in
    the Sahel (CILSS)

Commodities
African Groundnut Council
African Petroleum Producers' Association
Inter-African Coffee Organization (IACO)
West Africa Rice Development Association (WARDA)

Development Financing
African Development Bank (AfDB)

Management of Water Resources
Gambia River Development Organization (OMVG)
Lake Chad Basin Commission (LCBC)
Niger Basin Authority
Organization for the Development of the Senegal River
    (OMVS)
Organization for the Management and Development of the
    Kagera River Basin

ASIA AND THE PACIFIC

General Economic Competence
UN Economic and Social Commission for Asia and the
    Pacific (ESCAP)

Economic Co-operation and Integration
Asia–Pacific Economic Co-operation (APEC)
Association of South East Asian Nations (ASEAN)
Colombo Plan, The
Economic Co-operation Organization (ECO)
Pacific Basin Economic Council (PBEC)
Pacific Economic Co-operation Council (PECC)
South Asian Association for Regional Co-operation
    (SAARC)
South Pacific Commission (SPC)

Commodities
Asian and Pacific Coconut Community (APCC)

Development Financing
Asian Development Bank (AsDB)

Fisheries
Asia-Pacific Fishery Commission (APFIC)

Management of Water Resources
Mekong River Commission

Political Co-operation
South Pacific Forum (SPF)

Science and Technology
North Pacific Marine Science Organization

Security and Defence
ANZUS Pact
ASEAN Regional Forum (ARF)

EUROPE

General Competence
Council of Europe
Nordic Council

General Economic Competence
UN Economic Commission for Europe (ECE)

Economic Co-operation and Integration
Barents Euro-Arctic Council
Benelux Economic Union
Black Sea Economic Co-operation (BSEC)
Central European Free Trade Agreement (CEFTA)
Central European Initiative (CEI)
Council of the Baltic Sea States (CBSS)
European Free Trade Association (EFTA)
European Union (EU)

Development Financing
European Bank for Reconstruction and Development
    (EBRD)
European Investment Bank (EIB)

Fisheries
International Baltic Sea Fishery Commission (IBSFC)

Posts and Telecommunications
European Conference of Postal and Telecommunications
    Administrations (CEPT)
European Telecommunications Satellite Organization (EU-
    TELSAT)

Science and Technology
European Organization for Nuclear Research (CERN)
European Organization for the Exploitation of
    Meteorological Satellites (EUMETSAT)
European Space Agency (ESA)

Security and Defence
North Atlantic Treaty Organization (NATO)
Organization for Security and Co-operation in Europe
    (OSCE)
Western European Union (WEU)

Transport and Navigation
Central Commission for the Navigation of the Rhine
Danube Commission
European Conference of Ministers of Transport (ECMT)
European Organization for the Safety of Air Navigation
    (EUROCONTROL)

LATIN AMERICA AND THE CARIBBEAN

General Political Competence
Group of Rio
Organization of American States (OAS)

General Economic Competence
UN Economic Commission for Latin America and the
    Caribbean (ECLAC)

International Commission for the Conservation of the
   Atlantic Tunas (ICCAT)
North Atlantic Marine Mammals Commission
   (NAMMCO)
North Atlantic Salmon Conservation Organization
   (NASCO)
Northeast Atlantic Fisheries Commission (NEAFC)
Northwest Atlantic Fisheries Organization (NAFO)
Western Central Atlantic Fishery Commission (WECAFC)
Western Indian Ocean Tuna Organization (WIOTO)

Humanitarian Assistance
International Committee of the Red Cross (ICRC)
International Federation of Red Cross and Red Crescent
   Societies

International Arms Sales
Wassenaar Arrangement

Law
International Institute for the Unification of Private Law
   (Unidroit)

Monetary Co-operation
Bank for International Settlements (BIS)

Science and Technology
Agency for Cultural and Technical Co-operation (ACCT)
International Council for the Exploration of the
   Sea (ICES)

Trade and Customs
Customs Co-operation Council (CCC)

Whaling
International Whaling Commission (IWC)

Index of Acronyms

Italicized entries indicate organizations which are no longer in existence or have been reorganized and renamed.

Index of Names

Italicized entries indicate organizations which are no longer in existence or have been reorganized and renamed.